First Language Acquisition

First Language Acquisition

Method, Description, and Explanation

David Ingram

Department of Linguistics
The University of British Columbia

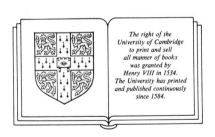

The right of the
University of Cambridge
to print and sell
all manner of books
was granted by
Henry VIII in 1534.
The University has printed
and published continuously
since 1584.

Cambridge University Press

Cambridge
New York *Port Chester* *Melbourne* *Sydney*

Published by the Press Syndicate of the University of Cambridge
The Pitt Building, Trumpington Street, Cambridge CB2 1RP
40 West 20th Street, New York, NY 10011–4211, USA
10 Stamford Road, Oakleigh, Melbourne 3166, Australia

First published 1989
Reprinted 1991

Printed at The Bath Press, Avon

British Library cataloguing in publication data

Ingram, David.
First language acquisition: method,
description and explanation.
1. Children. Language skills. Acquisition.
I. Title.
401′.9

Library of Congress cataloguing in publication data

Ingram, David, 1944–
First language acquisition: method, description, and explanation /
David Ingram.
  p. cm.
Bibliography.
Includes index.
ISBN 0 521 34109 4.   ISBN 0 521 34916 8 (pbk)
1. Language acquisition. I. Title.
P118.I44 1988.
401′.9 – dc19   88–16215   CIP

ISBN 0 521 34109 4 hard covers
ISBN 0 521 34916 8 paperback

For my mother,
Mary Strailman

Contents

Preface

This enterprise officially began in April, 1984, in the Dallas–Fort Worth airport while I was undergoing a seven-hour flight delay. The original idea, conceived a year earlier, was to present an exhaustive encyclopedic review of child language. My feeling at the time was that the field contained a massive literature which was being lost in recent years. In that year, however, my orientation changed rather dramatically. For one thing, my own work was concentrating on methodological issues in analyzing phonological and grammatical samples from children. Methodology took on a greater importance for me than it had ever done before. At the same time, the field began a self-assessment, which still continues, of its theoretical underpinnings. The collection of data for its own sake came under particlar criticism, and new theoretical issues came to the forefront regarding the learnability of linguistic constructions and the relevance of acquisition data for linguistic theory. By the onset of writing, therefore, my goals had changed considerably. I now saw my purpose as one of providing a more balanced view of methodology, descriptive review, and theory.

As should have been expected, this ambitious enterprise took a long time, slightly over three years, to complete. One problem, of course, was trying to maintain the balance between these three areas. With any particular study, I have tried to discuss the issues at stake, the relevant methodological decisions, and the most appropriate and insightful literature available. One consequence of this was a sacrifice in the area of descriptive review. It was impossible to provide exhaustive literature reviews while simultaneously giving in-depth methodological and theoretical information. Instead, I opted for a selection of representative studies in the areas covered. The belief was that the deeper coverage of selected studies would better prepare the reader to undergo his or her own reading of other works than would a superficial and incomplete treatment of a larger number of studies.

Despite the decision to restrict the literature review, the book still ended up being much longer than expected. Even so, it still only covers the core areas of phonology, morphology, syntax, and semantics. The potential effects of parental speech are discussed, but only in relation to these core areas. Relatively little is said about areas such as pragmatics and conversational patterns, and nothing appears on related areas such as second language acquisition, bilingualism, twin speech, language disorders, or spelling. Their inclusion would have led me into additional volumes. In addition, material originally intended for the text has since been eliminated, to be included instead in a separate accompanying Workbook. This material includes information on language sampling, bibliographies, review questions, and exercises.

This brings me to the potential audience. The book is directed towards those interested in the acquisition of the structure of language, rather than its use in everyday conversation. Further, it is for those who are relatively serious about the field of child language acquisition. Students who would use it are primarily those who are in either upper-level undergraduate or graduate courses. I have, for example, used it during the last three years in an undergraduate course for linguistics students which requires a previous course in linguistics. I also hope it will be of value to professionals in the field. One group might be researchers who would like a more detailed review of areas outside their primary research interests. Another potential reader is the practicing language clinician who would like to update his or her knowledge of normal language acquisition.

To acknowledge all those who contributed either directly or indirectly to the book would require pages. Certainly all the authors of the numerous works I have read over the last twenty years deserve recognition for their contributions to our field. I would like, however, to single out a few individuals who have played an important role in my thinking in some of the areas of language acquisition. Part of my continued interest in phonological acquisition is no doubt motivated by the wonderful colleagues I have in this area. These include Mary Louise Edwards, Larry Leonard, John Locke, Marcy Macken, Lise Menn, Richard Schwartz, Larry Shriberg, and Carol Stoel-Gammon. My understanding of grammatical and semantic acquisition has been greatly assisted by the opportunity to discuss the area, either briefly or at length, with people such as Elizabeth Bates, Lois Bloom, Martin Braine, Robin Chapman, Richard Cromer, David Crystal, Bruce Derwing, Paul Fletcher, Alan Kamhi, Judith Johnston, Stan Kuczaj, Brian MacWhinney, Jon Miller, and Catherine Snow. My knowledge of the more recent research from a nativist perspective owes a debt to discussions with, and the opportunity to hear presentations by, Stephen Crain, Helen Goodluck, William O'Grady, Marianne Phinney, Janet Randall, Tom Poeper, Larry Solan, and Ken Wexler.

I would like to single out four people for a special intellectual acknowledgement. During most of the writing of the book, I have had the unique opportunity to have regular interactions with four of the finest minds I have ever met – Guy Carden, Henry Davis, Heather Goad, and Cliff Pye. I cannot conceive of a richer enviroment in which to attempt such an undertaking. Guy, a theoretical linguist with an appreciation of the value of acquisition data, was always ready to drop what he was doing to go over a draft or discuss a particular difficult theoretical point. I have never met anyone so willing to give of his time to aid the work of others. Henry has a better combined grasp of theoretical linguistics and the child language literature than anyone I have ever met. I have enjoyed watching him play the devil's advocate, both with theoretical linguists and data-oriented researchers in child language. His 1987 doctoral dissertation is an outstanding theoretical contribution on language acquisition. Heather is a former undergraduate student in our department who is now studying for her doctorate in linguistics at the University of Southern California. She has a keen eye for detail and was very quick to push for evidence when theoretical claims were discussed in our seminars on language acquisition. Cliff came to UBC as a postdoctoral fellow after completing his excellent dissertation on the acquisition of Quiché. For two years I had the opportunity to discuss the text with him on a daily basis. More than to anyone, I owe him a special thanks for his constant input. When he left in 1986 to take up a position at the University of Kansas, he left as both a colleague and a close friend.

I would like to make a personal acknowledgement to my children Jennika and Daniel. During the last three years I have tried to allot my writing time so that it would not take away too much from time that I spent with them. Even so, there were occasions when things had to get done, or when the stress and preoccupation with the task no doubt left me less than energetic. They were always supportive, however, and their occasional arm around the shoulder, as we peered into the computer screen, gave me more support at times than they ever realized. Lastly, I want to acknowledge the lifelong support of my mother, Mary Strailman, to whom this book is dedicated.

1 Introduction

The study of children's language acquisition is a field that comprises a large body of literature, dating back well over one hundred years. To make sense of these works, however, is no easy task. One reason for this is that the topic is one without a discipline. There are virtually no university departments of language acquisition (or child language as it is often called), and only one major journal is devoted to it (*The Journal of Child Language*, since 1974). Instead, we have language acquisition subfields of other areas such as linguistics, psychology, education, and communication disorders. As may be expected, these disciplines approach the topic from very different perspectives. The result has been a handful of general texts from the view of one or another of these disciplines, often to the virtual exclusion of others.

This book is consistent with this trend in one sense – it will use as its foundation the current interests of the field of linguistics. It will differ, however, in that it will attempt to transcend a limited linguistic view, and discuss works and issues that have been produced in the other disciplines above. To do this, it will deal with three central aspects of the study of language acquisition: methodology, description, and explanation.

By METHODOLOGY I mean the ways in which one decides to approach the data of language acquisition. If there is any single void in the booklength treatment of language acquisition, it is the discussion of how to do or practice it. This dimension covers several topics, from data collection to the reasons for data collection. Here, the following methodological areas will be covered:

1. techniques of data collection – from spontaneous language sampling to experimental procedures such as elicited imitation, comprehension testing, and metalinguistic judgements;
2. techniques of linguistic analysis, focussing on grammatical and phonological analysis;
3. aspects of measurement – that is, how to decide on appropriate measures for the analysis of data from both experimental and naturalistic studies;

4.   approaches to data – from the formulation of testable hypotheses from linguistic theory to the establishment of inductive generalizations from the analysis of children's language.

These are the various procedures needed in order to collect reliable information on the language of young children.

A second characteristic of child language is that over the years it has accumulated a great deal of information on children's linguistic behavior. For example, we know a lot about when certain behaviors appear, such as the first words, the kinds of things children say, and the kinds of errors they make. This body of knowledge does not pretend to explain anything, in the sense of providing a theory of development, but it constitutes the facts to be explained. The presentation of the current state of what we know children do constitutes the DESCRIPTION of language acquisition. This book attempts to provide an in-depth review of these facts, and tries to separate facts from explanations. For example, to say that a child is at the two-word stage does not explain anything, but provides something to be explained.

The discussion of the descriptive aspect of language acquisition will be conducted by a presentation of the following traditional periods of acquisition:

1.   prelinguistic development – birth to end of first year;
2.   single-word utterances – from around 1 year to $1\frac{1}{2}$ years of age;
3.   the first word combinations – from around $1\frac{1}{2}$ to 2 years of age;
4.   simple and complex sentences – the third year of life.

By this point the normal child can be said to have mastered the rudimentary aspects of most aspects of language, and I do not discuss in any detail the subsequent development, from age 4 up to adulthood. That period is represented by a substantial literature that would require another book-length treatment of its own.

The above periods are described in terms of grammatical developments, but this is done only to provide a frame of reference. For each period, information will be provided on phonological, semantic, and syntactic development, and the child's linguistic environment. The discussion in these sections looks carefully at reported findings and selects just those that appear to result from reliable research. To do this, the focus will be on depth instead of breadth. Rather than just reporting superficially on the results of several studies, I will concentrate in more detail on selected studies of significance. This approach is based on the assumption that careful scrutiny of the studies on language acquisition is necessary to establish what is actually known.

The last and most difficult area of language acquisition is EXPLANATION, that is, the construction of a theory of language acquisition. Such a theory will account for how the child acquires language, based on the linguistic input. This discussion will include the following:

1. an examination of behaviorist, maturationist, and constructionist views of language acquisition;
2. the discussion of the notion of 'explanatory' stage, as contrasted with 'descriptive' stage;
3. the proposal of several assumptions about language acquisition that will allow us to formulate testable hypotheses;
4. the concentration on the relation between the child's linguistic competence and performance.

Very early in the book I lay out the theoretical assumptions underlying much of the methodological and descriptive information. It is taken for granted that the latter two pursuits are only interesting to the extent that they lead to principles which help explain how the child acquires language.

While these three aspects provide the focus of the book, they are not presented as separate sections, but are intertwined throughout. The actual structure of the book is as follows. Part I, 'Foundations', attempts to initiate the reader into the major methodological, descriptive, and explanatory issues. I discuss the primary methods used to study children's language, and concentrate especially on the method of the spontaneous language sample. The reader is encouraged to carry out an actual language sample if she or he has not yet done so in order to bring to the studies discussed later the necessary critical appreciation. This overview also includes a historical review of the field and of how various methodological and explanatory developments have occurred. The notion of 'stage' is carefully considered, since it is a term widely used in the literature.

Part II, 'Milestones', provides an introductory treatment of the main descriptive periods. As far as possible, within the limits of current knowledge, I give what is known about the child's receptive ability, followed by a discussion of expressive ability at the same point in development. This is done to show over and over how the child's receptive ability precedes and influences expression. In other books this aspect is often ignored or underemphasized, with the emphasis instead on expressive language only. This part also repeatedly examines the extent to which we can make claims about the child's rule system, based on linguistic behavior. As far as possible, we will assume that the child's behavior reflects competence, unless explicit performance factors can be isolated.

Part II also provides a detailed discussion of how to analyze children's language. Explicit suggestions are made on how to do phonological, morphological, and syntactic analyses. A recurrent theme will be the issue of 'productivity'. This is the concern with separating the child's linguistic forms which are rule-based from those which are imitated or rote-learned. It is the rule-based or 'productive' forms which reveal the most about the child's internal linguistic system.

A major goal of the book is to provide the reader with the ability to practice the field of language acquisition, not just learn about it. Such an ability requires awareness of all three areas discussed above. We need to establish principles that explain language acquisition, principles that are falsifiable through the description of children's behavior, behavior that reliably represents the child's linguistic knowledge. The course of the relation between these three can begin with any one and be traced to the others.

Further reading

There have been several introductory texts on the study of language acquisition of children. The two most used ones appear to be Dale (1976) *Language development: structure and function*, and de Villiers & de Villiers (1978) *Language acquisition*. A recent book of chapters contributed by different authors is *Language acquisition*, edited by Fletcher and Garman (1979, 2nd edn 1986). Still another recent book, Oksaar (1983) *Language acquisition in the early years*, has been translated into English from the original German of 1977. A recent text from a Piagetian perspective is *Language development from birth to three* by Anisfeld (1984). Earlier efforts at a text include McNeill (1970a), Menyuk (1971), Cazden (1972), and Bloom & Lahey (1978). There is also a highly readable introduction contained in Clark & Clark (1977).

Part I

Foundations

2   The history of child language studies

The field of child language acquisition is one that has gone through several changes over the years in both the methods and the theoretical orientation used. It is my belief that an understanding of the field requires an initial exposure to its history. My impression is that the field has lost this perspective and that many investigators are unaware of its rich literature. This chapter, then, is designed to provide a historical overview that will discuss the evolution of current methods, descriptive findings, and theoretical perspectives. It will proceed by discussing three major periods of child language studies. These periods are identified by the dominant method in each. They are:

1. The period of diary studies (1876–1926)
2. The period of large sample studies (1926–1957)
3. The period of longitudinal studies (1957–present)

For each period we will look at the major studies, the methodological approach, the most general findings, and the theoretical orientation.

2.1 The period of diary studies (1876–1926)

2.1.1 Methodological orientation

The first studies on language acquisition began to appear over one hundred years ago. These were a part of a general interest in child development that occurred at that time, led in many respects by the work of G. Stanley Hall in North America and William Preyer in Europe. For the first time in history, children became the focus of study to determine the way in which they develop in general. Child language was just one branch of this work.

The method selected for this enterprise was that of the *parental diary*. The linguist or psychologist parent would keep a diary of his/her child's learning over some period of time. These observations could be specifically on language, but often they were more generally on everything from motor development to musical awareness, e.g. Preyer (1889). These diaries were eventually published, sometimes in their raw form with little commentary (e.g. Roussey 1899–1900), but more commonly with selected entries and interpretations (e.g. Vinson 1915). These works came to be known as 'baby biographies', and they provide a rich descriptive foundation for the field.

The diaries show some common characteristics, though it is dangerous to think of them as homogeneous. They do vary tremendously in their quality and detail. One feature, already alluded to, is that they are usually the record of a parent observer. This feature has been considered as both a strength and a weakness of the approach. An undeniable strength is that the observer clearly knows the child well; behaviors noted, consequently, are not idiosyncratic, but presumably either common ones or ones that mark a new development. In language acquisition, for example, major milestones may appear and be acquired over a matter of days; the parent observer will be able to spot these and note their characteristics. By the same token, diaries have been criticized for being biased in that the parent observer will only record what s/he sees to be an important development – other important behaviors may go unnoticed. Without a theoretical orientation, the argument goes, how does one know what to record? One does not, so one randomly puts down what is noticed. Further, randomness is introduced by the fact that the diarist records events when possible. Many published diaries are full of gaps when either the parent or child was away for various reasons. Data on development during these periods, unfortunately, is gone forever. Despite these problems, many of the diaries of this period remain as some of our most detailed reports on language acquisition.

2.1.2 Major diary studies

While sporadic observations on children's language appear throughout the nineteenth century, the active publication of baby biographies can be dated from 1876 with the publication of H. Taine's paper that appeared translated into English the next year in *Mind*. Taine reported on his daughter's linguistic development from birth to the end of the second year of life, and his paper stimulated Charles Darwin to return to some notes he had made on his own son's language years earlier, as the basis for a report which he too then published in the following number of *Mind*. These papers led to much better and more intensive diaries in both English and other languages. In Europe, the most extensive general diary was by Preyer (1889) on the development of his son Axel, a work which contains excellent linguistic information and which was later translated into English. It was followed by the first classic work devoted exclusively to child language, Clara and Wilhelm Stern's *Die Kindersprache* (1907). This book, which unfortunately has never been published in English, reports on the language development of their two children, Hilde and Gunter. In English, we have only hints of this work through the authors' translated books dealing with general development, e.g. Stern (1924). *Die Kindersprache* is perhaps best known as the firstly widely accepted statement on the stages of language acquisition which all children are proposed to follow. This question of 'stage' will be returned to in the next chapter.

In North America, the main force of the work on language acquisition was stimulated by G. Stanley Hall of Clark University. While Hall wrote little on language acquisition, he stimulated work through his encouragement of baby biographies, such as the one done by Hogan (1898). Hall contributed also in two other ways. First, as editor of *Pedagogical Seminary*, he encouraged the publication of articles on language acquisition. During this period, the journal was constantly publishing reports on children's early language, e.g. Bateman (1916), Brandenburg (1915), Chamberlain & Chamberlain (1904, 1905, 1909), Nice (1917, 1920), Pelsma (1910). Lukens (1894) remains a very readable review of the findings to that date on children's language acquisition. These early works grew in number so rapidly that the first bibliography in *Pedagogical Seminary* by Wilson (1898) listed 641 entries, many dealing with language. Second, Hall planned to build at Clark University a Child Study Institute, with an entire floor devoted to child language. He had already begun a project to archive as much child language data as possible from other languages as well as English. Unfortunately, both the onset of the World War and a shift in theoretical focus aborted this ambitious plan.

The goal of the large majority of these works was descriptive. That is, the biographies were by and large concerned with plotting the facts of language acquisition, with little concern for theory construction. The result was an enormous descriptive literature, which unfortunately has been overlooked by many modern researchers. It would be unfair, however, to say that these studies were void of theoretical assumptions. When the question arose, the most frequent view was that the child brought a great deal of internal linguistic organization to the task. The child was perceived as being very creative, and capable of discovering the structure of language from its environment. Taine (1877:258) captures this feeling:

> We only help it [the child: DI] to catch them [general ideas: DI] by the suggestion of our words. It attaches to them ideas that we do not expect and spontaneously generalizes outside and beyond our cadres. At times it invents not only the meaning of the word but the word itself ... In short, it learns a ready-made language as a true musician learns counterpoint or a true poet prosody; it is an original genius adapting itself to a form constructed bit by bit by a succession of original geniuses; if language were wanting, the child would recover it little by little or would discover an equivalent.

While there was this view of the child, little effort went toward specifying the actual principles used by the child to construct a language system. While the dominant method of this period was the parental diary, this does not mean that diary studies ended with 1926. Rather, other methods came along and joined the diary approach. There have been numerous diary studies conducted since 1926, and the best ones in English have appeared since then. Clearly, the most cited is the four-volume work by Leopold (1939–49) on his daughter Hildegard from birth to age 2 years. While Hildegard acquired both English and German, most discussion has centered on Hildegard's acquisition of English. Perhaps the next most detailed book is that of Lewis (1936, 2nd edn 1951) who reported on the early language of a boy referred to as 'K'. Both these books are full of detailed observations. The most recent major diary is probably that of Smith (1973) on his son A's phonological development. The most novel diary is that of Weir (1962), who tape-recorded the pre-sleep monologues of her son Anthony from 2;2 to 2;4. Rich diary studies exist for other languages as well, e.g. French (Grégoire 1937, 1947), Russian (Gvozdev 1949), and Polish (Zarębina 1965).

2.1.3 The value of diary studies

The value of diary studies is enormous in providing a database for the field. The role these data play are quite diverse. In some cases, the data are rich enough to provide the basis for a study. In other cases, the data may be supplemental, that is, used in conjunction with newly collected data to substantiate a point. Also, the data may be merely suggestive, i.e. providing an interesting observation that can be followed up with original research. The studies that are reported on later in the book will sometimes show all these uses of diary data.

In any research project, the first step is an in-depth review of the literature. In acquisition, we have one additional step, the careful evaluation of available diaries for relevant data. One of the skills needed for the study of language acquisition, then, is the ability to extract data from diary studies. To do it requires careful reading and evaluation of the diaries relevant to one's interest. For example, we need to assess the parent observer's qualifications to observe certain aspects of language. It is difficult to get reliable phonological data, for instance, from a diarist with no phonetic skills; and the semantic study of early word meaning is of dubious value when we are only given word lists, with little mention of errors of usage. We are constantly rejecting or overlooking certain aspects in search of those points of importance.

There is no doubt that the difficulty of pulling out relevant data from a

Table 2.1 *A summary of Axel Preyer's language at 1;5, taken from Table VI in Ingram (1978), itself a summary of Preyer (1889).*

Production:	only two words since 1;1; 'atta' which meant 'going' and 'heiss' (hot).
Comprehension:	(a) since 1;1, responds correctly to: 'where is papa? Mama?'
	(b) consistently understands the following words: 'clock, ear, shoe, chair, shoulder, foot, forehead, chin, nose, blow, beard, hair, hat, meat, eye, arm, hand, cheek, head, mouth, table, light, cupboard, flower'.
	(c) obeys the following verbs: 'run, kick, lie down, cough, blow, bring, give, come, kiss'.

diary has led to either total avoidance of the approach or emphasis on just one or two highly reliable sources. We would like to argue, however, that the gains are worth the effort. For one thing, the diaries usually provide a comprehensiveness that is impossible to replicate starting from scratch. The collection of daily observations for one or more children for up to several years is a tremendous undertaking. One can benefit from a parent observer's years of effort in a few hours of reading. Second, children vary greatly and it may only be the occasional child who shows a particular pattern. An examination of a cross-section of diaries may reveal one such child, and provide clues for what to look for in seeking another for careful study.

Let us look at an example of how useful data can be extracted from a diary record. It is a common observation that children seem to comprehend more than they produce. What is the database for this observation? Preyer (1889) is an early study that provides explicit data on this point. In Ingram (1978), I extracted linguistic data from this diary on Preyer's son Axel as part of a general discussion of the relation of language and cognition. Table 2.1 here summarizes the data from Table VI of Ingram (1978) on Axel's comprehension and production at age 1;5.

We can see that Axel has around 50 items in his comprehension while only producing two words. As far as his production goes, Preyer observes (p. 131): 'Characteristic for this period is the precision with which the various moods of feeling are expressed, without articulate sounds, by means of the voice . . .' The general findings that might be classified as the conventional wisdom on language acquisition are based on data such as these.

2.2 The period of large sample studies (1926–1957)

2.2.1 Methodological orientation

While diary studies continued on after the First World War, a major shift in the field occurred around this time. It was the result of the emerging form of psychology that has come to be known as 'behaviorism'. Just as the earlier period was traced to G. Stanley Hall, this has been associated with the work of Thomas B. Watson. The immediate meaning of behaviorism is simple enough – a focus on behavior. Isn't this what has been going on in the baby biographies?

Behaviorism differed from the previous observations of behavior in two respects: the role of the child in the learning of language, and the measurement of observable behavior. Behaviorists wanted to develop a theory of learning where the child's changes in behavior were traced back to, or explained by, observable conditions of the child's environment. The emphasis was on observable events in the interaction of the child and its surrounding linguistic community. Within this view, the child is seen as passively controlled by the environment; this is in contrast to the belief of the earlier diarists that the active spontaneous behavior of the child is central. Taine and others supplied the internal structure and abilities of the child, i.e. its 'genius', that were rejected by the behaviorists as unmeasurable.

Examining the actual work done on language acquisition during this period, we find that most of it was devoted to measurement of language change rather than to a study of the controlling factors of the child's environment. That is, as in the period of diary studies, most of the emphasis was on description rather than explanation. The way this description proceeded, however, was much different. This difference is captured starkly by the following remark by McCarthy on diary studies:

> Although this wealth of observational material proved stimulating and suggestive for later research workers, it has little scientific merit, for each of the studies employed a different method; the observations were for the most part conducted on single children who were usually either precocious or markedly retarded in their language develop-ment; the records were made under varying conditions; and most of the studies were subject to the unreliability of parents' reports.
>
> (McCarthy 1954: 494)

The earlier works were of little value because they were unsystematic, focussed on single subjects, and provided little measurement of the child's behavior.

The result of the new emphasis of behaviorism was a series of studies which, though as varied as the diary studies, attempted to remedy their perceived deficiencies. The new accounts shared several characteristics. For one, researchers were interested in determining what could be described as normal behavior. To do this requires establishing norms through the observation of *large numbers of children*. It is the aspect of collecting data on a large number of subjects that has led me to call this the *period of large sample studies*. Here 'large sample' refers to the size of the sample of children used. (This needs to be kept distinct from the use of 'large sample' to refer to the amount of language selected from a single child. In this latter sense, several diary studies are 'large sample' studies.)

These studies also controlled for possible environmental influences by selecting subjects very carefully. The children came from similar socio-economic classes, and there were equal numbers of boys and girls. Whereas diary studies tend to be *longitudinal* studies, i.e. studies of single children changing over time, the large sample studies tend to be *cross-sectional* studies, i.e. studies of different children at distinct ages. If enough subjects are selected for each age group, presumably typical behavior is observed. We can then make inferences about the change of behavior over time without actually observing any one child change its behavior. There would usually be similar sample sizes for each age group, and the age intervals were usually separated by equal time periods, e.g. 2-year-olds vs. 3-year-olds vs. 4-year-olds.

Other factors distinguished these studies, besides the focus on large samples. A second one was the *systematic* observation of behavior, as contrasted with the unsystematic observations of diaries. All subjects would be studied for the same amount of time for the same behaviors. If a language sample were collected, it would be of some predetermined size, e.g. 100 utterances. If it were some specific behavior, a test would be constructed to be given to all the subjects. Further, the testing or data collection would be done by the same experimenter so that variations between children could not be traced to different experimenter styles.

A third difference between these and previous diary studies was the way in which the data were analyzed. Under the new experimental methodo-logy, there was an emphasis on *measurement*. While statistics was still being developed as a discipline, these studies are full of quantified results, usually in the form of numerous tables full of proportions and percentages. These measures were given mostly for grouped data rather than individual children, since the amount of data collected from any single child was usually quite small.

The content of these descriptive studies can best be seen by looking at a historical overview of the major work of the period. Table 2.2 gives a brief overview of some of the major studies in terms of sample size, the kind of data, and the topic under study. We date this period as beginning in 1926 because this is the date of the first study of this kind, by M. Smith (1926). Smith's study is typical of most. They concentrated on very superficial aspects of language. Most generally, there were three areas of concentra-tion: vocabulary growth, sentence length, and correctness of articulation.

Table 2.2 *Some general characteristics of some of the major large sample studies conducted between 1926 and 1957*

Study	Sample characteristics	Topic
Smith (1926)	124 children between 2 and 5; one-hour conversations	Length of sentences and general aspects of sentence development
McCarthy (1930)	140 children between 1;6 and 4;6 50 sentences each	Length of sentences and general aspects of sentence development
Day (1932)	160 children between 2;0 and 5;0 50 sentences each	Study of language in twins
Fisher (1934)	72 children between 1;6 and 4;6 three-hour samples	Study of gifted children
Davis (1937)	173 singletons, 166 twins, all ˉ ˎ between 5;6 and 6;6 50 sentences each	Comparison of twins with singletons
Young (1941)	74 children between 2;6 and 5;5 six hours of conversation	Comparison of lower- and middle-class children
Templin (1957)	430 children between 3;0 and 8;0 50 sentences each	Length of sentences and general aspects of sentence development

Smith's (1926) results on vocabulary growth, for example, are still cited today (e.g. Dale 1976:174) as the norms for English, and Templin (1957) remains the most common reference for norms of articulatory development (e.g. Ingram 1976a).

The study of sentence length is of particular interest. In the period of diary studies, Stern & Stern (1907) had developed stages of acquisition that were based on the observation that children's sentences get increasingly longer. Nice (1925) developed her own stages of sentence length (see further Chapter 3) that used an explicit measure which she called the 'mean sentence length'. This was calculated by counting the number of words in each sentence of a child's language sample and calculating the average number of words per sentence. This measure was used in virtually every study done during this period. In fact, in McCarthy's (1954) major review of this period, there is an extensive table that gives the mean sentence length from several studies across several ages.

The other emphasis of these studies was to apply the results on these three general areas to different groups of children. The first studies were concerned with normal children, e.g. Smith (1926), McCarthy (1930), and Wellman *et al.* (1931). Soon, however, other groups were analyzed, e.g. twins (Day 1932; Davis 1937), gifted children (Fisher 1934), and lower-class children (Young 1941). This natural development can be traced to the fact that most of these studies were conducted by students or colleagues of Smith and McCarthy. Madorah Smith was at the University of Iowa and one series of research came out of there, published in the *University of Iowa Studies in Child Welfare*. Dorothea McCarthy was at the University of Minnesota and

Table 2.3 *A summary of the methodological design of Templin (1957)*

Subjects: 430 total
eight subgroups of 30 boys and 30 girls at each of the following age intervals:
    3;0 3;5 4;0 4;6 5;0 6;0 7;0 8;0

Tests: (1) *Articulation* – 176 sounds tested in selected words ages 3;0–5;0, with separate
word test for those 6;0–8;0.
(a) 3;0–5;0 repeated words after the examiner or spontaneously identified
pictures.
(b) 6;0–3;0 read the text words or repeated them after the examiner.

(2) *Discrimination* – pairs of syllables were spoken by the examiner and children
had to judge them as 'same' or 'different'.
(a) 3;0–5;0 used pairs of real words of objects that were identifiable (59 pairs,
e.g. 'keys' to 'peas').
(b) 6;0–8;0 used pairs of nonsense syllables (50 pairs, e.g. [sā vs. zā].

(3) *Sentence development* – 50 utterances were elicited and transcribed on site using
toys and picture books.

(4) *Vocabulary* – receptive vocabulary was assessed through standardized tests.
(a) 3;0–5;0 Ammons Full-Range Vocabulary Test
(b) 6;0–8;0 Seashore-Eckerson English Recognition Vocabulary Test.

---

directed several studies that appeared in the *Monograph Series* of the
University of Minnesota Institute of Child Welfare.

The character of these studies can be captured by looking at one of the
best of them, Templin (1957), which also, coincidentally, marks the end of
these studies as conducted over this 31-year period. Table 2.3 summarizes
its basic methodology. The subject size is the largest of all the studies, and
suggests that it was designed to be the definitive one of its type. The four
aspects examined include the three mentioned above plus a discrimination
task. The results are given, by and large, through extensively quantified
data. There are, for example, 71 tables and nine figures. Here is just a
sample of the table headings for the analysis of sentence structure:

(2.1) a. Table 39. Mean number of words per remark of boys and girls,
upper and lower socioeconomic status groups, and total subsamples by age (p. 79).
b. Table 44. Mean percentages of total remarks in each sentence
construction category for boys and girls by age as found by
McCarthy, Davis, and Templin (pp. 86–7).
c. Table 48. Number and percentage of various types of subordinate
clauses used by boys and girls, upper and lower socioeconomic
status groups, and total subsamples, by age (p. 93).

Just as diary studies continued on after 1926, large sample studies have
continued beyond 1957. The change, however, has been a change in focus to
a new methodology. In the case of large sample studies, there has been a

noticeable drop in their number since 1957. Perhaps the major one since then has been Olmsted's (1971) study on the phonological development of 100 children.

2.2.2 Strengths and weaknesses

To benefit from the extensive data collected by these studies, we need to be aware of their strengths and weaknesses. They have three glaring weaknesses that have led to their virtual rejection by modern linguists. One is their lack of linguistic sophistication, a fact that led to superficiality of content. Language, for example, is much more than vocabulary, sentence length, and speech sounds. It is a system of rules, and insights into the acquisition of these rules is at the core of the study of language acquisition. An example of this linguistic naiveté is found in the work of Irwin, who between 1941 and 1952 published numerous articles on the development of speech sounds in infants from birth to 2 years (see McCarthy 1954 for references). In many of these papers, Irwin refers to the 'phonemes' of the young infant between birth and 1 year; the term phoneme, however, refers to a linguistic unit that is meaningless when applied to the prelinguistic vocalizations of infants.

A second weakness is the focus on grouped data rather than on the patterns of individual children. Language functions as a system of rules or units that interact with each other. It is usually impossible to see these interactions in grouped data unless it was planned for ahead of time. For example, data on what auxiliary verbs appear at what age do not tell us much about how rules that affect auxiliaries, such as Subject–Auxiliary Inversion, are acquired; and norms of sound acquisition do not reveal much about how the individual child acquires a system of phonological rules.

A third weakness, ironically, is a methodological one. Most of these studies, like the diary ones, were done without the aid of modern recording equipment. Instead, most language samples were done by someone writing the child's sentences down as quickly as possible. One should be highly worried about data gathered in this fashion. The problem is worse when we consider phonetic transcription. Templin transcribed all of her data herself with no other transcribers, and without the use of a tape-recorder. She says (1957:19): 'The use of recording equipment is not efficient when recording must be done in many places under varying and often unsatisfactory acoustic conditions.' With diary studies, at least, we are dealing, in the better ones, with a linguistically trained person who is familiar with the child. It is for these three weaknesses that modern investigators tend to reject these descriptive studies, and if they look at any data, it is from one or two selected accounts.

As with the earlier diary studies, the weaknesses in these accounts are not sufficient to lead us to disregard them outright. Rather, they need to be examined with these concerns in mind, for despite the above problems they have strengths that need to be considered. Normative data can be helpful in several ways. For professionals who need to identify children as either precocious or delayed, the norms are a useful step in that decision. The norms help give researchers an idea of just how typical a particular child is. It is easy in a diary study to assume that a child is usual when in fact it is not. Let me give two examples of this. In Leopold's famous diary of Hildegard, he observed that Hildegard replaced adult initial /f-/ in words like 'fall' with a [w] or [v]. We could assume this is a typical pattern in English acquisition. Ingram *et al.* (1980), however, did not find a single instance of this in their study of 73 children! Velten (1943) observed that his daughter Joan produced only two vowels, [a] and [u], for a very long time. An examination of any reasonable number of children (e.g. Ingram & Mitchell to appear) will show that this is highly unusual. Normative data will place any individual child within a larger picture of development. Normative data also give researchers an idea of where to begin in the study of a particular topic. For example, we may wish to study the acquisition of auxiliary verbs. The large sample studies can tell us what ages will be the most fruitful for our study.

Besides norms, large sample studies provide data that themselves can be used for analysis. One approach, which has been sparingly used, is to go to the original data. Take, for example, the data collected by Young (1941). Recall from Table 2.2 that she collected six hours of language samples from 74 children between 2;6 and 5;5. Despite our reservations about the data themselves, they could be used to yield initial results on a tremendous range of questions.

Another way to use these studies is to reanalyze the data to suit one's own goals. Throughout this book, we will emphasize the need to work with data and to manipulate them in various ways. Even though a particular diarist or experimentalist presents and interprets data in a certain way, we are not obliged to accept his/her analysis or interpretation. In some cases, we may find new results for these data by trying out new measures. In other cases, we may even conclude that the interpretations do not follow from the data as presented. We can return to the large sample studies and view them in relation to issues not actually considered by the original researcher. Examples of this process will appear throughout Part II.

The emphasis of the large sample studies on *methods* is one that is important and valid. We can learn from their concerns an awareness of the kinds of problems we face when we do not consider questions of subject selection and research design. In particular, they have made an invaluable contribution with their emphasis on *measurement*. A continuing weakness of the linguistic analysis of a single child is that the analyses will vary tremendously depending on which sentences we decide are produced by rules. While measures do not tell us the nature of a rule, they will allow us to decide when a rule exists in some form. It is a basic premise of this book that some form of measurement is a prerequisite to our linguistic analysis of a child. The ways in which the large sample studies scrutinized data through various measures are important in showing how new patterns can be isolated. Once identified, the linguistic patterns can be subjected to linguistic analysis.

2.2.3 Theoretical orientation

While most work during this period was descriptive, it would be unfair to leave it without a discussion of some attempts to explain acquisition from the behaviorist viewpoint. The behaviorists wanted to explain acquisition by assigning to the child very little innate behavior. On this view, the child would be born with a few very general skills; let us consider what these may be. First, it would be able to vocalize. Second, it would be able to process auditorily the vocalizations of others, and presumably be able to recognize similarities between these and its own. Thirdly, it would be able to pair a vocalization with some context, for example, it would have the ability to relate the vocalization 'mommy' with the context of the parent. Let us call this the ability to form *associations*. Fourth, the child is born with basic drives that will motivate it to form associations. For example, one of these drives is the drive to nourish itself. The actual associations that are formed, such as the one between the word 'mommy', the internal state of hunger, and the person who is the child's mother, are the result of its experience. They can occur because the child has one further ability, the ability to be *conditioned*, i.e. to build up associations by being exposed to events juxtaposed to internal drives.

To explain language acquisition for the behaviorist, then, is to determine the set of environmental conditions that lead the child to identify and associate events with internal states. There were a few attempts to do this during the period of large sample studies. Probably the first to receive attention was the attempt of Bloomfield in his classic book *Language* (1933: ch. 2). Table 2.4 gives the five steps Bloomfield proposes to account for the child's acquisition of word meaning. The child recognizes similarities between its vocalizations and the adult's, and then associates a particular speech event with a context. These five steps center on the child's production of speech. Bloomfield points out that the child also develops the role of a hearer. The child will become reinforced to act in certain ways when he hears certain speech forms, such as 'Wave your hand to Daddy.'

Table 2.4 *Five steps in the acquisition of language, according to Bloomfield (1933: 29–31)*

---

1. Child innately vocalizes, and can recognize sounds which are similar and which are different. He develops the habit of repeating a familiar speech sound, e.g. [da].
2. When someone such as the mother produces a word similar to one of his babblings, e.g. 'doll', he will imitate it with his closest speech form, e.g. [da].
3. The mother's use of 'doll' in the context of dolls will lead the child to associate the sounds with the event of seeing the doll. The sight of the doll becomes a stimulus for saying [da].
4. The habit of saying [da] in specific contexts, e.g. seeing one's doll after one's bath, will lead the child to say [da] in that context when the doll is absent. That is, speech becomes displaced.
5. His successful attempts at speech are reinforced, leading him to adult-like pronunciation. His imperfect attempts are lost.

This account of acquiring early word meaning attempts to combine the role of speaking and listening. Bloomfield states (p. 31):

> After he has learned a number of such twofold sets, he develops a habit by which one type always involves the other: as soon as he learns to speak a new word, he is also able to respond to it when he hears others speak it, and, vice versa, as soon as he learns how to respond to some new word, he is usually able, also, to speak it on proper occasion. The latter transference seems to be the more difficult of the two.

He sees the child as first acquiring a word separately in comprehension and production, and only later connecting the two.

There are several aspects of this view of learning that should be noted. For one, it certainly accounts for some part of early word acquisition. The child needs to imitate adult words in some sense of the word 'imitate'. Also, children do repeat speech a great deal, suggestive of some form of practice on the part of the child. Furthermore, it is common to see children who have been conditioned to act to language, for example, taught to wave bye-bye or say thank you. The crucial question, to which we will return, is whether or not it is sufficient. For example, Bloomfield says (p. 30) that children do not ever invent words, but only have imperfect exposure to the correct range of meanings. Is the process described above sufficient to explain the complex set of meanings that the adult speaker of a language possesses? As we will see later, others have argued that much more innate knowledge needs to be proposed to account for this.

A second aspect of this theory is the important fact that it is testable: that is, it makes predictions about acquisition that can be falsified. We can observe young infants and their mothers to see if children imitate adult words with utterances from their own phonetic repertoire. Or, we can see if there is a one-to-one relation between the conditioning of the child and its word acquisition. We can see if the child acquires words in comprehension and production separately at first and only later simultaneously. Or, for word meaning, we can compare the use of a child's word to the contexts in which it was first taught. Throughout the book, we will emphasize the importance of developing testable theories of acquisition.

A third aspect of Bloomfield's view is that it appears to be focussed on pronunciation and early word use. How does he account for the child's acquisition of grammar? Here Bloomfield has less to say. He has no theory that explains how the syntax of the language is acquired, although he does make mention of the role of analogy in historical change (p. 275). He does, however, emphasize the role of correction by the parent. For example, he says (p. 31): 'if he says *Daddy bringed it*, he merely gets a disappointing answer such as *No*! You must say *"Daddy brought it"*.' This does not tell us how the child establishes the grammar for the correct utterance, but it proposes that parents must do a tremendous amount of language teaching. As we shall see later, this prediction is not borne out by current evidence.

The major attempt during this period to explain language acquisition is that of Skinner (1957). As pointed out in its Preface, the book covers his research from 1934 to 1955. It is the culmination of his theoretical work during these years and it is ironic that it was published the same year as Templin's study. These two works constitute two of the reasons I place the end of this period in 1957. Skinner's proposals are an elaborate development of the basic notions of stimulus, reinforcement, and association, introduced above. They do include, though, some attempts to account for the learning of syntax. To oversimplify: the structure of a sentence consists of a chain of associations between the words in the sentence. Suppose, for example, that the child knows the words 'dog' and 'run', and hears them in the sentence 'The dog is running.' The child may imitate this as 'dog run' and be positively reinforced or rewarded. The word 'dog' becomes a response by the child to some stimulation, say seeing a dog run; and 'dog' in turn becomes a conditioned stimulus for the word 'run'. The development of grammar for the child, then, is the learning of a set of associations between words that can lead to classes of words. A grammar will be a set of classes that occur in a predicted serial order, based on these associations.

As is apparent from even as brief an account as this, Skinner allows for very little innate language structure. This point of view, so prevalent during this period, was attacked heavily by linguists in the next period who emphasized the hierarchical complexity of language. Nonetheless, behaviorism has continued on through today although most of the research has been on associations between words apart from syntax. There is a major work by Mowrer (1960) to account for language in behaviorist terms, and an early attempt by Jenkins & Palermo (1964) to develop Skinner's ideas on how syntax could be acquired without resorting to innate linguistic principles. An important question, which we will return to in later chapters, is the following. The attempt to account for early two-word utterances by imitation and word association is possible, although it becomes subject to massive difficulties as an attempt to explain more complex, adult-like language. When, in the development of language, does the child show language structure that is too complex to be explained by simple principles of association and imitation?

2.3 The period of longitudinal language sampling (1957 to present)

2.3.1 Methodological orientation

The third method used in collecting data on language acquisition is what we call *longitudinal language sampling*. In longitudinal language sampling, the child is visited at predetermined intervals for a reasonable length of time with the purpose of collecting a representative sample. It can be seen as a natural outgrowth of the two methods discussed. Diary studies are longitudinal, but they usually consist of notes rather than complete language samples for some predetermined length of time. (It should be added, though, that some one-day language samples were conducted, e.g. Brandenburg 1915.) Large sample studies took language samples, but they were normally quite short, and not longitudinal.

In the late 1950s, three independent groups of investigators developed a renewed interest in studying language acquisition in children. These were Martin Braine at Walter Reed Hospital in Bethesda, Maryland, Susan Ervin and Wick Miller at the University of California, Berkeley, and Roger Brown at Harvard University. They each developed their own method of longitudinal language sampling. Their work was followed by that of Lois Bloom of Columbia University. We will begin by considering the shared features of their methods of data collection, then discuss each individually.

The longitudinal language samples differ from the diary studies in that the subjects are usually not the offspring of the investigators. Instead, they are children who are selected specifically because they meet predetermined criteria; for example, they are usually on the verge of beginning multiword utterances and are talkative. Also, more than one child is studied; in three of the four studies above, three children were selected. This number is used as an absolute minimum necessary to determine general features of acquisition: if one is chosen, we do not know if the child is typical or not; if two, we do not know which of the two is typical and which is unusual; with three, we at least have a majority that can be used to make such a decision.

Table 2.5 *General information on four major studies using longitudinal language sampling*

Investigator	Children (age range in months)		Sampling schedule
Braine (1963a)	Andrew	(19–23)	parental diary of all multi-word utterances pro-
	Gregory	(19–22)	duced. For Steven, there were tape-recordings for
	Steven	(23–24)	four hours over a four-week period (12 sessions.)
Miller & Ervin (1964)	Susan	(21–)	initially weekly in 45-minute sessions; later every
	Lisa	(24–)	two months for 2 or 3 sessions for 4–5 hours.
	Christy	(24–)	Sampling over a two-year period.
	Harlan	(24–)	
	Carl	(24–)	
Brown (1973)	Adam	(27–44)⎫	two hours every two weeks; two observers present.
	Eve	(18–27)⎭	
	Sarah	(27–44)	half-hour every week.
Bloom (1970)	Eric	(19–26)	eight hours over three or four days, every six
	Gia	(19–27)	weeks.
	Kathryn	(21–24)	

The longitudinal language samples incorporate some of the experimental concerns of the large sample studies. The children are visited on a regular schedule at predetermined times for a predetermined amount of time. There are sometimes two visitors, one to take notes and one to interact with the child. All sessions are tape-recorded for later transcription.

There is one additional feature which separates these studies from the large sample ones. In the latter, sampling was often very short, up to the collection of 50 or 100 utterances (see Table 2.2). With longitudinal sampling, however, much larger samples are sought, so that a more representative sample of the child's general language ability is obtained.

Table 2.5 presents some general information on the four studies mentioned above. Braine (1963) used a method that is between the diary study and the collection of longitudinal samples as described. He asked the mothers of his three subjects, Andrew, Gregory, and Steven, to write down every unique two-word utterance they produced. This was done during the time when two-word utterances are not very common. Later, he initiated systematic tape-recording. The use of a parental diary combined with longitudinal sampling is a sensible technique which, interestingly enough, has not been used very frequently.

The studies of Miller & Ervin (1964), Brown (1973), and Bloom (1970) all involved systematic visits. Miller and Ervin started with short, frequent visits in the early months, then switched to longer, infrequent visits. The latter schedule is similar to the decision by Bloom. A six- to eight-week interval presumably allows the child to show considerable change. It misses, on the other hand, possible crucial periods of change which may occur over a day or two: such changes can only be captured by having a flexible schedule that allows emergency visits when alerted by the parent of changes.

These studies provided a database that is quite unlike that of the other two periods. We can understand this shift in the method when we examine the motivation for these studies. In 1961 there was a famous conference on first language acquisition in Dedham, Massachusetts. The papers from that meeting, including ones by Bloom and Miller & Ervin, were published in 1964, edited by Ursula Bellugi and Roger Brown. The editors say the following about this new wave of studies (p. 5):

> Quite recently, investigators in several parts of the United States have begun research on the acquisition of language as-it-is-described-by-linguistic-science. This new work is concerned, as the earlier work usually was not, with phonemes, derivational affixes, inflections, syntactic classes, immediate constituents, and grammatical trans-formations.

Many of the previous diary and large sample studies were not only descriptive, but often looked at only superficial issues, such as when particular features appeared in the child's speech. In these later studies researchers wanted to look for the emergence of rules, and to describe the developing grammar of the child. They wanted, for example, to go beyond dating the appearance of two-word utterances to writing rules of their structural properties.

The shift of interest in language acquisition toward rule-based descriptions of child language coincides with a paradigmatic change in linguistics stimulated by the publication of Noam Chomsky's *Syntactic structures* (1957). In that book, Chomsky redefined the goal of linguistics from one of description to one of explanation, with a theory of grammar which placed syntax at its center. This new field of transformational grammar stimulated research on syntax where previous linguistic research had concentrated more on phonemics and morphology. Chomsky defined grammar as a set of rules which generates the grammatical sentences of the language. In language acquisition, the goal became to establish how the child acquires rules of sentence formation. The primary focus of the Dedham meeting was the nature of the child's early grammar, and it was the primary interest of all of the investigators listed in Table 2.5.

It is of interest that Chomsky was invited to attend the Dedham conference as a discussant. His brief comments on the meeting (Chomsky

1964) remain an important comment on the field of language acquisition. In his discussion, Chomsky pointed out the important distinction between performance and competence, one elaborated upon in Chomsky (1965). The role of the linguist is to describe linguistic *competence*, that is, the underlying rule system that every native speaker of a language has. This rule system manifests itself in *performance*, i.e. when a speaker talks and listens to language. He states: 'It should be clearly recognized that a grammar is not a description of the performance of a speaker, but rather of his linguistic competence' (p. 35). Language samples, of course, are examples not only of performance, but of performance through speaking only. Because of this, Chomsky was highly critical of the use of only language samples for writing grammars for children.

It is important to look at some length at his comments on methodology. Here is a paragraph which sums up his general suggestions (p. 36):

> ... it seems to me that, if anything far-reaching and real is to be discovered about the actual grammar of the child, then rather devious kinds of observations of his performance, his abilities, and his comprehension in many different kinds of circumstances will have to be obtained, so that a variety of evidence may be brought to bear on the attempt to determine what is in fact his underlying linguistic competence at each stage of development. Direct description of the child's actual verbal output is no more likely to provide an account of the real underlying competence in the case of child language than in the case of adult language ... *not that one shouldn't start here* [emphasis mine: DI], perhaps, but one surely shouldn't end here ...

There are two central points made by Chomsky that need to be emphasized and which constitute central themes of the present book. One has to do with the kind of data used to make claims about the child's language. I emphasize the last remark about language sampling because I believe it is an important and necessary starting point. It is with this in mind that the above studies were conducted. Both Brown (1973) and Miller & Ervin (1964) talk about using other means of testing to supplement the language sample. One can start with language samples of various kinds to get an initial insight into some linguistic topic. Then, most likely, it will be necessary to switch to another procedure such as comprehension testing or elicited imitation. Unfortunately, this has not always been the practice. One reason is that it can take so long to transcribe data that the child has often changed its grammar by the time we return; this is a practical problem, though, that can be resolved by doing shorter initial transcriptions. Alternatively, we can use completed transcripts to get an initial idea of where to look, and then begin original elicitation that focusses on the issue being studied. As we will see in

Part II, there are a number of creative techniques that have been developed in recent years that go beyond language sampling.

The second point Chomsky makes in this extract concerns the difference between a child's competence and its performance. To what extent can we say that a child's performance, as reflected in a language sample, reflects a child's competence? If there is a tremendous difference, then child language research is left to study the performance factors that limit the child in speaking, such as memory, attention, processing time, etc. In this case, language acquisition is very much a branch of psychology. If they are close together, i.e. if we can determine a great deal about the child's competence or rules from its performance, then it is much more a branch of linguistics, in that we can talk about the form of the child's rules, the way they become more adult-like, etc. Chomsky is rather pessimistic on this point and thus, not surprisingly, has seen little that language acquisition can contribute to linguistic theory (see Ingram 1985a). In Chapter 4, however, we will argue that language acquisition can contribute to linguistics if we assume a closer relation between competence and performance. Throughout Part II, this will be demonstrated in the discussion of the acquisition of particular linguistic subsystems.

2.3.2 Theoretical orientation

It has already been mentioned that the studies of this period have been driven by an interest in the development of linguistic rules. The assumption that the child has systematic behavior, however, still leaves a great deal of latitude regarding the extent to which linguistic structure is learned and the extent to which it is innate. Here we give a simplified overview of the major theoretical positions that can be taken.

So far, we have considered briefly *behaviorism* which assigns very little internal structure to the child except general abilities such as the ability to form associations and be conditioned. In *Aspects of the Theory of Syntax* (1965) Chomsky expressed a completely different position, which we will refer to as *nativism*. In this view, language is seen as an extremely rich and complex system, certainly more than a series of associations between words that are linearly ordered. Language consists of hierarchical structure and at least two levels of representation, a deep or underlying structure (or D-structure, Chomsky 1981) that is mapped by transformations onto a surface structure (or S-structure). Universal principles of language apply to restrict what can be a possible grammar of any language. The collection of these universal principles which determine the form of any humanly possible language is referred to as *Universal Grammar* (UG). Nativism argues that these universal principles (or UG) are innate, that is, they are part of the genetic program the child is born with.

There are two major arguments put forth for this position. One follows from the fact that language is highly creative. We continually produce sentences that we have never heard before, and our grammar can potentially generate an infinite number of sentences. If the child learned language using rote learning and imitation, we could never account for the rate of acquisition that occurs. By a very young age, children are capable of producing a range of sentence structures that is nearly comparable to that of the adult. It is argued that this ability could not be attained without highly complex innate ability. Second, the language the child hears is 'degenerate' in the sense that it does not provide the child with the information necessary to acquire linguistic structure. Take, for example, the sentence 'Is the boy who left happy?' It consists, among other things, of a moved auxiliary 'is' that agrees in number with a noun phrase 'the boy', which in turn is modified by a relative clause 'who left'. There is nothing in the phonetic string of the sentence, [ɪzðəbɔɪhulɛfthæpi], that tells the child about the structure, or the nature of possible rules that move constituents. This kind of knowledge about the possible structure of the language is part of the child's Universal Grammar.

Another example of this can be given in reference to our earlier discussion of the acquisition of the meaning of the word 'doll' (cf. Table 2.4). Bloomfield proposed that the child learns this by pairing the vocalization of 'doll' in the context of the object doll. What stops the child from thinking 'doll' means 'a doll seated', or 'a pink thing', etc., in fact an almost infinite range of possibilities? There will need to be some innate limitations on what 'doll' could mean in that context, these being restrictions on possible relations between cognitive and semantic categories (cf. Jackendoff 1983).

Within nativism, we suggest that there are two possible positions, the *maturationist* vs. the *constructionist*. These two views have to do with the way in which the principles of Universal Grammar became available to the child. The maturationist view, which can be assigned to Chomsky, states that the principles are released or become available to the child at some genetically determined time. They could come quite early, like the ability to walk, or later, like puberty. The constructionist view, on the other hand, does not allow linguistic behavior to change due to maturation, but rather accounts for all changes by a building up of structure. What occurs later does not replace what occurred earlier, but rather builds upon it. The constructionist view, then, is a more restricted view of development in that it allows less change over time than a maturationist view. The point will be returned to in detail in Chapter 4.

The constructionist view has been most clearly articulated in psychology by Piaget (e.g. Piaget 1971). It focusses on the importance of determining sequential stages of development. Piaget (1971) has discussed the fact that his view is nativist, but emphasizes that it is nativism with a focus on development. For example, he states (p. 16): 'one still needs to explain in detail how, in the field of knowledge as in that of organic epigenesis, this collaboration between the genome and the environment actually works'. Much of the research on language acquisition done in this period seems to have a constructionist slant, although it is not always explicitly articulated.

The distinction between these two views can be used to isolate what appear to be two distinct fields of language acquisition that have evolved in the last decade or so. So far, we have used the terms 'child language' and 'language acquisition' interchangeably. Wasow (1983:191), however, has preferred the following distinction:

> There has been, for some years now, a fairly sharp split in the field of developmental psycholinguistics between what I will call researchers in 'child language' versus those in 'language acquisition'. Child language research is concerned primarily with what children say; that is, it focusses on the *data*. The central concern of most child language research is on data collection and classification, with correspondingly close attention to data collection *techniques*, and relatively little concern for abstract theoretical issues. Language acquisition specialists . . . regard child language data as interesting only to the extent that it bears on questions of linguistic theory.

Henceforth, I'll use this distinction by Wasow, and use capitals when doing so, i.e. Child Language vs. Language Acquisition.

It is now possible to characterize the theoretical approach of the longitudinal studies cited above. They can be called part of Child Language in that they focus on the data, and are concerned with data collection techniques. They also, however, have a theoretical orientation that tends to be constructionist, that is, they attempt to determine stages of acquisition that follow from the analysis of data. Wasow (1983) comments on this in a footnote (p. 91), stating that this kind of theorizing tends to be inductive, i.e. 'the hypotheses are generated from patterns observed in the corpora'. Wasow makes one further point about the theoretical work in Child Language. He states that its hypotheses are *local*, i.e. investigators 'posit strategies for dealing with particular phenomena at a specific stage of development, rarely attempting to relate to general issues in linguistic theory' (p. 191). For purposes of reference, I'll call those people who pursue Child Language in this fashion *psycholinguists*.

The field of Language Acquisition, on the other hand, starts with linguistic theory and then turns to questions of language acquisition. It considers language development in two ways. One, it views theories of adult language and isolates *predictions* those theories make about language acquisition. For example, a theory might say in one area that one construction or kind of rule is more basic or unmarked than another. This leads to a prediction that the child will acquire the unmarked case earlier than the marked case. For example, a theory might say that adjective + noun constructions like 'red apple' are more basic than relative clauses like 'the apple that's red'. The fact that children acquire adjective + noun constructions early can be said to be confirming data from acquisition. As currently articulated, however, Language Acquisition does not allow data from acquisition to disconfirm a linguistic theory. As an illustration, suppose that our theory states that relative clauses are less marked or simpler than adjective + noun constructions. The fact that adjective + noun constructions are acquired first does not disconfirm this, because one can always say that the principle which states that relative clauses are less marked has not matured yet. The maturationist view of Language Acquisition will always allow one to reject acquisition data as counterevidence. In Chapter 4 I will argue for a constructionist view that will allow us to use acquisition data as counterevidence.

The second way in which Language Acquisition discusses acquisition is in its consideration of the logical problem of *learnability*. Again, we begin with theories of grammar and concern about how we may restrict them. This approach may be demonstrated by looking at the sentences below (2.2a–d). The (d) sentence has an asterisk in front of it because it is ungrammatical in English.

(2.2) a. I gave a book to Mary
     b. I gave Mary a book
     c. I reported the crime to the police
     d. * I reported the police the crime

We can propose a theory that says there is a rule of English called Dative which moves an indirect object next to the verb, producing a sentence like (2.2b). Dative has not applied in sentences (2.2a) and (2.2c). We need to restrict the Dative rule so that it does not apply in (2.2d). To do this, we can mark the verb 'report' as an exception to our Dative.

This is a possible analysis for these English sentences. The problem, however, is this. How does the child ever learn that (2.2d) is an ungrammatical sentence? The child cannot learn it from *positive evidence*, i.e. the sentences that it hears, because it will only hear sentences like (2.2a–c). These three provide the child with the evidence for the rule. The next possibility is that the child learns it from *direct negative evidence*, i.e. the parent corrects the child. This was, in fact, the proposal discussed earlier by Bloomfield. There is, however, no evidence that this occurs, and Braine

(1971a) has produced several arguments against it: (i) transcripts like those collected by the studies in Table 2.5 indicate that parents correct mostly for semantic appropriateness, not grammaticality; (ii) even if we did correct the child, how does the child know in some cases what was wrong? Also (iii) transcripts studied to date indicate that children seem to be oblivious to corrections when they are made (see also Zwicky 1970). Below is an example of the last point from Braine (1971a: 161):

Child: Want other one spoon, Daddy.
Father: You mean, you want THE OTHER SPOON
Child: Yes, I want other one spoon, please, Daddy.
Father: Can you say 'the other spoon'?
Child: Other ... one ... spoon.
Father: Say ... 'other'.
Child: Other
Father: Spoon
Child: Spoon
Father: Other ... spoon
Child: Other ... spoon. Now give me the other one spoon.

The third possibility is that the child may learn that (2.2d) is ungrammatical by what is called *indirect negative evidence*. This is knowledge that is obtained by noting that something has never occurred. For example, the child would need to calculate the number of times it had heard sentences like (2.2a–c) and decide that (2.2d) must be ungrammatical because it has never been heard. This seems an implausible possibility because it would require the child to do a tremendous amount of calculating. Further, it goes contrary to the creative dimension of the grammar where the child is predicted to generate new utterances never heard.

Baker (1979) has proposed that we only consider linguistic analyses that are learnable from positive evidence. If so, then our Dative analysis is unlearnable and therefore rejected. The analysis he proposes in its place is one in which the child must learn the structure underlying (2.2a) and (2.2b) separately, and not relate them by rule.

The issue of learnability, as formulated and used in Language Acquisition, does not require looking at acquisition data. We return to this in Chapter 4, however, and show the relevance of acquisition data in Language Acquisition, reconciling the two divergent enterprises identified by Wasow within a field we can call Child Language Acquisition.

Further reading

Bibliographies

The first bibliography on language acquisition was that of Wilson (1898) which covers much of the period of diary studies. The next is that of Leopold (1952). This is a very useful reference source which gives brief descriptions of many of the studies. For example, on Taine (1877), he states (p. 94): 'The famous philosopher's observations of his two children . . . originality of the child emphasized too much . . .'; and on Chamberlain & Chamberlain (1904, 1905, 1909): 'interesting case study of daughter to 3;11, mostly third year. Careful observers; selected observations, not systematic, but thorough. "Phonetic" transcription unsatisfactory, but improves somewhat as the study progresses' (p. 15). Slobin (1972) is an updating of Leopold's bibliography. Slobin deletes Leopold's brief descriptions, and also some of the earlier references. It is important, therefore, to double-check Leopold (1952) with regard to the earlier literature. Besides adding new references, Slobin also provides appendices specifically on non-English studies. He also provides three valuable indices: 1, according to language spoken by child (44 language groupings are given); 2, according to content of reference (e.g. babbling, phonology, syntax); and 3, content of reference according to language spoken by child, that is, cross-listing the first two. The most recent bibliography is Abrahamsen (1977). Abrahamsen has selected over 1500 entries in the literature that she felt were relevant to child language research as of 1977. The organization is topical, with the main divisions as follows: I: general resources; II: syntactic development; III: semantic development; IV: grammar; and V: phonology and orthography. All references are for English (so that Slobin 1972 remains the primary reference for non-English studies) and the studies thought to be most important are set apart with asterisks.

Readers

There are currently three books of selected readings. Bar-Adon & Leopold (1971), Ferguson & Slobin (1973), and Bloom (1978). Bar-Adon & Leopold is the richest for selections from early researchers. It contains a selection from Taine (1877) and Darwin (1877) as well as items from other diary works. Ferguson & Slobin concentrate on non-English studies and provide the only translations available for some of these, particularly for some important ones in Russian. Bloom (1978) concentrates on recent work in English although there are selections from the work of M. Smith (e.g. Smith 1933).

Suggested reading

A feel for the nature of the research done during each of these three periods can be obtained by reading a sampling of each. A minimum introduction would be the following: Taine (1877), Templin (1957:3–18) 'I: Introduction, II: The experiment', Brown (1973:51–9) 'The study of Adam, Eve, and Sarah'. The earliest form of the behaviorist view can be found in Bloomfield (1933:28–37). Bar-Adon & Leopold's book (1971) *Child language. A book of readings* contains selections from several early works; each selection is preceded by a brief explanation which helps to set the work in its place in history.

3 Stages of language acquisition

The word 'stage' is possibly the most used term in language acquisition. The literature is rich with its use, and an article or book rarely comes along without its appearance. Unfortunately, few people attempt to define the way in which they are using it. In one respect this is understandable. Unlike other technical terms, stage is part of our everyday vocabulary, and we have grown up using it. It is easy to use it with the misleading assumption that our hearer understands the word in the same way that we do.

In a scientific enterprise such as language acquisition, however, we need to be careful to define what requirements we set in order for a stage to be proposed. As will be shown, there are various ways in which the term can be used, each with different implications. We need to define 'stage' in order to describe the facts of child language, and these facts are a necessary data base for the explanation of different stages. Careful analysis of the use of 'stage' is crucial to the constructionist view, since we ultimately want to use stages of acquisition as evidence for a theory of language acquisition.

This chapter will discuss 'stage' by first looking into some of the ways in which it can be used. Next, it will provide a general review of the stages of acquisition that have been put forward in the literature. Lastly, it will return to 'stage' and define it in two ways, distinguishing between *descriptive* and *explanatory* stages of acquisition.

3.1 Some possible meanings of 'stage'

We will see throughout the Child Language literature a multiplicity of uses of 'stage'. This section discusses just a few ways in which it may appear, with the goal of raising our consciousness about this word. In reading research, it will usually be up to the reader to determine any particular author's use of the term, since it is rarely defined. Later in this volume more precise definitions for its use will be developed.

3.1.1 Single behaviors

One way in which we may use 'stage', and probably the simplest, is in the sense of a point on a continuum. This will be referred to as the *continuity* requirement for the use of 'stage'. A continuous stage is one where a single dimension of behavior is being observed, and the difference between stages is only between the points along the continuum that are being selected for observation. We can provide simple examples from time and space. For time, we can say a child is at the '2-year stage' or '3-year stage' where the only change being described is one of changing time. Sometimes we see that these labels say little more than that there is a difference. Or, during one's work day, we can say we are at the 'noon' stage, or the '4:53 pm' stage. Spatially, children can be placed at different stages based on their height: we can say, for example, that a child is at the '2 foot' stage, or the '3 foot' stage.

The continuity stage can also be proposed for the measurement of some behavior that is either on the increase or decrease. We can look at both non-linguistic and linguistic behaviors. Suppose, for example, that a child's use of thumb-sucking increases from 20 percent at age 0;2 to 50 percent at 0;4. We could decide that 20 percent is not much thumb-sucking, but that 50 percent is a lot. Then we conclude that the child was not at the thumb-sucking stage at 0;2, but is at the thumb-sucking stage at 0;4. Notice that this claim does not sound as bad as our earlier '4:53 pm' stage of working, but it really does not claim much more: it only focusses at some point on a continuum. A linguistic example can be given in relation to single-word usage by young children. Suppose that a child at 1;0 uses one-word utterances such as 'mama' or 'bye-bye' as 100 percent of its meaningful vocalizations. At 1;6 the child may use one-word utterances as 70 percent of its meaningful vocalizations, since it is also now using two-word utterances. We could conclude that the child at 1;0 is at the 'one-word' stage, but the child at 1;6 is not. This use of stage is only based on continuity; as might be anticipated, we would suggest that it does not tell us much about the child's organization.

A second use of 'stage' is one where we build upon the continuity requirement and add a new requirement that the continuity has been halted. We will refer to this as the *plateau* requirement. Let us first examine some obvious examples, and then some less obvious ones. We can look at death as a stage of this sort. For example, we can say that someone who has died is in his 'death' stage. A behavior that was under change, i.e. life activity, has been halted, in this case permanently. Or, we can look at someone's growth which has now ceased, where the person will remain at a certain height, say 5 feet 6 inches. We could then say that she is at the '5 foot 6 inch' stage, meaning she will not change any more. There are less obvious linguistic examples where we can use stage in this sense. For one, we could describe a child who is severely retarded, and whose language is permanently arrested at a point where only one-word utterances are used. We could say that the child is at the 'one-word' stage where 'stage' refers to a behavior that is permanently halted at a point on the continuum. Another linguistic example, which is common, is to use 'stage' to refer to the attainment of the adult behavior on some linguistic feature, such as the use of relative clauses. This use of 'stage' sounds insightful, but does not say much more than does the continuity requirement above.

A third use of 'stage', one that approaches common use, is to add a third restriction to the two already mentioned, i.e. a *transition* requirement. The transition requirement restricts 'stage' to cases where the behavior that has plateaued is expected to change again at some later time. A child who is at the thumb-sucking stage under this use is a child who has reached some maximal use of thumb sucking, and will continue on for some time until it drops. A drop in rate, of course, is not the only direction in which the change may occur, although it is the most common use. We could have a plateau, and then an increase. It is common in learning a new skill, for example, that there is an increase in ability, followed by a plateau, followed by an increase. The period of the plateau can be referred to as a stage. In learning to juggle, we may eventually move on to four balls, but our ability is limited to three balls for the time being. A linguistic example would be the mean length of the child's utterances. We might find that the child's utterances have been increasing steadily, but that for several weeks their mean length has been constant, say around three words per utterance. We could then say the child is at the 'three-word' stage, meaning that there is a temporary halt at this point.

Our third definition of 'stage' is a static one, in that it describes a time when no change has occurred. We can shift this perspective, and instead limit 'stage' to a point where there is active change. In learning, there are occasions when the changes that occur seem more rapid than others. In physical growth, these are those periods when the child is said to be 'shooting up'; in language, these are those periods when the child seems to have made a breakthrough and makes rapid progress. In these changes, there is a sudden increase in use that then remains constant. This can be captured by adding an *acceleration* requirement. A 'stage', then, is a period of rapid acceleration in the development of a linguistic ability that will end in a plateau, i.e. a steady rate of use (possibly final acquisition) afterwards. A linguistic example is the way children acquire words in production. At first there is a slow period of growth from around 1;0 to 1;6, and then a rapid

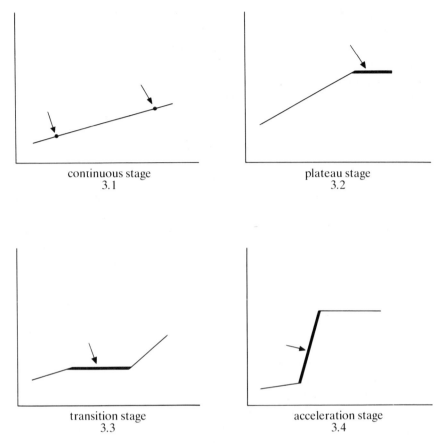

Figures 3.1–3.4   Graphic representations of four definitions of stage over one behavior, where the vertical axis measures rate and the horizontal axis measures time. Arrows indicate the stages.

spurt in the size of the child's vocabulary. We could refer to this spurt as a stage of acquisition. Figures 3.1–4 show each of these possible uses of 'stage' in terms of how they would appear upon measurement.

3.1.2 Multiple behaviors

These four kinds of 'stages' all refer to a single behavior. We may, of course, wish to stop here, and say that stages can only be proposed for single behaviors, and that we do not wish to relate behaviors to each other, i.e. we may not wish to countenance general stages of development. In developmental psychology, for example, Jean Piaget has suggested the Sensorimotor Period from birth to around age 2 years as consisting of six general stages. Each stage consists of a cluster of behaviors that are related by general principles. Uzgiris & Hunt (1975), however, have argued against these general stages, and say that we can only discuss stages of specific behaviors such as imitation or knowledge of the spatial relations of objects. In language, we could reject the idea of general stages of acquisition and concentrate on the stages of specific topics, like the stages of acquiring the meaning of 'cat', or the stages in learning how to pronounce a sound like /t/.

It is common, however, to see researchers go beyond single behaviors and to use 'stage' to refer to the relations between behaviors. The simplest relation that can hold would be where one behavior has succeeded another. Let us call this a *succession* requirement and such a stage a 'succession stage'. Imagine someone who likes to dabble in crafts and spends one year doing painting, and the next year doing pottery. He has gone through two such stages, a 'painting stage' and a 'pottery stage'. Or, there are certain reflexes that infants show for a short time and then lose: these could each be considered a stage. In language acquisition there is a period of time where children will overextend the meanings of their words, for example calling all four-legged animals 'dog'; it lasts from around 1;6 to 2;6. This behavior could be isolated and referred to as the 'overextension stage'.

While some behaviors may drop out, many appear for a first time, develop over time, and stay in the child's repertoire of behaviors. We can then add a *co-occurrence* requirement, i.e. a requirement that a stage is defined as the point at which at least two behaviors exist together. For example, there is a time from around 1;0 to 2;0 when children use single-word utterances such as 'mama'. From 1;6 to 2;0 these occur along with some usage of two-word combinations such as 'see mama', 'my cookie', etc. We can talk about a 'two-word stage' as the period when one- and two-word utterances co-occur. This kind of stage can be called a 'co-occurrence stage'. The name of each stage can be assigned by labeling it according to the dominant or new behavior that appears. In the above example, the label 'two-word stage' is taken from the new behavior. Suppose that one-word utterances are dominant (i.e. more frequent) from 1;6 to 1;9, and that two-word utterances are dominant from 1;9 to 2;0. If we used the dominant behavior as the label, then only the latter time period would be called the 'two-word stage'.

There are two further kinds of use of 'stage' that can be distinguished. We will add a third requirement to succession and co-occurrence, which we will call the *principle* requirement. This requirement states that a stage only exists if we propose a principle that accounts for the co-occurrence of the behaviors. For example, children walk and pronounce their first words around the same time. It is not likely, however, that we would want to refer to these two as a stage, since there seems to be no causal relation between

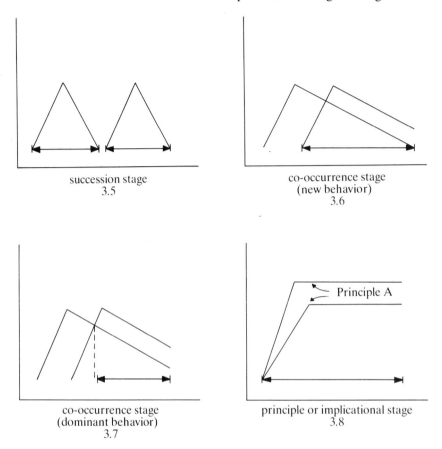

Figures 3.5–3.8 Graphic representations of four definitions of stage that relate two or more behaviors, where the vertical axis measures rate and the horizontal axis measures time. Arrows indicate the stages.

them, that is, their co-occurrence is *correlational*. Other behaviors may look similar enough that we may propose a principle to relate them.

The addition of the principle requirement leads to two further kinds of stage. One kind is what we shall call an 'implicational stage'. This stage occurs when the principle we propose to relate behaviors is such that the occurrence of one behavior necessarily implies the occurrence of the other. For example, we could propose that children acquire general phonological features before more specific ones. This claim implies by logical necessity that the stage in which the child acquires the difference between /p/ and /t/ will follow the stage in which children distinguish between /p/ and /l/ (assuming that class features like [± sonorant] are more general than place features like [± alveolar]).

The second is what we shall call a 'principle stage'. This occurs when the behaviors being explained are such that one does not by necessity imply the other. For example, children appear to begin to play symbolically with objects, as in pretending that a block of wood is a car, around the same time that they begin to acquire language (see Part II, Chapter 6). Piaget has proposed that these two behaviors are related by a general principle which is that the child has developed the symbolic function. This could be referred to as the 'symbolic stage' of development. The stage would be named for the principle that underlies the behaviors. Figures 3.5–3.8 present a graphic representation of these possible definitions of stage.

As hopefully is obvious by now, there is a multiplicity of ways in which 'stage' can be used. The student of language acquisition will probably find all the above uses and more when reading works in the field. The above discussion was provided to present the difficulties with the term. Section 3.2 will provide an overview of the better-known attempts to describe stages of language acquisition, and section 3.3 will attempt to limit our use of the term in future work.

3.2 Some proposals on stages of acquisition

There are numerous proposals for stages of acquisition in the Child Language literature. Here we will select just three, one from each of the periods described in Chapter 3, to give an idea how they have developed over time. As can be seen, they tend to focus on characteristics of grammatical development. This section provides an overview to the more detailed treatment in Part II.

3.2.1 Stern (1924)

Stern & Stern (1907) is generally considered to be the first real classic in child language. Oksaar (1983:8), for example, states: 'Child language research done by psychologists reached its climax with the work of Stern & Stern (1907). It initiated modern paedolinguistics.' Though their book *Kindersprache* was never translated into English, Stern (1924) provides a comprehensive statement of their view of the major stages of language acquisition. Table 3.1 gives an overview of these. Stern varies between the terms 'stage' and 'period'. He sees development as scanning five time periods. One he calls a Preliminary stage, the other four he calls periods and numbers them 1 to 4. He starts his periods of acquisition at 1;0, with the onset of the first word, because he feels that speech really begins 'from the moment in which the child, for the first time, utters a sound with full consciousness of its meaning and for the purpose of communication' (p. 143).

Table 3.1 *Summary of Stern's (1924) Preliminary stage and four periods of language acquisition*

Preliminary stage (first year) This stage consists of three behaviors: (i) babbling, (ii) unintelligible imitation, (iii) preliminary understanding.

First period (1;0–1;6) The child acquires a small number of sounds with special meanings, which express the ideas of an entire sentence. There is, however, no evidence that the child understands grammar.

Second period (1;6–2;0) The child realizes that everything has a name, with: (i) a subsequent spurt in word acquisition, (ii) questions about the names of things. Soon after, the first multi-word utterances appear, first hesitantly, then more fluently.
There are three stages of vocabulary growth:
(a) substance – increase in nouns;
(b) action – increase in verbs;
(c) relation and distinction – increase in qualifying and relational words.

Third period (2;0–2;6) Sentences become well-formed in that they contain words for the major grammatical relations, like 'subject and object'. The acquisition of inflections begins, and may last for years. Syntax consists of the loose linking of words together where word order may vary. The range of questions expands.

Fourth period (2;6 on) The simple juxtaposition of words in syntax is replaced by hierarchical structure and the acquisition of embedded or subordinate sentences. The acquisition of some grammatical morphemes still continues. The child's questions now include those of time and causality.

While there is no language during the first year, Stern sees it as an important precursor for later acquisition. There are three major activities during this year: babbling, imitation or 'echo babbling', and rudimentary understanding. At first, these three are independent of one another, but gradually merge together. When they do, around 1;0, real language begins. We can see this stage as one of the co-occurrence of these three behaviors, where the conclusion is marked by their coordination.

Babbling occurs because the child is innately disposed or programmed to babble. Stern does not use these exact words, but talks about 'impulses' and 'inner energies'. There are two inner drives behind babbling, one the drive to express oneself, and the other the drive to socialize with others. The drive to express oneself leads to practice which is necessary for later facility with words. It also allows the child to establish associations 'between certain states of feeling and the sound-forms belonging to them' (p. 143). The child's imitations or 'echo babbles' are also the result of an 'impulse' or innate disposition. This activity also allows the child to practice speech. Rudimentary understanding refers to the child's responses to certain utterances such as the clapping to 'pat-a-cake' or waving 'bye-bye'. These acts do not show understanding of the structure of language, but only an association of a sound or set of sounds with certain actions and contexts. Stern is very explicit in his belief that the beginning of language is with the first words produced, not with comprehension: 'This first understanding of speech has at first nothing to do with an intellectual grasp of the logical significance of words, in fact months pass before this stage is reached' (p. 143, fn. 4).

The *first period* begins when the child consciously produces a word with meaning, around 1;0. For this stage to begin, then, active production is required. The main behavior of this period is the slow growth of *one-word sentences*. Stern emphasizes the gradualness of the development of the child's productive vocabulary, and defines the end of the period by a spurt in vocabulary usage (p. 145):

> The child's power of speech, however, after it has begun, does not then increase at equal speed from day to day ... Periods of stagnation ... are suddenly replaced by periods of rapid development, to be followed in their turn by very slow development.

As an example, he cites Axel Preyer who only acquired two words in his production, 'atta' and 'ta' over six months. This stage can be seen as a 'transition stage' (Figure 3.3) between no words and rapid development.

The selection of words during this period is not random, but is determined by several factors. First, many words used around the child are beyond its current cognitive level of understanding. They are more likely to come within its understanding if they consist of sounds that are part of the child's babbling repertoire. There is thus the influence of the child's articulation capabilities. Secondly, the words selected tend to be onomatopoeic, that is, phonetically similar to the sound of things, e.g. 'moo-moo', 'meow', etc. Stern addresses the interplay of the words presented to the child by its environment and the desire of the child to express inner needs and ideas with its own phonetic repertoire. He denies the exclusive operation of either factor and introduces the notion of *convergence*:

> Here again our idea of 'convergence' must come to our aid. Early speech is the combined result of aptitudes and speech impulses, inherent in the child's nature, and of stimulus offered for his imitation from without. It seldom occurs that a child quite independently raises a descriptive sound or a natural sound-expression to a real designation in speech, for he cannot, as a rule, reach such a stage because his environment deprives him of any opportunity, by offering him ready-made expressions (*wow-wow*, etc.).   (p. 149)

He allows the child, however, to be quite creative with its first words. For example, his son Gunter at 1;5 used 'fff' to refer to all lights and lamps, presumably the result of the imitation of blowing them out.

Stern presents a common view of the time when he calls the one-word utterances of this first period *one-word sentences*. These utterances have certain properties: (a) they convey more than just a word – they convey a whole idea; (b) one word may be used to express several ideas, e.g. 'mama' may mean 'mother, come here', 'mother, give me', or 'mother, set me on the chair' (p. 151); (c) they do not have grammatical structure; (d) they are not purely statements of propositions but are the inseparable union of the expression of a concept and the child's internal needs; (e) they are not members of classes such as specific nominals (e.g. 'mama' for one's mother) or general nominals (e.g. 'dog' for all dogs), because the child is not yet cognitively able to generalize from its experiences; and thus, (f) their use is determined in large part by associative reactions to some present experience. While he uses the term 'sentence', Stern nonetheless denies the existence of any grammatical structure. This point is in agreement with others who studied language acquisition during this historical period, e.g. Jespersen (1922).

The first period ends and the second begins with the child's rapid development of vocabulary. In the *second period*, vocabulary growth goes through an 'acceleration stage' (Figure 3.4). Around the same time, another behavior occurs, an interest in learning the names of things by asking for names with a question like 'that?' (p. 164). Sometimes these two events may occur together as they did with his daughter Hilde around 1;6, or they may occur quite separately. His son Gunther asked for the names of things around 1;7 but took several more months before his word spurt. At first glance this appears to be just a co-occurrence stage (Figure 3.6), but Stern wants to go further than this. He offers a principle to relate these two; the child has realized that 'every thing has a name'. He does not label this principle, so let us call it the *Principle of the Linguistic Sign*, i.e. the realization that phonetic events can be paired in a conventional way with concepts. The rapid acquisition of vocabulary and the desire to seek names are both the result of this underlying principle.

One feature of this principle is that it is an 'awakening' in Stern's terminology. This suggests that it is an internal ability that has been triggered by the previous experience of the earlier first period which was presented as a transition stage. The child goes beyond the limits of its earlier associative links between sounds and real-world events.

> The insight into the relation between sign and import which the child gains here is something fundamentally different from the simple dealing with perceptions and their associations. And the demand that some name must belong to every object, whatever its nature, we may consider as a real – perhaps the child's first – general thought.

> (p. 165)

Another feature of the period is that the word spurt may occur *first* in comprehension, only later to be evidenced in production. Recall that Gunther asked for the names of things several months before his productive word spurt. Presumably his receptive vocabulary was increasing greatly during this time, although Stern does not say much about it.

Stern goes on to analyze the nature or categorization of the vocabulary developed during this period and beyond. He proposes three stages:

(a)   substance stage
(b)   action stage
(c)   relation and attribute stage

Since he did not attribute classes of this type to the first period (at least not in their adult form), we can presume that the Principle of the Linguistic Sign also contains some guidelines on how to classify. These three stages appear to be 'co-occurrence stages' (Figure 3.6) focussing on new behaviors that enter the child's language. In the substantive stage, most of the words are referring to nominals, i.e. the names of things. Later, in the action stage, terms for actions enter the vocabulary and grow. These are a new behavior that co-occur with the nominals. Unfortunately, Stern does not give us much information on how the stages progress, or what principle or principles determine them. Nor does he tell us how to classify words into these categories – a potential problem, given the holistic meaning of the child's utterances.

The above developments all refer to vocabulary. A second major characteristic of the second period is the onset of multiword utterances. Although he is not very explicit, Stern appears to want to separate these from the milestones in vocabulary, i.e. the vocabulary spurt and the onset of multiword utterances co-occur, but they are not caused by the same principle. The latter appears to occur later than the former, so that we could interpret from this sequence that the Principle of the Linguistic Sign is a necessary, but not sufficient, cause of multiword speech. Since they bear this relation, we can do one of two things, either treat the two separately, so that the vocabulary is in the second period, when the syntax (i.e. one-word sentences) is still in the first, or treat them as both in the same period, but define the second period as one composed of two principles, the Principle of the Linguistic Sign followed by the principle that leads to early word combinations. We will assume that Stern takes the latter course, although this is not obvious from his writing.

We can look at the cause of the early multiword combinations and their structural properties, but as for the cause, again we have to search a bit for Stern's position. Three potential causes can be located. One is that the child's cognitive advances are so great that the child needs more language structure: 'The general cause of all this working-up is a certain "language famine". For normally the wealth of experiences and the need of expression grows far more quickly than the supply of forms of words . . .' (p. 161). That is, the child's needs to express itself lead it to seek or develop new, more complex expression. Another possible cause could be the child's comprehension, which is in advance of production. Stern comments that his children understood multiword utterances during the last months of producing one-word sentences. For example, Hilde at 1;4 showed understanding of 'Touch your nose with your foot' one month before her first multiword utterances in production. The third possible cause is the child's growing imitative ability. Stern distinguishes between *direct imitation*, which comes immediately after hearing, and *indirect imitation*, which is delayed or internal. He states (p. 155): 'with increasing age direct imitation . . . falls more and more into the background and leaves indirect imitation to do most of the work'. If these three aspects come to be coordinated, as the three factors at the end of Stern's preliminary stage, then we can say that their interaction leads to early multiword speech.

Stern is very reluctant to give these first multiword utterances any structure. Rather, he sees them as loosely juxtaposed, initially in the form of successive one-word sentences:

> It is true that these word collections were not all so fluently spoken as are our sentences; their characteristic rather was a jerky utterance (often interspersed by pauses) of the isolated words; in such a case it is really more a question of a short chain of one-word sentences as: Hilde – cocaa (come Hilde, the cocoa is here), ater – dolly (Father look, I have a dolly). It is only by degrees that such loose juxtapositions pass into the firm union of a really coherent sentence.   (p. 166)

Stern has little specific to propose on the structure of these non-syntactic combinations, except that they are somewhat limited in their creativity. For example, he states at one point: 'For a year the words the child uses are fixed forms only' (p. 168).

The first major gains in syntax occur in the *third period* around 2;0. There are two major grammatical changes: (i) the onset of the acquisition of inflections, and (ii) the combination of words by syntactic rules, not just juxtaposition. He does not cite a specific cause, but implies it is a principle that leads the child to syntax: 'The two-year-old child begins to acquire all this in the different forms of inflection (declension, conjugation, comparison) fairly simultaneously, so that, in reality, we are dealing with united psychic progress along the whole line' (p. 168). Let us call this the *Principle of Syntactic Structure*, one which directs the child to formulate rules of sentence structure within the restrictions of Universal Grammar and some theory of acquisition. The fact that Stern believes the source of this principle is internal is clear from the following remarks:

> Now, it can be readily understood that, in spite of great individual differences in speech-development, *certain regularities in the sequence of speech-capabilities* are to be found in the child, for general laws of mental growth are at work here, and it is the consequence of these that every phase acquires the necessary supply of words and phrases . . . Since many of these laws act more or less independently of the kind of speech that influences the child or of any other conditions of environment, it is evident how strong must be the part played by the inner faculty and its gradual growth in the development of the child's speech.
>
> (p. 158)

Despite these innate abilities, the child's development is still quite slow. It takes children several years to complete the acquisition of inflections. Also, the increase in sentence length with greater productivity around age 2–3 years still goes through a great deal of non-fluent production. He gives the following sequence from Hilde (1;10) as a request for her mother to go get some pickles (p. 169):

(3.1) Mama. Want pickies. Room. Wanty pickies. Back. Dada, mama fetch.

Also, the child will move certain words to the sentence-initial or final position in order to give them prominence. Regarding inflectional development, there is just one mechanism that is proposed to account for the child's development, the ability to use *analogy*. This mechanism shows up in other discussions around this time, as in Jespersen (1922). The child will notice the regular inflections and apply them to irregular forms, e.g. 'drinked' for 'drunk' or 'badder' for 'worse'. There is no discussion of how the child unlearns these, or of how the child's syntactic rules change over time. Given the lack of a major syntactic theory at the time, however, this is not surprising.

Stern's *fourth period* starts from around 2;6. It is marked by three changes. The first is the appearance of subordinate sentences. At first, the complementizers, relative pronouns, and adverbials that mark the subordinate clause may be absent. For example, at 2;6 Gunter said the sentence in (3.2a) with the meaning of (3.2b) (as translated from German):

(3.2) a. Mother say, builded has Gunter
       b. I want to tell mother what Gunter has been building

At 3;0 Hilde used each of the sentences in (3.3), again translated from German (p. 171):

(3.3) a. *indirect question*   I will look in the kitchen and ask if she is coming here

b. *temporal clause*   Will whip the doll till it hurts her

c. *causal clause*   That moves so today because it is broken

d. *conditional clause*   You'll get no bread and butter if you're so naughty

e. *final clause*   You must take away the beds so that I can get out

f. *consecutive clause*   Dolly has disturbed me, so that I could not sleep

While these may appear around 2;6, their acquisition will vary from type to type and may take up to 5;0 to be acquired. For example, he cites hypothetical conditional clauses as quite late. He gives the following example (p. 171) from Gunter, which was used at 4;8 in reference to a friend who had an operation: 'If he were (not) cut at once, then he had died.'

Stern, as earlier, does not discuss the principle behind this, nor its relation to the earlier syntactic development of the third period. Since it is given as a separate account, we will assume it is a separate principle, and shall call it the *Principle of Subordination*. Further, we will assume that the Principle of Syntactic Structure is a necessary precursor. In this sense, Stern's fourth period is a 'co-occurrence stage' labeled for the new behavior that has appeared (Figure 3.6).

A second and apparently independent change of the fourth period concerns the use of questions. Up until now, the child has asked concrete questions like 'what?' and 'where?'. Now, the child begins to use the more abstract questions of 'why?' and 'when?'. These early 'why' questions can be quite persistent, as is evidenced by the following dialogue between Hilde and her mother at 3;7 (p. 172):

(3.4)

Child: What is he eating?
Mother: Fish.
Child: Why does he eat fish?
Mother: Because he is hungry.
Child: Why doesn't he eat rolls?
Mother: Because we don't give him any.
Child: Why don't we give him any?
Mother: Because bakers only make rolls for people.
Child: Why not for fishes?
Mother: Because they haven't enough flour.
Child: Why then haven't they enough?
Mother: Because not enough corn is grown.

Table 3.2 *A summary of the major characteristics of Nice's (1925) stages of acquisition*

---

1. *Single word stage*   The child uses single-word utterances.

2. *Early sentence stage*   (1;5.5 at onset). The first multiword utterances appear, although single-word utterances are still most frequent utterances at onset. Most sentences are incomplete, and consist of mostly nouns, verbs, adjectives, and adverbs.

3. *Short sentence stage*   (commonly around age 3;0). The acquisition of inflections and grammatical words begins. The ALS ranges from 3.5 to 4.5. Incomplete sentences become less frequent, yet compound and complex sentences are rare. The ratio between word classes becomes stable.

4. *Transition stage*   A period of change where the child moves from incomplete to complete sentences. The ALS is around 5.0. Little is known about this stage.

5. *Complete sentence stage*   (around age 4;0). Most sentences are well-formed, and complex and compound sentences become more common.

This change is apparently a separate co-occurring behavior in the area of cognition that is not related to the onset of subordinate clauses by any unifying principle.

A third major behavior that appears in this stage is the creative construction of new words by the child. Stern emphasizes that this varies greatly from child to child, with some hardly doing it at all. German is known for its extensive use of compounds, and Stern found his children each creating 40–50 of their own by age 5 years. Some examples of these compounds from his children, as translated, are given in (3.5):

(3.5) a. fire box   [a fireproof casserole over a stove]
      b. child-soldier [an officer who looked short]
      c. grey-red   [in reference to a color]
      d. muffiner   [someone who sells muffins]
      e. the smoke   [a cigar]
      f. raggy   [torn]
      g. splashiness   [result of splashing water]

Stern does not discuss the principle behind these changes either. We can isolate it as separate one from those discussed earlier and for reference purposes call it the *Principle of Derivational Morphology*.

Stern's stages capture behavioral milestones that are described by other diarists during this historical period. There are some attempts to relate these behaviors to each other through the proposal of unifying principles, although this is not done consistently. Some behaviors are related and others simply co-occur.

Table 3.3 *The basic measures used by Nice (1925) for five stages of language acquisition*

Measures	Stages				
	1	2	3	4	5
Average Length of Sentence (words)	1.00		3.5–3.5	5.0	
Number of subjects					
(a) English speaking	18	20	13	2	15
(b) non-English speaking	17	20			
Range of duration (in months)					
(a) English speaking	4–9	4–7			
(b) non-English speaking	4–12				
Average duration (in months)					
(a) English speaking	6				
(b) non-English speaking	6.6				
Range of ages at onset (in months)					
(a) English speaking		13–27			
(b) non-English speaking		12–23			
Average age at onset					
(a) English speaking		17.5 mos	3 yrs		4 yrs
(b) non-English speaking		18.3 mos			
Vocabulary size at time of first utterances		14–180	475–1135		
Proportion of incomplete sentences	1.00	below 0.6	0.2–0.6		below 0.2
Proportion of vocabulary					
(a) nouns		0.65+	0.5–0.6		
(b) verbs			0.2–0.24		
Proportion of complex sentences			very low	more	adult-like

3.2.2 Nice (1925)

In 1925 Margaret Nice introduced the measure of the Average Length of Sentence (ALS) as a means for dividing acquisition into stages. The ALS is the mean number of words used by the child in its spontaneous language. Nice wanted to build upon the traditional approach to stages, as exemplified by Stern, by adding a quantified measure to them. She also added a name to each stage, typically that for the new behavior which occurs (see figure 3.6). Table 3.2 provides a summary of Nice's stages.

Nice's stages are typical of the kind of work done during the period of large sample studies. Instead of intensively studying one or two children as Stern did, she seeks data from several children. The work is by and large descriptive, with virtually no attempt at hypothesizing general principles.

Further, there is the emphasis on the development of measures of superficial linguistic behaviors. Table 3.3 gives a listing of the measures reported for the five stages; they are not consistently given for each, but are randomly presented.

There is nothing given us on Nice's *single word stage* except figures on its average duration. For both English and non-English children, it lasts around six months. This stage is comparable to Stern's first period, which begins around the end of the first year of life.

The second stage, the *early sentence stage*, looks similar to Stern's second period. Nice states that it normally starts around 1;6. At the onset, the child uses mostly single-word utterances even though multiword utterances are appearing. For example, a 1042–utterance sample of Nice's fourth child, H, at 2;0 revealed an ALS of 1.35, consisting of 683 single-word utterances, 352 two-word utterances, and only seven three-word utterances. The size of the child's vocabulary may vary greatly at the time of the onset of the first multiword utterances. For the 19 children she sampled, the range of vocabulary at the start of this stage went from as low as 14 to as high as 180. This range is interesting because it is suggestive of a very loose relation between the word spurt and the onset of multiword utterances. Recall in our review of Stern that we suggested different principles behind each. Nice has less data on the typical duration of this stage, but states the lengths for three of her children as three, seven, and 13 months respectively. Curiously, she has not told us how she measures its end! Lastly, Nice talks about the vocabulary of the child in this stage. She uses the term *baby ratio* to refer to the fact that 65 percent or more of the child's words are nouns. This is consistent with Stern's proposal of a substance stage.

The *short sentence stage* looks like Stern's third period, although Nice's data suggest that it may occur later than suggested by Stern's dates. She assigns to it an ALS of 3.5 to 4.5. Nice describes this stage as one in which the child begins to develop inflections and grammatical words. There are as yet virtually no complex or compound sentences. She provides three measures for these developments. One is the *proportion of incomplete sentences*. An incomplete sentence is one which is lacking either a subject or verb. At the onset of the stage this will be as high as 0.60, and at the end, as low as 0.20. Stated differently, the ratio of incomplete sentences drops from 3/5 at the onset to 1/5 at the end. It could be viewed as a stage in which the child acquires well-formed simple sentences. The other measures are the *proportion of complex sentences* and the *proportion of compound sentences*. As with several of her measures, they are not defined. At this stage, they are expected to be quite low. She cites the example of her child R who at 4;0 with an ALS of 3.9 had the proportion of 0.01 and 0.00 respectively for a 350-sentence sample.

A potentially important new development happens around this time in regard to vocabulary. When the child has acquired around 400 to 600 words, it shows what Nice calls the *stable ratio*. That is, there is now a stable ratio between the proportions of the various word classes in the vocabulary. Nouns comprise 50–60 percent of the vocabulary, and verbs around 20–24 percent. The event presumably marks the end of the three vocabulary stages proposed by Stern for the second period (see Table 3.1).

The next stage of any consequence is the *complete sentence stage*, with an average length of sentences of 6.0–8.0. Between it and the earlier short sentence stage there is a *transition stage* that is barely worth mentioning. It is apparently a stage with an ALS around 5.0. Nice, however, had not been able to find enough children with that ALS to say anything of much consequence. The complete sentence stage is one where most sentences are well-formed, i.e. the proportion of incomplete sentences drops below 0.20. Further, complex and compound sentences are more common, although little normative data are provided. This stage looks similar to Stern's fourth period. In fact, if we ignore the transition stage, the two sets of stages line up relatively neatly.

In examining Nice's stages in comparison to Stern's, we see a loss of interest in explanation, and in certain respects, description. There are no principles proposed to account for changes that occur. For most of Nice's observations, the stages are merely 'continuous' (Figure 3.1), with the onset of the stable ratio revealing a 'plateau' stage (Figure 3.2). Nice also has observed fewer behaviors than Stern, with no discussion of the prelinguistic stage, word spurts, comprehension, or questions. Nice does contribute, however, some useful notions of measurement. It is useful to know, for example, the typical age when a behavior begins, as well as its normal duration. Also, when we talk about the onset of subordination, a measure of its distribution will give us some ideas about its productivity. The introduction of measurement is an important contribution of this historical period that has been improved upon in subsequent research.

3.2.3 Roger Brown (1973)

The most frequently cited general stages of grammatical development in recent years have been those proposed by Brown (1973). Brown's work has already been mentioned in Chapter 2 (see Table 2.5) in relation to the longitudinal development of Adam, Eve, and Sarah. As mentioned, he collected longitudinal language samples on the three children from the beginning of multiword utterances until their language was quite advanced. Given the enormous amount of data that was eventually collected, he wanted to select in a rational way some portion of the data for more detailed

Table 3.4 *A summary of Brown's (1973) five stages of grammatical development*

Stage	Range of MLU (morphemes)	Upper Bound	Midpoint	Stage name and description
	1.00			*The period of single-word utterances* The use of single words without any grammatical knowledge
I	1.00–1.99			*Semantic roles and syntactic relations*
early	1.00–1.49			The onset and acquisition of the basic semantic
late	1.50–1.99	5	1.75	relations used in language like Agent, Patient. Word order is first syntactic device acquired.
II	2.00–2.49	7	2.25	*Modulation of meaning* The child begins to acquire inflections and grammatical morphemes. Most are actually acquired in subsequent stages.
III	2.50–2.99	9	2.75	*Modalities of the simple sentence* The active acquisition of the English auxiliary as it appears in yes–no questions, *wh-*questions, imperatives, and negative questions.
IV	3.00–3.99	11	3.50	*Embedding of one sentence within another* Complex sentences appear with object noun phrase complements, embedded *wh-*questions, and relative clauses.
V	4,00 and up	13	4.00	*Coordination of simple sentences and propositional relations* The active development of sentence, noun phrase, and verb phrase coordination with the use of conjunctions.

analysis. It was with this selective process in mind that he originally proposed his stages.

Like Nice, Brown decided to use the average length of sentences as a means to divide up the developmental continuum. To calculate this, he chose to count the number of morphemes in sentences, instead of words, because he felt that it would be a more sensitive measure. For example, the utterances 'boy play dog' and 'boys playing dogs' have the same number of words, but the latter has three more morphemes. Nice had just counted words as had most of the previous researchers. Brown also developed a set of criteria (p. 54) to use to determine what gets counted as a morpheme. This way of measuring sentence length was referred to by Brown as the child's Mean Length of Utterance (or MLU).

Next, Brown arbitrarily divided up the MLU continuum into five stages (see Table 3.4), by a range of MLUs. For example Stage I is when the child's MLU falls between 1.0 and 2.0. Each stage is labeled by a successive Roman numeral. At this point, then, these are an example of continuous stages (Figure 3.1). Brown was aware of this and did not at this point claim any more than that. To study each of these arbitrary stages, Brown selected an MLU that represented the midpoint of each stage. He believed that samples from the children at those midpoints would be typical of the kinds of linguistic behaviors shown for that range of MLUs. The midpoints are far enough apart that the separate samples should also show change from one another. Since many of his samples tended to fall into the latter part of Stage I, he subsequently divided Stage I into two substages, early and late Stage I. The midpoint for Stage I for his analysis was thus the midpoint for late Stage I. Lastly, he selected all the samples for Adam, Eve, and Sarah that were around the midpoints selected. The smallest of these samples contained 713 utterances. He selected this number and subsequently analyzed 713 utterances from each of the three children at each of the five midpoints.

Upon analyzing his data, Brown found distinct linguistic behaviors for each stage. He states (p. 59):

> A stage is named ... either for a process that is the major new development occurring in that interval or for an exceptionally elaborate development of a process at that stage. However, the whole development of any one of the major constructional processes is not contained within a given stage interval.

The stages with this addition become co-occurrence stages in the sense of either Figure 3.6 or Figure 3.7. It also suggests that Brown may wish to relate these behaviors by principles, moving then to principle stages and a theory of acquisition. Brown stops short of doing this. Instead, he retreats to a more descriptive position (p. 58): 'The stages are not known to be true stages in Piaget's sense; that is they may not be qualitative changes of organization forced on the investigator by the data themselves.' The use of 'may' here, though, suggests that he is optimistic that they may turn out to be so.

Stage I is one which is marked by the onset of multiword utterances. Brown emphasizes two properties of these early word combinations: (i) they show the consistent use of word order, and (ii) the sentences reveal a basic set of ten semantic relations, such as Agent + Action or Action + Object. Word order is proposed as the child's first syntactic device. The relations are semantic, however, rather than syntactic. While this stage looks like Stern's second period, it differs in that it assigns more grammatical structure to the child. Stern described these early sentences as loosely juxtaposed with little structure. In Part II we shall return to this discrepancy, and focus on the possible differences between German and English acquisition.

In *Stage II*, the child begins to acquire grammatical morphemes and inflections, just as it does in Stern's third period and Nice's short sentence stage. The stage is marked by the onset of these, with most acquired later. To study grammatical morphemes, Brown developed a new measure of acquisition, the *percentage of obligatory occurrence*. This measures the number of times that a morpheme occurs in sentences where it would be required by adult rules of grammar. For example, if a child says 'two shoe' and 'two shoes', the percentage of obligatory occurrence for the plural morpheme would be 50 percent since it occurs in one of two obligatory contexts. Brown reports on 14 grammatical morphemes that can be scored by this measure. He finds that they occur in a regular order of acquisition, and attempts to explain the order by considering the syntactic, semantic, and phonological complexity of the individual morphemes. His study of these first two stages is more detailed than either Stern's or Nice's, both in terms of descriptive information and in the attempt to explain their development.

The next stages are only briefly described in Brown (1973), and one must look elsewhere for details on them. *Stage III* appears to be a substage of Stern's third period and Nice's short sentence stage. It focusses on the acquisition of the English auxiliary in different sentence types. In particular, it draws upon work done on the acquisition of questions and negation by Klima & Bellugi-Klima (1966). *Stages IV and V*, both dealing with sentences with more than one clause, are substages of Stern's fourth period and Nice's complete sentence stage. While Nice proposes that these two constructions occur together, Brown finds that sentence embedding at least begins before sentence coordination with conjunctions. While he gives examples of these constructions in the grammar of English, he gives no data at all on their pattern of acquisition.

In outlining these five stages, Brown purposely does not attempt to construct a theory of acquisition. He does, though, discuss two basic theoretical points that are part of such a theory. One, he looks at the form of the child's grammar in some detail. This is done by looking at both the categories used and the rules of combination. The first categories are proposed to be semantic, linked by rules of word ordering. The semantic grammar of Stage I will in Stage II begin to become a syntactic one. All three of the first stages deal with simple sentences. A second theoretical concern is the relation of the child's performance, as evidenced in spontaneous speech, to its actual competence. I propose that we need to consider the two to be relatively close together (and this will be discussed in greater detail in Chapter 4). Brown, on the other hand, gives a *rich interpretation* to the child's sentences, supporting the view that the child's grammar is much better than indicated by its performance. Given this

Table 3.5 *Five major periods of language acquisition and their relation to proposals by Stern, Nice, and Brown*

Period		
Stern's term	Nice's term	Brown's term
The period of prelinguistic development (0–1;0)		
Preliminary stage		
The period of single-word utterances (1;0–1;6)		
First period	Single word stage	Period of single-word utterances
The period of first word combinations (1;6–2;0)		
Second period	Early sentence stage	Stage I: semantic roles and syntactic relations
The period of simple sentences		
Third period	Short sentence stage	Stage II: modulation of meaning
		Stage III: modalities of the simple sentence
The period of complex sentences		
Fourth period	Complete sentence stage	Stage IV: embedding of one sentence within another
		Stage V: coordination of simple sentences and propositional relations

position, he discusses the *performance factors* which may restrict the child from showing this ability. He also looks into the performance factors that may help the child discover the structure of the adult language, for example, guidelines such as paying attention to the ends of words. There is, however, little attention to the principles that would be part of Universal Grammar and used to construct a grammar, i.e. a set of linguistic rules.

Before leaving Brown, there is one last point that needs to be addressed, i.e. his view of development before his five stages. He does discuss briefly his ideas on the *period of single-word utterances* which precedes the five stages. He sees this period as pre-grammatical, i.e. as not having any of the structural properties of Stage I. Thus, Brown gives this period's utterances a lean interpretation, as does Stern. Since Brown switches to a rich interpretation for Stage I, however, he needs to propose a marked qualitative change between the two. He needs to give single-word utterances a lean interpretation because he bases much of his inference on early structure on the child's use of word order.

3.2.4 Summary

The three proposals of stages of acquisition given above provide some preliminary facts about the child's early linguistic behavior. They also reflect the style of language acquisition research reported in Chapter 2. The stages proposed define 'stage' in a variety of ways, including those outlined in Figures 3.1–3.8. When general stages are given, they tend to describe co-occurrence rather than principles, although some attempts have been made at the latter.

It is not clear that any one approach is superior to the others; despite variation, they overlap a great deal in their general features. Until such a time as we have a principled set of stages, I propose that we emphasize as much as possible the limited theoretical importance of our current proposals about stages of acquisition. Rather, we should recognize that these general stages do little more than isolate co-occurring linguistic behaviors with a focus on the newest or most prominent. Table 3.5 gives five 'periods' I have derived from a comparison of the work of Stern, Nice, and Brown, to be used as descriptive labels for the more elaborate discussion of language acquisition to be given in Part II. To help separate the multiple use of 'stage', we restrict its use henceforth to cases where some *cause* is proposed for the stage, as in the case of the 'principle stage' of Figure 3.8.

3.3 Descriptive vs. explanatory stage

We can substitute various terms for 'stage' in Figures 3.1–7: 'points', 'periods', 'plateaus', etc. My concern is to narrow the use of 'stage' to those cases where we are referring to behaviors that are being explained in some way. To explain a behavior is to offer a cause for its occurrence. In Figures 3.1–8 only the last introduces some notion of explanation. In fact, we can add explanation to any of the uses of 'stage' in Figures 3.1–7 if we propose some cause for the designated stage. For example, we could talk about the 'word spurt stage' of acquisition when the child's vocabulary suddenly increases around 1;6: as such, it is only an 'acceleration stage' as in Figure 3.4. In our discussion of Stern's stages, however, we have proposed the Principle of the Linguistic Sign as the cause of this change, and this proposed cause allows us to call this change a 'stage'. Without this proposed cause, we can only call it 'the word spurt', 'the word spurt period', 'the time of the word spurt', etc., i.e. we must use some term other than 'stage'.

Brainerd (1978) provides an important treatment of the use of 'stage' in developmental research. He makes a distinction between two kinds of stages. The first is a *descriptive stage* which has two characteristics: (i) it consists of behaviors that undergo change, and (ii) there are antecedent variables proposed that are responsible for the change. The first characteristic is comparable to the continuity requirement that we discussed at the onset of section 3.2 which underlies all eight stages in Figures 3.1–8. The second characteristic is similar to the requirement we have just made to restrict the use of 'stage' to cases where a principle or cause is proposed.

Henceforth, we will use the term 'descriptive stage' in the way just defined. The 'word spurt stage', consisting of the behavior of rapid vocabulary acquisition and the Principle of the Linguistic Sign, is a descriptive stage in this sense.

The second kind of stage that Brainerd discusses is the *explanatory stage*. An explanatory stage is one which has the two characteristics above, plus (iii) the antecedent variables or causes must be subject to independent measurement. As Brainerd sees it, most of the proposed stages in the psychological literature, such as those of Freud or Piaget, are descriptive rather than explanatory. Without some independent measure, the so-called explanations are nothing more than circular definitions. Brainerd gives as an example Freud's oral stage of development. The behavior being observed in this case is thumb-sucking. Its proposed cause is the 'oral stage', i.e. a stage when the child centers on oral gratification. The child sucks its thumb because it is in the oral stage. Our evidence for the oral stage is that the child sucks its thumb. As Brainerd says (p. 174): ' "he sucks his thumb because he is in the oral stage" is simply a paraphrase of "he sucks his thumb" '. We can say the same thing about our descriptive stage 'the word spurt stage': the word spurt is caused by the Principle of the Linguistic Sign. How do we know the latter exists? Because the child is undergoing a word spurt. There is no independent measure of the principle.

The postulation of descriptive stages is a first step in eventually reaching explanatory stages. It is important, however, to develop ways to provide independent measurement of our proposed causes. Since Brainerd is a behaviorist, he uses terms like 'variables' and 'measurement'. For our study of language acquisition, we would like to replace these words with *principles* and *evidence*. That is, our hypothetical principles behind the child's specific linguistic changes should be supported by independent evidence. The kinds of evidence could be behavioral, but they often will not be. For example, suppose that we propose the *symbolic function*, which is a more general ability to deal with symbols. Independent evidence for this principle would be provided if all children show symbolic play with objects, e.g. pretending that a block of wood is a car, at the same time as the word spurt. Independent evidence for our proposals for language acquisition can come from some other branches of linguistics such as historical change, language disorders, or linguistic theory. Our principles may lead to claims about complexity that predict certain linguistic behaviors in other domains. Or, our principles may predict that certain kinds of linguistic analyses may be better than others. The most important advances will be those made at the higher levels when we talk about the structure of language, not just the occurrence of some linguistic event.

Brainerd is very careful in his consideration of what might constitute independent evidence. One potential form of independent evidence is the kind of predictions a stage makes about invariant sequences of behavior. Suppose, for example, that we propose a stage of acquisition that is like Brown's Stage II. This hypothetical stage is one where the child builds upon a previous development with a new one. Let us say the old behavior is the development of basic semantic relations like Agent + Action as in 'daddy go' in Stage I. In Stage II, the child adds inflectional morphology such as in 'daddy going' where the progressive morpheme '-ing' is added. Stage II consists of the old behavior plus a new one. The stage predicts that children will always show an invariant sequence, i.e. that two-word lexical combinations will always precede the use of lexical morphemes with inflectional marking.

To the extent that such predictions are testable (i.e. measurable), the invariant sequence will constitute independent evidence. That is, we may find out, in studying children, that some children acquire some inflectional morphology in the period of single-word utterances. Such a case, in fact, has been observed (see Munson & Ingram 1985). If so, then these cases are counterevidence to the stage being proposed. Brainerd, in fact, is reluctant to allow such data to be considered, on the grounds that we may make the mistake of letting the predictions of the stage *determine* our analyses of the relevant data. For example, we could say that the child who says 'going' as a single-word utterance before two-word combinations like 'daddy go' does not have an inflectional suffix *because the theory does not allow it.* In such a situation, we are letting our hypotheses determine our analyses of the observed behavior. Brainerd refers to such cases as a 'measurement sequence'. He states (p. 176): 'A measurement sequence consists of the immediately preceding item plus some new things. When behaviors are related in this manner, the only way they can be acquired is in an invariant sequence.' I suggest we call these *logical measurement sequences*.

Measurement sequences may result from the form of our theory, or they can result directly from the measures we select for the analysis of data. For example, we can say that there will be three divisions to our analyses: (i) children who never do some adult-like behavior, (ii) children who sometimes do some adult-like behavior, and (iii) children who always do the adult behavior. This measure yields three stages of acquisition that are totally determined by the measure selected. Thus, they have no evidence for their existence apart from the measure used. Let us call these *quantitative measurement sequences*.

We have to be careful because of the problems mentioned above in evaluating evidence for explanatory stages of acquisition. When we propose analyses of data that are logical measurement sequences, we cannot take these as evidence for an explanatory stage. This does not mean that such analyses are of no value, because they support the descriptive stage under consideration. It may be that in some cases our construction of a logical measurement sequence is not possible without being totally ad hoc. A serious problem, however, is that logical measurement sequences can lead researchers to use quantitative measurement sequences. That is, they select measures that support their predictions, while ignoring those that do not; we will refer to such mistakes as *stage errors*, i.e. stages that result exclusively from a quantitative measurement sequence. A specific example of such a case will be discussed later in Part II in relation to the acquisition of *before* and *after*. (This example is also discussed in Ingram 1981b.)

While we have focussed on stages here, a similar problem arises when we compare children with the purpose of distinguishing *types* of children. We can suggest that children at some stage will fall into two types, so that the child's language acquisition system will allow it two options. One such typology might be that some children focus on learning mostly substance words in the period of single-word utterances, while others concentrate on social words like 'hi', 'bye', etc. In fact, such a suggestion appears in Nelson (1973). We will call such a position, in parallel with the terminology above, a *logical measurement typology*. This can lead to the selection of a measure that automatically measures children into the two groups. This I will call a *quantitative measurement typology*, again in parallel with the above terms. In our example, one such measure would be to find the average number of social words used by children, then divide those using more than the average as 'expressive' learners, and those that use fewer as 'referential' learners. The measure determines the typology because the children are just showing a normal distribution of behavior. Another possibility is that the children differ because they are at different 'stages' of acquisition. We shall call decisions like these *type errors*, and point out actual cases in Part II.

Further reading

General literature
The literature on general stages is surprisingly restricted, with the efforts of Stern, Nice, and Brown constituting three of the major attempts. The proposals of all three are in a form that is readable for the beginning student; specific readings are: Stern (1924: 143–70), Nice (1925), and Brown (1973:6–32). In Part II, we will consider one other approach for early grammar proposed by Halliday (1975). Two other general attempts are not in English. One is that of Kaczmarek (1953) in Polish; the only discussion of this in English is a brief treatment in Bar-Adon & Leopold (1971:133–4). Interestingly, there appears to be a rich literature on acqui-

sition in Polish (e.g. Zarębina 1965) which is virtually unknown to English researchers. Other attempts at stages are those of Malrieu (1973) in French, and Guillaume (1927). The latter article has been translated and appears in English in Bloom (1978). Ingram (1976a: 10–15) compares grammatical stages as discussed in this chapter with phonological and cognitive stages. A more extensive discussion of cognitive stages in relation to linguistic stages during prelinguistic development can be found in Anisfeld (1984). A critical treatment of stages can also be found in Brainerd (1978), while an earlier version of my discussion of the topic is in Ingram (1981b).

4 Explanation and language acquisition

4.1 Introduction

In Chapter 1 it was stressed that language acquisition is an area of study that crosses a variety of disciplines. Because of this, the goals of investigators vary tremendously, and, thus, the extent and domain of explanation sought. As already noted, much of the research in the field has led to descriptive observations. This has been the consequence in some cases of an atheoretical orientation, or else of a belief that theorizing must follow from a strong data base. Much of the work of those in education or in language disorders is descriptive in nature, with the primary goal of establishing norms of acquisition. This is a useful practical goal, yet it does not take us very far in understanding why acquisition proceeds as it does. Much of the data from the diaries of linguists also lacks attempts at extensive explanation. As N. V. Smith (1982) has said somewhat facetiously (p. 471): 'by providing a plethora of factual observations, it [child language: DI] offers a rich field for the taxonomist and anecdotalists'.

So far I have addressed the issue of explanation in two contexts. In Chapter 2, I presented the theoretical orientation of the three major historical periods in the study of child language. It was pointed out that each of these three periods had its own theoretical orientation, with the nativism of the last period being divided into constructionism and maturationism. These two were contrasted with behaviorism, which assigned very limited innate ability to the child. In the last chapter, I dealt with the question of stages of acquisition and finished with the suggestion that our ultimate goal in determining stages is to limit ourselves to explanatory stages, i.e. changes in the child's ability that can be accounted for by principles that themselves are testable.

In the present chapter, I treat explanation in more depth, as a framework for the rest of the book. First, returning again to the distinction between Child Language and Language Acquisition, I discuss the way each differs in its approach to explanation in language learning. I will argue that each needs to adjust its approach in the direction of the other to improve upon some current difficulties in orientation. Once adjusted, the two approaches are less distinct, and become for all intents one discipline of Child Language Acquisition. This unified field has the following properties: (i) it requires the study of children's language; (ii) it examines children's data with well-defined theories of grammar; and (iii) it concentrates on methods that establish when a child's linguistic behavior is rule-based.

The goals of Child Language Acquisition are therefore two-fold: (i) to provide a testing ground for current theories of grammar; (ii) to develop a theory of acquisition. To pursue both these goals requires a careful look at the information obtainable from data from children. The feasibility of these two goals is discussed through the examination of the relation between the child's linguistic performance and its linguistic competence. To accomplish these goals we need to be able to make statements about a child's linguistic competence from its performance. We also need to relate the child's comprehension to its production within a theory of performance. That is, what are the factors which limit the structure of language? This chapter presents a set of assumptions that enable us to pursue these goals. Without these assumptions, there would not be any potential for explanation in the first place, and the field would need to restrict its goals tremendously.

4.2 Child Language vs. Language Acquisition

At present, these two approaches to the study of children's language are going in very different directions. On the one hand, we have those who pursue Language Acquisition who, for referential purposes, we will refer to as *linguists*. (It does seem that, with many exceptions, those who do Language Acquisition tend to be trained in linguistics, while those who do Child Language tend to be trained in psychology. As we will suggest, however, their goals should be the same, basically the development of a theory of grammar and a theory of learning.) They are concerned almost exclusively with developing a theory of grammar, and tend to minimize the role of data from children in this enterprise. Further, they tend to view Child Language as primarily descriptively oriented with little interest in theory (see comments by Wasow in Chapter 2, on page 27). On the other side, there are those who pursue Child Language, who we will refer to as *psycholinguists*. They focus on children's data, propose various stages of acquisition, tend toward inductive statements about the nature of language, and focus on performance factors in acquisition (e.g. constraints on memory, processing limitations, etc.). They tend also to be sceptical of linguistic theorizing about children's language as being too removed from the data. Here I will point out some problems with these approaches and suggest changes for each.

Linguists are rather dubious about the role of language acquisition data in the process of developing a theory of grammar. One reason for this is that language acquisition data are often not used in ways that are of interest to the linguist. It is not clear, for example, that many linguists are aware of the rich database that exists in the field. When theoretical issues are raised where acquisition data may be relevant, it is usually assumed that no data exist when in fact they do.

Most psycholinguists, however, seem to have misunderstood the goal of linguistics, and often are unaware of current linguistic issues. The linguist is concerned with testing hypotheses about language, so that a theory of grammar, be it Chomsky's work (1965, 1981), or that of others, such as Fillmore's case grammar (Fillmore 1968), is just an interim step along the way. Theories of grammar are constantly changing as we come to understand better the structure of language. In this context, child language data are only interesting to the extent that they may be used to prove or disprove a particular theory. For example, suppose we have two distinct theories that explain a structure, let us say relative clauses, in very different ways. They may each lead to very different predictions about how a child acquires relative clauses. Acquisition data on relative clauses, then, will only be of interest to the linguist to the extent that they provide a means to help choose between the two theories. The linguist will only be interested in acquisition data when he is convinced that this contribution is possible.

Psycholinguists have not seen their enterprise as a contribution to linguistics in this sense. Rather, they have seen linguistic theory as a field that provides Child Language with a method of description that can be applied to children's language. That is, linguistics is expected to provide the 'correct' theory for the psycholinguist to use to understand the child. This perspective, however, can only lead to frustration. One of the best statements of this is given by Roger Brown (1970a: vii, viii):

> I used to think that psychology took from linguistics because linguistics was the more advanced field, 'advanced' perhaps meaning here nearer the truth about its subject matter ... I do not think this anymore. Linguistics has, after all, solved very few practical problems ... The fact that linguistic theory changes, and does so at a rapid clip, poses real difficulties for the psychologist who wants to use linguistic theory in his own work.

This misunderstanding of the goal of linguistics led to the virtual cessation of grammar writing in the 1970s. Most of the work, in the view of the linguist, was consequently descriptive and taxonomic. It did not contribute to our understanding of the nature of language.

It is important for the psycholinguist to recognize the goals of the linguist, and to understand the potential contribution of acquisition data to them. There are two ways the psycholinguist may proceed. First, he can become conversant with a linguistic theory of one kind or another, and examine children's language for evidence that may support or suggest revisions in that theory. Lightfoot (1979:18) makes this point when he says: 'Data from acquisition, say, will simply constitute one more argument for or against the theory, one more area where the theory makes predictions, and will help to reduce the indeterminacy of the linguistic description.'

An alternative way to proceed is for the psycholinguist to construct a theory of acquisition, again within some general theoretical guidelines. This approach would start with a careful analysis of stages of acquisition. It would construct a theory that consists of principles which are proposed to explain the child's language at each stage, and also the changes from stage to stage. For example, it is well known that children at some point overgeneralize the plural morpheme and say 'foots' instead of 'feet'. A theory of acquisition (or learning) will be needed to explain the above form. Much of the theorizing, in fact, has been along these lines.

In summary, the linguist has yet to be convinced of the role of acquisition data in theory construction. When acquisition is discussed, as in the area of learnability (see 2.3), actual data from children are not seen as relevant. The psycholinguist has not always understood this role, and has looked instead for a final theory that can be used as a tool to understand the child. A reconciliation will require more awareness of the goals of linguistic theory, and the issues in theory testing. One way is to develop evidence for the role of acquisition data in theory construction; the other is to develop a theory of acquisition which will yield information on how the child formulates rules.

While Child Language focusses on data, it is unfair to suggest that it is atheoretical. There has been a good deal of theorizing, although it tends to vary from domain to domain, and often does not relate to findings in other areas. It is a discipline, however, which is rather impatient with theorizing that ignores and inaccurately cites data. For example, Baker (1979) talks about the possibility of a Dative Movement rule in English to relate sentences (4.1a) and (4.1b). (See Section 2.3.)

(4.1) a. I gave a book to Mary
      b. I gave Mary a book
      c. I reported the crime to the police
      d. * I reported the police the crime

He points out that if children acquire such a rule, it should result in sentences like (4.1d). Baker goes on to say (p. 570): 'What little evidence I have seen on the performance of children suggests that they do not make errors of the expected types in connection with these putative rules.' He goes on to assume that children do not make such errors and subsequently rejects the Dative Movement rule as unlearnable.

This is a peculiar research strategy indeed! The psycholinguist doing Child Language has developed techniques that allow him or her to answer questions like this one. The approach would be to resolve *first* what children actually do, then go on to discuss the rule under consideration: Ingram (1985c), for example, has found that children do make mistakes like sentence (4.1d), suggesting that there is a Dative Movement rule. (See also Mazurkewich 1982, 1984, Mazurkewich & White 1984.) Evidence like this alters one's analysis tremendously. Much of the research on learnability in Language Acquisition is of this kind, where claims are made about what children do, with little, if any, confirming evidence. It is from this perspective, then, that psycholinguists criticize linguists for a lack of awareness of the data.

Various techniques that can be used to see what children do or do not do have, as we will see in Part II, been effectively used to examine how children acquire particular structures of English. In particular, elicited production and comprehension tasks, metalinguistic judgements, and elicited imitation have contributed to our findings on the young child's knowledge of grammar. The linguist, then, needs to become more aware of the data base of Child Language and its methodological developments over the years.

If these two branches of language acquisition move in the directions suggested, it becomes clear that we are discussing one field with two different aspects emphasized. One works from the theory down, the other from the data up. Both, however, share two major features. First, each works from a theoretical basis, with the goal to explain the nature of language, both in its adult and developing state. Second, both recognize the need to examine children's data to ascertain what children actually learn. The latter will only be possible through the use of well-developed techniques of data collection or analysis. With these shared assumptions, we have a unified endeavor of Child Language Acquisition with two subbranches that are capable of dialogue.

4.3 A theory of acquisition

We have been using the term 'theory of acquisition', as distinct from 'theory of language' (or 'theory of grammar'). Chomsky, in various places (e.g. Chomsky 1965, 1981), has described the theory of language as one which consists of a set of principles (or Universal Grammar, UG) that underlie language:

What we expect to find, then, is a highly structured theory of UG based on a number of fundamental principles that sharply restrict the class of attainable grammars and narrowly constrain their form, but with parameters that have to be fixed by experience.

(Chomsky 1981: 4)

A theory of language is affected by language learning in that the grammar must be learnable, i.e. be obtainable by listening to the surrounding language. The child hears a certain pattern and 'fixes a parameter', i.e. it decides that the language operates one way rather than another.

This theory of language, however, does not deal specifically with the possibility that the final grammar may result only after a series of stages of acquisition. The above view sees acquisition as essentially 'instantaneous' (Chomsky 1975) in that the child's grammar is adult-like once the parameter is set. We use theory of acquisition as a set of principles, distinct from those of UG, that account for the stages the child goes through to reach the adult grammar. If there are only two stages, pre- and post-parameter setting, then the change is virtually uninteresting. In such a case, the theory of learning is rather simple – fix the parameter. If there is a series of stages (and data at this point suggest this to be true), then the theory of acquisition will explain how each stage is structured and how it develops from the previous stage and into the next one. Historically, Language Acquisition has concentrated on the theory of language, while Child Language has concentrated on the theory of acquisition.

The theory of acquisition will have two distinct components. One will be the set of principles that lead to the construction of the grammar, i.e. those that concern the child's grammar or linguistic competence. These principles will deal with how the child constructs a rule of grammar and changes it over time. The focus is on the nature of the child's rule system; it is concerned with *competence factors*. The second component looks at the psychological processes the child uses in learning the language. These are what we shall call *performance factors*. Performance factors enter into the child's comprehension and production of language. In comprehension, performance factors deal with how the child establishes meaning in the language input, as well as with the cognitive restrictions that temporarily retard development. In production, these factors describe the reasons why the child's spoken language may not reflect its linguistic competence. They also describe mechanisms the child may use to achieve the expression of their comprehension. Much of the Child Language literature is on the specification of performance factors in acquisition.

Let us look at some examples of the kinds of principles that will be part of the theory of acquisition, beginning with competence factors. I will present two possible principles that have been proposed, one dealing with the acquisition of morphology, the other with the acquisition of syntax.

Earlier, I mentioned the long-observed fact that children overgeneralize morphological inflectional suffixes in English to irregular forms, saying things like 'foots' and 'breaked'. Stern, as pointed out, referred to these as 'child etymologies'. We also mentioned that these overgeneralizations are not accounted for by a theory of language, which only accounts for the form of the rule. The occurrence of these overgeneralizations and their subsequent loss must be explained by a theory of acquisition.

Dresher (1981) has proposed a principle to account for these overgeneralizations as part of a detailed analysis of the learnability of Old English morphology. He states (p. 192): 'a learner adopts the most highly valued rules (i.e. rules requiring the fewest features) consistent with, and sometimes overriding the available data'. A rule that states that the plural of 'foot' is 'feet' is more complex, i.e. has more features, than the rule that says that the plural is made by affixing '-s', since 'foot' is exceptional and requires more marking than nouns like 'cat', 'dog', etc. I will call this the *generalization principle* and leave its exact formulation open. This principle accounts for cases like 'foots' which occur even though the child never hears 'foots'. As discussed by Dresher, this principle is part of the child's program to acquire rules of grammar. It restricts the form of the child's rules at some intermediate point in development.

There are some features of this principle that deserve consideration. First, it makes predictions about the child's grammar for comprehension as well as production. If the child's rule is general, then the young child should at the time of producing 'foots' also have 'foots' in comprehension as an acceptable utterance. Should the young child reject 'foots' as ungrammatical, yet produce 'foots', we would need to adjust our theory of acquisition to account for this, possibly accounting for the latter case by a separate performance factor. (The testing of these predictions, of course, will be no easy matter!)

Another point is that the generalization principle is not sufficient to account for the acquisition of morphological endings. As we shall see in Part II, children do not produce overgeneralizations like 'foots' at the onset of plural acquisition, but instead, either omit the plural or else use it correctly. To account for this, we need another principle which elsewhere (Ingram 1985a) I have called the *lexical principle*: learn individual paradigmatic alternations as separate lexical items. This principle claims that the child first acquires paradigmatic variants like 'cat, cats', 'dog, dogs' as separate words, and only later realizes that there is a separable plural morpheme '-s'. The lexical principle predicts that the child will initially get 'foot, feet' correctly, and only later change the latter to 'foots'. (This is in fact, as we will see, true.) If so, our theory of acquisition will contain the lexical principle and the generalization principle, and it will need to specify the conditions under which the one yields to the other.

These two principles are still not sufficient to account for the acquisition of the adult rule of plural formation. The child could conclude that there are two forms of the plural for 'foot', these being 'foots' and 'feet'. Wexler & Culicover (1980), who have led the research into principles of language acquisition, propose the *uniqueness principle* to make this last step. The principle, in its most general form, will tell the child to select only one of the above forms, the one that is used in the child's linguistic environment. As with the other principles, we will leave its exact formulation open. These three principles, the lexical principle, the generalization principle, and the uniqueness principle, are examples of the kinds of principles that will be part of the theory of acquisition that attempts to explain morphological acquisition.

An example of a principle of acquisition in the area of syntax is the principle discussed in Chomsky (1975:32). There, he presents the sentences in (4.2), where sentence (4.2b) is the correct question form of (4.2a):

(4.2) a.   The man who is tall is in the room
      b.   Is the man who is tall in the room?
      c. * Is the man who tall is in the room?

(4.2b) is the result of the rule in English of Subject–Auxiliary Inversion which moves the auxiliary to the front of questions. Chomsky refers to this rule as a *structure-dependent* rule, meaning that it requires a structural analysis of the sentence to apply it. It moves the auxiliary of the main clause. The rule would be *structure-independent* if it ignored structure, and simply said 'move the first auxiliary'. If the rule were such, it would produce the ungrammatical (4.2c), where the first auxiliary is the 'is' in the relative clause 'who is tall'.

Chomsky goes on to claim (with no evidence cited) that children never form questions like (4.2c). The reason is that the child has a principle which we shall call the *principle of structure-dependent rules* which blocks the child from ever having a rule that is structure-independent.

> The only reasonable conclusion is that UG contains the principle that all such rules must be structure-dependent. That is, the child's mind ... contains the instruction: Construct a structure-dependent rule ignoring all structure-independent rules. The principle of structure-dependence is not learned, but forms part of the conditions for language learning.   (Chomsky 1975:32–3)

We see this as a principle of language acquisition. The corresponding principle of UG is that *all* rules in language are structure-dependent. Such a principle restricts a possible rule of language, but it does not restrict the child from using structure-independent rules at some early point in acquisition. To do this, we need the separate principle of structure-dependent rules.

As with our earlier principles, this one will need to be revised in the face of acquisition data. Like Baker (1979), Chomsky has no data to support his claim about what children do, apart from experience in hearing children speak. Elsewhere (Ingram 1985a) we have pointed out examples where children do seem to form a structure-independent rule before a structure-dependent one. One example concerns the acquisition of the English rule of Subject–Verb Agreement. This rule operates in English to make a verb agree in number with its subject, as shown in (4.3):

(4.3) a. The man is in the room
      b. The men are in the room

We could formulate two forms to the rule, one structure-independent, the other structure-dependent. These two are stated in (4.4):

(4.4) a. *structure-independent rule*: a verb agrees in number with a preceding noun
      b. *structure-dependent rule*: a verb agrees with its subject

Sentences like (4.5) show why the rule for adults is structure-dependent, in that (4.a) and (4.b) are ungrammatical because the verb is agreeing with the preceding noun instead of with its subject:

(4.5) a. * Which balls are the boy throwing?
      b. * Which ball is the boys throwing?
      c.   Which balls is the boy throwing?
      d.   Which balls are the boys throwing?

I am currently studying the acquisition of Subject–Verb Agreement in English, using sentences like those in (4.5), asking young children to judge sentences as either 'good' or 'silly', using the technique of metalinguistic awareness. Interestingly, early results indicate that younger children will accept sentences like (4.5c) and (4.5d) as bad. That is, the younger children are using the structure-independent rule of (4.4a), rather than the adult structure-dependent rule. In Ingram (1985a), I suggest that we need another principle to precede the principle of structure-dependent rules. This principle, which I shall call here the principle of linear sequence, states that the child should first establish rules based on structure-independent linear order, such as 'precede' or 'follow'. This principle yields to the one proposed by Chomsky when the child eventually correctly processes sentences like (4.5) which trigger the later principle.

Our theory of acquisition will aim at finding a set of principles that allow the child to acquire rules of language in stages before acquiring the complete adult grammar. The above examples have led to five possible principles so far: the lexical principle, the generalization principle, the uniqueness principle, the principle of linear sequence, the principle of structure-dependent rules. At this point, they are only being described, though I will attempt to specify them and others more accurately in later chapters. They are seen as competence factors in language acquisition.

While some research has sought competence factors like the above, much of Child Language has concentrated on performance factors. These are factors that affect the processing of language in either comprehension or production. They may be facilitative, i.e. aiding in accessing the relevant data necessary to activate competence factors, or prohibitive, i.e. temporarily masking the child's competence. Let us look at some examples of each.

Slobin (1973) has proposed several performance factors in the acquisition of language under the label of 'operating principles'. In comprehension, one such principle, which he calls Principle A, is 'Pay attention to the ends of words' (p. 412). We will refer to such principles as *performance principles*, to distinguish them from competence factors. Slobin uses Principle A to account for the fact that the acquisition of suffixes is easier than the acquisition of prefixed morphemes. A principle like this may be peculiar to language, or it may also be a general cognitive operation that describes a recency effect in auditory processing. Another such principle would be one which instructs the child to pay attention to stressed words. Presumably, recency or prominence will enhance the child's ability to process the incoming signal for analysis.

It is possible to see such principles as prohibitive. For example, a child may know several words, but may have trouble in retrieving them. Problems with word retrieval may give the impression that the child has a smaller vocabulary than it actually has. Some prohibitive performance factors may be beneficial, in that they may allow the child to avoid some features of the input so that they may concentrate on others. For example, the principle 'Ignore unstressed syllables' could be a reverse of the prominence principle which would allow the child to concentrate on stressed material. The unstressed material could be returned to later when better understanding is achieved.

Performance factors will also be crucial in our understanding of the child's produced utterances. At the time the child is producing two-word utterances, it may in fact understand longer utterances, possibly with three or four words in them. If so, we would need to consider the operation of a restriction on sentence length. Memory factors and planning factors such as false starts are also possible performance factors. These factors will mask the child's underlying knowledge of grammar. In some cases, the factors may be facilitative. For example, young children often repeat themselves over and over again, as if practicing language; such self-repetitions are not particularly adult-like, but they seem an important part of the child's acquisition of language. Another facilitative performance factor is 'chaining', where the child starts a new sentence with the last word of the previous sentence, e.g. 'see cat. cat big.' Francis (1969) has discussed several factors of this kind that facilitate acquisition.

While it is important to isolate performance factors like those above, it is also necessary to remember that they are only part of the language acquisition process. They provide us with insight into how the child obtains information and expresses itself, but they do not tell us about the structure of language. Even though they reveal a lot about the processing of language, they do not reveal information about the child's rule system. A description of only a child's performance, then, is not in itself a theory of acquisition.

4.4 Theoretical assumptions about language acquisition

Earlier, we talked about three positions on the nature of language acquisition: behaviorism, constructionism, and maturationism. These three positions differ in the extent to which they assign innate structure. So far, we have implicitly assumed that the child has a good deal of innate structure beyond that necessary to form the associations and reinforcements described in behaviorism. This is apparent in the discussion of inherent principles that occurred in the previous section. Also, by concentrating on stages of acquisition, as in Chapter 3, we have implied a constructionist perspective. In this section, we shall discuss this position more directly and express some assumptions about the method of inquiry into language acquisition that will be pursued through the remainder of the book.

In section 4.2 we characterized Child Language as an area that tends to look at the child's language at some point in time, with relatively little interest in the final adult state, that is, the child data are not always seen as evidence for or against a theory of grammar. Further, the child's grammar at some point in time may be quite different from the adult's. Language Acquisition was described as a field which looks at theories of grammar and questions of learnability, rather than data from children. It leads to a tacit assumption that the child's language is not particularly different from the adult's, except where the difference is due to the effects of performance factors. We subsequently proposed a reconciliation into Child Language Acquisition, a field which works from acquisition data *and* a theoretical perspective. On the one side, it is a part of the effort to construct a theory of grammar; on the other, it is concerned with developing a theory of acquisition. We need to look more carefully now at how child language data can be used in both these endeavors. We need to see how acquisition data can be used to: (i) provide evidence for or against adult theories of grammar, and (ii) provide insight into the child's linguistic competence.

4.4.1 Acquisition data and linguistic theory

To accomplish the first task, we need to examine carefully the relation between the child's grammar and the adult's grammar. Specifically, we want to develop a theory which defines the extent to which the child may change or *restructure* its language system. If the child can change its grammar quite drastically, then acquisition data will be of little value to linguistic theory. If, however, we can limit restructuring, we will be providing a role of acquisition in linguistic theory. These points will be explained below.

The three theories described in Chapter 2 differ greatly in their claims about the child's restructuring of its language. Behaviorism sees learning as incremental, in that habits are established gradually over time. Changes that occur are gradual so that restructuring is highly restricted and subject to the environmental conditions. Once a habit is established, it is fixed and can only be lost bit by bit. While behaviorism restricts change greatly, it provides no linguistic principles that are part of the changes that take place.

More interesting are the views on restructuring from the two nativist positions. Maturationism, oddly enough, predicts two extreme possibilities. One of these states that the principles of UG appear early, possibly as early as the period of one-word utterances, so that restructuring is virtually non-existent. The child's grammar from the onset is seen as essentially adult-like, with only performance factors accounting for the differences between it and adult language. This was referred to years ago by Watt (1970) as the *strong inclusion hypothesis*.

The other possible maturationist position, which I will call the *restructuring hypothesis*, allows restructuring under two conditions. In one case, restructuring occurs late in acquisition because the sentences that the child needs to hear to trigger the appropriate principle are not heard. There are several structures of English that are rare in spoken language and virtually non-existent in the speech to children. A few examples are given in (4.6):

(4.6) a. *Backwards pronominalization*: When he$_i$ arrived, Mickey$_i$ was hungry

b. *Subject complement clauses*: That he is late is possible

c. *Passives with 'by'-phrases*: The cat was chased by the dog

Restructuring would occur later in development when the child experienced the appropriate sentences. The other possibility is that some principles simply mature late, regardless of the input – for example, (4.6c) above. Carol Chomsky (1969) studied the acquisition of pronominalization and found that it consistently was acquired around 5;6. She could not find a non-linguistic explanation for the uniformity of the date of acquisition and concluded that the necessary principles mature around 5;6.

Whether one takes one of these two positions, or a combination of both, their acceptance renders acquisition data irrelevant to linguistic theory. The reason for this is different in each case. If we take the strong inclusion hypothesis, then all changes are due to changes in performance, not competence. The child's grammar is adult-like from the onset; thus, no interesting insights into the adult grammar will be available from the child. If we take the latter position, which allows extensive restructuring later in development, it also leads us to the rejection of child language data, since the change in the child's grammar is not due to the nature of the child's earlier grammar, but rather to other factors, i.e. new input or maturation. Acquisition data will only be relevant if we can relate later changes to the child's system.

The latter point can be exemplified by looking at the acquisition of English adjectives within noun phrases. One common analysis of English prenominal adjectives, as in (4.7a), is to say that they are moved into prenominal position from a relative clause. Let us call this rule Adjective Preposing. If the rule of Adjective Preposing does not apply, then we get a relative clause as in (4.7b):

(4.7) a. the red dog
　　　b. the dog which is red

Data from child language indicate that children acquire prenominal adjective structures like (4.7a) before they acquire relative clause structures as in (4.7b). The analysis above, however, claims that the preposed adjective structure is more complex, i.e. it involves all the structure necessary for (4.7b) plus the rule of Adjective Preposing. Do the child language data, then, constitute evidence against the above analysis of English adjectives?

Both the maturationist positions can argue against the child language data. The strong inclusion hypothesis would say that the child who produces 'the red dog' already has the relative clause structure, and the rule of Adjective Preposing, but does not produce relative clauses due to performance factors. One such factor could be a restriction on sentence length. The other position can argue that the child restructures later, so that the first adjective+noun structures are different from the later ones. The child will only reanalyze 'the red dog' later on. One reason why Adjective Preposing does not exist might be that the child has not yet heard enough relative clauses to formulate the correct version of the rule. Another possibility is that the ability to embed sentences has not yet matured, and needs time to do so. Major restructuring will occur, whether as a result of hearing the appropriate input or as a result of a maturational event. In all cases, the child language data are explained, and hence are irrelevant to the adult analysis.

Under the maturationist positions, the goals of Language Acquisition are limited. Under the strong inclusion hypothesis, it becomes a field concerned with performance factors. Under the restructuring hypothesis, it focusses on one of two things. For one, it can document when children hear specific sentence structures in acquisition. Part of this task also involves determining the amount of time necessary with a particular structure before a principle necessary to acquire it is triggered. That is, what is the necessary trigger experience? Some research on this question can be found in Nelson (1981). The other area is to determine the relative times when principles mature. The strong inclusion hypothesis, of course, assumes early release of the principles, as its program of research will be concerned to prove the existence of adult principles as early as possible. The restructuring hypothesis, however, will allow for later appearance, so it will be concerned with relating the appearance of each of the principles in time.

It may turn out, ultimately, that the maturationist view is correct, and that we need to limit the goals of language acquisition in the ways just described. It is possible, however, to restrict the extent of restructuring in ways that will allow acquisition data to play a role in linguistic theory. This is possible if we take a constructionist view of acquisition. In its simplest form, constructionism proposes that a rule at any particular stage always adds to or builds upon the earlier forms of a rule. The final form of the rule in the adult grammar will result from the final addition to the rule. This view restricts change, in that the rule at stage $n+1$ can never be qualitatively completely different from stage n.

This position can be exemplified in our discussion of Adjective Preposing. Acquisition data indicate that the first structures are of the form adjective + noun as in 'red dog'. If there is evidence that this is productive (a point to be returned to), we can propose a phrase structure rule to produce it. Once proposed, however, it will always be a part of the child's grammar. The position does not allow the restructuring necessary to have Adjective Preposing once the child is exposed to relative clauses. It does allow, however, three other analyses of the relation between the two structures in

(4.6): (i) the two structures are generated separately, i.e. there are no principles of UG to relate them in the syntax; (ii) the adjective + noun structures are of two kinds, those generated by a phrase structure rule only, and those that result from Adjective Preposing; or (iii) the underlying structure for all proposed adjectives is adjective + noun + relative clause, and the Adjective Preposing rule moves an adjective from the relative clause into an empty adjective category. The rule would be structure-preserving in the sense of Emonds (1976). The adjective data in this case do not dictate a simple solution, but they limit the range of possibilities.

There has been some extensive debate as to whether the correct approach is constructionism or maturationism (e.g. Piattelli-Palmarini 1980), although the debate has never been formulated quite in the form just given. Here I would like to give two arguments for the selection of constructionism over maturationism as the correct underlying theory of acquisition. The first is an argument based on the potential contribution of each. If we select maturationism, our view of acquisition research is limited to the goals mentioned above. That is, it restricts the field to a highly descriptive discipline. If we select constructionism, however, it expands the role of acquisition to include a part of a theory of linguistic competence. All things being equal, i.e. the internal arguments for one do not settle the issue ahead of time, then the position that expands the scope of a discipline is preferable to one that limits it. If constructionism is proven false, i.e. that it does not lead to generalizations about the nature of linguistic competence, then we will be no worse off than if we had chosen maturationism. If true, we will add new data to linguistic theory.

The second argument concerns the testability of the two positions. As has been argued before, the maturationist view is not testable, in that acquisition data cannot be used either to prove or disprove it. Constructionism, however, predicts that the principles it develops should lead to generalizations about language that will be consistent with independent analyses of historical change and linguistic theory. The inductive generalizations should play a role much the same as that discussed for historical change in Lightfoot (1979).

The selection of a constructionist view leads us to our first assumption about language acquisition that will underlie the discussion throughout the book. It is summarized as follows:

> *The Constructionist Assumption*: The form of the child's grammar at any point of change which we shall call stage *n* will consist of everything at stage *n* plus the new feature(s) of stage *n + 1*.

This assumption adds to the other features of 'stage' discussed at the end of Chapter 3, namely that there has to be a change, and that a principle be proposed to cause the change.

4.4.2 The determination of the child's linguistic competence

So far, we have selected a view of acquisition where acquisition data may play a role in linguistic theory. This will only be possible, however, to the extent that we can establish something about the child's linguistic competence or rule system. We need to be able to make statements about the psychological reality of our analyses of the child's language.

The importance of this fact can be exemplified by discussing the emergence of a phrase structure grammar. In (4.8) I give five hypothetical productions of a young child over two years. Let us assume that these were all produced in exactly the same context as requests for a cookie:

(4.8) a. time 1: (grunt)
b. time 2: cookie
c. time 3: want cookie
d. time 4: want eat cookie
e. time 5: I want to eat a cookie

For purposes of discussion, let us assume, like Chomsky (1981), that the underlying phrase structure of the equivalent sentence in adult English is as given in (4.9):

(4.9) I want [$_\bar{S}$COMP [$_S$PRO [$_{VP}$to eat a cookie]]]

Here COMP is the category filled by 'that' in the sentence 'I know that Bill ate a cookie'. In (4.9) the COMP is empty, i.e. there is no lexical item for it. The PRO is also an empty category that will be interpreted in the grammar to be the same referent as the subject of the main clause, 'I'. An ungrammatical English sentence that is close to (4.9) would be 'I want that I eat a cookie'. The question to be posed is this: at which time, if any, in (4.8) can we say that the child has the phrase structure of (4.9)?

If we return temporarily to the maturationist view, we can see that the issue is untestable. We could say that it has matured at any one of the times, and that performance factors restrict evidence in the output for it. One may be intuitively less comfortable with the claim at time 1 than at time 4, but the claim is the same for both times. One's discomfort (if it exists at all!) stems from a tendency to assume such structures around the time the child appears to use relevant structures. If we wish to pursue analyses of child language, however, we will need to make this assumption more precise.

Let us call the structure bracketed by $\bar{S}$ in (4.9) a tenseless clause, and say it consists of a COMP category, a PRO, and a VP. Our dilemma, stated differently, is to decide when we can conclude from the child's language use that a tenseless clause has been acquired. As an initial attempt, we can say that the child does not have PRO until sentences are produced with overt embedded subjects, as in (4.10a). Further, he or she does not have COMP until sentences like (4.10b) are produced with overt COMPs:

(4.10)   a. I want Bill eat cookie
         b. I want that Bill eat cookie

Such a proposal, in fact, has been made by Maratsos (1978).

The facts from acquisition studies (e.g. Ingram 1972) indicate that sentences like 'want eat cookie', i.e. time 4 in (4.8d), appear earlier than those with overt embedded subjects and COMPs, as in (4.10). Maratsos (1978) has argued from these facts that the child at time 4 then cannot be said to have the structure in (4.9). Instead, he proposes that the underlying structure of 'want eat cookie' is that of aux + verb + noun, parallel to adult structures like 'can eat cookie' or 'do eat cookie'. Chomsky (1981:9), however, has argued for the maturationist position for time 4, stating that the tenseless clause is the unmarked case. Presumably, this means that it either matures earlier, or else is less affected by performance factors. He does not explicitly state which is the case.

These alternative analyses exemplify the two views discussed. Chomsky's view is essentially untestable, in that child language data cannot be used for or against it. Without an independent theory of markedness, what is unmarked will be what the child uses first. This circularity is comparable to that pointed out by Brainerd (see Chapter 2) about some stages proposed as explanatory. Maratsos's analysis, however, is testable. As pointed out by Davis (1983), it predicts that children should produce sentences like (4.11a, c) in parallel with other sentences with auxiliaries like (4.11b, d):

(4.11)   a. * want I eat cookie?
         b.   can I eat cookie?
         c. * want not go now
         d.   can not go now

Examples (4.11a, c) are asterisked to indicate that children do not seem to produce these (see Davis 1983 for details). Davis (1983) concludes that Maratsos's analysis of 'want' in 'want eat cookie' as an auxiliary is thus wrong. Elsewhere (Ingram 1985a) I have argued it is a serial verb construction, as in English sentences like 'Go get a cookie' and 'Come see me'. There are no studies on the acquisition of these, but serial verb analyses predict they should occur around the time of 'want eat cookie'.

This extended discussion of the sentences in (4.8) demonstrates the need to include some restrictions on when we can say that a child has a particular category or construction. If we allow the child to have rich underlying structures in relation to its output, then we are again in the area of seeking out performance factors. If we limit the distance between the child's performance (in either comprehension or production) and its competence, then we can make testable claims about the child's rule system. Toward this end, I propose the *Competence Assumption*, as stated below:

> *Competence Assumption*: Assume that the child's linguistic perform-
> ance is relatively close to the child's linguistic competence. That is, do
> not propose a linguistic construct until there is evidence for it in the
> child's performance.

This is, of course, a very preliminary formulation of this assumption. To make it more precise, we will ultimately need a more detailed understanding of the performance factors operating in child language, and of the relation between comprehension and production.

The Competence Assumption helps resolve the problem of how we can go about making claims about the child's underlying linguistic competence. There is, however, one further problem to resolve before we can do this with some degree of confidence. The Competence Assumption will isolate the child's data that *potentially* could have a particular structure, but it does not allow us to decide if the structure is rule-based for the child. For example, the child who says 'I know that Bill ate' provides data suggestive that there is a COMP category, since 'that' was produced. However, the child could have memorized part or all of the sentence. Therefore, we need a further assumption about when a child has a *productive* rule of grammar.

In Ingram (1981d), I discuss the point that children's utterances only gradually become rule-based or productive. There, we found four steps towards productivity brought about by rule (see also MacWhinney 1982):

step 1: unanalyzed whole utterance
step 2: analyzed utterance without productivity
step 3: partially productive utterance
step 4: productive utterance

An unanalyzed whole utterance is one where the child simply learns the utterance without any knowledge of its internal structure. An example with adults would be learning phrases in a foreign language for a vacation with no knowledge of the structure of the language. In the next step to understanding, the child may know the words as individual items, but still memorize their combination without rules. Idiomatic expressions for adults are often like this. For example, 'What's up?' is an expression where we know the individual words, but it is probably not generated by rules. A partially productive utterance is one where only part of the utterance appears to allow replacement or novelty. In the game 'Simon says', 'Simon says' in a sense is non-productive in that it cannot change, even though the speaker may. As will be presented in Part II, children will learn some specific word and combine others with it. The fourth step, or productive utterance, is one produced by a rule which combines categories of grammar. It is the productive utterance that we want to analyze to establish principles about the child's linguistic competence.

Unfortunately, establishing productivity has not always been a goal in the use of acquisition data. It is possible to find discussions where claims about the child's competence are made on the basis of a small number of utterances, as few as one or two. In such cases, it may be that the utterances were not rule-based, but rather were partially memorized speech or even speech errors. To avoid the suggestion, we add the *Productivity Assumption* to our assumptions about children's data:

> *Productivity Assumption*: Assume that the child's utterance was produced by a rule only when there is evidence that the rule is productive, i.e. that it creates new instances of the structure under discussion.

Ways to establish the productivity of children's utterances are discussed in Part II.

These three assumptions, the Constructionist Assumption, the Competence Assumption and the Productivity Assumption, will restrict the extent of restructuring and also the data available to make claims about the child's rules. They allow, however, for acquisition data to be used in linguistic theory. Further, they restrict us to analyses leading to predictions about the child's language that are falsifiable.

4.5 Sources of variation among children

It does not take much exposure to children to realize that they can vary greatly in their language use. This *individual variation* among children is a feature that is emphasized by some and minimized by others. Child Language with its extensive experience with child data tends to emphasize the extent of variation, often without explicit theoretical explanation. It is common in Child Language, therefore, to see taxonomies of types of language learners. Language Acquisition, on the other hand, with its focus on a highly restricted theory of UG, tends to minimize variation. Since all children are born with the same set of universal principles, they will be similar in their linguistic competence. The variation that does occur will need to be explained by other factors.

Elsewhere (Ingram 1981e) I have proposed three sources for variation between children:

> *Performance variation*: variation due to biologically determined individual capacities or abilities of the child that lead to preferences for, or better skill at, particular linguistic subsystems.

Environmental variation: variation due to environmental effects, from obvious ones such as the need to hear a language to speak it, to more subtle ones such as the effect of frequency on specific language forms. *Linguistic variation*: variation due to the range of structural possibilities allowed by Universal Grammar.

The theory of acquisition we construct will need to incorporate all three kinds of variation.

Performance variation is a general category to cover all the kinds of variation that result from individual capacities and preferences. A non-linguistic example would be running, where we can all do it, but some may do it much better than others. While we can talk about runners vs. non-runners, we do not wish to imply that running itself is only genetically determined for some of us. Rather, it is the degree of ability to perform that leads to the typology. Or, we can call people runners who like to run, even though they may not be very good at it. Fun runs are filled with runners who prefer to run, i.e. they enjoy it, even though they may not be gifted. These individual capacities and preferences can lead to tremendous variation between people.

It should not be surprising that similar factors are at work in language acquisition. Some children may simply be better at language learning than others, and acquire it faster. In some cases, a child may be better at one aspect of language, e.g. phonology, and subsequently have a more advanced phonology in relation to syntax than another child. We might expect to find some children more cautious than others, so that their production of language has few errors. Other children may be more daring and show several errors indicative of an incomplete mastering of some aspect of language. The latter children will show their production closer to their comprehension than others, and probably be better subjects for acquisition studies. Differences can also result from specific preferences in the child, for example, for certain sounds, sentence structures, or performance principles. These various differences are important to isolate, but at the same time they will not tell us anything about linguistic competence. They will not, therefore, contribute to our knowledge of UG.

Environmental variation will occur as a result of the differing linguistic environments of the child. The most obvious effect is that the child only learns the language that it hears. Ochs (1982a), for example, has shown that children in Samoa will not learn certain grammatical morphemes if their dialect of Samoan does not contain them. Maturationists often lose interest in environmental effects at this point. For maturationists who accept the restructuring hypothesis, there is an added interest in when certain structures appear in the input language, and how often they need to be used. Presumably, variation will appear if principles can be triggered independently of each other. Research in Child Language has indicated that there may be other effects, such as earlier or more frequent use of a structure by the child due to more frequent use by the parent. The extent of such effects is still being argued, but we need to acknowledge their possibility in the analysis of variation that we find.

The last kind of variation, linguistic variation, is the kind that is predicted by Chomsky and others to be limited. We know from linguistic studies that languages can vary greatly from one to another. Chomsky (1981) has proposed a theory of UG whereby language will differ on certain parameters, e.g. those that require subjects, as in English, and those that can drop their subjects, as in Italian. The latter are called *pro drop languages*. Once the child notices this parameter, an entire set of assumptions about the language follow. The child, in this theory, does not discover each fact about a language independently, but would only need to discover a small set of important parameters. Within any aspect, there will be a typical or *unmarked* way to do things, and an unusual or *marked* way. The unmarked way is expected by UG and thus will be the first guess by the child about the language. The child will only reject the unmarked case when the language the child hears presents evidence that it does things in the 'marked' way.

The extent of linguistic variation allowed by this theory is very limited. Suppose that on the pro drop parameter, pro drop languages are the unmarked case and therefore English is the marked case. We could envision instances where one child has realized English is different or marked, whereas another has not. These two children would appear quite different from each other since one will be assigning a different set of principles to its grammar from the other. This possible kind of variation does not seem likely, however, given the extensive amount of exposure to language that children have by the time they begin to form sentences. Given that children are predicted to establish parameters from minimal exposure to the language, the thousands of sentences heard by the normal $1\frac{1}{2}$-year-old should be more than ample to set such a basic parameter as pro drop.

Another possibility is that the child may be learning an unmarked language, but mistake it as the marked language, that is, the child would set the wrong parameter. This possible variation is also questionable, on the grounds that the unmarked language would not be likely to show aspects that look like the marked alternative. Also, it would require an additional ability in the child to retreat from a wrong parameter. It is not clear how this could happen: more primitive kinds of innate release mechanisms do not show such reversals, e.g. new goslings following the first moving object.

The current theory about UG predicts rather limited variation between children. The assumptions about language acquisition presented in the previous section will allow us to see if either of the above possible linguistic variations occur. If so, it will increase our knowledge of the parameters presented by UG and how they are set. If not, they will reduce the study of individual variation to one that concentrates on linguistic performance and the effects of the environment.

Further reading

General literature

The basic ideas in this chapter were first expressed in Ingram (1985a). White (1982) discusses explanation from a different perspective. Her major assumption is that the child's language at any stage of development is a possible human language. This is a weaker assumption than the Constructionist Assumption, but it forces linguistic theory to account for acquisition data. Chomsky's position can be found in Chomsky (1975). It was first adapted to issues of learnability by Wexler & Culicover (1980). An extremely critical discussion of the attempts to explain acquisition to date is Atkinson (1982).

The following are suggested excerpts from the above: Chomsky (1975:3–35), White (1982: chs. 1–3), Wexler & Culicover (1980:1–29), Atkinson (1982:1–26).

Part II

Milestones

5 The period of prelinguistic development

5.1 Introduction

Most generally, this is the period of the infant's development that extends from birth to the onset of the first word. The discussion of this period begins with an attempt to define its boundaries more carefully.

At first glance, the selection of birth as the beginning of the study of the infant appears uncontroversial. Even here, however, it is necessary to realize that an arbitrary point on the continuum has been imposed. In a more extensive study, it would also be desirable to explore the nature of the infant's prenatal development, for there are important issues concerning the fetus's physiological development, particularly regarding the auditory system and the vocal tract. There are also the possible effects of in utero auditory experiences. We assume, however, that birth represents the infant's readiness to begin the experiences we normally associate with human development.

The other boundary of the period needs to be set by narrowing down what we mean by the acquisition of the first word. As will be seen in section 6.1, defining this milestone is no easy matter. Recall from Chapter 3 that Stern defined the end of prelinguistic development as the onset of the first word in production. Throughout Part II, however, I will begin whenever possible with the child's receptive ability. The end of this period, therefore, will be marked by the onset of the first words in comprehension.

The description of prelinguistic development will concentrate on three major areas of development. The first is the infant's ability to perceive linguistic stimuli. This is the area of *infant speech perception*, which is defined as the ability to perceive speech *before* the recognition that such speech conveys meaning. This ability will later be compared to *child speech perception*, which refers to the perception of meaningful speech, or language. Child speech perception, then, begins with the period of single-word utterances. (I will use the term 'infant' for the first year of life, and 'child' thereafter; this appears to be a common practice, with no theoretical implications.)

A second area is that of *infant speech production*. Similar to the above, this refers to the infant's ability to produce speech-like vocalizations before they are given linguistic meaning by the infant. Infant speech production is commonly referred to by terms such as 'cooing' or 'babbling'. This chapter will make these terms more precise. In the period of single-word utterances, infant speech production is followed by *child speech production*, which is the production of meaningful speech, or words.

The third area to be covered is *infant–adult interaction*. This concerns the kind of language addressed to the infant, as well as the infant's response. This area is of importance in that it focusses on the nature of the infant's linguistic environment.

Given that the goal is the study of the child's language acquisition, why would we even want to look at development before language begins? The reason is that we need to examine this period to see what precursors to language may exist. If there is a discontinuity between prelinguistic and linguistic development, then the importance of looking at prelinguistic development is minimized. If, however, important continuities occur, then we will need to identify them and incorporate them into our theory of acquisition. A constructionist theory, of course, will predict the existence of such continuities.

5.2 Infant speech perception

Until recent years, the young child was considered to have little innate ability. This certainly appears to be true to the casual observer: the young infant responds to sound, but shows no recognition that it is in any way meaningful. As will be shown, however, the infant has been found to have an ability to perceive speech beyond anyone's original expectations. Before examining this ability, however, we will look at the theoretical implications of studying the infant's speech perception, and also some of the methods used to investigate it.

5.2.1 The explanation of speech perception

The general theories of behaviorism and nativism, with the latter divided into constructionism and maturationism, were discussed in Part I. These approaches can be examined in relation to the infant's ability to perceive speech. Each theory makes very specific predictions about the infant's ability.

Aslin & Pisoni (1980), developing the ideas of Gottlieb (1976), propose four possible theories of speech perception. The first of these, the *perceptual learning theory*, is basically a behaviorist theory. It proposes that the child's perception is undeveloped at birth. During the first year of life, however, the infant's experience with auditory input will lead him to recognize or perceive individual speech sounds. This theory, then, predicts that the young infant will be very poor at speech perception, and that he will only be able to perceive the distinctions of the language he is learning.

Nativist theories, on the other hand, propose that the child has innate perceptual abilities. Aslin & Pisoni provide three distinct nativist theories. One of these is the *attunement theory*, which is similar to a constructionist theory. The attunement theory proposes that the infant is born with the ability to perceive some of the basic sounds of language: other sounds, however, will develop as the result of experience with the language being acquired. There will be three directions to the infant's development. The sounds that the infant can perceive at birth will either be maintained, if they are in the language being acquired, or lost, if they are not in the language. Other sounds will be added if they are in the language but not part of the innate set. This theory predicts that all infants will have the same initial ability, and that linguistic experience will play a role in subsequent development. The fact that the infant uses experience to develop new perceptions, built upon a preliminary innate set, makes this theory a constructionist one.

The other two nativist theories are versions of the maturationist view. One of these is the *universal theory*, which claims that the infant is born with the ability to perceive all the speech sounds found in human languages. This theory claims that the young child maintains those sounds that occur in the native language, and eventually loses the ability to perceive the others. The universal theory is roughly comparable to the strong inclusion hypothesis proposed for syntax in Chapter 4. Both of these positions suggest that the child's ability is very adult-like from an early age.

The last theory discussed by Aslin & Pisoni is the *maturational theory*. It claims that the infant's perceptual ability appears according to a biologically determined schedule that is virtually unaffected by experience. This theory predicts that all children will show these new perceptual abilities at approximately the same times. The maturational theory is similar to a version of the restructuring hypothesis of Chapter 4. The latter position proposes that grammatical principles will simply appear at some consistent point in grammatical development, again unaffected by the linguistic environment. Both approaches allow the child's abilities to be quite different from one point to another.

An important point about these four theories is that they make empirically testable predictions; that is, they make distinct predictions about the infant's perceptual ability. These four theories and their predictions are summarized in Table 5.1.

Table 5.1 *A summary of four theories of infant speech perception, based on Aslin & Pisoni (1980), and their predictions about the ability of infants to perceive specific speech sounds*

Speech sounds	THEORIES			
	Perceptual learning theory	Attunement theory	Universal theory	Maturational theory
Ability at birth	none	basic sounds	all human speech sounds	some or all sounds
Ability to perceive non-native speech sounds during 1st year of life	will never be perceived without experience	will only perceive them if part of basic sounds	will perceive all of them	will perceive them at point at which ability matures
Effects of linguistic experience	determines entire course of child's ability	determines the acquisition of non-basic sounds	no role, therefore no cross-linguistic differences in infant's ability	no role, therefore no cross-linguistic differences in infant's ability

Until recent years, however, the testing of these predictions was only logically possible. How is one to find out if a 4-month old infant, for example, can hear or perceive the English fricative [ʃ]? We certainly cannot ask them, as we do adults. The ability to test these predictions requires new and creative methods of investigation for use with infants. In the last 15 years there have been several major developments in the methods used to test young infants that have enabled scientists to begin to test these theories. The next section presents an overview of the most important methods that have been developed.

5.2.2 Methods to test infant speech perception

Eilers (1980) describes three general procedures to study the speech perception ability of infants. These are the high-amplitude sucking paradigm, the heart-rate paradigm, and the visually reinforced infant speech discrimination paradigm. Each seems to be suitable for children at certain ages only.

The *high-amplitude sucking paradigm* (henceforth HAS) was first used successfully by Eimas, Siqueland, Jusczyk & Vigorito (1971). In this task, the infant is given a pacifier which contains a wire attached to a computer which measures the child's rate of sucking. As the infant sucks the pacifier, he hears auditory stimuli, usually in the form of single syllables such as [ba], [ba], [ba], etc. During an *acquisition phase*, the infant learns that he may increase the amplitude (or loudness) of the auditory stimulus by increasing the rate of sucking. When an increased rate of sucking occurs, the infant enters the *habituation phase* of the experiment. After hearing the same stimulus for several minutes, the infant gets used to (or habituates to) the sound and subsequently decreases the rate of sucking. When this happens, the infant is presented with one of two conditions. If the infant is in the control group, he continues to hear the same stimulus item while his sucking rate is recorded. If the infant is in the experimental group, however, he will be presented with a new stimulus item. When the infant perceives that a new stimulus has appeared, he will increase his sucking rate to make the stimulus more audible. The new stimulus interrupts the habituation to the old stimulus, and hence its appearance marks the *dishabituation phase* of the experiment. If the rate of sucking for the experimental group is significantly greater than that of the control group at this point, then it is concluded that the infants perceived the difference between the stimuli. Eilers (1980) suggests that this approach works primarily with infants from birth to 3 or 4 months of age.

The *heart-rate paradigm* (henceforth HR) was developed around the same time as the HAS (see Moffitt 1971). It differs from the HAS primarily in that the infant does not control the presentation of stimuli. The infant is monitored through the attachment of electrodes which record his heart rate. When the experimenter is assured that the rate is normal she presents the child with a series of auditory stimuli. e.g. [pa], [pa], [pa] etc. The infant's heart rate will decelerate as he listens to the stimuli. The stimuli are halted then repeated several times until deceleration is minimal. At that point, a new stimulus is introduced and the heart rate is followed to see if deceleration occurs. If so, the experimenter infers that the child heard the difference between the stimuli. The age range for use of the HR is greater than for the HAS, being applicable from birth to 6–8 months. The upper range occurs because the increased mobility of the older infant makes the procedures difficult to complete.

The third technique, the *visually reinforced infant speech discrimination paradigm* (referred to as the VRISD by Eilers, Wilson & Moore, 1976), is the most recent, and was first reported in that publication. It represents a major breakthrough as it can be used with older infants from 6 months up to 18 months of age. The description presented here is adapted from Kuhl (1981) who has refined the technique.

The infant is seated on the parent's lap and faces a research assistant; the latter holds the attention of the infant by presenting a variety of toys. Meanwhile, to the other side there is a visual reinforcer, which consists of a toy animal in a dark plexiglass box. The toy animal is not visible to the infant. Both the mother and assistant wear earphones so that they do not hear the auditory stimuli and unconsciously prompt the infant. In the background, the infant hears a series of auditory stimuli, e.g. [pa], [pa], [pa], etc. Initially, the stimuli are changed and the toy animal (visual reinforcer) is lit up by lights inside the box. The infant eventually learns to turn his head to look at the box each time the stimuli change. The experimenter and assistant both record all instances of the infant's head turns. A correct score would be if the infant turned his head at the time the stimulus was changed. Eilers, Wilson & Moore (1977) used a criterion of at least five out of six correct responses during stimulus changes to conclude that a discrimination had occurred.

These three techniques have been adapted in a variety of ways to investigate infant speech perception. As will be seen, the result has been much better grasp of the infant's ability. Unfortunately, the field has also had its share of methodological difficulties and debates; nonetheless, there are findings that are worthy of serious consideration.

5.2.3 Experimental results

To study an infant's speech perception, we need to decide at the onset the nature of the speech stimuli to be tested. Ideally, we would like to present

Table 5.2 *The voice onset times for Spanish and English labial stop consonants*

VOT	English	LANGUAGE DIFFERENCES Spanish	Phonetic symbol
Fully voiced: voicing begins through entire production of the consonant.	does not occur	occurs as /b/	[b]
Partially voiced: voicing begins during the articulation of the consonant.	occurs as /b/	does not occur	[b̜]
Voiceless unaspirated: voicing begins at release of consonant.	occurs as stop after /s/, e.g. 'spa'	occurs as /p/	[p]
Voiceless aspirated: voicing occurs after release of consonant.	occurs as /p/ e.g. 'pa'	does not occur	[pʰ]

subjects with a string of speech and have them tell us what they hear, perhaps through making phonetic transcriptions and providing phonetic commentary. While difficult to do with adults, this is of course impossible to do with infants. Consequently, we must select a highly restricted set of auditory stimuli, usually single syllables differing in just one phonetic dimension, for example [pa] vs. [ba]. The techniques outlined above will enable us to see if infants hear the two sounds as the same or as different. Given the need to control for the interference of other acoustic cues, most of the stimuli used have been artificially made.

Probably the most frequently studied acoustic feature in infant speech perception has been *voice onset time*, or VOT. VOT refers to the moment at which voicing occurs in relation to the release of a prevocalic consonant. Table 5.2 demonstrates the VOT for labial stop consonants in English and Spanish. While both of these languages contain consonants that are written as 'b' and 'p', their phonetic properties are quite distinct. The Spanish distinction is between a fully voiced and voiceless unaspirated stop whereas the English one is between a partially voiced and a voiceless aspirated consonant. In addition, English has the voiceless unaspirated allophone [p] that only occurs after /s/ (see Ladefoged 1975 for details).

One reason that stop consonants have been studied is that VOT can be manipulated in the phonetics laboratory. Another, more important, reason is that we have clear evidence which shows how adults perceive these consonants categorially. To see this, we need to look for a moment at how VOT is measured. We can assign a zero at the point at which a consonant is released, and measure a consonant's VOT from that point in milliseconds (msec). The voiceless unaspirated consonants in Table 5.2 will have a zero VOT, since voicing in these begins at the point of release. Those consonants that have prevoicing (for example, fully voiced or partially voiced) will be assigned minus VOT values, and those with voicing lag, e.g. voiceless aspirated, will be assigned positive values. Experimentally, we can construct artificial speech stimuli that differ systematically in their VOT values, e.g. a [ba] will have a VOT of −10 msec, or a [pa] a VOT of +10 msec. We can then play these artificial (or synthetic) consonants to adults and ask them if they hear a /b/ or a /p/. If perception were continuous, speakers should gradually begin to hear a /b/ as the minus values increase. Studies like those of Lisker & Abramson (1967) show that this is not the case. Around a VOT of +25, English speakers suddenly hear the stimuli as /pa/. Before this, they hear them as /ba/. This result, which has been replicated, is referred to as *categorical perception*.

We can study infants to see what specific acoustic parameters they can perceive. One such parameter is VOT. Another aspect we can examine is whether or not infants can perceive categorically as adults do. In 1971, Eimas *et al.* published the results of an initial inquiry into both of these issues. It has since become a classic study that initiated the field of infant speech perception.

Eimas, Siqueland, Jusczyk & Vigorito (1971)   This study was done to examine two issues: (i) if infants can hear the difference between voiced and voiceless stop consonants, and if so, (ii) if their discrimination is categorical. To do this, they used the HAS with two groups of infants: 1-month olds and 4-month olds. There were 26 infants in each group, with equal numbers of boys and girls.

The stimuli they used were synthetic speech sounds prepared at Haskins Laboratories, the primary research center for much of the research on adult perception of VOT differences. The stimuli were even prepared by Lisker and Abramson, the investigators who reported categorical perception in adults. There were six speech stimuli used, with VOT values of −20, 0, +20, +40, +60 and +80 msec. The consonants in the first three of these are perceived by adults as /b/, i.e. an English voiced consonant. The consonants in the last three speech stimuli are perceived by adults as /p/. Recall from above that English adults place the boundary for English /b/ vs. /p/ around +25 msec. The infants in both age groups were assigned to experience one of three experimental conditions. In one condition, called the 20 D condition, the infants were to hear the speech stimuli that had VOT values of +20 and +40 msec. The '20' represents the fact that the stimuli differ by 20 msec in VOT and the 'D' refers to the fact that the difference between the two crosses the adult boundary for categorical perception, and thus the sounds are different. Another group of infants was to experience two stimuli that were 20 msec apart in VOT, but which

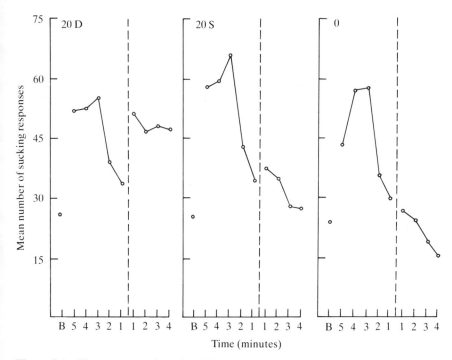

Figure 5.1   The mean number of sucking responses per minute for three groups of 4-month-old infants, taken from Eimas, Siqueland, Jusczyk & Vigorito (1971: fig. 2).

were within an adult category. That is, if the infant heard these pairs as adults do, they would sound the same. Thus, this was called the 20 S condition, with 'S' for 'same'. The two stimuli used for /b/ were −20 and 0, and the two for /p/ were +60 and +80. Half the infants in condition 20 S would hear the /b/ stimuli, and the other half would hear the /p/ stimuli. A third group of infants was assigned to the control condition. These infants would hear *only one* of the six speech stimuli, instead of two. This group was needed to check that infants did not increase or change their sucking rate even when no changes in stimuli were presented. There were eight infants from each age group in each of the 20 D and 20 S conditions, and ten of each in the control condition.

When the infants entered the laboratory, they were given a pacifier which would record their sucking rate. At first, their sucking rate was recorded to determine their normal (or baseline) rate. This was generally about 25 sucks per minute. Next, the child would hear a stimulus item. The infant's increased sucking would result in an increase in the loudness and rate of the stimulus. The infant would hear repeated instances of the sound until his interest wavered, as measured by a decrease in the sucking rate. For the infants in the 20 D and 20 S conditions, it was necessary to decide when habituation to the first stimulus was sufficient to introduce the second stimulus. The experimenters decided to shift to the second stimulus when the decrease in sucking rate was at least 20 percent for two consecutive minutes when compared to the rate for the immediately preceding minute. This is an arbitrary measure that proved to be effective. The infant would then hear the second stimulus item for four minutes, after which the experiment was terminated. The control group infants, of course, would hear only one stimulus over the entire experiment.

Figure 5.1 gives the results of the study (Figure 2 in Eimas *et al.*, 1971). The numbers along the vertical axis give the mean number of sucking responses (or sucks) per minute at different times during the experiment. The vertical line in dashes for each of the groups represents when the sucking response had decreased according to the measure described in the previous paragraph. At this point, the infants in the 20 D and 20 S conditions were presented with a new stimulus. The control infants, however, continued to receive a single stimulus sound. First observe the control group responses to the far right, indicated with a zero. The sucking rate continues to drop for this group, which is expected since this group is still hearing the same sound. For the 20 D group (far left), however, there is a sharp increase at this point, indicating that they have heard the change of sounds. What about the 20 S group? As shown in the center of Figure 5.1, they show a slight increase at this point. Statistical analysis of the data revealed that only the 20 D infants showed a significant increase at the point of stimulus change. The 20 S infants, however, did not show a significant increase, that is, the slight increase they showed could have been due to chance variation. These infants did not appear to hear the within-category change of VOT. The experimenters conclude from this that infants have categorical perception the same as adults do.

As you might imagine, the effects of these results were enormous. They initiated a wide range of studies to examine the other speech sounds that infants can hear. The results of these studies are impressive (see the reviews mentioned at the end of the chapter). For example, it was found that English children could discriminate a variety of non-English sounds at an early age, sounds that even adult English speakers could not hear. At first it was felt that this was a unique characteristic of the human auditory system until Kuhl & Miller (1975) found similar results after testing chinchillas. It now appears that the mammalian auditory system in general is able at birth to perceive categorically the range of human speech sounds.

Eimas and his colleagues concluded from this and subsequent studies that children are born with the perceptual abilities to perceive speech. The role of experience, therefore, is primarily to help children maintain the distinctions that occur in their language. Their research, then, is in support of the universal theory of Table 5.1. During the mid 1970s, the bulk of research expanded the list of the infant's discriminable speech sounds (see the review in Butterfield & Cairns 1974). Curiously, little thought has been given as to when the infant loses the ability to make distinctions that are not in the native language.

While the universal theory is still held by many investigators, it has been challenged more recently by a series of studies that argue for an attunement theory. Recall that this theory does not deny the impressive early abilities of infants, but proposes that some more peripheral distinctions in language require linguistic experience. To prove it, one needs to demonstrate that certain distinctions are acquired only after linguistic experience with that language. Some of the first studies to argue this position were Lasky, Syrdal-Lasky & Klein (1975) and Streeter (1976). Here we will take a closer look at one of the more recent of these studies by Eilers, Gavin & Wilson (1979).

Eilers, Gavin & Wilson (1979)   This study was undertaken to compare the speech discrimination ability of English and Spanish infants on pairs of synthetic stops that differ in VOT. Recall from Table 5.2 that English and Spanish differ in the VOT values for the voiced vs. voiceless distinction: Spanish places the distinction in the prevoicing range, while English places it later (around +25 msec). The researchers decided to present the infants with pairs representative of the contrasts in both languages. If the Universal Theory is true, the infants should hear both distinctions. If the Attunement Theory is true, then the infants should do better on just that distinction in their native language. For the latter situation to occur, however, one of the distinctions will need to be a basic one, in the sense of Table 5.1, and the other to be a non-basic one. The non-basic one should show the effects of experience.

Like Eimas *et al.* (1971), Eilers, Gavin & Wilson used synthetic speech stimuli prepared at the Haskins Laboratory. The pair selected to test the English contrast of /ba/ vs. /pa/ have VOT values of +10 and +40 msec. The Spanish pair VOT values were −20 and +10 msec. The subjects were eight Spanish and eight English infants, all between 6 and 8 months of age. They selected older children than did Eimas *et al.* because they wanted to allow for the possibility of experience having an effect.

Since the infants were older, they used the VRISD already discussed. The infant sat on the mother's lap and was entertained by the assistant while speech stimuli were presented over a speaker. The infant was first conditioned (see 2.2.2) to turn to look at the visual reinforcer (a toy animal) that would light up when the stimulus changed. In this study, the initial conditioning was done with the pair [bit], [bɪt]. All the infants were able to hear this pair and turned their heads toward the visual reinforcer when there was a change from one to the other. Then they were presented with the test stimuli. The infants were tested six times for each pair. Three times the stimulus item changed, and three times it did not. A head turn was scored as 'correct' when it coincided with a change in stimulus. The infant was scored 'wrong' if he turned his head when the stimuli did not change, or if he did not turn his head when the stimuli did change. An infant was judged able to perceive a discrimination if he was correct five out of six times.

There are two further details of the study that are worth emphasizing. First, there is always the possibility that the mother or assistant might unconsciously alert the infant to a sound change. To avoid this, both the mother and assistant wore earphones and listened to music. Second, there is the problem of judging what constitutes a head turn. The assistant and experimenter, who watched through a one-way window, would judge independently. If they felt that a head turn had occurred, they would push a button. If both pushed their buttons, the electronic equipment would then cause the visual reinforcer to light up. In this study, the assistant and experimenter agreed 96 percent of the time on what constituted a head turn.

The measure used in the analysis was the percentage of correct head turns on each pair of stimuli for each group of infants. The English infants were correct 92 percent for the English pair, but only 46 percent for the Spanish pair. When subjected to statistical analysis this difference proved to be significant, i.e. greater than what would be expected due to chance variation. The English infants, therefore, were better on the English contrast. The Spanish infants, on the other hand, did well on both contrasts. They got 80 percent correct on the Spanish pair and 86 percent on the English pair, i.e. they did equally well on both pairs.

These results support the attunement theory if certain assumptions are made. One is that the boundary for the English contrast needs to be a basic contrast in languages, that is, one which all infants are born to discriminate. Eilers, Gavin & Wilson (1979) suggest this, arguing that there are acoustic reasons for this contrast being more salient. If so, this explains why the Spanish infants were able to make this discrimination without any experience of hearing it. Another assumption is that the Spanish contrast is not a basic contrast, and is therefore one which requires linguistic experience. This will explain why only the Spanish infants were able to perceive this contrast, while the English infants were not. This study, then, provides suggestive evidence that experience may be necessary for certain less salient speech discriminations.

5.2.4 Some controversial issues

The two studies described above represent the universal theory and the attunement theory respectively. Both views assign the infant excellent perceptual ability at birth, with the latter allowing some development over time. Over the last few years, the disagreement between proponents of these two views has polarized into a vitriolic debate. Possibly the best place to view this is the *Journal of Child Language*, one issue of which offers a direct confrontation between the two views (see Jusczyk, Shea & Aslin 1984 vs. Eilers, Oller, Bull & Gavin 1984). The basis of the controversy has been on method and interpretation. For example, Eilers, Gavin & Wilson have been criticized for accepting five out of six correct responses as sufficient to conclude perception. Or, the claim is made that certain results are not supportive of the interpretation they are given. It is important, therefore, to realize that there is no universal consensus on the results of speech perception studies to date.

Some of the controversial issues can be summarized as follows. (i) *The role of experience*: the universal theory concludes from numerous studies that the infant's ability is excellent at birth and only some fine tuning is necessary. The work of Eilers and her colleagues, however, suggests that some contrasts may only be perceived after some linguistic experience. (ii) *Method of inquiry*: each of the three methods used to date has been criticized. For example, it has been argued that heart rate responses may be too gross to use to test certain contrasts. The measures used to conclude accurate perception have also been criticized. (iii) *The level of analysis*: the fact that infants can make fine distinctions was initially interpreted as the result of a unique human ability for speech perception. Kuhl & Miller (1975), however, have shown that chinchillas can also categorically perceive speech. The latter study suggests that this ability is not uniquely human, but a characteristic of the mammalian auditory system. (iv) *The loss of discriminatory ability*: both of the above theories will need to account for the loss of innate speech discriminations. One position is that these are lost for ever, and that adults, therefore, will not be able to perceive contrasts that do not occur in their language. An opposing position is that the contrasts are not lost, but that they will only be more difficult to discriminate. Recent work by Werker & Tees (1984) indicate that some loss may occur by as early as 10 months of age. (v) *The relation between physiological maturation and speech perception*: while much of the auditory system is physiologically developed at birth, some changes continue to occur over the first year of life (see Eilers & Gavin 1981: 192–4 for a review). The issue is whether or not this development may contribute to a possible increased ability to perceive certain speech discriminations.

Despite these controversies, there are some general conclusions we can draw about the infant's speech perception. The major one is that the young infant is born with much greater ability than was ever thought just a few years ago. This fact makes the child's rapid linguistic development a year later less difficult to understand (though no less impressive!). It appears that this innate ability combined with a year's listening experience is sufficient for the young child to begin to recognize language-specific words around the end of the first year. Further, it appears that these perceptions are categorical in that the discriminations are more abrupt at specific acoustic parameters than at others. These two findings make the young infant's speech perception much more adult-like than was ever anticipated.

5.3 Infant speech production

At first glance it might appear that infant speech production should be easier to study than perception, since it is more overt. This, however, is not necessarily the case. Lewis (1951), in his classic study of the child K, states in very human terms the difficulties this area poses (p. xi):

> The sounds that a child makes during his first few months are so elusive and apparently so remote from anything that might be called language that any observer – however interested in speech – might well be pardoned for waiting until the noises become, at any rate, a little more obviously human. To persist in making observations one must be interested in the variety of human sounds merely as sounds, one must have faith in the continuity of growth, and in addition, perhaps, one must have something of that insensitiveness to ridicule which is found at its highest level in the truly devoted parent.

The difficulty of recording the young infant's sounds is such that it is an area with a very small, but devoted group of researchers. As in the preceding section, the discussion here will be concerned with the theoretical explanations available, methods used, and lastly the findings to date.

5.3.1 The explanation of speech production

Using the theoretical possibilities from section 5.2.1, adapted to speech production, the following theories (at least) can be considered:

> *Universal theory*: the infant begins with the ability to articulate all human speech sounds, then loses those that do not occur in the linguistic environment.

Articulatory learning theory: the infant is born with virtually no articulatory ability. Early speech sounds will consist of those heard in the environment.

Maturational theory: the onset of human speech sounds will be gradual, that is, according to a biological predetermined program. Infants in all linguistic environments will show the appearance of specific sounds at the same approximate ages.

Refinement (vs. attunement) theory: the infant begins with a preliminary or basic set of speech sounds to build upon. He then acquires or adds other less basic sounds from the linguistic environment.

These four theories make predictions that are testable. It should be possible (assuming adequate methodologies) to collect the infant's vocalizations across language groups and see which of these theories is supported. The primary evidence will consist of two bodies of data: the infant's prelinguistic vocalizations and the child's early word productions. In this chapter we will examine the current evidence from the former, in order to draw some preliminary conclusions. The topic will be returned to in the next chapter when the structure of the child's early words is examined.

To pursue these theoretical possibilities, it is important to specify what will be considered to be the onset of speech production. I selected birth as our starting point with regard to speech perception. This was done despite the fact that there may be perceptual development prenatally, and despite the fact that the auditory system does undergo some physiological change during the first year. Birth, however, proves to be a point where we can assume that the physical structure is sufficiently intact to get clear evidence of processing. Further, it is a point where our methods of inquiry are applicable. We need to select a similar point from which to begin to test theories of speech production.

Most investigators begin their study of speech production at birth. While I will also look at the infant's productions from that point, I suggest that the above theories can only begin to be appropriately examined with data from infants at around 6–8 months of age. The reason for this is the tremendous physiological development that takes place in the infant's speech apparatus after birth, especially during the first year. These changes will continue in fact up to 14 years of age. It is at approximately 6 months, however, that the child's vocal tract begins to approximate to its adult shape, and that the vocal behavior generally referred to as 'babbling' begins.

The infant's vocal tract is quite different from the adult's; Lieberman (1975), for example, has noted that the infant vocal tract is actually more similar to that of the adult chimpanzee than it is to that of the adult human.

Kent (1981: 106–7), citing the work of Goldstein (1979), gives four major differences between the two: '(1) the infant's tract is appreciably shorter, (2) the pharynx is relatively shorter in the infant, (3) the infant's tract is wider in relation to its length, and (4) because the infant does not have erupted dentition, the oral cavity is flatter than in the adult'.

One consequence of these structural differences is that the resonant cavities are quite different for speech production. The size of the oral cavity is much more restricted than the adult's, with the tongue filling most of it. Further, the tongue's movement is also limited by incomplete maturation of its complex set of muscles. Besides a narrow oral cavity, the infant does not yet have a pharyngeal cavity (the area behind the back of the tongue in the adult). Lastly, the operation of the velum is designed so that the infant can breathe predominantly through the nasal cavity. Kent points out that the transition to possible oral breathing occurs around 6 months of age. Before this, the infant's vocalizations are thus highly nasalized.

These differences combine to demonstrate that the infant's vocalizations will be heavily influenced in the first six months by physiological properties of the developing vocal tract. While these changes do not stop at age 6 months, the infant develops enough by then to produce sounds that are more easily recognizable to adults as human speech sounds. I propose, then, that the development of these sounds over the last half of the first year of life will constitute the testing ground for the theories just outlined.

There have been proponents for variants of each of the possible theories of early speech production. Possibly the first to gain popularity during the period of diary studies was a form of the *universal theory*. Due to the restricted capacities of the infant's vocal tract (as just described), the infant will begin with many velar-like vocalizations. Early diarists saw in these sounds the exotic sounds of the diverse languages of the world being described by the new discipline of descriptive linguistics. Ignorant of their physiological determinants, the diarists would hear an assortment of sounds not heard in their native languages. As these diverse sounds were compiled from more and more diaries, they came to be an extensive list of non-native forms.

The expression of the universal theory is most often identified with the Russian linguist Roman Jakobson. In 1941, Jakobson published in German a book entitled *Kindersprache, Aphasie, und allgemeine Lautgesetze*, which was translated into English in 1968 as *Child language, aphasia, and phonological universals*. In this book, and in several of his other writings, Jakobson made the proposal that infants babble the wide range of sounds that may occur in the languages of the world. This position resulted from his review of a large number of diary studies on children acquiring different languages – Jakobson himself never actually collected data from children directly.

The following lengthy extract, taken from his presentation at the Fifth International Congress of Linguists in 1939, presents Jakobson's basic views on babbling:

> During the babbling period the child easily produces the widest variety of sounds (for example, clicks, palatalized, rounded or pharyngealized consonants, affricates, sibilants, etc.) almost all of which he eliminates upon passing to the 'few words' stage . . . It is true that some of these disappearing sounds are not maintained by the child when they do not occur in the speech of those around him, but there are other sounds which suffer the same fate despite their presence in the adult speech, and the baby reacquires them only after much effort. Such is frequently the case with velars, sibilants, and liquids.

An important feature of Jakobson's version of the universal theory is his proposal for the transition from babbling to words. The universal theory as stated earlier simply allows the infant to maintain the sounds that will occur in the language, while dropping others. Jakobson, however, restricts these sounds further by suggesting an abrupt discontinuity between babbling and the first words. The latter will be constrained by a theory that predicts the order of appearance of phonological oppositions. Only the sounds that participate in the first phonological oppositions (or contrasts) will be maintained. Other sounds that are part of the language being acquired, however, will be lost temporarily only to be reacquired later. The details of Jakobson's theory of the emergence of phonological oppositions will be presented in Chapter 6. Here the important point is that the infant is given the ability to babble or produce all possible speech sounds. Jakobson's theory had a tremendous impact on the field of child language and has been frequently cited as a fact about the infant's babbling, even in recent years.

Since the advent of behaviorism, there have been several theoretical proposals made that could be described as variants of an *articulatory learning theory*. Examples of these can be seen in Skinner (1957), Mowrer (1960), and Winitz (1969). The last contains a particularly in-depth review and elaboration of such theories. Most generally, acquisition proceeds in the following way. First, since the mother will occasionally vocalize while feeding the infant, her vocalizations become associated with a primary drive (feeding). Since the infant's vocalizations sound similar to the mother's, they too acquire reinforcing properties. Further, the infant's vocalizations will be reinforced or rewarded by the mother, especially if they sound like the mother's. That is, the mother (or parents) will reward or encourage the infant to produce vocalizations like the adult language (e.g. 'mama', 'papa'). This leads the infant to imitate actively the speech he hears.

While such theories rarely discuss the acquisition of different languages, it seems that they predict potential linguistic variation. The infant's need to be reinforced for sounding adult-like suggests that the infant's babbling will soon begin to sound like the adult language, if only at first in general features like rhythm and timing. If this is so, the infant's babbling should sound different from language to language. Further, there should not be any use of non-native sounds in the infant's later babbling or first sounds since these would not be reinforced by adults. For these theories to work, the infant's motor speech development at the end of the first year should be sufficient to allow the child to imitate specific adult sounds.

A version of the *maturational theory* can be found in Locke (1983). Locke proposes that infants in all linguistic communities will show the appearance of certain basic, or what he calls 'repertoire', sounds at biologically predetermined times. There is, therefore, no effect of the linguistic community on the infant's vocalizations. He states (p. 84):

> I will suggest that no genuine accommodations to the adult system will be evident until the child reaches the *systemic stage* of phonological acquisition, which probably occurs at some time after the first 50 words are in use.

He therefore predicts that the babbling of infants in different linguistic communities will all be the same.

Locke's theory, however, is not completely maturational. At the point when phonological acquisition begins, presumably around the 50th word produced, the child shifts to a different procedure. Locke says that 'it seems reasonable to ascribe the child's articulatory progress for nonrepertoire sounds to an environmental interactive process we might inelegantly term *learning*' (p. 87). I know of no one who has proposed a complete maturational theory of speech production. We can of course hypothesize one, which predicts that all sounds, not just basic or repertoire ones, occur at approximately the same time for all children.

The *refinement theory* is basically a constructionist theory. That is, it proposes that the infant will go through well-defined stages of vocalization where the earlier stages provide the building blocks of later ones. To be consistent with constructionism, these stages will also require interaction with the environment for their development. A theory of this kind can be found in the work of Oller (1980, 1981). We will go through the details of his theory in section 5.3.3. Generally, he outlines five stages of infant vocalization which each contribute to the infant developing adult-like speech production. He proposes four major parameters that develop: pitch and voice quality, resonance, timing, and amplitude. The emergence of adult-like speech does not appear reflexively, however, but as a result of the infant's exploration of his speech ability and selective imitation. Oller's model, however, does not have a strong interactional component. He believes that the infant in the first year is primarily focussing on the basic inventory of speech abilities. Infants in different linguistic communities, therefore, are all coming toward the same point and will sound similar to one another. In this sense, Oller's viewpoint is similar to Locke's in regard to predictions about cross-linguistic babbling. A more constructionist model would predict some cross-linguistic differences, either in the later babbling or at least in the structure of the early words.

5.3.2 Methods to study infant speech production

Initially, the traditional method of *phonetic transcription* was used to record infants' vocalizations. As in recording a new language, the International Phonetic Alphabet (IPA) would be used. There have been numerous studies which have used this method. As was pointed out in 5.2.1, however, the vocalizations of the very young infant, up to around 6 months at least, are not very adult-like. Many of the infant's early sounds, unfortunately, cannot be transcribed by the IPA. This method, therefore, is more suited to studies with older infants. It does allow, however, some preliminary observations on the infant's earlier vocalizations.

In recent years, attempts have been made to analyze the infant's vocalizations by submitting tape-recordings to *spectrographic analysis*. The spectrograph is a machine which provides a visual copy of the primary acoustic features of utterances. The first major discussion of the attempt to do this can be found in Lynip (1951). Unfortunately, this approach does not always make the study of infant vocalizations any easier. Often the spectrograms are so difficult to read that it is impossible to judge certain acoustic parameters, at least with very young infants. Lieberman (1980) has been able to do spectrographic analysis of infant vowel productions with infants only as young as 4 months old.

With infants below 3 or 4 months of age, the most efficient technique has been developed by Stark, Rose & McLagan (1975). They made spectrograms of selected vocalizations, then used multiple interpretations. Each analyst would read the spectrogram *and* hear the vocalizations, then describe whether or not certain features were present. Table 5.3 gives a summary of the features they looked for. Stark, Rose & McLagan refer to this as an *auditory judgement–spectral feature system*, and argue that it is the most effective approach currently available for studying the earliest vocalizations of infants. In using this system, the analyst does not need to identify a segment as a recognizable one of some human language, but instead only needs to identify some more noticeable features. Even with this amount of caution, Stark (1980) points out that certain features cannot be identified in

Table 5.3 *The auditory and spectral features used by Stark, Rose &
McLagan (1975) to study the vocalizations of two infants from 1 to 8
weeks of age*

Category	Feature
Features of breath direction, voicing, pitch and loudness	egressive vs. ingressive airflow silence in mid-segment voicing: voiced, voiceless or breathy voicing change forceful expulsion of air pitch: absent, normal, high pitch contour: flat, rise, fall or combination raised pitch glide loudness: faint, normal to loud
Degree of constriction of vocal tract above glottis	open (vowel-like) or closed (consonant-like)
Features of vowel-like sounds	glide glottal stop voice quality features: harsh, vocal fry,[1] pharyngeal friction, subharmonic break[2]
Features of consonant-like sounds	friction noise, trill, nasal, liquid, stops, click, fricative

[1] sometimes referred to as 'creaky voice'
[2] a doubling of the harmonics of the fundamental frequency, giving a roughness of the voice without a change in pitch

these first vocalizations with any inter-judge reliability. These difficult features are place of articulation, for consonants, tongue height and position for vowels, and nasality of vowels.

   Besides recording techniques such as the above, some studies have used *recognition* techniques. I use the latter term to refer to cases where listeners are played segments of infants' vocalizations and asked to identify them in some manner. This kind of technique is often used in studies trying to see if infants in different linguistic communities babble the same or not. Typically, the listener will hear two segments of babbling and judge whether the infants come from the same language or different ones. Indeed, most of the studies which have tried to investigate the effects of the linguistic environment on babbling have used a version of this technique.

5.3.3 Studies on infant speech production

The studies on infant speech production range from diary studies using IPA to modern studies applying spectrographic analyses. Here we will look at

Table 5.4 *M. M. Lewis's results on the vocalizations produced by infants during the first year of life, taken from Lewis (1936/51: Table 1)*

Sound class	Sounds uttered in discomfort	Sounds uttered in comfort
I. Vowels	(i) Onset: immediately after birth (ii) Limited mainly to sounds ɑ, a, ɛ, e (iii) Often nasalized	(i) Onset: when the discomfort cries have already begun to appear (ii) a wider range, much less well defined in quality (iii) very rarely nasalized
II. Early consonants	The semi-consonant ŭ appears early, followed by h, l, and ŋ	The back consonants γ, x, g, k, r
III. Later consonants	The front consonants, almost exclusively nasal: m, n	The front consonants, both nasal and oral: m, n, p, b, t, d

two classic studies that constituted the primary references in the area for several years, and then turn our attention to more recent work.

Lewis (1936/51)   Lewis's classic work, originally a Ph.D. dissertation at the University of London, remains one of the richest diaries ever recorded on development during the first two years of life. It is also the only English source for the primary data reported by Stern & Stern (1907) on the acquisition of German by their two children. Lewis combines his observations on a young boy, K, with those collected by other diarists. Much of these data are reported in a rich collection of appendices.

Lewis kept a record in IPA of K's vocalizations during the first year, and subsequently compared it with diary data from three other children: Axel Preyer (Preyer 1889), Gunter Stern (Stern & Stern 1907), and Hoyer (Hoyer & Hoyer 1924). Lewis divided the sounds of these four children into comfort and discomfort sounds, since he considered that they were different from each other. Table 5.4 gives his summary of his analysis.

One of the major findings was that the infants' early consonants were back or velar sounds, with more typical labial and dental consonants not occurring until later. It is because of these early velar articulations that the early months of the infant's development have been referred to as a 'cooing' stage. (Stark 1980, in fact, retains this traditional term in her typology.) Another important finding was that the vowel-like vocalizations were difficult to identify, and appeared to occur as lower or more fronted vowels. Given what we now know about the physiological properties of the infant's vocal tract, these results are not surprising. They were seen, however, as the first serious attempt to identify the young infant's vocalizations.

Table 5.5   *A summary of the major characteristics of the series of studies on infant speech production done by O. Irwin between 1941 and 1949, based on McCarthy (1954)*

Subjects: Earlier studies (1941), based on 40 infants during first 10 days of life; small groups of 10 to 15 infants in the first six months.
Later studies (1946–1948) 95 infants in the first 30 months, originally to be visited twice a month longitudinally; there was a significant attrition rate.

Method: Vocalizations were tape-recorded and transcribed. The sample for each child consisted of all the vocalizations that occurred within 30 breath groups. Multiple transcribers were used and reliability was claimed to be over 90%.

Measures: 1. Simple frequencies[1] of the occurrence of vowel and consonant tokens
2. Simple frequencies[1] of vowel and consonant types
3. Ratios of token frequencies of vowels to consonants
4. Ratios of type frequencies of vowels to consonants
5. Type to token ratios, i.e. how often were specific types used
6. Comparison of adult and child frequencies of occurrence.

---

[1] All frequencies are given for each child's sample for 30 breath groups.

Irwin (1941–49)   As might be expected, the behaviorist oriented research-ers in the United States were not satisfied with a diary account of this topic. A researcher at the University of Iowa, Orvis Irwin, initiated a series of large sample studies on infant vocalizations, and his studies remain the most extensive ever undertaken to study early infant speech production (an insightful treatment of his work can be found in McCarthy 1954: 507–11).

Irwin began his research by taking every phonetics course available at the University of Iowa, and then extensively studying with several phoneti-cians. He subsequently trained two assistants, Curry and Chen, the latter eventually completing both a master's thesis and doctoral dissertation on the topic. Either alone or with one of the above, Irwin published approxi-mately 30 articles on his research from 1941 to 1949.

Table 5.5 gives a general overview of Irwin's studies. His subjects fall into two groups, one followed for the earlier studies, the other for the later ones. The later group of 95 infants was originally to be visited twice a month for $2\frac{1}{2}$ years. For various reasons, not all of the infants were visited for the entire period. The data from these latter infants were analyzed in seven major reports from 1946 to 1949. These studies are the ones most often cited (e.g. in Winitz 1969). Irwin is not always clear on the method by which data were collected and transcribed. In one early report, he does claim that observer reliability was above 90 percent. Given the difficulties found by Stark, Rose & McLagan (1975), however, one needs to view these studies with a certain amount of caution. The sample size for each infant consisted of all the vocalizations produced within 30 breath groups. These breath groups could

Table 5.6 *Major results of O. Irwin on infant vocalizations during the first year of life, adapted from McCarthy (1954: Table 2)*

Measures	Age (in months)					
	1–2	3–4	5–6	7–8	9–10	11–12
No. of subjects	62	80	75	64	62	62
No. of records	125	181	166	170	147	149
1. Mean number (tokens)[1] of						
vowels	49	53	56	55	56	58
consonants	11	14	18	21	25	34
2. Mean number (types)[1] of						
vowels	5	7	7	8	8	9
consonants	3	5	5	7	8	10
Percentage of consonants						
glottal, velar	98	90	87	75	53	41
dental, alveolar	1	6	5	12	26	36
labial	1	4	8	13	21	32
Percentage of vowels						
front	72	61	62	63	62	62
central	25	26	24	20	17	16
back	2	14	14	17	21	22

[1] Per 30 breath groups per subject.

include both crying and non-crying sounds: presumably the younger the infant, the greater number of crying vocalizations were included. The measures most frequently reported were frequency of vowels and consonants, for both types and tokens, and various ratios between these frequencies.

In Table 5.6 I give some of the data from the seven major studies between 1946 and 1949 that are behind the findings in Irwin's work. This table reflects four findings. First, vowel-like vocalizations are much more frequent than consonant-like ones at the onset, and the number of vowel-like segments remains constant over the year while the number of consonants nearly triples. Second, the differences between vowels and consonants are not so great when types are observed. In fact, by 7 to 8 months of age, there are as many types of consonants as vowels in the infant's vocalizations. Third, the distribution of consonants reveals that virtually all of the consonants up to 6 months are either glottal or velar. A shift begins at 6 months, however, so that by 12 months the majority of consonants are either labial or dental/alveolar. Fourth, the data on vowels indicate that back vowels are infrequent in the first months, but increase gradually throughout the year.

Despite methodological problems, Irwin's studies provide an extensive body of data that in essence support and add to Lewis's results. Together, they present a picture of the young infant using a predominance of vowel-like vocalizations that sound like front or low vowels. Further, the early consonantal productions are either velar or glottal. A shift towards more back vowels and front consonants begins around 6 months of age. These results were commonly cited in the literature over the subsequent years. Of some consequence is the fact that these available data were quite in opposition to the claim by Jakobson (1941/68) that children babble all possible sounds. Despite this, Jakobson's position continued to be stated, in the face of available findings.

Oller (1980) Sporadic diary studies continued to appear after Lewis's work (e.g. Cruttenden 1970; Stockman, Woods & Tishman 1981). Major projects, however, were initiated in the 1970s by two investigators, Rachel Stark at Johns Hopkins University in Baltimore and Kim Oller, initially at the University of Washington and subsequently at the University of Miami. Both have proposed stages of development based on their findings. Here we will focus on Oller's results and his subsequent theoretical interpretations.

Oller (1980) presents an analysis of infant speech production which divides the infant's development into five stages. His overview of this analysis is presented in Table 5.7. First, we will look at the descriptive characteristics of his stages.

The first stage, the *phonation stage*, is one characterized primarily by crying and generally reflexive vocalization (e.g. grunts, burps, etc.). During these first few weeks, however, some non-reflexive vocalizations do appear. Oller (p. 95) labels these first sounds as QRNs, or 'quasi-resonant nuclei':

> these elements have been categorized by previous authors as vowels, syllabic consonants, and/or 'small throaty sounds.' Quasi-resonant nuclei include normal phonation (not vocal fry, not breathy voice, etc.) but do not seem to involve any systematic contrast between opening and closing of the vocal tract, and do not make use of the full potential of the vocal cavity to function as a resonating tube.

Oller points out that these often sound like syllabic nasals or nasalized vowels. When producing QRNs, the infant will often have the mouth closed, or nearly closed.

The second stage, at 2 to 3 months, is the *GOO stage*, and is the one when the velar-like sounds reported by Irwin appear, and occur along with QRNs. GOOs are back consonant-like sounds, often velars, and often voiced fricatives. They comprise the sounds [ɣ, x, k, g] proposed by Lewis (see Table 5.4). Oller points out that the occurrence of GOOs in his subject L at 2 months ranged from 13 percent to 49 percent of the infant's non-reflexive sounds. They may combine with QRNs to produce

Table 5.7 *Oller's stages of infant speech production, taken from Oller (1980: Table 2)*

Normal infant's age	Characteristic vocalization types	Metaphonological characteristic of mature languages
0–1 month phonation stage	QRN (quasi-resonant nucleus)	Normal phonation in non-reflexive vocalizations
2–3 months GOO stage	GOO (QRN plus velar or uvular consonant-like element)	Vocalizations with closure: alternation between opening and closure of the vocal tract
4–6 months expansion stage	FRN (fully resonant nuclei)	Use of resonance capacity providing possibility for contrasts of resonance types
	RSP (raspberry)	Front as opposed to back (GOO) closures Further manipulation of vocalizations during closure Pitch contrasts
	SQ (squeal) GRL (growl) YEL (yell) IES (ingressive–egressive sequence) MB (marginal babble)	Amplitude contrasts Further control of vocal breath stream Alternation of *full* opening and closure of the vocal tract
7–10 months canonical stage	BB (canonical babbling)	Syllabic timing constraints on relationship of openings and closures (vocalic transitions)
11–12 months variegated babbling stage	VAR (variegated babbling)	Contrasts of consonantal and vocalic type
	GIB (gibberish)	Contrasts of stress

syllable-like sounds, but the timing of the opening and closing of these syllables is irregular and not particularly adult-like.

Around 4 months of age the *expansion stage* begins, a period characterized by the addition of a range of vocalizations to the infant's phonetic inventory. These do not appear in any particular order, and the infant may go through periods of concentration on one or the other. Table 5.7 lists seven such sounds. Four of these are obvious from their labels: RSP (raspberry), bilabial or labiolingual trills; SQ (squeal), high-pitched sounds; GRL (growl), low-pitched creaky sounds (the opposite of squeals); YEL (yell), high-amplitude or loud vocalizations. In any particular sample from an infant at this stage, the occurrence of any of these may vary tremendously. This is also true for another of the new sounds, IES, or ingressive–egressive sequences. These are vocalizations that concentrate on varying ingressive and egressive breathing.

The two other new vocalizations merit special attention. FRNs, or fully-resonant nuclei, are vowel-like vocalizations that sound more like adult vowels. They have stronger resonances than the QRNs. For Oller's subject L, they comprised less than 10 percent of the vocalizations between 4 and 5 months. However, when adjacent to consonant-like elements, they accounted for 59 percent of L's vocalizations. MB, or marginal babbling, begins in this stage, but is infrequent, less than 5 percent of L's vocalizations between 4 and 8 months. Marginal babbling consists of 'sequences in which a closure of the vocal tract is opposed with an FRN' (p. 98). These sequences are not reduplicated like later babblings, and they do not have regular timing to the syllables.

The *canonical stage* around 7 months is the one usually identified with the onset of babbling. To distinguish the babbling at this time from the earlier marginal babbling, Oller refers to canonical babbling, or BB. 'BB includes both consonant-like units and FRNs (vowels) in a timing relationship that conforms to mature language restrictions' (p. 98). Oller points out that the onset of the stage is relatively sudden, and that many of these units are reduplicated, e.g. [bababa], [dadada]. He distinguishes two kinds of canonical babbling: reduplicated babbling (RB) and single-consonant babbling (SCB), e.g. [ba]. At this stage the latter is as frequent as reduplicated babbling.

The last stage of infant vocalization for Oller is the *variegated babbling stage*. There are two new types of vocalizations that appear: VAR (variegated babbling) and GIB (gibberish). Variegated babbling consists of sequences of consonants and vowels that differ. These vocalizations appear to overcome the restrictions on the earlier canonical babbling. Gibberish refers to 'phonetic sequences with contrasts of syllabic stress. In GIB, fully canonical syllables occur in the same utterances with low-stressed, often slurred syllables that seem to have QRNs as nuclei' (p. 99). These sequences sound as though the infant is producing an adult sentence with no recognizable words.

As just described, Oller's stages are only co-occurrence stages in the sense of Chapter 3, Figure 3.6, defined by the occurrence of new vocal behaviors. Oller wants, however, to go beyond this and to describe these stages as construction stages. That is, he wants the stages to build upon each other toward adult-like speech. To do this, he outlines what he calls 'metaphonological parameters'. There are four of these general parameters that need to be developed and coordinated before adult-like vocalizations can be achieved:

Pitch and voice quality parameter: the development of the control of pitch is practiced through squeals and growls; the emerging ability to control pitch is seen later in development through the pitch variations found in variegated babbling and gibberish.

Resonance parameter: the development of the articulation of fully resonant vowels. The frequent quasi-resonant nuclei of the first months give way to fully-resonant nuclei in the later stages.

Timing parameter: the development of control over the breathing cycle in order to produce smooth consonant–vowel transitions. The emergence of reduplicated babblings initiates adult-like timing of syllables.

Amplitude parameter: the development of the control of amplitude or loudness. The concentrated use of yells is an example of manipulation of this parameter.

Table 5.7 lists the development of these parameters over Oller's five stages.

Oller's stages are constructionist in that the earlier developments of these four parameters build upon each other toward more adult-like speech. To make these stages descriptive, in the sense of section 3.3, we also need to propose causes for the changes the infant undergoes. Here we will consider three possible causes: physiological change, maturational growth, and intentional exploration.

We have already discussed the extensive physiological or structural changes undergone during the first year of life. Kent (1981) has explored the possibility that these changes may account for the stages described by Oller. Table 5.8 gives the anatomical developments suggested by Kent as possible causes of the infant's vocalizations from birth to 6 months of age. Kent is careful, however, not to conclude that these are the causes. He states (p. 111):

Table 5.8 *Parallels between Oller's first three stages of phonetic development and physiological development, from Kent (1981: Table 1)*

Age of infant	Phonetic development	Anatomic–physiologic correlate
0–1 month phonation stage	quasi-resonant nucleus	Nasal breathing and nasalized vocalization because of engagement of larynx and nasopharynx. Tongue has mostly back-and-forth motions and nearly fills the oral cavity.
2–3 months GOO stage	quasi-resonant nucleus plus velar or uvular constrictions	Some change in shape of oral cavity and an increase in mobility of tongue; but tongue motion is still constrained by larynx–nasopharynx engagement.
4–6 months expansion stage	fully resonant nuclei	Disengagement of larynx and nasopharynx allows increased separation of oral and nasal cavities, so that non-nasal vowels are readily produced.
	raspberry (labial)	The intra-oral air pressure necessary for fricative-like productions can be developed with some regularity because of larynx-nasopharynx disengagement. Raspberry results from forcing air through lips, which close after each air burst because of natural restoring forces.
	squeal and growl	Contrasts in vocal pitch are heightened perhaps because descent of larynx into neck makes the vocal folds more vulnerable to forces of supralaryngeal muscles.
	yelling	Better coordination of respiratory system and larynx, together with prolonged oral radiation of sound, permit loud voice.
	marginal babble	Alternation of full opening and closure of vocal tract is enhanced by larynx–nasopharynx disengagement.

Although a causal relationship has not been firmly established, the evidence certainly invites the tentative conclusion that major discontinuities in vocal behavior in the first year are related to significant remodeling of the oropharyngeal anatomy. This is not to argue for a physiologic–anatomic determinism of early vocalization, but merely to stress the importance of physiologic and anatomic factors in evaluating early vocal behavior.

Oller (1980) acknowledges these changes as a contributing factor, but wishes to go beyond them, pointing out that they do not account for certain developments. For example, a purely physiological explanation would predict a gradual increase in fully-resonant nuclei as the vocal tract develops. Their occurrence, however, is relatively abrupt. Oller argues (p. 108): 'Such a result would suggest that an infant's introduction of FRNs is motivated in part by central (nonanatomical) factors. One possibility is that the infant is attempting to produce sounds like those heard in his or her environment.'

A second possibility is that these stages are the result of a biologically predetermined maturational schedule, a position argued for in Locke (1983), and presented earlier in this section. There are two major characteristics of a maturational model of development. One is that the infant is seen as a passive participant in the process, in the sense that it does not explore, discover, seek out or otherwise operate on the environment to achieve the skill involved; instead, there is a natural unfolding from within. The second is that the role of the environment or experience is minimal. These two characteristics are interrelated. As long as the infant's environment is normal, the sequence of development will be the same for all infants, with no observable effects of linguistic experience.

Oller (1981) discusses the possibility that the infant's stage of production could be explained by a maturational or biological model. As with the physiological explanation, he does not deny that maturation plays some role. He does not, however, want these to be the only two factors. Given that maturational models are not always easy to test (see the discussion in Chapter 4), it is important to look carefully at Oller's discussion of this. His arguments are relevant not just here but also to later chapters where this model is raised to explain other areas of language acquisition.

Oller (1981) discusses a biological explanation in which the infant's vocalizations are innate reflexes which, when they are ready (i.e. matured), appear in response to some environmental stimulus. He proposes three components to this model: (i) the reflexive behavior should be elicited whenever the appropriate stimulus occurs, (ii) any stimulus within the class of appropriate stimuli should elicit the behavior; (iii) the reflexive behavior does not change its physical form across time. He argues that infant vocalizations do not have any of these properties. There does not appear to be any environmental stimulus that will consistently elicit infant speech. Further, infants are very selective in the adults they are willing to vocalize with. Lastly, as shown in Table 5.7, the infant's vocalizations change structure. Oller concludes that the infant's vocalizations cannot be reflexive behaviors of a passive being. Rather, the infant is said to play an active role in development.

Locke's model (1983) does not have all the properties of the biological model described above. He allows the infant's vocalizations to change, and he considers that the vocalizations do not occur as a result of external stimuli (that is, through hearing adults), but of internal stimuli. His evidence for this is data suggesting that deaf infants babble the same way as hearing infants, even though they do not hear speech. Importantly, he argues that deaf children babble the same sounds as normal children, and cites this as evidence that linguistic experience plays no role in development.

Oller (1981) offers the third possible explanation for infant production, that the infant is intentionally exploring his speech capacities. In this proposal, the infant is an *active* participant in the process, and he is sensitive to the linguistic environment. He gives the following arguments in support of his position, granting that current research is insufficient to confirm them at this point in time. First, young infants appear to engage in *selective vocal imitation*, that is, they appear to enter into prelinguistic dialogues with adults. Second, their production of specific types of vocalizations goes through active cycles that look like practice or *vocal play*. For example, the infant may produce a series of vowels, like [i] [a] [u] as if practicing the extreme capacities of the vocal tract (Ingram 1981d:101). 'Such a systematic alternation behavior suggests that the child is literally engaged in *practice* of phonetic contrasts and of combinatorial possibilities of an emerging vocalic system' (Oller 1981:96).

These arguments concentrate on the claim that the infant is an active participant in learning. Experience, however, also plays a role. He argues, therefore, against Locke's claim that deaf children babble the same as normal children. Gilbert (1982) has pointed out that this finding, originally given in Lenneberg, Rebelsky & Nichols (1965), was based on scanty evidence. In a detailed study of one deaf child, Oller *et al.* (1985) have found that the deaf infant's babbling never became canonical, that is, she never developed beyond the expansion stage. They conclude that linguistic input is necessary for the infant to develop fully resonant vowels. If this claim can be substantiated by further research, it would constitute a major argument in favor of Oller's constructionist-like view of development.

Even stronger evidence would exist if we could demonstrate that the infant's active involvement in its own speech and that of those around it leads to differential babbling. That is, cross-linguistic differences in the babbling of infants would constitute major support of Oller's model, and counterevidence to the maturational explanation. To date, attempts to demonstrate cross-linguistic differences have led to contradictory results. Locke (1983) concludes from his review of this research that all infants babble alike. Oller & Eilers (1982) compared the babbling of English and Spanish infants at 12 months and found no differences. The latter study is particularly important since these authors were looking for differences to support their model.

A recent study by de Boysson-Bardies, Sagart & Durand (1984), however, suggests that the issue is not yet settled. They argue that the comparison of segmental inventories of infants may not be the best way to see cross-linguistic differences, given that there is a basic set of segments across languages. They suggest that linguistic differences may be more obvious if there is focussing on the acquisition of supralinguistic features (such as intonational variations). Further, they feel that more attention needs to be given to selecting for comparison languages that are so different as to lead to predictable differences between the infants learning them. They selected French, Arabic, and Cantonese Chinese, since these languages differ on specific non-segmental parameters: for example, Arabic differs from French in having (i) an emphatic voice quality, (ii) a more posterior tongue position, and (iii) more sharp contrasts in pitch. They then collected samples of babbling from infants exposed to each of the three languages. The infants were 6, 8, and 10 months old. There were 15-second samples selected from all the samples to be used in the experiment. They used the recognition technique described in 5.3.2. Adult speakers of French were played pairs of babbled sequences and asked to identify the French infants. Their results suggest that the adults could do this for infants at 8 months of age. For example, when paired with samples of Arabic infants, the French infants were correctly identified, 76 percent for the 8-month-old samples and 75 percent for the 10-month-old samples. While this is only a preliminary finding, it suggests that more subtle research may yield cross-linguistic differences in infant babbling.

5.3.4 The relation of speech perception and production

We saw that two views are currently being proposed concerning speech perception: there is the universal theory, which claims that the infant can make all the necessary perceptual distinctions at birth, and the attunement theory, which grants extensive ability at birth, but proposes that non-core or peripheral perceptual features require linguistic experience to be acquired. As for speech production, there is the maturational theory which sees the cause of speech production as totally determined by biological factors, and the refinement theory which sees the infant's active interaction with his linguistic environment as an important additional factor.

When we compare these positions, there are two natural alignments that occur, if we assume that any theory in one domain should be logically consistent with one in another domain. One alignment is what I shall call the *universal–maturationist* position. It proposes that the infant is born with the basic capacity to perceive and produce speech. The perceptual maturation is ahead of production, so it is basically complete at birth. Production skills require the first year of maturational growth. The infant's role in the process is minimal, as is the role of experience. The second alignment is that of an *attunement–refinement* theory. This theory is constructionist in essence, seeing the child as an active participant in his development. The child begins with some basic abilities, then builds upon these as he interacts with the linguistic environment. Experience will play a role in development, and the stages that occur will be related to the structure of the earlier stages.

The evidence to date does not clearly support one of these theories over the other. The key research will be to demonstrate the importance of linguistic experience, as well as to develop a logically consistent theory of the stages that the infant follows. Some research indicates that experience plays a role in perceptual development, but we need to know more about what constitutes the salient and non-salient acoustic parameters of development. Also, we have yet to see any proposals of stages of infant speech perception that look anything like those for speech production. The stages for the latter proposed by Oller are constructionist stages that are descriptive in the sense of Chapter 4. There are behaviors under change, and the causes are physiological growth and active exploration by the infant. To make them explanatory, we will need independent evidence that the child is an active explorer. Support can come from the speech perception research, and from what we know of the infant's cognitive development, a topic we turn to in the next section. The evidence for the role of experience in speech production is also only suggestive at this time, at least for the infant's babbling. We shall argue in the next chapter that there is evidence that the cross-linguistic differences predicted by the attunement theory are more evident in the sound system of the child's early words.

In Chapter 4 we discussed certain assumptions about how we may proceed to develop a theory of language acquisition. One of these, the Constructionist Assumption, can be adjusted for our discussion here. This assumption states that theories that are constructionist are in the long run more subject to being falsified than maturational theories. Based on this assumption, we proposed that we start with such theories and examine their predictions. The attunement–refinement theory of infant speech development makes specific predictions about the role of experience that have been partially supported by research. Using the Constructionist Assumption, we will continue to evaluate its viability in the next chapter when we examine its predictions about the young child's ability to perceive and produce his first words.

5.4 Early cognitive development

An aspect of the infant's prelinguistic development which is no easier to study than speech is that of cognitive development. By cognitive development we mean the infant's growing knowledge of the world around him. In order to understand the meanings of the child's first words and subsequent sentences it is important to have an awareness of the child's knowledge of the world in general. The study of the infant's cognition is important in two specific ways: to understand what the child means by its words, and to explore the role that cognitive growth may play in language development. For example, must certain cognitive developments occur before certain linguistic ones may occur? Stated differently, does the child's cognitive ability limit or constrain semantic development just as early physiological structure limits the infant's speech production?

We could discuss early cognitive development as we did speech, by exploring various theoretical approaches and their predictions for early behaviors. This, however, could take us far away from our main concern of language acquisition. Consequently, we will concentrate on one theoretical approach to early cognition, that of the Swiss psychologist, Jean Piaget. Piaget's work on cognitive development constitutes an enormous undertaking which holds a central place in child development research.

In the early 1900s, Piaget followed the development of his three children, Jacqueline, Lucienne, and Laurent. His study of his children was in the spirit of the early baby biographies of his day, as were discussed in Chapter 2. He reported the results of his observations in three books, originally published in French and only years later in English. (The dates given below for Piaget's books will be those of the English translations.) The first book, *The origins of intelligence in children* (1952), presented a general theory of what he called 'sensorimotor intelligence', his term for the child's cognitive ability during the first two years of life. In it, he outlined the characteristics of six stages of sensorimotor development. This was followed by *The construction of reality in the child* (1954). In this work Piaget presents his observations on four areas of cognitive development: the object concept, the spatial field, causality, and time. He shows how the child's knowledge of each changes through the six sensorimotor stages. The third book is *Play, dreams and imitation in childhood* (1948) which is the most important of the three for the study of language acquisition – its original French title, *La formation du symbole*, is more directly indicative of this. The book follows three major developments that lead to the ability to have symbols (and hence language): imitation, play, and mental representation.

Piaget's work is important for the study of language acquisition for three reasons in particular. First, it is an impressive *body of facts* about the child's early development. Like other baby biographies, his observations tell us a great deal about what infants do. Second, his work is important because he goes beyond description and attempts to explain early development. In particular, he developed a constructionist view of development that has been the model for several subsequent theories of language acquisition. Here it is important to emphasize that we are talking about the *form* of the theory, not its content. By form I mean that stages are actively constructed by the child, building upon earlier structures, and influenced by the environment. Third, Piaget's theory is important for its *content*. That is, Piaget's theory offers one explanation of language acquisition, proposing that it is the result of general symbolic growth. His claims about the relation of language to cognition have led to a larger body of studies in recent years.

We will eventually look at all three of these aspects of Piaget's work. Here, however, I will restrict myself to a general introduction to his theory, and a brief description of his observations on cognitive development before the first words.

5.4.1 General aspects of Piaget's theory

When Piaget talks about infants, he uses the term *sensorimotor intelligence*. The infant does not have the ability to represent objects, that is, to recall them in their absence. Rather, the infant's knowledge is restricted to the ways his senses have responded to objects or to his own manipulations of them. As Anisfeld (1984:15) has described this: 'the knowledge that young infants have of objects is in terms of the sensorimotor impressions the objects have on them and the sensory and motor adjustments the objects require'. The infant will not begin to have concepts as adults do until the second year of life, around the time language begins. Until then, he only knows objects primarily through his actions on them. The young infant does not have abstract concepts but sensorimotor schemata, which are the action patterns associated with objects. The development of the first year is a gradual move away from schemes to eventual abstract classification.

The infant begins knowledge with basic reflexes and two functional processes: *assimilation* and *accommodation*. Assimilation occurs when the infant processes incoming events by adjusting those events to its internal structures. An example from speech perception would be to perceive a sound that we are not familiar with to be the same as one with which we are familiar. We assimilate it to, or treat it the same as, a unit in our internal system. Also, assimilation will allow the infant to realize a familiar sound or event. Accommodation is the opposite process. In accommodation the infant changes the internal structure to become more like the external event. For example, the Spanish infant who learns to perceive a difference between [b] and [b̪] has accommodated his perceptual system to the linguistic input he learns. Development, then, is seen as the constant interaction of assimilation and accommodation to the sensorimotor input. Once that change becomes part of our system, we assimilate other events to it. For example, the child who acquires the English past tense '-ed' has accommodated to the linguistic input. When he proceeds to say 'eated' and 'breaked', he is assimilating the past tense of these verbs to his new structure. Only after a period of assimilation or exercise is the new structure sufficiently established to begin a new accommodation. Eventually these two processes lead to a third one, *organization*. These processes allow the child to 'construct' its reality, hence the term 'constructionism'.

Piaget's theory emphasizes the innate nature of the three processes of assimilation, accommodation and organization, and how they build upon innate reflexes to construct knowledge. It is in this emphasis on the processes that he differs from stronger nativist or maturationist positions. Maturationists have argued that there is no difference in the positions, in that what has the potential to exist must be said to be innate. Piaget (1971: 16) has conceded this point to a degree, but argues that one still has to account for how the collaboration between the innate potential and the environment actually works. This point was described in somewhat different terms in Chapter 4. The above processes will prove useful when later other milestones of language acquisition are considered.

5.4.2 The first four stages of sensorimotor development

Piaget's six stages of sensorimotor development are proposed to cover development from birth to around 18 months to 2 years. (There is a problem in determining the end of the period in relation to the onset of language, and that will be returned to in the next chapter.) For the period we are examining, that is, birth up to the first word understood, only the first four stages are relevant. The description of the fifth and sixth stages will be considered in the next chapter.

The first stage is characterized by the appearance of reflexes. These provide the basis upon which subsequent developments are built. In speech perception, the reflex would be the innate ability activated by the initial exposure to sound. In speech production, these are the vegetative sounds associated with the process of eating discussed by Stark, Rose & McLagan (1975). Most of Piaget's actual discussion focusses on reflexes of sucking and vision.

The first adaptations or accommodations appear in sensorimotor stage 2. The following selection from Piaget's observation 40 in Piaget (1952:78) on his daughter Jacqueline discusses this for crying behavior:

> Around 0;1 it seems as though crying stops simply expressing hunger or physical discomfort (espectially intestinal pains) to become slightly differentiated. The cries cease, for example, when the child is taken out of the crib and resume more vigorously when he is set down for a moment before the meal. Or again, real cries of rage may be observed if the feeding is interrupted. It seems evident, in these two examples, that crying is connected with behavior patterns of expectation and disappointment which imply acquired adaptation.

Piaget describes at this stage the appearance of the *primary circular reaction*. This term refers to basic repetitive behavior by the child to exercise newly acquired behaviors. Observation 40 also points out some instances of these regarding crying and babbling (p. 78):

> It is then that the first 'circular reactions' related to phonation may definitely be observed. Sometimes, for instance, the wail which precedes or prolongs the crying is kept up for its own sake because it is an interesting sound: 0;1(22) ... At 0;2(15) the crying is transformed into playing with the voice, 'aha', 'ahi', etc. At 0;2(15) she even interrupts her meal to resume her babbling.

This stage coincides with the GOO stage in Oller's framework (Table 5.7). Circular reactions are also referred to as 'reproductive' assimilations, that is, the reproduction or repetition of the new structure. These are complementary with *recognitory* assimilation, that is, the recognition of a known or acquired schema.

The primary circular reactions of stage 2 are activities of the infant that focus on his body, such as thumb-sucking, babbling, grasping things to exercise the grasping activity, or shaking his arms or body. In all of these activities, the end or goal of the activity is the same as the means to achieve it. An initial separation between ends and means occurs in stage 3 with the onset of the *secondary circular reaction* (around age 0;5). These activities are secondary in that the action of the infant's body is used as a means which achieves a result outside of the activity itself. The infant's shaking his arms, for example, may cause the mobile attached to the crib to move. The infant repeats the body act in order to see the outside event once more. Piaget states (1952:154): 'after reproducing the interesting results discovered by chance on his own body, the child tries sooner or later to conserve also those which his action bears on the external environment'. Because of this preliminary separation of ends and means, Piaget emphasizes that these are the first instances of intentional behavior by the infant. He acknowledges the difficulty of defining intention, and emphasizes that these early behaviors are still far from being like the intentions of the adult. He states (p. 148): 'intentional adaptation begins as soon as the child transcends the level of simple corporeal activities (sucking, listening and making sounds, looking and grasping) and acts upon things and uses the interrelationships of objects'.

Recall that the infant does not have concepts at this time, but rather sensorimotor schemata. Primary circular reactions help establish primary schemata (e.g. grasping, shaking, vocalizing, etc.). The secondary circular reactions lead to secondary schemata, which are sensorimotor impressions of the properties of objects. These are the precursors to later classes or concepts: 'The secondary schemata constitute the first outline of what will become "classes" or concepts in reflective intelligence: perceiving an object as being something "to shake", "to rub", etc.' (Piaget 1952:183). These schemata will become even more complex in the next stage. We see at stage 3 the onset of possible intentional behavior and the first roots of later classification.

During stage 3, the infant's use of a circular reaction is to prolong an event which he discovered or caused by chance. These acts consequently only involve the continuation of a primary circular reaction (e.g. shaking). In stage 4, however, the distinction between the ends and means becomes more pronounced. The infant appears to want to cause some activity, and will try out his available circular reaction to accomplish this. Suppose, for example, that the infant wants to grasp an object, but that object is not accessible because of some obstacle – let's say the infant wants to grasp a box which the parent is holding. The infant can use one of its other schemata, such as pushing objects, or striking objects, to achieve the end, which is to grasp the box. Importantly, the infant will not attempt to discover new means; this will not occur until the next stage.

Piaget has used these stages to follow the development of the major conceptual domains of intelligence. In his second book (1954), he presents his findings on the development of the object concept, spatial displacement of objects, causality, and time. This was followed up in his third book (1948) with a treatment of imitation and play behavior. His observations on the major behaviors in these areas through the sensorimotor stages constitute an important database on the infant's cognitive development. Table 5.9 presents a summary of some of these behaviors for stages 3 and 4. These observations give a general picture of the infant around the time of the first words.

The infant's knowledge of objects is becoming advanced by the end of sensorimotor stage 4 (or the end of the first year). The infant indicates that he recognizes people and objects, and will explore the properties of new objects. He even shows an awareness that certain events anticipate others, for example, that standing up indicates someone is about to leave. The coordination of actions, e.g. removing an obstacle to be able to hold an object, provides the infant with an early form of causality.

The area of *object permanence* is probably the most known area of Piaget's observations on infants. The infant only gradually indicates awareness that an object exists when it is no longer in sight. In stage 4, the infant for the first time will actively search for an object that is suddenly removed from its sight. This development of object permanence along with the growing awareness of objects appears to occur just before the advent of word comprehension.

Lastly, imitative ability is also increasing. In stage 3, the imitation is limited to acts already done previously by the infant. Piaget states that the stage 3 infant will only imitate sounds that he recognizes as ones that he has already produced (or babbled). Attempts at novel sounds do not appear until stage 4. The latter, of course, will be essential for the acquisition of the adult language.

5.4.3 The development of meaning

We might expect the discussion of meaning to wait until the infant begins to acquire words. It is crucial in Piaget's theory, however, for later developments to have their roots in earlier developments. This is true for the growth of the awareness of meaning, where Piaget outlines prelinguistic developments that prepare the infant for word acquisition.

We can simplify the infant's task by emphasizing two major goals: to develop the notion of 'word', and to acquire the meanings of the words in the native language. Logically, the former development necessarily precedes the latter. In our preliminary discussion of the acquisition of meaning, we will concentrate on the first of these two. That is, how does the infant arrive at the realization that vocalizations may be meaningful?

To begin, Piaget discusses the notion of the linguistic sign, proposed earlier by the French linguist Ferdinand de Saussure. The linguistic sign is the result of the *signifier–signified* relation where the signifier is some group of sounds and the signified is the concept these sounds stand for or

Table 5.9 *Some behaviors of young infants which are typical during stages 3 and 4 of sensorimotor development from selected areas of cognition, selected from appendix in Ingram (1978)*

Cognitive domain	Stage 3	Stage 4
Knowledge of objects	*reproductive assimilation* (secondary circular reactions): shaking objects stacking objects with hand hitting two objects together putting object in mouth *recognitory assimilation* fear of strangers recognizes footstep, door opening, bottle knows presence of someone when touched	*coordination of secondary schemas:* removal of objects that are obstacles, e.g. moving another's hand to grasp object intentional rejection of object *prevision* recognizes that someone who gets up plans to leave *active exploration for properties of new objects* visual and tactile exploration
Object permanence	attempts to follow trajectory of a fallen object recognizes object by seeing only part of it.	for first time, will search for an object that is hidden from him, e.g. under a blanket
Spatial field	has interrupted prehension, i.e. will grasp for object that has been dropped or taken away lacks ability to follow trajectory of an object or to rotate objects	has reversible operations, i.e. hands objects back to adult studies the constant shape of objects by moving them to and from eyes
Imitation	systematic imitation of sounds that he has already made systematic imitation of movements seen by infant, e.g. clapping hands, opening and closing of hands, waving bye-bye	imitation of new sounds imitation of non-visible movements already made by child, e.g. opening and closing of mouth, putting out tongue imitation (with effort) of new visible models, e.g. bending and straightening finger

represent. For example, the English word 'tree' is a phonetic string [tri] paired with the concept TREE that we recall when we hear these sounds. (I'll indicate the concepts referred to, as distinguished from the word, in capitals, e.g. TREE vs. 'tree'.) The linguistic sign has two important properties in particular. One is that the relation is *arbitrary*. There is nothing about the signified that requires a particular signifier. The French sound [larbr] for 'l'arbre', for example, does just as well as the English sounds to represent the concept TREE. Second, the concepts are *abstract* representations. We do not see the tree to understand the word, and some of the concepts can be quite abstract, e.g. LOVE. The young child, then, needs to develop the signified–signifier relation, abstract concepts, and the arbitrary nature of the relation. (Additional developments include the ability to recognize the perceptual form of the adult words.)

Piaget argues that the signifier–signified relation of the linguistic sign has its roots in more primitive relations of signifiers and signifieds of the sensorimotor period. Piaget (1952: 185–96) proposes steps that the signifier-signified relation goes through from birth to the time when the linguistic sign is developed. The first three sensorimotor stages are each characterized by their own type of *signal* or *elementary indication*. Stage 4 is marked by the appearance of the *indication* (or *index*, Piaget 1948; the translations for this term vary across Piaget's books). Stage 5 shows the advent of *symbols*. Arbitrary *signs* do not occur until the end of the sensorimotor period. A discussion of the emergence of symbols and signs will be postponed until the next chapter. Here, we will briefly look at the development of signals and indices (or indications).

It is important to realize that the signifier–signified relation can apply to sensory impressions. To use one of Piaget's examples, we may observe a tree while sitting in a park. We may not see all of the tree and certainly we do not observe it from all angles or perspectives, yet we know that we are watching a tree. The signified, then, is TREE, the intellectual concept, not the sensory attributes. The latter are the signifiers that allow us to recognize the concept that represents the object. Piaget states (1952:190):

> The signified of a perception – that is to say, the object itself – is therefore essentially intellectual ... In order to perceive their individual realities as real objects it is essential to complete what one sees by what one knows. Concerning the 'signifier', it is nothing other than the few perceptive qualities recorded simultaneously and at the present time by my sensory organs ...

In the infant, we can not yet speak of concepts, but instead of sensorimotor schemata. Nonetheless, we can describe the relation between the infant's perceptions and the early schemata as one of signifier–signified. These are what Piaget means by 'indications' (of which 'elementary' indications are a subcategory): 'In a general way we shall call indication every sensory impression or directly perceived quality whose signification (the 'signified') is an object or a sensorimotor schema' (Piaget 1952:191).

Elementary indications characterize the first three stages of sensorimotor development. Stage 1 elementary signification refers to the connection between a reflex act (e.g. sucking) and the sensory feeling the infant has while exercising it: 'In such a case the signifier is the elementary sensory impression accompanying the play of the reflex . . . and the signified is the sucking schema' (Piaget 1952: 192). In reflexive crying, the signifier would be the motor impression of crying as well as its auditory impression. The signified is the crying schema itself.

The elementary indication of stage 2 is not far removed from that of stage 1. At stage 2, the first habits are being acquired. Sensorimotor impressions associated with a schema will set the schema in motion. For example, being placed in the position for nursing may be a signifier to the infant to begin to suck: 'The consciousness of the position for nursing does not signify anything more . . . than the awaiting and the beginning of the sensory images connected with sucking' (p. 193). In such cases the relation is not arbitrary, as it will be later for the linguistic sign. Rather, the signifier is one aspect of the real-world events associated with the schemata. Another example is the mother's voice as a signifier of the presence of the mother.

The stage 3 elementary indication is the last of the three types of elementary indications. It is the one which is part of the infant's secondary circular reactions. Just as the secondary circular reaction entails an initial development of the infant's own actions for their own sake toward their use to cause other events, so too the signifier will now suggest a series of events:

> In effect, the significations of the second type remain essentially functional and related to the subject's own activity. That which the sensory signals announce is that a certain thing is to be seen, heard, grasped, etc. On the contrary, the significations of this third type comprise from the beginning an element of foresight related to the things themselves: the string hanging from the bassinet is not only to be seen, grasped, and pulled, it serves to swing objects from a distance, etc. (1952:194)

An important restriction of this new foresight is that it is limited to activities of objects or people tied to the infant's activities; that is, they are always part of the infant's secondary circular reactions.

Here are some examples of stage 3 elementary indications (or signals):

At 0;7(10) he [Laurent: DI] cries in the morning as soon as he hears his mother's bed creak. Until then, although awake, he did not show his hunger. But at the slightest creak, he moans and thus demands his bottle . . .

At 0;8(3) Jacqueline smiles and says *aa* as soon as the door to her room opens, before seeing the person who enters. She therefore understands by this sign that someone will enter.   (1952:195)

Piaget refers to the significations (or signals) of the first three stages as primary. He reserves the term 'indication' (or 'index' in the translation of Piaget 1948) for stage 4. Remember that in stage 4 the infant for the first time coordinates schemata with separate objects. As such, the separation between means and ends becomes more pronounced:

. . . a fourth type of sign is now constituted . . . which permits the child to foresee, not only an event connected with his action, but also any event conceived as being independent and connected with the activity of the object.   (1952:248)

He calls this *prevision*, meaning that the child can anticipate the next event which is separate from the one in progress.

Table 5.9 gives one example of prevision, the recognition that the act of standing up indicates another action, which is the act of leaving. Jacqueline, for example, at 0;9(15) would cry if the person next to her moved or stood up, since this gave the impression of leaving (p. 249). Piaget states (p. 251): 'prevision becomes possible in connection with facts rarely or very recently observed, or even in connection with the actions of other people. Thus to foresee the departure of a person when he rises or even turns away is a prevision which is already very much detached from the action in progress.'

By the end of sensorimotor stage 4, around age 1 year, the infant has made some noteworthy gains. He has acquired a variety of sensorimotor schemata, auditory as well as visual and motor, in a variety of areas. There is an impressive growing knowledge about actions and objects, with increasing ability to operate upon people and objects. Importantly for language, activity is becoming more clearly intentional, as the gradual separation between means and ends occurs. Vocalizations will become in the next stages one of the means to achieve ends, just as secondary schemata are at stage 4. In addition, the separation between signifiers and their signifieds is occurring. This separation will eventually lead to the acquisition of the arbitrary linguistic signs characteristic of human language.

5.4.4 Piaget: pro and con

Piaget's work stands out as the major effort to date on cognitive development in both the areas of description and explanation. As stated earlier, the work is substantial even if our only interest is to obtain an extensive body of facts on what infants and children do. A small sampling of these facts has been presented above. In addition, it provides a theoretical statement of tremendous breadth on the cause of development. Indeed, his theory has had such an impact that its vocabulary characterizes much of the discussion in child development.

Both of the above observations can be used to justify the choice here of Piaget's theory as a vehicle for discussing cognitive development in the first year of life. There is, however, a more substantive reason for its selection: his work in a very general way provides the model for the approach taken in this text toward language acquisition, that is, his research on development is characterized by the constant interaction of method, description, and explanation, with an awareness of the importance of each.

Piaget's method is usually referred to in his own terminology as a *clinical method*. It is defined as an approach where there is experimentation, in that the experimenter has a hypothesis to pursue, and may vary conditions to test it, but there is also careful observation of the child's actions in the context of the child's total ability or mental states. One is constantly attempting to understand the nature of the child's behavior. Here the important point is that Piaget was always discussing the importance of method and what the best method might be to study a particular point. For example, as early as Piaget (1929) he made the point that the study of children is a difficult enterprise that requires extensive experience. He states (pp. 8–9): 'it is our opinion that in child psychology as in pathological psychology, at least a year of daily practice is necessary before passing beyond the inevitable fumbling stage of the beginner'. His is a far cry from the rather casual treatment of method discussed in 4.3, when Chomsky (1975) concludes that children do not produce a particular construction because he has never heard them produce it.

A second characteristic of Piaget's work is its descriptive force: he has provided a plethora of facts to be explained about cognitive development. This is the obvious consequence of a concern to work extensively with data. The observations cited in his three books on sensorimotor development are striking in the careful detail taken. They probably represent the most careful diary ever done. While these books followed three children in detail, others show his awareness of the occasional need to verify results with larger populations: Inhelder & Piaget (1964), for example, presents results from

2,159 children. His appreciation of the need to work closely with children's data reflects the general orientation of the Child Language field. For example, in Piaget (1955:20) he states: 'for teachers and all those whose work calls for an exact knowledge of the child's mind, facts take precedence over theory'.

Despite the flavor of this last quotation, it is nonetheless obvious that Piaget was very much committed to the development of a core explanation of child development. Indeed, it is his theory, rather than his method and descriptive work, that has proven the central focus of both supporters and critics. The assumptions I presented in Chapter 4 in regard to the exploration of language acquisition are very heavily influenced by specific features of Piaget's theory. Most central is the Constructionist Assumption, which was made with the hope it could yield a developmental theory for language as extensive as Piaget's for cognitive development. Piaget's constructionism is a position that deserves careful consideration. It is one that has been presented in depth in several places, especially in Piaget (1971). It is also a position, unfortunately, that has not even been considered by those who approach language from a maturationist perspective. Recent books by Lightfoot (1982), Chomsky (1975) and Jackendoff (1983), for example, treat issues that have been discussed by Piaget at great length – none, however, contains a single reference to Piaget. To discuss cognition without a serious treatment of Piaget is as fallacious as attempts to study modern syntactic theory without ever reading Chomsky. The Competence Assumption is also implicit in all of Piaget's work. He consistently only attempts to assign to the child knowledge that can be ascertained from his behavior. The Productivity Assumption is also implicit, in that Piaget is very cautious in assigning a rule or schema to the child until there is consistent evidence for it in the child's behavior. This concern for productivity is a permanent part of the clinical method.

When discussing Piaget's work, it is also necessary to mention the place of this work from one's own viewpoint. Piaget has managed to create very strong reactions to his theory. There are those who support it carte blanche, and others who attack it vehemently. It is important for the student to be aware of this and to weigh writings by each group accordingly. In this book, Piaget's work plays the following roles: (i) it provides the model for our general orientation to language acquisition (in the sense of providing an integration of method, description, and explanation); (ii) the form of his theory leads to three assumptions that have been proposed here in Chapter 4 for the study of child language acquisition; and (iii) his discussion of the emergence and structure of meaning will be used here as a demonstration of a constructionist attempt to account for the emergence of meaning. This volume is not, however, an attempt to present and defend

Piaget's view of the relation of cognition and language. In fact, as will be discussed in Chapter 7, it will present a position more in support of autonomous syntax.

Before concluding this section, it is important to present the major criticism of Piaget's description of sensorimotor development as presented here. This concerns his description of general stages of sensorimotor development. In probably the first extensive experimental attempt to replicate Piaget, Uzgiris & Hunt (1975) found that infants did follow the invariant sequences of behaviors found by Piaget, but not in well-defined general stages. For example, the infant would show the stage 4 behaviors of object permanence in the right sequence to other object permanence behaviors, but he would not necessarily also show stage 4 behaviors in causality. Their work, as well as that of several others, has led many investigators to reject the idea of general sensorimotor stages. This is coupled with the problem, pointed out by Brainerd (1978), that Piaget never explained *how* to place a child into a general sensorimotor stage.

This issue is important for our study of language acquisition when we turn to the relation between language and cognition. If there are general stages, then we can see if those stages correlate with specific linguistic milestones. If not, we need to concentrate exclusively on the relation of specific domains to language, such as imitation, causality, etc. The general criticism above, in fact, has led to work of the latter kind. It is my impression, however, that this general critique is based on a misunderstanding of Piaget's view on how general stages are attained. The following statement of Piaget, in relation to Laurent's application of familiar schemata to new situations, suggests that the attainment of a sensorimotor stage is no simple matter:

> ... it is perfectly normal that these first behavior patterns of the fourth stage are constituted sporadically from the middle of the third stage except that these episodic productions are only systematized and consolidated one or two months later.   (1952:214)

That is, there is a spiralling effect that is not going to be evident from strictly experimental results like those in Uzgiris & Hunt (1975). Because of this, I have maintained the original Piagetian descriptions in the text above.

5.5 The linguistic environment

So far, we have considered the infant from the point of view of the development of its internal abilities. The infant, of course, does not acquire language in a vacuum. In order to appreciate the language acquisition process, it is also necessary to look at the infant's interaction with the linguistic environment. We need to examine the nature of the language presented to the infant, or the *linguistic input*, and the characteristics of adult–infant interaction.

5.5.1 The cultural influence

To begin, we need to be aware of the fact that cultures vary from each other in their view of the infant and the way he should be treated. These cultural attitudes can influence the nature of infant–adult interaction and thus the language heard by the infant. Much of the work done in recent years on how adults speak to infants has been on English-learning infants. In our culture, to oversimplify, an infant is seen as someone to interact with actively, and thus he can receive a great deal of linguistic input. Further, it is common to see parents actively involved in linguistic stimulation of their infants as if teaching them. This attitude is captured very nicely in the following excerpt from Piaget (1971:19–20):

> ... very rarely have I been able, in America, to expound any aspect of my stage theory without being asked, 'How can you speed up their development?' And that excellent psychologist, J. Bruner, has gone as far as to state that you can teach anything to any child at any age if you go about it the right way.

We have to be careful not to generalize too quickly from our own cultural biases to universal claims about how parents speak to their infants.

Pye (1983b) has recently discussed cultural attitudes that may exist towards the young infant. Table 5.10 gives a brief summary of examples he has found. The bulk of Pye's discussion, however, concentrates on the attitudes of the Quiché, a language group located in the western highland region of Guatemala. The Quiché infant is seen as being born with a soul that must be protected from being lost. The infant is treated with great care so that the soul does not leave the body. Two of the possible ways to lose one's soul are excessive crying and falling down. Such views then lead to expectations in the parents as to what constitutes appropriate infant behavior.

In the Quiché case, the parental attitude is to ignore the infant until it is producing recognizable adult-like language, as if addressing the infant would jeopardize its soul. Pye states that Quiché parents direct very little speech to their babies, and only begin to engage in conversational-style interaction when their children are around 18 months to 2 years. Even then, the parents continue to protect their child from outsiders. Pye found that the mothers would even attempt to speak for their children when addressed by an outsider. For example, one case he observed was when Pye's assistant said to a Quiché child 'Do you know what you are holding?' Before the child

Table 5.10 *Some examples of cultural attitudes toward infants, based on the summary in Pye (1983b)*

Language group	Cultural attitude	Reference
Mundugumor	Infants are seen as a threat, causing loathing and jealousy; they are consequently kept in isolation.	Mead (1963)
Mohave	The fetus is born capable of understanding the adult language.	Devereux (1949)
Japanese	Infants are extensions of the parents; their needs are obvious and do not require extensive interpersonal communication.	Caudill & Weinstein (1969)
Samoan	Rules of etiquette restrict parents from speaking to young infants.	Ochs (1982b)
Javanese	Infants are not yet human.	Goertz (1973)

could answer, the mother responded (translations are mine): 'He says "girl".' To child: 'You say "little horsie"' (2 times). To experimenter: 'Play. He says "little horsie plays".' In a later paper, Pye (1986) has found similar 'to say' routines in other cultures, but with different purposes. For example, they occur in Kaluli (Schiefflin 1979) as teaching devices for developing language.

Another effect of the Quiché attitude toward their infants is that the culture has no developed linguistic routines for interacting with infants. Pye says (1983b:18): 'Quiché parents spend their time working, not entertaining their children. I did not observe (nor could I elicit) any traditional games or songs which parents engaged in with their young children.' This is in marked contrast with English parents, for whom such routines abound. Several of these routines have been subjected to careful study:

give-and-take games (Ratner & Bruner 1978)
peekaboo (Bruner & Sherwood 1976)
book reading (Ninio & Bruner 1978; Snow & Goldfeld 1983)

Given this contrast in cultural attitudes, it is striking that the studies just cited seek to explain the onset of later language milestones by the occurrence of these play routines.

In the rest of this section, I will be reviewing data primarily on the language addressed to English infants. At this point, however, we should be reminded that the results *are* for English-learning infants. Thus, generalizations will need to await more careful studies in other cultures.

5.5.2 Possible effects of the infant's linguistic environment

We could, of course, be content with describing how parents speak to children. This is, however, only one of the reasons for looking at this issue. The major concern is to determine the possible effects of the linguistic environment on the child. That is, to what extent can we say that the environment has caused a particular milestone for the child? This issue brings us back to the theoretical possibilities discussed in Chapter 4; here I want to try to separate the predictions each makes.

The behaviorist view, with its emphasis on the role of the environment and incremental learning, would expect a tremendous influence from parental interaction with the child, beginning with the period of prelinguistic development. In fact, the work on early infant–adult interaction by Bruner (e.g. Bruner 1975; Ninio & Bruner 1978) is very behavioristic. It sees the parental interaction with the infant as the basis of later linguistic developments. The cross-cultural facts described above, however, create some difficulties for this position, though it could be maintained by moving the environmental influences to a later stage.

The maturational view places much less importance on input, especially for the prelinguistic child. In this period, the child would need to hear language, but the parent would not need to be involved in elaborate simplifications of his or her own language. This view predicts a range of possibilities, from no speech adjustments to children, to elaborate ones due to cultural factors. The crucial point would be that parental speech adjustments, should they occur, would not be done to teach language. The possible cultural effects discussed above are not a problem for the maturationist view, and could even be cited as some support for it. For example, Quiché children do eventually begin to talk, despite what appears to be a minimal amount of input.

The constructionist position is difficult to separate from the maturationist one in this regard. In Piagetian work, the child is seen as developing his cognitive capacities through interaction with the environment. Nowhere, however, does Piaget propose that the environment needs to adjust itself to the child. In fact, it is the child who needs to be flexible in order to deal with a changing environment (Piaget 1971). In this sense, then, the child needs to be able to acquire language within a range of varying environments. There seems to be very little difference between the maturational and constructionist views regarding the kind of language addressed to children.

Why, then, study the infant's linguistic input, given the nativist orientation of the text? The reasons are two-fold. First, as recorded in Chapter 4, nativism, either in the form of Chomsky's or Piaget's theory, has never denied some role in acquisition to behaviorist principles. It is important to know the extent to which parental reinforcement and shaping influences language acquisition. The second reason is the one expressed in section 4.5: there may be differences in the way children differ within and across languages in their language acquisition that can be traced back to the environment, not to the child's internal programming. If we are going to understand the nature of the child's developing linguistic competence, we need to separate out the non-linguistic factors that lead to variation. Our Quiché discussion can provide a trivial example. Based on the ages in Pye (1983a), Quiché children appear to acquire language slower than their English counterparts. The fact that Quiché parents direct relatively little speech to their children can account for this cross-linguistic variation.

5.5.3 Baby talk in English

For reference purposes, the language addressed to children is often called *motherese* or *baby talk*. Neither term is particularly helpful. Motherese is not adequate, since the infant is also addressed by fathers, other adults, and children. Baby talk is also inadequate because it is used in the literature in a negative sense as a form of language which uses a restricted set of features such as changing [r] to [w], e.g. 'wabbit' for 'rabbit'. Here I will use the following broad definition of baby talk:

> *Baby talk*: the language used by anyone in the linguistic community when addressing a child

Thus, even if an adult spoke to a child in the same way as to an adult, we would call this language baby talk. The set of features that distinguish the person's baby talk from non-baby talk in this case would be zero. Also, baby talk as defined may vary from speaker to speaker and language to language. The purpose initially will be to see if individuals speak differently to children and, if so, what the distinguishing features are. These can then be examined for their possible effects on the child's language. This section will begin the inquiry into baby talk by looking at how adults address infants. There will be further discussion in subsequent chapters.

While there are numerous studies of language addressed to English children, there are relatively few on the language addressed to infants. The studies on baby talk to children have found features that are characteristic of it. Kaye (1980a) divides these features into five general categories, summarized here in Table 5.11. While the details behind them will be given in subsequent chapters, they are presented here in order to provide an initial general picture of what English baby talk looks like.

Here we will look at the language used by English parents to address their prelinguistic infants. One possibility is that they do not talk to their infants –

Table 5.11 *Five kinds of characteristics of English baby talk, taken from Kaye (1980a: 489–90)*[a]

Characteristics	Specific examples and references
1. prosodic features	higher pitch, greater range of frequencies, more-varied intonation (Garnica 1977; Sachs 1977)
2. lexical features	special forms like *potty* and *nana* (Ferguson 1964)
3. complexity features	shorter utterances, fewer embedded clauses, fewer verb auxiliaries, etc. (Snow 1977a; Furrow, Nelson & Benedict 1979)
4. redundancy features	more immediate repetition and more repetition of the same words or phrases over a period of time (Snow 1977a)
5. content features	restriction to topics in the child's world (Snow 1977b)

[a] This is a direct quotation from Kaye (1980a: 489–90) reorganized into the form of a table.

as Pye has claimed for Quiché parents. As we will see, English parents have a very different view of their infant from Quiché parents. As you might expect, English mothers (the parents in the studies to be discussed) do talk quite a lot to their infants. That being so, the next question is the purpose of this language. One possibility is that they are directly teaching them in the sense of behaviorism, as discussed in section 2.2.3 in relation to Bloomfield. Or, they could be involved in indirect teaching by presenting a model of how the infants should talk. If so, we would expect that parents' language should be quite simple during the period of prelinguistic development, possibly dominated by single-word utterances. This would be supportive evidence of a claim that the child's single-word utterances follow from such modeling. Still another possibility is that parents reserve attempts to teach children language until they show some evidence of acquiring language during the period of single-word utterances. If this is so, then the language used to the prelinguistic infant may look quite different from that used later.

To study these possibilities requires observing parents addressing children at two time periods and comparing their language at each. Here we will review two studies which have used this methodology: Snow (1977b) and Kaye (1980a).

Snow (1977b) Snow conducted her study with the hypothesis that English baby talk would begin to show features like those in Table 5.11 when children were around 1 year and beginning to use language. For example, it was predicted that tutorial types of questions like 'What's that?' or requests would not be used before that time since they would serve no teaching purpose.

To study this hypothesis, Snow collected longitudinal samples using video- and audio-tapes from two mother–child dyads. The infants, Ann and Mary, were firstborn daughters of middle-class English parents. The tapes were 20 minutes long, and included a feeding session and a play session. The ages of the samples were as follows (in weeks):

	1st year (in quarters)				2nd year (in quarters)		
	1st	2nd	3rd	4th	1st	2nd	3rd
Ann:	12	(none)	29	49	(none)	(none)	79,87
Mary:	13	22	29	38,44,52	(none)	75	81

As can be seen, the samples are not exactly comparable, but they are sufficiently close.

Snow's quantitative analysis applied several measures to the mother's language in each of the above sessions. The main measures were MLU and percentage of interrogative sentences. The results of both of these are presented in figures, so no specific numbers are available. Neither figure showed any abrupt changes during the second year of life. For both mothers, MLU remained constantly around 4.0 throughout the samples. This short MLU indicates that the complexity features of Table 5.11 are probably part of baby talk even during the period of prelinguistic development. The occurrence of interrogatives was also relatively constant, around 30 percent. Interestingly, the most frequent occurrence of interrogatives was during the first session where these were around 40 percent for Mary's mother, and 60 percent for Ann's. Snow concludes from this that the data do not support the hypothesis that the features of baby talk in English are used in response to the child's needs for a simplified model of language.

There were other measures applied by Snow which did show change over the study period. These were percentages of declaratives, imperatives, and contentless utterances (for example, verses, songs, sound-play). Table 5.12 gives these percentages for those times when samples were available for both girls. At first glance, these appear to support the hypothesis that baby talk changes around 1 year. For example, we would expect a mother to use more contentless utterances during the period of prelinguistic development if she felt that the infant was not learning language at that time. Or, we would expect the increase in imperatives when the child becomes able to understand and follow them. These data, then, appear to provide some support for the claim that English parents adjust their speech as their infants begin to acquire language. Unfortunately, the data also lend themselves to other interpretations. For example, we could claim that they show that the

Table 5.12 *Percentages*[a] *of Ann's and Mary's mothers' utterances that were imperatives, declaratives, or contentless utterances, at four sessions, extracted from Snow (1977b: table 2)*

	Age in weeks			
Type of utterance	12–13	29	49–52	79–81
Imperatives				
Ann	10	6	25	23
Mary	15	7	28	5[b]
Declaratives				
Ann	9	22	29	35
Mary	19	13	29	38
Contentless				
Ann	22	38	26	16
Mary	26	32	18	17

[a] Percentages are rounded off.
[b] This is a rather mysterious figure in light of the other data.

adult adjusts in order to provide a simplified model for language learning. Or, they could show that the adult changes in response to the child's level as allowed by restrictions of the grammar of English. This adjustment would be solely for the purpose of communication. In all the possible interpretations of the data, the independent evidence is usually lacking.

Snow's explanation of her data is neither of the above. Instead, through a qualitative analysis, Snow concludes that mothers treat their children as conversational partners. Stated differently in the perspective of this section, our culture perceives children as potential conversational partners, even though they cannot speak or understand. Indeed, our culture allows such a view of various animals, cars, lucky charms, and televisions. The changes in Table 5.12, then, result from the content changes that occur as the infant matures. For the youngest infants, conversation will be limited to grunt, burps, and smiles. For older children, the content may even include motor acts and some meaningless vocalizations.

We can appreciate Snow's perspective by looking at some of the examples she provides. Here is an example of an exchange between Ann and her mother at 3 months (p. 12):

> *Mother*
> (Ann smiles)
> Oh, what a nice little smile!
> Yes, isn't that nice?
> There.
> There's a nice little smile.

(Ann burps)
What a nice wind as well!
Yes, that's better, isn't it?
Yes.
Yes.
(Ann vocalizes)
Yes!
There's a nice noise.

Snow comments on this period (p. 13) '... it is possible to identify a fairly restricted class of infant behaviors which at 0;3 qualify as unit-types: smiles, laughs, burps, yawns, sneezes, coughs, coo-vocalizations, and looking attentively at something.' While all cultures will need to recognize the potential for children to be conversational partners, ours apparently assumes this to be the case from the very onset of life. (It would probably be possible to find such conversations preceding birth, with the topic being kicking activity in utero.)

Snow observes that mothers can be quite insistent on the child taking a turn in the conversation. Here is an example (p. 16) of one such episode:

Mother
What can you see?
What are you looking at?
What are you looking at?
What are you looking at?
What are you looking at, hmm?
Hmmm?
(Ann says 'haaa')
Haaa.

These earlier conversations lead eventually to real-looking conversations around 18 months, a topic we shall return to in the next chapter. For the data for the present period, Snow concludes (p. 21): 'The way mothers talk to their babies is one reflection of their belief that the babies are capable of reciprocal communication.'

Kaye (1980a)   The preliminary data on baby talk to infants in Snow's study has been expanded by a much larger study by Kaye (1980a). Kaye examined the language addressed to 37 infants by 36 mothers, one mother having fraternal twins. Samples of 4–7 minutes were videotaped when the children were 6, 13 and 26 weeks of age; samples of 22 of the mothers were compared to later samples collected at 26 months and 30 months as reported in Kaye & Charney (1981). While the infant sample sessions were small, they still produced a large total sample of 13,574 utterances from the mothers.

Kaye used six measures to analyze the mothers' utterances. Here, we shall look at four of them:

number of utterances per minute
words per utterance (an MLU measure)
percentage of phatic utterances
percentage of exact repetitions

The term *phatic utterance* requires an explanation. These are (p. 493): 'a class of one-word greetings, consisting of the following utterances: Huh, Uhhuh, Right, Sure, OK, Yes, Yeah, Yeh, Yep, Yay, Hello, Howdy, Hm, What, Well, Ah, Oh, and Ooh.'

Like Snow, Kaye does not find that speech adjustment waits until the child begins to acquire language. His data indicate, however, that adults speak even shorter utterances to infants than to children acquiring language. The short MLU to infants (2.76), high percentage of phatic utterances (21 percent) and exact repetitions (16 percent) show even simpler language than that used later. To the 2-year-olds the mothers' MLU increased to 3.68, and though the percentage of phatic utterances is not given, exact repetitions reduced to 3.8 percent. Kaye states (p. 497): '...the mothers said many two-word utterances, as well as one-word utterances not in the phatic category (e.g. No, Hey, Lookit, and the baby's name)'. While the mothers' speech adjustments to infants may not be intended to provide a teaching model of language, the highly repetitive and simple language presented does provide what should be a helpful model for acquisition.

Kaye also noticed that there were important individual differences between mothers. He does not give a detailed analysis, but does provide an example of two mothers who were very different from each other. Here are partial samples of the language of these two mothers (p. 503):

Mother 1	*Mother 2*
1. Come on.	1. Is that a burp?
2. Talk.	2. Huh?
3. Talk to me.	3. Or are you going to get the hiccup
4. Can you talk to me?	4. Huh?
5. (laugh) say something.	5. You going to get the hiccups?
6. Come on.	6. Huh?
7. Talk.	7. Yeah.
8. Can you talk?	8. Hi there.
9. Can you say something?	9. You look like you're just
10. Well, talk.	concentrating too hard.
	10. Roseann.

Mother 1 was highly directive, and used a lot of imperatives and direct requests; for example, she used 44 percent requests in the sample as compared to 0 percent for Mother 2. She also had over twice as many exact repetitions (15 percent vs. 6 percent for Mother 2). Mother 2, on the other hand, had a more narrative style with few requests made to the infant. She also had twice as many fragments like 'huh?' (utterances 2, 4, 6) than Mother 1 (56 percent vs. 24 percent). Also, she was more apt to drop an auxiliary verb in questions, as in utterance 5, than Mother 1 (50 percent vs. 20 percent of all questions). When we return to the role of the linguistic environment in later chapters we will examine more carefully the possible effects of these individual differences.

Kaye concludes that the language addressed to infants reflects the mother's expectations of the infant. He agrees, then, with Snow that English mothers perceive their infants as possible conversational partners. He takes this one step further, however, by allowing for mothers to vary in their perceptions of their infants. He states (pp. 504–5):

> The individual differences in maternal language input to the infants and children in this study were less a matter of linguistic differences among the mothers, and still less of different attitudes about linguistic instruction, than they were differences in expectations of the baby as a person and expectations about how one ought to relate to a baby (Kaye 1980 [=1980b, DI]). Authoritarian vs. ego-building vs. egalitarian attitudes have consequences in the complexity and structure of the child's linguistic environment from birth.

There are two points to be emphasized here. First, there are linguistic differences that result from these different attitudes, as exemplified by Mothers 1 and 2. The effects of these differences need to be observed. Second, the kinds of perception will vary from culture to culture, as mentioned in 5.5.1. We need to be careful not to draw universal conclusions in this area of research based solely on work in English. Both of these issues will be returned to in the next chapter.

Further reading

Infant speech perception

There is quite a large, and controversial, literature that has appeared since 1971. The bibliography in this chapter is a selection of some of the more frequently cited works. Periodically, books have appeared containing review papers of the field; the major ones are: Schiefelbusch & Lloyd (1974) with reviews by Morse, Eimas, and Butterfield & Cairns; Yeni-Komshian,

Kavanaugh & Ferguson (1980b) with reviews by Eilers, Kuhl, and Aslin & Pisoni; Schiefelbusch & Bricker (1981) with a review by Trehub, Bull, and Schneider.

Infant speech production
Overviews of stages of articulatory development can be found in the articles by Oller and Stark in Yeni-Komshian, Kavanaugh & Ferguson (1980a). Descriptive data are provided in Lewis (1936/51), Cruttenden (1970), Blount (1972), the studies by O. Irwin, and Oller *et al.* (1976). Summaries are available on behaviorist views (Winitz 1969), maturationist views (Locke 1983), and constructionist views (Oller 1981; Elbers 1982).

Cognitive development
There are numerous introductions to Piaget's theory; a simple one can be found in Ginsberg & Opper (1969), also in Piaget & Inhelder (1969). An in-depth coverage is provided by Flavell (1963). The serious student should take a look at Piaget's own researches on sensorimotor development which are contained in his three books on the topic (Piaget 1948, 1952, 1954). The best treatment of Piaget in a language acquisition text is Anisfeld (1984).

Linguistic input
Like infant speech perception, infant–adult interaction has been an area of active research in recent years. While there are several papers on the topic, few focus on the linguistic aspects of the mother in relation to later development and the theories discussed in 5.5. The cultural differences that may occur can be seen in Schiefflin (1979). The summary of the English view of the infant as a conversationalist can be seen in Snow (1977b). Bruner (1975) presents a strong statement on the role of the parent.

6 The period of single-word utterances

6.1 The definition of word acquisition

As we have just seen, the young infant has progressed through several developments during the first year of life. In a constructionist perspective, these advances lay the foundation for later growth. In one sense, then, there is no prelinguistic development, since the origins of the infant's language rest in its first reflexes. This point was raised several years ago by Kaplan & Kaplan (1971) in a paper entitled 'Is there such a thing as a prelinguistic child?'. Despite this, language is most commonly seen as beginning with the acquisition of the first words.

At first glance, it may appear that marking the onset of language by the child's first words should be an easy task. In her classic review of child language, however, McCarthy (1954) pointed out how difficult it is to discuss the acquisition of words. Adapting her discussion, we can propose that a word is acquired in any one of the following definitions:

(i)   a word of the adult language that is understood with some meaning, however variable, by the child;
(ii) a word of the adult language that is understood in approximately its adult meaning;
(iii) any vocalization of the child that is used in a consistent context;
(iv) a word of the adult language that is produced in a consistent context;
(v)   a word of the adult language that is understood and used in an adult-like manner;
(vi) a word of the adult language that is understood and used in an adult-like manner, and is pronounced correctly.

There are several factors that need to be considered. First, there is the issue of comprehension vs. production. Second, we need to decide between adult and non-adult vocalizations as in definition (iii). Third, there is the issue of correct pronunciation. If we take definition (i), then word acquisition occurs around the end of the first year. If we take definition (vi), the first words will not be acquired until much later.

Recall in Stern's stages, the first period begins with the onset of single word utterances in production, presumably through definition (iv) above. Here, however, this period will be shown as beginning with the onset of consistent understanding of adult words. Thus, I will use definition (i) to establish the boundary between what is prelinguistic and what is linguistic. Nothing of import should be made of it, however, since it is primarily a descriptive decision. It will only be important within a theory of acquisition which attempts to propose principles for the transition of one infant ability to another.

6.2 Early word comprehension and production

6.2.1 Onset and rate

Most of our information on word comprehension until recently came from diary studies. The general picture was that children begin to respond meaningfully to words around 1 year of age, and increase their receptive vocabulary for several months before any noticeable gains in production. This led to a general conclusion that comprehension precedes production. In Table 2.1, for example, we gave data on Axel Preyer from Preyer (1889) indicating that Axel at 17 months had a receptive vocabulary of 35 words but a productive vocabulary of only two words. This impression was confirmed by several other diarists, despite discrepancies in their methodologies.

Given the current findings on the infant's perceptual abilities, it is not surprising that the child should begin to identify adult vocalizations by 10 months or so. This ability, combined with its growing knowledge of the world, enables it to pair the recognizable vocalizations with consistent contexts, and eventually with concepts. The observation that the child's abilities lead the child to do this, of course, does not reduce the amazing nature of the event.

Several studies during the period of large sample studies attempted to go beyond the individual data of diaries to provide norms for the acquisition of words. Most of this work focussed on production, to the neglect of comprehension. In one of the most cited studies, Charlotte Buhler (1931) looked at the age of the onset of the first word in production for 46 German children. She found the following age distribution:

Age of first word acquisition	No. of children
0;8–0;9	10
0;10	19
1;0–1;1	10
1;2–1;3	5
1;4–1;5	2

From this, she concluded that the first words in production occur around 10 months.

Onset, of course, provides little information about the cause of development. In the first, and for a long time most widely accepted, study on English children, M. Smith (1926) looked at the average vocabulary size for children at several age periods. I give here a simplification of her data for the early months of development:

Age	No. of words in vocabulary
0;8	0
0;10	1
1;0	3
1;3	19
1;6	22
1;9	118

These simple figures show that the onset of a productive vocabulary at 10 months does not lead to rapid growth. Instead, there is a period of several months before the word spurt in production sometime around 18 months.

We were left with these rather general findings until Benedict (1979) provided the first controlled study comparing the onset of comprehension and production.

Benedict (1979) Benedict followed the vocabulary acquisition of eight children longitudinally for approximately a six-month period. By comparing several children through the same method of inquiry, she was able to overcome the difficulties inherent in trying to compare different diary studies. At the same time, by limiting her subjects to eight, she was able to do a more in-depth study of individual children than previous large sample studies.

To score the acquisition of her subjects' vocabularies, Benedict determined the ages at which each child acquired predetermined numbers of words for comprehension and production. She presented her results for each child in a way which allows for some rearranging of the data. Table 6.1 presents her general results for all her subjects. The advanced development of comprehension is quite striking. First, the onset of comprehension was nearly four months in advance of production. Second, the rate of acquiring the first 50 words in comprehension was twice as fast as that for production. The children needed approximately two weeks to acquire 10 words in comprehension, but four weeks in production. These results in a carefully controlled study confirm the initial findings of diary studies. There is one discrepancy with the earlier findings in that the onset of the first words was later for Benedict's subjects than for Buhler's, although the vocabulary

Table 6.1 *The mean age at which Benedict's (1979) eight children acquired their 20th, 40th, and 50th words in comprehension and production*

| Comprehension | | Production |
No. of words acquired	Mean age	No. of words acquired
0	0;10(14)	
20	0;11(15)	
30	1;0(3)	
40	1;0(19)	
50	1;1(5)	
	1;1(21)	0
	1;3(6)	20
	1;4(14)	30
	1;5(16)	40
	1;9(15)	50

sizes for Benedict's subjects at 18 months were larger than those found by Smith. Given differences of method and Benedict's small sample, however, one should not make too much of these differences.

Benedict's results are particularly interesting when we go beyond the general findings and look at individual children. Table 6.2 provides a simplified view of her results for four of the eight subjects, comparing the age at which specific numbers of words were acquired in comprehension and production. It shows two aspects of the data: the relation between the sizes of the comprehension and production vocabularies, and the rate of acquisition in each.

The results show four apparently very different children. Michael shows a relatively small gap between comprehension and production. When he has 100 words comprehended, he already has 20 words produced. David shows an even smaller gap, with 40 words produced with only 80 comprehended. Diana and Elizabeth have a wider gap, with the latter showing 150 words understood before *any* words produced. Clearly, the gap between the sizes of the child's receptive and productive vocabularies can vary tremendously.

Even though Michael and David have small gaps between the vocabularies comprehended and produced, their patterns of development are by no means the same. Looking at the rate of acquisition, based only on the first 50 words in each vocabulary, Michael acquires his first 50 words in comprehension and production at about the same rate, which is approximately two days per word. David, on the other hand, acquired the first 50 words in comprehension five times faster than in production, with rates of one day per word vs. five days per word respectively. Stated differently, David acquired his comprehension vocabulary twice as fast as Michael did, but his productive vocabulary twice as slowly. Regarding rate, Elizabeth

Table 6.2 *The number of words acquired in comprehension (C) and production (P), and the number of days per word for the first 50 words in comprehension and production, for four subjects taken from Benedict (1979)*[a]

Age	Michael C	Michael P	Elizabeth C	Elizabeth P	David C	David P	Diana C	Diana P
0;9	0							
0;10	20		0		0		0	
0;11	30		30		20	0	30	
1;0	80	0	60		40	1	40	0
1;1				80	50	20	50	
1;2	100	20	150	0		30	80	
1;3		30		20	80	40	100	20
1;4		50		30				30
1;5				40		50		
1;6				50				40
1;7								50
Rate[b]	2.3	2.0	1.6	2.0	1.0	5.0	1.8	3.7

[a] Vocabularies at specific ages are approximate in that the data were not presented in this manner originally.
[b] Mean number of days needed to acquire a new word.

is very similar to Michael, in that her rate of acquisition for the two vocabularies is similar, around two days per word for each. Diana, on the other hand, is more like David in that her rate of acquisition of receptive vocabulary is twice as fast as her acquisition of productive vocabulary.

These results show that we have to be very cautious in applying the norms of Table 6.1 to individual children. Further, the results in Table 6.2 reveal that rate of acquisition and the gap between comprehension and production are, to a certain extent, independent. Two general conclusions are: (i) the rate of comprehension acquisition is the same as or greater than that for production; and (ii) the gap between the two varies greatly, with a norm of approximately 100 words understood at the time of the first words produced.

6.2.2 General semantic categories

In the period of large sample studies, investigators looked at the general meanings of the child's first words by classifying words into syntactic categories such as noun, verb, adjective, etc. While these are categories of the adult's language, we have to be cautious about assigning such categories to the child's. Our Competence Assumption, in fact, requires us to do so only if there is evidence in the child's linguistic behavior for such classes.

Table 6.3 *Nelson's (1973) semantic categories for early word meaning, as defined and adapted by Benedict (1979:192–3)*

1. *Specific nominals*: words that refer to only one exemplar of a category, but are not necessarily limited to proper names, e.g. 'Daddy', 'Coppy' (name of pet).

2. *General nominals*: words which refer to all members of a category. It includes inanimate and animate objects, and pronouns like 'this', 'that', 'he'.

3. *Action words*: words that elicit specific actions from the child or that accompany actions of the child. It includes social-action games, e.g. 'peekaboo' and 'what does doggie say?'; event words, e.g. 'eat'; locatives, e.g. 'where's ___?'; general actions, e.g. 'give'; and action inhibitors, e.g. 'no', 'don't touch'.

4. *Modifiers*: words that refer to properties or qualities of things or events. It includes attributes, e.g. 'big'; states, e.g. 'allgone', 'hot'; locatives, e.g. 'there'; possessives, e.g. 'mine'.

5. *Personal-social*: words that express affective states and social relationships. It includes assertions, e.g. 'yes', 'no', 'want'; and social-expressive actions, e.g. 'bye-bye', 'hi', 'nite-nite'.

In the very important monograph entitled *Structure and strategy in learning to talk*, Katherine Nelson (1973) developed a more semantically oriented taxonomy to replace the earlier syntactic ones. Table 6.3 provides Nelson's taxonomy, as modified by Benedict (1979), who was a student of Nelson's. Benedict's adaptation was done to make the categories more compatible for analyzing comprehension.

Nelson followed 18 children longitudinally, starting when they were around 1 year. Below I give the three arbitrary age groups she divided her subjects into:

Group	(Age)	No. of children
I	1;2–1;3	7
II	1;0–1;1	5
III	0;10–0;11	6

She asked the parents of each child to keep a parental diary of their word productions. In addition, she visited each child once a month. We saw above that Benedict altered this methodology by visiting every two weeks, and also by studying comprehension vocabulary. Nelson followed her children until they had acquired their 50th word in production.

Nelson analyzed the words acquired by her 18 children according to the categories in Table 6.3. Table 6.4 gives a summary of her major findings. First, for all children, general nominals were the largest class of words, with 51 percent of the children's words falling into this category. This confirms Stern's earlier claim of a substance stage at the onset of vocabulary development. She also found that the acquisition of the nominals changed

Table 6.4 *Percentage of vocabulary that fell into six categories for 18 subjects in Nelson (1973) and for two groups of expressive and referential children*

Category	Referential (%)	Expressive (%)	Combined (%)
Specific nominals	3	7	14
General nominals	38	17	51
Action words	4	6	13
Modifiers	2	6	9
Personal-social	1	12	8
Other	1	2	4

over time; general nominals increased in class size, while specific nominals decreased:

Category	No. of words acquired		
	1–10	21–30	41–50
Specific nominals (%)	24	14	9
General nominals (%)	41	46	62

In addition, Nelson divided her children into two groups which differed in their acquisition of these categories. These were called *expressive* and *referential* children. As seen in Table 6.4, the expressive children had half as many general nominals as the referential ones, but had many more personal-social words – the referential children had very few of these.

There are at least two points that need to be discussed about this finding. One is that while the children could be placed into these groups, their use of these categories appeared to fall on a continuum. That is, except for a few children at the extremes, children only *tended* toward one type or the other. It may be that children may follow a normal distribution in the extent to which they use general nominals or personal-social words. This is important to state, since otherwise one may conclude that children fall neatly into one category or another. Observe that we could set an arbitrary measure such as saying that all children with 6 percent or more personal-social words are expressive. If so, we have imposed a measurement sequence in the sense of Chapter 4.

A second issue concerns the cause for this variation. In Chapter 4 we explored three possible causes for variation. First, it could result from performance differences, i.e. that some children focus on naming while others focus on self-expression. Nelson, in fact, seems to prefer an explanation of this kind. A second cause could be the effect of the linguistic environment. It is possible, for example, that some parents concentrate on getting their children to learn names, while others allow them to concen-

Table 6.5 *Percentages of occurrence of words in three semantic categories for the first 80 words in comprehension (C), and the first 50 words in production (P), for eight subjects studied by Benedict (1979)*

| Category | No. of words acquired | | | | | | |
	0–10 P (%)	C (%)	0–30 P (%)	C (%)	0–50 P (%)	C (%)	0–80 C (%)
Specific nominals	24	30	17	19	11	17	15
General nominals	38	14	41	33	50	39	43
Action words	22	53	26	44	19	36	36

trate on self-expression. Nelson does not support this interpretation, in that she describes cases where the adult may have one style while the child has the other. A third possibility is that the difference reflects two distinct ways children may choose to acquire language. We could say that the referential child selects to acquire nominals and will use these as cues to sentence structure, while the expressive child is concentrating on the pragmatics of utterances. I am unaware of anyone who has interpreted the results in this latter fashion. If Nelson is correct, we have found an interesting pattern of individual variation in lexical development that tells us little about the child's language acquisition system.

Benedict (1979) wanted to replicate the developmental changes suggested by the data on acquisition of general and specific nominals and to expand it to the emerging comprehension vocabulary. Table 6.5 provides information on the three most frequent categories for her eight subjects across the acquisition of the first 80 words in comprehension, and the first 50 words in production. Benedict noticed that the distribution of these vocabularies was quite different for comprehension than for production. In comprehension, the most frequent class at first was action words, followed by specific nominals. In production, on the other hand, general nominals are more frequent at the onset. She concludes from this that comprehension and production are different in their propensity to focus on action words.

There is, however, a much simpler explanation. Figure 6.1 presents my reanalysis of Benedict's data in Table 6.5. The distribution of the three categories in comprehension and production is shown along the time axis. As can be seen, the distribution of the three classes at the onset of productive vocabulary around 15 months is the same as the distribution of the comprehension vocabulary *at that time*. The production data, therefore, simply reflect the fact that the children are producing lexical types in a comparable proportion to their receptive vocabulary. If so, the data do not support qualitative similarities between production and comprehension. In

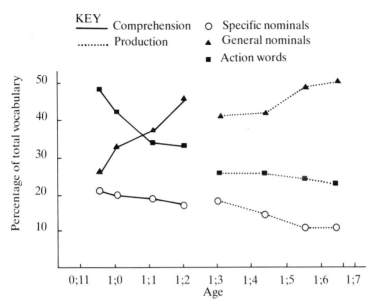

Figure 6.1 Percentages of occurrences for specific nominals, general nominals, and action words, in comprehension and production, in the vocabularies in Benedict (1979).

a more recent simple subject study, Hoek, Ingram & Gibson (1986) have found a similar result.

6.2.3 Acquisition of individual lexical items

I began this chapter by defining word acquisition in a very loose way in reference to the assignment of some meaning. Ultimately, of course, the child will need not only to use a word with meaning, but also to use it with the same meaning as that assigned by the adult language. That is, we will eventually need to push our definition of acquisition to correct usage.

At the onset of acquisition, the words first acquired in comprehension have a strong tendency towards actions. Table 6.6 provides Benedict's data for the most frequent early words understood. Here frequency refers to the percentage of subjects who understood a word as one of their first 50 words. As can be seen, several of these are part of social-action games that are very limited in their meanings. The young child does not have a wide range of activities when it responds to terms like 'pat-a-cake' and 'peekaboo'. 'Dance', 'give kisses', and even 'bye-bye' are for the young child very restricted acts. This limited context for words is characteristic of the first meanings of the child's words. This observation has been supported in a

Table 6.6 *The most frequent action words found in the first 50 words comprehended and produced by eight children, based on the percentage of subjects who acquired each word, from Benedict (1979)*

Categories	Comprehension	(%)	Production	(%)
Social-action games	bye-bye	88	bye-bye	63
	pat-a-cake	88	woof-woof	63
	dance	63	nite-nite	50
	peekaboo	63	peekaboo	50
	do nice	63		
	give kisses	50		
General actions	give	100	no	75
	get	88	see	63
	no	83	go	38
	kiss	63	out	38
Locatives	where's	100	get down	38
	come here	88		
	look at	75		
	put in	63		
	get down	50		

study by Snyder, Bates & Betherington (1981). As part of a more elaborate study, they analyzed the contextual flexibility of the first 50 words comprehended for 32 children who had a mean age of 1;1(7). They collected their data through the use of parental diaries. They devised an elaborate set of rules (their Table 1) to score words as either *contextually restricted* or *contextually variable*. Their children had vocabularies that averaged 45 words in comprehension and 11 words in production. Of these, 60 percent and 48 percent respectively were defined as contextually restricted. I will refer to cases where the child uses a word for a more limited range of meanings than does the adult as *underextensions*.

We can get an idea of the more specific categories that children use in their early words by returning to Nelson's study. Table 6.7 gives my summary of what appear to be the most common words used by her subjects. Nelson broke down the general nominals into several classes, which are listed in Table 6.7 in order of descending class size. In other words, food/drink words were the largest class, followed by animals, etc. Of course, these are descriptive labels, and we cannot assume from these figures that the children had such general classes.

If we examine Table 6.7 carefully, we see that the words acquired refer to inter-categories of meaning. For example, they use the term 'dog' rather than the more general term 'animal', or a more specific one like 'collie' or 'poodle'. This observation was first pointed out by Brown (1958b), and has been studied in depth with older children by Anglin (1977).

Table 6.7 *A composite of the most frequent words to occur across selected semantic categories, taken from Nelson (1973). Percentages are for the number of subjects who acquired a word in its first 50 words in production*

Category	% of subjects with word production
Specific nominals[a]	'daddy', 'mommy' (at least one proper name) 100
General nominals	
Human[a]	'baby' 63
Non-human[b]	
food/drink	'juice' 67, 'milk', 'cookie' 56
	'water' 44, 'toast' 39, 'apple', 'cake' 28
animals	'dog' 89, 'cat' 78, 'duck' 44, 'horse' 28
clothes	'shoes' 61, 'hat' 28
toys	'ball' 72, 'blocks' 39
vehicles	'car' 72, 'boat', 'truck' 33
furniture	'clock' 39, 'light' 33
other	'bottle' 44, 'key' 33, 'book' 28
Action words[a]	'up' 50, 'sit', 'see' 38
	'eat', 'down', 'go' 25
Modifiers[a]	'hot' 75, 'allgone', 'more' 38
	'dirty', 'cold', 'here', 'there' 25
Personal-social words[a]	'hi' 88, 'bye(bye)' 63, 'no', 'yes(yeah)' 50
	'please', 'thank-you' 38

[a] These are taken from Appendix A where Nelson gives the first 50 words for eight children.
[b] These are taken from Table 8 where Nelson gives data for all 18 children.

Information like that in Table 6.7 is the first step in trying to determine the nature of word meaning in young children. Besides knowing the specific words children acquire, we need to look carefully at their contexts of usage. This is, of course, no easy task. Most of the work in this area comes from diaries and from the more recent studies which combine parental diaries with naturalistic language sampling – even then our data are often incomplete. Some generalizable findings, however, have emerged.

As cited above, the earliest uses of words appear to be cases of underextensions. Shortly after, however, there is evidence that the child's use of the word becomes generalized, not only to new appropriate instances, but to inappropriate ones. For example, Braunwald (1978), in her diary of her daughter Laura, provides the following data on the production of 'ball':

(6.1) 1;0(9)   picture of a ball in a book
    1;0(9)–1;4 (i)   a ball
                (ii)   round objects, e.g. grapefuit, orange, seedpod, doorbell buzzer
                (iii)   request for the first and second servings of liquid in a cup

What started out as an underextension at 1;0(9) became overextended for several months after. These instances of inappropriate usage have come to be known as *overextensions*.

Overextensions have intrigued investigators for years, especially because the word's meanings can spread so far from the original context. Braunwald gives a particularly striking example of Laura's use of 'cookie':

(6.2) 1;0(9)   used for cookies
1;0(9)–1;4 (i)   novel round foods, e.g. cheerios, cucumber
(ii) 'record players' and/or 'music' on hi-fi or car radio
(iii) rocking and/or rocking chair
(iv) ice cream

The first overextension was to round new food items. Next, the perceptual feature of roundness took over, where the round record turntable led to its reference as a 'cookie'. Soon she associated the music of the record player with the word. Eventually the rocking chair motion was associated to the movements made in response to music. Vygotsky (1962) years ago commented on these occurrences, which have come to be referred to as *associative complexes*. As the above example has demonstrated, they can get quite far from the original meaning.

The first systematic study of overextensions was done by Eve Clark (1973a). Aware of the rich data contained in diary studies, Clark found as many cases as she could in a survey of several early diaries. Her analysis of these anecdotal examples found that most were due to perceptual similarities between the objects. The perceptual features she found were shape, size, sound, movement, taste, and texture. Her study shows the value of using a review of diary studies as a first step in the study of a particular topic. In this case, however, additional study is needed since the diaries did not report on comprehension, and of course one cannot test the diary data to find the full range of possible overextensions. A more comprehensive treatment of the topic is Rescorla (1980).

Rescorla (1980)   Rescorla, another student of Katherine Nelson's, followed six children longitudinally through the acquisition of the first 75 words in production. Like Nelson (1973) and Benedict (1979) she relied heavily upon diaries kept by the parents. The children were also visited for a one-or two-hour session every two weeks. The children were approximately 1 year at the onset and were followed for at least six months.

Since six children each acquired 75 words, there was a total of 445 words acquired. Of these, 149 or 33 percent were observed as being overextended. The 149 words overextended occurred so 190 times, indicating that many words were only overextended once. These data are quite important in

Table 6.8 *Three types of overextensions, as defined by Rescorla (1980)*

Category	Definition	Examples
Categorical overextensions	'the use of a word to label a referent close to the word's standard referent in some clear higher-order category of adult usage' (pp. 325–6)	'dada' for mother 'truck' for bus 'apple' for oranges
Analogical overextensions	a non-adult referent for a word where it bore no clear categorical relation to what would have been an appropriate referent. The similarity could be: 1. perceptual, 2. functional, or 3. affective (see examples)	1. 'ticktock' for the sound of dripping water 2. 'hat' for basket on child's head 3. 'hot' for glassware that the child was prohibited from touching
Predicate statements	when the child would 'convey some information about the relationship between the immediate referent and some absent person, object, property or state, rather than labelling the referent itself' (p. 326)	'doll' said in absence of doll to refer to the place in the crib where the doll was normally found

showing that overextensions only occur for a subset of the child's vocabulary, despite the fact that they are noticeable when they do happen. They also reveal the difficulty in using unsystematic diaries to study overextensions, since such diaries tend to concentrate on unique or novel events with no comments on more regular behaviors.

The analysis of semantic categories indicated that certain categories were more likely to have words overextended than others. Words within categories that were overextended were as follows: letters 100 percent; vehicles 76 percent; clothing 62 percent. Only 28 percent of animal words were overextended, which is interesting in that many of the examples of overextensions in the diary literature are animal terms. There were 12 words in particular which were overextended: 'baby', 'apple', 'car', 'truck', 'shoe', 'hat', 'dada', 'cheese', 'ball', 'cat', 'dog', 'hot'. These were words which (i) were used by at least four children, and (ii) were overextended by at least half of the children who used them. All but 'cheese' appear among the first words acquired by English children in Table 6.7. These 12 words were overextended 55 times, and thus represent 29 percent of the 190 overextended cases. Overextension, then, appears to be a salient characteristic of a small part of the child's lexicon.

Rescorla next divided overextensions into three types. These types were labeled and defined as shown in Table 6.8. The *categorical overextensions* are what we typically think of when we think of overextensions. These occurred in 105 cases or 55 percent of the total number of overextensions.

Table 6.9 *Four patterns of associative complexes found by Rescorla (1980)*

Pattern	No. of words	Description
1	18	The associative complex occurred only for about one month, e.g., one child used 'baby' for himself, his toys, other children, and for mother and father when they pretended to cry. It only happened during the first month of the word's acquisition.
2	14	Use of the associative complex for a longer period of 2 to 4 months. 71% of these occurred after 1;3.
3	18	The associative complex developed gradually over time, with new meanings added sequentially. For example, one child's use of 'daddy' went through these stages: (1;1–1;2) for her mother; (1;3–1;4) for all fathers; (1;4–1;5) pictures of men or animal fathers.
4	8	The associative pattern showed a mixed or complex temporal pattern.

People words were most frequently overextended, followed by vehicles and animals. *Analogical overextensions* were much less frequent, with 36 cases or 19 percent of all overextensions. The most common example was the use of 'ball' for round objects, which was done by five of the children. Lastly, *predicate statements* occurred 47 times or 25 percent of the overextensions. These are particularly interesting in that they are suggestive of later two-word sentences. This point will be returned to in section 6.3.

Our characterization of overextensions has been that they follow earlier underextended applications. Rescorla's longitudinal analysis supports this. The percentages of words overextended during the last seven months of her study were 11, 9, 24, 29, 28, 28, 24. The rate of overextensions increased over the first four months and was still 24 percent at the end. Importantly, all the children were beginning to produce multiword sentences by the last month of the study. Thus, overextensions continue on into the next period and are not unique to the period of single-word utterances. Further, Rescorla found that the words that were overextended tended to be the earliest ones acquired:

Words acquired	*% of words overextended*
1–25	45
26–50	35
51–75	20

That is, nearly half of the words that were overextended in the study were among the first 25 words acquired. Rescorla states (p. 329): 'Most of these words denoted some highly valued, familiar and salient object.'

Lastly, Rescorla analyzed the occurrence of *associative complexes*. She defines the word (p. 330) as 'a collection in which each referent shares some common attribute with the standard but no single feature characterizes all exemplars of the complex'. A word which showed an associative complex would be one with overextensions that combined the categories of Table 6.8. There were 58 words, or 30 percent of the overextended words, which were used as associative complexes. At least three children used the words 'daddy', 'key', 'hot', 'mommy', 'hat' and 'cheese' as associative complexes. Rescorla found four patterns of associative complexes, summarized in Table 6.9. We should not place too much importance on these, since they look very much like a measurement sequence. The fourth pattern, for example, appears to be just a category for everything that will not fit into the first three. Nonetheless, the patterns show the variability that characterizes associative complexes.

While data on overextensions in production are numerous, the facts on overextensions in comprehension are less clear. Huttenlocher (1974), in a naturalistic study on four children at around 1 year, was the first to observe that words overextended in production were nonetheless understood correctly. She states (p. 357): 'With respect to comprehension, however, I have noticed no overgeneralization. The children typically did not respond to a word unless they knew its referent.' This comment was made after following her children over a six-month period. More recently, several studies have indicated that some comprehension overextensions do occur, but they are less frequent and obvious (Thomson & Chapman 1977; Kuczaj 1982a; Mervis & Canada 1983; Hoek, Ingram & Gibson 1986). The claim is that the overextensions in comprehension will only be apparent if the child is presented with a sufficient array of objects. For example, if the child thinks 'bear' means four-legged animal, he will still perform correctly if offered a choice of a bear, a bird, and an apple.

The first systematic study on comprehension and overextensions was done by Thomson & Chapman (1977). They tested five English children with mean age of 22.4 months, and with an average MLU of 1.55. Thus, their subjects were beyond the period of single-word utterances. Since data from other studies with younger children are less robust (e.g. Mervis & Canada 1983; Hoek, Ingram & Gibson 1986), I will discuss Thomson & Chapman's study here rather than returning to it in the next chapter. The results from Rescorla indicate that overextensions continue into the next period, and that no qualitative changes occur. I assume then, without direct evidence, that Thomson & Chapman's results on slightly more advanced children are generalizeable to children at least at the latter part of the period of single-word utterances.

Thomson & Chapman selected four words that were documented as being overextended from each diary report of the five children. General information about the subjects and their test words is given in Table 6.10. Thomson & Chapman collected a wide range of photographs and pictures to use in testing for overextensions, as, for example, those used to test the subject K:

(6.3) *Test word*

Test materials

'Daddy' }
'Mommy' }
- 5 Polaroid pictures of mother
- 5 Polaroid pictures of father
- several Polaroid pictures of familiar men
- several Polaroid pictures of unfamiliar people, varied by sex, age, facial features, and clothing
Total of 42 pictures

'woof'
- 10 pictures of different kinds of dogs
- 1 picture of K's toy dog
- pictures of familiar animals (2 of bears, cat, duck, cow, lamb, horse, toy horse, bird, toy rabbit)
- pictures of less familiar animals (buffalo, reindeer, wolf, donkey, kangaroo, giraffe, elephant, hippopotamus, fox, koala bear, penguin, tiger, llama, sea horse)
Total of 35 pictures

'apple'
- 11 pictures of different kinds of apples
- pictures of familiar objects (pumpkin, 2 of tomatoes, peas, orange, strawberry, 3 of balls, 2 of footballs, lamp, lemon, banana, carrot)
- pictures of less familiar objects (whole onions, 2 of soap, plain green oval paper)

First there was a production task in which the child was shown pictures until he labeled at least five pictures correctly and ten pictures incorrectly. Next, there was a comprehension task in which each of the four words was tested 16 times. On ten trials, the child was shown an appropriate picture along with an inappropriate one. On five trials, an overextended picture was shown with an inappropriate one. The last trial had two unrelated pictures together. The child had to respond to either 'Show me the X' or 'Where is X?'. A word was scored as overextended in comprehension if a correct picture was selected on the first ten trials *seven times or less*. Stated differently, a child was credited with having the word understood correctly if it got eight or more correct on the first ten trials.

Table 6.10 *Subject, age, MLU and test words for five children studied by Thomson & Chapman (1977)*

Subject	Age	MLU	Test words
D	1;11	2.46	*doggie, *cow, *fish, *ketchup
F	2;3	1.66	Daddy, Joey, *kitty-cat, apple
I	1;9	1.32	Daddy, bow-wow, banana, ball
J	1;8	1.09	Daddy, *dog, apple, *ball
K	1;9	1.20	Daddy, Mommy, woof, *apple

* Words overextended in comprehension.

Table 6.10 indicates the words that were overextended in comprehension according to Thomson & Chapman's score. Only eight of the 20 words tested were overextended. Curiously, the one child who overextended all four words was the most advanced child, D. The other three children showed much less evidence for overextensions. The results indicate that some overextension may occur in comprehension, but that it is much less widespread than in production.

6.3 The explanation of early word meaning

The presentation so far of the acquisition of word meaning has been primarily descriptive. I have tried to present what appears to be some of the more reliable information on how the child's early vocabulary develops. There was no attempt, however, to offer an explanation of what underlies these behavioral changes. There are now two separate theoretical questions that need to be addressed: what is the theory of semantics that accounts for the adult's language, and what is the theory of acquisition that accounts for the child's errors, i.e. overextensions?

It is my impression that linguists are in much less agreement about what constitutes a theory of semantics than they are about what constitutes a grammar. For example, in syntax we can propose that the child must acquire at least a phrase structure grammar that contains certain properties, e.g. categories such as NP, VP, and rules that relate antecedents to pronouns or moved NPs to their initial positions. What are the parallels to these examples in semantic theory? Current theories make quite distinct claims from each other. For example, feature theories assign word meanings binary features such as [± human] while prototype theories assign meanings according to proximity to some typical exemplar of the word's meaning. I suspect the beginning student could become quite bogged down just understanding these theoretical alternatives without learning anything more about the child's language acquisition. Stated differently, it appears that child data can be manipulated to support any of the current theories, in the sense that the independent evidence is difficult to find.

In this section I will focus on the second question raised above concerning our theory of acquisition, using this discussion to set up a later discussion on theories of semantic acquisition, to be presented in Chapter 7. I am taking, therefore, an inductive approach, beginning with an analysis of what aspects of the child's linguistic behavior constitute evidence relevant to a theory of semantics.

The Competence Assumption instructs us to consider the child's performance to be indicative of its competence. In the case of word overextension, the assumption will apply when we have evidence that the child overextends (or underextends) a word *in the same way* in both comprehension and production. For example, in (6.1), we gave the example where Laura Braunwald used 'ball' for the meaning of round objects. Suppose that she also understood 'ball' as meaning round objects. If so, her performance leads us to assume that 'ball' means round objects for Laura. It is data like these that are directly relevant for the construction of theories of acquisition. Certain theories, in fact (e.g. Clark 1973) have been constructed on this assumption. The mechanism for such linguistic behaviors will be the child's linguistic (or semantic) system.

Unfortunately, such data are rare in language acquisition. Those few studies that have followed overextensions in both so far suggest that the majority of overextensions in production do not occur in comprehension. For example, Huttenlocher (1974: 339) states in her important study: 'I don't know how to test whether the child knows that "hi" is said as people arrive and "byebye" as they leave.' It appears then that the data from word acquisition during the current period of acquisition do not easily lend themselves as evidence for the nature of the child's semantic system. This state of affairs is further complicated by the influence of the child's cognitive development, to which we now return.

6.3.1 Cognitive factors in word acquisition

In section 5.4 we outlined the first four of Piaget's six sensorimotor stages. These four stages cover the period of development between birth and approximately 1 year of age. The next six months (1 year to 18 months) are described by Piaget as sensorimotor stages 5 and 6. As presented in 5.4.3, the onset of concepts of the kind that underlie word meaning as in the adult language do not appear until around 18 months or after the sensorimotor period. The signifier–signified relationship develops through several stages. Up to sensorimotor stage 5, the first relation that occurs is that of the *signal* or elementary indication. During sensorimotor stage 5, the first identifiable word-like vocalizations appear, but Piaget argues that they are not yet words or *linguistic signs*. That is, they do not yet pair vocalizations with concepts. Instead, they are *symbols*, a relation that exists between signals and signs. Here we will take a brief look at sensorimotor stages 5 and 6, and examine the notion of symbol.

The major gain around 1 year is the appearance of the *tertiary circular reaction*. In the fourth stage, the child is restricted to coordinating familiar schemata to solve a novel problem. In stage 5, the child begins to discover new ways that were not used before, although it happens through trial and error. Piaget states (p. 264) that the fifth stage 'is characterized, in effect, by the formation of new schemata which are due no longer to a simple reproduction of fortuitous results but to a sort of experimentation or search for novelty as such'. Here the ability to control the means to reach an end is increased. The child can begin to use objects as means, e.g. a stick to move or get an object. As we will see in section 6.4, this achievement coincides with the pragmatic use of vocalization, that is, language becomes one of the means the child can use to obtain ends, either through understanding or speaking.

Another development is more active exploration of objects, as well as better ability to locate hidden objects. The child becomes more interested in aspects of objects such as the sounds they make and their trajectory when they fall. When he sees an object hidden in one place, such as under a cup, and then in another, such as under a plate, he will look directly under the plate. During stage 4, he would go to the cup if it were the previous place where the object was hidden. At stage 5, however, the child still cannot succeed in an *invisible displacement*. For example, if we hide the ball in the cup, then put the cup behind our back, leaving the ball behind us, then return the cup, the child does not look behind us for the ball. The child's involvement with objects and its interest in seeking objects has been suggested as a prerequisite for establishing the signifier–signified relation. I will return to this point below. If it is necessary, the child's incomplete achievement of object permanence would be a further argument for the lack of the linguistic sign at this period.

A third development in stage 5 is the appearance of symbols. Piaget (1948) proposes that these occur in stage 6, but his own data (cf. Ingram 1978) suggests their appearance in stage 5, with a continuation into stage 6. In fact, Piaget (1948: 53) states in reference to the growth of imitation: 'It was, as a matter of fact, during this fifth stage that J., L., and T. began to make their first clumsy efforts to reproduce the words of adults.' He sees these words, however, as symbols or 'motivated signifiers, i.e. those which are related to the signified by some resemblance, as distinct from "signs", which are "arbitrary"' (Piaget 1948: 68). They are still associated with the contexts they occur in, and even represent for the child part of that context.

(6.4) is an example from Piaget (1948: 216) of one such symbol used by Jacqueline:

(6.4) 'bow-wow' 1;1(20) – to indicate dogs
                         – to indicate landlord's dog
                         – to geometrical pattern on a rug
                         – to two horses
          1;2(3)   – to baby in a pram
          1;2(4)   – to hens
          1;2(8)   – at sight of dogs, horses, prams, and cyclists
          1;2(12)   – everything seen from balcony – animals, cars,
                           landlord, and people in general
          1;2(15)   – trucks being pulled by porters
          1;3(7)   – pattern on rug
          1;4   – only for dogs

Piaget comments (p. 218): '. . . these first verbal schemas are intermediary between the schemas of sensory–motor intelligence and conceptual schemas', or 'the words applied by the child to these schemas are themselves intermediary between symbolic or imitative signifiers and true signs'. This description of 'bow-wow' is typical of what was called earlier an associative complex. Piaget's position, then, is that associative complexes are the result of the incompletely established relation between signifiers and signifieds.

As evidence for his position, Piaget cites examples of children's symbolic play behavior. The first instances of symbolic play occur during stage 6, but they are very much restricted. The child is not yet ready to pretend that any object can be any other, and behaviors are very much tied to the activity being symbolized, for example focussing on the child's activities, such as pretending to sleep, or pretending to wash oneself. It is only gradually that the child reaches the more advanced play behavior of having one object represent another, such as having a block of wood be a truck.

Regarding overextensions then, Piaget would say that they represent, in their earliest occurrences, the underdeveloped relation between signifiers and signifieds. They do not so much reveal information about the child's concepts, however, as about the child's sensorimotor schemata. There are, however, some problems with the incomplete linguistic sign argument. One is the striking finding of Rescorla that only a small percentage of the child's words overextend, even in the earliest records. If the relation is supposed to be only partially developed, one would expect that all words would be uniformly affected. Second, Thomson & Chapman's data suggest that some overextensions occur in comprehension in slightly older children. Even more extensive data to this effect can be found in Anglin (1977). Thus, at some point the data do become revealing of the child's system. Further, our evidence on word comprehension (Benedict 1979) suggests something like a word spurt in comprehension before word production begins. This word spurt is hard to explain without some reference to the Principle of the Linguistic Sign. These factors make it difficult to eliminate the possibility that some of the overextensions during the period of single-word utterances may directly reflect the child's organization of its semantic system.

Even if a child has reached the level of linguistic signs, it is still possible to offer an alternative to the claim that overextensions result from the child's *incomplete semantic system*. As suggested in Bloom (1973) and Thomson & Chapman (1977), it may be that the child overextends due to *limited vocabulary*. That is, the child is presented with an unknown object, and calls it by a word that is known. This may result purely from perceptual similarities between the known and unknown objects. In Hoek, Ingram & Gibson (1986), we tested for this in a diary study of a young girl, Claire, by seeing if overextensions in production would occur for cases where the correct word was not part of the child's receptive vocabulary. There indeed proved to be several cases of this kind. When this factor operates, we could conclude that the child has adult-like knowledge for the words it has acquired, but must resort to other means when presented with new objects. Even adults probably have to resort to this strategy at one time or another.

6.3.2 Other factors behind overextensions

There is a reasonable amount of data which shows that for at least some words children will overextend in production but not in comprehension. For example, Rescorla (1980) refers to this situation for one of her subjects, Rachel (p. 230):

> During the period when she overextended *car* to a wide range of vehicles, she was able to pick out all the same objects in response to their correct name; these included *motorcycle, bike, truck, plane*, and *helicopter*. Once she acquired productive labels for these concepts, they began to emerge from the *car* cluster. Indicative of how the process operated, her first label for *airplane* was *sky car*.

What, then, is the cause of such cases?

One possibility, as stated in Thomson & Chapman (1977), is that there may be a retrieval problem, i.e. the child may be unable to recall the correct word, so he uses a more familiar one. Some evidence for this can be found in

Rescorla (1980) where she observes that overextended words tend to be frequently used ones that are acquired early. In Hoek, Ingram & Gibson (1986), we operationalized this into a prediction that overextensions in production would more likely be an earlier acquired word used for a recently acquired word instead of vice versa. Our analysis of the parental diary of a young girl bore out this prediction. Lastly, there may be phonological factors at work. That is, the child may use a phonologically simpler word for one that is more complex. Schwartz & Leonard (1982) have found that children tend to avoid temporarily words that are beyond their present phonological system (see section 6.5). In Hoek, Ingram & Gibson (1986), there was some evidence for this in our analysis in which Claire was taught nonsense words that were either in or outside her phonological system. Overextensions occurred in the direction of 'in' words for 'out' words.

Summary   It appears, then, that several factors may be at work when children overextend their early words. It is therefore simplistic to say that overextensions during the acquisition of the first words reveal a great deal about the child's semantic system. If anything, given the limited data on overextensions in comprehension, the data indicate that children are reasonably good at getting the meanings correct for their early words, at least in regard to simple lexical items. The overextensions that do occur may be the result of the child's incomplete vocabulary.

6.4 Pragmatic and grammatical development

So far, we have discussed the meaning that underlies the child's earliest words. Besides the child's word meaning, it is also possible to study the child's intentions when it speaks. What is the child's intended effect when it utters a word? Also, we will consider the possibility that the beginnings of grammatical structure may have their origins during the period of single-word utterances. Discussion of these topics begins with the child's comprehension of multiword utterances during this period, and will be followed by a discussion of the characteristics of the child's early one-word sentences.

6.4.1 The comprehension of multiword sentences

We know from Benedict's (1979) study that the child has a number of words understood before the first word produced, possibly as many as 100. Further, we know that the acquisition of the first 50 words in production can take some time. Most attempts to follow receptive vocabulary after the first 100 words are given up because acquisition is so rapid. By the end of the

Table 6.11 *Estimated size of receptive vocabulary for Craig and Amy in Benedict (1979) at the time of the acquisition of the 50th word in production*

Measures	Craig	Amy
Comprehension		
(a) Age at 100th word comprehended	1;0(17)	1;0(26)
(b) Age at 200th word comprehended	1;3(24)	1;3(16)
(c) No. of days to acquire 200th word after 100th word comprehended[a]	97	80
(d) Rate of acquisition (days per word)	0.97	0.80
Production		
(e) Age at 50th word produced	1;5(2)	1;6(29)
(f) No. of days between 50th word produced and 200th word comprehended	38	103
(g) Estimated size of receptive vocabulary at time of 50 words produced	239 words	329 words

[a] This calculation assumes 30 days per month.

period of single-word utterances, then, the child has a relatively large receptive vocabulary. Benedict, for example, gives data on two subjects for the first 200 words in comprehension. Table 6.11 estimates the size of their receptive vocabulary at the time of the 50th word produced. (We know from Nelson 1973 that the latter figure tends to coincide with the first multiword utterances in production.) The table assumes that the rate of acquisition is that of the development between the 100th and 200th word understood, probably a conservative estimate, and the estimated receptive vocabularies are thus 239 and 329 words. Given this size of vocabulary, is it possible that the children are also beginning to be able to comprehend utterances beyond a single word? We know, for example, from section 5.5 that mothers speak sentences, not words, to their young children. We will look into this issue by first discussing methods of testing comprehension and then presenting some research findings.

Method of testing comprehension It cannot be overemphasized that testing comprehension, even of single words, in children around 1 year to 18 months is quite difficult. How do we know, for example, that the child understands 'dog' in the way we do? The typical procedure is to present the child with alternatives that are systematically varied. This was done in the study by Thomson & Chapman (1977). Even so, children at this age are often not obliging: they may not attend, crawl off, or start to cry. When they do attend, we still have problems of scoring a response. They may touch one object, then another, or only look at the object. Careful scoring procedures need to be developed and consistently followed. It is important, therefore, if possible to have several scorers.

These problems are even greater when we investigate the understanding of sentences. For example, suppose we wish to test the child's understanding of the Possessor–Possessed structure as in 'Mommy's shoe'. How do we do this? If we say 'Give me Mommy's shoe' we are actually testing a greater comprehension, which includes the verb 'give'. Just saying 'Mommy's shoe' does not direct the child to any scorable response. Suppose, however, that we teach the child a game, so that we name something, and the child hands it to us. We know from Benedict (1979) (see Table 6.6) that social-action games are among the child's earliest acquired Action words. If we say 'Mommy's shoe' and the child hands us its mother's shoe, does this mean that the child understands the structure of the sentence? Not necessarily. For one thing, it could have been the only shoe around. We need to be sure that there are alternatives to choose from. Suppose the choice is Mommy's shoe and baby's shoe. This tells us that the child recognizes two words in the sentence, but that's all. Of course, recognizing the two words is an important start in grammatical development. We still do not know, however, if the child recognizes the importance of word order or the grammatical inflection ''s'. It also does not tell us if the child can generalize the pattern to novel situations like 'Mommy's glove' or 'Mommy's sock'.

There are ways that are available to try to get around some of these problems. One is to use novel stimuli that are unlikely to have been heard previously, e.g. 'Kiss the apple' or 'truck's shoe'. To test for grammaticality, we can give the child ungrammatical structures, e.g. 'Mommy shoe' or 'shoe Mommy' to see if the child responds differently. We can not ask directly for the child's grammatical intuitions as we can with adults. Particularly with children at 18 months, we can only try to get responses in controlled circumstances, and interpret them with great caution.

Studies on sentence comprehension　There has been a small number of creative studies in recent years on the receptive ability of children who are only producing single-word utterances. This section will look at four of them which are suggestive of some comprehension of multiword utterances before the production of multiword utterances.

Shipley, Smith & Gleitman (1969)　This study, as the authors stressed later (Gleitman, Shipley & Smith 1978), was not directly a study of comprehension. Rather, it tested whether children would prefer to respond to language from their parents that was at the child's level of production, or in advance of it. That is, it was indirectly a study of the young child's notions of grammaticality or well-formedness. Nonetheless, their data suggest some information about children's understanding of structure.

Shipley, Smith & Gleitman studied two groups of children which they called the *holophrastic group* and the *telegraphic group*. Here we will look just at their data in regard to the holophrastic group. There were four subjects in the group:

Name	Age	MLU
Mike	1;6	1.06
Karen	1;8	1.10
Linus	2;0	1.09
Jeremy	2;0	1.16

These children are older than 18 months, but they were still using mostly one-word utterances. Shipley, Smith & Gleitman state (p. 325): 'Although there were instances of two-word utterances in these children's speech, these were so rare as to suggest that they may represent merely benefit-of-the-doubt decisions by the transcriber.' I assume that they were at the very end of the period of single-word utterances.

The children were tested individually in a room where they were allowed to play freely while the mother and an experimenter talked to each other. Then, periodically, the mother would turn and direct a command to her child. There were three main types of commands directed to the child (where V = verb, N = noun, F = functors):

(6.5) a. well-formed (VFN)   'Throw me the ball!'
     b. telegraphic (VN)   'Throw ball!'
     c. holophrastic (N)   'Ball!'

The object was to see if the children would prefer one of these three kinds of structures over another.

Shipley, Smith & Gleitman used several measures to score the children's response. Here I will discuss just one, which they called *touch*. This was when the child came into physical contact with the toy named in the command. They say (p. 328): '... we took this behavior as an indication that the child had accepted the utterance as a "good" command and was making the natural response'. Table 6.12 gives the results for the four children on the three sentence types.

Shipley, Smith & Gleitman analyze their data statistically and draw the following conclusions (p. 329): '... all holophrastic speakers obey more often with single-word commands than with well-formed commands'. Their statistics include other response measures such as looking at the object and providing a verbal response. Even so, one would expect *touch* to show this same pattern since it was probably the most reliable measure. They also claim that the responses on VN were less frequent than with N. They conclude that holophrastic children prefer commands at their own level of production.

Table 6.12 *Percentage of times each of four children in Shipley, Smith &* *Gleitman (1969) would touch an appropriate toy in response to each of* *three constructions*

		Structures	
Subjects	N (%)	VN (%)	VFN (%)
Mike	33	50	16
Karen	80	75	83
Linus	46	16	42
Jeremy	16	33	0
Mean	52	44	35

The data in Table 6.12, however, invite closer examination. Only one of the children, Linus, shows the pattern for preferring N over VN (though Karen has a slight preference), but he also prefers VFN over VN. Two children, Mike and Jeremy, show a clear preference for VN over N. Despite statistical tendencies, these data suggest that children at the end of the period of single-word utterances are beginning to respond to VN and VFN structures. That is, the data are suggestive of an emerging ability to process VN structures. The following studies more directly address this possibility.

Huttenlocher (1974)   Huttenlocher reported preliminary results on her longitudinal study of four children over a six-month period. The children were between 10 and 13 months of age when the study began. They were visited every few weeks and observed on their development of receptive and productive language. Some of Huttenlocher's remarks on lexical development were discussed in section 6.3.

Huttenlocher not only recorded lexical development but wanted to determine the children's grammatical comprehension. For Wendy, only two frequent words occur in her production at 1;2 (17), these being 'see' and 'hi'. Huttenlocher says (p. 345): 'Wendy does not at present, at 17 months, give any evidence of comprehension of relational meaning based on syntax, nor indeed of any comprehension of more than one word at a time.' Her receptive vocabulary, however, is still quite small, around a dozen items. She is still, therefore, in a very early period of word acquisition. Similar results occurred with Thomas, who had even less language at 17 months.

The other two children, however, were more advanced in their comprehension. The most extensive and revealing data are presented for Craig. At 1;4(2) Craig had two words in production: 'di' and 'uhuh'. His comprehension vocabulary was larger, with at least a dozen words. At this point, Huttenlocher makes the following observation (p. 347):

. . . he follows commands involving three differentiable elements. The first time this increase occurs is when I notice that Craig will follow a command of the form 'Show the X to Mommy' vs. 'to Jane' vs. 'to Candy' vs. 'to Julie'. Within a week he also differentiates 'give' from 'show' so that by 16 months he can follow the command 'Give Jane the cookie' vs. 'Show Jane the cookie'. I test this capacity many times, contrasting each of the three critical elements.

This ability supports the Shipley, Smith & Gleitman (1969) data on VN, and adds a third lexical item to the child's receptive ability.

At 1;5(3), Huttenlocher found differential responses to the Possessor–Possessed relation in 'your bottle' vs. 'baby's bottle', and 'your diaper' vs. 'baby's diaper'. She tested this further with Craig at 1;5(30) by giving him the eight commands, listed here:

(6.6) a. Give me baby's bottle
    b. Give me your bottle
    c. Give Mommy baby's bottle
    d. Give Mommy your bottle
    e. Show me baby's bottle
    f. Show me your bottle
    g. Show Mommy baby's bottle
    h. Show Mommy your bottle

A further distinction occurred at 1;6(16) when Craig would respond differently for 'Get diaper' and 'Where's diaper?', where the latter question elicited pointing. Other indirect evidence for questions occurred at 1;3(5) where 'uhuh' would be made in response to 'Do you want X?' but not to 'Where's the X?'. The data from Kirsten are less extensive, but show responses to Possessor–Possessed structures like 'your' vs. 'Mommy's' 'shoe' or 'nose'. This was at a time when no words were being produced.

These results indicate that Craig, at least, was able to recognize four lexical words in a sentence and carry out a command in an appropriate context. They do not indicate, however, syntactic processing. We do not know if a scrambled word order would have produced similar responses or not. We also do not know if the possessive suffix 's' was being processed. Even so, they indicate early processing of multiple words in the input. Craig still seemed far from the point where he would be producing multiword utterances.

Sachs & Truswell (1978)   Sachs & Truswell (1978) examined in more detail the ability of children to process two semantically contrasting items in a sentence. They tested 12 children between 16 months and 2 years who were still only producing single-word utterances. The children were visited in the home and presented with Action + Object sentences that consisted of words found in their own receptive vocabulary. The test items, then, varied from child to child. The sentences were constructed in a way that they would describe novel or unique situations which the child probably would not have experienced. Eleven of the 12 children received four-way minimal contrasts as exemplified in (6.7); the twelfth child was uncooperative and only received two-way contrasts.

(6.7) a. Smell truck   (Leslie 1;6)
      b. Smell dolly
      c. Kiss truck
      d. Kiss dolly

They scored the children's responses as either '1' correct (the child carried out the command); '2' incorrect or partially correct (wrong action and/or object), or '3' no response. They were able to present each child an average of 16 commands.

   Sachs & Truswell found that 58 percent of the responses were correct, 16 percent incorrect or partially correct, and 6 percent elicited no response. Further, of the 11 children who received four-way minimal contrasts as in (6.7), ten got at least one such set correct. The one who did not was the youngest child (1;4), who did get a two-way contrast correct ('Kiss horsey' vs. 'Kiss teddy'). They conclude that children who use single-word productions can at least understand novel Action + Object commands.

Miller, Chapman, Bronston & Reichle (1980)   This account provides some indirect evidence about the emergence of the understanding of two- and three-term sentences by children. This study is summarized in Chapman (1981a). As part of a general study on the development of cognition and comprehension, Miller et al. tested comprehension on eight items, which are given in Table 6.13. There were 12 children in each of the following age groups: 10–12 months, 13–15 months, 16–18 months, and 19–21 months. While there is no mention of the children's language production, we will assume that at least the first three groups were primarily children in the period of single-word utterances.

   Table 6.14 gives the number of children who passed a particular comprehension test item at least once. We can see at least four children in the 16–18 months group passed the items Possessor–Possession and Action–Object. These results are consistent with results of Shipley, Smith & Gleitman (1969), Huttenlocher (1974) and Sachs & Truswell (1978). Interestingly, even in the 19–21 month group, only one child got an item correct on the Agent–Action–Object structures. If Huttenlocher's results

Table 6.13 *Eight comprehension items tested in Miller, Chapman, Bronston & Reichle (1980) for 48 children between 10 and 21 months of age, based on Chapman (1981a: Table 4)*

Item and examples	Passing response
1. Person name e.g. 'Where's Mama?'	Child indicates correct person in response to question.
2. Object name e.g. 'Where's X?', 'Go get X', 'Give me X' (where X = words supplied by mothers)	Child looks at, gets, shows, or gives the appropriate object among several present in visual field.
3. Absent person or object (item passed from no. 1 or no. 2)	Child searches for a person or object when it is out of view.
4. Action verb, 'V it; wanna V it' or 'can you V it?' (V = verb supplied by mother)	Child complies by carrying out action. If child is already attending to object, then action should be one not conventionally associated with it.
5. Possessor–Possession e.g. 'Where's Mama's shoes?' (items are ones passed in no. 1 or no. 2)	Child appropriately locates the correct person's objects twice.
6. Action–Object e.g. 'Kiss the shoe', 'Can you hug the ball?', 'Wanna pat the book?'	Child complies for the appropriate object among several present. He cannot already be attending to the object.
7. Agent (other than child)–Action e.g. 'Horsey eat', 'Make the doggie kiss', 'Wanna make the horsey eat?'	Child selects toy among several present and demonstrates action with the toy serving as agent.
8. Agent (other than child)–Action–Object e.g. 'Horsey kiss the ball', 'Can doggie eat the diaper?'	Child selects appropriate toy and object among those present and demonstrates appropriately.

are correct, these data suggest that it is not the number of words which is important, but the function of these. Recall that Craig's early success was with structures of the form Action–Object–Recipient. Unfortunately, Miller *et al.* did not test items of this kind.

Data suggest that children toward the end of the period of single-word utterances begin to understand some structures which contain two or three lexical items. Those that appear understood around this time are Action–Object and Possessor–Possessed, and possibly Action–Object–Recipient. No study yet has demonstrated sensitivity to word order or grammatical morphemes. One general problem is the difficulty of testing for children's comprehension at this age. One possible methodology, which has not yet been applied to this area, is the VRISD paradigm discussed in section 6.2.2.

Table 6.14 *Number of subjects[a] in Miller, Chapman, Bronston & Reichle (1980) to pass a comprehension item at least once, based on Chapman (1981a: Table 5)*

Age group (in months)[a] Comprehension item	10–12	13–15	16–18	19–21
1. Person name	12	12	11	11
2. Object name	5	12	12	12
3. Action verb	1	4	9	10
4. Possessor–Possession	0	1	5	10
5. Absent person or object	0	2	4	8
6. Action–Object	0	1	5	8
7. Agent–Action	0	0	1	7
8. Agent–Action–Object	0	0	0	1

[a] Number of subjects in each group was 12.

6.4.2 Some characteristics of single-word utterances

Since the onset of diary studies Child Language has predominantly defined word acquisition in production as beginning when some vocalization was produced that sounded like an attempt at a word that was in the adult language. Typically this would be 'mama' and 'dada'. Some of the better diaries avoided this, and looked for words, defined as child vocalizations that appeared to have a consistent meaning despite not sounding like the adult words to be acquired later. For example, Leopold (1939) observed that his daughter Hildegard used a vocalization [ʔə] that coupled with a pointing gesture served as a kind of demonstrative. A month later, Leopold interpreted this vocalization as a volitional term, as if it meant 'There is something, and I want it.' Still later, it acquired a rising intonation which made its use similar to that for a 'what's that?' question. It appeared that a small number of vocalizations would come to be used in a meaningful way around 1 year of age in a variety of pragmatic contexts. They appeared to vary according to the child's intentions in speaking.

Recall from our discussion on cognitive development that the first words appear to be used around sensorimotor stages 5 and 6. This observation has been supported in studies by Bates (1979), Harding & Golinkoff (1979) and others. The child in these stages is beginning to develop its ability to achieve ends through novel means. Vocalization appears to be one such means to achieve ends such as obtaining objects, food, etc. Bates, Camaioni & Volterra (1975), for example, refer to these vocalizations as 'performatives', meaning they are direct reflections of the child's intentions rather than the child's concepts. This, of course, is consistent with the Piagetian claim that the child does not have concepts at that point. Bates, Camaioni &

Table 6.15 *A summary of some of the major studies on the acquisition of single-word utterances*

Investigator	Subject(s) (Age in months)	Orientation
Bloom (1973)	Allison (9–22)	Diary and four 40-minute video tape-recordings of daughter. Argues against existence of syntax before multiword utterances.
Halliday (1975)	Nigel (9–18)	Diary study of son, divided into six sample periods, and two phases of development; proposes taxonomy of six functions for Phase I.
Carter (1975a,b; 1978a,b)	David (12–16)	Ten one-hour play sessions. Proposes taxonomy of eight communicative schemata.
Dore, Franklin, Miller & Ramer (1976)	4 children (11–16 at onset)	Monthly videotapes for an eight-month period; proposes stages of development of grammatical structure, and a taxonomy of pragmatic functions.
Greenfield & Smith (1976)	Matthew (7–22), Nicky (8–21)	Diary notes plus nine (Matthew) and eight (Nicky) formal sessions; proposes a taxonomy of 12 semantic functions.

Volterra go on to divide the performatives into two types: proto-declaratives, as in the Hildegard demonstrative at 8 months, and proto-imperatives, i.e. vocalizations intended to get the adult to satisfy some need on the child's part. These kinds of vocalizations are small in number and precede the more adult-like words acquired shortly after, as described in Table 6.7.

Since the early 1970s there have been several detailed studies on the acquisition of single-word utterances during the period of single-word utterances. Table 6.15 gives a summary of some of the more extensive ones, resulting in a set of observations and proposed taxonomies of the speech of children during this period. To present these works descriptively and critically would take us far beyond the scope of this text. Instead, we will select some of the salient observations, proposals, and issues, beginning with an outline of two of the proposed semantic taxonomies of this period. These are the proposals by Halliday (1975) and Greenfield & Smith (1976).

Halliday (1975)   Halliday kept a detailed diary of his son Nigel from 9 to 18 months. To study these data, he divided Nigel's development into six-week intervals that he labeled as Nigel (NL) 0 through 6. The actual ages for these are as follows, in months:

Table 6.16 *Definitions for six functional concepts that underlie early word use, according to Halliday (1975) and the number of words belonging to each for samples NL 1 to 5*

Functional category	NL 1	No. of words				
		NL 2	NL 3	NL 4	NL 4	NL 5
(1) *Instrumental* function: used to satisfy the child's needs to obtain goods or services, the 'I want' function		2	3	5	5	10
(2) *Regulatory* function: used to control the behavior of others; the 'do as I tell you' function		2	2	6	6	7
(3) *Interactional* function: used to interact with those around child; the 'me and you' function		3	7	7	7	15
(4) *Personal* function: used to express the child's own uniqueness; the 'here I am' function		5	9	9	11	16
(5) *Heuristic* function: used to explore the environment; the 'tell me why' function		—	—	—	?	?
(6) *Imaginative* function: used by child to create its own environment; the 'let's pretend' function		—	—	2	3	4
Totals		12	21	29	32	52

In the table '—' indicates that there were no instances, whereas '?' indicates that the data were difficult to determine.

NL 0:9   NL 3:13½   NL 6:18
NL 1:10½   NL 4:15
NL 2:12   NL 5:16½

The notes combined phonetic transcription with careful contextual observations.

Halliday divides Nigel's development into three phases. *Phase I* refers to the period from NL 0 to NL 5, or development up to 16½ months of age. During Phase I, Nigel used only single-word utterances, and acquired a small set of words (approximately 50). Halliday argues that Nigel had no syntax during this phase, but only a direct mapping from sound to meanings. The meanings in this case are ones that Nigel created for his utterances, not ones he acquired from the linguistic environment. He sees the child, much as Taine did in his (1877) classic diary study, as creating language at this point. Halliday refers to the language created by the child during Phase I as a proto-language, and the vocalizations *proto-words*. A proto-word is basically the third definition of word in McCarthy (1954), given on page 139, with the meaning coming from the child's internal ability to express intentions.

Halliday discusses the emergence of six *functions* during Phase I for Nigel. These are briefly defined in Table 6.16 along with the number of words that belonged to each function for NL 1 through 5. Four of these functions, *instrumental*, *regulatory*, *interactional*, and *personal*, are frequent during Phase I. The other two, *heuristic* and *imaginative*, develop more during Phase II. Table 6.17 gives Halliday's analysis for NL 3 for the 29 proto-words acquired around $13\frac{1}{2}$ months of age.

Halliday wants to argue that these functions are the foundation upon which later development is based. While the descriptions of each are straightforward enough, there are no operational definitions of how anyone can apply these to data from another child. The only method available is an understanding of the definitions combined with a very careful reading of his actual analyses from Nigel, focussing on the meanings as in Table 6.17.

A look at the data at NL 3 should provide insight into the basic features of Halliday's taxonomy. First, I have italicized under 'meanings' in Table 6.17 those words in Halliday's description that look like possible models for Nigel's productions.

'Powder' is questionable and is thus indicated with a question mark. 'What's that?' is my own guess for utterance numbers 16, 17 and 18 and is therefore not included. Were this a diary by a less careful, nonlinguistic observer, the claim would probably be that Nigel had acquired nine or ten words. Probably over 60 percent of the words noted by Halliday would not be proposed. This reflects Halliday's claim that these are proto-words, that is, created by the child to express itself, not adult words acquired from English. Even the italicized words in the table, Halliday would claim, are taken by the child and given their meaning. The meanings of proto-words do not come from the adult language. A micro-analysis is highly suggestive of intentional communication earlier than normally expected.

Another feature of Halliday's analysis is that a few vocalizations serve more than one function at NL 3. Examples are utterance numbers 18 and 19, and 27 and 28. Also, we have pairs that differ in intonation, e.g. utterances 7 and 25, 4 and 26. These data represent two claims: that the function for a limited number of proto-words may vary, and that the use of tone may be contrastive at a very early age.

In NL 6, just six weeks after NL 5, Nigel entered what Halliday labels *Phase II*. This phase has the following features: (i) there is a word spurt – Nigel's vocabulary grew from 52 words to 145 words in this short period; (ii) Nigel begins to enter into dialogue; (iii) shortly after, there is the onset of syntax in the form of multiword utterances; and (iv) there is a change in

Table 6.17 *A summary of Nigel's proto-language at NL 3 (or 13½ months), based on Halliday (1975: Fig. 3)*

Utterance no. Proto-word (and tone)	Gloss	Meaning
Instrumental		
1. ʔnã̄––– (mid)	'give me that'	initiation of a general demand
2. yi (high level)	'yes I want that'	response to a general demand with object present
3. a: (high rise-fall)	'yes I want what you just offered'	response to a general demand for a service or nonvisible object
4. bʷga(–) (mid) buġ(–) (mid)	'I want some powder'	specific demand for *powder*
5. tǩa(–) (mid) tǩɔ(–)	'I want (to go and get) clock'	specific demand for *clock*
Regulatory		
6. a:3;3̃ (mid)	'do that (again)'	normal imitation of a general command
7. m̃ñ (wide; ff)	'do that right now!'	intensified imitation of a general command
8. ɔ̃––– (low)	'yes (let's) do that'	positive response to a general command
9. ã ã (mid on both)	'no don't (let's) do that'	negative response to a general command
10. ʔ––	'let's go for a walk'	specific command to go for a walk
11. pʷi––––; peʷ (high level)	'let me play with the cat'	specific command to *play* with cat
Interactional		
12. na; an:a (high level)	'Anna!'	greeting *Anna*
13. da; dada (high level)	'Daddy!'	greeting *Daddy*
14. ʔɛ: (long low)	'yes it's me' 'yes I see'	response to interaction

No.	Transcription	Gloss	Description
15.	ø (low)	'don't be cross with me'	response to regulation or reproof
16.	aːːda (high rise and mid fall)	'look, a picture; you say what it is'	normal initiation of object-oriented interaction; [*what's that?*]
17.	aːːda (high rise and mid fall)	'another picture; now you say what that one is'	subsequent initiation of object-oriented interaction [*what's that?*]
18.	æ(dæ——)dæː proclitic and (high level and high fall)	'nice to see you, shall we look at this?'	initiation of person-oriented interaction [*what's that?*]

Personal

No.	Transcription	Gloss	Description
19.	æ(dæ——)dæː (mid)	'look, that's interesting!'	expression of personal interest
20.	da (mid low)	'a dog!'	specific interest in a *dog*
21.	ba (mid low)	'birds!'	specific interest in a *bird*
22.	ba (mid low)	'a bus!'	specific interest in a *bus*
23.	ɶʷɶ (mid low for both)	'an aeroplane'	specific interest in an *aeroplane*
24.	eʸiː / æʸiː (mid)	'that's nice'	expression of pleasure
25.	m̄n̄ŋ̄ (high rise-fall)	'that's funny (look where it's gone!)'	expression of surprise
26.	bʷga(-) / buɡᵃᵗ(-) (low fall)	'a lot of talk'	expression of disgust
27.	ġwyi——— (narrow low)	'I'm sleepy'	expression of desire to withdraw

Imaginative

No.	Transcription	Gloss	Description
28.	(same as no. 27)	'let's pretend to go to sleep'	pretend play
29.	bʷɛ——— (high sung)	'tra la la'	song

——— indicates repeated syllable; (–) (––) indicates number of optional repetitions; [ ] indicates my own guess.

functions. The six functions of Phase I merge into two general functions, the mathetic and the pragmatic.

Some of the features of Phase II are part of the period of early word combinations, so we will leave a discussion of them until the next chapter. We can see, however, that Phase I contains very specific claims about the nature of single-word utterances. To summarize, they express a set of basic communicative functions that have the child as their source. Further, the phonetic form of these is taken from the child's vocalization, not borrowed from the adult language. These words are referred to as proto-words, and the child's language during this period as a proto-language.

Several of the investigators cited in Table 6.14 have noted some of the same features of the child's early intentions. Carter (1979) refers to proto-words as *sensorimotor communicative schemas*, preferring to use terms that map the child's phonetics onto schemata, the Piagetian term for the child's structures at this stage. Dore *et al.* (1976) prefer to focus on their unique articulatory structure. They call them *phonetically consistent forms* (PCFs), i.e. child vocalizations that are not adult words in the normal sense, but which are fairly consistently produced, with some phonetic variation, and which appear to have intentional meaning. With some minor discrepancies, these terms appear to be interchangeable. The real differences, it seems, are in the theories that underlie each.

Greenfield & Smith (1976)   The study by Greenfield & Smith presents a slightly different description of the child's early vocalizations, and demonstrates how susceptible these utterances are to variable interpretations. To understand their proposals, it is important to review the data which they analyzed. They studied two children, Matthew and Nicky, over several months. The data consisted of diary notes and several formal sessions with each child during which language sampling took place. Table 6.18 gives the formal sessions, ages, and distribution of single-word and multimorphemic utterances for both children during those sessions.

In examining Table 6.18, we can see that the data on single-word utterances are taken from both the period of single-word utterances and the period of early word combinations. In fact, most of the data on the earlier period is from Matthew, sessions I–V. Only Nicky's first session has no instances of multimorphemic utterances – it is important to realize this in comparing their analyses to others like Halliday's, who was looking only at the period of single-word utterances in proposing his functions for Phase I. Further, given that at least Halliday sees Phase II (or roughly speaking, the period of early word combinations) as qualitatively distinct, we need to be cautious in expecting single-word utterances after the onset of multiword utterances to be the same as those before them. I have argued elsewhere

Table 6.18 *The formal sessions for Nicky and Matthew, giving their ages and number of single-word and multimorphemic utterances at each, based on Greenfield & Smith (1976: Tables 2, 3, 5)*

| | Matthew | | | Nicky | | |
| | No. of utterances[a] | | | No. of utterances[a] | | |
Session and age	Single-word	Multimorphemic	Session and age	Single-word	Multimorphemic
I 1;0(15)(22)	13				
II 1;2(10)(18)	25				
III 1;3(5)(17)	66				
IV 1;4(2)					
V 1;5(13)	83				
			I 1;6(4)	66	
VI 1;6(18)	99	12			
			II 1;6(27)	130	7
VII 1;7(21)	91	17			
			III 1;7(29)	96	38
			IV 1;8(23)	98	42
VIII 1;8(26)	108	72			
			V 1;9(17)	118	28
IX 1;10(1)	32	87			
			VI 1;10(21)	170	80
			VII 1;11(21)	119	119
			VIII 2;0(23)	42	321

[a]These are token frequencies; no information is given on types of words within these categories.

(Ingram 1979b) that overlooking this fact has led to a misunderstanding in some places of some of the claims in the literature on the nature of single-word utterances.

A second feature of the data in Table 6.17 is that the numbers represent number of utterances, not vocabulary, which is presumably much smaller. Further, frequent use of individual words may accentuate the numbers in any session. Unfortunately, Greenfield & Smith do not provide any overviews of the children's receptive and productive vocabularies.

Greenfield & Smith propose 12 semantic functions for the children's one-word utterances. They also give an order of acquisition for these, based on *both* the diary data and the formal sessions. The latter point is important since some of these (e.g. Agent and Dative) appear early in their diary data but are not attested in the formal sessions until much later. Here, I will only present those relations which occur in at least five utterances during the sessions when the children are in the period of single-word utterances (i.e. sessions I–V for Matthew, and I, II for Nicky. Session II is added to expand Nicky's data for this period even though a small number of multiword utterances occur).

Greenfield & Smith find that their 12 semantic relations are acquired in a

Table 6.19 *The first semantic relations acquired by Nicky and Matthew during the period of single-word utterances, adapted from the data in Greenfield & Smith (1976: Tables 8, 9, 10, 11) and the subsequent text*

PERFORMATIVES	
Performative:	use of nonstandard sounds to accompany actions; e.g. Matthew used 'dat' at 0;8(6) to accompany clapping and playing pat-a-cake. Later, more recognizable words would be used in similar ways.
Indicative Objects:	calling attention to objects by naming them, usually accompanied by pointing; e.g. Nicky at 1;0(7) would use 'dada' as he went around the house and pointed to various objects.
Volition:	appears *after* the above function. It occurs when the child wants something, and focusses on the desired object; e.g. Nicky's use of 'mama' at 1;1(19) for general requests; Nicky's use of 'no' to express desire not to go to the backyard at 1;6(4).
Volitional Object:	expression of desire for an object by naming the object; e.g. Matthew at 1;5(13) says 'bottle' with a whine, looking for his bottle.
ACTION–ENTITY RELATIONS	
Action or State of Agent:	reference to an action or state that requires an agent; e.g. Nicky at 1;6(27) says 'down' as he gets down from a chair; Matthew says 'night-night' at 1;2(5) while getting ready for bed.
Object:	reference to an object which is directly involved in an action or change of state; e.g. Nicky at 1;4(19) says 'fan' wanting the fan to be turned on; at 1;1(0) Matthew says 'ball' after throwing a ball.
Action or State of Object:	focus on the change of the object, rather than the initial or resultant state; e.g. Nicky at 1;6(27) says 'down' after pulling his train down, where the focus is on the state of the train; Matthew at 1;4(17) says 'dirty' in reference to milk in a dirty baby bottle.

sequence consisting of four general groupings. The first two of these groups are acquired by Matthew and Nicky while they are still in the period of single-word utterances. The first group of semantic functions acquired are *performatives*. The second group are functions that show relations between *Actions* and *Entities*. Table 6.19 gives definitions and examples of the semantic relations that fit in each of these two general groupings, subject to the restrictions cited at the end of the previous paragraph.

The first group of performatives look similar to Halliday's categories in the sense that they may consist of nonstandard vocalizations, and that they are pragmatic, i.e. they focus on the purpose of the speech act. An exact pairing of the two systems, however, is difficult. The Action–Entity relations move from speech acts to the content of the child's utterances. The four relations shown are based on the assumption that the child has an awareness of the concepts of Agent, Action, State, and Object. Given that these categories follow the Performatives, their appearance is occurring around the end of the period of single-word utterances, and it continues into the next period.

The Action–Entity relations resemble to an extent the semantic relations that appear to be understood at the end of this period, based on the evidence presented in the previous section. The Object and Action or State of an Object function could be related to the child's ability to understand Agent+Action sequences, yet Greenfield & Smith (1976) have an Action or State of Agent. When we look at the examples used by Greenfield & Smith, however, we find that the words the child uses are usually Action or State words. One could relate these single-word productions to the comprehension of Action words, as defined in Table 6.12.

The second discrepancy concerns the Possessor–Possessed relation. Both Huttenlocher and Miller *et al.* found evidence for the comprehension of this semantic relation during the period of single-word utterances. Greenfield & Smith, however, do not include it among their 12 semantic relations. There are, however, two relations that look comparable. These are:

(a) *Object associated with another Object or Location*: this involves naming one object in relation to another, e.g. Nicky at 1;7(29) says 'apple' while holding the refrigerator door; Matthew at 1;2(29) says 'caca' (cookie or cracker) while pointing in the direction of where cookies are kept.

(b) *Animate Being associated with Object or Location*: when a child points to an object and names its absent owner, e.g. Nicky at 1;6(19) says 'Lauren' while pointing at her empty bed; Matthew says 'fishy' at 1;3(19) while pointing at the empty fish tank.

The (b) example is like the Possessor–Possessed relation defined in the comprehension task described in Table 6.13. The task itself does not separate 'association with' from 'possession'. The first cases of Animate Being associated with Object or Location appear for Nicky at sessions IV and V, but never become frequent in the subsequent sessions. For Nicky, there are two instances at 1;6(27), but it only becomes frequent at 1;8(23). The emergence of some form of a Possessor–Possessed relation, therefore, is only weakly supported by the Greenfield & Smith data.

There is, however, some other support for the production use of something like Possessor–Possessed in the data reported by Rescorla. Recall that Rescorla defined one kind of overextension as a *predicate statement* (see Table 6.8). Predicate statements look quite similar to the function in (a) and (b) above. Rescorla notes the following (p. 330): 'for the four children using some word combinations by the end of the study, the peak in new predicate statement applications occurred in the month preceding the onset of word combinations'. Such data can be taken as indirect evidence of some parallels between the child's receptive and productive ability at the end of the period of single-word utterances.

The data from studies like Halliday's and Greenfield & Smith's suggest some general characteristics of early meaningful vocalizations. The first ones may not look very much like adult words in the language, yet they appear to express speech acts of wishing and noticing objects and events in the environment. As the vocabulary expands to include more identifiable adult words, the child's words become more classifiable semantically. The classification of these utterances into semantic categories appears to bear some resemblance to the semantic categories that children comprehend around the same time.

The theoretical implications of the specific proposals by the researchers cited in Table 6.15 is critically discussed in Atkinson (1982). One concern of Atkinson's is that the taxonomies proposed are often not related to any theory of language or, in most instances, theory of speech acts. Halliday is an exception, in that he does have his own functional theory of adult language. As we will see in Chapter 7, his functional categories must undergo relatively extensive restructuring in Phases II and III. The Greenfield & Smith semantic functions are not related to any theory of adult language, and so they lack any explanation of how these lead to the grammar of English. Another concern of Atkinson's is at the other end of development, that is, the relation of these taxonomies to some explanation for their appearance. On this issue Greenfield & Smith fare better in that they attempt to relate the semantic functions to earlier acquired concepts and cognitive developments. It is less clear where Halliday's functions originate.

This discussion has concentrated on description, isolating what looks like important observations. These observations will need to be part of any attempt to explain the developments of this period. At the end of the chapter I will address generally the Constructionist Assumption in regard to the child's ability to understand and produce language during the period of single-word utterances. Before that, however, we need to consider the possible effects of the child's linguistic input during this period, as well as his phonological development.

6.5   The onset of phonemic perception and production

The child has begun to develop a semantic system during the period, and by its end shows some evidence of comprehending multiword utterances, at least in terms of their major semantic categories. In this section we turn now to the child's emerging phonological system. The discussion will begin with a look at perceptual development, followed by a treatment of the phonological characteristics of the child's first 50 words or so in production.

6.5.1 Child speech perception

In Chapter 5 we began by defining infant speech perception as that ability of the infant to perceive meaningless acoustic stimuli. The stimuli are meaningless in that the infant does not yet see these sounds as parts of words. Child speech perception, however, is operationalized here to refer to the child's ability to perceive speech sounds that are part of what the child identifies as a word. Barton (1980: 87) discusses this same distinction with the term *phonemic perception*. There are two components to phonemic perception. One is the ability to discriminate speech sounds, that is, to hear them as distinct. The other is the ability to classify the sounds discriminated into phonological categories. The research with infants indicates that the first of these abilities is quite developed in the first year of life; the second, however, adds a great deal of complexity to the child's task.

We have suggested earlier that the infant's perceptual ability and developing cognitive ability enable him at around 1 year of age to recognize words in the linguistic input. While this milestone, referred to as the Principle of the Linguistic Sign in our discussion of Stern, is a unique genetic feature of humans, it appears to be dependent in part on earlier developments. Its operation becomes particularly noticeable in comprehension during this period, where the vocabulary grows to an impressive size before much productive vocabulary appears. Given the size of this receptive vocabulary, it seems reasonable to propose that phonemic perception is occurring during this period. That is, the child is beginning to identify and categorize the speech sounds in his words into linguistic categories.

We can briefly explore possible explanations of the child's speech or phonemic perception ability at this point in much the same way we did in Chapter 5, section 5.3.1. First, we could propose a universal–maturationist view. In its strongest form, this view states that the infant's precocious discrimination ability, combined with some linguistically programmed milestone such as the Principle of the Linguistic Sign, triggers the innate ability to develop phonological categories. We would expect then that the child's perceptual phonemic ability would be quite good, with little need for development. Linguistic experience would be necessary to set the phonological categories of the language being acquired. Assuming the child is exposed to the range of speech sounds in the language, combined in words with simple syllabic structure, then the child's ability should be well-developed after the acquisition of a relatively small vocabulary.

The attunement–refinement theory of Chapter 5 makes different claims. It states that the child may begin with some initial structures as part of the genetic program, but that these will be built upon through linguistic experience. The child, in other words, needs to discover the phonology of the language being acquired. As with infant speech perception, this theory makes specific predictions about the emergence of phonemic perception: (i) the development will go through stages, where the categories discovered at one stage are built upon into greater differentiations at later stages; (ii) there will be an effect of experience. Basically, the child who is exposed to a phonological system of a certain kind will develop perceptual phonemic abilities that will not be shown by children acquiring a different phonological system.

Unfortunately, there has been little research on child speech (or phonemic) perception as compared to that on infant speech perception, and what has been done is mostly on children in later periods than the one under discussion. The resolution of these predictions, therefore, will require future cross-linguistic research. There is, however, one study that has pioneered this area, that of Shvachkin (1948/73). In fact it remains today as one of the truly classic studies in language acquisition. Because of its richness, in method, description and explanation, we will look at it in some depth.

Shvachkin (1948/73)   Shvachkin is just one of several Russian psycholinguists who have worked on language acquisition. The 'Further reading' section at the end of this chapter gives a guide to the relevant literature.

Method.   Shvachkin's (1948) paper would be of value even if he had done no more than develop a method to test children's speech perception. The problems involved with testing comprehension with children around 1 year are formidable; they are increased when we attempt to focus on the perception of individual segments. Shvachkin's own remarks on this problem are insightful. He states (p. 99; all page references for Shvachkin's work are from the translation in Ferguson & Slobin 1973): '. . . it was necessary to work out a method which would correspond to the actual course of development of phonemic perception in the child. This problem proved to be quite difficult and *required a great deal more time and effort than the actual study of the facts themselves*' (my emphasis: DI).

When linguists seek the existence of phonemes in languages, one of the primary methods is to find *minimal pairs*, i.e. words that differ in only one segment, for example 'pit' vs. 'bit', or 'tea' vs. 'toe'. When pairs like these are found, it is concluded that the sounds that differ are contrastive, and the pair itself is a *contrast* or *opposition*. For example, English has a contrast (or opposition), of [p] vs. [b] or [i] vs. [o]. We can further conclude that the sounds that contrast are phonemes, and can be shown in slants (e.g. /p/ vs. /b/ and /i/ vs. /o/). Also, it is proposed that the contrast is not just marked by sounds, but by the *distinctive feature* in the opposition, e.g. [±voice] or [±round]. Our goal in studying the phonemic perception of the child is to see how the child recognizes oppositions in the language being acquired.

Table 6.20 *Six steps followed by Shvachkin (1948/73: 100–1) testing for phonemic perception*

1. Day 1. Spend time with the child teaching a nonsense word, e.g. 'bak', until the child shows evidence of knowing the word.

2. Day 2. Teach the child a second word, e.g. 'zub', until the child shows evidence of learning the word.

3. *Test for non-minimal opposition:*[a] Ask the child to respond to two nonsense words that have non-minimal oppositions, e.g. 'bak' vs. 'zub'. Do this until the child shows evidence of hearing a difference.

4. (Next day? Time unclear). Teach the child a third nonsense word that contains a minimal opposition to one of the earlier words, e.g. 'mak'.

5. *Tests for new non-minimal opposition:*[a] Ask the child to respond to the newest word taught with the second word taught, e.g. 'mak' vs. 'zub'.

6. Test for minimal opposition: Place the objects for all three nonsense words in front of the child. Test for perception, particularly in the cases where the child must perceive a minimal difference, e.g. 'mak' vs. 'bak'.

[a] Examples in the text suggest that occasionally minimal oppositions would be tested in step 3.

Shvachkin's proposal is that we seek minimal pairs in the child's perception in order to be able to say with any confidence that a contrast exists. For example, suppose we determine that the child hears the difference between 'pig' and 'cake'. Since the words differ in all three segments, we do not know if the child processes all three segments, or focusses on only one. We can conclude something, however, by showing the child perceives 'tea' vs. 'toe'.

Shvachkin's method was to teach the young child who is at the onset of acquisition nonsense words that are minimal pairs. Each nonsense word was assigned to an object that the child did not know. He used mostly solid geometric figures such as wooden pyramids and cones. The steps that Shvachkin followed are presented in Table 6.20. His method is strikingly similar to Piaget's clinical method discussed in section 5.4.4. He worked with the child until he was confident the word was acquired, and adjusted the teaching to the interests of the child.

A crucial part of this procedure is knowing that the child hears a minimal contrast. Shvachkin was very aware that children may have contextually based knowledge, that is, ability to do something in one context but not in another. He used six methods, therefore, to test for the comprehension of a test pair. The child would only be given credit for the acquisition of an opposition if he succeeded in at least three of these methods. These methods are given in Table 6.21. Unfortunately, Shvachkin does not

Table 6.21 *Six methods used by Shvachkin (1948/73: 101–2) to test phonemic perception of a minimal contrast*

1. *Pointing to the object*: The child would be asked to point out the object among a selection of objects. The position of the object would be altered systematically.

2. *Giving of the object*: The child would be asked to hand the object to the experimenter, under similar circumstances as in 1.

3. *Placement of an object*: The child would be asked to place several objects in different places in the room.

4. *Finding the object*: The child would be asked to find one of the objects.

5. *Operation of one object in relation to another object*: The child would be asked to seek out the object to put one object upon the other.

6. *Substitution of objects*: The child would be asked to get an object in a particular place, but another object would be there instead. The child was observed to see if there was a reaction of disappointment.

provide information about the number of times in a row that the child must get a contrast correct before being assigned success on the method, a characteristic of the clinical method.

There was apparently a long period of pilot testing until a word list was decided upon to test the emergence of Russian contrasts. This word list deserves a brief mention. It consisted of monosyllables that were CVC or VC. The contrasts tested were: (i) between vowels in CVC syllables when the consonants were the same; (ii) between initial consonants where the vowels and final consonants were the same; (iii) CVC or VC where the vowel and final consonants were the same. In other words, he worked with a very specific set of contexts, not looking at final consonants or multisyllabic words. This point will be important when we look at the generality of his results.

Description.   Shvachkin's study had two phases to it. In the preliminary phase, he worked carefully with individual children to establish what appeared to be the earlier acquired contrasts. These results were then checked in a more extensive study on other children, bringing the total number of children studied to 19. All children were studied longitudinally for approximately six months. The following is a profile of Shvachkin's subjects:

Shvachkin's subjects
Age at onset: range 0;10–1;6, mean: 1;3
Age at end: range 1;0–2;0, mean: 1;9
Sex: 14 girls, 5 boys

Unfortunately, Shvachkin gives us little specific information on the children's language abilities. If the children were normal, the mean age of 15 months at the onset suggests that they would only be producing single-word

Table 6.22 *Shvachkin's stages in the acquisition of Russian phonemic contrasts, adapted from Shvachkin (1948/73: 124, Table 2)*

Stage/Distinction	Substages and contrasts
1. Between vowels	1. a vs. other vowels 2. i–u, e–o, i–o, e–u 3. i–e, u–o
2. Presence vs. absence of consonant	e.g. bok–ok, vek–ek
3. Sonorants vs. articulated obstruents[a]	e.g. m–b, r–d, n–g, j–v
4. Palatalized vs. non-palatalized consonants	e.g. n–n', m–m', b–b', v–v', z–z', l–l', r–r'
5. Distinction between sonorants	1. Nasals vs. liquids and /j-/ e.g. m–l, m–r, n–l, n–r, n–j, m–j 2. between nasals m–n 3. between liquids l–r
6. Sonorants vs. non-labial fricatives	e.g. m–z, l–x, n–ž
7. Labials vs. non-labials	e.g. b–d, b–g, v–z, f–x
8. Stops vs. spirants	e.g. b–v, d–ž, k–x, d–ž
9. Velars vs. non-velars	e.g. d–g, s–x, š–x
10. Voiced vs. voiceless consonants	e.g. p–b, t–d, k–g, f–v, s–z, š–ž
11. Palatal vs. alveolar fricatives	e.g. ž–z, š–s
12. Distinction between liquids and j-	e.g. r–j, l–j

[a] These are those obstruents that can actually be produced by the child at the time of testing. Their membership will thus vary from child to child. See discussion in text under *Explanation*.

utterances at the beginning of the study. The 21-month final age in turn suggests that they were probably beginning to produce multiword utterances by the end. The predominance of girls in the study is an interesting fact that Shvachkin does not comment upon.

It is helpful to look at some results from the preliminary phase before presenting the general results. The first discrimination Shvachkin found was between vowels. The data for this were as follows:

	Success	*Failure*
Nina K. (1;3)	'kot' vs. 'kit' 'zuk' vs. 'zak'	'bak' vs. 'mak' 'bak' vs. 'pak'
Zina P. (1;6)	'kot' vs. 'kit' 'zuk' vs. 'zak' 'bak' vs. 'mak'	'bak' vs. 'pak'

Nina could only successfully respond to contrastive pairs that differed only in their vowels. She failed both 'b' vs. 'p' and 'm' vs. 'b'. Zina, on the other hand, could succeed in all the cases that Nina could, plus the 'b' vs. 'm' opposition.

Next, Shvachkin wanted to see when the ability to perceive CVC was acquired in relation to the above sequence. To do this, he gave Nina K. the words 'os', 'mos', 'pos', 'bos'. She succeeded on 'mos' vs. 'os', 'bos' vs. 'os' and 'pos' vs. 'os', but failed on 'mos' vs. 'bos' and 'mos' vs. 'pos'. He concluded then that the contrast of presence vs. absence of consonants occurs after differentiation of vowels and before the differentiation of consonants. In this way, he proceeded to develop a series of stages for the order in which contrasts are perceived by Russian children. These stages were developed in their final form after the data from all 19 children were analyzed.

Table 6.22 gives Shvachkin's results on the stages his children followed. To understand this table, it is useful to take a brief look at the phonemes of Russian, based on the appendix in Shvachkin. The vowels and non-palatalized consonants are given below:

Vowels	*Consonants*		
i, e, a, o, u	p t		k
	b d		g
	f s	š	
	v z	ž	x
	m n		
	l		
	r		
	w		j

Each of the consonants, except j, s, z, š, and ž has a palatalized counterpart (for a description of palatalization, see Ladefoged 1975). It is a complex system, and there is controversy concerning its exact nature. For example, other descriptions of Russian include a ts and č, but Shvachkin makes no reference to these in his data. Importantly, Shvachkin claims that children show the acquisition of all the Russian contrasts by age 2 years at least in simple CVC or VC syllables, and in initial position for consonants. The findings show relatively rapid phonemic perception between 1 year and 2 years that parallels the rapid phonetic perceptual development between birth and 1 year of age. They do not, however, show that perceptual acquisition is complete at 2 years; rather, they indicate that the basic perception of Russian oppositions is available to the young child to use in later development of more phonologically complex words. As we shall see in the discussion of production, most child words during the period of single-word utterances are simple CV and CVC syllables.

We can get some ideas of age in relation to these stages by reworking some of Shvachkin's data. In his Table 1, he gives data showing that six of the children only achieved stage 7 by the end of the study. These six children ranged in age from 18 to 21 months at the end of the study, with a mean of 19 months. Again, if we assume the children were normal, this would be about the time that most children begin to produce multiword utterances. The data suggest that children begin the phonological analysis of words perceptually during the period of single-word utterances, and that they develop many of the basic contrasts (presumably in Russian children at least to stage 7).

The sequence of acquisition for Russian in Table 6.22 merits two specific comments. First, observe that the distinction of palatalized vs. non-palatalized consonants occurs relatively early, in stage 4. This distinction does not occur in English, and it might appear to the English speaker learning Russian to be a difficult one. We need to be careful, however, not to be Anglomorphic in our ideas about what will be difficult for a young child who has not yet acquired language. For example, tones in Chinese are considered difficult to hear by many English speakers yet Chinese children acquire them quite early (Tse 1982). Second, the voiced–voiceless opposition is very late (stage 10), yet we know from the infant perception studies reviewed in the previous chapter that it is phonetically perceived early. We will want to look for an explanation for this late appearance. As we will see, Shvachkin has his own explanation to offer.

Explanation.   Before looking at Shvachkin's explanation of his results, consider his use of 'stage'. We need to extract his meaning for the term from Table 6.22 since he offers no definition. If we compare the stages in 6.22 to the kinds of stages presented in Chapter 3, several appear to be co-occurrence stages, defined by a new behavior (Figure 3.6). Compare, for example, stages 1 and 2. At stage 2, the vowel distinctions from stage 1 remain, and a new behavior is added, the ability to recognize the presence or absence of an initial consonant. The new behavior is not directly the result of an earlier one, and there is no logical relation between them. We need, therefore, some principle to relate the two behaviors. This would make the stages descriptive, in the sense of section 3.3. Shvachkin, in fact, offers some principle to relate these behaviors, but to make them explanatory we will also need some independent evidence for the principles. Shvachkin also makes a preliminary attempt to do that; we will consider his proposals below.

Other stages of Table 6.22 are implicational stages in the sense of Figure 3.8, of Chapter 3. Compare, for example, stages 2 and 3. The new behaviors of stage 3 are not independent from stage 2. In fact, the occurrence of a distinction between sonorants and stops and labial fricatives implies the awareness of the presence of consonants (a stage 2 behavior). The sequencing of implicational stages does not require principles to relate the change and is in a sense uninteresting. An implicational relation also exists between stages 3 and 5. Most of the relations between the stages, however, are non-implicational and therefore require an explanation. For example, why should the distinction between palatalized and non-palatalized consonants precede that of voiced and voiceless consonants?

Shvachkin begins his explanation of phonemic perception by contrasting two general periods or stages, the *prephonemic period* and *phonemic period*. The prephonemic period is not what it might appear to be, that is, all the development that occurs between birth and the first words; instead, it refers to the period when the child first assigns meanings to sounds. The child does not analyze the parts of the vocalization but maps meaning directly onto the word. Shvachkin states (p. 94):

> The unique phonemic features of the initial period in child speech development correspond to the unique semantic features . . . it is not the phoneme (a phonetic unit of speech) but the intonation, the rhythm, and later a general sound picture of words which bear a semantic load at this stage.

From the examples, this period occurs around 6 months to 1 year and characterizes the child's understanding of its earliest words. There are two features to the stage: there is a correspondence between semantic differences and phonetic differences, and there is direct mapping of meaning onto a general phonetic characteristic of the words. His use of 'semantic differences' looks similar to Piaget's discussion of 'symbol'.

The phonemic period is the time when the child acquires the phonemic contrasts of the language, as shown in Table 6.21. Shvachkin directly addresses the possible cause of this change, which he argues to be the acquisition of the semantic system of the language. He states (p. 96):

> Thus, under the influence of semantic change the child moves toward the phonemic perception of speech, which is connected with a radical reconstruction of both articulation and speech perception. The elements of this transformation are seen in the beginning of the second year of life.

Linguistic organization, according to Shvachkin, begins very early, starting with semantics.

There are a number of crucial aspects to Shvachkin's proposal. One is that he is proposing a radical reorganization around age 1 year. The transition between prephonemic and phonemic development is one of discontinuity, and there is no attempt to relate the developments of the phonemic period to those of the prephonemic period. Ironically, his stages for the phonemic period are developmental and imply a Constructionist Assumption. This is not true for the onset of phonemic perception, however, which would need some innate principles unrelated to previous development. This is similar to Stern, who argues for a developmental perspective and yet proposes a series of discontinuities.

Another aspect of this claim is that the proposal of semantics as the cause of the onset of phonemic perception is not developed. It seems to me that the claim is that the child's receptive vocabulary grows and the semantic system becomes organized in some way that triggers phonemic organization. We could reinterpret Shvachkin and argue that the Principle of the Linguistic Sign precedes and triggers another linguistic principle. Let's call the latter the *Principle of Phonemic Organization*. If so, we should realize that the relation between the two is implicational; that is, a phoneme is a unit that speakers use to differentiate words that differ in meaning. This raises the question, then, as to whether or not there is any way to test this claim.

I would like to propose the following. While the Principle of Phonemic Organization implies the Principle of the Linguistic Sign, there is nothing in this implication that requires the former immediately to follow the latter. The child could function for at least some time with a notion of linguistic signs without yet phonemically organizing words. Shvachkin's claim, however, is that the two occur closely together, with phonemic perception developing gradually. If this claim is true, one should expect evidence of early phonemic perception in both perception and production. Shvachkin is very clear on this point. He believes that the child begins acquiring a psychological representation of words that underlies his perception and production.

The onset of the ability to organize phonetic segments into psychological units or phonemes (the Principle of Phonemic Organization) only accounts for the onset of the phonemic stage. Shvachkin still needs to account for the sequence of stages in Table 6.21. Unfortunately, his account of this is not always clear. A major reason for this is that his stages reflect a process of differentiation: the child differentiates the most general classes of sounds, and gradually discriminates between lower classes. To do this, however, requires some theorizing about what are the natural classes in language and their defining or distinctive features. Nowhere does Shvachkin discuss this question. He could have proceeded in one of two ways: he could have taken a proposed theory of phonological features and tested its predictions (a study in Language Acquisition); or he could have analyzed his results into classes and proposed a set of natural classes based on his results (a study of Child Language). If anything, Shvachkin appears to be doing the latter.

Let's assume that Shvachkin is proposing that there is a sequence of acquisition that follows from some theory of phonological features. The child will discriminate down the set of features, going from the most general to the most specific. This is a viable proposal, and one that could be seriously pursued today, given the range of theories we now have on phonological features. Shvachkin's own classes are in some cases unusual. For example, in stage 3 he distinguishes between articulated and non-articulated consonants. The examples in his table contain stops and labial fricatives, which are not normally considered to be a natural class. For reference, let's call this proposal the *Principle of Phonemic Differentiation*.

Shvachkin argues that differentiation is directly affected by two factors: perceptual salience and articulation. Neither of these is discussed satisfactorily, but his remarks are suggestive. *Perceptual salience* means that some distinctions are easier because they are in some sense easier to hear; he uses this factor to explain why vowels are discriminated first. Apparently two aspects of vowels lead to their salience: they are the loudest or most audible segments and they are frequent (i.e. in Russian they are about five times more frequent than consonants). We are not given any suggestions, however, on how these two factors interact. He uses these same factors to explain the early differentiation of /a/ from other vowels.

Importantly, Shvachkin attempts to provide independent evidence in the form of patterns found in adult language. For example, he cites languages that only have a vocalic difference between /a/ and other vowels, and others that only have /i/, /a/, /u/. The point appears to be that the stages the child goes through should correspond to possible systems in the adult language. This is very similar to White's condition (1982) that the child's language at any stage should be a possible human language. Shvachkin does not, however, provide evidence of this kind for his stages.

The second factor that aids differentiation is *articulation*. The point appears to be that sounds that are easier to articulate tend to be discriminated earlier. He uses this factor to explain why children could at stage 3 discriminate between sonorants and so-called articulated consonants. Examples of articulated consonants are /b/, /d/, /g/; of non-articulated /z/, /ž/, /x/. (He is unclear in regard to /v/, treating it sometimes as articulated, sometimes as non-articulated.) He says (p. 114):

> The facts noted above reveal an *interaction between hearing and articulation* in the process of phonemic development. Discussing whether hearing determines the development of articulation or articulation determines the development of hearing, the ontogenetic facts speak for a two-way interaction of hearing and articulation.

Given the gap between receptive and expressive vocabulary, one would expect this factor to become greater as development proceeds. It is not the only factor, however, in that he acknowledges that there are cases where the child will be able to discriminate but not produce a difference.

There is one last factor that Shvachkin mentions briefly (p. 115), the role played by the language that the child is acquiring:

> The Russian child discriminates palatalized and non-palatalized consonants comparatively early; however, this cannot be explained simply in terms of articulation and hearing. Here the linguistic peculiarities of these phonemes in the Russian language manifest themselves. First, in Russian (unlike English, French and German) this distinction is of semantic significance. Second, the frequency of alternation of palatalized and non-palatalized consonants plays a role in Russian. Peshkovskiy's data (1925) show that in most cases the child encounters one palatalized consonant for every two non-palatalized consonants.

If true, this shows a very early effect of the child's linguistic environment. We already discussed this possibility for infant speech perception. Here, we see the suggestion of the development of an early phonological system that is determined in part by the frequency of phonological oppositions in the adult language. I will refer to contrasts that are prominent in a language as having *phonological salience*. Such influence is, in fact, expected from a theory of acquisition where the child's linguistic system is the result of the constant interaction of assimilation and accommodation. It is also in this sense that Shvachkin's study is Piagetian in nature.

6.5.2 Child speech production

Data from Shvachkin's study suggest the onset of phonemic speech perception during the period of single-word utterances. While this may be a controversial claim, it is not an implausible one, given the size of the child's receptive vocabulary. The alternative would be that the child recognizes and stores its 300 or so words by isolated acoustic cues. Apart from the difficulty that arises when one tries to specify this disparate set of cues, there is the problem of discontinuity; that is, when does phonemic categorization begin, if not at this time? Given the current lack of counterevidence, I will assume that Shvachkin's position is the most viable one to pursue at this time. It meets both the Constructionist Assumption and the Competence Assumption. It only partially meets the Productivity Assumption. It does so to the extent that the child's ability was tested in a variety of contexts; but it does not do so to the extent that contrasts were only tested between single lexical items, e.g. 'bak' vs. 'mak' and not multiple items, e.g. 'mak' vs. 'mik' vs. 'bak' vs. 'bik'.

The next question is the nature of the child's produced words during this period. First, do they show phonological organization of the kind proposed for perception? They should, if we follow Shvachkin's suggestion that phonemic organization underlies both perception and articulation as a more abstract psychological level of organization. Second, do they follow an orderly sequence of stages of the kind proposed by Shvachkin for perception? Shvachkin's proposals can be interpreted as predicting such a sequence. They suggest some further predictions:

(a)   they will not be isomorphic to the ones in perception, since the articulatory factors are not always the same as perceptual ones;

(b)   there will be some individual variation, just as there was in the perceptual stages; and

(c)   there should be cross-linguistic differences, since the phonological salience of specific phonemes will differ from language to language.

This section will explore these proposals, first by examining the major theory of phonological acquisition ever proposed, that of Jakobson (1941/68). As will be discussed later, this theory probably provided the stimulus for Shvachkin's research. Despite arguments by some to the contrary, it remains the most useful theory ever proposed to account for early phonological development. Its difficulty is that it was never developed sufficiently, and also was never adequately tested. After a discussion of Jakobson, I will outline a method that can be used to analyze the child's early words for phonological contrasts. Lastly I will present some of the findings in recent years on the nature of the child's early words. The current data are preliminary, but provide some support for the proposals just cited.

Jakobson (1941/68) and Jakobson & Halle (1956)   It is rare to find any discussion of phonological acquisition that does not refer to the work of the late Russian linguist Roman Jakobson. In 1941 he published in German a short book (*Kindersprache, Aphasie und allgemeine Lautgesetze*) that outlined a theory of phonological acquisition. This theory was initially accepted in the 1940s and 50s without question, but recently it has gone through a period of evaluation and criticism (see Menn 1980 for a discussion). In fact, in some places it is felt that the theory has been refuted (Atkinson 1982: 1). Here, however, I will propose that the reports of the death of Jakobson's theory are greatly exaggerated; its demise will require more elaboration of the theory to render it more testable, and better methods to test it. We will begin with an outline of his theory, then turn to methods of analysis in the next section.

Jakobson's theory is most extensively described in Jakobson (1941/68; page references are to 1968, the English translation). It is altered somewhat in Jakobson & Halle (1956), and I discuss these changes later in this section.

Unlike Shvachkin, Jakobson (1941/68) begins with a theory of phonological features. This theory, which is widely accepted in its most general form, is that the phonemes of languages can be divided into a universal set of distinctive features. (Changes in Jakobson's theory can be frequently traced to changes in his proposals concerning the set of universal features.) These features can be seen as part of the child's innate linguistic capabilities. The child's acquisition of a phonological system consists of his acquiring these features in a consistent and predictable sequence.

In section 5.3.1 it was noted that Jakobson proposes a discontinuity between babbling and language; we also noted that this discontinuity does not appear to be supported. The counterevidence to that claim, however, does not necessarily constitute counterevidence to his claims about development during the period of single-word utterances. We can think of his proposals about the child's phonological system as linguistic constructs imposed upon the child's articulations.

Jakobson sees phonological acquisition as the result of the interaction of the child's internal structure (or innate knowledge) and the linguistic environment. The child actively imposes structure on the linguistic input, then alters this structure in response to the input. That the interaction is very much like the processes of assimilation and accommodation proposed by Piaget is shown by the following remarks, which also make clear that the similarity is not accidental. The Genevan scholar referred to is de Saussure (1922), who was writing at the same time as Piaget was doing his research on infancy:

> Accordingly, we recognize in the child's acquisition of language the same two mutually opposed but simultaneous driving forces that control every linguistic event, which the great Genevan scholar characterizes as the 'particularist spirit', on the one hand, and the 'unifying force', on the other. The effects of the separatist spirit and the unifying force can vary in different proportions, but the two factors are always present.   (Jakobson 1941/68: 16)

The child's system at any point in time, then, is the result of its internal organization of the linguistic input and its adaptation to that input.

While he emphasizes this interaction, Jakobson nonetheless concludes that the child constructs an *invariant sequence* of phonological contrasts. This is an apparent contradiction in that one would expect some effects of the nature of the linguistic input as a result of the interaction. He does not discuss when the child's phonology of Language A will begin to look

Table 6.23 *The first stage of phonological development, adapted from Jakobson (1941/68)*

Substages
1. The acquisition of vowels and consonants develops from a basic CV syllable which contains a forward articulated stop, and a wide vowel; it may appear singly, e.g. 'pa', or reduplicated, e.g. 'papa'.
2. The appearance of the first consonantal opposition, nasal vs. oral, e.g. 'papa', 'mama'.
3. The appearance of the second consonantal opposition, labial vs. dental, e.g. 'papa' vs. 'tata', 'mama' vs. 'nana'.
4. The appearance of the first vocalic opposition, narrow vs. wide vowel, e.g. 'papa' vs. 'pipi'.

5. The appearance of the second vocalic opposition, either:
 (a) splitting of narrow vowel into front vs. back
   e.g. 'papa' vs. 'pipi' vs. 'pupu'
 (b) splitting of narrow vowel into a more open vs. narrow opposition
   e.g. 'papa' vs. 'pipi' vs. 'pepe'

Minimal consonant system: m – n
                             p – t

Minimal vowel system: i   u   (or)   i
                           a   e
                                            a

different from another child's phonology of Language B. As we will see, however, his most specific predictions are only about the earliest words.

Another feature of Jakobson's theory is that it is directed toward, and based upon, speech production. Jakobson gives data from acquisition for 15 languages, based on published data. Most of the data is production data on Czech, Bulgarian, Russian, Polish and Serbo-Croatian. While based on spoken language, the theory makes the claim that the child's words are being restricted by an underlying linguistic system, not just by articulatory constraints. For example, he cites data from Ament (1899) whose daughter first varied in attempting words with /k/ between [k] and [t]. She eventually settled on [t], not because she could not produce [k], but because the linguistic system imposed it upon her.

The child's linguistic system is under the influence of linguistic laws that regulate the order of acquisition of oppositions. Table 6.23 presents a summary of the proposed order of acquisition of the first phonological oppositions, based on Jakobson (1941/68). These are part of what he calls the *first stage*. The child develops the minimal consonant and vowel systems upon which all further development is based. The CV syllable is seen as the starting point in acquisition for both vowels and consonants. Two consonantal features are first acquired: nasal vs. oral, and labial vs. dental. For vowels, there are also two oppositions acquired. The second one allows alternatives, one resulting in a triangular system, the other in a linear one. In the first stages all children will sound the same. He states (p. 50): 'the child possesses in the beginning only those sounds which are common to all the languages of the world, while those phonemes which distinguish the mother tongue from the other languages of the world appear only later'.

To understand the developments for the next stage, we need to look briefly at Jakobson's methodology. First, Jakobson never states the data-base for these substages of stage 1. Presumably his reading of the diary studies suggested that these forms were characteristic of early phonological acquisition. His study, however, is not inductive in the sense of Child Language, or even in the manner of Shvachkin's study; that is, he is not studying child language data and drawing conclusions from them. Remember that he is starting from a theory of phonological features. Further, as part of his study of linguistics, Jakobson had studied the distribution of his universal features across languages in the world. (The most impressive work in this regard had been just completed by his close colleague Trubetzkoy, translated into English in 1969.) This led him to propose what he called laws of *irreversible solidarity*. Jakobson uses these laws to make predictions about the child's acquisition in the next stage, that is, the acquisition of specific languages.

Laws of irreversible solidarity are claims about the distribution of phonological features among the world's languages. Presumably, these laws are part of phonological theory. They state that, in the unmarked or normal state, certain relations exist between the phonological features within a language. These are implicational laws which state that the occurrence of one feature (or class of sounds) implies the occurrence of another. For example, Jakobson found in his survey that all languages had front consonants but not all had back consonants: the law of irreversible solidarity for this fact is that the presence of back consonants presupposes the existence of front consonants.

Jakobson proposed that the laws of irreversible solidarity can be seen as making predictions about the order of acquisition of phonological oppositions. The laws together indicate features or oppositions that are more basic (or less marked). Children will acquire the basic or unmarked features before the more marked ones: for example, children will acquire front consonants before back ones. Table 6.24 gives some of the laws cited by Jakobson and their predictions about acquisition.

As can be seen, these predictions are limited to a few classes of sounds that occur in languages. There are a great number of further laws and specific relations that are not given. For example, what about liquids?

Table 6.24 *Some laws of irreversible solidarity and their predictions for language acquisition (Jakobson 1941/68)*

Laws of irreversible solidarity	Predictions for acquisition
CONSONANTS	
1. The existence of fricatives implies the existence of stops (p. 51).	Stops are acquired before fricatives; fricatives are changed into stops, e.g. /f/→/p/.
2. The existence of front consonants (labials and dentals) implies the existence of back consonants (palatals and velars) (p. 53).	Front consonants are acquired before back consonants, back consonants are replaced by dentals, e.g. /k/→/t/.
3. If a language has only one fricative, it will be /s/.	The first fricative acquired is /s/ (a variable articulation between [s] and [ʃ]); other fricatives will be changed to /s/.
4. The existence of an affricate in opposition to a stop implies a fricative within the same series, e.g. /pf/ vs. /p/ implies /f/ vs. /p/.	An affricate is acquired in opposition to a stop after the acquisition of the fricative in the same series; affricates are changed into stops or fricatives, e.g. /ts/→/t/or/s/.
VOWELS	
5. An opposition of two vowels with the same degree of aperture implies the existence of an opposition with a narrower aperture; e.g. /æ/ vs. /a/ implies /a/ vs. /e/.	The opposition between vowels of similar aperture is acquired late.
6. An opposition between rounded vowels implies the same opposition between unrounded vowels, e.g. /u/ vs. /o/ implies /i/ vs. /e/.	Oppositions between unrounded vowels are acquired before those between rounded vowels.

Jakobson states that many languages will have a single liquid (usually /l/), and that the acquisition of a second liquid is late. We are not told, however, when the first liquid is acquired, nor its first opposition. One needs to realize, therefore, that we are dealing with an incomplete theory, or actually the outline of a theory. These laws will need to be elaborated, altered and joined with other ones before a complete theory can be proposed. Also, Jakobson is sometimes careless in the way he states his predictions. For example, he states that front consonants precede back consonants, as if he were dealing only with the acquisition of sounds. Given that he is really concerned with distinctive features or oppositions, this is quite misleading. What he actually means is that oppositions between front consonants precede oppositions between back ones. For example, labial vs. dental appears before palatal vs. velar, or even dental vs. velar.

Since Jakobson gives no analysis of child data, but only anecdotal examples, we have no idea of when children acquiring different languages will begin to sound different from each other. Since the child has to acquire the oppositions of a specific language, however, one would expect some differences before very long, but the processes that merge oppositions should look similar across languages. The child's oppositions, though, are always acquired in relation to some adult language. This point is worth emphasizing because it has sometimes been misunderstood in the literature.

Jakobson is not always clear on the level of representation of distinctive features, but it appears that he recognizes a *level of linguistic representation* that is distinct from the phonetic level. This level often appears to correspond to the perceived surface structure of the adult word. There are two kinds of examples which indicate a level of linguistic representation. One is his discussion of the early merger of /k/→/t/. He states (p. 54): 'Occasionally, an intermediate stage is introduced . . . in which, although the velar series is not established, the two phonemes are already distinguished. In this case, a glottal stop corresponds to /k/ (or velars, in general) of the mother tongue.' In other words, a phonetic distinction between [t] and [ʔ] represents an underlying dental vs. velar contrast. The second example concerns a French child who said 'papa', [dédé] (for 'téter') and [de] (for 'bé') (p. 49). Jakobson proposes that the child has only one vowel phoneme /a/ with a rule that /a/→/e/ after dentals. The phonological representation of the last two words 'téter' and 'bé' would be /dada/ and /da/. This example differs from the first in that the child's phonemic representation is distinct from the perceived adult form. The second example is similar to the first, however, in showing that there is a linguistic representation that is distinct from, but related to, the perceived and produced form of words.

In Part III of his book, Jakobson attempts to explain the laws of irreversible solidarity by reference to the acoustic and articulatory properties of speech sounds. The style of explanation is similar to that discussed by Shvachkin in that there is gradual differentiation. When discussing Shvachkin I called this the Principle of Phonemic Differentiation. Jakobson's term for the same general principle is the 'principle of maximal contrast'. In reference to his stages, he says (p. 68): 'This sequence obeys the principle of maximal contrast and proceeds from the simple and undifferentiated to the stratified and differentiated.' He discusses possible explanations for the early oppositions acquired by the child and these are summarized here in Table 6.25. They develop in this fashion, moving to lesser degrees of contrast. This term is less than satisfactorily defined but appears to refer to differences between features that are as acoustically distinct as possible. This is similar to Shvachkin, except the latter also discusses the role of frequency. In his later work, particularly Jakobson, Fant & Halle (1963), Jakobson attempts to refine these acoustic differences

Table 6.25 *The principle of maximal contrast applied to the first oppositions acquired by children (Jakobson 1941/68)*

Opposition	Principle of maximal contrast
The basic CV syllable	The maximal contrast in the syllable is between closure and opening. The maximal closure is a labial stop (which seals the entire vocal tract); the maximal opening is the vowel /a/.
Nasal vs. oral consonants	The maximal contrast within consonants is the obstructed oral cavity in contrast to the open nasal cavity.
Labial vs. dental consonants	Both of these involve pitch contrasts; dental consonants and narrow vowels are greater in pitch than wide vowels and labials.
Front vs. back consonants	Back consonants contrast with front consonants by having greater resonance (or loudness).

through spectrographic analysis. The important point here is that the sequence of development is explained by marginally distinct acoustic properties of the human repertoire of speech sounds.

Lastly, Jakobson attempts to provide independent evidence for his laws of irreversible solidarity, citing predictions the laws make about language acquisition and data from language disorders. He proposes that the laws also predict the order in which language is lost in cases of language disturbance, such as aphasia; in which case, however, we see the reverse process – the last contrast acquired is the first lost. This hypothesis, although controversial, has nonetheless stimulated a great deal of discussion (see Caramazza & Zuriff 1978). The important point here is that Jakobson attempts to make predictions in different domains to support his theory on the nature of phonological universals.

Jakobson did not spend much effort in elaborating or altering the basic theory presented in 1941. The most extensive development took place in the refinement of his theory of distinctive features, as found in Jakobson, Fant & Halle (1963). These new feature specifications were the primary topic in the book *Fundamentals of language* by Jakobson & Halle (1956). In that work, he also altered some of his claims about language acquisition, though these alterations appear more in response to his changing view of features than his response to language acquisition data, that is, his revised features led to different predictions about the order of acquisition of phonological contrasts.

The major changes are as follows:

(i)   a revision of stage 1 into what is referred to as the acquisition of the primary triangle; the primary inventories that result from the primary triangle are [p, t, k] for consonants, and [i, a, u] for vowels.

(ii)   division of distinctive features into three general classes: eight *sonority features* (including [± vocalic], [± consonantal], [± nasal], [± compact], [± voice]); *protensity features* [tense] vs. [lax], and three *tonality features*. Importantly, the acquisition of features within a class will follow a sequence, but there is independence between the classes. For example, nasal vs. oral, an early sonority feature, may precede or follow the acquisition of labial vs. dental, the first tonality feature (the specific feature is grave vs. acute).

(iii)   the universal syllable CV may contrast early with V or VC, i.e. /pa/ vs. /a/ or /pa/ vs. /ap/.

The major innovation in these changes is the separation of the features into three major classes. One result of this change is that the theory introduces the possibility of variation between children at the earliest stages. For example, some children may acquire nasal vs. oral first, while others may acquire labial vs. dental first. By doing this, however, the theory runs the risk of possibly becoming too powerful, i.e. being able to account for any possible sequence of development. It is an essential condition of any theory of phonological acquisition to be comprehensive enough to account for individual variation without becoming a measurement sequence.

As pointed out by Atkinson (1982), the importance of Jakobson's theory, despite its incompleteness, resides in its attempt to provide a principled theory of acquisition. Even though it has attracted widespread attention, the theory has not been subject to rigorous development. It has either been used without criticism or criticized without attempts to develop it. It is obviously the influence behind Shvachkin's later study, even though the latter never refers to it. The lack of such a reference, however, is not surprising when one realizes that Jakobson was vilified in the Stalinist period after World War II. According to Kučera (1983: 878): 'It was during the harshest years of Stalinism that Jakobson was viciously attacked, for his linguistic theories as well as his literary opinions, both in Moscow and Prague.' He was also denounced by the Moscow Linguistic Circle. Shvachkin's attempt to extend Jakobson's work, under such circumstances, is truly remarkable.

6.5.3 Methods of phonological analysis

Theories like Jakobson's need to be tested by the careful analysis of children's early word structure. In our discussion of Shvachkin we have seen a method that can be used for phonemic perception. Most research, however, has been limited to the analysis of spoken words. The problem then is how to analyze the child's early productive vocabulary for the development of phonological categorization.

One of the most innovative ways would be to follow a child and actually attempt to teach him specific phonological oppositions. This was, in fact, attempted once by Braine (1974a), with his son Jonathan. Jonathan's first words were as follows:

(6.8) 'that, there'   [da ~ dʌ ~ dæ ~ dɛ]
       'see'   [di]
       'no'   [do]
       'juice'   [du]
       'hi'   [ʔai]

Braine hypothesized that Jonathan had only vocalic oppositions, and the 'd' was noncontrastive. That is, he was at Shvachkin's stage 1 (Table 6.22). To test this, he attempted to teach Jonathan two words that would require Shvachkin's stage 2, that is, a contrast between the presence and absence of a consonant. Braine made up two words: [i] meaning 'cat' or 'food', and [dai] with a certain toy. If Jonathan had acquired 'd' contrastively, then the pairs [di] vs. [i] and [ʔai] vs. [dai] should be learnable. Jonathan readily acquired both words, but changed them to [di] and [da ~ dʌ] respectively. Braine concluded that Jonathan was not yet acquiring consonants contrastively. The rule was that 'd' was placed automatically on simple vowels.

Ideally, the study of phonological development could be pursued in a manner like Braine's brief experiment. That is, we could continually analyze the child's system and teach words to test our analyses. In most cases, suitable English words would be available. If not, nonsense forms could be used. The viability of using nonsense words was recently shown by Schwartz & Leonard (1982). In their study, Schwartz & Leonard sampled 12 children between 1;0(21) and 1;3(15) who were producing only single-word utterances. They analyzed their data for each child's more common segments and syllables. They then composed two lists of eight nonsense words, one with words like their own words (IN words), and one with words not like their own words (OUT words). They taught the nonsense words to the children over ten bi-weekly experimental sessions. They found that the children showed a superior ability to acquire IN words, i.e. words near their own phonological level.

Most analyses of child's phonologies, however, are done on data collected either through diaries or spontaneous language samples. Unfortunately, it is not apparent that such data will ever be sufficient to test a theory such as Jakobson's and our only available data on most languages will consist of diary material.

Given such restrictions, we need to develop ways to analyze the young child's phonological system through spontaneous data. Until recently, most analysts have 'done their own thing' so to speak, thus making comparisons

Table 6.26 *Phonological lexicon for T at VI, taken from Ferguson &*
Farwell (1973: 34)

Lexical type	Spontaneous phonetic type	Imitated phonetic type
1. allgone	1. ʔaʊgʰo	
	2. ʔaʊwo	
	3. ʔokʰõ	
	4. ʔokʰu	
2. baby	5. əβeβi	
	6. əbi	
	7. bibi	
3. ball	8. baʊ	
4. blanket		9. bijæ bjæ
5. book	10. əg	
	11. bʌʔ	
6. bounce	12. bʌ	
	13. bɛ	
	14. bwæ	
7. byebye	15. pʰædi	16. bæˈbæ
8. cereal		17. ʰoʂuɪʃ
9. cheese	18. çi	
10. dog	19. ⁿdæ (2 tokens)	
	20. da	
	21. daɪʰaɪ	
11. hi	22. haɪ	
12. ice	23. aɪç (2 tokens)	
	24. ʔə	
13. nightnight		25. nəɪnə
14. no	26. nõnõ	27. nʌʰ
	28. nõ	
15. paper	29. øetʃə	
	30. bædu	
16. pat	31. pʰæt (3 tokens)	
	32. pʰæ	
17. please	33. pʰe (2 tokens)	
18. pretty	34. pɹ̥hi	
19. purse	35. pʰe	
	36. pʰe	
20. rock	37. wakuak (2 tokens)	
	38. uakwak (2 tokens)	
	39. uakuak	
	40. wak	
21. shoe	41. ɪʃu	
	42. ʃˈu	
	43. ʃu	
	44. tʰuʰ	
22. tea	45. t̪ʰi	
	46. tʰi	
23. thankyou	47. tʰat̪ʰi	
24. up	48. ʔaʔ	
25. yeah	49. ijʌʰ	

of different analysts difficult. In recent years, however, two distinct approaches have appeared which attempt to analyze the child's emerging phonological system. Here we will take a brief look at each.

Phone classes and phone trees   This method was originally proposed by Ferguson & Farwell (1975). It has been used since by several other researchers, in particular Shibamoto & Olmsted (1978), Leonard, Newhoff & Mesalam (1980), and Stoel-Gammon & Cooper (1984). A reading of the literature requires an understanding of the phone class/phone tree methodology.

The study by Ferguson & Farwell limited itself to word-initial consonants. The definition of phone class, however, can be extended to all word positions (as is done in Shibamoto & Olmsted 1978) and this should be kept in mind when we look at their definition of phone class. A *phone class* (Ferguson & Farwell 1975: 424) is determined as follows:

> Then all words beginning with the same phone or set of variant phones were put together. The set of initial-consonant variants of each of these groups of words constitutes a 'phone class', and is represented by the appropriate phonetic symbols in a box, or between vertical lines. Thus a phone class [d ~ t^h] consists of the initial consonants of all those words whose initial-consonant sound varied between [d] and [t^h].

Phone classes, then, are primarily determined by the distribution of segments across words.

In an earlier version of their paper, Ferguson and Farwell provide an appendix giving the data which is the basis of their analysis. Table 6.26 gives a phonological lexicon of their data for one of their subjects, T, at the sixth sample session. The phone classes for this session were as follows (subscripted numbers refer to the number of tokens):

(6.9) *Phone classes for T at session VI*

1. [b ~ β ~ bw ~ p^h ~ φ ~ ø]   for 'baby', 'ball', 'blanket', 'book', 'bounce', 'bye-bye', 'paper'
2. [p^h]$_4$ for 'pat', 'please', 'pretty', 'purse'
3. [w]$_1$ for 'rock'
4. [d]   for 'dog'
5. [t^h]$_2$ for 'tea', 'thankyou'
6. [n]$_2$ for 'nightnight', 'no'
7. [j]$_1$ for 'yeah'
8. [ʂ ~ ç ~ ʃ ~ t^h]$_3$ for 'cereal', 'cheese', 'show'
9. [h]$_1$ for 'hi'
10. [ʔ ~ ø]$_3$ for 'allgone', 'ice', 'up'

First of all, there is a problem concerning how words are assigned to phone classes. Here it appears that words are grouped into phone classes if some of the variants are the same. For example, 'ball' and 'baby' are grouped together because the former's [b] is a variant of the latter [ø ~ b]. Shibamato & Olmsted (1978: 421–2), however, point out that for some data this can result in some analyses that produce a very small number of phone classes with very large membership. This happens in Ferguson & Farwell (1975: 426), in fact, when T at VII has a phone class of the following: [ʃ ~ tʃ ~ ʒ ~ j ~ tʰ ~ s ~ h ~ ç ~ tç ~ d̪].

The next question, then, concerns the purpose of phone classes. Ferguson & Farwell (1975: 425) state it as follows:

> The notion of 'phone class' here is similar to the notion of 'phoneme' of American structuralism, in that it refers to a class of phonetically similar speech sounds believed to contrast with other classes, as shown by lexical identification.

Phone classes, by this definition, are isolated in order to follow the development of phonemic oppositions.

Ferguson & Farwell determine the phone classes of a longitudinal series of language samples, and then connect the classes across time. These longitudinal connections are *phone trees*. They state (p. 424):

> If successive phone classes did not contain the same word but were related to phone classes which did, dotted lines were drawn connecting them. For example in T's /m/ class:
>
> /m/   (mama)
>   ⋮
> /m/   (milk)
> |
> /m/   (milk, mama)

Figure 6.2 gives T's phone classes for nine longitudinal sessions, over 13 weeks, beginning at 11 months.

As stated earlier, this approach has become quite popular in recent years for the phonological analysis of children during the period of single-word utterances. In 6.5.4 we will present some results of these analyses. Here, however, we would like to point out some concerns with this method. First, there is a minor methodological point. These trees like Figure 6.2 are hard to devise, since the procedures are not often clear, and they are difficult to read. More elaborate phone trees look like the wiring diagram of a television set. This would be worth the effort, of course, if they reflected the child's emerging phonological system. There are difficulties, however, in arguing that they do.

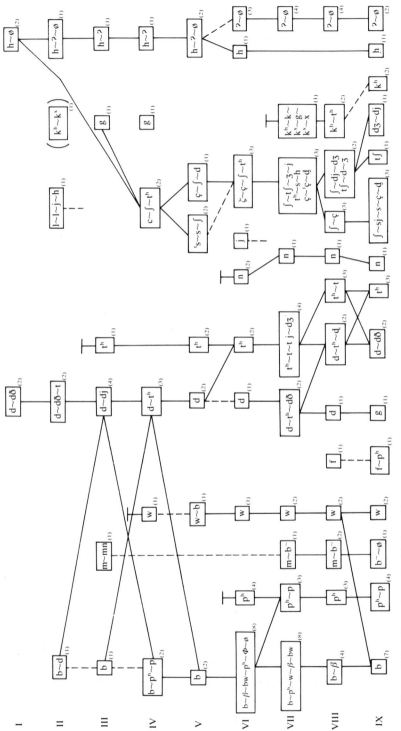

Figure 6.2   Phone trees for T, from Ferguson & Farwell (1975: fig. 1).

The most serious problem with phone trees is that they are extremely sensitive to the phonetic variability of a single lexical item. Suppose, for example, that a child's attempt at English /b-/ were as follows:

(6.10) 'ball' [ba] 'button' [bʌ] (6 tokens), [ʌtʌ], [tʌtʌ]
       'bike' [baɪ]
       'book' [bʊ]

The phone class would be [b ~ ø ~ t] suggesting extensive variability where, in fact, only one out of four lexical types shows this variability. Further, the variability of 'button' is not as great as it might appear, since six of the eight phonetic tokens begin with [b]. The phone class analysis, however, misses this point. This approach places tremendous emphasis on variability that may result from performance factors, yet uses the results for conclusions about the child's phonological competence, i.e. his emerging phonological oppositions. Still further, this variability is enhanced the more narrow the phonetic transcription. The phone class given above for T at session VII is an example of this. My general conclusion is that phone class/tree analyses are awkward to do, and they predispose the analyst to focus on the surface variability of lexical items, variability that is subject to sampling conditions and performance factors in general. It is useful as a method to draw attention to such variation. As a measure of competence, however, it is a measurement sequence in the sense of Chapter 3, that is, it can only lead to conclusions that development is variable from lexical item to lexical item.

Phonetic inventories and phonological contrasts In a series of works (Ingram 1981a, 1988; Ingram & Mitchell to appear), I have attempted to develop a method of analysis that eliminates some of the variability in production data due to performance factors. This method consists basically of three steps: the determination of (i) a phonetic inventory, (ii) patterns of substitution, and (iii) a set of phonological contrasts. Here I will briefly outline the features of each of these steps. To reiterate, the process is designed to reduce variability in order to determine evidence for underlying linguistic competence.

First, we need to establish the child's *phonetic inventory*; these are the sounds that the child uses to construct his words. The analysis begins with an abbreviated phonological lexicon. There are two initial steps to this process: enter data in a broad phonetic transcription to eliminate transcriber variability that occurs when fine phonetic transcriptions are done, then select a typical phonetic type for each lexical type. The first step simply eliminates diacritics and raised elements that were faintly heard or questionable in the transcription. The second step requires some comment. The idea is to eliminate some of the data by selecting a phonetic type that is

Table 6.27 *An abbreviated phonological lexicon for T at VI, with only the most typical phonetic types indicated*

Lexical type	Phonetic type
1. allgone	ʔokʰo
2. baby	bibi
3. ball	baʊ
4. blanket	bijæ bjæ (imitated)
5. book	ɔg
6. bounce	bɛ
7. bye-bye	pʰædi
8. cereal	ʂuɪʃ
9. cheese	çi
10. dog	dæ
11. hi	haɪ
12. ice	aɪʃ
13. nightnight	nəɪnə (imitated)
14. no	no
15. paper	ɸetʃə
16. pat	pʰæt
17. please	pʰe
18. pretty	pr̥hi
19. purse	pʰe
20. rock	wakuak
21. shoe	ʃu
22. tea	tʰi
23. thankyou	tʰatʰi
24. up	ʔaʔ
25. yeah	ijʌ

most typical of all the phonetic types for a lexical type. The following rules seem to work most of the time:

(a)   If a phonetic type occurs in a majority of the phonetic tokens, select it.
(b)   If there are three or more phonetic types, select the one that shares the most segments with the others.
(c)   If there are two phonetic types, select the one that is not pronounced correctly.
(d)   If none of the above work, select the first phonetic type listed

We can see how these rules work by attempting to select the most typical phonetic types in Table. 6.26. Rule (a) will apply in 'ice', which has the phonetic types [aɪʃ] (two tokens) and [ʔə]. Since the former occurs in more phonetic tokens than the latter, it is selected as the phonetic type. Rule (b) will operate for 'allgone'. The medial consonant that is most typical is 'k' because three out of four phonetic types have a stop, and two out of three of the stops are [k]. Three of the phonetic types end in [o], so it is the most typical vowel. The only phonetic type with both of these is [ʔokʰo]. There are no examples where rule (c) would apply in Table 6.25. An example

Table 6.28 *The criterions of frequency for marginal, used and frequent consonants at selected sample sizes*

VOCABULARY SIZE	CATEGORY		
No. of lexical types	marginal[a]	used	frequent
1–37	1	2,3	4 and up
38–67	0	2,3	4 and up
68–87	2	3,4	5 and up
88–112	2,3	4,5	6 and up

[a] Normally, we want to avoid including a sound that only occurs once, even as marginal. An exception is made for samples with 37 or fewer lexical types because the database is so small.

would be if 'dog' were [dag] and [da]. The latter is selected by rule (c), for we want to be conservative in our claims about the child's ability. Lastly, rule (d) will operate if the other rules do not apply. For 'paper', for example, it would select [etʃə]. Table 6.27 gives the abbreviated phonological lexicon for T at session VI. (Imitations are included.)

The child's phonetic inventory is determined separately for word-initial and final consonants. Example (6.11) gives the initial and final consonants that occur in Table 6.27 along with the phonetic forms in which they occur:

(6.11) *Initial consonants*   *Total phonetic forms*

b-	bibi, baʊ, bijæ bjæ, bɛ	4
p-	pʰædi, pʰæt, pʰe (2 tokens), p̥ɻhi	4
d-	dæ	1
t-	tʰi, tʰæ tʰi	2
ʔ-	ʔokʰo, ʔaʔ	2
fricative-	ʂuɪʃ, çi, ʃu	3
h-	haɪ	1
n-	nəɪnə; no	2
ɸ-	ɸetʃə	1
w-	wakuak	1

Final consonants

g-	əg	1
-fricative	ʂuɪʃ, aɪʃ	2
-t	pʰæt	1
-k	wakuak	1
-ʔ	ʔaʔ	1

The child's phonetic inventory is determined by the frequency with which consonants occur in distinct phonetic forms. In (6.11) 24 phonetic forms are shown. According to their frequency, consonants are assigned to the phonetic inventory as either marginal, used, or frequent. Marginal sounds are placed in parentheses, and frequent sounds are marked by an asterisk, while used sounds are shown without any marking. Table 6.28 gives the number of times a sound must occur in samples of various sizes in order to occur in one of these three categories. (These figures are arbitrary, based on the expectation that used words should occur at least twice; see Ingram 1981a for details.) Each phonological sample, based on the number of phonetic forms, has a *criterion of frequency* that is used to assign consonants to the phonetic inventory.

The phonetic inventory for T's session at VI is shown in (6.12).

(6.12) T's phonetic inventory at session VI

Initial			*Final*		
	n-			(-g)	
*b-	(d-)		(-t)	(-k)	(-?)
*p	t-	?	-ş ~ -ç		
(ø-)	s ~ ç ~ ʃ	(h-)			
(w-)					

There are two frequent initial sounds, [*b] and *[p], and three used ones [t, ?, n] and the fricative group. The latter are placed together because they would probably be given a single symbol in a broad phonetic transcription.

The second step is the determination of *patterns of substitution*. This is done from Table 6.27 by looking at the single consonants only, in the adult models. (Clusters are analyzed separately.) Example (6.13) gives the substitution analysis for initial consonants, where correct productions of a consonant are indicated with a 'C' (for correct), and substitutions are given:

(6.13) *Lexical types*   *Proportion correct*

	C C ø C pʰ	
b-	baby, ball, book, bounce, bye-bye	3/5
	ø C C	
p-	paper, pat, purse	2/3
	C	
d-	dog	1/1
	C	
t-	tea	1/1
	C C	
n-	nightnight, no	2/2
	ş	
s-	cereal	0/1
	ç	
tʃ-	cheese	0/1
	C	
ʃ-	shoe	1/1
	C	
h-	hi	1/1
	w	
r-	rock	0/1
	tʰ	
θ-	thankyou	0/1
	C	
j-	yeah	1/1

Once we have the substitution patterns, we need to decide when the child has matched the adult model. I propose that we call a child's attempts at an adult target a *match* if they are correct over 50 percent of the time. Further, we can specify a *marginal match* when there is only one attempt. In our data, we have three matches, [b-, p-, n-], and five marginal matches, [d-, t-, ʃ-, h-, and j-].

These data are an example of the difficulties in working with spontaneous samples. We have no data on adult words with /m-/, and we have five cases of marginal matches. We would like to be able to visit this child at this point and attempt to elicit more words in this area. These problems are somewhat ameliorated when longitudinal data are involved.

The third step is to determine the child's *phonological contrasts*. Unfortunately, it appears that we can never do this with much confidence with a single sample of this kind: even so, we can suggest the following criteria:

> A sound is considered part of the child's phonological system (i.e. becomes a phoneme in the child's phonology) when
> (i)   it is frequent; or
> (ii) it is used, and it appears as a match, or substitute.

We thus need to compare the initial phonetic inventory in (6.12) with the patterns of substitution in (6.13). By these criteria [n-, b-, p-, t-] and fricative are part of the system. If we include these as marginal (in parentheses), we get the following phonological system for T's initial consonants:

(6.14)   n-
       b-   (d-)
       p-   t-
             ʂ
             ʂ ~ ç ~ ʃ (h-)
       (w-)

It is proposed that data like these are more amenable to analysis to test Jakobson's theory than those of Figure 6.2 which are full of performance factors.

The strongest evidence for the emergence of contrasts is obtained through comparisons of analyses like the above at different time periods. Table 6.29 gives such an analysis for T's data in Ferguson & Farwell (1975) across all nine sessions. For the longitudinal data, the analysis was altered as follows. The phonological lexicon consisted of all the typical phonetic types at a session, plus all previous typical types that were not altered at the current session. For example, the phonological lexicon for session VI (Table 6.27) contains one phonetic type beginning with a [d]: [dæ] for 'dog'.

Table 6.29 *Phonetic inventories, matches, substitutions, and proposed phonemes (in circles) for T*

Phonetic inventories

Session	m	n	b	d	g	p	t	k	f	s	ç	ʃ	tʃ	h	w
I				ⓓ											
II				d				(k)							
III	(m)			d	(g)		(t)							h	
IV	(m)		ⓑ	*d			(t)				(ç)				
V	(m)		b	*d			(t)			Ⓢ	(ç)	ʃ		(h)	(w)
VI	(m)	(n)	*b	d		ⓟ	t			s	(ç)	(ʃ)		(h)	(w)
VII	m	(n)	*b	d		*p	ⓣ	(k)			(ç)	ʃ		(h)	w
VIII	(m)	(n)	*b	d		p	*t	(k)	(f)		ç	ʃ		(h)	w
IX	(m)	(n)	*b	d	(g)	*p	*t	ⓚ	(f)	s	(ç)	(ʃ)	(tʃ)	(h)	w

Matches and substitutions

Session	/m	n	b	d	g	p	t	k	f	θ	s	ʃ	tʃ	dʒ	w	j	r	h/	Sample size
I				d															4
II				d				(k)			(h)							(?)	5
III	(m)		(d)	d			(t)	(k)		(d)	(h)	(g)						(h)	9
IV	(m)		b	d			(t)			(d)	(ç)	(ç)		(ø)				(h)	12
V	(m)		b	d						(d)	s	(ʃ)			(w)			(?)	15
VI	(m)	(n)	b	d	(φ-p)	p (φ)	(t)				s	(ʃ)			(w)	(j)		(h)	25
VII	m	(n)	*b (p)	d		p	t	(k)	(t)		(ç) (s)	(ʃ)	(t) (ʃ)	(w)	(w)	(j)		(h)	34
VIII	(m) (b)	(n)	*b (β-p)	d		p	t	(t) (k)	(f)		ç (ç)	(ʃ)	(t) (ʃ) (tʃ)	(w)	(w)	(j)		(h)	39
IX	(m) (b)	(n)	*b (p)	d	(p)	p	t	k	(f) (p)	(t)	s (ç)	ʃ	(t) (dʒ) (tʃ)	(w)	(w)	(j)	(b)	(h)	45

[a] Only sounds are shown that occur in more than one session, except for IX.
[b] Imitations are not included in the analysis.
[c] Parentheses indicate a single occurrence of a sound.
[d] Criterion of frequency for sessions I–VII was 2(1); 2 for sessions VIII, IX.

A phonetic type beginning with [d] was also carried over from a previous session, i.e. [dædi] 'daddy' (V). Thus, [d] meets the criterion of frequency of two for used sounds. We refer to such analyses as *cumulative phonological analyses*, in that they carry data from previous samples over to the one under analysis. A second feature of the analyses is that imitations were not used. These were dropped because it was felt that claims about the child's emerging phonological system should only be made in reference to spontaneous language. The criterion of frequency for marginal and used sounds was one and two respectively for all nine sessions, a departure from the guidelines in Table 6.28 in that there should have been no marginal sounds for sessions VIII and IX, due to the sample size. This was changed in order to present as much data as possible in Table 6.29.

Longitudinal data allow us to add one more important criterion for defining an opposition:

A phoneme is acquired in the first session in which the criteria (i) and (iii) are met, if they are also met in all further sessions.

We have circled those sounds in Table 6.29 that meet these criteria. As we can see, /d/ is acquired right from session I. /b/ is next at session V, followed by /p/ at VI, and /t/ at VII. /t/ is not circled at session VI because it is a match in only one lexical type. The last session shows evidence for a /k/, although it would be nice to see data from subsequent sessions. The data on /s/ are not as neat. It does not meet criterion (iii) in that there are no [s]s in sessions VII and VIII. During these sessions, and IV for that matter, [s] and [ç] are phonetic alternants. We can circle /s/ at V, then, if we define this phoneme as having two alternants for the child. The right side of the table shows that these two are consistently used for adult words with /s/.

T's data show the following developments:

(6.15) *Sessions*

I		d	dental
IV	b	d	labial vs. dental
V	b	d	dental stop vs. dental fricative
		s	
VI	b	d	voiced vs. voiceless labial stop
		s	
	p		
VII	b	d	voiced vs. voiceless stop
	p	t	
		s	
VIII	b	d	
	p	t k	velar vs. non-velar stop
		s	

It is data like these which can be used to test and elaborate Jakobson's theory, as well as others.

6.5.4 Some characteristics of early phonological development

We can now use the data from T, as analyzed by phone classics and phonetic inventories, to discuss some of the general characteristics of the child's phonology during the period of single-word utterances. To do this, we will focus on the study by Ferguson & Farwell (1975), using my reanalysis of the data on T in Table 6.28 for parts of the discussion.

The use of phone classes in Ferguson & Farwell (1975) enables the authors to identify some of the specific features of early phonological development. The major conclusion of their analysis is what they refer to as the *lexical* parameter. (The term 'parameter' was of no theoretical importance here, and should not be confused with the parameter-setting model discussed in Chapter 4.) The course of early phonological development is heavily influenced by the properties of individual words. One aspect of this is that the first contrasts may only be between individual words. This is particularly clear in Table 6.29 for [m-] and [n-]: through most of the sessions, [m] occurs in 'mama', and [n] occurs in 'no'. I will refer to such cases as *lexical contrasts*. Other lexical contrasts occur for T with 'he' for [h] and 'where' for [w]. None of these contrasts becomes generalized over the nine sessions; thus, not only do some contrasts first appear as lexical, but they may remain so over a long period of time.

Ferguson & Farwell also propose that the lexical parameter operates when a contrast begins to generalize. They argue that it will spread gradually word by word rather than suddenly to all relevant words. Velten (1943) noted a lexical influence of a similar kind in his study of his daughter Joan. In her case, a new contrast would be used for new words being acquired, but older ones only changed gradually.

Table 6.29 shows some evidence for the gradual emergence of contrasts. Look, for example, at T's acquisition of /t/. For sessions III, IV, and V it is marginal, i.e. it is only a lexical opposition. At VI it becomes used, but it is only at VII that it becomes frequent and meets the criteria for an opposition. It is important to point out, however, that not all oppositions begin lexically, as suggested by Ferguson & Farwell; /p/, for example, suddenly emerges as a productive phoneme for T at VI. Ingram & Mitchell (to appear) find several other examples of this in a study of three English-learning and three French-learning children. There seem to be three patterns, then, in the emergence of oppositions: (i) extended lexical oppositions, (ii) gradual lexical spread, and (iii) sudden emergence. T's acquisition of /m/, /t/, and /p/ are examples of each pattern.

Another aspect of the lexical parameter pointed out by Ferguson & Farwell is *phonetic variability*. While young children tend to show alternative pronunciations for lexical types, Ferguson & Farwell claim that some words are more variable than others. They refer to those words which are fixed in their pronunciation as *stable forms*. Unfortunately, they do not provide a measure of stability. As examples, they provide T's use of 'baby' as a variable form contrasted with 'book' as a stable form. As can be seen in (6.16), however, both are only variable within certain limits. For example, if we look at the shared features of the two words, it appears that their underlying representations are something like /bebi/ and /bǝk/ respectively:

(6.16) 'book'   VI ǝg, bǝʔ; VII bak; VIII bǝ; IX bʊ
       'baby'   III de; VI bebɛ; V beβɪ, ba, bebi; VI ǝβeβi, ǝbi, biβi;
                 VII bebi; VIII bebi; IX bebi

In fact, in some ways 'baby' is less variable than 'book' in that it shows a repeated phonetic form [bebi], and it becomes stable at session VII whereas 'book' does not. Therefore, while there may be a lexical dimension to variable pronunciation, we need to be cautious until stronger documentation is provided. (See Leonard, Rowan, Morris & Fey, 1982 for an attempt to pursue this further.)

Besides the lexical parameter, Ferguson & Farwell observe other characteristics which seem the result of what we will call the *phonological parameter*. This term refers to the restrictions imposed by a limited phonological system. One of these characteristics is what is called a *phonological idiom*, a term first used by Moskowitz (1971). This refers to the child's first pronunciations of some words which are superior to later pronunciations. It is as if the first attempts were direct reflections of the child's perceptual and articulatory skills, without the interference of the phonological system. Once they are incorporated into the system, they get a simpler pronunciation. As an example, they cite Hildegard Leopold's acquisition of 'pretty' which was phonetically accurate at ten months (although whispered), reduced to [pɪti] at 21 months, and eventually became [bɪdi] at 22 months. They say (p. 432):

> Progressive idioms suggest that a child's perceptual and productive abilities are more advanced than the phonological system seemingly exemplified by most of his words.

They do not provide, however, an operational definition of how to determine a phonological idiom, nor information on when they occur or their frequency.

The proposal of something like a phonological idiom has been around for some time. Jakobson (1941/68: 23) discussed this at some length:

First, one often secures the 'parrot-like' repetition of single sounds and syllables from children, even though the very same sounds continue to be absent when they talk spontaneously. Second, these sounds are sometimes used correctly in the first acquisition of words, and with the progressive acquisition of vocabulary, they disappear from use without a trace.

He cites Abrahamsen (1938) and Ament (1899: 51ff.) as references on this. Their occurrence is one reason why Jakobson argues for a phonological level of representation in the child, distinct from the articulatory level.

Another characteristic of early phonological development that comes under the phonological parameter is Ferguson & Farwell's reference to *salience* and *avoidance*. The claim is that children will tend to produce or acquire words that contain sounds within their system, and avoid those that do not. For one example, they cite T's acquisition of [p]. Up to session IV, she avoided saying any English word that began with [p]. At IV, however, it became part of her system, and it was used frequently. The study cited in 6.5.3 by Schwartz & Leonard (1982) has experimentally supported the observation that selection and avoidance occur. The fact that they do, of course, raises our confidence level about the use of diary data, as long as they are complete. We must remember, however, that these processes are concerned with production. In Hoek, Ingram & Gibson (1986), for example, we found that OUT words were acquired as easily in comprehension as were IN words, even though IN words occurred earlier in production. (Recall that IN words are nonsense words similar to the child's own words, and OUT words were ones that were relatively different in their phonological form.)

The last aspect discussion by Ferguson & Farwell that is part of the phonological parameter is the sequence of acquisition of contrasts in the child's system. As mentioned, Jakobson suggests that there is a universal sequence, at least in his stage 1. While admitting some initial uniformity among the children (p. 435), Ferguson & Farwell go on to emphasize how different the children are from one another. They say, for example (p. 437), '...each of the three children is exhibiting a unique path of development with individual strategies and preferences and own idiosyncratic lexicon'. This, then, is about as opposite to Jakobson as one can get. Their study has since been seen by many (e.g. Atkinson 1982) as the ultimate counter-evidence to Jakobson's theory. Further, it has been the basis for subsequent studies which also focus on individual variation between children (e.g. Stoel-Gammon & Cooper 1984). It is important, then, to take a close look at their claims and the data on which they are based.

First, there are the problems cited in the previous section on the measurement sequence that results from using phone class analyses as evidence for claims about lexical influences and individual variation. I would offer the qualification that their data show that children are quite different from each other in their phonological development *when perform-ance factors are emphasized.* The children will be acquiring different vocabulary (to a degree at least), in varying contexts, with individual preferences for certain objects and, probably, sounds. Further, the data will be collected in varying circumstances. For example, in Ferguson & Farwell, the data from T, a child sampled by the authors in a systematic longitudinal study (in the sense of Chapter 2), are compared to Hildegard Leopold, a bilingual English–German child who was observed in a diary study by her father, Werner Leopold. Given this, it is not surprising that there are individual differences.

The phonetic inventories/phonological contrasts method, designed to minimize performance factors, can yield a rather different picture of development. For example, Ferguson & Farwell state (p. 435): 'T develops her /m/ class just before her /w/, although the /w/ forms appear more stable.' As Table 6.29 indicates, however, neither of these moves beyond lexical contrasts. Further, T is contrasted with Hildegard because Hildegard 'on the other hand, seems to gain control over certain classes and then to prefer to add new words to them'. As Table 6.28 suggests, T did this also at least with /b/, /d/, /p/ and /t/. It is the claim here, then, that claims about the individual variation between children regarding their phonological com-petence, as opposed to performance, will need to await more studies, using a method more like the one of phonetic inventories/phonological contrasts.

Besides these methodological questions, there are theoretical issues to be addressed. To understand Ferguson & Farwell, it is important to see their initial orientation. They are very much part of Child Language, as discussed in Chapter 4:

> Our approach is to try to understand children's phonological develop-ment in itself so as to improve our phonological theory . . .
>
> . . . some linguists at the present stage of the art might be well advised to turn away from the fascination of writing rules of maximum generality and conciseness for whole languages, and undertake instead highly detailed analyses of the idiosyncratic paths which particular children follow in learning to pronounce their languages.
>
> (Ferguson & Farwell 1975: 457, 438)

They are inductive, letting the data from children contribute to theory, rather than vice versa. Interestingly, they also cite (p. 438) a form of the Competence Assumption.

Given all of this, it is not surprising that they emphasize individual variation and performance factors, both important aspects in Child Language. In doing so, they need to explain how the child even reaches a non-lexical, systematic phonology. They are consistent in that they suggest that phonological theory may need to be altered to be more lexical and individualistic. They even hint at the possibility that all speakers may in a sense have their own unique phonology.

Most important, however, is the need to explain what is meant by individual strategy. This term is used throughout the Child Language literature, but it is not often defined. Ferguson & Farwell never define the term. They acknowledge (p. 435) that some differences between children may be due to the linguistic environment, but propose that others are due to individual strategies. Their definition is by example (p. 436):

> Such individual strategies include preferences for certain sounds, sound classes, or features ('favorite sounds'); extensive use of reduplication; special markers for certain classes of words . . . ; preferences for lexical expansion or phonological differentiation at the expense of the other; and persistent avoidance of particular 'problem sounds'.

Some of these may possibly be instances of linguistic variation (in the sense of section 4.5); most, however, seem to be cases of performance variation.

To summarize, Ferguson & Farwell have demonstrated through their phone class analysis the role of the lexical parameter. At the same time, though, they also provide evidence through phonological idioms and salience and avoidance that there is a phonological parameter at work. Their study, due to the limitations of their method, concentrates on performance factors and individual variation. We are still waiting, however, for extensive evidence for or against Jakobson's theory as a theory of phonological competence.

Despite numerous studies on languages other than English we know relatively little about phonological development in other languages. Some recent research, however, applying the phonetic inventories/phonological contrasts method to other languages has indicated support for cross-linguistic differences, and a linguistic level of representation (e.g. Ingram 1988, 1985b; Ingram & Mitchell, to appear). Here I conclude the section with a brief look at one of these studies which has compared the acquisition of English with Quiché, a language which is phonologically quite different.

Pye, Ingram & List (1987) Quiché is a Mayan language spoken by half a million people in the western highland region of Guatemala. Its phonological inventory is quite different from that of English. Table 6.30 provides the

Table 6.30 *The word-initial consonants of adult Quiché*

	Bilabial	Alveolar	Palatal	Velar	Uvular	Glottal
Plosives	p	t, ts	tʃ	k	q	ʔ
Ejectives	b'	t', ts'	tʃ'	k'	q'	
Fricatives		s	ʃ	x		
Nasals	m	n				
Liquids		r, l				
Glides	w		j			

initial consonants that occur in Quiché. Stops and affricates are grouped into a category labeled plosives. Quiché initial consonants differ from English in the following ways: (i) there is a series of ejectives (or glottalized stops; see Ladefoged 1975); (ii) there are uvular and glottal stops /q/ /ʔ/; (iii) there is no /f/, but there is /x/, the voiceless velar fricative. This system is sufficiently different from English to lead to some interesting tests of predictions about phonological development. In section 5.3.1 we examined Locke's (1983) maturational theory which predicted that there would be no effects of the child's linguistic environment until some time after the first 50 words acquired (Locke 1983: 84). On the other hand, a constructionist position such as Oller's (1981) suggests that some modifications due to the linguistic environment should occur. In particular, Jakobson's theory predicts linguistic effects after his stage 1 (the very earliest words) since the child is proposed to have a phonological level of representation.

Phonological data from Quiché children were collected by Cliff Pye as part of a longitudinal study on acquisition (Pye 1980). He visited Quiché children in their homes over a nine-month period, approximately every two weeks, for a one-hour play session. All sessions were tape-recorded and transcribed by Pye with the help of two native Quiché speakers. In Pye, Ingram & List (1987) the initial consonants from five of the children were analyzed using the phonetic inventories method described above. The sample sizes ranged from 23 to 115 lexical types with a mean of 68. The children's vocabularies were larger than those of the children studied by Ferguson & Farwell. According to Pye's morphological analysis (Pye 1983a), however, they were still primarily using single-word utterances.

Table 6.31 presents the phonetic inventories for the five children. Pye, Ingram & List then determined a composite inventory for the five children, using procedures for composite transcriptions. This composite phonetic inventory was taken as representing a basic or core set of consonants that

Table 6.31 *Phonetic inventories of five Quiché children, taken from Pye, Ingram & List (1987)*

QUICHÉ CONSONANTS

Child	Age	Nasals		Stops		Affricates		k	q	ʔ	Glottalized stops						Fricatives			Liquids		Glides	
		m	n	p	t	ts	tʃ	k	q	ʔ	bʼ	tʼ	tsʼ	tʃʼ	kʼ	qʼ	s	ʃ	x	l	r	w	j
A Tu:n	1:7		n	(p)			tʃ	(k)		ʔ**										l*		w*	(j)
A Li:n	2:0	m	n**	p	t		tʃ*	k*	q	ʔ**	(bʼ)								x*	l**		w*	
Al Tiya:n	2:1		n*	p	t*		tʃ	k*		ʔ***	(bʼ)								x*	l***		w**	
Al Cha:y	2:9	m	n	p*	t		tʃ*	k		ʔ*								ʃ*	x	l***		w*	
A Carlos	3:0	(m)	n	(p)	t*	(ts)	tʃ*	k		ʔ*	(bʼ)				kʼ		s*	(ʃ)	x*	l		w	
Composite		(m)	n	p	t		tʃ*	k		ʔ*	(bʼ)								x*	l*		w*	

Quiché children acquire early. It was then compared to a core set of initial consonants for English proposed by Ingram (1981a), where 15 children were analyzed by the same procedure. This comparison is shown in (6.17), where marginal sounds are given within parentheses:

(6.17) *The basic phonetic inventories of Quiché and English*

Quiché					English			
(m)	n				(m)	n		
(b')					b	d	(g)	
p	t	tʃ	k	ʔ	p	t	k	
			x		(f)	(s)		h
w					w			
	l							

While there are some similarities, particularly regarding nasals and voiceless stops, there are more differences. Clearly Quiché and English children are acquiring very different sets of initial consonants. The first Quiché fricative acquired is [x], whereas English children begin with [f] and [s]. One could argue that English children do not show an [x] because it does not occur in English. This is not true for [l] and [tʃ], however, which occur in English, but do not appear among children's early initial consonants. These two sounds, however, are two of the most used initial consonants by Quiché children.

These data indicate that children will show the effects of linguistic input in their phonetic inventories, at least toward the end of the period of single-word utterances. In some ways this is not surprising, in that Shvachkin's study has indicated that phonemic perception is well on its way by that point. Importantly, the data show that articulatory constraints are not as strong as one might expect, certainly not as strong as predicted by Locke's maturational theory.

Pye, Ingram & List give two possible explanations for the differences shown in (6.17). First, they consider the articulatory learning theory discussed in 5.3.1. This theory would predict that the child acquires the sounds that are most frequently heard. The problem of correlating onset of acquisition and frequency of occurrence in adult speech has been discussed for English by Moskowitz (1970). Using the data from Wang & Crawford (1960), Moskowitz points out that the most frequent English fricatives are, in order of frequency, /s/, /ð/, /z/, /v/. Only one of these, /s/, is early in acquisition. Pye, Ingram & List conclude that absolute frequency does not seem to be a primary factor.

They then explore the possibility of *functional load* on phoneme frequency. This has to do with the extent to which a phoneme is necessary to the phonological system. The functional load of a phoneme is measured by

Table 6.32   *The rank order frequencies for initial consonants common to Quiché and English*

Language	Sounds											
	/tʃ/	w	k	p	t	l	n	s	m	r	ʃ	j/
Quiché	1	2	3	4	5	6	7.5	7.5	9.5	9.5	11	12
English	10	7	1	2	6	11	8	3	9	12	13	4.5

the number of oppositions or minimal pairs it occurs in. English /ŋ/, for example, has a smaller functional load than /m/ because /ŋ/ does not occur initially. Wang & Crawford (1960) have found that English /ð/ is the second most frequent fricative. This is because it occurs in a small class of frequent words, like 'the', 'this', etc. Its functional load, however, is quite small in that these words are a small class and subsequently enter into a small number of minimal pairs. We could change all English /ð/ into [d]s and still communicate.

To get an indirect measure of functional load, Pye, Ingram & List looked at the frequency of English and Quiché initial consonants in terms of lexical types. For English, we used the 500 most frequently used words of 5- and 6-year-old children in Birmingham, England, based on Burroughs (1957). Since no adult data are available on Quiché, we had to resort to looking at the frequency of Quiché initial consonants in the adult word types attempted by the children. Table 6.32 gives the frequency rank order for those sounds shared by the two languages. These frequencies seem to account for the differences quite well. For example, /tʃ/ occurs in many more words in Quiché than in English, while the opposite is true for /s/; /l/ is also nearly twice as frequent in lexical types in the words Quiché children use as in English.

This preliminary study provides some suggestive data on the effects of the input language on early phonological development. Similar analyses on children acquiring other languages will need to be done before more definitive conclusions can be drawn. If valid, the data indicate that children begin during the period of single-word utterances to acquire the phonological system of their language. While there may be some articulatory effects that restrict the child's production, these effects may be less than previously expected. The primary factor behind the appearance of a sound in the child's early system appears to be its importance in the phonological system which underlies the words that the child hears. It would not be surprising to find that languages also tend to assign these highest functional loads to sounds that are easier to say. We need to be cautious, therefore, in concluding that the sounds that are acquired later in English are in some sense harder to say. In some cases, such as /l/ and /tʃ/, they may just be not as important phonologically.

6.6 The linguistic environment

We saw in Chapter 5 that the language addressed to infants may be influenced greatly by the culture in which the infant lives. Western culture sees the infant as a potential conversational partner, and its burps and smiles are accepted as turns in the conversation. Further, as found by both Snow (1977b) and Kaye (1980a), this language to the child does not change abruptly once the child begins to produce words. Adults continue to use a simplified form of English which contains the features given in Table 5.11.

In this section I look first, during the period of single-word utterances, at the child beginning to engage in what looks like conversation – while the child still has relatively little to say, he begins to respond to adult speech with language of his own. Second, I discuss the methodological means for examining how the adult language directed to the child may influence his language. Lastly, I look into the possibility that some individual differences noted between children may be the result of their linguistic environment.

6.6.1 The onset of conversation

In section 5.5.3 an extract was given from Snow (1977b) of a conversation between a mother and her infant. Later, two other examples were given from Kaye (1980a). In each case, the mother was clearly the initiator and controller of the conversation. During the period of single-word utterances, the child begins to play a more important role in the process.

One of the first people to examine the development of conversation was Lewis (1937) as part of his study of K. Lewis proposed that K went through the following three stages of development (p. 67):

> *Lewis's three stages of conversational development*
> 1. *Earliest months*: the child responds to the adult's *acts* by *acts* and some utterance of sounds.
> 1. *Towards the end of the first year*: the child responds to the adult's *speech* by *acts*; and to his *acts* by *speech*.
> 3. *About 1;6*: the child responds to the adult's *speech* by *speech*.

Conversations for K, then, began toward the end of the period of single-word utterances.

Table 6.33   *Four examples of K's early conversation, taken from Lewis (1937; Series 2: 73) (format amended)*

Example no.	K's utterance		Mother's utterance
Age	Orthography	Phonetics	
1.	(Mother is dressing K in front of the gas fire; K points to fire and speaks)		
1;5(10)	'Aha'	aha	
	'Fire'	fa	
	(Mother points to fire)		
			'What's that?'
	'Fire'	fa	
2.	(Around bath time, K climbs upstairs, with his mother following him)		
1;6(3)			'Where are you going?'
	'Bath'	ba	
3.	(The mother is standing by the bureau in which chocolate is kept)		
1;6(9)			'I've got something nice for you.'
	'Chocolate'	gɔga	
	'Chocolate'	gɔga	
4.	(Mother is wheeling K's carriage toward a bed of tulips)		
1;6(16)			'What can you see?'
	'Flower'	fafa	

Table 6.33 gives four examples of K's first conversational exchanges. In three of the examples, K responds to his mother's speech. It is only in the first example that K actually initiates the conversation. Lewis emphasizes that the transition of his stage 2 to stage 3 is very gradual, although no frequency counts are given. Further, he stresses the important part played by K's mother in eliciting K's conversation. He states (p. 68): 'The adult, by gestures and intonation, continually incites the child to speak, and encourages him with signs of approval when he has spoken.' Again, we have to remember that this is a feature of Western culture.

More recently, Lewis's observations have been elaborated by Halliday (1975) in his study of his son Nigel. Like Lewis, Halliday observed that his son did not begin to engage in dialogue until around the end of Phase I (or the period of single-word utterances) or 18 months. During Phase I, Nigel engaged in what Halliday calls *proto-dialogues*. He could do the following (p. 48):

(i)   give three specific responses to calls, greetings and gifts;
(ii) answer questions of the type 'Do you want . . . ?'; 'Shall I?', i.e. ones where the answers required were instrumental, regulatory, or interactional in function;
(iii) say 'yes' and 'no' in instrumental and regulatory ways (these were not used to answer questions seeking information, e.g. 'Did you see a car?').

Table 6.34 *Nigel's five ways to engage in dialogue, taken from Halliday (1975: 49)*

(1) Respond to *wh*-question (provided the answer was already known to the questioner), e.g. 'What are you eating?' Nigel: 'banana'.

(2) Respond to a command, e.g. 'Take the toothpaste to Daddy and go and get your bib.' Nigel does so, saying: 'daddy . . . noddy . . . train', [i.e. 'Daddy (give) noddy (toothpaste to him, and go and get your bib with the) train (on it)]

(3) Respond to a statement, e.g. 'You went on a train yesterday.' Nigel signals attention, by repeating, and continues the conversation: 'train . . . byebye' [i.e. 'Yes, I went on a train, and then (when I got off) the train went away.']

(4) Respond to a response, e.g. Nigel: 'gravel' Response: 'Yes, you had some gravel in your hand.' Nigel: 'ooh' [i.e. 'It hurt me.']

(5) Initiate dialogue, e.g. Nigel: 'what's that?' Response: 'That's butter.' Nigel repeats: 'butter'.

Proto-dialogue is restricted to the child's communicative functions at the time. Halliday does not see these events as dialogues, however, because Nigel cannot initiate the dialogue and he cannot respond to information-seeking questions.

Nigel's first dialogues appeared around 18 months, over a two-week period. At the end, he could participate in dialogue in five different ways. These are provided with examples in Table 6.34. As with K, Nigel is mostly limited to responses to the adult language. This is similar to Lewis's stage 3. The only means that Nigel has to initiate conversations is the question 'what's that?'. As we will see in the next chapter, the onset of dialogue for Halliday is an important event which marks the end of Phase I and the start of Phase II.

Some further examples of the restricted dialogue of the child in this period are given in Ingram (1981c). There I report on the early language of a girl referred to as K. Like Nigel, K had a small number of proto-words that assisted her in maintaining conversations with adults. One of these was 'huh?', which was not used to get the adult to clarify her remarks, but simply to keep talking. Example (6.18) gives one such dialogue (p. 277; E = Experimenter), at 1;2(15):

(6.18) E;   What are those? (buttons in a jar)
       K: huh?
       E: What are those?
       K: huh?
            huh?
            (pause)
            huh?
            tata please (three times)

E: Can't you get them out?
K: huh?
      huh?
E: You do it?
K: huh?

The session contained 61 uses of 'huh' out of 199 utterances. Two other such words were 'tata', which was used when handing items back and forth, and 'oooh!', which indicated excitement.

Another aspect of K's language was that she and her mother (M) would practice discourse routines. The most striking example occurred in a session when K was 1;0(26) (p. 276):

(6.19)   K: 'Uncle Ben' (ak^{h}aba]
              (I don't understand and turn to her mother)
         M: 'Uncle Ben' (whispered to me)
         M: 'Uh huh. Ask her where he is' (to me)
         Me:'Where's Uncle Ben?'
         K: 'huh?'
              'Norway' [i:wei]
         M: 'Norway' (to me)
         K: 'Norway' [ni:wei]
         Me:'What's that?' (to M)
         M: 'Norway' (to me)
         Me:'Norway?'
         M: 'Yeah, that's where he is.'
         K: 'yeah' [jæ]

In this example, K is clearly too young to have any idea of where Norway is or even what such an answer would mean to an adult. K's mother felt that Uncle Ben's departure was an important event, and had discussed this at length with K. Such discourse dialogues allow a mother and child to have brief conversations, albeit one-sided ones.

6.6.2 Methods used to study the effects of linguistic input

In this period, we see that the child is beginning to understand language, and can begin to engage in at least proto-dialogues in the sense of Halliday (1975). From Chapter 5, we also know that at least English mothers are speaking in a simplified fashion to their children. What effects, then, does the mother's input have on the child's emerging linguistic system?

In Section 5.5.2, we briefly discussed predictions made by the behaviorist, constructionist and maturational views of acquisition. We pointed out that the latter two views place the primary emphasis on the child adjusting to a changing environment. Even so, it was felt that some environmental effects may exist, due to the fact that some behaviorist principles will be part of a theory of acquisition, even if they do not constitute the entire theory. Also, such effects will need to be determined in order to separate those aspects of the child's linguistic behavior from others which are due to the child's internal language acquisition system.

The need to examine the role of the linguistic environment, even without a nativist orientation, is not always acknowledged by those with a maturational orientation. A primary reason has been Chomsky's claims throughout his writings about the inadequacy of the linguistic environment for the acquisition of language. For example, in Chomsky (1968:88) he refers to the language that the child hears as 'degenerate'. There are two ways in which this term has been used: (i) it indicates that the language the child hears is full of errors and false starts such that it could not possibly be an adequate model for acquisition – research on English, at least, has proven this aspect false, as indicated in section 5.5; (ii) it suggests that the linguistic input does not provide sufficient information to allow the child to induce the rich structural properties of human language. For example, a well-formed, clearly spoken simple sentence is still nothing more than a string of words, with no information in the signal about phrase boundaries, the sites of moved NPs, the existence of empty categories, etc. The claim that the child's linguistic input is degenerate from this viewpoint is still valid.

In recent years, there has been a return to the issue of the child's linguistic environment within the maturational view. In Chapter 4, there was a discussion of Chomsky's parameter-setting model which claims that the child establishes certain key features of the language being acquired which enable a whole other series of assumptions to be made about the language. These parameters will be triggered by specific linguistic events in the child's environment. The question then arises: what is a trigger experience for the child? This issue has been raised recently by Lightfoot (1982) and Roeper (1981), among others. To summarize, then, we now have three goals in examining the linguistic input to the child: (i) to establish the effects that are due to the behaviorist principles that will be part of the theory of acquisition; (ii) the isolation of these effects in order to determine those aspects of the child's language that are due to the innate properties of the child's acquisition device; and (iii) to specify more clearly what constitutes the relevant linguistic input for the child to formulate a linguistic rule (or, within the parameter-setting model, to 'set a parameter').

There are several ways in which one might proceed to look for effects of the linguistic environment. Most studies fall into one of the three following general categories: (i) experimental studies; (ii) Time 2 studies, and

(iii) Time 1 vs. Time 2 studies. Here I will briefly discuss the general features of these three types of studies, and then report in 6.6.3 on some findings for this period. The major studies, however, have been done with more advanced children; their results, therefore, will be presented in Chapter 9.

The *experimental* studies use the traditional psychological procedure of controlling the child's linguistic environment, and then monitoring the effects of that control. One can see the difficulties this presents with children, since total control of their environment would be impossible except through unethical procedures. There are, however, two ways in which this may be done with a minimum of problems. One way is to present the child with artificial data, which may be in the form of nonsense words, or even an artificial language. Since these data are created by the experimenter, there is not the concern that the child may get additional experience during the period of the study through normal linguistic interaction. Another way is to select natural language forms, but only ones that are rare in the child's linguistic environment. For example, passive sentences such as 'The cat was chased by the dog' are not frequent in the speech of adults to children. The presentation of such sentences could be controlled, say through their inclusion in selected reading materials given to the child. Pre- and post-tests of the child's receptive or productive ability on the selected structure could then be studied.

In experimental studies there are at least three aspects that can be controlled. One is the frequency of presentation: it is useful to know how often a child in any given stage needs to hear something before it is acquired. The second aspect, which is related to frequency, is rate of presentation: is acquisition enhanced more by frequent exposure over a short period, or infrequent (but regular) exposure over a longer period? Third, it is possible to look for generalizations from the presented stimuli to other stimuli. For example, linguistic theory may claim that two structures, S_1 and S_2, are related by rule. We could present the child with only S_2, and then see if S_1 is also acquired; if so, the data could be used in support of the linguistic theory which relates S_1 and S_2.

The second type of study is what I refer to as *Time 2* studies. In these studies, the mother's and child's language are compared at a selected time of development on some feature or set of features. The studies attempt to correlate the frequency of use of some aspect of the mother's language with its use in the child's language. Such studies are also called *correlational* studies. They typically examine a large number of mother–child pairs, and select a controlled sample from each pair. For example, we could collect samples from mothers of 3-year-olds and their children to see if the frequency of use of passive sentences by mothers correlates with their use by the children. There are three possible correlations: (i) positive, i.e. mothers who use more passives have children who use more passives; (ii) negative, i.e. mothers who use more passives have children who use fewer passives; and (iii) no correlation. In this example, if we get a positive correlation, we might conclude that the data suggest that the mother's frequent use of passives has caused the child to acquire passives. These studies are called Time 2 studies since they imply an effect that presumably would have occurred at an earlier time, say Time 1.

There are obvious difficulties with Time 2 studies. The major one is that we can never conclude causal effects from correlations – it could be that the mother is using more passives because her child has acquired them. Time 2 studies, therefore, can only be suggestive at best. Even a result of no correlation does not mean that there may have been some effect at an earlier time. Further, such studies imply that the mother has been the primary linguistic influence on the child. Such studies therefore need to be quite explicit about the general linguistic environment of the child.

The third type of study, *Time 1 vs. Time 2* studies, has been developed to overcome the problems of Time 2 studies. To explain them, consider the following design:

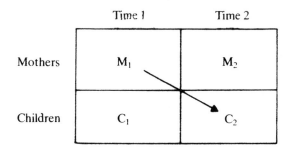

Assumption: all children are the same at Time 1 (C_1)

Basic design of Time 1 vs. Time 2 studies

The general orientation of such studies is to observe the child's language before and after the acquisition of some feature of language. Their use of the feature at Time 2 (where C_2 = the child's language at Time 2) is then examined in relation to their mothers' use of the feature at Time 1 (M_1). If there is a correlation between M_1 and C_2, then it is concluded that a causal relation exists.

The first major study of this kind was conducted by Newport, Gleitman & Gleitman (1977). In their design, C_1 consisted of three age groups of children: 1 year to 15 months, 18–21 months, and 2 years to 27 months. This design was later criticized by Furrow, Nelson & Benedict (1979: 425) as being based upon two unwarranted assumptions. First, it assumes that possible effects of the linguistic input will be similar at different ages and levels of development. Second, it assumes that changes in the use of particular forms by children will be the same regardless of age or stage. These are two very strong assumptions. It seems possible that effects, if any, may differ dependent on the child's level of development, and that they may differ dependent on the structure being acquired. To get around these assumptions, Furrow, Nelson & Benedict add the assumption that the children must all be linguistically the same at Time 1; I have added this assumption to the design above.

There is a further aspect of the Time 1 vs. Time 2 study which needs to be pointed out. Suppose that we get a M_1, C_2 correlation that is the same as the M_2, C_2 correlation. According to Campbell & Stanley (1963), such a result weakens the causal effects since the C_2 data are equally interpretable as being caused by M_2. If the M_2, C_2 correlation differs from the M_1, C_2 one, however, then the only possible cause of the child's language at Time 2 is the mother's language at Time 1. The arrow in the design above implies that the M_1, C_2 correlation differs from that of M_2, C_2.

Furrow, Nelson & Benedict point out that there may be confounding third variables that might lead to the correlations found in a Time 1 vs. Time 2 study. The possibility of such confounding variables makes it difficult to conclude a cause and effect relation. Even so, the design at least provides one means to begin exploring the possible effects of the child's linguistic environment.

6.6.3 Some possible effects on lexical development

Most of the research looking for effects of the linguistic environment on the child's language has looked at grammatical development beyond the current period of acquisition. A review of this research will be presented in subsequent chapters. Here we will briefly examine two studies which attempt to look at the possible effects of the most obvious milestone of this period, lexical development.

An important aspect of the linguistic input that is inadequately understood is the effect of *frequency* of exposure. That is, how often must a child hear a particular aspect of language before it is acquired? There are several points that need to be considered in studying this topic. The most important point is that of readiness. Most likely the role of frequency is minimal until the child is linguistically ready to develop particular linguistic features. At the current time we have little understanding within either maturational or constructionist orientations of readiness. In the area of language disorders in children, the issue of readiness is a central one since the language clinician needs to make assumptions about what the child is most ready to acquire. In that field, such decisions are made by assuming that the normal child's order of acquisition reflects sequences of readiness (e.g. Miller & Yoder 1974). We do not have, however, a well-defined theory of linguistic readiness.

Given a child's readiness, there are still the issues of number and rate of exposures. Using the terminology of Schwartz & Terrell (1983), we can separate *massed* presentations from *distributed* presentations. Massed presentation refers to a situation where the item under acquisition occurs very frequently over a short period of time. Moerk (1980), for example, has proposed that children are very sensitive to short periods of increased usage by their parents of selected linguistic features. Such an explanation puts a great deal of responsibility on the parent to recognize the child's readiness and present the linguistic feature at the appropriate level of frequency. Distributed presentation refers to some minimal pattern of exposure. For example, daily exposure over a particular period of time, say a week, may be more important to acquisition than massed presentation in a single day. Besides these two types, we can also propose *single event* presentation, which means that the child will acquire an item after just one, clear example. A strong biological theory should contain predictions about single-event presentations. It will need, however, to account for how the child deals with input that contains grammatical errors.

Schwartz & Terrell (1983) make a preliminary attempt to examine the effects of frequency and rate of exposure on early lexical development, using the experimental approach described in the previous section. Twelve children (1;0(21) to 1;3(15) at the onset) were taught 16 nonsense words (divided into objects and actions) during ten experimental sessions over a four-month period. All of the children had five or fewer words in production at the onset of the study. Each nonsense word was taught through exposure to four exemplars. For example, one nonsense word was 'objects at the end of a string or chain' which was taught with the following exemplars: 1. a nose clip, 2. a yoyo, 3. a key chain, 4. a drain stopper on a chain. Within each word, two exemplars were assigned to a frequently presented condition (or FP condition), and two to an infrequently presented condition (or IP condition). Exemplars in the FP condition were presented twice each session, whereas those in the IP condition were presented once. Thus, across the ten sessions IP exemplars were collectively presented 320 times whereas FP exemplars were presented 640 times.

Table 6.35 presents the results for the three measures applied to the data

Table 6.35 *Summary of results from Schwartz & Terrell (1983) on input frequency*

Measure	Condition FP	IP
1. Percentage of exemplars named at least once	44%	29%
2. Mean number of presentations before naming:		
(a) object exemplars	12.77	7.59
(b) action exemplars	12.19	7.33
3. Mean number of exemplars named during first ten presentations	4.33	9.42

by Schwartz & Terrell. The first measure shows that the child named more of the frequently presented exemplars than the infrequent ones. There was then a significant effect of *frequency* regarding naming. The next two measures are particularly interesting. They show that the infrequently presented exemplars were still acquired around the same rate as the frequent ones, even though they were presented only half as often. This can be seen by a reanalysis of measure 2. Measure 2 gives the mean number of presentations that an exemplar needed to be first named. For the infrequently presented exemplars, they need approximately seven-and-a-half sessions (since one exemplar was given per session). The frequently presented exemplars needed approximately six-and-a-half sessions (a number obtained by dividing the mean of 12.77 and 12.19 by two, the number of presentations per session). That is, even though the frequently presented exemplars were presented twice as often, they were only first named approximately one session before the infrequent exemplars. In these data, then, *rate* of presentation appears to be nearly as important as frequency.

The Schwartz & Terrell study is an insightful attempt to examine the interaction of frequency and rate. Two reservations, however, need to be made. First, they did not look at comprehension, only at production: the next step would be to examine these factors in relation to the child's growth of receptive vocabulary. Second, the difference between frequent and infrequent presentations within exemplars was not particularly great, and the study, therefore, cannot be taken as definitive evidence against Moerk's proposals concerning the short-term effects of massed presentations. Different results might have occurred if frequent presentations were increased, say to four presentations per exemplar per session.

While Schwartz & Terrell studied the acquisition of nonsense words, Della Corta, Benedict & Klein (1983) looked for environmental effects on the acquisition of English vocabulary. In Section 5.5.3, there are examples from Kaye (1980a) of two mothers, one of whom was very directive while the other was more narrative. In this chapter, section 6.2.2, we have presented Nelson's (1973) analysis of children in this period falling into the groupings of referential and expressive learners (see Table 6.4). Della Corta, Benedict & Klein report on a study undertaken to see if the expressive vs. referential distinction can be accounted for by environmental factors.

To study this issue they conducted a Time 2 study in the sense of the previous section. They collected 50-utterance samples from 16 mothers during caretaking situations (diapering, dressing, bathing) with their children. The children were between 1;3(15) and 1;7 and were divided into either expressive or referential children. The samples from the mothers of the five most referential and five most expressive children were then separated for further analysis. Unfortunately, the authors provide no information about the measures applied to the children to make this separation. Presumably the children were only using single-word utterances at the time.

The mothers' samples were subsequently analyzed for general structural and pragmatic characteristics; an overview of the aspects measured is given here:

General measures
(a) MLU; yes/no questions; common nouns; 3rd person pronouns; noun/pronoun ratio; noun type/token ratio
(b) number of utterances per caretaking event

Pragmatic measures
(a) *communicative intent* (13 measures): labeling; requests for information; suggestions; prescriptives; proscriptives; phonological corrections; referential corrections; description; displaced speech; conventional social expressions; social play; fillers; other
(b) *focus of attention*: child- vs. mother-oriented speech; task- vs. context-oriented speech; indeterminant

Evaluation: approval; disapproval; neutral

For communicative intent, the two categories of prescriptives and description are particularly important as possible sources for the referential and expressive difference in the children. These two were defined as follows (p. 38):

Prescriptives: Commands made in an attempt to direct the child's behavior or verbalizations, e.g. 'Put the doll over here', 'Say Daddy'.
Description: Statements that describe a person's behavior, actions, feelings, appearance, etc. or an object or an event that is present in the immediate situation, e.g. 'Mommy's getting your diaper', 'You look sleepy'.

Table 6.36 *Selected findings from Della Corta, Benedict & Klein (1983) on the language of mothers of expressive and referential children*

	Mothers	
	Referential children	Expressive children
Measures		
General measures		
MLU	4.30	4.03
no. of utterances per caretaking event	*20.8	*6.2
other measures	no significant effects	
Pragmatic measures (mean no. of each category per 50 utterances)		
(a) *Communicative intent*		
description	*19.6	*13
prescriptives	*6.8	*12.6
requests for information	8.0	8.8
fillers	6.6	6.6
(b) *Focus of attention*		
child-oriented speech	26.0	31.4
task-oriented speech	8.4	4.98
(c) *Evaluation*		
approval	31.2	24.4
neutral	13.2	20.6

* Indicates significant differences between the two types of mothers.

Table 6.36 presents the major results of the study. Concerning general measures, there were no significant differences between the speech of mothers of referential and expressive children except for the number of utterances per caretaking event. Even though both groups of mothers had comparable MLUs (around 4.0) the referential mothers produced three times as many utterances. Unfortunately, the study was not designed to see if this difference would lead to a greater rate of acquisition for the referential children. (We also do not know if the expressive mothers would have spoken more to referential children.) Regarding the pragmatic measures, there were no differences between the mothers on focus of attention or evaluation. There were, however, significant differences on two of the 13 measures of communicative intent, these being prescriptives and description. The mothers of referential children used more description, whereas the mothers of expressive children used more prescriptives. The authors see the high use of description as a possible source of the high proportion of general nominals in the speech of referential children. They do not comment on how the high use of prescriptives would lead to the relatively high use of personal-social words in expressive children (Table 6.4).

The study by Della Corta, Benedict & Klein is an example of the difficulties in doing a Time 2 study in order to determine causal effects. The authors are aware of this problem, but say nonetheless: 'Although a causal inference cannot be made, the findings lend some support to the notion that the mother's speech has some influence on that of the child' (p. 42). Of course, we can also conclude that their mothers are simply responding to differences in their children. A more definitive answer will require a Time 1 vs. Time 2 study. In such a case, Time 1 would be at some point around the onset of word comprehension. To date, such studies are quite small in number; they will be looked at in Chapter 9.

Further reading

Lexical development
The early research on word acquisition (reviewed in McCarthy 1954) concentrated on onset and rate for the purpose of determining norms of acquisition. In recent years the research has been interested in developing a theory of semantic acquisition, in large part inspired by Clark (1973a). Much of the recent research has concentrated on early word over-extensions.

McCarthy (1954: 523–34) provides a useful overview of the early studies on word acquisition. Nelson's (1973) study has provided the frequently discussed distinction of referential vs. expressive children, and has inspired a number of studies. A reading of the first three chapters (pp. 1–56) will provide the major aspects of the study. Also read two of the studies that follow Nelson's study, Benedict (1979) and Rescorla (1980). Lastly, Piaget's observations on early lexical acquisition can be found in Piaget (1948) for Stage V (pp. 52–4), Stage VI (pp. 62–72) and the emergence of signs (pp. 215–24).

Pragmatic and grammatical development
General characteristics of single-word utterances were frequently discussed by early investigators, with Jespersen (1922) and de Laguna (1927) most frequently cited. The period was often referred to as the 'holophrastic' stage to indicate that a whole idea was being expressed. A renewal of interest occurred around 1970 (see Ingram 1971) and has led to an extensive literature. This effort occurred after several years of concentrated study of early word combinations (see Chapter 7), for the 1960s were directed toward precursors to language in the periods of prelinguistic development and single-word utterances.

A major debate on single-word utterances has been the extent to which they can be said to contain structure. Some have argued that there is semantic structure underlying single-word utterances which surfaces later in two-word utterances (e.g. Ingram 1971; Greenfield & Smith 1976), while others have denied this (e.g. Bloom 1973). Most of the studies have concentrated exclusively on production data. The text has discussed some of the small number of studies on comprehension. Shipley, Smith & Gleitman (1969) only examined four children in this period, and is better known for its results on older children (see Chapter 7). Huttenlocher (1974) was the first study to concentrate exclusively on this period, although it is only a preliminary report of a study that was never reported elsewhere. Miller *et al.* (1980) is one of the few attempts to study comprehension in this period for a relatively large number of children.

Huttenlocher (1974) provides a very insightful treatment of the problems of testing comprehension in young children, as well as some important preliminary results. Halliday's approach can be seen in Halliday (1975: 8–36), and Greenfield & Smith (1976: 31–65). Reviews which argue for or against structure at this period are Ingram (1979b) and Barrett (1982) respectively.

Phonological development

Perception.   While relatively little research has been done on phonemic perception, even less has treated this period of acquisition. Elkonin (1971) provides a summary in English of the rich literature on research in language acquisition by Russian psycholinguists. Abstracts of 32 Russian studies are provided by Slobin (1966) and comprise the major English summary of Russian research. Most of the literature, however, is unavailable in English at this time. Most of what is translated can be found in the collection of articles in Ferguson & Slobin (1973). Thanks to the work of Dan Slobin, the volume contains seven articles translated from Russian. One of these is an overview by Elkonin of the famous Russian diary of Gvozdev (1949) of his son, Zhenya. Another is the study (discussed in this chapter) by Shvachkin on the development of phonemic perception. Shvachkin's original study on Russian children remains the major contribution. Unfortunately, little is known about Shvachkin. The bibliography done by Slobin (1972) lists four articles by Shvachkin between 1947 and 1954. According to the index at the end, the first two articles are on the development of phonemic perception. Since the latter of these was translated, we can assume that it was the more important of the two. The last two papers, both published in 1954, are indexed as studies on syntactic and semantic comprehension. Neither is summarized in Slobin (1966). Shvachkin's 1948 paper is valuable for its creative methodology, descriptive findings, and theoretical proposals. In the 1970s, a group at Stanford attempted to adopt Svachkin's method and applied it to English children. A brief report of this effort is found in Garnica (1973). The method was also tried with older children in Edwards (1974). A different method for the study of phonemic perception was developed by Eilers & Oller (1976). A general review of the topic for this period and later ones is Barton (1980).

Production.   There is a large and diverse literature on the child's early production of words – the text has been restricted to works focussing on the acquisition of the first 50 words. Much of the literature in the field concentrates on children with larger vocabularies than this, usually in the 50 to 150 range.

It is necessary to read Jakobson directly to gain an appreciation of his proposals for phonological development. Jakobson (1941/68) remains the major place to begin. The following sections give the most important discussions of child language: pp. 12–31, 46–59, 66–81, 84–91. The revisions to this original theory are in Jakobson & Halle (1956), section 4 'Phonemic patterning', pp. 50–5. (A good summary of Jakobson's theory can be found in Ferguson & Garnica 1975: 162–9.) The lexical orientation of recent years can be seen in Ferguson & Farwell (1975), and Stoel-Gammon & Cooper (1984). An alternative point of view can be found in Goad & Ingram (1988).

Linguistic environment

The 1970s have seen the emergence of the study of the child's input. In this time there has arisen an extensive body of works on how adults speak to their children. We will look at this literature in subsequent chapters. The Bibliography here is restricted to studies which focus on speech to children during the period of single-word utterances, and attempts to establish effects. This limitation results in a much smaller list. The major collection of articles on linguistic input is that by Snow & Ferguson (1977). An overview of the topic can be found in Chapman (1981b).

7 The period of the first word combinations

7.1 Defining the period of the first word combinations

The onset of the period of the first word combinations is indicated by several developments. First, there is a noticeable increase in the child's spoken vocabulary. In Smith's (1926) classic study, for example, the vocabulary size for her subjects expanded from a mean of 22 words at 18 months to 272 words by age 2. I give here a summary of this jump:

Age	No. of subjects	Mean no. of words
1;6	14	22
1;9	14	118
2;0	25	272

Further, recall that the child's receptive vocabulary at 18 months is much larger than the productive one. The estimate in Table 6.11 indicated that it was as much as five times larger. There is active semantic development, therefore, at this time.

A second important development is the gradual onset of multiword utterances. Table 7.1 gives some general information on the emergence of multiword utterances for five children. (Similar data are presented in Table 6.18 for Matthew and Nicky from Greenfield & Smith 1976.) These data show the gradual emergence of unique syntactic types over a four or five-month period. Overall, the striking increases begin when the number of these approaches 100, around 22 months, based on the grouped data. The early multiword utterances go through a time of slow growth just as lexical development did during the preceding period. We will refer to the marked increase in syntactic types around the end of the second year as the *syntactic spurt.*

Bloom, Lightbown & Hood (1975) provide MLU measures for two of the children in Table 7.1, Eric and Peter. Eric's MLU was 1.42 at 22 months and 1.69 at 23 months. Peter's MLU was 1.33 at 23 months and 1.75 at 2 years. That is, for these two children the syntactic spurt coincided with an MLU of approximately 1.5. As indicated in Table 3.4, Roger Brown (1973)

234

Table 7.1 *The number of unique syntactic types for four children over the first few months of multiword utterances. The children are Gregory (Braine 1963a), Jennika (author's diary), Eric and Peter (Bloom, Lightbown & Hood 1975)*

| Age | Children | | | | Mean |
	Gregory	Jennika	Eric	Peter	
1;5		5			1
1;6		10			3
1;7	14	36	10		15
1;8	24	72	37		33
1;9	54	130	—	7	57
1;10	89	256	108	70	131
1;11	350	—	401	81	272
2;0	1,400	—	—	243	575
2;1	2,500+	—	902	458	1,029

refers to the development from MLU 1.0 to 1.5 as early Stage I. Here, we will retain Brown's term for this subperiod of the period of the first word combinations, but alter its measurements. Somewhat arbitrarily, I will specify this period as having the following boundaries. It begins when the child has produced 25 recognizable syntactic types (i.e. multiword utterances). This measure is used because of the difficulty, to be discussed, of identifying the child's first multiword utterances. It ends with the syntactic spurt, which is operationally defined as occurring when the child either has an MLU of 1.5 or has used 100 syntactic types. At this point there is nothing of theoretical importance in making these boundaries: their purpose is to enable us to identify children at this stage in our review of relevant studies. Most generally, I describe this first subperiod of the child's first multiword utterances as one during which the child very gradually develops the ability to use words in novel combinations.

As with the spurt in vocabulary development, the syntactic spurt does not necessarily indicate that the child's linguistic system is now adult-like. Bloom, Lightbown & Hood (1975) report on two patterns of syntactic–semantic acquisition that their subjects followed after the syntactic spurt up to approximately MLU 2.00 when their systems converged. Results like these suggest that the syntactic spurt is followed by another formative period in which fundamental aspects of the *grammatical system* are being established. This subperiod roughly coincides with what Brown has referred to as late Stage I when the child's MLU is between 1.5 and 2.0. Here we will define this second subperiod of the period of the first word combinations as beginning at the end of early Stage 1 (as defined above), and ending when the MLU reaches 2.0 or when there are at least 250 unique syntactic types.

The latter number is based on the figures in Bloom, Lightbown & Hood (1975) when the individual patterns seemed to merge. We speculate that the child begins this second period with possibly an idiosyncratic grammar, and ends it with a grammar that is much more adult-like.

7.2 Grammatical development: an overview

7.2.1 The major studies

This overview of early grammatical development begins with a brief look at some of the major studies on the topic. As reported in Chapter 3, the first extensive data were collected by Bloom, Brown, and Braine in the early 1970s. While other studies have followed, many have been reanalyses of these original data. Given the importance of the claims one would want to make about the child's development during this time, it is crucial that we be aware of the data used to make them. As will be argued, most of the claims about early grammatical development are based upon a rather small number of children. This, no doubt, is the result of how difficult and time-consuming it is to collect extensive data from young children. It will be necessary, however, to be quite cautious about claims of acquisition which are based upon such a small sample size.

Of all the investigators in the field, Bloom and her colleagues have clearly conducted the most extensive data collection and analysis in the area. These studies cover subjects such as single-word utterances, early syntactic–semantic relations, imitation, individual variation, discourse, and question acquisition. They are based not only on Bloom's original data, but also on later data on several other children, including Bloom's daughter Allison. Together, they represent a formidable body of research that is necessary reading for any serious student in the field.

Another important series of works have appeared as a result of analyses conducted by Brown and his colleagues on the original data from Adam, Eve, and Sarah. A related work is Bowerman (1973a) who was part of the Brown project and subsequently recorded similar data from a young child named Kendall. Brown has been quite generous in sharing his data with other investigators, and Bowerman (1973a) presents the data from Kendall in an appendix. A recent theoretical work of importance, Pinker (1984), is in large part based on Brown's original data.

Lastly, Braine has followed his original study of Andrew, Stephen, and Gregory with the collection of additional samples from other children. In 1976 he published an influential monograph on early grammatical development in which he presented new data from two subjects, David and

Table 7.2 *Summary of the more frequently cited published data on English children during the period of early word combinations*

Child	Age	Source	Form of data
Eric II Gia I	1;8 1;7	Bloom (1970)	Most of the syntactic types used are presented with discussion for Eric II and Gia I.
Gia II Kathryn I Kathryn II	1;8 1;9 1;10		Examples of the 226 syntactic types produced in Gia II, and of the 226 and the 767 syntactic types in Kathryn I and II respectively.
Allison IV	1;10	Bloom (1973)	Entire language sample of 271 utterances is given in the Appendix.
Kendall I	1;10	Bowerman (1973a)	Lists in the Appendix are given for 102 syntactic types for Kendall I (MLU = 1.10) and 152 syntactic types for Kendall II MLU = 1.48).
Andrew Gregory Steven	1;7–1;11 1;7–1;11 1;11–2;0	Braine (1963a)	List of 102 first syntactic types for Andrew, of 33 of the first 89 syntactic types for Gregory, and of 82 first syntactic types for Steven.
David I David II	1;9 1;10	Braine (1976)	List of 60 first syntactic types (MLU = 1.3) for David I, and 149 syntactic types for David II.
Jonathan I Jonathan II	1,11 2;1		List of 73 first syntactic types for Jonathan I, and 187 syntactic types for Jonathan II.

Jonathan, and also reanalyses of data from several other published works. It is both a useful source of data and an important attempt to present a lean interpretation of children's early utterances. Braine's work has included a series of experimental studies in addition to the observation of spontaneous speech.

The subjects of these studies represent a large part of the data used to make observations on the child's acquisition of grammar during this period. Table 7.2 gives a summary of the available published data on these children. Two points are worth making. First, few attempts have been made to divide development of this period into subperiods, as is done above. When this is attempted, it is usually based solely on MLU or age. One has to be very cautious, however, in comparing a child like Gia II (where the II refers to the sample time) with an MLU of 1.34 with Eric II with an MLU of 1.19, when both children were twenty months old. While they appear similar on these superficial measures, Eric II used 37 unique syntactic types while Gia II used 226. By our definition, Eric II is at the onset of early Stage I while Gia II is at the end of late Stage I. Such comparisons are vulnerable to type errors, as discussed in Chapter 3.

A second point concerns the small amount of data on children in early Stage I as defined above. Many of the samples are for children who already have 100 syntactic types, e.g. Kendall (see Table 7.2). Bloom (1973) exemplifies the problem in getting data on this subperiod. She presents data for her daughter Allison at four ages, and the numbers of syntactic types for these four samples are 11, 4, 19, and 94 respectively. We see that the first three samples are before this subperiod, and the last one is at its end. Allison's data, therefore, tell us little about development up to the syntactic spurt. Much of the data on this subperiod are from Braine's subjects. Unfortunately, they are presented without any information about daily longitudinal changes. We can only conclude, therefore, that our data on this period remain relatively meager, despite the incredible amounts of effort expended on collection.

7.2.2 The transition to multiword utterances

The period of the first word combinations has been defined as beginning when the child has shown evidence of 25 syntactic types in its productive language. This has been suggested because the first multiword utterances are not easy to identify, since they are difficult to distinguish from *sequences of single-word utterances*. Through the period of single-word utterances, the child will bring its single-word utterances closer and closer together. This is true for the contextual aspects of the utterances as well as their acoustic properties. We begin by describing the facts of this situation, then turn to possible explanations.

Description   Bloom (1973) observed this gradual approximation of single-word utterances in her study of her daughter Allison, and separates them into two types: chained, and holistic. *Chained* successive single-word utterances are ones in which each utterance refers to its own event or activity. An example adapted from Bloom (1973:47) is given in (7.1).

(7.1) *Allison at 16 months, 3 weeks*
    Allison: 'cow' (three times, reaching under a chair and picking up a toy cow)
             'chair' (twice, trying to put the cow on its hind legs on the chair)
    Mother: 'What's that?'
    Allison: 'Mama' (giving cow to mother for help)

Each of Allison's utterances has its own contextual reference. 'Cow' is used referring to the act of picking up the toy cow, as if it meant 'here's the cow'. 'Chair' is spoken as Allison puts the cow on the chair with a meaning such as 'I'll put it on the chair.' Lastly, 'Mama' is a call to her mother to help her.

Holistic successive single-word utterances differ from chained ones in that the utterances are both referring to the same activity. An example from Bloom (1973:51) is shown in (7.2):

(7.2) *Allison at 20 months, 3 weeks*
    Allison: 'up' (twice, while wearing her coat and pointing to her neck)
    Mother: 'What?'
    Allison: 'neck'
              'up'
    Mother: 'Neck? What do you want? What?'
    Allison: 'neck'
    Mother: 'What's on your neck?'
    Allison: 'zip' (three times, pointing to her zipper and lifting chin)

Here Allison is referring to a single activity, which is her desire to have her mother zip up Allison's coat. The words 'up', 'neck', and 'zip' are all used in reference to this one act. The holistic sequences show an advance on the child's part, since the utterances are more closely bound to each other contextually. Bloom points out that the holistic sequences only appear toward the end of the period of single-word utterances, a few weeks before the first multiword utterances. She sees these as important precursors to the eventual development of grammatical structure which underlies multiword utterances.

The gradual proximity of single-word utterances has also been demonstrated acoustically in studies by Fónagy (1972) and Branigan (1979). Fónagy is a well-known Hungarian phonetician who tape-recorded the early development of his two children, Eve and Pierre, and acoustically analyzed selected utterances. The first single-word utterances were clearly separate utterances. There was a noticeable time between them and they each had their own intonational contour and stress. The intonational contour consisted of an initial rise in pitch to a peak, and then a terminal fall. He states that between the use of single-word utterances of this kind and later multiword utterances 'there is a more or less long period of *transition*. During this period single-word utterances show a tendency to group together to form sequences, especially in pairs' (p. 65; my translation). These successive single-word utterances differ from multiword utterances in having one or more of the following features: (i) a brief pause between them, (ii) identical intonational contours on each word, (iii) primary stress on both words. Fónagy measured his children's successive single-word utterances for these features and concluded that there were four stages to the transition period. These are given in Table 7.3, with 'stage' here in the sense of the co-occurrence of new behaviors with old ones. That is, sequences of single-word utterances do not neatly follow through these four stages as successive events; rather, new types will coexist with old ones.

Table 7.3 *Four stages of successive single-word utterances proposed by Fónagy (1972)*

Stage 1: Each word has the same intonational contour and a primary stress. It is only their closeness in time which suggests any relation.

Stage 2: There is still a pause between the words, and each has a primary stress. The terminal falling pitch of the first word, however, is not as great as that for the second one.

Stage 3: The stress on the first word is weaker than that of the second one, and the pause between them is reduced (from examples, apparently to less than 500 msec).

Stage 4: There is no longer a pause between the two words. A succession of two words is still indicated because of: (i) the force of the two accents; (ii) frequently a glottal stop occurring between the two words; and (iii) the terminal falling pitch of the first word.

Further, it appears that Fónagy presents these as a simplification of the facts he observed. For example, his analysis of the types of utterances used by his son at 20 months shows more kinds than suggested by the stages in Table 7.3. Nonetheless, his analysis provides important information about the gradualness of the change from single- to multiword utterances.

Fónagy's initial insights have received support in Branigan (1979). Branigan acoustically analyzed the successive single-word utterances of three children during the period leading up to the first multiword utterances. Using a range of information, Branigan found that adults perceive two words as successive single-word utterances when the pause is between 400 and 1100 msec. He then measured the falling pitch level of words that were in single-word utterances, successive single-word utterances, and multiword utterances. The results confirmed the observation made by Fónagy about his stage 2, i.e. he found that the falling contour of the first words of successive single-word utterances was less than that of the second word. Importantly, he also found that these contours were similar to those in the child's multiword utterances. Branigan concludes from this that the successive single-word utterances are therefore closer in nature to multiword utterances than to single-word utterances. While an interesting conclusion, it needs to be viewed with some caution because of the measure he has used to divide utterances into successive single-word utterances vs. multiword utterances. By categorizing successive words with an interval of less than 400 msec as multiword utterances, he is placing most of the utterances of Fónagy's stages 3 and 4 into this category. We know from Fónagy's study that the first words in these stages do not yet have the terminal pitch of later multiword sequences. It appears, therefore, that the results are confounded by a measurement sequence of the kind discussed in Chapter 3.

Explanation The fact that successive single-word utterances come to refer to one context as well as sharing acoustic properties has been used by some investigators as evidence that these sequences share a common grammatical structure (e.g. Scollon 1976; Branigan 1979; Ingram 1979b). The proposal is something like this. During the period of single-word utterances, the child begins to have some rudimentary understanding of the grammatical structure of the adult language. As discussed in the previous chapter, there is little evidence of understanding syntactic structure, but there is some indication that some semantic relations are understood. During at least the latter part of this period, this knowledge underlies the child's single-word utterances. For example, the child who says 'cow' in referring to picking up a toy cow may be using that with the underlying structure of Action + Object. Later, holistic sequences are further expressions of this same semantic structure. The child at this point may say the sequence 'up' 'cow' in the same context. Later still, a multiword utterance such as 'up cow' will also reflect this knowledge.

This viewpoint is what has come to be known as a *rich interpretation* of single-word utterances. It has been argued for in Ingram (1971), Greenfield & Smith (1976), and Scollon (1976), among others. Scollon (1976) has used the terms 'vertical construction' and 'horizontal construction' to discuss this issue. A *horizontal construction* is a construction which has its constituents represented in a single sequence of words as in the English sentence 'I want a cookie'. Adult grammar is typically a series of horizontal constructions. Scollon argues that children acquire structures as horizontal constructions only after they first appear as vertical constructions. A *vertical construction* is a construction which has its constituents appearing in a sequence of utterances. Holistic sequences of single-word utterances would be called a vertical construction by Scollon's definition. An important feature of Scollon's claim is that it is not just restricted to the discussion of the transition from single-word to two-word utterances. Using data from his subject Brenda, he gives cases where three-word horizontal constructions arise from earlier vertical constructions consisting of a sequence of a single-word utterance and a two-word utterance. For example, the semantic structure Agent+Action+Object of the utterance 'baby eat cookie' may occur at an earlier time as 'baby' 'eat cookie'.

The rich interpretation of single-word utterances has been a controversial issue since its first inception. A major feature of this interpretation is that it is consistent with a constructionist view of acquisition where development of linguistic knowledge is seen as beginning in comprehension. In this case, the primitive semantic relational knowledge emerging in comprehension first appears as underlying single-word utterances, then successive single-word utterances, and eventually multiword utterances. Further, it proposes that new grammatical forms, such as successive single-word utterances, are used with already acquired (or 'old') meanings. The idea that new forms mark old meanings and that old forms mark new meanings is a basic Piagetian notion that has been applied to child language by Slobin (1973).

The rich interpretation is in opposition to what can be called the *lean* interpretation of successive single-word utterances. This position has been expressed in Brown (1973), Bloom (1973), Dore (1975) and Barrett (1982), among others. It has several sides to it which we will first introduce here and then discuss. First, one version claims that the young child in this period is mapping conceptual representations directly onto its single-word utterances (Bloom 1973; Brown 1973). Allison's expression of 'cow' in (7.2), for example, is mapping the child's knowledge of the toy cow in this context, not a linguistic category like Object or Agent. Bloom (1973) relies heavily on Piagetian theory in taking this position, emphasizing the limits of the child's cognitive ability at the end of the sensorimotor period. We have discussed this aspect of development in the previous chapter, and have pointed out its use to account for word overextensions. The argument is that the sensorimotor child is unable to categorize and represent reality, abilities necessary for the use of a grammatical system.

A second aspect of the lean interpretation is that it restricts the child's meanings at this time to pragmatic functions such as expressions of desires and demands, as discussed in the previous chapter. For example, Barrett states (1982:62) that these utterances consist 'of a lexical item serving a particular communicative function, this function being communicated to the listener by the intonation and gestures of the child'. Third, it argues that predictions of the rich interpretation are not supported by the data. Two predictions in particular are challenged: (i) that the child does not use two-word utterances initially because of an inability to produce utterances longer than a single word; and (ii) that successive single-word utterances should show the word order of later multiword utterances.

In comparing these latter alternatives, it is important to point out at the onset that they are not as opposed to each other as may initially seem. The first rich interpretations appeared in the early 1970s as an exploration of the hypothesis that features of two-word utterances may have their origins in single-word utterances (e.g. Ingram 1971). These early analyses focussed on single-word data independent of multiword utterances. In Ingram (1979b), I looked at these data and found that most studies which are claimed to have a rich interpretation divided the development of single-word utterances into two periods. The first one lasts from around 1 year to 16 months and has the characteristics of the lean interpretation. That is, the child's single-word utterances do not show structural properties, and their meaning appears to be primarily functional in nature. The sequences of single-word utterances that do occur are chained at this time. There is no substantive disagreement, therefore, concerning this initial period.

The next period is one around 16–18 months when the single-word utterances are analyzed as reflecting semantic categories like Action and Object. As pointed out in Ingram (1979b), this period has the following characteristics: (i) it occurs just a few weeks before the first multiword utterances begin; (ii) it is characterized by holistic sequences of single-word utterances; and (iii) it appears to coincide with other behaviors characteristic of the onset of representation (i.e. the end of the sensorimotor period) such as 'what's that?' questions, symbolic play, references to past events, and the onset of dialogue. It is in the description of this period where the primary issue of a rich vs. a lean interpretation exists.

Since the critics of the rich interpretation tend to lump these two periods together, it is not clear how they would directly support the lean interpretation for this second period. The general argument would probably be a narrow interpretation of the Competence Assumption, as suggested in the following statement from Bloom (1973:19–20):

> Whether or not children do have pre-syntax knowledge of grammar may well be unknowable; that is, it is not clear that any amount of or kind of evidence can demonstrate convincingly that children know about sentences before they say sentences.

A similar note of caution appears in Barrett (1982). It is still the case, however, as pointed out by Bloom (1973:19), that 'The most persuasive argument in favor of this position is that it offers a strong explanation for the transition to syntax.' While the lean interpretation may show a certain methodological caution, it needs to answer some very difficult questions. For example, how does it account for the discontinuity in development between single-word and multiword utterances? Can the single-word utterances and holistic sequences that occur after the onset of multiword utterances be given a rich interpretation, and if not, why not?

The most serious arguments against the rich interpretation appear to be the two stated above concerning the predictions it makes that do not appear to be supported by the data. The first prediction is that the child has some performance factor such as a physiological restriction of the length of utterances which restricts him/her to single-word utterances or sequences. The data from Fónagy certainly suggest that this is the case, but Bloom (1973) refers to data from her daughter Allison which seem to contradict this position. During the period of single-word utterances, Allison produced a number of utterances which consisted of one of her words and a phonetic form transcribed as /widə/. Bloom concluded that this form was an empty form that could occur with any word in Allison's language. 'It has been concluded that "widə" apparently referred to anything and everything, and thus it "meant" nothing' (Bloom 1973:34). These utterances with

/widə/ are taken as evidence that Allison could put two words together, but didn't because she had no grammar to allow her to do so.

Ingram (1979b:273) discusses some problems with these data; for example, they contradict all the data such as Fónagy's which indicate that multiword utterances follow after a gradual approximation of single-word utterances. Also, if this type of behavior is possible, it is surprising that none of the many diary studies over the years have observed a similar case, i.e. it is a unique characteristic of Allison's language. Most important, there is a much simpler explanation possible. With some very reasonable assumptions, it can be shown that /widə/ was probably Allison's pronunciation of her own name. To begin, /widə/ most often occurred as the variant form /əwidə/. (7.4) shows how these two forms could result from the name Allison by a series of common phonological processes of simplification which will be discussed in the next chapter.

(7.3) Allison

ælısən		
əlısən	æ → ə	vowel neutralization
əlisən	ɪ → i	vowel tensing
əwisən	l → w	gliding
əwisə	n → ∅	final consonant deletion
əwitə	s → t	stopping
əwidə	t → d	voicing
widə	ə → ∅	syllable deletion (optional)

There is even support for this interpretation in Bloom's own discussion of this phenomenon. '. . . it occurred often in action events, as Allison either did something or something happened; and it often occurred in situations where Allison wanted to have or do something' (Bloom 1973:34). If the phonological explanation is correct, it removes this argument against the rich interpretation, since these utterances with /widə/ would then be multiword utterances.

A more serious challenge is the claim that the rich interpretation predicts that sequences of single-word utterances will show the restrictions on word order that are evident in the child's first word combinations. As will be discussed later, early word combinations appear to adhere to restrictions on the order of their constituents. No such ordering, however, has yet to be reported for sequences of single-word utterances. This is a problem, though, only if we can demonstrate that order is also a feature of the child's knowledge at the time when successive single-word utterances are occurring. Evidence so far is lacking in this regard. It may be that children first understand some basic semantic relations and only later work out their ordering for the language. Also, there is some evidence (e.g. Braine 1976) that not all early word combinations show such ordering. It may be that the ordering is really the result of adults imposing adult interpretations upon children's utterances, as pointed out by Howe (1976). Even with this response, it remains the case that the lack of ordering in these sequences is a potential problem for the rich interpretation as currently presented.

Before concluding this section, there is one last point that needs to be made about the rich interpretation. While we have used the term 'rich', the view presented is by no means the richest interpretation that could be given. We could propose, for example, that there is an underlying syntactic structure, or even that the underlying structure is the grammatical structure of the adult language being acquired. This is, however, far from the case. The rich interpretation discussed above is actually quite conservative, and conforms to the Competence Assumption of Chapter 3. That is, the competence assigned to the child is based on behaviors such as the child's understanding and its use of sequences of single-word utterances. It only claims that there is some evidence for primitive semantic structures under-lying the child's utterances during the weeks before the first multiword utterances.

7.2.3 Some general characteristics

The discussion of early word combinations often starts from a list of unique syntactic types that are used as data for the analysis being presented. While this is a reasonable place to start an analysis, it can distort the picture of the child's data at this time. Children during this period do not speak in a sequence of clear, unique syntactic types, and in fact the data used consist of a short list of sentences that had been put together after several hours of data collection. This section, then, presents a general discussion of what the child's actual language looks like during this period.

One aspect to keep in mind about this period is that it is named after the new behavior which appears, that is, word combinations. Throughout it, however, the most frequent production of the child is the single-word utterance. This can be exemplified by looking at the data from one of Bloom's subjects, Eric. Based on data given in Bloom, Hood & Lightbown (1974), Eric had an MLU of 1.42 at 22 months of age. This was calculated on a sample of utterances collected during nearly seven hours. During this time, 1,043 utterances were elicited. According to Bloom, Lightbown & Hood (1975) only 165 of these were multiword utterances. Further, only 108 of these were unique syntactic types. Clearly, Eric's predominant pro-duction at this time near the end of early Stage I is the single-word utterance. It is also striking that it took seven hours to collect 108 sentences for a grammatical analysis. This fact alone is highly suggestive that Eric must not yet have a very productive grammar, or else that severe perform-ance factors are at work.

The limits of the child's productive grammar can be seen by looking at a sample of multiword utterances for a child during early Stage I. Table 7.4 gives all of the word combinations produced by Andrew over the first five months of multiword usage, based on Braine (1963a). As mentioned in Chapter 2, these data were collected by the mother through a parental diary. The fact that it took five months to obtain the sample is another example of the limited productivity of the grammar at this time. When we examine this sample, we see that there is a small number of words that are especially frequent, e.g. 'all', 'no', 'more', 'there'. Also, they tend to occur consistently in one sentence position: 'no', for example, occurs initially while 'there' occurs finally. Braine emphasized these two facts in his observations of this period and incorporated them into his explanation of the child's early grammar. This theory, which is referred to as 'pivot grammar', will be discussed in 7.3.2.

Another feature of Andrew's sample is its lexicon and how it enters into word combinations. In Table 6.7 of the last chapter, we gave the semantic categories proposed by Nelson for the child's early words. When we look at Andrew's combinations, we see that they are predominantly nominals combining with either action words, modifiers, or personal-social words. This tendency in early grammars has been found in several studies, e.g. Bloom (1970). While nominal+nominal combinations do occur, they do not seem to be frequent in the earliest word combinations. A crucial issue in explaining such early utterances is the interplay of the distributional features of these words with their semantic properties. As we will see, some accounts emphasize the distributional aspects of these words while others concentrate on their semantic properties.

While most analyses usually work from lists like the one in Table 7.4, it is important to realize that there are also contextual aspects of these utterances that can aid in understanding their structure. For one thing, children do not produce a sequence of unique lexical or syntactic types. The samples during this period are full of repetitions and variations upon some idea being com-municated. Although adults express a proposition within a single sentence, the equivalent child thought may span several utterances. The various sen-tences are connected for the child in the sense that they are combining to express what appears to an adult speaker to be a single proposition. Such sequences are similar to what Scollon (1976) has called vertical construc-tions. Since this term implies the existence of a single structure, we will not use it here. Instead, we will refer to such sequences as *sentence paragraphs*. This is a strictly descriptive term which refers to a sequence of child utteran-ces that could be expressed as a single adult sentence.

Table 7.4 *Andrew's pivot grammar, as given in Braine (1963a: Table 2)*

Pivotal constructions				
all broke	no bed	more car[d]	other bib	airplane by[f]
all buttoned	no down[a]	more cereal	other bread	siren by
all clean	no fix	more cookie	other milk	
all done	no home	more fish	other pants	mail come
all dressed	no mama[b]	more high[e]	other part	mama come
all dry	no more	more hot	other piece	
all fix	no pee	more juice	other pocket	clock on there
all gone	no plug	more read	other shirt	up on there
all messy	no water	more sing	other shoe	hot in there
all shut	no wet[c]	more toast	other side	milk in there
all through		more walk		light up there
all wet	see baby		boot off	fall down there
	see pretty	hi Calico	light off	kitty down there
I see	see train	hi mama	pants off	more down there
I shut		hi papa	shirt off	sit down there
I sit			shoe off	cover down there
			water off	other cover down there

Other utterances			
airplane all gone	byebye back	what's that	look at this
Calico all gone	byebye Calico	what's this	outside more
Calico all done[g]	byebye car	mail man	pants change
salt all shut	byebye papa	mail car	dry pants
all done milk	Calico byebye	our car	off bib
all done now	papa byebye	our door	down there
all gone juice		papa away	up on there some more
all gone outside[h]			
all gone pacifier			

[a] 'Don't put me down'
[b] 'I don't want to go mama'
[c] 'I'm not wet'
[d] 'Drive me around some more'
[e] 'There's more up there'
[f] 'A plane is flying past'
[g] Said after the death of Calico the cat
[h] Said when the door is shut: 'The outside is allgone'

Weir (1962) was one of the first to identify different types of sentence paragraphs. She observed these in the presleep monologues of her son Anthony between the ages of 26 and 28 months. The three types she found are build-ups, breakdowns, and completions. In (7.4) these three types are presented, with examples taken from Bloom's (1973) corpus of Allison at 22 months of age. Allison had an MLU of 1.73 at this time, placing her in late Stage I.

(7.4) a. *Build-ups*

'baby eat'	'baby doll ride'
'baby eat'	'baby doll ride'
'cookie'	'truck'
'baby eat cookie'	'baby doll ride truck'

b. *Breakdowns*

| 'walking around' | 'there baby' |
| 'around' | 'there' |

c. *Completions*

| 'mommy' | 'cow' |
| 'comb hair' | 'stand up' |

In Allison's data, the build-ups where the child shows the parts of an utterance before eventually getting them all together seem to be the most common type. Breakdowns are similar to build-ups except that they are going in the opposite direction. Both types indicate some awareness of the parts of the longest sentence produced. There are two extreme explanations that can be offered as to why the child is producing these. Using the terms in Peters (1977), we could propose that the child is learning language either analytically or synthetically. The child is being *analytic* if she is using rules of combination to produce longer sentences. The other possibility is that she is acquiring language *synthetically*, by learning an entire sentence and then breaking it down into its different parts. Unfortunately, data like these do not alone help us to determine which of these is happening. The completions show less evidence for a single underlying structure. Such an assumption would be supported, however, if a single utterance such as 'mommy comb hair' and 'cow stand up' were found elsewhere in the sample.

Although we write the child's sentences in adult orthography, it is important to realize that the child is not actually pronouncing most words 'correctly'. Later we will look at some of the kinds of phonological patterns children use in this stage, but first we need to examine the implications of these imprecise speech forms for the child's speech and for our attempts to analyze it.

One obvious effect of the child's incomplete phonology is that there are a number of child utterances which will be unintelligible. Bloom (1970:106), for example, reports that she was only able to elicit 490 intelligible utterances from Eric in a six-hour visit when he was 20 months, 2 weeks old. This can be contrasted with the 1,043 intelligible utterances she collected from him during a comparable sampling six weeks later. His MLU was 1.19 and 1.42 for these two samples respectively, suggesting a noticeable increase in intelligibility by the end of early Stage I. Also, during the time of the first word combinations, some children show consistent uninterpretable vocalizations alongside interpretable words. For example, Bloom (1970) transcribed several sentences from Eric which contained an element given as [ə]. She was not able to identify a specific morpheme for this, although possible candidates included 'I', 'a', and 'the'. It was simply impossible on the basis of its occurrence to decide the issue. Elsewhere, Dore, Franklin, Miller & Ramer (1976) have observed a similar phenomenon and call these *phonetically consistent forms*. They claim that these do not have any content at this stage, but only reflect some awareness on the child's part of some phonetic elements occurring before the nouns and verbs it hears in adult speech. We will return to this point in 7.2.4, when we discuss the child's comprehension ability during this period.

A last general aspect of the first word combinations is the question of interpretation. Even when we can identify the words in the child's sentence, we need to attempt to determine what the child meant by it. In Table 7.4, for example, Braine gives us in the footnotes several interpretations of sentences. These interpretations are crucial in making judgements about the underlying structure of the child's sentences, but unfortunately there is no totally satisfactory way of assigning meanings. There is always the danger, as pointed out in Howe (1976), that we may impose our adult ideas of meaning onto the child – the child could be intending something totally different from what we think. One needs to be quite cautious, therefore, in assigning meanings to children's first sentences.

Even with this warning, it is possible to establish some guidelines for interpreting children's sentences. Bloom (1970) discusses three kinds of evidence that can be used. First, there is the non-linguistic context of the utterance. The child who says 'mommy eat' while watching the mother eat a cookie is more likely to be referring to the mother as an Agent than as an Object. Second, there are the preceding adult utterances. For example, when Bloom (1973:246) says 'What are you doing?' to Allison, and she responds 'chewing', it is likely she means 'I'm chewing' rather than 'he's chewing'. Third, there are also the child's subsequent utterances. These may be build-ups or completions as shown in (7.4) which clarify the intended meaning. Even with these guidelines, it is still not always clear what the child intends. Bloom (1970:53) gives a useful taxonomy of the kinds of problems in interpretation that may occur. These are given in Table 7.5.

7.2.4 The onset of syntactic comprehension

In section 6.4.1 data were presented which suggested that during the period of single-word utterances children are capable of understanding more than

Table 7.5 *Four categories of interpretation for children's sentences, taken from Bloom (1970:53)*

Ambiguous: a form having two (or more) possible interpretations that can be distinguished or resolved – for example, 'Mommy sock' meaning 'Mommy's sock' or, alternatively, 'Mommy (verb) sock';

Equivocal: a form having two (or more) possible interpretations that cannot be distinguished – either one or the other interpretation being acceptable in the particular situation, for example, 'Mommy iron';

Indeterminate: a form for which an interpretation cannot be made, most often because of insufficient evidence;

Anomalous: a form that appears to have no interpretation – the occurrence of an utterance in a situation to which the linguistic expression bears no apparent relation – for example, Gia eating peaches and saying 'no more'.

---

one word in a sentence, and that they may even relate these semantically. There was, however, no convincing evidence that they understand grammatical morphemes. In the period of the first word combinations, there is some evidence which suggests that syntactic understanding is taking place. As with the studies on the earlier period, these studies need to be interpreted cautiously, owing to the inherent difficulties in testing comprehension in young children. Here we will review four studies which indicate syntactic processing of grammatical morphemes in advance of their appearance in spoken language. In one of these, we see another method for determining a child's grammatical knowledge, that of elicited imitation.

Shipley, Smith & Gleitman (1969)   The major features of this study have already been given in 6.4.1. To summarize: they asked parents of young children to direct a series of commands to their children which varied in their syntactic structures. There were three main commands: well-formed (VFN) 'Throw me the ball!'; telegraphic (VN) 'Throw ball!'; and holophrastic (N) 'Ball!' The children's responses to these commands were monitored to see if they would show a preference for one type over the others. Chapter 6 presented the results of this study with the four holophrastic subjects. We interpreted these results as suggestive of some preference for well-formed and telegraphic commands over holophrastic commands, although this was only a statistical tendency which did not prove significant.

Here we will present the more clear-cut results that were found for the second group of subjects who were tested. This second group, referred to as the telegraphic group, consisted of seven children between the ages of 19 and 32 months, with a mean age of 25 months. Their MLUs ranged from 1.40 to 1.85 with a mean of 1.57. This measure places these subjects in the middle of the period being discussed in this chapter.

Table 7.6 *Percentage of times each of seven children in the telegraphic group in Shipley, Smith & Gleitman (1969) would touch an appropriate toy in response to each of three constructions*

Subject's Name	Age	MLU	N(%)	Structures VN(%)	VFN(%)
Carl	23	1.85	33	33	58
Dottie	19	1.75	15	27	36
Eric	25	1.65	25	28	38
Fran	29	1.48	21	54	64
Gregory	28	1.43	37	25	57
Helen	21	1.41	33	38	62
Ira	32	1.40	50	33	54
Mean			31	34	53

Table 7.6 presents the percentages of times each of the telegraphic children touched an appropriate toy,in response to each of the three types of commands. These results can be compared with those for the holophrastic group as presented in Table 6.12. While the holophrastic children showed a preference for the simpler commands, the telegraphic ones showed the opposite preference. A statistical analysis of the data revealed that 'all telegraphic speakers obey more often with well-formed commands than with single word commands ... The results for VN are similar but less sharp' (p. 329). Even though the children were producing predominantly single-word and simple word combinations, they showed an awareness that adult speech required more than what was occurring in their own output.

As pointed out in Gleitman, Shipley & Smith (1978), this result does not mean that the telegraphic children understood the syntactic role of the grammatical morphemes in the well-formed commands. It is, however, a first step in demonstrating that they do. Also, even if they didn't, the fact that they recognized that 'something' needs to occur between lexical morphemes provides some information on why they might use phonetically consistent forms in their own speech, as mentioned at the end of the last section. The next study, however, suggests that the children may process these morphemes as more than meaningless noise.

Katz, Baker & Macnamara (1974)   We know from Benedict's study (1979) discussed in 6.8.2 that specific and general nominals are a prominent part of the receptive vocabulary of the holophrastic child. The paper by Katz, Baker & Macnamara is a brief report on research into the question of whether or not young children know that the difference between proper and common nouns in English is normally marked by the absence or presence of an article. In normal usage, proper nouns such as 'John', 'Mary', and

'Rover' occur without either an indefinite article 'a' or a definite article 'the'. These are required, however, for common nouns, except in cases where the plural is used for the class as a whole, e.g. 'Dogs like to bark'.

Katz, Baker & Macnamara developed a clever experimental design to test for this distinction. The children in the study were assigned to either the common-noun or the proper-noun condition. The idea was to show the children in both conditions a pair of dolls. The dolls were assigned labels which were nonsense syllables, e.g. 'zav', 'mef' and 'jop', among others. In the common-noun condition, one of the dolls was introduced to the child as 'a zav' (or whatever nonsense name had been assigned to it. Here we will use 'zav' for purposes of demonstration). In subsequent references, it was called 'the zav'. The other doll was never named or referred to. The proper-noun condition was similar except that the doll was introduced as 'Zav', with no article ever used in referring to it.

During the learning period of the study, the experimenter attempted to familiarize the child with the dolls. Each of the dolls was mentioned to the child at least five times. The unnamed doll was referred to only as 'the other one' or 'this one', whereas the named one was referred to according to which of the two conditions was being tested. After this was done, testing began. Both dolls would be placed within reach of the child, and he was asked 'to dress, undress, feed, hold, or bring the named doll to his mother' (p. 470). The experiment was flexible in nature, using Piaget's clinical method discussed previously. The important thing was to determine which doll the child selected for the requested activity. In the proper-name condition, the child should select just the named doll if he knew that proper nouns occur without articles. In the common-noun condition, the child could select either doll, since the named doll was only introduced as 'a zav', i.e. one of the class of 'zavs' which could presumably include the other unnamed doll. Every child was tested at least seven times, and many were tested as many as 15 times.

This procedure was used in two experiments. The second experiment differed from the first only in the nature of the dolls and in the subjects used. In the second one, the dolls were made more distinct than in the first to see if this would encourage a greater experimental effect. Information on the subjects in the two experiments is given in Table 7.7. Unfortunately, we are not given any information on the linguistic level of the subjects. The mean ages, however, were typical of children in the period of the first word combinations. Also, the youngest group in experiment 2 was quite young, with a mean age of only 17 months, which would probably place them at the beginning of early Stage I.

Table 7.7 gives the percentage of times that the subjects in the two experiments selected the named doll when prompted to act upon the dolls.

Table 7.7 *Mean percentage of times each experimental group selected the named doll in Katz, Baker & Macnamara (1974)*

			Condition	
Experiment	Subjects	Mean age	Common-noun	Proper-noun
1	30 girls	22 mos.	48	75
	25 boys	24 mos.	47	51
2	10 girls	17 mos.	42	76
	15 girls	22 mos.	53	72

Statistically significant differences were found between the two conditions for the three groups of girls. The authors suggest that the boys did not yet have the distinction, either because they were developmentally slower, or because they were less experienced with dolls. Importantly, the results with the girls, particularly with the 17-month-olds, indicates that they had some awareness of the grammatical role of articles.

There is one further aspect of this study that needs to be mentioned. Katz, Baker & Macnamara were not just interested in proving understanding of one of the functions of articles. They also were interested in how this acquisition takes place. There are two possible explanations that they considered. One explanation, which we will call the *cognitive explanation*, is that the child cognitively categorizes the world into classes that differ in the importance of the individual members. Since people (and presumably dolls) are named and individually stand out, children distinguish between specific and general references, and thus labels. This distinction is then used to determine the role of the articles. The alternative explanation, which we will call the *distributional explanation*, is that the child's syntactic processing distinguishes the distributional properties of the articles. He then looks for semantic properties for these grammatical morphemes.

To test these alternatives, they also tested the subjects above on the same procedure, but with blocks instead of dolls. None of the groups showed any differences between the two conditions with blocks. They argue that the distributional explanation would predict that there should be a difference, since the distributional analysis would precede the semantic one. The cognitive explanation, however, predicts the results since the children would not have had the same experience with naming blocks as they would with dolls. Again, these conclusions should be viewed with some caution. A proponent of the distributional explanation could argue that the child's first rule is semantically restricted at first, based on his linguistic experience with naming practices. The importance of raising this issue here is that it is a central one that will come up later. That is, we need to explain the interaction between the child's cognitive organization of the world, its discovery of the semantic properties of individual languages, and the distributional properties of grammatical categories of the language.

De Villiers & de Villiers (1973a) This study focusses on acquisition of active and passive sentences by children at each of Brown's five stages of acquisition (see Table 3.4). They divided their subjects in Stage I into early and late Stage I; thus, part of their results are relevant to the period we are currently examining. Research into the comprehension of active and passive sentences can provide us with information on children's knowledge of two aspects of English sentence structure: first, the ability to process active sentences will indicate when children use word order to understand sentences; second, the ability to process passive sentences tells us about their knowledge of English verbal morphology.

In designing their study, the de Villiers had to face two problems in particular. One was how to get the child to respond to the test sentences. To do this, they introduced each sentence with the command 'Make', for example 'Make the dog bite the cat'. Despite using a sentence structure which was relatively complex, the procedure appeared to work, except for the youngest group. Another problem was how to get around the possibility that the children might use semantic probabilities in responding to the sentences. For example, the child could correctly act to the command 'Make the cow eat the flower' because of its knowledge of 'eat', not because of word order – the child knows that cows eat flowers but flowers do not eat cows. To avoid this factor, they used what are called *reversible sentences*. These are sentences where the subject and object are capable of being interchanged, for example 'The boy hit the girl' vs. 'The girl hit the boy'. If children process such sentences correctly, it is assumed it is because they have learned the English rule that the unmarked word order in English is Agent, Action, Object.

The subjects included seven children in early Stage I (MLU 1.0–1.5), with an age range of 19 to 24 months, and three in late Stage I (MLU 1.5–2.0), with an age range of 19.5 to 27 months. The latter small number is unfortunate, in view of the importance of the results to be discussed. (7.5) gives the basic set of sentences that was used:

(7.5) a. Make the dog bite the cat
     b. Make the truck push the car
     c. Make the mommy touch the daddy
     d. Make the boat bump the train
     e. Make the boy hit the girl
     f. Make the horse kiss the cow

Table 7.8 *Mean percentages of four kinds of responses for two test groups on the understanding of active and passive sentences, taken from de Villiers & de Villiers (1973a: Table 1).*

	early Stage I		late Stage I	
	actives	passives	actives	passives
Correct	31.0	28.6	75.5	28.9
Reversed	21.4	26.2	5.6	30.0
Child as Agent	33.3	30.9	12.2	28.9
Refusals	14.3	14.3	6.7	12.2

These are what we will refer to as the *active sentences*. A second set was created from these, which we will call the *reversed active sentences*. These are the same as those in (7.5) except that the subjects and objects are reversed, e.g. 'Make the cat bite the dog'. Two further sets were created, the *passives* and *reversed passives*, which were the 12 active sentences made into passives, e.g. 'Make the dog be bitten by the cat', and 'Make the cat be bitten by the dog'.

Each child was tested in two experimental sessions. In each session, the child was shown 12 toys and asked to act upon them. Each session was restricted to the testing of either active or passive sentences – pilot testing indicated that mixing the sentences was difficult for the children. Half of the children received the active sentences in the first session, and half received the passives first. Six sentences were tested in each session, with the presentation of reversed alternates being counterbalanced across children.

Table 7.8 presents the results in terms of the mean percentages of the four different responses given by subjects in the two groups. 'Correct' indicates that the child processed the sentence as an adult would; 'Reversed' indicates that they reversed the subject and object, i.e. treated actives as passives and vice versa. 'Child as Agent' is a response mode which was not anticipated. Here the child would do the act itself on either the subject or object, treating itself as the Agent of the sentence. 'Refusals', as expected, is when the child did not respond to the test sentence.

The results indicate that the early Stage I children are understanding neither the basic word order of English, nor the passive morphology. Given the design of the study, we should restrict this to the claim that they could not understand the constructions embedded in a sentence command beginning with 'Make'. It is still possible that they could process word order in a simpler structure, such as 'The cat is biting the dog'. The high number of Child as Agent responses suggests that this structure might be having some effect on their processing. Another possibility, however, and a very reasonable one, is that this response is used when the child cannot process the grammatical structure of the sentence. The 75.5 percent correct responses of the three late Stage I children indicate that they have acquired the English word order rule. This leads the authors to conclude that the 'ability to use word order information in reversible active sentences first appears in late Stage I' (p. 338).

De Villiers & de Villiers do not comment on the responses of the subjects in these groups on the passive sentences, except to say that there was little evidence that they had acquired passives. It seems to us, however, that the data in Table 7.8 indicate clearly that they are at least aware that there is something about passives that is different from actives. The last three measures, in fact, show evidence to this effect. Our interpretation is as follows. If the children were treating the passives as actives, then the percentage of reversals for passives should have been comparable to the percentage of correct actives. This, however, was not the case, with only 30 percent of the passives being reversed. Instead, they just as often responded to the passives with Child as Agent responses. This response occurred twice as often for the passives as for the actives. We saw that this response type occurred in the data for the early Stage I children as a strategy which was used when they didn't yet have the construction being tested. We take this increased use of the Child as Agent response for passives as evidence that they recognized these as a form they didn't know. Lastly, there were twice as many refusals for the passives as for the actives.

In sum, the data from de Villiers & de Villiers indicate that children are receptively aware of the role of English word order by late Stage I. Further, the data suggest that the same children distinguish passives from actives. The children know that passives are a form that they have not yet acquired, and respond differentially to it. They show three separate ways to respond to such a dilemma: (i) treat passives as a form they have acquired, i.e. actives; (ii) use a non-linguistic strategy such as Child as Agent, i.e. when in doubt, do the action yourself; or (iii) refuse to respond, i.e. ignore the utterance.

The studies on comprehension which we have reviewed in the last two chapters share a feature in common – they present the child with sentences and then monitor the child's response. The last study we will examine on this topic uses a very different method, known as *elicited imitation*. It has been observed in a range of studies that young children, when given a sentence to imitate, often alter its form. In particular, they seem to change it to conform to their grammatical system at the time. This has been referred to as the 'filter effect', which claims that the child, when asked to imitate a sentence beyond its current short-term memory ability, will encode it through its own grammar. Like comprehension studies, this method has its own problems – how do you get a child to imitate, and how can you be sure that the sentence has been processed if it is correctly imitated? Because of such problems, no doubt, there are relatively few studies which have used this method. Those that have, however, have been highly suggestive. The method has the virtue of providing us with information that is not available from either comprehension studies or from the study of the child's spontaneous utterances. This should be evident from our discussion of the next study, which was one of the first to use this method.

Rodd & Braine (1970)   This study examined three main areas of the child's grammar during the period of the first word combinations: (i) the grammatical morphemes which occur between verb+noun constructions; (ii) the word order of subjects and predicates; and (iii) subject pronouns. We have already looked at some information on the first two of these areas of development, with Shipley, Smith & Gleitman's research on the first, and de Villiers & de Villiers' research on the second. Here, we will address each topic separately.

As stated, the method used was that of elicited imitation. The sessions took place in the child's home, where the experimenter and at least one parent were present. The parents were instructed as to the nature of the sentences to be tested, and asked to present them to the child, interspersed with normal conversation. Rodd & Braine state (p. 432): 'The model offered for imitation was most often a question with a rising intonation, intended to encourage relevant comment or assent from the child; such comment often took the form of imitation.' As might be expected, this method takes time and a certain amount of patience. They found that the children would imitate approximately one-third of the model sentences, with variation between children in their interest to imitate. There were two general kinds of data that were anticipated: they expected that the children would selectively imitate, avoiding sentences that were not part of their competence, and that they would show different kinds of imitations to different constructions.

The first study was with a young boy, Owain, who was 23 months old. Unfortunately, Rodd & Braine do not tell us much about his productive language, except that he, as well as the other subjects, 'had been producing multi-morphemic utterances for at least a few weeks before the study began' (p. 432). Owain was presented during two sessions with five kinds of verb+noun constructions, which are shown in Table 7.9. Two of these, verb+noun and verb+'it'+noun, are ungrammatical phrases in English, but occur in the speech of young children. They state, for example, that the latter construction occasionally was used by Owain. Owain's responses

Table 7.9 *Percentages of occurrence of six kinds of intermediate elements for five constructions in the imitations of Owain, based upon Rodd & Braine (1970: Table 1)*

Construction	No. presented	No. imitated	Intermediate elements[a]					
			$\emptyset$	[də]	[ə]	[ɪn]	[ɪt]	other
Verb noun	74	21	38	38	19	—	—	5
Verb 'a' noun	53	13	38	23	23	—	—	16
Verb 'the' noun	64	26	—	65	11	—	8	16
Verb 'it' noun	45	14	7	57	14	—	—	21
Verb '-ing' noun	12	7	14	—	14	72	—	—

[a] $\emptyset$ indicates no intermediate element.

were placed into three categories: complete imitations, when the noun and verb were both repeated with or without additions; partial imitations, with either the noun or verb omitted; and no imitation. Only complete imitations were used in the analysis.

Table 7.9 presents the results of this first study, given in the form of the percentage of times each of six kinds of imitation took place. These six types are defined by the element whch Owain inserted between the verb and noun. The first finding was that Owain did not show selective imitation, as expected. He imitated all models to about the same extent, which was approximately 33 percent of the time. He did, however, show differential patterns of imitation. Statistical analysis revealed the three patterns summarized in (7.6):

(7.6) *Pattern*   *Dominant element inserted*

    1. verb '-ing' noun   [ɪn]

    2. verb 'the' noun   [də]
        verb 'it' noun

    3. verb noun $\emptyset$, [ə], [də]
        verb 'a' noun

That is, Owain treated the five constructions as if they were three, with neither $\emptyset$ and 'a', nor 'the' and 'it', distinguished from each other. This supports Shipley, Smith & Gleitman's finding that children in this period have some grammatical awareness of the occurrence of morphemes between verbs and nouns, as well as bearing out their caution that such awareness does not necessarily mean adult grammatical knowledge. It also suggests that 'the' rather than 'a' is the important article in the results of Katz, Baker & Macnamara.

Table 7.10 *Number of times that Owain and Carolyn maintained or changed the word order of two kinds of constructions in their imitations, based on Rodd & Braine (1970: Tables 3 and 4)*

Subject and construction	No. presented	Response type	No. imitated	Order same	Order changed
Owain					
NP + VP	185	substitution	10	10	0
		complete	25	23	2
VP + NP	175	substitution	10	0	10
		complete	25	2	19
Carolyn					
NP + VP	153	substitution	11	11	0
		complete	41	39	2
VP + NP	24	substitution	0	0	0
		complete	14	3	11

The second study turned to the issue of the word order of intransitive verbs and their subject noun phrases. Two types of constructions were used, as exemplified in (7.7):

(7.7) 1. NP+VP   e.g.   (The) bird's flying
                          Is the bird flying?
                          (The) bird flying?

      2. VP+NP   e.g.   (He's) flying, the bird
                          Is he flying, the bird?
                          Flying, the bird?

There were two children used, Owain and Carolyn. Owain was 24–25 months old for this study, and was tested over three sessions. Carolyn was 25 months old and tested in two sessions. The method was similar to that of the previous study. The responses were categorized as in the first study, except that substitutions were included in the analysis with complete imitations. A substitution was when the child repeated the NP and VP but replaced one or the other with a syntactically suitable substitute. The results are given in Table 7.10, and are very straightforward. Both children maintained the word order of NP+VP constructions, but changed it in the VP+NP ones. The results support the findings of de Villiers & de Villiers that children have acquired some knowledge of word order around 24 months of age.

The third study reports on the imitation of sentences with subject pronouns. The test sentences were similar to the type 2 constructions in (7.7), except that the following NP was missing, e.g. 'He's flying'. These were elicited from Owain and Carolyn during the same sessions that were used for the second study. They were also given to Owain again when he was 28 months old. This later data is referred to as Owain2, and the earlier data Owain1. There was also a third subject used in this study, Christine, who was tested on the sentences in (7.7) and the subject pronoun sentences during four sessions at 21–22 months of age.

The analysis of the data for the four sets of sessions (Carolyn, Christine, Owain1, and Owain2) revealed three patterns of acquisition of the subject pronouns. These are summarized below, with some relevant percentages which were used to determine them.

> *Pattern 1*: no pronouns. Both pronoun+VP and VP test sentences elicited most often VP responses, i.e. VPs without a subject (77% and 86% for Owain1, and 61% and 72% for both for Carolyn).

> *Pattern 2*: optional subject prefixes. Pronouns occur with equal frequency for both pronoun+VP and VP sentences (e.g. around 36% and 27% respectively for Christine), with virtually no NP subjects for either one.

> *Pattern 3*: obligatory subject pronouns. Pronoun+VP sentences elicit a subject, either an NP or pronoun (33% and 38% respectively for Owain2), and even VP sentences elicit either an NP or pronoun in 33% of the test sentences.

These patterns are presented in a way that suggests a developmental sequence. The sessions for Owain1 show little evidence of any knowledge of subject pronouns (pattern 1). Christine seems to place the subject pronouns on both VP and pronoun+VP constructions, suggesting to the authors the following conclusion (p. 439): 'A plausible interpretation of her total response pattern is that Christine's 'pronouns' are optional prefixes to isolated VPs, without referential function.' While quite an interesting speculation, it needs to be taken cautiously for at least two reasons. First, if this were true, one would expect uses of the pronoun in NP+VP test sentences also, e.g. as 'NP+pronoun+VP', which apparently did not occur. Second, there is no discussion of what would ever lead the child to this grammar; the English child does not hear optional pronouns. This point is one that we will return to later. As they stand, however, the data on pattern 2 provide some evidence for English as being marked for the pro drop parameter, a point discussed briefly in section 4.5. Pattern 3 is the pattern expected for the English-learning child. Since we have little information on Owain's language at time 2, we don't know when this change took place. It seems that he is acquiring some knowledge of the status of English subject pronouns around the end of this period.

The discussion of pattern 2 by Rodd & Braine contains a particularly useful exploration of its explanation. The authors propose pattern 2 by assuming something very close to the Competence Assumption of Chapter 4. They discuss the alternative that the child may have obligatory subject pronouns at this time, but that there are performance factors which inhibit their use. Two possible performance factors are considered. One is that the child may be constrained to repeat after the adult verbatim, thereby reflecting the nature of the stimulus sentences rather than its own grammar. They point out that all the data suggest that the three subjects altered the model sentences in systematic ways rather than repeating them as presented. A second factor is that the subjects may have been constrained by the length of the model sentences. Upon analysis, however, they found no effect of length of model sentences on the use of pronouns. After excluding these possible performance factors, they support the analysis of data for the four sets of sessions as given above.

7.3 The grammatical analysis of early word combinations

The literature on attempts to characterize the grammars of children during this period is one of the largest, if not the largest, in the field of child language. This is due probably both to a desire to understand the onset of grammar and to the practical fact that the lists of syntactic types for this period are somewhat less intimidating than later samples. Here we will begin with some general issues in attempting to account for the child's early grammars, and then review the major studies.

7.3.1 General issues

The proposals that have been made about the young child's early grammar differ from one another on a number of dimensions. Most of these have been mentioned at one point or another earlier in this volume, and this section will outline several to be used in characterizing the various approaches that have been attempted.

One aspect which sets off several approaches is the nature of the child's first grammatical categories. We have talked earlier about the young child's possible understanding of categories like Agent and Action. Such categories are part of most adult theories of grammar in some way, and are referred to as *semantic* or thematic categories. We have also referred to grammatical or *syntactic* categories like noun and verb. The question that needs to be answered is when and how each of these categories emerges in the child's language. Some have argued that the child has syntactic categories from the onset, and that the nature of these is highly constrained by Universal Grammar. Others have argued that the child's first categories are semantic, and that these are used by the child to discover the syntactic ones in the language. The interaction of syntactic and semantic categories, then, is one aspect that needs to be part of any theory of grammatical development.

Besides specifying the child's categories as either semantic or syntactic, child grammarians also differ in the degree of generality that is granted for these categories. Categories can be claimed to be either *specific* or *general*. To claim, for example, that a child has the category of Agent is to assign a general semantic category to the child. An alternative is to say that the child's category is much more specific, for example, 'people who play with toys'. Or, that instead of Object, there are 'things which can be eaten'. This distinction can also be applied to syntactic categories. We can have, going from most to least general, NP, noun, or nominals which occur only sentence-initially or finally.

Another important distinction to be accounted for is that between *lexical* and *grammatical* categories and their corresponding properties. Lexical categories are those such as noun and verb, with their corresponding semantic features. Grammatical categories are those such as number, gender, tense, etc. which specify information about lexical categories. There are two ways that the child could learn these two types of categories. One way, which is commonly referred to as *semantic bootstrapping*, is for the child to first determine the lexical categories, then use these to acquire the grammatical ones. We saw an example of this when reviewing the paper by Katz, Baker & Macnamara. Their proposal is that the child has the cognitive distinction for the equivalent of common and proper nouns, and then uses this to discover the way it is marked in English. The opposite view is that of *distributional learning*, which is the claim that the child first notices the regular occurrence of some morpheme, e.g. the presence or absence of the article, and then seeks the corresponding semantic/syntactic properties. Theories differ in the importance they assign to each of these properties during early acquisition.

Child grammars also differ from one another concerning the amount of *productivity* assigned to the child's grammar. By productivity, I mean the extent to which the grammar can generate sentences which have not been attested for in the child's spoken language. The grammar could have *limited* productivity, in the sense that it mostly generates the sentences upon which it was written. On the other hand, we could allow for *extensive* productivity whereby the grammar generates many more sentences than have been heard. This important point was emphasized in one of the first discussions of grammatical development of the period of longitudinal studies, that of Brown & Fraser (1964). At one point they wrote two grammars for 89 two-word utterances from Eve. One grammar only generated the 89 utterances recorded, while the other generated the original 89 utterances plus 469 others. In their discussion of how to choose between such grammars, they emphasize that the true test is the grammar's ability to make predictions. We will return later to the problem of testing predictions of these kind.

The converse of productivity is a grammar's *observational adequacy*. Here I use this term to refer to a grammar's ability to account for all of the attested data. Some grammars may be *lean* in observational adequacy in the sense that they only account for a subset of the data. Such grammars are proposed by those who set strict criteria on what is a productive utterance in the child's language. These theories allow for nonproductive utterances for a variety of reasons, e.g. because of imitation, memorization, emerging constructions which are not yet productive, performance errors. Other grammars may be *rich* in that they propose rules to account for all of the child's utterances.

As with adult grammars, child grammars also differ in their *complexity*. Some are written to be as *simple* as possible, with a small number of rules and categories. Others tend to be *complex*, with a large number of rules and categories. This aspect of grammars is not necessarily correlated with productivity. Some simple grammars can be quite productive, while others are not, depending on the kinds of categories used in the grammar.

In Chapter 4 we discussed at some length the issue of continuity vs. discontinuity in development. One's view on this affects one's grammar for the young child in two further ways. If one allows for a discontinuity in development, this often leads to the postulation of *non-adult* categories in the child's language. This is in contrast to the view that the child's categories are constrained by Universal Grammar to be adult-like, or *universal*. Within these distinctions, there is the further question of *individual* variation. That is, to what extent can any one child's grammar be different from that of any other child? That is, we can propose *individual* grammars, or non-individual or *common* grammars.

A last feature of the grammars to be discussed is their degree of *formality*. There was a time in the early 1970s when it was common to see formal grammars written for language samples. This was followed by a move away from formalism toward taxonomic descriptions of the child data. Such descriptions often take the form of lists of common constructions found in the data. Recent signs indicate a move back toward more formal accounts.

7.3.2 Pivot grammar: Braine (1963a)

The first attempt to capture the young child's grammar which gained a wide appeal was that of Braine (1963a). We have already discussed Braine's work in the overview in Chapter 2. To summarize, he asked mothers to keep parental diaries of the first word combinations of Andrew, Gregory, and Steven over a four- to five-month period. Braine's paper gives most of the data for the three children, which we summarize in Table 7.2. Table 7.4 gives Braine's organization of the data from Andrew according to its grammatical classification. By our definition, the children are in early Stage I.

Pivot grammar is a theory that assigns a great deal of importance to distributional learning. The child begins acquisition by selecting out a small group of words for grammatical acquisition. Presumably from its receptive knowledge, the child recognizes that certain words are quite frequent in the input language. These words also are consistent in their position, usually occurring before or after a wide range of other words. Braine does not specify how the child selects these words, but the prosodic system of the language and the language of the parents would have to play some role. For example, the child might hear 'Hi' stressed before a range of words and notice its frequency and constant position. Or, the parents might have some verbal games such as 'see'+'X', where X might be a series of objects being pointed out. This small class of words identified by the child is called the *pivot class*. All other words are defined negatively in relation to the pivot class, and are thus simply the other class, or what was called the *open class*. Since each child's linguistic experience will differ from that of other children, each child's pivot class will also differ.

The pivot class is then used to acquire other classes. When only two-word combinations are being produced, there are only two kinds of possible pivots, sentence-initial pivots or sentence-final pivots. A pivot class word is always restricted by its position. If it is a sentence-initial pivot, it must always occur in only that position. The child begins by learning which words can occur with each pivot word. At the onset, the child might simply put potentially any open class word with any pivot word. After a while, however, he will recognize that certain open words only occur with certain pivots. Gregory, for example, used distinct open words after initial, and before final, pivots. Primarily English nouns and adjectives appeared after initial pivots, while English verbs appeared before final pivots. Braine used these observations to suggest that Gregory was beginning to acquire the substantive–verb distinction in English. Since pivots are being used to acquire word classes, they serve no purpose in occurring either alone or with each other, so both of these distributions are disallowed by the theory. Further, combinations of open+open class words are predicted to occur only after the open class words have begun to differentiate into finer classes.

Table 7.11 *The defining features of a pivot grammar*

Feature	Pivot class	Open class
size	small class	large class
frequency	frequent	infrequent
position	restricted	not restricted
co-occurrence	cannot co-occur	may co-occur
isolation	do not occur alone	may occur alone

The possible combinations in a pivot grammar are summarized below. Nonpermitted combinations are marked with an asterisk (*):

> *Possible word combinations of a pivot grammar*
> (a) P1+X (where P1 = initial pivot and X = open class words)
> (b) X+P2 (where P2 = final pivot)
> (c) X+X (after types a and b have occurred for some time)
> (d) *P+P
> (e) *P

To summarize, there are five criteria which define the pivot and open classes; these are given in Table 7.11. Unfortunately, Braine does not provide any procedures for determining them. For example, how frequent must a word be before it is a pivot? Or, which of these is more important than the others? To learn how to write a pivot grammar requires looking at Braine's grammars and learning from example. As will be seen, this lack of precision has led to criticisms on the theory on the grounds of internal inconsistencies, since some of Braine's proposed pivots seem to violate one or more of these criteria. Braine does, however, provide a distributional criterion for defining a word:

> Those segments are considered 'words' which are the longest segments that cannot be divided into two or more parts of which both are English morphemes that occur in the corpus independently of the others. Thus 'ice cream' and 'all gone' are each classified as one word in Gregory's speech, since neither 'ice' nor 'cream', nor 'all' nor 'gone', occur in other contexts or alone. However, for Andrew 'allgone' is classified as a combination of two words since 'gone' occurs by itself, and 'all' occurs independently in 'all wet', 'all dressed', etc.
> (Braine 1963a:3)

This criterion is important as one of the first attempts to define productivity. We will discuss other ways to do this in section 7.5.

We can now look at the pivot grammar for Andrew, based on the data in Table 7.4. Example (7.8) presents Andrew's pivot grammar:

(7.8) S →   P1+X
      S →   X+P2
      P1 →   'all', 'I', 'no', 'see', 'more', 'hi', 'other'
      P2 →   'off', 'by', 'come', 'there'

We can see that this is a very simple grammar, with a small number of rules and only three classes of words. Andrew has a long way to go to get from this grammar to that of adult English. There are also 29 of Andrew's utterances which are placed into the 'other utterances' category. Braine does not address this problem, but it is one that needs explanation. It is possible that these utterances are indicative of future advances, or the result of performance factors. Any theory will need to account for the child's productions which are outside the predictions of the proposed grammar. Braine's pivot grammar is quite 'lean' in the sense used in the previous section.

Braine's analysis also gives some insights into the relative importance of the defining characteristics of the pivot class. Two pivot words, 'by' and 'come', only occur twice, and three others, 'I', 'see' and 'hi', only occur three times; frequency does not appear to be as important as positional consistency. The data also show some internal inconsistencies in the analysis. One sentence, 'I see', is a combination of two pivot words, which is a violation of the theory. Also, the distribution of 'byebye' is peculiar. This is a frequent word which is a likely candidate as a pivot word, yet it appears to occur in free variation with open class words. Even 'off', a final pivot, can be found in the list of 'other utterances' in initial position.

Assessment.   At first glance, a pivot grammar has a certain appeal due to its simplicity and apparent success at characterizing the child's early utterances. In the years after its first appearance, however, several investigators began to challenge its validity. Substantial criticisms appeared in Bloom (1971), Bowerman (1973a), and Brown (1973). By the mid 1970s pivot grammar was generally considered to be discredited. Here we will briefly review the arguments against it, and then provide a defence on its behalf.

Brown (1973:97–111) presents three arguments against pivot grammar as an adequate account of the child's language at the onset of syntactic acquisition. The first argument is that it doesn't even account for Braine's original data. We have already commented on the internal inconsistencies in the data for Andrew. The second argument is against its universality. Both Bloom (1971) and Bowerman (1973a) found that it was too lean to capture the grammars of the children they studied. Brown concludes that the only data that show some support for it are those from children at the very onset of acquisition. The third argument was on its grammatical adequacy. As we will shortly see, Bloom (1970) pointed out semantic regularities in early speech that are missed in the pivot account. In particular, she emphasized the existence of ambiguous sentences like 'mommy sock' which occurred in different contexts with different meanings – one as 'mommy is putting on your sock', and the other as 'mommy's sock'.

Investigators have generally been convinced by these arguments but some reservations are necessary. First, it is not clear that the theory itself could not be revised to deal with some of the problems with the internal consistencies in the original analyses as well as with its application to other data. This would need to take the form of better criteria for determining the defining features and their interaction. Also, it needs to be emphasized that the theory was only designed to apply to the earliest sentences of young children. Much of the data shown to be inadequately described by pivot grammars are actually from children who are relatively advanced. The 'mommy sock' example, for instance, comes from Kathryn I who, by our definition, was at the end of late Stage I with 226 unique syntactic types in her sample. The data that seem most like pivot grammars, e.g. those of Eric II, tend to be at much earlier points of development.

The strength of the pivot approach is that it offers an account of certain distributional facts about the child's early word combinations. It also offers some idea, albeit imprecise, on how the child might achieve such a grammar from the adult input. The suggestion that the child looks for positional consistency in frequent words as a basis for building word classes and presumably rules of word combination is a possible initial learning heuristic. To make it work, however, requires additional specification about how the classes and rules get established. In particular, it needs to include the role of semantic information, and how the child gets from this primitive system to the adult grammar. Braine (1976), in fact, attempts some revisions along these lines, and we will look at these later in this chapter.

7.3.3 Transformational grammar: the Standard Theory

Around the time of Braine's article on pivot grammar, other distributional analyses were also being done (Brown & Fraser 1964; Miller & Ervin 1964). These analyses were typical of child language research as presented in Chapter 2. The focus was on the child data and there was little reference to any theories of the adult language. In the 1960s, however, Chomsky's work in syntactic theory (Chomsky 1957, 1965) began to influence not only grammatical theory, but also work in child language. This model was seen as capable of providing a powerful means of describing and explaining children's early grammatical development. Grammatical research in the period from 1965 to 1975 was dominated by the theory of syntax presented in Chomsky (1965), which has since been referred to as the 'Standard Theory'.

In examining this research, it is important to realize that the study of syntactic development was just beginning. The extensive child language literature to that point had concentrated on data collection, and lexical, morphological and phonological development. There were few data available on the child's early word combinations, much less theories to account for them. It was with some excitement that investigators brought the descriptively powerful theory of transformational grammar to the study of children's language. It was applied in two distinct ways. On the one hand, the theory was taken as the basis for an explanation of acquisition. On the other, it was used as a descriptive device, a method to use in characterizing the speech of young children.

McNeill (1970b)   The first to use transformational grammar as an explanation of language acquisition was McNeill (1966a). This paper was a lengthy attempt to provide a nativist account of syntactic development, using the Standard Theory. McNeill's writings from this perspective include McNeill (1966b), Miller & McNeill (1969), McNeill (1970a,b, 1971). As expected, this view was striking in its contrast to the behaviorist orientation of Braine's pivot grammar, and had quite an impact at the time. Most of the discussion here, and all references are taken from McNeill (1970b).

According to McNeill, the child has genetically available at the onset of language acquisition a highly constrained universal grammar. The foundation of this grammar is the basic set of grammatical relations that underlie all languages. The major ones are shown, with examples, in (7.9). The first feature specifies its grammatical category, and the second its subcategorization. For example, the relation 'predicate' is represented by a VP, and it occurs after an NP which is its subject. The brackets in the examples set off the domain of each relation, since each one enters into a relation with one of the others. The constituent which represents each relation is italicized in the examples.

(7.9) *Relation*	*Feature*	*Example*
predicate	[+VP, +NP___]	[The dog *ate the apple*]
subject	[+NP, +___VP]	[*The dog* ate the apple]
main verb	[+V, +___NP]	The dog [*ate* the apple]
object	[+NP, +V___]	The dog [ate *the apple*]
modifier	[+Det, +___N]	[*The* dog] ate [*the* apple]
head	[+N, +Det___]	[The *dog*] ate [the *apple*]

The child's task is to identify these relations in the language being acquired. The child's early grammar does not manifest all of them simultaneously; rather, they appear in a predictable order. McNeill discusses this point in regard to Brown's subject Adam. Adam's sample included the following relations, with examples: predicate 'change diaper', direct object 'see truck', indirect object 'write paper', modifier 'dirty paper'. McNeill (p. 1090) makes the following comment:

> It is impossible to say from Adam's evidence whether or not these relations had equal tenure in his grammar at 28 months. All four conceivably existed at the holophrastic stage. But it is equally possible that originally Adam's utterances expressed only predication, to which was first added modification (including possessives), then direct objects of verbs, then subjects, and finally indirect objects of verbs – this being the order of the frequency of these relations in Adam's speech at 28 months.

McNeill thus acknowledges that there is possibly an order of appearance of these over the period of the first word combinations.

Importantly, McNeill accepts the superficial features of the early pivot grammar. The child begins this period with a grammar which looks much like the pivot grammars just discussed, but has, by its end, a basic phrase structure grammar with the universal grammatical relations. The initial pivot class, however, is not a random collection constrained by their frequency and positional constancy. Rather, it is constrained by the hierarchical nature of the universal grammatical relations. McNeill wants to propose that the relations predicate, main verb, and modifier are grouped together at a higher level of organization. In particular, they share the feature of occurring with NP. The pivot class, therefore, is initially a class of words that enter into relations with nominals.

The child begins grammatical acquisition by assigning relations to the language it hears, presumably beginning in the holophrastic period. McNeill states (p. 1096): 'It is important to note that these features are automatically made available whenever a child obtains *any* meaning from adult speech.' To make these distinctions, it seems that the child would need to use semantics. McNeill seems to imply this, since he refers to them as 'logical relations'. Our discussion from the previous chapter indicates that children have a range of semantic categories at this time. The universal grammatical relations can be interpreted as constraints on how these semantic categories can be related in speech. Table 6.8 gave the semantic categories of specific and general nominals, action words, modifiers, and personal-social words. We can rephrase McNeill's claim as something like this: the most general grammatical relation is between nominals and the other semantic classes, which are initially organized into a general class of general predicates. Assign all members of the first class some feature, say [+N], and all those of the latter class another feature, let's say [+V]. These initial semantically motivated distinctions immediately lead to syntactic categories. The child assigns to each word it acquires the relevant grammatical features from (7.9). Andrew's pivot class, for example, has two subclasses – one with the features [+V +____NP], the other with the features [+V, +N____]. Universal Grammar will require a set of principles that specifies the phrasal structure of a sentence. It will require that any constituent which has a lexical feature like [+N] or [+V] is also part of a phrase which is an NP or VP. Such speculations are part of current theory and are referred to as X-bar syntax (Jackendoff 1977).

Further development during the period leads to the emergence of the other grammatical relations besides the initial one distinguishing general predicates from nominals. For example, general predication will begin to divide into other relations such as main verb by similar semantic guidelines. The child's acquisition device will know that objects affected by actions are [+N] categories which also bear the grammatical relation of object to the action. Words so identified are then assigned the features [+NP, +V____].

The assignment of grammatical features to the individual lexical entries of words is an important part of McNeill's theory. This assignment occurs in a systematic fashion. At first, each word 'has one and only one classification' (p. 1096). A pivot class word, for example, cannot belong to both the P1 and P2 classes simultaneously. Another example comes from Brown's data. Two of his subjects used only animate nouns as subjects, and inanimate nouns as objects. McNeill assigns these two classes the features [+NP, +____VP, +animate] and [+NP, +V____, +inanimate] respectively: 'Eventually all words are classified in several ways, thus enlarging the distributional range of each word' (p. 1096).

This picture of development leads the child to a grammar which at an early age is very adult-like regarding its representation of grammatical relations. It also claims that the grammars of young children should look very similar from virtually the onset of acquisition. McNeill, in fact, makes this very claim (p. 1099): 'Insofar as the basic grammatical relations reflect the innate abilities of children, the type of grammar just outlined will be developed regardless of the language to which a child is exposed. It is a universal child grammar . . .'

The grammar which McNeill wrote for Adam's language sample at 28 months is given in (7.10). Adam has an MLU of just under 2.0 at this time so is just at the end of the period which we are discussing. The 'P' here stands for a modifier:

(7.10)   rule 1   S⟶   (NP)   (VP)

       rule 2   NP⟶   (P) $\begin{Bmatrix} N \\ N & N \end{Bmatrix}$

       rule 3   VP⟶   V   (NP)

Table 7.12 *Information of the two-word utterances expressing grammatical relations for Adam at 28 months of age, taken from McNeill (1970b; Table 3)*

Pattern	Frequency	Corresponding grammatical relations
P + N	23	modifier, head noun
N + N	115	modifier, head noun; subject, predicate
V + N	162	main verb, object
N + V	49	subject, predicate

This grammar has features in common with other grammars written for this period of development. First, there are a number of optional elements, since the child's actual productions are much shorter than the longest utterance which this grammar can generate. Adam, for example, produced 349 two-word utterances at this time, but only 49 three-word utterances. Table 7.12 gives information on the grammatical relations which were attested in Adam's sample. The grammar is very powerful, therefore, in the sense that it predicts a lot of utterances which were not attested. Second, there are no grammatical morphemes, such as prepositions or articles, represented; the theory implies, in fact, that these will be acquired after the basic grammatical relations.

Assessment. McNeill's theory is the first extensive theory on syntactic acquisition to be proposed. It relies on the child's innate ability to have and determine the basic grammatical relations in language by the end of the period of the first word combinations. It has a developmental component to it in that it allows for the relations to emerge gradually over several months. The theory also claims that all children will form the same universal grammar at this point. It is less clear whether children will necessarily also show the same order of emergence, but it implies that they will.

The theory has been attacked as assigning too much structure to the child. If true, it would be in violation of the Competence Assumption. If we look at the grammar proposed for the end of this period in (7.10) however, we are hardly looking at the adult grammar of English. We would argue that McNeill's proposals are not nearly as rich in their assignment of structure to the child as has been claimed by some critics. Also, this grammar is not the one which he would write for early Stage I. He seems willing to accept the surface patterns that Braine observed for the first multiword utterances. The difference in Braine's and McNeill's grammars for the early data is not in the number of categories and rules, but in their nature: McNeill wants to constrain them in ways that make them closer to the adult ones which will occur later.

We already have some evidence for syntactic processing from our review of comprehension studies. The arguments for syntactic relations will need to fall in large part on internal arguments of McNeill's theory. That is, the theory accounts for the emergence of syntax, and in part for the development of an adult grammar in a way that pivot grammar does not. Later we will look at a more recent theory by Pinker (1984) which is similar to McNeill's in many ways, but which addresses many of the issues left open.

The use of the Standard Theory as a descriptive tool was probably first attempted by Menyuk, who wrote transformational grammars for a large sample of children. The results of these analyses appeared in a series of articles which are pulled together in Menyuk (1969), which provides a useful introduction to the kinds of errors and omissions children show across several years in acquiring the structure of English. The samples from individual children, however, were relatively small, and no individual grammars are presented. The first in-depth attempt to write individual grammars was that of Bloom (1970).

Bloom (1970)   The extensive data collected by Bloom have already been discussed in a general way in Chapter 2 and again at the beginning of this chapter. Bloom was interested in providing detailed analyses of the early word combinations from the three children she studied. To do this, she used the Standard Theory as a method to describe the child's data. Her concern was more with describing the children's grammars, however, than testing the predictions about language acquisition that follow from transformational grammar. As a result, she changed the formal features of the theory when necessary to enable it to account for the children's patterns of acquisition. The result was a set of grammars for the three subjects which looked different from one another, and unlike that for adult English.

Superficially, Bloom's grammars appear to fall somewhere between those of Braine and McNeill. Those on data from early Stage I bear resemblances to the pivot grammars of Braine, while those from late Stage I data look more like McNeill's grammar for Adam. Bloom's early Stage I grammars, however, assign more structure than that of a pivot grammar, while those for late Stage I are less adult-like than McNeill's, and require more restructuring to reach the adult model. We will argue that Bloom's grammars are more similar to those of Braine and McNeill than is normally credited.

Before looking at a sample of these grammars, however, we need to examine Bloom's procedure for selecting data for analysis. She was very concerned about keeping close to the data and not assigning structures to children on the basis of one or two examples. All sentences were assigned to one of three categories.

Generally, a structure was *unique* if it occurred only once in the corpus of a speech sample, *marginal* if it occurred fewer than five times with different formatives in different situations, and *productive* if it occurred five times or more.

(Bloom 1970: 17)

The grammars presented usually excluded unique and marginal structures, although these were often referred to in the discussion.

We begin by looking at Bloom's grammar for Gia I. This sample, collected when Gia was 19 months, 2 weeks old, yielded 1,015 utterances, with an MLU of 1.12. Bloom, Lightbown & Hood (1975) give 55 syntactic types for Gia I, probably not counting the constructions with [ə] to be discussed. Gia I appears to be in early Stage I, at a point comparable to Braine's subjects. One would expect, therefore, that Gia's grammar would be a pivot grammar.

Bloom considers two phrase structure grammars for Gia I both of which are given in (7.11). Examples of the constructions for the first grammar are listed in Table 7.13 (Bloom uses VB for V, so I follow that practice here).

(7.11)   *Grammar 1*   *Grammar 2*

$$S \rightarrow \left\{ \begin{matrix} [\text{ə}] \\ Q \\ \text{`Hi'} \\ N \end{matrix} \right\} \begin{matrix} \text{VB} \\ N \end{matrix}$$

$$S \rightarrow \left\{ \begin{matrix} P \\ N \end{matrix} \right\} \left\{ \begin{matrix} \text{VB} \\ N \end{matrix} \right\}$$

$$Q \rightarrow \text{`more', `another'}$$

$$P \rightarrow \text{`more', ``nother',}$$
$$\text{`hi', [\text{ə}]}$$

A large number of recognizable words occurred with a preceding [ə]. This was a phonetically consistent form which had an indeterminate interpretation. Braine, for example, would have excluded these from his analysis. Two other words, 'more' and ''nother', were used in the sense of *recurrence*. It was because of this consistent semantic usage that Bloom groups these under the category Q. It is also productive by Bloom's criterion since it occurred at least five times. 'Hi' occurred in the context of Gia's looking out the window and waving. Bloom acknowledges the positional consistency of these four forms and groups them as an initial pivot class in her alternative grammar, shown above as grammar 2.

Bloom is more reluctant, however, to write a totally pivot grammar and relegate the rest of the data to the category of 'other utterances'. She feels that the N+N and N+VB sentences suggest emerging semantic relations. Since these are not frequent, she is cautious in concluding that they exist at this time. The N+N constructions suggest a 'locative' relation, and also either a 'subject–object' or 'genitive' one, as in the sentence 'Gia eyes', said while reaching for her doll named 'Blueyes'. The even less frequent N+VB

Table 7.13 *Gia I's word combinations*

| [ə] + N
29 *combinations*
e.g. '[ə] pen'
'[ə] car'

[ə] + VB
6 *combinations*
e.g. '[ə] ride'
'[ə] write'

'Hi' + N
10 *combinations*
e.g. 'Hi Jocelyn'
'Hi Eric' | Q + N or VB
'more rabbit'
'more clown'
'more write'[a]
'more byebye'
''nother /bæbə/'<br>''nother bang'

'hi' + VB
none attested | N + N
conjunction
'wowwow car'[b]

subject–object
'Gia eyes'
'Gia Blueyes'
'lamb ear'
'girl fish'
'truck wheel'
'girl ball'

locative
'block bag'
'fly block'
'fly blanket'[c] | N + VB
N subject
'girl write'
'Mommy back'[d]
'out Daddy'
'go Mommy'

N object
'slide go'
'balloon throw'
'block 'way' |

[a] Used in two contexts, one when she wanted to scribble again after her book was taken away, the other when she was scribbling after she had scribbled before.
[b] Used while looking at a picture of a dog running alongside a boy in a toy car.
[c] Used twice, once when fly landed on her blanket, the other when it did so again.
[d] Used twice, once waiting for mother to come back, the other as mother came through the door.

sentences show emerging evidence for both 'subject+verb' and 'verb+object' relations.

When we compare these data and their analysis to those for Andrew, we see that there are noticeable similarities. Andrew's sample also shows evidence for emerging relations. For example, the pivots 'more' and 'other' could be grouped as a Q marking recurrence. The final pivots 'off', 'by' and 'come' could be classed as verbs in N+VB constructions. The issue becomes not so much a difference in the data as in one's emphasis on the role of context in interpreting the child's sentences. Both sets of data show the use of a small class of words in positionally consistent ways, as well as some evidence of consistent semantic patterns.

The advances which are made over this period can be seen by looking at Bloom's grammar for Kathryn I. This sample yielded 1,225 utterances over seven-and-a-half hours. Bloom states (p. 40) that there were 397 multimorphemic utterances, presumably tokens, and that the MLU was 1.32. Bloom, Lightbown & Hood (1975) identify 226 syntactic types in five-and-a-half hours of the sample. While the MLU suggests that she is in early Stage I, the high number of syntactic types places her at the end of late Stage I, and shows how MLU can be misleading as a measure of syntactic development. The phrase structure rules for Kathryn I are presented in (7.12):

(7.12)
1. $S_1 \longrightarrow$ $\qquad$ Nom (Ng) $\left\{ \begin{array}{c} NP \\ VP \end{array} \right\}$

2. $S_2 \rightarrow$ $\qquad$ Pivot+N

3. $VP \longrightarrow$ $\qquad$ VB $\left\{ \begin{array}{c} NP \\ Part \end{array} \right\}$

4. $NP \longrightarrow$ $\qquad$ ([ə]) (ADJ) N

5. Nom $\longrightarrow$ $\qquad$ $\left\{ \begin{array}{c} N \\ Dem \end{array} \right\}$

Pivot $\longrightarrow$ $\qquad$ 'hi', 'oh', 'OK', 'thank you'

Ng $\longrightarrow$ $\qquad$ 'no'

The grammar for Kathryn I is actually relatively similar to McNeill's grammar for Adam, shown in (7.10). One difference is that there is a rule here to generate pivot-like constructions. A look at the proposed pivots, however, reveals that these are items that even occur in a pivot-like manner in adult English. An example of this is 'hi', although Bloom mentions that it was not used as a greeting, but more in the sense of 'taking notice' of something (p. 41). It is possible that Adam produced constructions like this, but that they were considered peripheral to the grammar. The grammar also includes a phonetically consistent form [ə] whose distribution is more restricted than the one in Gia I. Here it only appears in NPs. There were 36 constructions of the form [ə]+N, and 13 of the form [ə]+ADJ+N. The [ə] in this context looks like an emerging article which cannot be specified as either 'the' or 'a' according to its pronunciation. The elicited imitation technique used by Katz, Baker & Macnamara might have helped to clarify the status of this element. Bloom also has an optional negative morpheme, Ng for 'no', and a verb particle shown as Part, for sentences such as 'throw away'. Neither of these is mentioned in McNeill's grammar.

There are two noticeable formal differences between this grammar and the one for Adam. One is that, McNeill has restricted his categories to those which appear in the adult grammar of English. This followed from his theoretical position that the child's universal grammar restricts the range of possible categories from the onset of acquisition. Bloom, however, has created the category Nom which includes N and Dem, but has done so in an attempt to limit the generative power of the grammar. Nom is equivalent to the subject NP of McNeill's rule of S$\longrightarrow$ (NP)(VP). The problem with having NP in this position is that it generates ADJ+N constructions as subject NPs which are not attested in the data. As has been noted by others, e.g. Ingram (1972), adjective phrases such as 'more cereal' first occur in isolation, then inside of isolated VPs, e.g. 'eat more cereal', and only later as subjects. Bloom's Nom category avoids this problem, but creates the one of accounting for (i) what allows the child to form such a category, and

(ii) how the child gets from it to the adult one. For purposes of discussion, we will avoid this difficulty by revising Bloom's first rule to read:

$$S_1 \longrightarrow \left\{ \begin{array}{c} N \\ Dem \end{array} \right\} (Ng) \left\{ \begin{array}{c} NP \\ VP \end{array} \right\}$$

The second formal difference is the NP in Bloom's first rule for Kathryn I. This is needed to generate possessive constructions, e.g. 'mommy sock' meaning 'mommy's sock', as will be shown below, and subject demonstratives such as 'this book' meaning 'this is a book'. McNeill captures these by generating two Ns inside of the NP for possessives, and using P+N for demonstratives, where P is the category symbol for modifiers. He points out, however, that the latter construction may not be adequate if children use demonstratives in two meanings, one as a subject of a predicate nominative, the other as a modifier of a noun. Again, Bloom wishes to avoid writing a grammar that is too powerful.

Despite being generatively weaker than McNeill's grammar for Adam, Bloom's grammar for Kathryn generates basically the same grammatical relations as does McNeill's. For example, there were several cases of the subject–predicate relation as in 'mommy push'. Bloom discusses at length (pp. 62–7) the inadequacy of a simple rule such as S $\longrightarrow$ N+N to account for the child's early N+N constructions. She argues that there were five distinct kinds of N+N sentences, based on the context of their use and their consistent word order. They are each given a distinct underlying structure, presented here in Figure 7.1. The $\emptyset$ indicates underlying constituents which do not appear in the surface structure of the sentence. Two of these relations, conjunction and locative, are not actually generated by the rules in (7.12) because they did not meet the productivity criterion of occurring at least five times.

McNeill's arguments for the importance of grammatical relations were based primarily on logical grounds, that is, the innate nature of grammatical relations provides the child with a starting point for acquisition of the adult grammar. Bloom, however, was mostly concerned with proving the existence of these relations on the basis of the child's data. They arrived at the same conclusions via deductive and inductive methods respectively, as these terms were used in Chapter 4.

Bloom (pp. 50–62) describes five tests for proving the existence of these relations in the child's language. Each of these tests is summarized below; as will be indicated, some proved to be better than others.

1. *Sentence patterning.* If a construction occurs in the same place as its head without a change of meaning, then there is evidence of a constituent. For example, if both 'sock' and 'mommy sock' occur as an object of the same verb with the same meaning, then they are the same constituent, e.g.

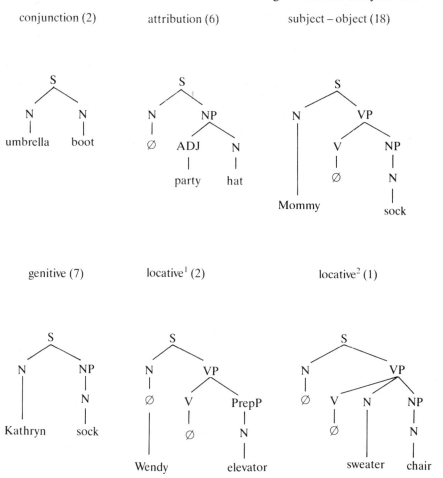

Figure 7.1 The underlying structure of five kinds of noun+noun construction for Kathryn I, along with their frequency (in parentheses), adapted from Bloom (1970).

'give sock', 'give mommy sock'. This argument was also used by McNeill (1970b:1079), but was not very helpful for Kathryn's data because most of her multi-morphemic utterances were restricted to two words.

2. *Linear order.* If a construction shows the order of the adult construction, then it has the same grammatical relation. This proves to be a weak test because some relations have the same order, e.g. subject-object and genitive, and conjunctions in random order, yet these could be misinterpreted as another relation. Another problem with this test, not mentioned by Bloom, is that adults tend to interpret child speech with the meanings they would use as adults (Howe 1976).

3. *Replacement sequences.* If the child produces two or more sentences in a row in the same context, and one is an expansion of the other, then the shorter sentence has the same relation as the longer one. An example is the sequence 'mommy milk', 'mommy's milk', where the expansion indicates a genitive relation. This test was first proposed by Braine (1973). These constructions were not, however, very frequent in the data.

4. *Replacement and deletion.* This is a variation of the previous test where expansion and simultaneous deletion indicates the relation. An example is 'Baby milk', 'touch milk' where the second sentence suggests that the first one is subject-object. This proved to be the most valuable linguistic test.

5. *Non-linguistic context.* The use of the non-linguistic context to infer the child's intended meaning. This includes the child's overt behavior and aspects of the environment at the time of the utterance.

While Bloom's grammar is more restricted than McNeill's, it still generates structures where constituents are proposed which do not occur in the surface structure of the sentence. This is evident in the cases where 0 occurs in Table 7.14. While there was evidence that three or more categories were underlying a sentence, most showed only two at one time. Only four actual three-term utterances occurred in the data: 'me show Mommy', ''chine make noise', 'man ride [ə] bus', and 'I comb pigtail'. These sentences and the patterns in two-word sentences led Bloom to conclude that Kathryn had an underlying subject-verb-object order.

The problem arose, then, of how to account for this discrepancy between the surface and underlying order. McNeill accounted for this by generating optional subjects and predicates. Bloom does not do this because she wants to represent the missing elements in the underlying structure of the sentence. As the grammar in (7.12) currently operates, however, it will generate surface strings with more categories than are appearing in Kathryn's language. Bloom adds an additional rule, called the *reduction transformation*, which deletes one of the categories when three are generated by the grammar. The selection of the category to be deleted is random, thereby allowing for the various two-word combinations which appeared.

As pointed out in several places (e.g. Wall 1972; Brown 1973: 234–9), this rule has several questionable characteristics; here we will briefly mention two of them. One problem is that it is inconsistent with the formal properties of transformations. Deletion transformations, for example, apply in cases where information about the constituent deleted can be 'recovered' through other constituents in the surface structure. For example, subject pronouns in languages like Spanish and Italian can be deleted because information about the person of the sentence can be found in the agreement affixes on the verb. No such recoverability, however, operates in the case of the reduction transformation. Another problem is that the rule violates the Constructionist Assumption. It is a rule that is unique for this period, and which will be lost in later acquisition. Brown (1973: 239) points out the peculiarity of having development proceed 'from the more complex to the less complex'. The rule's real effect is not to map from deep to surface structure, but rather from surface structure to speech. That is, it is really a description of a performance factor which limits the number of constituents that the child can say at one time. As a performance factor, its eventual loss also becomes easier to understand.

Assessment. Bloom's grammars are an important empirical attempt to verify the existence of basic grammatical relations underlying children's early word combinations. They show that these relations are difficult to establish in the earliest data, but that they exist at a more advanced level such as that of Kathryn I. Importantly, this finding is based on evidence found in the child's language, not just of logical arguments following from the theory of transformational grammar.

These grammars are also a serious attempt to restrict the generative power of grammars for children in this period. While they go beyond the restrictiveness of pivot grammars, they are less powerful than the grammars of McNeill. As such, they are the first extensive attempt to implement the Competence Assumption in writing formal grammars for children. Likewise, postulating the reduction transformation is a pioneering attempt to provide some justification for the discrepancy between the child's proposed underlying grammar and its surface manifestation. The fact that the formal properties of these grammars may be criticized should not take away from the importance of their contribution.

7.3.4 Semantically oriented approaches

Establishing consistent relational meanings in the first word combinations led to research exploring the relations in detail. In Child Language, at least, the 1970s became absorbed with this question. A major impetus to this work was the development of generative semantics in linguistics (see Newmeyer 1983). Generative semantics, in its most general form, was an attempt to redefine the underlying relations in grammatical theory as *semantic primes* such as Agent and Patient.

One of the first expressions of this approach was the case theory expressed in Fillmore (1968). Fillmore noted that the notion 'logical subject' covers a variety of semantic relations. Take, for example, the sentences in (7.13) where the subject of each sentence is italicized.

(7.13) a. *John* opened the door
     b. *The door* opened
     c. *The key* opened the door

The semantic role of the subject of each of these sentences differs. In (a) it is an Agent, in (b) an Object, i.e. the object affected, and in (c) the Instrument. Fillmore proposed a list of such basic semantic primes or 'cases' to underlie all sentences. The underlying structure of a sentence in this theory is not an NP and VP which bear the syntactic relation of subject–predicate, but rather a verb and its semantic roles or cases.

These semantically oriented theories produced a great deal of debate within the linguistic literature. The issue was whether these semantic roles were primitive, as argued by Fillmore, or derived. They can be considered derived in the sense that the semantic component of the grammar can determine them from the underlying syntactic structure of the sentence and the lexical features of its nouns and verbs. In such theories, they are considered redundant. A response to case theory can be found in Chomsky (1972). The general result of this debate has been a gradual incorporation of such semantic relations into grammatical theory. One of the first attempts to do this within the Standard Theory is Jackendoff (1977). Chomsky's more recent theory, known as Government and Binding Theory (Chomsky 1981), includes a subtheory known as theta-theory to deal with them. Within current literature, these roles are referred to as *theta roles* (see Radford 1981 for a useful summary). Recent theoretical work such as Marantz (1984) and Culicover & Wilkins (1984) even have a separate linguistic level where such roles are represented, distinct from the level where syntactic ones occur.

Semantically oriented theories had an instant appeal to those working in Child Language. It was noted that the range of semantic roles in children's early sentences was quite restricted. Sentences like (7.13b,c) did not look like the sentences which occur in early language samples. The idea that a grammar begins with semantic primes and later groups these into syntactic relations looked like a viable model for explaining early language acquisition. Further, it was suggested that such primes had as their roots the child's early concepts which appear at the end of the sensorimotor period (e.g. Sinclair 1971). Child Language research in the 1970s explored these ideas by examining the kinds of semantic relations which occur in early child speech, and exploring the possibility that they are the result of the child's level of cognitive development.

Bowerman (1973a)   The transition to more semantically oriented views of early grammatical development began with comparisons of Standard Theory grammars with case grammars. Two studies in particular stand out in this regard. One of these is Bowerman (1973a), who examined the acquisition of Finnish by two children, Seppo and Rina. Bowerman wrote pivot, Standard Theory, and case grammars for her two Finnish subjects,

Table 7.14 *Data used in Bowerman (1973a) for the comparison of pivot grammar, the Standard Theory, and case grammar*

Child	Sex	Age (months)	MLU	No of utterance types[a]	Language	Investigator
Seppo	M	23	1.42	297	Finnish	Bowerman (1973a)
Seppo	M	26	1.81	437	Finnish	Bowerman (1973a)
Rina	F	25	1.83	338	Finnish	Bowerman (1973a)
Kendall	F	23	1.10	136	English	Bowerman (1973a)
Adam	M	27	2.06	505	English	Brown (1973)
Eve	F	18–19	1.68	309	English	Brown (1973)
Sarah	F	27–28	1.73	265	English	Brown (1973)
5 subjects				49	Luo	Blount (1969)
Sipili	M	30	1.52	not given	Samoan	Kernan (1969)

[a] Total of unique types of syntactic and single-word utterances.

then compared these to comparable grammars written for selected other subjects. One of these was an English child, Kendall, whose data were collected by Bowerman. These were also compared with other English data from Adam, Eve, and Sarah, and other non-English data from Luo (an African language) and Samoan, collected by Blount and Kernan respectively. The former investigator had a difficult time obtaining language samples, discovering that Luo children are not usually addressed by adults, much less foreign visitors. These data, therefore, needed to be grouped. Table 7.14 gives a summary of relevant information about the samples.

Bowerman criticizes both the pivot grammars, for reasons already discussed, and the Standard Theory grammars. While the Standard Theory grammars improve upon pivot grammars in capturing more of the complexities of the child's grammar, they fail by assigning more structure to the child than Bowerman feels is warranted by the data. Since these arguments have proven to be the central ones against early syntactic grammars, we will look at them more carefully (they are also discussed in Bowerman 1973b, 1975). First I present the patterns observed in the data, then discuss their interpretation.

As is evident from Table 7.14, the first sample from Seppo at 23 months was the least developmentally advanced of the Finnish samples. The analysis of it indicated that the construction N+V was by far the most frequent construction, occurring in 30 syntactic types. The next most frequent one was N+V+N which occurred in only six types. All other constructions appeared in four types or fewer, and would have been considered marginal by Bloom's criterion of productivity. These two constructions also consistently occurred with the word order indicated, although some of the less frequent ones showed some variability. Although Finnish has a highly variable word order, due to its rich morphological system, the unmarked or most frequent one is N+V+N, as in English. An analysis of the mother's use of word order indicated that she most often used the unmarked order at the time of the sample. Bowerman concludes that the mother's word order is probably the source of the consistent order used by Seppo. Another feature is that subject and object NPs were always just an N. The only NPs that consisted of a modifier and an N occurred in isolation. Seppo's Standard Theory grammar is given in example (7.14). 'Proloc' refers to a class of grammatical morphemes called 'prolocatives', which are pronouns with case endings which have meanings such as 'here' and 'there'.

$$(7.14)\ S^h1 \longrightarrow \quad (M)(N) \quad (\text{Select at least one})$$
$$S^h2 \longrightarrow \quad (N)\ VP$$
$$M \longrightarrow \quad \left\{ \begin{array}{c} \text{Adj} \\ \text{N} \end{array} \right\}$$
$$VP \longrightarrow \quad \left\{ \begin{array}{c} \text{V(N)} \\ \text{Loc} \end{array} \right\}$$
$$\text{Loc} \longrightarrow \quad \left\{ \begin{array}{c} \text{N} \\ \text{Proloc} \end{array} \right\}$$
$$\text{Proloc} \longrightarrow \quad \text{'tuossa' ('there')}$$

The later grammar for Seppo at 26 months showed a number of advances over the earlier one. Some of the more noteworthy are as follows: (1) while the previous grammar was primarily restricted to two-word strings, three-word strings became more frequent; (ii) modifier–noun strings could now be embedded within subject and object NP; (iii) locatives could now co-occur with object NPs; and (iv) new constructions that appeared included (a) the use of adverbs with the previous constructions, and (b) copular sentences. There was still no evidence of the development of inflectional morphology. The flexible word order of adult Finnish also became more evident. Bowerman includes optional transformations which allow for each of the following reorderings of constituents from their unmarked orders: reversal of prolocative and object NP; reversal of verb and direct object, locative, or adverb; reversal of subject and verb; and movement of adverb or prolocative to front of sentence. Rina's grammar at approximately the same MLU showed several, but not all, of the same features. Rina did show the same degree of variable word order. Importantly, the distribution of the varying orders of constituents for both children correlated with that of their mothers.

Bowerman uses these data to argue against the existence of two grammatical aspects of the child's grammar at this time. Specifically, she wants to argue that there is no evidence for the existence of either the constituent

Table 7.15 *A summary of Bowerman's (1973a) arguments against the existence of a VP in children's grammars*

Argument for	Argument against
Children should respond to questions like 'What's it doing?' with VPs.	No evidence exists that this is the case.
V and V+N utterances in child speech should show the same privileges of occurrence.	The data indicate that V shows the same privileges of occurrence with V+N and N+V.
The use of 'do' as a pro-verb for VP, e.g. as in 'daddy like cake. mommy does too.'	Such sentences are not found in the language samples of children during this period.
V+N utterances are more frequent in the speech of children at this time than N+V strings.	The data from Rina, Seppo, and Kendall show the opposite (Table 16 in Bowerman 1973a).
In replacement sequences with verbs, children will first expand to an object NP before adding a subject NP.	The data from Rina, Seppo, and Kendall show both kinds of replacement sequence.

VP, or the relation 'subject'. The árguments are built upon a version of the Competence Assumption. The first set of arguments are against the postulation of a VP. These are summarized in Table 7.15. These arguments claim that there is no valid test available to establish the existence of a VP. Those tests based on frequency are inadequate, because they would lead to the conclusion that subject and verb form a constituent for Seppo, Rina, and Kendall, since subject+verb constructions for these children were more frequent than verb+object ones.

A second set of arguments are made against the existence of the grammatical relation 'subject of'. Bowerman considers two reasons why the notion of subject is needed in a grammar, and argues that neither of these yet exist for the developmental data. One reason for subject is that it is needed for certain grammatical transformations like Passive, where the underlying subject becomes the surface object. This is not the case for this period, because children at this time are not producing constructions like the passive which require this category. The second reason is for the operation of rules like Verb Agreement, Subject Pronominalization, and Case Marking (in Finnish). Again, there is no evidence yet in the child's sentences for the operation of these rules. She comments that the assignment of subject to the child's early sentences is imposing our adult knowledge of the language upon the child. She concludes that the data only support the postulation of sequenced semantic categories.

Brown (1973) A second work which compared the various approaches to the grammatical description of children in this period is Brown (1973).

Table 7.16 *Definitions and examples of eleven semantic relations proposed for Stage I grammars, taken from Brown (1973: 187–98)*

Relation	Definition and examples
1. Nomination	The naming of a referent, without pointing, usually in response to the question 'What's that?' Often indicated with words such as 'this', 'that', 'here', 'there'. (Also see Demonstrative and Entity below.)
2. Recurrence	The reappearance of a referent already seen, of a new instance of a referent class already seen, or an additional quantity of some mass already seen, e.g. 'more' or 'another' X.
3. Non-existence	The disappearance of something which was in the visual field, e.g. 'no hat', 'allgone egg'.
	Semantic Functions
4. Agent + Action	The agent is 'someone or something, usually but not necessarily animate, which is perceived to have its own motivating force and to cause an action of process' (p. 193), e.g. 'Adam go', 'car go', 'Susan off'.
5. Action + Object	The object is 'someone or something (usually something, or inanimate) either suffering a change of state or simply receiving the force of an action' (p. 193).
6. Agent + Object	A relation which uses the two definitions above. It can be considered a direct relation without an intervening action.
7. Action + Location	'the place or locus of an action' (p. 194), as in 'Tom sat in the chair.' Often marked by forms like 'here' and 'there'.
8. Entity + Locative	The specification of the location of an entity, i.e. any being or thing with a separate existence. These take a copula in adult English, e.g. 'lady home' meaning 'the lady is home'.
9. Possessor + Possession	The specification of objects belonging to one person or another, e.g. 'mommy chair'.
10. Entity + Attribute	The specification of 'some attribute of an entity which could not be known from the class characteristics of the entity alone' (p. 197), e.g. 'yellow block', 'little dog'.
11. Demonstrative and Entity	The same as Nomination except that the child points and uses a demonstrative.

Brown also provided an in-depth review and critique of pivot grammar, the Standard Theory, and case theory. Like Bowerman, he took the position that the primary development during this period is the acquisition of a basic set of semantic relations, which are the building blocks of later development. His work extended that of Bowerman, however, in attempting to determine the set of semantic relations that children have.

Brown's study of children's semantic relations consisted of analyzing the data from 24 language samples collected from 18 children. While the bulk of the data are from English, there are also samples from Finnish, Swedish, Samoan, and Mexican Spanish (see Brown 1973: 66, Table 9 for details). He also used a second set of data from 17 children acquiring American English, French, German, Hebrew, Japanese, Korean, Luo, and Russian. These data are secondary in that there is less information on these samples than the others. The two sets of data together constitute a broad base from which some general statements can be made.

Brown's analysis resulted in the claim that there are 11 kinds of semantic relations that underlie the child's early word combinations, divided into two subtypes. First, there are the *operations of reference*. These are relations where one term defines a property for a set of arguments. Brown specifies three of these, which are defined here in Table 7.16. An example would be Gia's category of 'recurrence' discussed above for the grammar in (7.11). The words marking recurrence, such as 'more', define a property of nominals, in this case that they are repeated or occur in several instances. Brown proposes that these are the relations that create the pivot look of early grammars. The second subtype is a set of eight prevalent *semantic functions* or relations. These relations consist of the categories that semantically underlie the grammatical relations such as those in (7.9). These are called 'prevalent' because these are the ones that occurred in the samples discussed above; Table 7.16 also gives definitions and examples of these.

In Brown's analysis, all of the multi-morpheme types used by the first group of subjects were categorized according to their semantic relations, using the kind of evidence discussed above for Bloom. For purposes of analysis, he collapsed Nomination with Demonstrative and Entity. The data were scored according to the percentage of each child's multi-morphemic types which fell into each semantic relation. Brown found that the eight 'semantic functions' or 'prevalent relations' accounted for approximately 70 percent of children's utterances (Brown 1973: 174, Table 22). Two of the relations, Agent+Object and Entity+Locative, were somewhat marginal, in that neither constituted over 9 percent of any child's sentences by this measure.

Brown goes on to propose that this particular set of relations occurs because they represent the knowledge acquired about the world during the period of sensorimotor development. He states (p. 200): 'Representation starts with just those meanings that are most available to it, propositions about action schemes involving agents and objects, assertions of nonexistence, recurrence, location, and so on.' Since they are part of every child's early representation, they are also proposed as being universal. That is, every child acquiring language will show the same relations.

Another important feature of Brown's study is his comparison of two-term and three-term multi-morpheme relations. He found that there were two ways in which his subjects expanded their constructions. These are what he calls concatenation-with-deletion and expansion-of-one-term. *Concatenation-with-deletion* is the case where two appear to combine, with the shared term being deleted in one of them. An example would be the combination of Agent+Action with Action+Object to form a new Agent+Action+Object construction. *Expansion-of-one-term* is the case where categories that are NPs are expanded. For example, the Object in an

Action+Object construction will expand to also mark Possessor+Possession, as in 'hit ball' expanding to 'hit Adam ball'. The latter type is particularly of interest because such utterances can be taken as evidence of an emerging NP structure. Brown's analysis of these indicates that they are relatively rare, only appearing toward the end of Stage I.

The above analysis led Brown to propose the *law of cumulative complexity*:

> It predicts that any child able to construct x+y will also be able to construct either x or y alone. It does not predict . . . that a child able to construct both x and y, severally, will be able to construct x+y. There is evidently, and this is simply an empirical discovery, some additional knowledge involved in putting the component items of knowledge together to make a more complex construction.   (Brown 1973: 186)

The fact that Brown does not want to make this law predict the existence of *x+y* on the basis of the separate occurrences of *x* and *y* shows the conservative stance which Brown takes about the child's grammatical knowledge. For example, he does not want to propose that the child has an Agent+Action+Object structure (*x+y*) on the basis of observing Agent+Action (*x*), and Action+Object (*y*). In this way he is more cautious than Bloom, who does just that. A further feature of this law is that it is also quite similar to what we have called the Constructionist Assumption. It relates the structures at one point in acquisition to those which have preceded them.

Brown's study is representative of a wide range of research done in the 1970s. This research had the following characteristics. It was concerned with accounting for the child's early word combinations on the basis of semantics rather than syntax. The only syntactic ability assigned to the child was usually word order, although even this was not always found to be consistently used. Further, these semantic relations were explained as coming from the child's sensorimotor knowledge. Language acquisition, then, was seen as being closely tied to, and even the result of, cognitive ability. Paradoxically, this continuity with early cognitive development was juxtaposed with a discontinuity with later syntactic acquisition. That is, few of these studies attempted to account for how the child ever got from a semantic grammar to a syntactic one. One of the leaders in this area was Schlesinger (1971), who developed his own theory on the acquisition of semantic relations. A detailed account of his research on early grammatical development appeared in Schlesinger (1982). While Brown and Schlesinger tended to be conservative in the amount of semantic structure assigned to the child's sentences, others (e.g. Antinucci & Parisi 1973; Leonard 1976) proposed quite rich semantic grammars. Leonard (1976) includes a comprehensive review of this literature (Appendix B, pp. 189–44).

While other investigators proposed similar sets of semantic relations, they were by no means the same. Howe (1976) reviewed the ones presented in Bloom (1973), Brown (1973), Schlesinger (1971) and Slobin (1970), and pointed out a number of discrepancies between them. She also examined what she saw as the two general methods or 'strategies' used to determine them. These methods were needed since the meanings of early word combinations are difficult to determine from their surface structure alone. One method was to observe the referents of each word and then infer their relation. The other was to rely heavily on the word order and expand the child's sentence into a grammatical adult one. Howe argued that these strategies share one basic flaw – they assume that the adult and the child share the same cognitive view of the world. Her conclusion about these studies is therefore radically different:

> Their most significant, though unintentional, contribution to the study of child language development could be their demonstration of the strategies parents use to interpret their children's speech. Parents assume that the two-word utterances of their children express one of the meanings they would express. Parents use word order and their perceptions of the relation between the referents of their children's utterances as clues to interpretation. (Howe 1976: 45)

Howe went on to suggest her own method for the study of the meaning of children's early sentences. This method has the following characteristics: (i) 'begin with the possibility that the two-word utterances of young children refer to situations to which adults would never refer' (p. 45); (ii) 'specify those situations which children can conceive and observe how they refer to them'. She predicts that the categories that result from such an analysis will be more general and fewer in number. She mentions three likely ones – Actions, States, and Names of concrete objects.

Howe's criticisms are useful in warning us against the pitfalls of imposing aspects of the adult grammar onto children's sentences. Her comparison of the various semantic taxonomies of the time also points out the difficulty in coming up with an acceptable set of semantic relations. Disagreements of this kind have also appeared recently in the area of linguistic theory in attempting to characterize thematic (or semantic) relations or roles. It is not a problem, therefore, that is restricted to child language research. The method she suggests is too general in its presentation to determine its feasibility. It has, however, one useful feature to it. It begins with the assumption that the child is not like the adult, and puts the onus on the analysis to prove otherwise. This, we will argue, is an important methodological assumption which should underlie research on child language acquisition. It does not logically exclude the possibility that we may ultimately conclude that the child and the adult are the same, but it makes that point the result of the analysis, not its premise.

Braine (1976)   Another study which takes issue with the semantic relational analyses of that time is Braine (1976). Like Howe, Braine feels that the number of semantic distinctions in child speech at the onset is much smaller than those proposed by others such as Brown (1973). Unlike Howe, he believes that these meanings are more specific, rather than more general. In Braine's view, the child sentences first express a small set of very specific meanings that will vary from child to child. This position looks very much like a revision of pivot grammar which takes into account the intended meanings of the child's sentences. Due to the extent of the data analyzed and the methodological care taken, Braine's study has had a major impact on the analysis of early grammars. Here we will look at the results of his study, as well as his methodology.

Braine conducted grammatical analyses on 16 corpora from 11 children acquiring either English, Samoan, Finnish, Hebrew, or Swedish. Several of these corpora have been discussed already. Collectively, they are children who tended to be in early Stage I in our definition of this stage. The fact that these children were at a relatively early point in grammatical acquisition becomes important when we compare the results with the other studies we have reviewed. Table 7.17 provides some information about the children studied.

Of particular importance are the methodological procedures Braine used in his analysis. First and foremost, Braine was very strict in setting criteria for the existence of rule-based behavior. He examined two properties in making decisions of this kind – positional consistency and productivity. *Positional consistency* refers to the requirement that a proposed pattern reflect a strict ordering of its constituent parts. This property is never fully justified but presumably follows from the assumption that children acquiring languages with strict word order will use that in their first rules. In specifying this, Braine also was responding to the earlier criticisms of pivot grammar that no criterion was used to determine if a morpheme was occurring in a fixed position or not. Positional consistency is operationally defined as follows:

Criterion for positional consistency
No. of utterances with
(a) dominant order   6,7   8   9   etc.
(b) opposite order   0   1   2   etc.

First, the criteria require that at least six sentence types must occur before a pattern can be considered. In addition, if there are only six or seven types, then they all must show the dominant order, where dominant order means the order of the rule producing them. If one sentence violates the appropriate order, then eight instances of correct order must appear (see Braine 1976:12 for details).

Productivity refers to the requirement that there be evidence of the production of sentences that could not be accounted for by adult modeling. Andrew, for example, produced sentences like 'no wet' meaning 'I'm not wet', and 'more hot' meaning 'another hot thing'. Such sentences, Braine believed, would be evidence for an underlying rule. No absolute criteria were set for this property, and it appeared to be determined by scanning the child's sentences. In addition to positional consistency and productivity, there is also the requirement of *semantic consistency* which is never operationalized, but is presumed to be obvious from the data.

The application of these properties to data from children resulted in the following kinds of possible patterns:

(a) *positional productive patterns*: patterns that meet the criteria of positional consistency, productivity, and semantic consistency;

(b) *positional associative patterns*: patterns which meet the criteria of positional consistency and semantic consistency, but not the one of productivity. These are so called because they combine positional learning and the association of a word or words with a set of words with which they have never been heard to occur;

(c) *groping patterns*: patterns which only meet the criterion of semantic consistency, and which are (i) small in number and (ii) produced with some uncertainty. The child is attempting to express a new meaning and is 'groping' for a way to do so;

(d) *free order patterns*: patterns where productivity and semantic consistency are met, but not positional consistency. These are also different from groping patterns in that they do not meet both the criteria in (ci) and (cii).

In addition to these patterns, there are approximately 25 percent of the data which cannot be assigned. Braine proposes that such residual data are probably imitations of adult models with no analysis yet done on them.

Braine used the data from Andrew, presented earlier in Table 7.4, to illustrate the first three of these patterns. The positional productive patterns include 'no'+X, 'more'+X, and 'other'. Examples of its meeting the productivity criterion are 'no wet', 'more hot' and 'other milk'. The constructions with 'all' are analyzed as a positional associative pattern.

While they meet the criterion of positional consistency, they do not meet that of productivity. Braine states (p. 8):

> It is unlikely, however, that the pattern is productive for the following reason: because the set of English words that can co-occur with 'all' is rather small . . . it would follow that, if Andrew had some formula for making combinations with 'all', one should expect that his use of the formula would yield some . . . strange combinations he could not have heard.

Since this is not the case, however, Braine places these into the positional associative category. Lastly, Braine analyses the sentences with 'all gone' and 'all done' as examples of a groping pattern. They are small in number and show variable word order. He also claims that they were uttered 'hesitatingly' (p. 11).

Braine did not write grammars for his data, but presented his results in the form of lists of utterances grouped according to their semantic consistency. Table 7.17 presents a summary of these semantic taxonomies. It gives the meanings Braine proposed for each of the 11 children he studied along with its pattern. This somewhat lengthy summary is given because his analysis remains the most rigorous cross-linguistic grammatical study conducted on this period. Also, the results of his analysis indicate the extent of individual variation that appears to characterize early grammars once strict criteria on productivity are applied.

When we compare the meanings used, we see that certain ones are more frequent than others. Actor/Action, Possession, Location, and Identification are the most frequent, followed by Recurrence and Requests. This is a shorter list, however, than the one given by Brown. Importantly, Brown was putting together a composite list, not trying to specify which patterns would occur with individual children. Brown's own data, in fact, show variation of this kind, which Brown discusses. Each child appears to differ in the meanings it selects for expression. Even though the labels suggest comparable meanings, Braine also emphasizes that individual children may restrict these in their own ways. These meanings are not universal for Braine in the way that they are for Brown. Braine states (p. 57): 'Children differ considerably in the kinds of contents expressed by their productive patterns and in the order in which they acquire them.' He points out, for example, that there is virtually no overlap between Andrew's patterns and those in Kendall II.

We have already discussed the issue of individual variation in regard to phonological acquisition in 6.5.4. We pointed out then that the individual differences claimed after analyses using the phone classes and phone trees approach could be explained as a measurement sequence, i.e. that

Table 7.17 *Summary of the subjects, meanings, and patterns found in Braine (1976)*

Children and information[1]	Meanings	Patterns
Andrew, Steven, and Gregory[2] (Braine 1963a)		
Kendall I (Bowerman 1973a)	Actor/Action	positional productive
	Possession	positional productive
	Location	groping
Kendall II	Actor/Action	positional productive
	Possession[3]	positional productive
	Locatives with 'here', 'there'	(uncertain)[4]
	Locatives (with other words)	positional productive
	Actor/Action/Locative	(uncertain)
	Identification[5]	
	1. 'that' + X	positional productive
	2. X + Y	positional productive
	??Verb/Object[6]	??groping
Seppo (23 months) (Finnish) (Bowerman 1973a)	Actor/Action	positional productive
	Locatives with 'tuossa' ('there')	groping
	Locatives (with other words)	positional productive
	??Verb/Object[6]	??groping
Sipili (Samoan) (Kernan 1969)	article-like Identification	
	1. 'le' (the)	positional productive
	2. ''o' (sign of nominative)	positional productive
	Possessives	
	1. X + 'a'u' ('me')	positional productive
	2. X + ''oe' ('you')	positional productive
	3. 'ma'[7] + X	positional productive
Tofi (26 months) (MLU 1.6) (Samoan) (Kernan 1969)	movement-to Locative (Verb + Location)	positional productive
	Action/Actor (V + N)[8]	positional productive
	Act/Patient (V + N)[9]	positional productive
	Request	
	'fia' ('want') + X	positional productive
Jonathan I (see Table 7.2) (Braine 1976)	Possessive	positional productive
	size-Attribution	
	1. 'big' 2. 'little'	positional productive
	Recurrence 'more'	positional productive
	color-word + Object name[10]	(uncertain)
Jonathan II	Possessives	
	Property-indicating	
	1. 'big' 2. 'little' 3. 'hot'	positional productive
	4. 'old' 5. 'hurt' 6. color	positional productive
	7.'(all) wet'	groping
	Recurrence 'more', 'other'	positional productive
	Number 'two'	positional productive
	Disappearance 'allgone'	positional productive
	Locatives	
	1. object/location	positional productive
	2. X with 'there'	groping
	?Actor/Action[11]	positional productive

Table 7.17 (*cont.*)

Odi	Identifying patterns	
(Hebrew)	1. 'ze' (that) + X	positional productive
(23–26 months)	2. 'tire/tiri' (see) + X	positional productive
(MLU 1.4)	3. 'hine' (here) + X	positional productive
(Braine 1976)	Requests	
	1. 'ten' (give) + X	positional productive
	2. 'efo' (where) + X	positional productive
	Locatives	groping
	Possessives	groping
David I	Identifying form 'here' + X	positional productive
(Table 7.2)	Requesting expression	
	'want' + X	positional productive
David II	Identifying forms	
	'here', 'this', 'that'	positional productive
	Requesting expression	
	'want', 'Can-I',	positional productive
	'I-can't', 'gimme'	positional productive
	Recurrence 'more'	
	Verb + 'it'	positional productive
Embla 1[12]	Actor/Action	
(Swedish)	Locating or Identifying	
(Lange & Larsson 1973)	'dar' (there) + X	positional productive
	'den' (it) + X	positional productive
Embla 2	Actor/Action	positional productive
	Locatives 'ga' (go)	positional productive
	Actor + 'ga' + Locative	positional productive
	Locative with 'dar'	
	1. 'dar' + X	positional productive
	2. X + 'dar'	positional productive
	Conjunction 'och' (and) + X	positional productive
	Negation 'inte' (not) + X	positional productive

[1] These are only given for children not previously discussed in the text.
[2] Data used to exemplify the kinds of patterns found. The meanings of individual patterns are not usually given.
[3] Braine actually labels these as Possessives for Kendall II, but states in the text that he uses 'Possessives' and 'Possession' interchangeably (p. 16).
[4] Braine speculates that 'here' was a positional (final) pattern at Kendall I, and that Kendall has now learned that 'here' and 'there' can occur initially and finally.
[5] Also called Class Membership.
[6] There are several action phrases in the data without an agent, and with the object either before or after the action word. Braine does not actually include these in his analysis because the semantic basis for it is unclear.
[7] Translated by Kernan as either 'and', 'with', or 'for'. Braine is not sure if these are one or several semantic patterns.
[8] The basic word order in Samoan is Verb-Subject-Object although it is variable. Braine combines Agent + Action and Noncausative Movement Verbs (e.g. 'pa'u:' meaning 'fall') + Object Moved in this pattern. He feels that the child makes a distinction between causative and noncausative verbs, with the nominals having some kind of agent role.
[9] This pattern includes Causative Movement Verbs + Object Moved, and other transitive Verb + Object sentences. The nominals are speculated as being Patients, i.e. objects affected.
[10] These were semantically peculiar in that the color words were not used correctly.
[11] Braine speculates that the nature of these sentences are such that they could be collapsed with the Object + Locative pattern on a semantic basis.
[12] Exact ages are not given, but the first samples were around 21–22 months, and the second ones around 22–23 months.

approach gives a lot of importance to infrequent and idiosyncratic data. We can now ask if Braine's method does the same. In fact, by setting strict criteria for what is considered a productive pattern, Braine has developed a method which should minimize individual variation. Given this, his finding of individual variation needs to be taken quite seriously.

Braine takes these grammars as an indication that children begin acquisition by developing a small set of meanings for expression. These meanings may be quite narrow, and have one member restricted to a single word, as in David I's Identifying form 'here' or his Request expression 'want'. Since these early patterns appear to be independent, he doesn't even want to call them 'rules', since the latter implies the features of a generative grammar. Instead, he calls them *formulae of limited scope*. They only become more general as formulae with similar meanings are acquired.

Braine also accepts Bowerman's criticisms against assigning a transformational grammar to the child at this stage, but adds a third argument. He gives the example of Kendall who acquired Actor/Action as one of his first productive patterns. According to the syntactic approach this should lead to the rules:

rule 1   S $\longrightarrow$ NP+VP
rule 2   VP $\longrightarrow$ (V)+(NP)

When the child acquires locatives, rule 2 would be then changed as shown:

rule 2′   VP $\longrightarrow$ $\left\{ \begin{array}{l} (V)+(NP) \\ \text{Locative} \end{array} \right\}$

Since the order of the subject in relation to the locative is done by rule 1, then locatives should appear with appropriate ordering. The data from Kendall and Seppo, however, indicate that Locatives were a groping pattern at the time when Actor/Action was acquired. These data, then, are taken as evidence against the syntactic explanation of early word combinations.

Assessment. Braine's monograph is an important methodological and descriptive contribution to our knowledge about early word combinations. Its methodology is a major step towards extracting the productive utterances from a spontaneous language sample. The results of his analyses are an impressive set of observations that require explanation. It appears that children can be quite different in their selections from the set of meanings which they could express. These data are quite a problem for any theory of acquisition which states that all children begin in the same way.

We see two major limitations to Braine's account of early word combinations. One concerns the restriction of the data being considered to spontaneous speech samples. While Braine is adhering strictly to his version of the Competence Assumption, our formulation of it does not restrict data in this way. Information about the child's receptive knowledge as well as other forms of expressive language can and should be used. We have already seen the viability of the imitation technique in Rodd & Braine (1970), and will explore still others in Section 7.5. The second limitation is that it avoids accounting for how the child ever gets from this kind of grammar to an adult one. Braine briefly discusses this fact toward the end of his study (pp. 88–9). He correctly points out that there is no inherent discontinuity in development in his proposals, should adult grammars be different from the current syntactic models being considered. Only additional research on later development will find if and when discontinuity occurs.

Bloom, Lightbown & Hood (1975) The last study done during this period of initial research into semantic relations is that of Bloom, Lightbown & Hood (1975). Like the previous studies, it was concerned with examining the language samples of young children for the kinds of semantic relations which occurred. Its goals in doing this, however, extended far beyond simply identifying a set of relations. They wanted to answer the last problem just expressed concerning Braine's study, i.e. how and when does the child go from a semantic grammar to a syntactic one? They make this point very clearly (p. 1) when discussing semantic relations:

> It should not be surprising that these are the kinds of things that children first learn to talk about. However, the linguistic means that children learn for the representation of such notions, the sequence of development in child grammar, and the relation of systems of child language to the adult model remain to be determined.

In essence, this was an attempt to reconcile the apparent difference between the proposals of McNeill (1970b) and Bloom (1970) with the results of the studies by Bowerman (1973a), Brown (1973), and de facto Braine (1976). That is, when does the child change from a semantic grammar to a syntactic one? Or, stated differently, when does the child shift from semantic categories (e.g. Agent) to syntactic ones (e.g. subject)?

The study was done by examining the spontaneous speech samples of four children: Eric, Gia, Kathryn, and Peter. The first three children were the ones studied in Bloom (1970), while Peter's data were collected in a similar fashion at a later time. Several samples were obtained from each child while they were approximately 19–25 months of age (see Table 1 in Bloom, Lightbown & Hood 1975: 7). Their MLUs across the samples ranged from 1.04 to 2.83. Based on the children's MLUs, the authors felt that the samples presented data from all four children on both early and late Stage I,

Table 7.18 *Number of syntactic types for each sample period of four children studied in Bloom, Lightbown & Hood (1975:7, Table 1); the number of the sample period, and its MLU, are shown in parentheses*

Ranges of syntactic types	Peter	Eric	Gia	Kathryn
0–50	7 (I, 1.04)	10 (I, 1.10)		
	5 (II, 1.09)	37 (II, 1.19)		
	70 (III, 1.37)		55 (I, 1.12)	
	80 (IV, 1.41)			
	81 (V, 1.41)			
101–150		108 (III, 1.42)		
151–200				
201–250	243 (VI, 1.75)		226 (II, 1.34)	226 (I, 1.32)
251–300			288 (III, 1.58)	
301–350				
351–400				
401–450		401 (IV, 1.69)		
451–500	458 (VII, 2.39)		457 (IV, 1.79)	767 (II, 1.89)
over 500		902 (V, 2.63)	842 (V, 2.30)	1443 (III, 2.83)

as defined by MLU values in Brown (1973), as well as Stage II. This is so, as can be seen by examining their MLUs, which are given in Table 7.18. Recall, however, that we have challenged this definition at the beginning of this chapter, and have defined the periods in Stage I by the number of syntactic types as it interacts with MLU. Table 7.18 presents the four subjects based on their number of syntactic types.

Table 7.18 reveals that these four children's samples do not equally represent both early and late Stage I, at least by our definition. There are nine samples with 108 or fewer syntactic types, placing them in early Stage I. Eight of these nine are from Peter and Eric. After a gap between 108 and 226 syntactic types, there are four samples between 226 and 288 which could be placed into late Stage I, assuming some flexibility in interpreting our measure. Three of these four are from Gia and Kathryn, and none are from Eric. The rest of the samples are beyond this range and are in Stage II from our perspective. In other words, most of the early Stage I data are from Eric and Peter, and most of the late Stage I data are from Gia and Kathryn. This observation is important when we come to analyze their data. We will only present their results regarding semantic relations for those samples which fall within these two periods by our definitions of them.

Bloom, Lightbown & Hood determined a semantic relation for each syntactic type in the data. They did not use a predetermined list of relations, but instead let the data reveal the meanings. Like Braine, they did not provide a set of explicit criteria for this task, but imply as Braine does that the meanings are in some way self-evident. They state (pp. 7–8):

> Each multi-word utterance was examined and the semantic–syntactic relations among words were identified by observing the relationship between the utterance and aspects of the child's behavior and the situational context in which the utterance occurred. Obviously, one cannot be confident that the semantic interpretation given to an utterance by an adult does indeed equal the child's semantic intent. At the least, it is necessary to establish that (1) any utterance can be identified as a separate behavior (from the other linguistic behaviors that occur) by observers, and (2) given the same information about the utterance and nonlinguistic context and behavior, different observers can assign the same interpretation to it.

The important advance here is that the validity of the relations is determined by comparing the independent judgements of observers. In this case, two interpreters were used and their judgements compared. This is an advance over the other studies, which used a single individual for all interpretations.

The analysis revealed over 20 semantic relations, although only a small number of these proved to be frequent. To separate frequent from infrequent relations, they used the same measure of productivity as in Bloom (1970), i.e. a relation was considered to be productive if there were at least five syntactic types for it. As mentioned in Bowerman (1975), this is not a particularly good measure since it will be highly influenced by sample size. Further, as pointed out in Ingram (1981d) and discussed here in Section 7.6, it does not take into consideration crucial information about the distributional properties of words. Five memorized phrases with similar semantic properties could qualify as productive under this definition. Here we will present their results with this measure with one proviso. A relation is considered productive in the session when it meets this measure and continues to do so on all further samples.

This adjusted measure reveals for the Stage I samples nine semantic relations which were productive for at least two children. Here we summarise Bloom, Lightbown & Hood's definitions of each.

1.   *Action*: sentences referring to movement where the purpose of the movement was not to change the location of an object of person. There were two subcategories – (a) transitive actions (our term for this), where the semantic relation was agent-action-object, with any two appearing in the sentence, e.g. 'open drawer', 'I made';

(b) intransitive actions, where only an agent and action were involved, e.g. 'Kathryn jumps'

2. *Locative Action*: 'movement where the goal of movement was a change in the location of a person or object' (p. 11). As in the previous relation, there were two kinds – (a) transitive locative actions (our term for this), where the semantic relation was agent-action-object-place, and at least two appeared in the sentence, e.g. 'put in box', 'tape on there'; (b) intransitive locative actions, 'where the agent and affected object or person were the same' (p. 11), e.g. 'I get down', 'Mommy stand up (ə) chair'. The semantic roles for this type were mover-action-place. (Note that 'mover' is being distinguished from 'agent'. This distinction will prove to be important later.)

3. *Locative State*: reference to a person or object and its location without an indication of movement. The relation is object-state-place, with at least two of these in the sentence, e.g. 'I sitting', 'sitting on chair';

4. *State*: 'reference to transitory states of affairs involving persons or other animate beings' (p. 112). There are three kinds of these – (a) internal states with verbs like 'like', 'need', 'want', e.g. 'I want pretzel', 'Caroline sick'; (b) temporary ownership, e.g. 'I have it'; and (c) external states, e.g. 'it's dark outside';

5. *Existence*: 'pointing out or naming an object' (p. 13);

6. *Recurrence*: 'reference to "more" or another instance of an object or event' (p. 13);

7. *Attribution*: 'counting, specifying or otherwise qualifying objects' (p. 13);

8. *Possession*: (not defined);

9. *Negation*: 'nonexistence, disappearance or rejection of objects or events' (p. 13).

These nine relations are remarkably similar to the frequent ones found by Braine (1976). The primary differences appear to be in name. Braine's Requests and Identifications are classified here as State and Existence respectively. Their terminology for locatives also differs. Braine refers to Locative Actions as Movement-to-Locatives. Lastly, Negation occurs with two of Bloom, Lightbown & Hood's subjects, but it is not as frequent in Braine's data. Generally, though, there is a great deal of overlap.

Table 7.19 presents the acquisition of these relations by the four children studied, divided into early and late Stage I. Like Braine's study, the data from Bloom, Lightbown & Hood reveal a certain degree of individual variation. Even so, there are patterns which emerge. We can see this by requiring that a relation exists when at least two children acquire it.

Table 7.19 *The productive semantic relations for early and late stage I for Eric, Peter, Gia, and Kathryn, adapted from Bloom, Lightbown & Hood (1975: 15, Table 2). Relations are shown with the sample in which they first appeared*

	Children			
Stage	Peter	Eric	Gia	Kathryn
Early I:	III, IV Action Recurrence Attribution V Locative Action	II Action Negation Existence III Locative Action State Recurrence Attribution	I Existence Recurrence	
Late I:	VI Locative State		II Action Locative Action Possession Attribution III Locative State	I Action Locative Action State Existence Negation Recurrence Possession Attribution

Applying this measure to early Stage I, the following patterns appear in this subperiod: Action, Recurrence, Existence, Locative Action, and Attribution. The fact that two of the children show developmental changes even allows us to impose an order to these. Action, Recurrence, and Existence appear first, followed by Locative Action and Attribution. Given the individual variation involved, however, we can only state this as a statistical tendency. In late Stage II, Locative State, State, Negation, and Possession also meet our criterion. The data also indicate that there is an acquisition order which is exceptionless in the data: Actions are acquired before Locative Actions, which are in turn acquired before Locative States.

Bloom, Lightbown & Hood discuss these data in terms of their implications for the child's grammar, particularly as evidence for the emergence of the grammatical category of 'subject'. First, several of these relations involved initial nominal categories, i.e. Action, Locative Action, Locative State, and Attribution. Further, the initial nominals of these particular relations occurred consistently in sentence-initial position. Each could be described syntactically by a rule of the form S ⟶ noun or pronoun+verb (or verb phrase). Recall that both Bowerman and Braine had argued that there was no evidence to support such a claim, and proposed instead that

Table 7.20 *The proportion of pronouns used to mark agents and affected objects (Object) in Actions for Peter, Eric, Gia, and Kathryn, calculated from Bloom, Lightbown & Hood (1975: Table 3)*[1]

Ranges of syntactic types	Peter		Eric		Gia		Kathryn	
	agent	object	agent	object	agent	object	agent	object
0–50	—	—	—					
	—	—	—	0.67				
51–100	—	—			—	—		
	0.86	0.74						
	0.75	0.89						
101–150			0.88	0.78				
151–200								
201–250	1.00	0.64			0.00	0.05	0.17	0.08
251–300						0.01		
301–350								
351–400								
401–450			0.75	0.49				
451–500	0.76	0.45			0.06	0.12		
over 500			0.77	0.39	0.77	0.30	0.08	0.34
							0.57	0.38

[1] Calculations are shown only for cases where five or more instances occurred.

children's initial rules were solely semantic. Bloom, Lightbown & Hood state (p. 28): 'The kind of evidence that both Bowerman and Schlesinger might accept in order to attribute such knowledge of grammatical relations to the child would be the occurrence of superordinate categories whereby words in the same syntactic position took on different semantic functions relative to one another.' They interpret the gradual and consistent spread of initial nominals to different semantic roles as evidence for the syntactic category of subject. In Kathryn I, for example, the subject of sentences could be either an agent (in Actions), mover (in Locative Actions), possessor (in Possessions), or object (in Locative States).

Besides examining the emergence of semantic relations, Bloom, Lightbown & Hood looked into the acquisition of pronouns and nouns by their subjects. They observed that the two boys, Eric and Peter, tended to mark the semantic roles accompanying actions with pronouns. The two girls, however, did so with nouns, and did not show pronouns until later in development. This pattern was consistent for Possession, Action, and Locative Actions. It was demonstrated by counting the number of times a possessor, agent, mover, affected object, or place was indicated by either a noun or pronoun in syntactic types. Here we will present their results somewhat differently, using the format of Table 7.20, and a different measure than absolute numbers. For each semantic role, I calculated the proportion of pronouns, which is the proportion of times that the child in any sample used a pronoun instead of a noun. These data are presented in Table 7.20 for the agent and affected object roles of Actions. Both Eric and Peter used pronouns predominantly until they were beyond Stage I. The opposite was the case for Gia and Kathryn who used predominantly nouns. All subjects eventually acquired the other category by the latest samples where their proportions are relatively similar.

Bloom, Lightbown & Hood interpret these results as indicating that there are two distinct strategies that children may use in acquiring an early grammar. One is the *categorization strategy* which was used by Gia and Kathryn. The girls used the semantic relations of early sentences to abstract grammatical relations such as 'subject' and 'predicate–object'. This strategy has come to be known in more current literature as *semantic bootstrapping*. We will examine this notion more carefully later, but essentially it claims that the child's language acquisition device looks for semantic roles which pattern together for the purpose of forming more abstract categories. As pointed out by Bloom and her colleagues (p. 32), these may not initially be adult-like. Gia and Kathryn's initial subject included possessors as well as agents and movers. Even so, it presumably will restrict the possibilities available in ways which are unknown at this time.

The second strategy is the *pronominal strategy* which was proposed for Peter and Eric. This strategy is one which bears similarities to the early pivot grammars and Braine's more current view of formulae. Here we will refer to it as an alternative to semantic bootstrapping which accounts for early development by *distributional learning*. The children's pronouns operated like pivots with each marking a particular meaning. Peter and Eric, for example, used 'I' to indicate agents, 'my' for possessors, 'it' and 'this one' for affected objects, and 'here' and 'there' as locations. If the children were acquiring pronouns semantically for the purpose of establishing grammatical relations, we would expect a very different pattern. Some pronoun such as 'my', 'me', or 'I', for example, would be expected to represent several semantic roles as the subject, much the same as 'Mommy' did for Kathryn. We would then expect mistakes in their use until the adult pronominal case system was acquired. This did not happen, however, and instead the pronoun functioned as a formal marker of the individual semantic role of the word with which it occurred.

If these pronouns are not leading to grammatical relations, what do they help the child to acquire? As given in our discussion of pivot grammar, they allow the child to acquire the grammatical classes of the language. For example, the child might begin by identifying 'it' as a frequent morpheme which occurs after a number of action words which it knows. 'It' then comes to define that particular class as 'words which occur with "it"'. Eventually, as other properties are added, this becomes the class of English transitive verbs. Another morpheme such as 'the' comes to identify the common nouns. Only later will more detailed information be acquired about these initially formal markers.

These two strategies lead to very different theories of early acquisition. The categorization strategy (or semantic bootstrapping) leads to early identification of grammatical relations, with subsequent distributional learning. For example, the early identification of lexical items which function both as agents and movers establishes an early category of subject. Presumably Universal Grammar or subsequent distributional learning leads to grammatical classes like noun or noun phrase. The pronominal strategy (or more general distributional learning) predicts early specific learning of positional word classes which develop eventually into grammatical categories, then grammatical relations. For example, words which occur with 'it' become verbs, and subsequently function as the predicate in the predicate–object relation. In Section 7.5 we will look in more detail at a recent proposal of this kind.

Assessment. The Bloom, Lightbown & Hood study was an important first attempt to reconcile the discovery of semantic relational meanings in children's early word combinations with earlier proposals for the existence of a syntactic grammar. They pointed out the need to account for the transition to an adult grammar, and provided a major argument in support of the existence of grammatical relations. This argument was empirically based, i.e. it came from the analysis of children's language. They also noted that the development of these relations could occur in two very different ways. One allowed for the early establishment of general semantic categories, the other for early formal ones. The effort to decide between these alternatives characterizes most of the subsequent theoretical research in the field.

Its weaknesses stem from both its method and its gaps in theoretical interpretation. The measure of productivity was too weak to establish with confidence what the children's grammars actually looked like. No formal grammars were written, and claims about the child's grammatical knowledge were usually in the form of taxonomies or lists of numbers. Even with this reservation stated, the numbers in the larger studies, with our added criterion, result in data that need to be explained by any serious candidate for a theory of grammatical acquisition. The theoretical interpretations do not deal with some important questions. One is how the child actually gets from the semantic relations to grammatical ones, i.e. what is the child's learning mechanism? Later we will examine a proposal by Pinker (1984) for one such mechanism. There is also little in the way of theoretical explanation as to why children would use two apparently opposing ways to acquire language. Bloom, Lightbown & Hood may be on the right track when they suggest it may be due to alternative hypotheses on what type of language English is. Most recent work attempts to select one or the other procedure as the one children follow. The presentation of the data, however, forces all present investigators who support one of these views to account for the development of the two children who seem to have used the other.

7.4 Current theoretical approaches

The research up to 1976 on early word combinations was characterized by an effort to collect and analyze data from young children. Because of the time-consuming nature of this effort, it resulted in data from a relatively small number of children. It has been pointed out that the subject pool for early Stage I, for example, is particularly small. Also, this research had only begun to work out the methodological problems in analyzing data from such young subjects. On the theoretical side, it laid out the basic alternative explanations, and discussed ways these positions might be proven through the analysis of child data. In the process, it concentrated on the child's creative role in acquisition. The research did not, however, focus on what is the child's learning procedure, given the primary linguistic data.

Much of the research since the mid 1970s has attempted to specify more exactly the steps the child follows to get from the linguistic input to its internal grammar. In doing so, it has concentrated on theoretical specu-lation, with virtually no data collection, at least for the period under discussion. As we will see, most of this research refers back to the data collected in the studies just reviewed, and it is largely because of this fact that these data were presented in relative detail. Much of the new data has been on children beyond this period, often in the form of experimental studies. This is not surprising, in that the concern to account for how the child reaches an adult grammar led people to look at slightly older children. It was influenced also no doubt by the apparent individual variation being shown by the younger children.

While the recent work shares a theoretical emphasis, it does not neces-sarily have a common theoretical orientation. Somewhat simplified, it can be said that approaches differ in the amount of formal grammar assigned to the child's early grammar. Several accounts which assign very little gram-matical knowledge to the child have developed from Braine (1976). One such approach, which is referred to as *functionalism*, proposes that not only does the child begin acquisition with a small set of restricted meanings, but that these meanings may actually evolve into a more elaborate set which underlies the adult grammar. It handles the problem of transition to an abstract syntax by denying the existence of the latter. Braine's later work, for example, attempts to explore the semantic relations of Fillmore's case grammar (Braine & Hardy 1982). Some people have tried to detail how the early restricted formulae lead to more general grammatical categories. We will refer to these as *distributional theories*. They vary from those which reject abstract syntax (Kuczaj 1982a), to others which allow for the possibility of its eventual emergence (Maratsos & Chalkley 1980). A major concern has been to determine a set of procedures which the child applies in acquisition. These procedures take the child through several steps before adult-like rules are established.

Others have argued for the early appearance of abstract syntax, and resemble McNeill's pioneering approach in this regard. These researchers assume the existence of an abstract grammar whose early existence can be predicted on theory-internal grounds. This general orientation was discussed in Chapter 4 under the label of Language Acquisition. One approach of this kind has been referred to as *semantic bootstrapping*. The child begins the acquisition of formal syntax by applying a set of procedures to the first semantic relations, resulting in essentially an immediate syntax. This was proposed in one form by Macnamara (1972, 1982), and by Grimshaw (1981) and Pinker (1984). Another rich interpretation is the *parameter-setting model* of Chomsky (1981), in which the child begins acquisition with a set of innate parameters about what is a possible grammar. Some are unmarked and presumed to exist in the language unless counterevidence is presented. The determination of a particular parameter is an important event for the child because it predicts a range of other characteristics about the language. This model has been applied to language acquisition by Hyams (1983, 1984, 1986), among others. Here we will look at each of these four approaches in more detail.

7.4.1 Functionalism

This is a term which can be traced back to the distinction between 'form' and 'function' in language, where form refers to grammatical properties such as verb agreement, and function refers to the role these play in communication. Functional properties cover a range of things, for example the semantic relations that underlie sentences, the pragmatic intentions of speakers, the influence of cognition on language, and communicative aspects such as informativeness. In its most broad use, functionalism can be said to be the emphasis on the functional properties of language in general, and in our case, in early acquisition. As such it can cover a diversity of studies. We have already discussed a number of works that come under this general use of the term – Halliday's (1975) analysis of the first words and

Brown's (1973) specification of universal semantic relations. Muma (1986) surveys the range of research which comes under this general definition of functionalism.

While a large number of studies can be considered functionalist, the term itself did not become consistently used until around 1979, when it appeared in the title of Karmiloff-Smith's (1979) study of the acquisition of determiners, and in a review of research by Bates & MacWhinney (1979). The latter two in particular have developed the use of the term, as seen in their subsequent review in Bates & MacWhinney (1982). In its broad or descriptive use, functionalism refers to a range of research on pragmatic aspects of language. The recent uses of it, however, are more as an explanatory theory of language.

Bates & MacWhinney (1982)   We can examine functionalism as an explanatory theory by looking at the discussion in Bates & MacWhinney (1982). They contrast two ways of doing psychological research into language. One is to take linguistic theories or models and test their psychological reality; such research, for example, would involve seeing if more complex structures of the grammar do predict greater processing time. Another way is to begin with the study of how people (adults and children) process language, and use this processing as the explanation of the structure of language; i.e., to say that the structure of language is such because of constraints imposed upon it by communicative needs. For example, we have discussed the point that English has a grammatical relation 'subject' which seems to conflate several semantic roles – see (7.13). The formalist may be satisfied with noting this correspondence, and then accounting for the properties of subjects within a formal system; the functionalist, however, wants to explain why such a conflation occurs in the first place. This use of functionalism emphasizes the processing of language, and how this processing determines the form of language.

Bates & MacWhinney offer their own form of functionalism, called the *competition model*. This preliminary model has been influenced by previous research both in linguistics (e.g. Givón 1979), and in child language (e.g. Slobin 1973, 1977; Karmiloff-Smith 1979). The term 'competition' comes from the claim that the functions which underlie language must compete for the small number of possible surface representations. For example, two functions may 'divide the spoils' or share 'peaceful coexistence' (p. 192). If they divide the spoils, then each function maps onto its own surface representation. If they show peaceful coexistence, then they share the same surface manifestation. The results on the use of pronouns and nouns in Bloom, Lightbown & Hood (1975) exemplify these alternatives. Recall from Table 7.21 that Eric and Peter used unique pronouns to mark each semantic relation. This would be a case of choosing to divide the spoils. Kathryn and Gia, on the other hand, show several semantic roles mapped onto the same surface positions in the sentence. This, then, would be peaceful coexistence. Presumably Bates & MacWhinney would account for these two types of pattern as cases where the children differed initially in the way to resolve the competition between their newly acquired functions.

The competition model presented in Bates & MacWhinney (1982), as they admit, is still in a preliminary form. Also, since much of it is devoted to outlining a model of human language processing, there is relatively little detail about the form of either the child's or adult's grammar. They do outline, however, how they see development proceeding from the onset of word combinations to the adult language (pp. 183–7). I will present these speculations in the form of a series of steps to the acquisition of 'subject', with our own labels for each stage:

Step 1: *Establishment of basic functions.* At least two functions seem to be acquired before the onset of syntax: topic–comment, and agent. Topic–comment is a fundamental function for Bates & MacWhinney which underlies much of their acquisitional research. They define these terms as follows (p. 199):

> Topic is defined as what is being talked about, and comment is defined as the point being made about the topic. In other words, the topic–comment system involves a single communicative function of point making, albeit applied in a variety of ways in the service of a variety of motives.

These functions exist in the holophrastic period before the onset of syntax, and thus word order.

Step 2: *Competition of surface representations.* The child seeks to represent these two functions by competing for surface forms. They eventually will either map onto different surface forms (divide the spoils), or the same one (peaceful coexistence). This step will reveal a certain amount of groping and problem solving. The surface forms available in any language are limited, due to acoustic–articulatory restrictions, to one or a combination of the following four choices (p. 190): 1. lexical items, 2. word-order patterns, 3. morphological markings, and 4. intonational contours. Research from Bates & MacWhinney (1979) indicates that the language being acquired influences the patterns of this step. For example, Hungarian and Italian children first show a comment-topic sequence, whereas English children show agent-action sequences. These two examples indicate an important claim of functionalism which is summarized as follows: *initially, maps single forms onto single functions.* This was argued for in Karmiloff-Smith (1979) where the multifunctional nature of determiners was only acquired after an initial period of assigning them to single functions.

Step 3: *Acquisition of the adult system of mappings.* True competition occurs as the child needs to map all functions onto the surface through either peaceful existence or dividing the spoils. Abstraction of the category 'subject' happens through a process to be determined.

A theoretical issue arises in step 3 as to whether or not this step also involves the abstraction of purely formal categories such as 'subject'. Bates & MacWhinney mention the theories that have tried to do this, and we will examine some of these later in this section. They are dubious, however, about the postulation of abstract formal categories in the first place. They discuss the discontinuity involved in shifting from semantic to syntactic categories, which they call the *developmental shift hypothesis*. Their own preference, however, is to form a fully functional adult grammar: 'In the final and most radical functionalist view, the categories of adult grammar retain their full functionalist definitions' (p. 187). This position is based upon an assumed Constructionist Assumption.

Much of the research on functionalism in recent years has been on children beyond the period of the first word combinations. Functionalist accounts of early word combinations tend to be somewhat general, as in the three steps just discussed. This account assigns little in the way of grammatical knowledge to the child, and accounts for the child's first sequences of words in terms of functional categories such as topic–comment. A similar view, for example, which argues for early sequences on the basis of 'informativeness', can be found in Greenfield & Zukow (1978). The functionalist view is also marked by a commitment to developing a theory of grammar which is quite distinct from those characterized by the postulation of abstract syntax.

As an account of early word combinations, there seems to be an important aspect that needs further elaboration. The theory claims that children begin acquisition with a set of basic functions. If so, one would expect that the functions would be constant across children, and thus also their early grammars. The example discussed above, however, indicates that there are cross-linguistic differences in this regard. For this to be the case, the child will need to have done some formal analyses of the input language to determine the formal means in it for marking a particular function. However, we are not told the procedures the child follows to select any particular formal means over another, nor anything about the potential individual variation that may occur, given the child's ability to grope for forms. The early appearance of cross-linguistic differences actually seems to support claims for early distributional analysis of the input.

Such apparently contradictory data also appear in Karmiloff-Smith (1979). As part of a large sample cross-sectional study of French children, Karmiloff-Smith examined children's ability to use the gender distinction in French articles. French articles distinguish two genders, masculine and feminine, although its use with nouns is more arbitrary than semantic. For example, tables, rain, and music are feminine while dogs, mountains, and milk are masculine. The appearance of the two classes of articles, however, is partly determined by phonological properties of the words, i.e. by formal means. One would expect from the functionalist view that children would first use the articles in a semantic way, and later learn their formal properties. The results, however, indicated that the first uses of the articles were formal rather than semantic. That is, the children showed awareness of the phonological properties of nouns which occur with the articles before an awareness of their semantic features. Results like these indicate that the interaction of distributional learning and functional mapping within this theory needs more clarification than exists to date.

7.4.2 Distributional learning

We need to be careful when discussing a model of acquisition as one which can be characterized by distributional learning; all theories will need to account for it in some way. The issue is one of when this learning begins and how it proceeds. Semantically oriented approaches like functionalism and semantic bootstrapping propose that semantic categories occur first and provide the basis for the onset of distributional learning. We are reserving the term distributional learning for those approaches which allow for distributional learning at the onset of acquisition, and which even allow for it to account for semantic development. Braine's models are examples of an approach of this kind.

Current approaches based on distributional learning have explored how the child might move from restricted formulae of the kind discussed by Braine to the categories of the adult language. These approaches character-istically propose procedures on how the child builds more general cate-gories out of more specific ones. As such, they propose models which probably could be incorporated into the semantically oriented ones, at least once the latter begin to allow for more formal acquisition. Here we will consider two studies which have tried to determine procedures of this kind: MacWhinney (1982), and Maratsos & Chalkley (1980).

MacWhinney (1982) In an earlier study, MacWhinney (1978) developed a computational model for the acquisition of morphophonology. The present paper was an attempt to extend those ideas to the acquisition of early word combinations. The earlier work even provided flow charts to demonstrate the learning procedure presented. The major feature of both approaches is the claim that the child follows an ordered set of strategies to acquire language. As is typical of computer models, these strategies are discussed in terms of the capabilities of the model, not necessarily of the child's psychological state. The success of such a model to account for the acquisition data, however, can be used to infer its psychological validity.

MacWhinney's model consists of three processing mechanisms: rote, analogy, and combination. The latter mechanism can be broken down further into four strategies, resulting in the six strategies which MacWhinney suggests allow the child to develop from very restricted to productive grammars.

The first strategy is *rote*. This refers to the claim which has appeared in various places in the literature that many of the child's first sentences are simply internalized imitations of parts of the adult language (e.g. R. Clark 1977, 1982; Peters 1983). These may range from obvious ones used in games and ritual situations to less obvious ones that could mistakenly be identified as productive sentences. It is the concern for possible rote sentences, in fact, which underlies some of the criticism of Bloom's (1970) productivity measure. MacWhinney argues that rote can also explain some of the well-known errors made by children, such as redundant pronouns, e.g. 'have it egg' (Braine 1976: 36) and redundant auxiliaries, e.g. 'what's that is' (Hurford 1975: 300). Examples such as these are often presumed to be rule-based and have led to claims about the nature of the child's grammar. It may also be, however, that they are simply the combination of a memorized unit such as 'have it' or 'what's that' with another word. The methodological procedures to be presented in section 7.5 attempt to isolate such rote forms in early samples.

While rote may play a role in holding forms in memory or for idioms in the adult language, it will yield to procedures for building up rules. The first primitive rules are developed in MacWhinney's model by the process of *analogy*. These are very limited in that they consist of breaking up a rote form into at least two parts and replacing one of them with another lexical item. MacWhinney cites an example from R. Clark (1974) of a child who said 'wait for it to dry', a purported analogy from 'wait for it to cool'. Another example given is the child who says 'I are' in response to the adult question 'Are you?'. These are distinguished from the combinations produced by the next procedures by being limited to pairs of lexical items, although MacWhinney acknowledges that the difference between analogies and combinations is not a sharp one.

The next four procedures all fall under the general category of combination. *Combination* refers to 'the set of principles that serves to transform an unordered string of lexical items into an ordered string' (p. 91). Four such procedures are presented in increasing order of generality.

MacWhinney proposes that the first causes for the ordering of lexical items in early word combinations are non-syntactic factors. Their order is determined by several functional *dispositions* which order words in particular ways. The claim that these are the first influences on word order reflects the functional influence on MacWhinney's work. Some of the dispositions that can affect word order in these early combinations are as follows:

(a) *informativeness* – the first item in the combination will be the one which is the newest or most informative;
(b) *complexity* – short, simple words precede long, complex ones;
(c) *agency* – nominals which are agents tend to precede other roles;
(d) *perspective* – the first item will tend to be an item with which the child can identify.

These and other dispositions are given with limited information on how they interact and affect any particular set of child data.

The next procedure creates *bound* or *item-based patterns*. These are the pivot-like combinations that were described as restricted formulae in Braine (1976). Our discussion of the latter work should be sufficient for providing an idea of what such combinations are like. Their occurrence in this set of procedures represents the onset of distributional learning. The implications are similar to those of Braine – they suggest that the child notes the positional properties of specific words and uses these to determine the grammatical patterns of the language being acquired.

Item-based patterns lead to more complex ones, which MacWhinney calls *free patterns*. These result from rules which combine words based on general semantic features such as Agent and Action. Unlike item-based patterns, these ones are not lexically restricted to specific words. Any word which has the semantic properties to be an agent can enter into such a pattern. The proposal that these patterns are seen to develop after more limited item-based ones is a major feature of distributional learning theories. The distributional properties of the previous patterns presumably aid in the eventual formation of the more general semantic ones. MacWhinney is not clear in how he sees the interaction of these two kinds of patterns in acquisition, but the discussion suggests that free patterns are the later development.

The last patterns are those which MacWhinney refers to as *class-bound positional patterns*. These are word combinations which result from rules which refer to grammatical features. Such rules take the distributional properties of a word into consideration, and presumably can refer to aspects such as 'subject'. Being a functionalist in orientation, MacWhinney is not overly enthusiastic about proposing that the child actually ever acquires rules of this sort. The point appears to be that such rules are more complex and should be acquired last, if such rules exist in language in the first place.

MacWhinney's presentation of these six kinds of pattern provides a useful taxonomy for the discussion of possible procedures for the acquisition of grammatical structure. As stated, the attempt to determine patterns which go from specific to general learning are characteristic of distributional models. Also, these patterns appear such, in that distributional patterns are suggested as preceding more general semantic ones. This approach differs from functionalism and semantic bootstrapping which see the acquisition of the general semantic categories as preceding any distributional knowledge. MacWhinney, however, does not elaborate on how the sequence of patterns emerges or interacts. A more detailed attempt to do this is the work of Maratsos & Chalkley (1980).

Maratsos & Chalkley (1980)   This long paper has become the most commonly cited approach attempting to outline how distributional learning can take the child from specific knowledge about individual lexical items to broad grammatical categories. A summary of some of its points can be found in Maratsos (1982). Its presentation here combines the views of both of these papers on the acquisition of rules of word combination and of grammatical classes.

Like other recent studies, Maratsos & Chalkley (1980) present a theoretical model based on their interpretations of data collected by the earlier studies. Much of the work deals with acquisition in older children, and particularly the acquisition of gender in German. There is, however, a reasonably detailed later section on early development. Maratsos & Chalkley do not work from a current model of grammar, but they do have definite ideas about the nature of the adult language. They see language as consisting of classes that are defined in large part by their distributional properties: 'It is probable that what are called syntactic categories, such as verb, adjective, or gender class, are so called because they rest on differentiation among themselves by partly distributional distinctions among the sets of correlated semantic-distributional patterns in which their members appear'. For example, a verb such as 'spill' is not just defined as an 'action' word, but also as a word which takes the progressive '-ing' suffix, the present tense suffix '-s', and the past tense suffix '-ed'. The child's goal, then, is the discovery of these distributional properties.

As with our discussion of functionalism, we will present what we see as the steps in this model for the acquisition of grammatical knowledge (the authors do not actually present numbered steps as here, although they do talk about sequences of development).

Step 1: *Identification of individual morphemes.* Use phonological, semantic, and lexical properties of sentences to identify the separate morphemes in utterances. Little is said as to how this takes place but it is an important step in all theories of acquisition.

Step 2: *Formation of the first semantic-distributional patterns.* The initial patterns have a form:

(7.15)

Pattern 1 (... Category X ...)

|

Word A

This states that the child has noted some property for an individual word (word A), and thus assigns this word to a preliminary category (category X). The specification of the category as X is important because the child's categories are not predetermined by Universal Grammar to be highly restricted at the onset to noun, verb, or some other universal category. Depending on the number of properties noted, the child may begin with several restricted patterns. The first properties of these early categories are likely to be positional ones such as 'occurs with "it"', or some other word. Each category which occurs is noted as a separate pattern. The first categories are restricted to individual words, that is, they are not general.

Step 3A: *The strengthening of patterns.* Patterns become strengthened in two ways. One is through the identification in the input of known words in their previously established semantic-distributional pattern. The other way is through the addition of new words to a pattern when those words are seen to have the same categorical property. This generalization can be represented as:

(7.16)

Pattern 1 (... Category X ...)

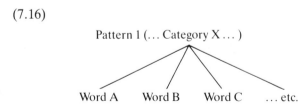

Word A   Word B   Word C   ... etc.

The idea of strengthening is an adaptation of an original idea in Braine (1971a).

Step 3B: *The establishment of pathways between patterns.* We label this step 3B because Maratsos & Chalkley claim that it occurs simultaneously with step 3A. At this time individual lexical items are being identified as belonging to more than just one category. The diagram in (7.17) shows the development of pathways in this fashion:

(7.17)

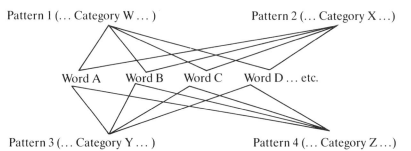

Pattern 1 (... Category W ...)   Pattern 2 (... Category X ...)

Word A   Word B   Word C   Word D ... etc.

Pattern 3 (... Category Y ...)   Pattern 4 (... Category Z ...)

These interconnected pathways become strengthened as more lexical connections occur, as in step 3A.

Step 4A: *Pattern generalization and overgeneralization.*   Once patterns are sufficiently strengthened or established, they 'continually seek for occasions for application, depending on their own proportional frequency of use' (p. 193). One way which this occurs is in overgeneralizations such as saying 'knowed' instead of 'know'. Suppose that the English past tense morpheme defines category W in (7.17). A new word such as 'know' may be first identified with categories X, Y, and Z, and thus enter into this network of connections. Once so identified, 'know' can then be connected with category W without previous experience with its having this property. An important part of this step is determining how many connections are necessary for a new word to become part of a network of connections. Maratsos & Chalkley believe that this eventually will happen even after just one connection, in large part due to the extensive redundancy that exists in such a system. Three factors interact to determine how words are connected to new patterns. These are (i) *frequency* – how often the established words in a network, e.g. words A to D in (7.17), are used in all the categories; (ii) *variety* – how many different pathways are shared by the categories; and (iii) *directness* – the extent to which categories are connected through the same lexical items.

Step 4B: *The inhibition of overgeneralizations.*   While the model will account for a large number of generalizations of words to new patterns, it also predicts a large number of overgeneralizations which are not part of the adult grammar. For example, noting that both 'spill' and 'call up' are actions could lead the child to connect 'call up' to the past tense category and say 'call upped'. Simultaneously with the generalization of patterns are restrictions or inhibitions. One factor which will restrict generalization is *accuracy*. This is the extent to which a pattern which is established for a new word has direct connections to another pattern. This is shown in (7.18):

(7.18)

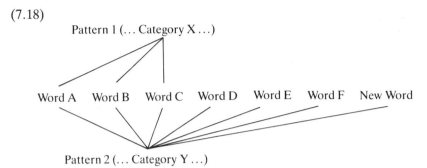

Here all the words, including the new one, have been connected with pattern 2. There are only three direct connections, however, between patterns 2 and 1 (words A, B, and C). The connection would not be accurate enough (by measures to be determined) for the new word to overgeneralize to pattern 1. The accuracy requirement predicts that certain overgeneralizations should never occur.

Step 5: *The correction of overgeneralizations.* Accuracy is not sufficient to prevent overgeneralizations from occurring occasionally: examples are well-documented in the child language literature, e.g. 'foots', 'knowed', etc . . . The child needs to correct those which occur. Maratsos & Chalkley propose that this is done through indirect negative evidence. That is, the child keeps track of the number of times he or she does or doesn't hear a word appearing with a particular grammatical property. For example, once the child never hears 'know' occurring in the past with '-ed', he or she records as part of the lexical information for this morpheme that it is restricted from doing so. They refer to these as *positive inhibitory blocks*.

Maratsos (1982) provides an example of how the child follows these steps through his early word combinations. Using a slightly modified terminology, Maratsos begins his example with the child acquiring the sentence 'daddy walk' with the meaning 'that daddy moves himself along by movement of the lower limbs' (p. 256). This would be step 2, when the child forms a restricted semantic-distributional pattern. The pattern consists of two 'sequential loci or slots' (p. 256), with each slot defined by the properties of the terms which can occur within the slot. (7.19) provides the structure of this initial pattern:

(7.19)   X   +   Y
           | |
         daddy   walk

This is somewhat different from the discussion in Maratsos & Chalkley where one of the morphemes would be the category (e.g. category X), and the other would be its defining property. Here the defining property is also assigned categorical status.

Step 3A occurs when the child next acquires 'mommy walk'. The words 'mommy' and 'daddy' become members of the emerging category of things that can walk. With the addition of other words, it can become 'an individual word formula' (p. 257) with the structure of 'walker+walk'. the Y class can also expand in this manner, so that the eventual pattern may have the meaning of 'mover+movement'. Maratsos points out that the child will be restricted in building a broader category from comparisons of 'daddy walk' and 'daddy chair' with a possessive meaning. Maratsos states (p. 258): 'The scheme thus builds grammatical categories on the basis of overall sequential similarity, but also on the basis of semantic function and analysis of parts of the sequence. It is hence not a purely distributional analysis.' No details are given, however, on the semantic properties that the child will use to restrict such broader categories, and the example is not carried on through any further developments.

Assessment.   The work by Maratsos & Chalkley is a relatively detailed attempt to follow acquisition after the early restricted formulae proposed by Braine (1976) and to see how the child could develop adult categories. Interestingly, it led them to a position that the adult grammar may consist of complex networks of semantic-distributional patterns, with general terms such as noun, verb, and subject being unnecessary: it is an ultimate example of using child language data and something like the Constructionist Assumption to develop a theory about the adult language.

Much of the demonstration of how such learning proceeds was done with examples of the acquisition of grammatical morphemes to define grammatical classes. For example, we discussed the proposed steps with examples of the acquisition of categories such as words which take '-ed', '-ing', etc. (i.e. potential verbs). There is relatively little discussion on how general sentential relations such as 'subject–predicate' (or the equivalent in their theory) are acquired in relation to the acquisition of grammatical classes. For example, do relations like agent–action precede, follow, or occur simultaneously and independently with emerging patterns like 'words which take "-ed"'? This is an important issue, as we will see in our discussion of semantic bootstrapping, where semantic relations are claimed to precede distributional learning. Maratsos (1982: 263) points out this problem, among others, for his theory at this point in its development. He states (p. 265): 'These problems indicate that considerable empirical and theoretical analysis is required before we can be said to have any good idea of plausible complete accounts of formal category formation.'

Pinker (1984) presents two arguments against the semantic-distributional model of Maratsos & Chalkley. The first is what he refers to as the *learnability argument*. This is the claim that the child in this model will require some form of negative evidence in order to acquire the adult language. We have already discussed the problems with negative evidence in Chapter 2, and how Maratsos & Chalkley propose it in Step 5. The problem of how children acquire language without negative evidence is a serious one for a number of approaches in both grammatical theory and acquisition (see Lightfoot 1982: Chapter 2). Pinker's second argument is the *efficiency argument*. Without better-defined measures of how patterns correlate with each other, the number of potential patterns is enormous. The theory as it now stands requires a tremendous amount of computation and thus memory for it to take place. Pinker's own solution to these problems, as well as many others, is to restrict the range of possible solutions in language acquisition to a limited number which are innately endowed. The next section examines the views of Pinker, as well as of others who assign a richer syntactic structure to the young child.

7.4.3 Semantic bootstrapping

At first glance, the term semantic bootstrapping looks like part of an acquisition theory which evolved out of the research on semantically oriented grammars. As we will see, however, this is far from the case. The latter work has attempted to develop theories in which the child acquires a set of semantic relations and functions, not a formal syntax. Semantic bootstrapping, however, is an acquisition procedure needed for theories which want to show the acquisition of abstract grammatical categories and relations. The acquisition problem for any theory of abstract syntax is how the child determines the language-specific features of the language being acquired. For example, how do children come to know what are the subjects and VPs in sentences? The answer to this dilemma for the preceding approaches which believe in abstract syntax is semantic bootstrapping. The formal grammatical properties are triggered by the appearance of certain semantic properties. Using terminology from computer technology, the claim is that semantics 'boots' the child's syntax into operation.

Until the term semantic bootstrapping was created, this process was more assumed than expressed. For example, McNeill's model of acquisition requires some way for the child to form categories like subject NP and VP from the early meanings of the child's utterances. The process of semantic bootstrapping is also implied in the work by Bloom, Lightbown & Hood (1975) where the category 'subject' emerges through the gradual broadening of the first subjects to more and more semantic categories. For this to occur, subject would have to be 'triggered' by the first one or two semantic relations acquired.

The most explicit statement of semantic bootstrapping in the older literature is in Macnamara (1972). Macnamara begins with the assumption that the child first acquires the meanings of individual words, much like step 1 in the discussion of Maratsos & Chalkley. This happens as the child seeks word forms to represent semantic notions like specific and general nominals. Then, the child develops combinations of meanings or semantic relations of the kind which we have considered at various points in this section. The child uses these meanings to acquire the syntax of the language. It is at this point that Macnamara makes a somewhat vague suggestion which could be interpreted as semantic bootstrapping. He states (p. 395) that the child '. . . might, for example, suppose that a single semantic relationship would always be expressed by means of a single syntactic device or structure'. The crucial question here is whether Macnamara wants to claim that all children are innately endowed to map the same single semantic relations into the same single or limited set of syntactic devices. For example, do certain semantic relations like 'Action' always map into a predetermined syntactic category such as VP? This point is never clarified or elaborated upon.

It is only in the most recent literature that the claims of semantic bootstrapping have been made more explicit, and even these attempts have not been widespread. Macnamara (1982), among many things, expands his original ideas on how semantics leads to syntax, focussing on the development of categories like noun and verb from semantic notions like object and action. Some preliminary ideas on how syntactic structures follow from semantic ones can be found in Grimshaw (1981). Marantz (1982, 1983) has discussed two routes in which semantic bootstrapping could logically proceed. Here, however, we will concentrate on what is clearly the most detailed effort to develop a model along these lines, that of Pinker (1984).

Pinker (1984) This is a major work which examines the acquisition of a wide range of grammatical phenomena including inflections, complementation, auxiliaries, and lexical entries. We will limit our treatment to his explanation of the first grammatical acquisition of the child, the acquisition of phrase structure rules for Stage I.

Pinker begins with laying out his assumptions about acquisition, the first of which is the *learnability condition*. Pinker states (p. 5): '. . . we may view the child's abilities at any stage of development as a way-station in a process that takes the child from a state at which he or she knows nothing about the target language to a state at which he or she has acquired the language completely'. The learnability condition has two parts. First, acquisition will need to occur through the interaction of an acquisition mechanism which begins with no knowledge about the target language and obtains this knowledge from the linguistic input. This aspect of the condition takes the position that acquisition must be accounted for by only positive evidence. Second, the acquisition mechanism will need to be able to arrive at the adult grammar through its exposure to the input. This condition expresses the concern of recent approaches to take the child beyond the apparently idiosyncratic features of the early word combinations to the adult grammar.

While the learnability condition requires continuity in development, it still could allow for some restructuring during acquisition. The second condition, however, the *continuity condition*, restricts this greatly. It states that the most highly valued or explanatory theory will be the one which posits the least number of mechanisms to get the child from the first stage of acquisition to the last. 'As Macnamara (1982) has put it, the null hypothesis in developmental psychology is that the cognitive mechanisms of children and adults are identical; hence it is a hypothesis that should not be rejected until the data leave us no other choice' (Pinker 1984: 7). Importantly, the condition does not eliminate the possibility that the child may have a grammar at some point which will be different from the adult one being acquired. This would be the marked case, however, requiring the investigator to propose a mechanism that manages to get the child back to the adult grammar. In practice, however, Pinker does not explore this possibility. Instead, he assumes that 'the child's grammatical rules should be drawn from the same basic rule types, and be composed of primitive symbols from the same class, as the grammatical rules attributed to adults in standard linguistic investigations' (p. 7).

These two conditions combine to define a theoretical approach which is similar to what was called in Chapter 4 the strong inclusion hypothesis. The child's grammar from the onset looks very similar to, and is a subpart of, the adult one. The conditions are also stronger than the Constructionist Assumption, which resembles the learnability condition. We did not make any assumptions at the onset, however, to restrict the extent of restructuring to the degree that the continuity condition does.

As is characteristic of maturational theories like Pinker's and others to be discussed, Pinker selects a current grammatical theory to describe the grammar that the child is acquiring. The theory selected is that of Lexical Functional Grammar (or LFG as it is commonly called), as developed in Bresnan (1978, 1982). One main feature of this theory is that it does not map deep structures onto surface structures via transformations as does Chomsky's Standard Theory (Chomsky 1965). Instead, each sentence has only one constituent structure which is generated by the phrase structure rules. To use the terminology of the Standard Theory, the surface structure is the deep structure. In such a theory, the notion of level of representation is meaningless. The phrase structure configurations are similar to those of the Standard Theory, except that grammatical functions like subject are indicated on categories like NP and VP. That is, the subject is not just the NP under S as in the Standard Theory, but it is indicated as NP_{subj}. A second feature of the theory is that there is also a separate functional structure which combines the functional information which is indicated on the grammatical categories of the phrase structure with the information in the individual lexical items in the sentence. The role of the lexicon is quite substantial in this theory, with the lexicon accounting for many of the grammatical aspects previously handled by transformations. For example, there is no longer a Passive transformation, but instead separate lexical entries for forms of verbs which can occur in passive sentences.

One appeal of LFG (at least to some people) is its psychological plausibility. Acquisition will consist primarily of establishing the phrase structure of sentences and the lexical features of words. Since the only structure to be acquired is that of the surface structure, the theory does not present the problem of how the child reconstructs a deep structure from a surface structure and acquires the complex set of transformations that operate between the two. Also, it places most of acquisition on acquiring information about words. Lexically oriented theories are relatively better at dealing with individual variation and the specific kinds of learning observed in Braine (1976). While children probably hear relatively similar distributions of construction types, their experience with individual words probably varies more. While Pinker selects LFG as his grammatical theory, he points out that the general features of his acquisition model are applicable to other grammatical theories as well.

In general terms, acquisition begins with semantic categories and relations. Semantic bootstrapping can be defined as follows (p. 40): 'The categorization of words can be inferred from their semantic properties, and their grammatical relations can be inferred from the semantic relations in the event witnessed.' Pinker's Table 2.1 gives a tentative list of some of the syntactic categories that are booted in this way. A selection of these is given in Table 7.21. These correspondences are innate in the child: that is, once the child acquires the relevant semantic notion, then the syntactic property appears. For example, the young child, possibly in the holophrastic stage, who says 'daddy' as a specific nominal will automatically assign the feature [+noun] to the word. This is true for all of the correspondences in Table 7.21. The child's semantic notion will also lead to phrase structure information. The example under configurations claims that once the child

Table 7.21 *Some syntactic properties and the semantic knowledge which leads to their inference, selected from Pinker (1984: Table 2.1)*

Syntactic properties	Semantic basis categories
Categories	
noun	Name of person or thing
verb	Action or change of state
adjective	Attribute
preposition	Spatial relation, path, or direction
sentence	Main proposition
Functions	
subject	Agent of action; cause of causal event; subject of an attribution of location, state, or circumstance
object	Patient or Theme
oblique	Source, Goal, Location, Instrument
Cases	
nominative	Agent of transitive action
accusative	Patient of transitive action
dative	Goal or Beneficiary
Features	
tense	Relative times of event, speech act, and reference point
aspect	Durativity
Configurations	
sister of X	Argument of X

relates two semantic notions such that one is an argument of the other, the child places them into a phrase structure configuration. For example, Agents are arguments of Actions. The corresponding syntactic categories, noun and verb, will therefore be sisters, i.e. attached to the node, in this case S. If this looks familiar it should be; we saw a similar claim in McNeill (1970b), exemplified in more detail in (7.9).

Up to this point, the approach looks very much like a combination of the insights on semantic bootstrapping of Macnamara (1972) and the claims about syntactic structure of McNeill (1970b), with supporting evidence in the data in Bloom, Lightbown & Hood (1975). Pinker goes on, however, to address the crucial issue of how the child acquires the particular grammatical properties in languages. Different types of languages are discussed, but we will limit the examples to two problems in acquiring English.

Two potential problems for the English-learning child are predicate adjectives and oblique preposition phrases. (7.20) gives examples of each with a simple phrase structure configuration of the adult structure for the italicized part of each sentence:

(7.20)   a. *Predicate adjective*   b. *Oblique prepositional phrase*
           'The dog is big'   'I went to the store'

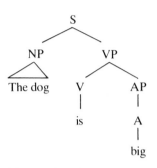

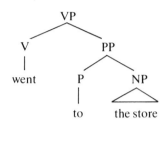

The problem pointed out by Pinker is how to describe the grammar of the child who says 'dog big' and 'go store' with the same intended meaning as the adult sentences. Since the child does not have either the copula 'is' or the preposition 'to', there is no evidence for the adult structures in (7.20). Based on the child's sentences, the child could just as well have the structures in (7.21):

(7.21)

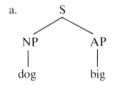

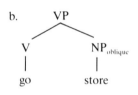

The sentence 'go store', for example, would be similar to the adult phrase 'go home' which would have the structure of (7.21b). We also need to account for how the child gets from categories like noun to phrases like noun phrase (NP).

Pinker proposes a series of procedures that take the child from the initial acquisition of semantics to syntactic structures. We will demonstrate these in the same way as earlier, by defining a series of steps. (Pinker does not provide labeled steps, but labels them as a series of procedures – P1 through P6. We will give his procedures in the appropriate steps.) These will be demonstrated by following through the acquisition of the structures in (7.20) by a child who has only 'dog big' and 'go store' at the onset.

Step 1: *Acquisition of basic semantic notions.*   This will be a subset of those shown in Table 7.21. We assume in our example that the child has acquired Proposition, Name of person or thing, Action, Attribute, Agent, Theme (the future subject of the sentence 'dog big'), Goal, and Argument of X.

Step 2: *Semantic bootstrapping.* The child assigns syntactic properties as shown in Table 7.21. The child has thus also acquired the syntactic properties of sentence, noun, verb, adjective, subject, object, oblique, and sister of X. These properties will allow the child to process a number of simple sentences as determined by the following procedures.

Step 3: *Application of existing phrase structure rules (P1).* Trees for sentences are understood and produced by the syntactic properties available from step 2. Presumably these may include rules for word order. The sentence 'dog go', for example, will have the structure in (7.22a):

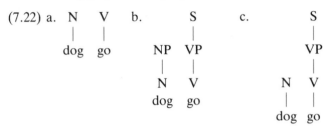

Step 4: *Apply X-bar theory (P2).* X-bar theory refers to work since Jackendoff (1977) to impose general conditions on grammatical categories. Simply stated, it proposes that all categories share the same phrase structure properties. For example, all Xs (where X=category) belong to a higher category X-bar (usually shown as $\bar{X}$). The X-bar for lexical categories like N and V are phrases such as NP and VP. Within this theory, the higher category of a VP is S. This step imposes this theory onto the child's grammar so that phrases are generated over the child's lexical categories in the tree. The results of this step for our example are shown in (7.22b). (See Radford 1981 for an introduction to X-bar theory.) While Pinker proposes this step, he does allow for the possibility of restricting it to apply only if there is evidence for the proposed phrases in the data (p. 108). If we apply this adjusted P2, then our child would still only have the structure in (7.22a) for NP since there is no evidence for the phrase, i.e. there are no adjective–noun or determiner–noun constructions. There is evidence, however, for the VP in that the child has the relation Object. Let's assume that such is the case and that she can produce sentences such as 'eat apple'. Also, we have evidence for S since the child has the notion of Proposition. This would then give us the structure in (7.22c).

Step 5: *The assignment of grammatical functions (P3).* Functions like subject and object are added to the syntactic categories in the tree, again based on the correlations from Table 7.21. These functions are used in the next step to connect categories to their appropriate nodes, for example subjects to the S node, and objects to the VP node. The application of this step to our example results in (7.23a):

(7.23) a.   b.

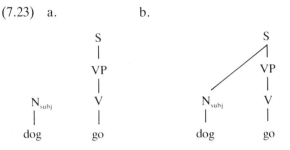

Step 6: *Connection of unattached branches (P4).* Connect all unattached branches to their appropriate categories based on their configurations. Subjects, for example, will attach to S. This gives us (7.23b).

It is at this point that our child runs into a problem with its sentences 'dog
big' and 'go store'. After step 5, they will have the structures in (7.24a) and
(7.24b) respectively (ignoring the broken lines for now). (Pinker represents
the critical nodes as AP and NP but the restricted form of P2 should leave
these as A and N in our example. We will use A and N, but the arguments
equally hold for AP and NP.) The problem is that the child does have more
than one option available for the attachment of the A and $N_{oblique}$ since
neither the copula nor the preposition are yet acquired to guide their
attachment. The A could attach to either S or VP, and the $N_{oblique}$ to either
VP or a newly created PP. Pinker refers to categories in this situation as
orphans. He does not wish to create lexically unfilled categories, for two
reasons: such categories would not be substantiated by the child's data (a
violation of the Competence Assumption), and, more seriously, they might
lead to the creation of categories which do not exist in the language.
Pinker's solution to this problem is to give orphans special marking (in our
example ?A? and $?N?_{oblique}$ respectively), and assign them temporarily to
an *ancestor* node. These connections are shown with the broken lines in
(7.24). We will return to the question of how orphans are assigned
eventually to the correct English nodes.

(7.24) a.   b.)

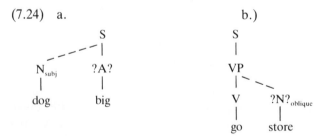

Step 7: *Creation and strengthening of phrase structure rules
(P5).* Create phrase structure rules that will produce the tree which has

been built. If rules already exist, then strengthen them. This latter process is similar to rule 3A in Maratsos & Chalkley. In our example, this step leads to the following rules:

(7.25)
  a. $S \longrightarrow \quad N_{subj} \left\{ \begin{array}{l} VP \\ ?A? \end{array} \right\}$

  b. $VP \longrightarrow \quad V \left\{ \begin{array}{l} ?N?_{oblique} \\ N_{object} \end{array} \right\}$

These rules will account for the four sentences that we have used so far: 'dog go', 'eat apple', 'dog big' and 'go store'. As can be seen, the orphans are marked differently from the other categories.

Step 8: *Lexical storage and strengthening (L1).*   Add new words to the lexicon with information about their grammatical properties. Verbs, for example, will be entered with information about the complements which they may take. Entries which already exist are strengthened.

Step 9: *The collapsing of rules (P6).*   This procedure operates when a new rule is added to the phrase structure which already has a rule which expands the same category. For example, if the new rule is as in (7.25a) and the old rule is (7.25b), then this procedure will collapse them to (7.26c). Pinker provides a number of proposals on how collapsing takes place.

(7.26)   a. $VP \longrightarrow \quad PP$
    b. $VP \longrightarrow \quad NP$
    c. $VP \longrightarrow \quad \left\{ \begin{array}{l} PP \\ NP \end{array} \right\}$

We can now return to a discussion of how the child will adjust the status of the orphans and reassign the orphans to their appropriate place in the tree. Using the acquisition of prepositions as our example, it will happen as follows. First, let's assume that our young language learner acquires the sentence 'go to store'. In step 2, he or she identifies 'to' as a preposition according to its semantic properties listed in Table 7.21. Step 3 (or P1) allows the child to make the tree in (7.27a), since it now has the rules in (7.25). Step 4 (or P2) then creates a PP (prepositional phrase node) above the P, as in (7.27b). Such an expansion is allowed on the grounds that there is a constituent present, i.e. 'store', which can function as the object of the preposition. This structure creates a problem, however, when we come to step 6 (or P4) and have to attach the PP to the VP. Since the ?N? is already attached to VP, it needs to be detached and placed within the PP. Pinker adds a condition to P4 (p. 104) that orphan nodes are replaced by a new node (in our case PP) when the new node has the same structural relation to the ancestor node (in our case VP) as the orphan. This then results in (7.27c).

(7.27) a.   b.   c.

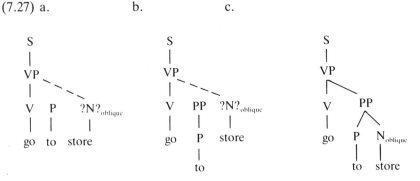

In my introduction to Pinker's assumption about acquisition, I reviewed his continuity condition which assumes that child and adult grammars are the same unless evidence shows otherwise. The orphans are such a situation, since the child needs to restructure its grammar once the prepositions are acquired. Such a restructuring would not be allowed under our Constructionist Assumption, which requires that rules be retained once they are formed. In this case we could claim that the rule in (7.25b) is retained for oblique NPs, and used for phrases such as 'go home'. Pinker considers, and rejects, the possibility that the child adds a new rule and maintains the old one. Instead, he argues that the child is constrained by a *uniqueness principle* from maintaining two rules to produce the same function. This, admittedly vague, principle claims that the child, when presented with alternative rules to represent the same function, will only use the one for which positive evidence exists. In his account, rule (7.25b) is deleted from the grammar, replaced with the one created from the structure in (7.27c) by P5. The uniqueness principle, an innate property of the language acquisition device, forces the child to do this. The new rules are shown in (7.28). P6 will collapse the new rule with the old rule which generates object NPs as in (7.28a).

(7.28)
  a. $VP \longrightarrow \left\{ \begin{array}{l} NP_{obj} \\ PP \end{array} \right\}$

  b. $PP \longrightarrow P\ NP$

The initial semantic bootstrapping is followed by what Pinker calls *structure-dependent distributional learning*. This is needed for acquisition of the aspects of the language which are not semantically transparent. For example, not all nouns are objects ('flight'), and not all subjects are agents ('John received a parcel'). Grammatical morphemes, like the articles and verb inflections, can in turn be used by the child to identify abstract nouns and verbs. This occurs through a procedure referred to as D1. Here we will label this step 10:

Table 7.22 *Pinker's LFG grammar for late Stage I, from Pinker (1984: 11), with examples of possible utterances*

Grammar			Examples
S ⟶	NP$_{subj}$	$\left\{\begin{array}{l} \text{VP} \\ \text{?P?} \\ \text{?A?} \\ \text{?NP?} \end{array}\right.$	$\left.\begin{array}{l} \text{'mommy fix'} \\ \text{'tree there'} \\ \text{'pillow dirty'} \\ \text{'that man'} \end{array}\right\}$
NP ⟶	$\left\{\begin{array}{l} \text{N}_{poss} \\ \text{A}_{mod} \\ \text{Q}_{quant} \end{array}\right.$	$\left.\begin{array}{l} \text{N} \\ \\ \\ \end{array}\right\}$	$\begin{array}{l} \text{'mommy soup'} \\ \text{'pretty boat'} \\ \text{'more tree'} \end{array}$
VP ⟶	V (NP$_{obj}$)	$\left\{\begin{array}{l} \text{P}_{adj} \\ \text{NP}_{obj2} \\ \text{N}_{oblique} \\ \text{N}_{adj} \end{array}\right.$	$\left.\begin{array}{l} \text{'put book here'} \\ \text{'give food doggie'} \\ \text{'put truck window'} \\ \text{'take baby downstairs'} \end{array}\right\}$

Step 10: *Distributional learning.* If a new word or phrase has the same distributional properties as an acquired word or phrase, assign the new word or phrase to the category of the acquired one. Pinker is purposely vague on when this operation begins. He says at one point that it could begin as soon as the second sentence heard (p. 53). More likely, however, 'one expects the accretion of rules (and possibly the strengthening of rules) to be slow enough that large amounts of structure-dependent distributional learning do not follow the very first acquisitions' (p. 56). It depends, in large part, on the acquisition of grammatical morphemes, yet, as we will see, Pinker does not see these as being part of the Stage I grammar. For this reason we have placed this learning as the last step in Pinker's sequence of mechanisms.

These procedures, Pinker argues, will lead the child to the basic phrase structure rules of the language. However, there are questions which arise concerning how they operate. For example, it is not clear from the presentation how the S is created for the sentence 'dog big' in (7.24), since the S results from the operation of X-bar theory on V, not A. Also, it is not clear how the child is going to distinguish sentences with verb particles from those with prepositions such as 'pick up ball' vs. 'sit on chair'. Other questions arise as other examples are tried out (see Pye 1985). The important point, however, is that Pinker has presented the most detailed attempt yet to account for such facts, and some adjustments and clarifications may reasonably be expected.

Pinker uses this approach to write an LFG grammar for late Stage I or early Stage II, using the data cited by Brown (1973) in his discussion of Stage I speech for Adam, Eve, and Sarah. Table 7.22 presents this grammar along with some examples of the constructions it generates. The grammar is a modified one which attempts not to assign structure to the child unless there is evidence for it in children's Stage I utterances. The examples are ones that we have either taken from the text or made up, since Pinker does not go through the grammar with examples.

We can compare this grammar to those proposed by McNeill, given in (7.10) and by Bloom for Kathryn, in (7.12). Both McNeill's and Pinker's grammars are attempts to characterize late Stage I in general, and both were based in large part on data from Adam. While less detailed than Pinker's, McNeill's grammar is the most powerful of the three, generating sentences with several terms. Pinker's and Bloom's grammars share an attempt to implement something like the Competence Assumption. Bloom restricts her grammar by avoiding subject NPs, using 'Nom' instead. Pinker restricts his by including orphan nodes and avoiding phrases unless there is evidence for them. Bloom's grammar generates a smaller range of structures than does Pinker's, but this is not surprising since she is writing it for just one subject. Overall, however, the grammars share some general features.

Pinker's discussion of his grammar consists of justification for five of its features: (i) order and composition in phrase structure rules, (ii) identity of categories across positions, (iii) use of syntactic categories, (iv) limitations on the length of sentences, and (v) the use of universal symbols. Since these are the major issues involved in writing grammars for young children, we will look at a defense of each.

Order and composition refers to the issue of how the linear order and composition of constituents is acquired by the child. For example, one of the rules in Pinker's grammar is VP—→ V+NP. This rule combines two aspects of the child grammar: that the verb precedes the NP (i.e. linear order), and that a verb phrase consists of a verb and a noun phrase (i.e. composition). Such a rule assumes that children acquire these two aspects together, but it is also possible that they are acquired separately; for example, the child could identify the composition of phrases, but not the linear order of their constituents.

Pinker points out that these two possibilities lead to different predictions about the acquisition of languages with strict or with free word order. Pinker's position that linear order and composition are acquired simultaneously predicts that children should have little problem in acquiring word order in languages (such as English) which have strict word order. It also predicts that children acquiring free word order languages should show a tendency to impose an order on them. The alternative theory predicts a very different pattern in the acquisition of these two kinds of languages. If order is not acquired until later, then children acquiring strict word order languages should show a variety of orders, particularly ones that violate the allowed sequences in the language. On the other hand, free word order languages should be no problem.

The currently available data by and large support Pinker's position. Although there are sporadic reports of children using free word order in the acquisition of English, most analyses show a high degree of accuracy. Pinker cites Brown's (1973) analysis in particular, which indicated very few violations of appropriate usage. Regarding the acquisition of free word order languages, Pinker cites Bowerman's (1973b) analysis of Finnish, Luo, and Samoan which revealed that children tended to use one order in particular, despite having a range of options. Pinker concludes that amalgamating word order and constituent combinations in one rule reflects the acquisition procedures used by children.

Another issue addressed by Pinker is the *identity of categories* across positions. Recall in Bloom's grammar for Kathryn that she used NP for objects but Nom for subjects. This was because the only subjects which Kathryn used were single nouns or demonstrative pronouns. Pinker, however, has an NP for both positions. The major argument for this is a logical one. If Universal Grammar specifies that there are a small number of general categories, and that they are triggered semantically, then the categories should exist once the trigger experience has taken place. Even though Pinker allows for a restricted P4 to limit the use of phrasal categories in the grammar before there is evidence for them, he feels that they need to be represented on logical grounds once the evidence exists for the category in any position.

The evidence for the claim that children do not have subject NPs is that most of the subjects in early sentences are either nouns or pronouns, not phrasal structures such as article+noun or adjective+noun. Also, the nouns that occur in subject position tend to be inanimates. Pinker's counterargument to these facts is that they are only tendencies. First, animates tend to be subjects because most of the child's early verbs are actions by people upon objects. When data are observed more carefully, there are usually examples of inanimate subjects, and nouns which can be found as both subjects and objects. This is also true for the claim that expanded NPs never occur in subject position. He cites examples from Adam such as 'Dale Panda march' and 'Dale shoe right there' which have subject NPs. This uneven distribution of type frequencies, then, is accounted for by pragmatic factors in speaking. A similar argument can be found in Limber (1976).

A third aspect of Pinker's grammar is the *use of syntactic categories and rules* instead of semantic and lexical ones. Pinker acknowledges that some of the main kinds of evidence to prove the existence of syntactic categories are not available yet at Stage I. Subject–verb agreement, for example, would be one form of evidence. One could postulate syntactic categories if the child showed that verbs agreed with the number of the subjects, regardless of their semantic roles. Conversely, semantic theories should predict that the first syntactic rules such as verb agreement should be semantically restricted. Since such forms begin to be acquired during Stage II, their study could be useful in resolving this issue. Definitive results on this, however, have not yet yet appeared. Pinker cites research in progress which indicates that the first verb inflections occur as often for action verbs as for non-action verbs. On the other hand, in a study not mentioned by Pinker, Antinucci & Miller (1976) have claimed that the first past tense affixes are only used on verbs which mark abrupt change.

One way that this issue can be addressed in Stage I data is to look at the interaction of NP expansions with semantic categories. If the child's categories were syntactic, one would expect that expanded NPs would occur across different semantic roles (Pinker refers to such a spread as 'promiscuity'). His analysis of Adam's speech showed such promiscuity. For example, possessive+noun expansions occurred in at least four semantic roles: patient of action 'pull Dale bike', object of experience 'see Daddy car', predicate nominal 'dat Dale baby', and locative 'spill Mommy face'.

In discussing this issue, Pinker responds to the argument given by Braine against syntactic categories. I gave this argument during the presentation on Braine (1976) in 7.3.4. To reiterate, Braine presented data from Kendall and Seppo which showed an ordered rule for Agent+Action, but an unordered rule or grouping pattern for Action+Locative. He used these data to argue that the children therefore couldn't have a rule of VP→NP or PP (Locative) because such a rule would require agents to precede actions. Pinker's response is that his rules do not produce this effect. The locative in this example would be an orphan, as in (7.24b), and produced by the rule $S \longrightarrow ?N?_{oblique}$. That is, the locative would not be generated in the VP at that point in development.

Pinker also provides a general discussion of his view on the work of Braine, MacWhinney, and Maratsos. He states (p. 146): 'Like the logician who saw a black sheep through a train window on his first trip to Scotland and would conclude nothing more than that at least one sheep in Scotland was black on at least one side, these theorists have offered a hypothesis that is difficult to refute, given available data.' He feels that his account describes the available data as well as theirs, and has the advantage of meeting the continuity condition presented at the onset. He also points out that these theories are difficult to attack because they do not present a detailed learning theory of the kind he has attempted (p. 151). Curiously, he does not mention the one older study which tried to argue for syntactic categories, that of Bloom, Lightbown & Hood (1975).

Pinker's grammar for Stage I is relatively powerful, not only because it generates a subject NP but also because it is shown as obligatory. The grammar then produces a number of constructions that are longer than those of the spontaneous sentences used in the analysis to construct the grammar. Pinker therefore has to account for the *limitations on the length of the child's sentences*. Four hypotheses are considered to account for this. The first is the solution used by Bloom (1970), that the child has *deletion rules* which eliminate constituents. This is rejected for four reasons: (i) such rules usually 'do not account for the full set of apparent deletions in the data (Braine 1976)' (p. 156); (ii) such rules violate the formal conditions on deletion rules in transformational grammar (Chomsky 1965); (iii) since adult speech does not have such deletions, there is no positive evidence for the child to use from the input to form such rules; and (iv) it requires that the child unlearn rules to acquire the adult grammar. The second hypothesis is that the child's *rules are incomplete*. This is essentially the solution taken by Brown (1973) in constructing his set of semantic relations (see Table 7.16). Separate relations were proposed like Agent+Action, Agent+Action, and Action+Object rather than one relation of Agent +Action+Object. Pinker argues that to have separate abbreviated rules misses the point that the children show these constructions in appropriate orders, and will even produce sequences where the missing elements are inserted. The third hypothesis is that the constituents in the *rules are optional*. This was McNeill's choice in his grammar. Pinker rejects this on two grounds: (i) it has all the same problems as the deletion rules hypothesis; (ii) if it were true, one would expect at least some sentences which show all of the constituents generated, but such sentences usually don't appear.

Pinker's solution is the last hypothesis that he considers, which is that there are *processing limitations*. As is typical of such proposals, there is no real psychological model of what the limitation is. Pinker speculates that there may be limitations of mapping from functional structure to constituent structure. No independent evidence is presented, however, to support that speculation.

The last issue that Pinker addresses is the use of *universal symbols*. We have already treated Bowerman's (1973a,b) arguments against the proposal of a VP node for her subjects. Pinker accepts her arguments, and acknowledges that 'the sort of evidence necessary even for making tentative hypotheses about a VP node for children, or other detailed aspects of their tree geometry, does not currently exist' (p. 162). He falls back on the logical argument that since they are part of adult grammar, then the child must have them innately (p. 165): 'The use of universal adult symbols in children's first rules, then, is simply the theoretical commitment that the child's early rules are continuous with their later ones and with adult ones.'

Assessment.   Pinker's work shows a clear historical connection with earlier work. The claim that the child begins with a syntactic grammar which contains adult-like categories is very similar to the position taken by McNeill (1966a, 1970b). It is also similar to McNeill in postulating that the child's lexicon plays a major role in the process. The attempt to tie the onset of the syntactic development to semantics is an extension on the original ideas in Macnamara (1972). Also, the argument that evidence can be found in children's speech for the existence of grammatical relations has its roots in the work of Bloom, Lightbown & Hood (1975).

The originality in Pinker's work is in the detailed speculation on the steps that the child actually follows in constructing its grammar. It is also a forceful demonstration of the kind of argumentation that needs to be done to advance our understanding in this area of study. He provides a wide range of arguments that can be the basis for future research.

While rich in theoretical ideas and argumentation, it has the same weakness as in virtually all recent research. Unlike the work prior to 1976, it does not provide detailed analyses of child data to support its claims. Often the examples to support an argument are from different children, and often from children at different points of acquisition. The arguments also seem to be more appropriate for some data than for others. For example, semantic bootstrapping appears to be a much more suitable account of the acquisition of Kathryn and Gia in Bloom, Lightbown & Hood (1975), than for Eric and Peter. (See Ramer 1976 and Ingram 1981d for more data on these two patterns of acquisition.) The next step is the collection and analysis of data through a new methodology that combines the theoretical advances of recent years with the interest in data of the earlier studies. An outline of what that methodology may look like is presented in section 7.5.

7.4.4 Parameter setting

As pointed out in Chapter 4, a major feature of language acquisition studies is the use of a theory of adult grammar for making predictions about child data. Most work done of this kind, however, has been either on acquisition in older children, e.g. papers in Tavakolian (1981a), or have not really used child data at all. The latter studies are those on learnability which restrict themselves to the logical problems of acquisition, e.g. Wexler & Culicover (1980) and Culicover & Wilkins (1984). Pinker's, then, is one of the few studies to apply a current theory to early word combinations. Even so, it is restricted to one particular theory, that of Lexical Functional Grammar. Some other current theories, for example Relational Grammar (Perlmutter 1983) and Generalized Phrase Structure Grammar (Gazdar, Klein, Pullum

& Sag 1985), have produced little in the way of proposals for theories of language acquisition. One current theory that is beginning to be applied in this way is the Government and Binding (GB) Theory of Chomsky (1981).

Until recent years, much of the work which could be characterized as Language Acquisition had been working from the *universal base* hypothesis. This is the claim that all languages share a single underlying 'base', or phrase structure grammar. This was the assumption in McNeill's work, as well as others around that time. For example, Gruber (1967, 1975a,b), who developed his own theory of acquisition, says the following (Gruber 1975a: 71):

> ... the child's grammar does not develop in terms of increasing complexity in the nature of his possible base structures, but rather in terms of an increasing ability to analytically lexicalize those structures. While the actual base structures produced may increase in complexity, this is a performance, not a competence, factor. That is, we have assumed that competence for the generation of base structures, being innate, does not undergo development.

Gruber's theory, in fact, is an excellent example of a strong innateness theory. Pinker's theory, by allowing more developmental change and the possibility of discovering language-specific properties, is a major movement away from the universal base hypothesis. The exact extent to which this is true, however, is speculative since Pinker does not provide analyses leading to the possible Stage I grammars of young children.

Another alternative to the universal base hypothesis is expressed in Chomsky (1981). Chomsky proposes a model of acquisition which he calls a *parameter-setting* model. We have already presented a brief discussion of this model in Chapter 4, section 4.5. Most generally, the child is born with a set of options or parameters about what is a possible language. These options are such, however, that they are linked to each other in predictable ways. The establishment of one parameter, then, informs the child that a series of other characteristics should be expected. This simplifies the child's task to determining a presumably small set of parameters in acquiring a language. Also, the child is born with an original or unmarked set of expectations.

An example of the application of this theory to acquisition is Hyams (1983, 1986). Hyams looks at the acquisition of one parameter discussed in Chomsky (1981) and numerous other works. This is the pro drop parameter which distinguishes languages like Italian and Spanish from those like English and German. Pro drop languages are characterized by several features such as the optional use of subject pronouns, the use of rich verbal agreement, and certain formal features of the GB model. Hyams proposes that the child is born with the pro drop parameter as the unmarked approach. English children, therefore, first treat English as a pro drop language. Hyams argues that this accounts for several features in the acquisition of English, including the early optional use of subject pronouns. While Pinker treats this as a performance factor, Hyams proposes that it is due to the child's original analysis of a language which has optional subject pronouns.

Since this theory is relatively recent, it is only now just being developed as a possible theory of language acquisition: for example, it is still not clear what the range of parameters is, nor how the parameters get set. The theory is also undergoing change at a very rapid pace, which makes its adaptation for child language somewhat difficult. I expect, however, that its use as an explanatory theory of language acquisition will become more frequent.

7.5 The methodology of grammatical analyses of children

All of the approaches for writing grammars for children which we have reviewed used spontaneous language samples for the analysis. This has been the case despite the strong warning against this from Chomsky in 1964. The lesson of the last twenty years is that such data are not sufficient to determine the grammatical knowledge of the young language learner. If a methodology exists which can, it will have to be of the form suggested by Chomsky, that is, 'devious kinds of observations of his performance, his abilities, and his comprehension in many different kinds of circumstances' (Chomsky 1964: 36). Also, we have not fully developed ways to use spontaneous data and extract from them the most useful data for examining grammatical competence. This section will outline some ways in which these problems could be overcome. The discussion will be limited to one goal – the collection of data from children in the period of first word combinations for the purpose of determining the child's grammar. It is generalizable, however, to the study of other aspects of language acquisition.

7.5.1 Spontaneous language samples

I do not suggest the elimination of spontaneous language samples; my claim, however, is that such samples need to be the starting point for data collection, not the end point. The typical use of such samples has been to collect an extensive amount of language from the child, and then spend an enormous time transcribing it. In principle, the transcription should occur immediately after the sampling; in practice, it often occurs weeks, and even months later, and this is not surprising, given the difficulty of the task. I propose that the first sample should be relatively short, as little as 100 utterances, in order to get a general picture of the child's current language level. Next, if a longer sample has been collected, a *selected transcription* can be done. We define a selective transcription as a transcription of a subpart of a language sample of just those utterances needed for the analysis being done. For example, the transcription could involve only the identifiable multiword utterances in the sample. We have already seen from Bloom's data how few of these can occur over several hours of sampling. Importantly, the transcription should be completed within a day or two of the sampling.

In making the above suggestions, it must be stressed that they are practical in nature. It is certainly preferable to have an extensive transcription of two or more hours of spontaneous language before beginning a grammatical analysis; such transcriptions, however, are rarely available immediately after a sampling. Here we place a higher importance on immediately obtaining initial insights into the child's language which can be used for further observations. This is also practical in that a complete transcription does not usually add that much more new information, relative to the time it takes to do one, than does a selective transcription. I feel that the time spent on a complete transcription can be better used planning experiments to pursue initial hypotheses about the child's grammar.

Of particular importance for grammatical analysis is the word index, the sentence index, and the syntactic lexicon. As pointed out in our review of the major analyses in the field, it is not enough to analyze a list of syntactic types. As suggested by MacWhinney (1982), sentences can vary as to the extent to which we can say that they are rule-based. For example, at one extreme, a child utterance may simply be a memorized phrase, while at the other it could be the result of a general combinatory rule. In other words, we need to establish the *productivity* of individual sentences as well as proposed patterns. Productivity is defined here as the extent to which a sentence or grammatical pattern can be said to be rule-based. The determination of such information is needed before a grammar can be proposed for the child.

While the need to establish productivity has been expressed in recent work, little has been done to develop a methodology. The simplest measure criterion is a frequency criterion, such as the one used by Bloom (1970). Recall that Bloom defined a pattern as productive if there were at least five syntactic types which fit it. This measure, however, has a number of flaws. It can (a) lead one to conclude that a pattern exists when the sentences which meet the criterion are all memorized wholes, or (b) it can exclude productive patterns which do not meet the criterion. Hypothetical examples of each of these are given in (7.29):

(7.29) a. ride horsey   b. eat apple
      eat apple   throw apple
      throw ball   throw ball
      drink water   .   eat cookie
      tie shoe

Example (7.29a) contains five sentences which could qualify as an Action+Object or verb+noun pattern by a frequency criterion of at least five sentences. They are also possibly five reduced forms of sentences that the child has frequently heard and has memorized. The sentences (7.29b) would not meet the criterion. The fact that 'eat' and 'throw' occur with different objects, however, is suggestive of a productive combinatory rule.

The first attempt to include co-occurrence in a definition of productivity was Braine (1963a), where it was used to distinguish between Gregory's and Andrew's use of 'all gone' (see above, section 7.3.1). Braine (1976) also refers to productivity, but as in his earlier work, stops short of providing an operational definition for it.

A more explicit attempt to define productivity is in Ingram (1981d). First, any word which occurs in a child's sentence is assigned to one of three categories: not lexically free, lexically free, and grammatically free. In principle, *lexical freedom* means that the child knows a word. Operationally, a word is lexically free if either it occurs alone, that is, as a single-word utterance (e.g. 'cookie'), or in at least two sentences with different words (e.g. 'cookie here', 'want cookie'). If neither set of data is found, then the word is 'not lexically free'. Words which are lexically free may also be grammatically free. *Grammatical freedom* means that the child knows the word and has identified it as belonging to a grammatical class. A word is operationally defined as being grammatically free if it is lexically free, by the above definition, and occurs in at least two sentences with the same relational meaning. In the previous example with 'cookie', 'cookie' is not grammatically free because it has different semantic relations in the two sentences. 'Cookie' becomes grammatically free if we add the example 'cookie on table', where 'cookie' can occur as a subject of locatives. (The definition of possible relations is kept purposely vague, and can be altered depending on one's grammatical theory.) There are also two degrees of grammatical freedom – weak and strong. Weak grammatical freedom occurs when the word enters into only one relation; strong grammatical freedom occurs when the word enters two or more relations.

The above definitions can be applied to every syntactic type in the data under analysis. They lead to one of two kinds of further classification of the data. First, they divide individual syntactic types into different degrees of productivity, which will be shown first by presenting a set of hypothetical data, and then using them to demonstrate the possible degrees of productivity. The adaptation of Ingram (1981d) found in Dale (1985) will also be used. The hypothetical data in (7.20) are the collection of examples we have used so far with some additions.

(7.30) a. ride horsey   f. see apple   j. cookie here
      b. eat apple   g. throw apple   k. cookie on table
      c. throw ball   h. see ball   l. want cookie
      d. drink water   i. eat cookie   m. table pretty
      e. tie shoe   j. table shoe   n. see [ə] cookie

The possible types of sentence are as follows:

> *nonproductive*: sentences in which no word is lexically free. Examples are 'ride horsey', 'drink water';
> *productive*: sentences in which all words are grammatically free. Examples are 'eat apple', 'eat cookie', 'see apple', 'see ball', 'throw ball', 'throw apple';
> *productive /X*: sentences in which all words are grammatically free, except for an unintelligible part. An example is 'see [ə] cookie';
> *partially productive*: sentences which fall between productive and nonproductive. Dale (1985) distinguishes three kinds:

> 1. sentences with at least one word which is lexically free. An example is 'table pretty' where 'table' is lexically free but 'pretty' is not;
> 2. sentences where all words are lexically free. An example is 'table shoe' (with the meaning 'table and shoe') where both words are lexically free;
> 3. sentences where at least one word is grammatically free. An example is 'want cookie' where 'cookie' is grammatically free as object of 'see' and 'eat', but 'want' is not lexically free;

> *Unclassified*: all other sentences.

This classification can also be used to examine the productivity of specific patterns proposed for the data, such as Agent+Action. Dale (1985) proposes that a relation be considered productive if there is at least one sentence in which both words are grammatically free for that relation.

    These criteria provide an initial attempt to operationalize the notion of productivity. They were applied in Ingram (1981c,d) to data from two children to show that their grammars were quite similar despite the fact that they were at different levels of cognitive development. The results were used to argue that grammatical development appears to have its own form, distinct from that cognitive development. Since the procedures are preliminary, they no doubt will need to be adjusted as they are developed. They provide, however, a useful way to begin an examination of the child's spontaneous sample.

The syntactic types obtained in the initial spontaneous sample from the child can be analyzed with some version of the criteria above to get a first impression of the productive aspects of the child's grammar. Again, this will need to be done within a day or two of the initial sample. While these analyses can be done by hand, a more efficient method would be the use of a program for a microcomputer. Dale (1985) and Pye (1987) have recently prepared programs that do analyses of just this kind. Given the availability of such programs, and the use of selective transcriptions, it is reasonable to expect to be able to revisit a child within a day or two of the first sampling to follow up the initial analysis of the child's grammar.

7.5.2 Multiple testing procedures

It is suggested that all subsequent data from the child be the combination of several procedures used to verify hypotheses about the child's grammar. These can be as numerous as practical and theoretical issues allow. Here I will specify what I see as a possible program to follow the hypothetical child whose data were given in (7.30).

First, we would want some information on the child's receptive and productive vocabulary. A parental diary technique of the kind used by Benedict (1979) could be initiated either a week or more before the spontaneous sample, or at that time. The parent's diary could then be checked by testing for the child's response to words that are especially relevant for the grammar suggested by the initial analysis. It would be important to distinguish those words which are only in the receptive vocabulary from those which are also produced.

Once some idea of the child's vocabulary is established, we could begin with more detailed study of the child's receptive grammatical knowledge. A useful test of receptive knowledge is that of Miller & Yoder (1984). Most likely, we will want to develop specific tests for aspects noted in the initial grammar. The techniques used by de Villiers & de Villiers (1973a) and Katz, Baker & Macnamara (1974) are examples of possible procedures to follow. For our subject, we would want to establish her receptive knowledge of word order across the semantic relations which appeared productive. We could also see if she shows some awareness of grammatical morphemes like the articles and verb inflection which are not yet in the productive language. The elicited imitation technique used by Rodd & Braine (1970) is another way to get at this information.

Besides receptive knowledge, the subsequent visits to the child can be used to test the predictive power of the grammar. A way to do this is to come with a list of sentences that might be predicted by the child's patterns but which are not attested. Our subject, for example, may have a productive pattern for location, with 'here'. The context of interaction with the child could then be set up to be exactly as it was in the first session, except with the replacement of an earlier item with a new one. For example, we could try to replicate the context of the sentence 'cookie here', but provide an apple instead, with the hope of eliciting 'apple here'. This could be controlled by also attempting to elicit previously produced sentences, and comparing our success in the two contexts.

If well planned, the multiple testing procedures could be implemented quickly enough that the child's grammar would not have changed much since the initial sampling. It is expected that such a procedure would provide the kind of information needed to resolve the kinds of issues discussed by Pinker concerning the nature of the child's grammar. Syntactically rich interpretations like Pinker's would be supported by success on comprehension tests and the elicitation of gaps in the data. The leaner interpretations could be supported by success at elicited attested, but not unattested, sentences in the data. More detailed analyses of productivity should also provide more information on the two kinds of learners found in Bloom, Lightbown & Hood (1975).

Further reading

The major studies
Despite their age, the early studies by Bloom (1970, 1973), McNeill (1970a), Braine (1963a, 1976), Brown (1973), and Bowerman (1973a) are still necessary reading in the area of child language. Descriptions of Bloom's subjects and goals can be found in Bloom (1970: 1–23, 1973: 11–15), and Bloom, Lightbown & Hood (1975: 1–8). Brown's subjects are described in Brown (1973: 51–8, 63–74), and I recommend the entire 'Unbuttoned introduction'. A brief introduction to Bowerman (1973a) can be gotten from the first two chapters.

Syntactic comprehension
The three new studies reviewed in the text are all relatively short and should be read: Katz, Baker & Macnamara (1974), de Villiers & de Villiers (1973a), and Rodd & Braine (1970).

Early studies on grammatical development
The first major publications in this area were the proceedings of conferences. Bellugi & Brown (1964) was the first, and contained the initial reports

by Roger Brown and Sue Ervin, as well as Chomsky's early comments on language acquisition. Two years later, two further collections appeared, Lyons & Wales (1966) and Smith & Miller (1966). There were two papers by McNeill in these works which provided an alternative to Braine's pivot grammar. The later collection had a particular impact and was required reading at the time. Two other of this early series of conference papers were Hayes (1970), and Slobin (1971) which contained Schlesinger's early attempts to develop semantically oriented grammars. The early 70s saw the first appearance of single-authored, book-length research reports, and also the first textbooks. Major works appeared by Bloom (1970, 1973), Bowerman (1973a), and Brown (1973). Other important collections of papers at the same time were Ferguson & Slobin (1973), which contained the first English translations of several classic works, and Moore (1973). A series of monograph-length research reports by Bloom and her colleagues and Braine's (1976) monograph completed this initial period of data collection and analysis. A useful set of review papers appeared in the same year by Morehead & Morehead (1976), reinforced by a lengthy article by Bowerman on early semantic development.

Suggested passages from the works reviewed in section 7.3 are as follows: Braine (1963a), McNeill (1970b: 1078–99), Bloom (1970: 34–79) 'Kathryn's grammar at Time 1'; Bowerman (1973a: 217–28) 'Summary and conclusions'; Brown (1973: 91–111) discussion and critique of pivot grammar, and pp. 169–98, 'The major meanings at stage I'; Braine (1976: 56–70) 'The structure common to all corpora'; Bloom, Lightbown & Hood (1975: 25–40) 'Discussion, and conclusion'; and Bowerman's (1975) commentary on Bloom, Lightbown & Hood (1975), and (1976a) commentary on Braine (1976). I also recommend Howe's (1976) critique, and Leonard's (1976) review of semantic approaches.

Current approaches
Two recent collections of articles, Kuczaj (1982b) and Wanner & Gleitman (1982) are major sources of information about several of the recent approaches. The first work contains papers by R. Clark, Kuczaj, and MacWhinney which all tend toward a distributional learning view of acquisition. The paper by MacWhinney (1982) is long, but provides a great deal of information on the linguistic behavior of children around this period of acquisition and beyond. Wanner & Gleitman (1982) contains the paper on functionalism by Bates & MacWhinney and the summary by Maratsos of his view of distributional learning. It also contains a summary by Wexler of the basic features of learnability research. Since 1980, Keith Nelson has edited six volumes of collected papers entitled *Children's language*. The most extensive book-length work by a single author is that of Pinker (1984).

A feel for Pinker's work can be gotten from the following sections: (pp. 1–12) 'Introduction', (pp. 34–47) 'The bootstrapping problem', (pp. 67–8) 'Acquisition mechanisms', (pp. 101–28) 'Three learnability problems for the Stage I grammar'.

8 The period of simple sentences: phonological and semantic acquisition

8.1 Introduction

Chapter 7 dealt exclusively with one topic, that of grammatical development. The reasons for this were twofold. First, the literature in this area is quite extensive and requires an unusually long discussion for comprehensive coverage. Second, that aspect of acquisition is usually broken down into a separate period coinciding with the period of the first word combinations (i.e. approximately from ages 1;6 to 2;0). It is, however, possible to combine our treatment of acquisition of phonology and semantics over the previous period and the current one.

There have been few attempts to provide general stages of acquisition for phonology. In one of the first attempts to do so (Ingram 1976a:11) the following are discussed:

1. *Prelinguistic vocalization and perception* (birth to 1;0)
2. *Phonology of the first 50 words* (1;0–1;6)
3. *Phonology of single morphemes* (1;6–4;0)

> 'Child begins to expand inventory of speech sounds. Phonological processes that result in incorrect productions predominate until around age 4 when most words of simple morphological structure are correctly spoken.'

These are very much descriptive stages in the sense of Chapter 3, i.e. they do little more than document changes over time. Nonetheless, they provide an overview of the major behavioral changes which occur.

I have already examined the first stage in Chapter 5, and the second one in Chapter 6. In the present chapter I will look at the period of the *phonology of single morphemes*, which is proposed to last usually from age 18 months to around 4 years. It is claimed to be a period during which the child goes from a small set of spoken words (approximately 50) to a large vocabulary of words that are relatively correctly spoken. These words are claimed to be simple in that they mostly consist of a single morpheme, except for inflectional endings which are also acquired during this time.

340

Later development, which I will only briefly discuss, includes the acquisition of (i) a small set of difficult sounds (e.g. English dental fricatives), (ii) the morphophonemic rules of the language, and (iii) the spelling system.

There have been even fewer attempts to divide semantic development into stages. Often it is simply divided into two periods, i.e. before and after the word spurt around 18 months. The interest in viewing semantic development in relation to cognitive development led us to follow it (in Chapters 5 and 6) in relation to Piagetian stages of cognitive development, up to the end of the sensorimotor period of development. Chapter 6 also included discussion of studies on word acquisition which covered data on children up to age 2 years.

In this chapter I review semantic acquisition between the ages of 18 months and 4 years, as with phonological acquisition. This time period is the first part of what Piaget has referred to as the *period of concrete operations*, which in his earlier work he divides into three subperiods. The first two subperiods are summarized below, based on Ingram (1976:11) where they are compared to phonological stages of acquisition:

1. *Preconcept subperiod* (1;6–4;0)
   'The onset of symbolic representation. Child can now refer to past and future, although most activity is in the here and now. Predominance of symbolic play.'
2. *Intuitional subperiod* (4;0–7;0)
   'Child relies on immediate perception to solve various tasks. Begins to develop the concept of reversibility. Child begins to be involved in social games.'

An important feature of this period is that the child is primarily involved with her immediate environment. This will be seen in the way she comes to understand temporal and spatial terms. The early attempts to do this will demonstrate the use of 'immediate perception', for example, in interpreting two clauses as reflecting the natural order of the events. Besides examining some of the semantic errors children make, we will also look at some of the theories that have been proposed to account for them.

The topic of grammatical acquisition will be returned to in Chapter 9, concentrating on the child's acquisition of grammatical morphemes, but also considering the child's developing ability to comprehend and produce more complex sentences.

8.2 The phonological acquisition of single morphemes

Based on our review of phonological development during the period of single-word utterances, the child around 18 months can be seen to have made the following gains. First, receptive vocabulary is around 200 words, and the productive vocabulary is around 50. During the present period, which follows the word spurt, the child's vocabulary undergoes a tremendous increase. Second, our review of Shvachkin (1948/73 and Jakobson (1941/68) suggests that some preliminary phonological analysis has begun in both perception and production, with the former leading the way. The child's perceptual ability appears such that she can identify differences between words which are marked by differences between single segments, although this ability appears to emerge only gradually. Preliminary data also suggest that the child's articulatory ability, although far from complete, is capable of producing at least a basic set of phonemes of the language being acquired.

Given the incomplete development that exists at the onset of this stage, it is not surprising that the word spurt should put a tremendous strain upon the child's primitive phonological system. The result is a period of time during which the child shows errors both in the perception and production of words. An attempt will be made, first for perception, then for production, to document the kinds of errors which occur and their extent. The explanations that have been offered to account for these errors will then be examined.

8.2.1 The growth of phonemic perception

Shvachkin claimed that his subjects showed acquisition of the phonological oppositions of Russian by the time that they reached 2 years of age. Despite proposing a development sequence which the children followed, this still is potentially a very strong claim for early acquisition. Given the results of the recent studies on infant speech perception (Chapter 5), it is not surprising that early perceptual development should be in advance of production. Here we will explore the extent to which this is true.

To examine this issue, we will first look at the implications of Shvachkin's study. While the creative nature of Shvachkin's method is acknowledged, the report still lacks sufficient information to allow unequivocal acceptance of the results. As pointed out in Barton (1980), Shvachkin does not provide details on the number of trials he used, nor his exact criteria for acquisition. Even if we accept the results, which we do in their general form, the claims that follow need to be closely tied to the stimuli used, i.e. they show perceptual acquisition of the Russian consonants in minimally paired CVC nonsense forms that were conscientiously and systematically taught to the children. The results still leave open the possibility that other oppositions or more complex words require longer acquisition time, or even that the sounds studied take more time to acquire under totally naturalistic conditions. Even Shvachkin's claim about acquisition is somewhat cautious. He does not say that the children know all the aspects of the phonological system of Russian, such as its diverse phonotactic constraints; he only states that the child has the basic oppositions for such acquisition to proceed.

If we examine Shvachkin's explanation for the order of acquisition of oppositions, we find three factors which interact – perceptual salience, articulation, and phonological salience (6.5.1). These can also be viewed as possible reasons for the later acquisition of an opposition. That is, an opposition could be late because of the fact that its acoustic properties are such that it is more difficult to process by the human auditory system (low perceptual salience); or because it is difficult to articulate (should we accept Shvachkin's claim that correct articulation aids perception); or because it does not have a central role in the phonological system; or some combination of these. As stated earlier, such factors are difficult to isolate without some independent measure of them. Even so, they provide a basis for discussion of the known results on phonological acquisition.

There has been a wide range of studies conducted on this topic. The initial enthusiasm wavers, however, on closer inspection. First, most of the research has been on English; the fact that there has been little in the way of cross-linguistic research limits the range of our conclusions from the onset. The most serious attempts to study the effects of phonological salience will need to wait until such studies are done. Second, much of the English research was done during the period of large sample studies and has all of its associated flaws. Templin (1957), for example, conducted a speech sound discrimination study on her subjects but does not give any results on specific words or phonemes – results are only given in the form of scores for particular age groups.

Even the more recent studies are questionable because of the many factors that may affect a perception study. Both Barton (1980) and Strange & Broen (1980) have discussed a number of such factors. Strange & Broen (1980) distinguish between stimulus variables and task variables. *Stimulus variables* 'refer to the choice and structure of the set of to-be-perceived items, or more precisely, contrasts between items' (p. 122). We know from research on acoustic phonetics that there are numerous acoustic features of a speech sound which can be possible signals of its phonemic status in the language. By using computer-generated synthetic speech, it is possible to manipulate the test stimuli along several dimensions. We can use only criterial aspects, i.e. those that are recognized by adults as separating phonemes, or can include non-criterial ones, i.e. those such as pitch and amplitude, which do not affect phonemic perception. While such stimuli allow one to control what is heard, they can also be criticized as not being natural sounds. Other stimulus variables pointed out by Strange & Broen

Table 8.1 *General methodology of studies on phonemic perception, presented in order of increasing ages of subjects*

Study	Subjects		Stimulus items[1]		Contrasts	Task
	No.	Ages	Shape	Words		
Garnica (1973)	15	1;5–1;10	Cvc	nonsense	?	select one of two objects
Barton (1976b)	10	1;8–2;0	Cvc	real	2	select one of four objects
Johnson, Hardee & Long (1981)	8	1;6–2;6	Cv	nonsense	11	select one of two objects
Eilers & Oller (1976)	14	1;10–2;2	varied	real & nonsense	8	select one of two objects
Barton (1978)	20	2;3–2;11	Cvc cvC	real	20	select one of two pictures
Garnica (1971)	8	1;9–3;5	Cvc	nonsense	?	select one of two objects
Edwards (1974)	28	1;8–3;11	Cvc	nonsense	18	select one of two objects
Strange & Broen (1980)	20	2;11–3;5	Cvc	real	3	select one of two pictures
Clumeck (1982)	31	3;1–5;10	varied	real	19	select one of three pictures

[1] The capital letter of the syllable shape indicates the syllable position in which the contrasts were tested.

are: (i) lexical status, i.e. whether a word is a real word or a nonsense word, (ii) frequency of usage, i.e. how well the child knows a word, and (iii) grammatical variables.

Task variables are those which have to do with 'the configuration in which the stimuli are presented and the method by which subjects respond to them' (p. 124). One common procedure is to use a *discrimination task* in which two items are presented and the child must decide whether they are the same or different. Barton (1980), in particular, is critical of this task on the grounds that the child could process the stimuli acoustically without using his linguistic (or phonemic) system, much in the way the prelinguistic infant does. The alternative is to use an *identification task* in which the child needs to match the stimulus to an internal model to identify something that represents the meaning of the word, such as an object or picture. Other task variables pointed out by Strange & Broen are the number of trials used, and if the subjects are given feedback on their responses. Barton also mentions the potential problems of experimenter effects when the stimuli are presented live instead of being recorded.

With so many variables involved, it is not surprising that the results from the literature in this field do not constitute a homogeneous body of findings. It is also possible to find fault with most studies on phonemic perception, for one reason or another, as has been done in Barton (1980). Table 8.1 presents a summary of the methodological features of a selection of these studies. The list is restricted to those studies which used an identification task, since these are felt to reflect linguistic processing more directly. Here I highlight some of these findings, claiming that they are actually more in agreement than has been thought by some – the controversy which exists seems rather to be tied to their interpretation.

Most of these studies were done in the early 1970s when there was a flurry of interest in this topic. The first were done at Stanford University by Garnica, who adapted the technique used by Shvachkin. This adaptation, which has been referred to by some as the Shvachkin–Garnica method, changes the testing procedure into a more strict experimental format. In particular, a criterion of acquisition was added that the child would need to respond correctly in seven out of ten trials before it was concluded that the contrast was acquired. This method was used in Garnica (1971, 1973), and Edwards (1974). It was first criticized in Barton (1975) on the grounds that the criterion of seven out of ten is not an adequate statistic. Barton also comments: 'approximately one in six of the results thought to be significant will in fact not be so' (Barton 1980: 100). The technique was subsequently adjusted by Clumeck (1982), who used the following criteria to judge a child's perceptual ability on a contrast:

Clumeck's criteria for phonemic perception
1. If the first five responses are correct, then conclude correctness and go on to next pair.
2. If not, give five more trials and conclude correctness if nine out of ten are correct; if five or fewer are correct, conclude that the child cannot discriminate the contrast.
3. If six to eight are correct, give ten more trials and conclude correctness if 15 out of 20 are correct.

This was an adaptation of Barton (1976a, 1978) who used criterion 1 and then if the first five were not all correct went on to 20 trials. In the latter case, 15 out of 20 needed to be correct. Other criteria used are nine out of ten in Strange & Broen (1980) and ten out of 12 in Johnson, Hardee & Long (1981).

Barton has also criticized the Shvachkin–Garnica method on the grounds that the use of nonsense words rather than real words makes the task more difficult. Barton (1976a) found, for example, that his subjects did poorer on words that they had to be taught than on ones they already knew before the experiment. The effects of familiarity were also found by Clumeck (1982). Such concerns have led some investigators to restrict their stimuli to real and familiar words. Since this choice restricts one's choice of possible test items, others by necessity have still used nonsense forms (e.g. Johnson, Hardee & Long 1981).

Before looking at some results of these studies, I would like to comment on the two above criticisms of the earlier studies. Regarding the statistical error of the early Shvachkin–Garnica studies, it should be pointed out that this error is in the direction of *overestimating* the child's perceptual abilities. The results of these studies can be examined with this direction of error in mind. They can be interpreted with more confidence, however, if their results turn out to be comparable to those in studies with stricter measures of acquisition. (It is somewhat ironic that Barton was the one to point out this error, given that his own theoretical view is that children have complete phonemic perception at the onset of acquisition.)

The second criticism about the use of nonsense forms raises a general issue about our definition of rule acquisition. Recall that Chapter 6 began with six definitions of what it means to say that a child has acquired a word. Defining acquisition continually returns to the question of the extent of a rule's productivity. In various domains of language acquisition, such as morphological development, productivity is typically defined as the ability to apply a known rule to a new or novel form. The same issue is at stake here. If a child has a general phonological opposition, then it should be applicable to new words being acquired. Indeed, when we consider it, the thousands of words that the child acquires after 18 months of age are nonsense forms to the child when first heard. Little in the phonemic perception literature has been concerned with the question of the productivity of the system. Most work with real words tests ones that are familiar to the child, often with oppositions tested in just one pair of words. The nonsense word studies are actually the only data we have that begin to address this issue. We suggest, therefore, that the nonsense word data are actually the most robust data we have on phonemic perception.

It is necessary to raise a further methodological problem before examining the results to date on phonemic perception, a problem concerning the selection of the contrasts used in the various studies. Even if we restrict ourselves to simple CVC syllables, we still have an enormous range of possible oppositions to test. Every English consonant and consonant cluster can be paired with every other, both in initial and final position (as well as medial position in longer words). Much of this selection is arbitrary, by necessity, even when the domain is restricted, as in Johnson, Hardee & Long (1981). As a result of the wide range of possible choices, few studies have examined the exact same contrasts. Here this problem will be attacked first by looking at one general study, then by examining the acquisition of contrasts within general classes such as fricatives and glides.

Table 8.2 *The contrasts tested, stimulus words used, proportions of response on all words and known words for 20 children between 2;3 and 2;11 tested in Barton (1976a), based on Figures 3.4 and 3.5*

Contrasts	Pairs used	Proportion of subjects to meet criterion	
		All pairs (no. of subjects)	Known pairs[1] (no. of subjects)
STOPS			
/p-,t-/	pie, tie	1.00 (15)	1.00 (13)
/-p,-t/	cap, cat	0.90 (19)	(1.00) (3)
/k-,g-/	coat, goat	0.81 (16)	0.85 (13)
	curl, girl	0.75 (16)	0.92 (12)
	card, guard	0.93 (15)	1.00 (10)
/-k,-g/	lock, log	0.92 (13)	(1.00) (3)
	back, bag	0.94 (16)	1.00 (15)
	frock, frog	0.47 (15)	— —
/b-,g-/	boat, goat	1.00 (17)	1.00 (15)
/b-,p-/	bear, pear	0.95 (19)	0.94 (17)
STOP-NASALS			
/b-,m-/	bat, mat	0.94 (16)	1.00 (11)
/-d,-n/	head, hen	1.00 (15)	1.00 (17)
	cloud, clown	0.50 (14)	0.83 (6)
FRICATIVES			
/s-,f-/	seat, feet	1.00 (20)	1.00 (8)
/-s,-θ/	mouse, mouth	1.00 (19)	1.00 (17)
APPROXIMANTS			
/l-,r-/	lock, rock	0.79 (14)	1.00 (8)
/w-,r-/	wing, ring	0.89 (19)	0.94 (16)
CLUSTERS			
/gr-,gl-/	grass, glass	0.83 (18)	0.83 (18)
/kr-,kl-/	crown, clown	0.77 (17)	1.00 (7)
/tr-,tʃr-/	train, chain	0.77 (17)	(1.00) (4)

[1] Parentheses are placed around those proportions where there were four or fewer subjects who knew the pairs.

Barton (1976a, 1978) Barton's work is generally considered to be the first major work to overcome some of the problems of the earlier studies. He actually conducted two studies on this topic, which are reported in detail in Barton (1976a) and much more briefly in Barton (1978) and (1976b). They are summarized in Table 8.1. Here we will look at the first of these, which is discussed in Chapter 3 of Barton (1976a) and in Barton (1978).

This study examined the ability of 20 children between 2;3 and 2;11 to perceive the difference between 20 pairs of English words. The contrasts and words used are presented in Table 8.2. Each word was audio-recorded on a card which could be played through a machine called a language master. The child would put the card through the machine, hear the word, and then identify a picture of the object named. The machine was used because it could provide a constant model for all children to hear, and because it created a task which interested the children.

The task consisted of two parts. First, there was an identification phase in which the child put each card through the machine with the sound off and was asked to identify its picture. The child's responses for each word were placed into one of three categories: (1) *named*, if the child appropriately named the picture, (2) *prompted*, 'if the experimenter named it only once ... and the child pointed it out and could later identify it' (p. 90), or (3) *taught*, if the experimenter had to name it more than once. Second, there was the discrimination phase. The child would run each card through the machine and be asked to identify one of the two pictures which represented the test pair. The criteria mentioned on page 345 were used to determine if the child received five or twenty trials.

Of the 20 subjects, 13 completed all 20 test pairs. The other seven only completed ten pairs each, for a variety of practical reasons. The results are given in Table 8.2 in the form of two measures. The first one, labeled 'all words', is the proportion of subjects on each pair who met the criteria for acquisition. The second measure, labeled 'known words', is the same except it excludes data on all pairs where the child's response during the identification phase was categorized as 'taught'. That is, the second measure is presumed by Barton to be more reliable in that it only treats words already known by the children.

At first glance, these results are quite impressive. Even on the 11 words measure, most sounds are correctly perceived by at least 90 percent of the subjects. Barton uses these results to conclude the generalization that phonemic perception is complete when words begin to be produced. This is an important conclusion in that it allows us to assume that the underlying representation of children's words is at least the adult surface form.

The results are less exciting, however, when we take a closer look at them. Recall that the subjects are children between 2;3 and 2;11, with a mean age of 2;7. Children at this age have acquired a fair amount of language already. According to Smith (1926), as cited in Dale (1976: 174), the average spoken vocabulary at 2;6 is 446 words. We have already considered data suggesting that the receptive vocabulary is much larger than the productive one. We would expect the child's perception to be reasonably good for at least a subset of English phonemes. The question then becomes: what is this subset? Since Barton has only examined some of the contrasts found in English, it is still possible that performance might not be as good on other ones. He may have selected those contrasts which are characteristic of the early vocabulary of young children.

This possibility is strengthened by looking at the actual contrasts that Barton tested. In (8.1), we give the phonemes tested by Barton in the form of a phonetic chart. Next to it, we repeat the phonetic inventory for the English child (6.17). This is the phonetic inventory determined in Ingram (1981a) to be that typical of the average 2-year-old English child, based on data from 15 children.

(8.1) English phonemes tested   Phonetic inventory at 2;0

m n		m n
b,p d,t g,k		b,p d,t g,k
f s		f s h
w		w

θ

l   r

clusters:

gr, gl, kr, kl, tr, tʃ r

We can see that eleven of the phonemes tested by Barton are typically acquired by English children by age 2 years (the shared sounds are indicated within boxes). Interestingly, those few sounds tested that aren't are the ones which received the lowest scores in the experiment. For example, all of the words with clusters appeared to create some difficulties. All of this suggests that the only conclusion we can draw from Barton's experiment is that children between 2;3 and 2;11 can perceive differences between sounds that they already have been able to produce since age 2. This limited conclusion is not surprising in that the study is actually a measurement sequence in the sense of Chapter 3. By selecting sounds to test that are among the first acquired by children, and restricting the stimuli to known words that can be named by the children already, the method predetermined its outcome.

The lesson to be learned from Barton's study is that perception research cannot be done without considering the child's articulatory abilities, for example, by using norms of acquisition as the basis for selecting stimuli. As we shall see in the next section, several large sample studies exist

Table 8.3 *Contrasts used and proportion of subjects to meet the criterion of acquisition in perception and production for 28 children between 1;8 and 3;11 to test four hypotheses in Edwards (1974)*

Hypotheses & contrasts	Proportion of subjects to meet criterion	
	Perception (no. of subjects)	Production (no. of subjects)
H1:		
/s/–/z/	0.50 (3/6)	0.00 (0/6)
/t/–/d/	0.67 (4/6)	0.50 (3/6)
/f/–/v/	0.57 (4/7)	0.71 (5/7)
/p/–/b/	1.00 (7/7)	0.86 (6/7)
/ʃ/–/z/	0.80 (4/5)	0.20 (1/5)
/tʃ/–/ʤ/	0.80 (4/5)	0.80 (4/5)
/θ/–/ð/	0.56 (5/9)	0.11 (1/9)
/t/–/d/	0.89 (8/9)	0.78 (7/9)
Totals	0.72 (39/54)	0.50 (27/54)
H2:		
/s/–/z/	0.50 (4/8)	0.00 (0/8)
/s/–/ʃ/	0.75 (6/8)	0.38 (3/8)
/d/–/ð/	1.00 (8/8)	0.25 (2/8)
/f/–/θ/	0.75 (6/8)	0.38 (3/8)
Totals	0.75 (24/32)	0.25 (8/32)
H3:		
/k/–/g/	1.00 (8/8)	0.88 (7/8)
/f/–/v/	0.75 (6/8)	0.75 (6/8)
/θ/–/ð/	0.75 (6/8)	0.38 (3/8)
/x/–/ɣ/	0.75 (6/8)	0.25 (2/8)
Totals	0.81 (26/32)	0.56 (18/32)
H4:		
/l/–/r/	0.90 (17/19)	0.32 (6/19)
/l/–/w/	0.90 (17/19)	0.47 (9/19)
/r/–/w/	0.79 (15/19/	0.21 (4/19)
/l/–/j/	0.74 (14/19)	0.32 (6/19)
/r/–/j/	0.68 (13/19)	0.32 (6/19)
/w/–/j/	0.84 (16/19)	0.79 (15/19)
Totals	0.81 (92/114)	0.40 (46/114)

which provide such norms. Sander (1961), for example, has found that the last sounds acquired by English children between 4 and 6 years of age are /č/, /š/, /ž/, /ǰ/, /v/, /θ/, /ð/, and /z/. Note that Barton only tested one of these sounds, /θ/, and only in opposition to an early one, /s/. Another option is to study the child's productive ability at the same time as perception. We will now turn to a few studies which have, in fact, attempted these options.

Edwards (1974) This study used the Shvachkin–Garnica technique to study the acquisition of a range of contrasts in 28 children from 1;8 to 3;11. The contrasts were organized so that four separate hypotheses about their acquisition could be examined. The testing of each of these four hypotheses constituted a separate study, and not all subjects participated in all the experiments. The four hypotheses (H1–4) are follows:

H1: Voice distinction in stops precedes voice distinction in fricatives.

H2: In acquisition of an unmarked–marked opposition, (i) perception precedes production and (ii) the unmarked member substitutes for the marked member in production.

H3: Velar spirants are 'acquired' at the appropriate point in phonological development even though they are absent in the model language.

H4: Phonemic perception precedes production in the acquisition of every opposition among the liquids and glides /l,r,w,j/.

The contrasts used to test each of these hypotheses are given in Table 8.3. This list also demonstrates the point about the range of possible contrasts that can be tested. Only three of these are the same as contrasts used by Barton: /k/–/g/, /l/–/r/, and /w/–/r/. Edwards's list provides much more information about both fricatives and glides.

Most generally, the results indicate that phonemic perception overall was good. All the contrasts were acquired by at least one-half of the subjects tested. The only one to show a relatively low score was /s/–/z/. A comparison of the results of this study with those of Barton's for the contrasts which were the same is given (8.2):

(8.2) Contrast   Barton   Edwards

    /k/–/g/   0.81   1.00
    /l/–/r/   0.88   0.90
    /w/–/r/   0.63   0.79

We can see that the results are similar, with Edwards's subjects showing better performance than Barton's. This could be due either to the fact that Edwards's subjects were older, or to the statistical problems already discussed.

The performance in perception was consistently better than that of production, indicating that the children were perceiving differences that they were not making in their speech. Even so, Edwards emphasizes that many children showed a lack of perception on some of the pairs tested. This can be seen by looking at the individual scores on the six contrasts used to test H4. Of the 19 subjects who participated, ten acquired all six, three acquired five, one acquired four, four acquired three, and one acquired one. Also, while a general pattern emerged, individual subjects would vary regarding the set of approximants which they had acquired.

The data provided only partial support for the four hypotheses tested. Since these hypotheses are not the primary reason for our review of Edwards's study, they will be only briefly discussed. H1 predicts that a voice opposition will exist within the stops at any point of articulation before it occurs between fricatives at the same point of articulation. For example, /t/–/d/ will be acquired before /s/–/z/. The results given in Table 8.3 generally support this prediction. For the four pairs tested, three out of four show better performance on the stops than on the fricatives in perception, and all four show better performance on the stops in performance. Oddly enough, Edwards does not interpret the data in production this way, because of substitution patterns for individual subjects such as those in (8.3) below, i.e. consonants are not always occurring in their correct phonetic form. ('Subject numbers' here are simple arbitrary numbers assigned to individual subjects.)

(8.3) Subject 119   Subject 114   Subject 111

/p/ ⟶ [p]   /t/ ⟶ [t]   /p/ ⟶ [p]

/b/ ⟶ [p]   /d/ ⟶ [ð],[ʤ],[z]   /b/ ⟶ [b]

/f/ ⟶ [f]   /s/ ⟶ [s]   /f/ ⟶ [f]

/v/ ⟶ [f]   /z/ ⟶ [s]   /v/ ⟶ [w]

It seems to us, however, that these data do not contradict the predictions of H1. Subject 199 has not acquired voicing in either pair, so it is irrelevant for H1. Subject 114 supports H1 in that voicing is acquired for the stops, but not the fricatives. Subject 111 is irrelevant because voicing has already been acquired for both pairs.

The first part of H2 predicts perception before production and is supported by the data in Table 8.3. The second part of H2 is a very strong claim about the interaction of perception, production, and the child's substitutions. Edwards proposes a four-stage model of acquisition of a contrast which she feels is predicted by H2(ii). This model is given here in (8.4) with hypothetical examples for the acquisition of /s/ and /z/. (The unmarked members of each pair tested are shown on the left in Table 8.2.)

(8.4)   *Stage*   *Perception*   *Production*

I.   Perception and production of   /s/ ⟶ [s]   /s/ ⟶ [s]
     marked member as being   /z/ ⟶ [s]   /z/ ⟶ [s]
     unmarked

II. Substitution of unmarked   /s/ ⟶ [s]   /s/ ⟶ [s]
     member for marked member in   /z/ ⟶ [z]   /z/ ⟶ [s]
     production

III. Variable production of the   /s/ ——> [s]   /s/ ——> [s]
      marked member   /z/ ——> [z]   /z/ ——> [s],[z]

IV.   Acquisition of both members in /s/ ——> [s]   /s/ ——> [s]
      perception and production   /z/ ——> [z]   /z/ ——> [z]

Edwards claims that the data support the prediction strongly for the pairs /s/–/ʃ/ and /d/–/ð/, and weakly for /f/–/θ/ (since one subject replaced /θ/ with [s] instead of [f]). They did not support H2 for /s/–/z/ where four subjects replaced /s/ with [z] instead of replacing /z/ with [s]. This kind of variability in fricative substitutions has been more recently substantiated in Ingram, Christensen, Veach & Webster (1980). Edwards also found that the children were variable concerning which stages were occurring for which pairs. Subject 110, for example, was in stage II for /s/–/ʃ/, but stage III for /d/–/θ/.

Of particular interest in this model is the prediction of stage I, i.e. a stage of incomplete perception. Unfortunately, few data are given to support its existence: the only case cited is Subject 113 who was found to be in stage I for the pair /f/–/θ/. It is such data which will constitute true counterevidence to Barton's claim that children have correct perception of words before they produce them. We will later report stronger evidence for stage I in the study by Eilers & Oller (1976).

H3 is of interest because it tests for the perception of a distinction that does not occur in English, that is /x/–/ɣ/. The prediction is that the acquisition of a voicing distinction in English fricatives should generalize to this non-English pair. The data in Table 8.3 support H3, although they did not fully support some other predictions about this set of contrasts, which Edwards discusses. Lastly, H4 on the acquisition of glides was strongly supported by the data, i.e. the subjects showed better perception than production of each of the pairs. Edwards also points out that the order of the scores differed for perception and production, leading her to conclude that the order of acquisition of contrasts may differ between perception and production. Since the numbers are so small, however, this can only be taken very tentatively.

Edwards draws seven conclusions from the results of her study (pp. 218–19; her own words are used here).

(i)   Phonemic perception develops in a gradual and patterned way;
(ii)   Phonemic perception of a given sound difference generally precedes correct production of the difference;
(iii) The order of acquisition tends to be uniform, but the details vary greatly;

(iv)   The order of development in phonemic perception may not be identical with the order in production;
(v)   Initial fricatives and glides (liquids and semivowels) are acquired as whole segmental units rather than by successive additions of individual features;
(vi)   Substitutions are usually less marked than the model but details vary greatly;
(vii) Factors not directly related to the content of features or feature combinations may be important in the acquisition process.
       (Edwards names frequency of occurrence as one such possible factor, although this factor is not explored.)

Despite its statistical problems and occasionally questionable interpretations of the results, the Edwards study is probably the most insightful study conducted on phonemic perception for the period under review. We will consider one further study which provides support for some of its speculations.

Eilers & Oller (1976)   Eilers & Oller were interested in studying the relationship between perception and production. In particular, they wanted to see if the common errors in children's productions were the result of articulatory or perceptual factors. As such, the study investigates the existence of stage I as proposed by Edwards. I have already pointed out that Edwards's data were not sufficient to conclude the existence of such a stage. If it exists, then at least some of the child's errors could be accounted for as perceptual errors. If there is no such stage, which is Barton's conclusion, then substitution errors could only be the result of articulatory or linguistic factors.

Eilers & Oller used three types of stimuli to study this question. Type 1 stimuli were pairs of words which differ in sounds which are often collapsed in the speech of young children. One such pair, for example, is /r/–/w/ which are often collapsed to [w] by children. Type 2 stimuli were pairs of words which differ in sounds that children do not usually collapse, e.g. /p/–/t/. Type 3 consisted of just one pair which differed in /k/–/p/. This was a control item to ensure that the children understood the task. If the errors on type 1 pairs are due to perceptual factors, then the children should find these more difficult than types 2 and 3. If there are no perceptual factors, then the type 1 pairs should be perceived correctly. For purposes of the later discussion, we shall refer to these predictions as the *perceptual hypothesis* and *articulatory/linguistic* hypothesis respectively.

The study is particularly interesting because of the stimuli it used. Instead of using either pairs of nonsense words or real words, they used real words

Table 8.4 *Information about stimulus items and the proportion of subjects to meet the criterion of acquisition in perception and production for 14 children between 1;10 and 2;2 tested in Eilers & Oller (1976), adapted from Tables 1 and 4*

| Stimulus items | | Proportion of subjects to meet criterion | |
| | | Perception | Production |
Gloss	Phonetic form	(no. of subjects)	(no. of subjects)
TYPE 1			
car–gar	[kʰar] [kar]	0.86 (12/14)	0.21 (3/14)
block–bock	[plɔk] [pɔk]	0.58 (7/12)	0.17 (2/12)
monkey–mucky	[mʌŋki] [mʌki]	0.20 (2/10)	0.00 (0/10)
fish–thish	[fɪʃ] [θɪʃ]	0.00 (0/10)	0.10 (1/10)[1]
rabbit–wabbit	[ræbɪt] [wæbɪt]	0.60 (6/10)	0.10 (1/10)
TYPE 2			
pig–tig	[pʰig] [tʰig]	0.50 (7/14)	0.86 (12/14)
block–lock	[plɔk] [lɔk]	0.83 (10/12)	1.00 (12/12)
TYPE 3			
cow–bow	[kaw] [paw]	1.00 (14/14)	1.00 (14/14)

[1] Production of subject was unstable.

paired with nonsense words. For example, the child would be shown a familiar toy object, e.g. 'car', and one unfamiliar nonsense toy, e.g. 'gar'. They decided on this method because it avoids the problem with real words of having a restricted number of possible minimal pairs, and the problem of nonsense words of having to teach them. Table 8.4 presents the stimulus pairs used in the experiment.

The subjects were 14 children between 1;10 and 2;2. The procedure was to show the child two objects which were each placed on top of a container, one with candy inside. The child was told that the candy was 'under the (name of one of the objects)'. Each subject was first tested on nonminimal pairs such as 'horse' and 'dog' until four correct answers in a row were obtained. Then the experimental sessions began. The testing of each pair began with a warm-up session during which the child was encouraged to play with the objects. Each pair of words was tested eight times, with the real word correct four times and the nonsense word correct four times. The orders of presentation and location were randomized to avoid biases due to hand or object preferences. The children's responses on the pairs were scored as correct if they got seven out of eight. The children's production of the test words was also recorded. A child was scored as correct in production if he imitated 'both the nonsense word and real object word in such a way as to maintain some clear phonetic contrast' (p. 325).

The results are presented in Table 8.4. They do not support fully either the perception hypothesis or the articulatory/linguistic hypothesis. The type 1 pairs were neither all correctly perceived nor all the most difficult to perceive. The statistical analysis of the perception data revealed three levels of difficulty. For purposes of reference, we will refer to these as 'difficult', 'moderate', and 'easy'. Example (8.5) shows how the pairs fell into these three levels.

(8.5) *Level*	*Pair*	*Type*
Difficult	fish–thish	1
	monkey–mucky	1
Moderate	rabbit–wabbit	1
	block–bock	1
	block–lock	2
	pig–tig	2
Easy	pig–tig	2
	car–gar	1
	cow–bow	3

We can see that the type 1 pairs fall into all three levels of difficulty. They constitute two of the most difficult pairs, as well as one of the easiest. The score for 'pig–tig' fell between 'moderate' and 'easy', so could not be assigned to a unique level.

Eilers & Oller also present results on how individual subjects performed on each of the pairs. For the difficult pairs, most of the subjects showed neither correct perception nor production (nine out of ten for 'fish–thish', and eight out of ten for 'monkey–muckey'). For the easy pair 'car–gar', on the other hand, nine out of 14 subjects showed correct perception without correct production. Subjects were more evenly divided between these two patterns of response for the moderate pairs. These data thus constitute much stronger evidence for Edwards's proposed stage I than that presented in Edwards (1974).

In the above analysis, one seemingly peculiar result emerged. On the two type 2 distinctions, several children showed incorrect perception but correct production (five subjects for 'pig–tig', and two for 'block–lock'). This result leads initially to the peculiar conclusion that production precedes perception. I would like, however, to offer an alternative explanation. Observe first that the criteria for correctness were more strict for perception than production (see above). Pairs of words which are articulatorily easy for children when compared to their perception will be likely to show the above pattern when an imbalanced scoring system is applied which favors production. We take these results to indicate that these two pairs are difficult to perceive relative to their likelihood of being imitated successfully. This is just one example of the general finding of this study that the relation of perceptual and articulatory difficulty is a complex one.

The results support the first conclusion drawn by Edwards about phonemic perception: its acquisition is gradual, with certain distinctions appearing earlier than others. They also support the speculation that the child may have a perceptual representation of a word which is not a correct perception of its adult surface form. They do not, however, support a view that all of the child's substitutions are the result of perceptual problems. At least one pair tested was perceptually easy but articulatorily difficult for the children.

Since both Edwards and Eilers & Oller are cross-sectional studies, neither can be taken as definitive evidence for the stages suggested by Edwards. They are suggestive, however, of distinctions first appearing perceptually, and then later in production. Nor do they provide an idea of the extent to which we can say that a child's perceptual development at any time is incomplete. Studies on phonemic perception, apart from Barton (1978) and Clumeck (1982) at least, tend to select stimuli that are likely to pose problems for the child. We still have little in the way of direct evidence on the extent to which incomplete perception characterizes the young child's total vocabulary.

So far, we have examined phonemic perception through reviewing experimental studies which directly pair words for the child to process. We would like to conclude our discussion of the topic by looking into a very different approach. This is the possibility of making claims about the child's perceptual ability on the basis of her productive language.

The general method is something like this. First we do phonological analyses of the child's matches and substitutions, presumably by methods such as those discussed in 6.5.3. Different theories about the relation between the child's perception and production lead to different predictions about the resulting analysis. I list here three possible theories (one with two subtheories) and the kinds of analyses that each predicts. The subsequent discussion will attempt to clarify their claims.

1. *Global perception theory.* The child only identifies general features of words without assigning them necessarily to individual segments. *Prediction*: analyses should show poor correspondences between adult and child sounds with variable pronunciations.
2. *Partial perception theory.* Segmental perception is good but incomplete for some more difficult sounds. *Prediction*: pairs of adult sounds that are not distinguished will surface with similar substitutions.
3. *Complete perception theory I.* The child perceives all adult sounds. *Prediction*: the child's substitutions are use of an unmarked for a marked sound, with variable articulation for the marked sound.

4.

> *Complete perception theory II.* The child perceives all adult sounds and
> keeps them distinct in his own speech. *Prediction*: the child sounds
> never correspond to more than one adult sound.

Waterson (1970, 1971) was one of the first to discuss the possibility of
drawing conclusions based on the child's productive language. She discussed this in relation to the analysis she made of her son P around the ages
of 1;6 to 1;8. At this time P had about 155 words, with approximately 100 of
them monosyllables (Waterson 1970: 9). She found that several of his words
couldn't be analyzed as simple correspondences between his sounds and
those of the adult language. She concluded that he was extracting only
certain features from the adult words which he used in his own. Since this
research is the strongest data in the literature in support of the global
perception theory, it will be examined more closely.

Example (8.6) gives a phonological lexicon of a subset of P's vocabulary
upon which Waterson based her arguments.

(8.6) angel [aɦɔ], [æhə], [æhə], [afiö] fish [ɪʃ], [ʊʃ]
    another [ɲaɲa] flower [væ], [væwæ]
    barrow [wæwæ], [bʌwu] fly [wæ], [bβæ], [βæ], [væ]
    biscuit [be:be:] honey [aɦu:]
    Bobby [bæbu:] kitty [tɪti]
    brush [byʃ] pudding [pupu]
    bucket [bæbu:] Randall [ɲaɲɵ]
    dirty [da̰:ti] Rooney [ehe], [hehe]
    dish [dɪʃ] vest [ʊʃ]
    fetch [ɪʃ] window [ɲe:ɲe]
    finger [ɲē:ɲē], [ɲi:ɲɪ]

In Table 8.5 we give two analyses of these data. The first is a substitution
analysis of P's initial consonants of the kind presented in Chapter 6. The
second is a summary of Waterson's analysis.

The segmental analysis in Analysis 1 supports the predictions for the
global perception theory. The correspondences look questionable in that
they are not what we would expect if the child were simply attempting an
adult sound. [ɲ] seems to occur for several sounds which it does not
particularly resemble. Also /f/ shows extensive variable pronunciations.
The fact that [t] occurs for both /t/ and /k/ suggests another possible
perceptual confusion. Waterson wants to suggest that such patterns are
indicative of the child's incomplete perception. Instead of matching individual segments, 'the child perceives only certain of the features of the adult
utterance and reproduces only those that he is able to cope with' (Waterson
1971: 181).

Table 8.5 *Two analyses of the data for P in (8.6). Analysis 1: a segmental analysis of P's initial consonants; Analysis 2: a summary of Waterson's (1971) analysis*

Analysis 1

Matches and substitutions for initial consonants

/p–	t–	k–	b–	d–	f–	h–	v–	w–	r–	n–	/
(p)	(t)	(t)	*b	d	ø	(ø)	(ø)	(ɲ)	(ɲ)	(ɲ)	
			(w)	v							
				(ɲ)							
				(bβ, β, w)							

Analysis 2: Five perceptual structures

I. Labial structure: wV(w(V)
barrow   [wæwæ], [bʌwu]
flower   [væ], [væwæ]
fly   [wæ], [bβæ], [βæ], [væ],

II. Continuant structure: VhV
angel   [aɦɔ], [æhə], [afiö]
honey   [aɦu:]
Rooney   [ẽfiẽ], [hẽfiẽ]

III. Sibilant structure: (C)V
brush   [byʃ]
dish   [dɪʃ]
fetch   [ɪʃ]
fish   [ɪʃ], [ʊʃ]
vest   [ʊʃ]

IV. Stop structure: CV
biscuit   [be:be:]
Bobby   [bæbu:]
bucket   [bæbu:]
dirty   [da̰:ti]
kitty   [tɪti]
pudding   [pupu]

V. Nasal structure: ɲVɲV
another   [ɲaɲa]
finger   [ɲẽ:ɲẽ:], [ɲi:ɲi]
Randall   [ɲaɲø]
window   [ɲe:ɲe]

As stated earlier, Waterson's data make a strong case for the global perception theory. There are, however, two reservations that stop us from accepting this position. First, the data in (8.6) constitute only 21 of P's 155 words. We are given little information about the nature of these other words. It may be that the other words demonstrated correspondences more consistent with segmental analyses. If so, then the data may be more consistent with the partial perception theory in that they point out a small number of the more difficult discriminations which P is still working out, such as initial /f/–/fl/ and medial nasals. A second concern is that extensive data of this kind are not widespread in other phonological diaries which have been reported. This will be apparent when we review some of them in the next section.

The opposite position to the global perception theory is the *complete perception theory II*. This would be the strongest claim for early perception, in that the child would never in its speech show mergers of adult categories. Such a situation is logically possible on the grounds that the child's language acquisition device would dispose the child to attempt to maintain distinctions of the adult language in his own language. We will, in fact, in our later discussion of homonymy provide some evidence that such constraints are at work. Current evidence indicates, however, that perceptual and/or articulatory factors still prevent this tendency from being totally successful.

This leaves us then with the *partial perception* and *complete perception I* theories. It is our impression that the above data from perception studies and data such as Waterson's favor at this time the partial perception theory. It is not possible to take a definitive position between these two, however, because the crucial research to decide the issue has not been done. This would be work which does phonological analyses on the child's spontaneous language, and then tests for perceptual awareness of those adult distinctions which are merged by the child. In taking this position, I wish to clarify that I do so with the feeling that the child's incomplete perception will be more noticeable in the child's earliest words, and that it may never be apparent for more than a few distinctions at any time.

The difficulty in determining which of these theories is at work can be exemplified by looking at our analysis of T in Table 6.29. There are no cases of two adult sounds being merged into one sound in T's speech where both cases involve non-lexical matches or substitutions. For example, /t/ is [t] and /θ/ is [t], but the latter only occurs in one word. Also, the cases of mergers which occur tend to fit the predictions of the complete perception theory I. For example, /t/ is [t] while /k/ appears both as [t] and [k], and /ʃ/ appears as [t] and [ʃ]. These are the variable pronunciations of Edwards's stage III when perception is good.

Summary.   We have explored the extent to which we can say that children during the current period of acquisitions have acquired phonemic perception. We have looked at both experimental studies and production data in attempting to find an answer to this question. The evidence to date suggests that children at this time have reasonably good perception of the words they know, but not necessarily complete knowledge. There may be particular distinctions which are inherently more difficult and which thus take longer to acquire. We have also seen from Schwartz & Leonard (1982), as discussed in Chapter 6, that children are selective in the words that they use. We need to establish the extent to which such selectivity contributes to this impression.

8.2.2 Phonological production

The discussion in Chapter 5 of early production for the first 50 words has suggested that children begin acquisition with a small phonological inventory which may show some influence of the native language. Despite this early system, the child's productive vocabulary is still quite small and variability both within and across children is quite noticeable. I proposed a method of analysis which reduced much of this variability to reveal the systematicity which led Jakobson to his original proposals on language acquisition.

The present period begins with the word spurt and provides more substantial data to make claims about phonological acquisition. While some researchers deny phonological organization during the acquisition of the first 50 words or so, most researchers will agree that the data of the period of simple sentences shows such organization. Here we will begin with a description of the kind of data available, and turn to some of the explanations that have been put forward to account for it.

Large sample studies
A number of large sample studies have been conducted on phonological acquisition in English, as well as in other languages (see the bibliography at the end of the chapter). Many of these were conducted early on, e.g. Wellman *et al.* (1931), Templin (1957), although there have been some others since then, e.g. Olmsted (1971), Prather, Hedrick & Kern (1975). Since the goal of most of them is to provide an overview of acquisition, they usually study as many sounds of the native language as possible. Some studies, however, have also concentrated on a single class of sounds, e.g. Ingram *et al.* (1980) on fricatives and affricates in English.

Templin (1957) We can get an idea of the general nature of these studies by examining the most frequently cited in Templin (1957). That this study is still perceived by many as the single most important normative study on English is supported by the fact that it is heavily cited for this purpose in the most recent text on phonological acquisition by Stoel-Gammon & Dunn (1985: 30–3). The general aspects of Templin's study have already been summarized in Table 2.3. To reiterate briefly, Templin tested 60 children at each of eight age intervals between 3;0 and 8;0 on 176 sounds in English. The younger children (3;0–5;0) were asked to identify a picture or asked to imitate the experimenter. The older children either read the words or repeated them.

Here we are particularly interested in how Templin constructed the test words, recorded the responses, and scored for acquisition. Table 8.6 lists the words used by Templin, distributed according to the consonants in them. Importantly, each of the 176 test sounds was tested in only one word. These test sounds are shown in Table 8.6 in capitals. For example, while there were six words which began with a /p/, only the child's response to 'pie' was scored for this sound. All responses were scored by Templin on site without the use of a tape-recorder. Only the test sounds in a word were

Table 8.6 *Test words used in Templin (1957) for children aged 3;0–5;0, arranged by the word position of their consonants. I = word-initial, M = word-medial, and F = word-final, based on Templin's analysis of these words. Test sounds in each word are capitalized*

STOPS

/p/   I: paGE, peaCH, peaS, Pie, piG, pIn, PRoMPT, playTHing, PLeaSure   M: oPen, o'poSSUM, Upon   F: CHip, SHip, soaP, sOUp, SLeep, SWeep, graSP, heLP, laMP, shaRP

/t/   I: tIE, Toes, tuB, TRain, tweLFTH, TWiNKLE   M: SKaTing   F: baT, Feet, Goat, Seat, WHite, biGGest, buRST, giFT, JumPED, neXT, PRoMPT, QUiLT, SQUiRT, condUCT, elePHaNT

/k/   I:caGED, caR, caRD, Cards, cOne, conduCT, ciOcks, clOUd, CLown, QUiLT, CRaCKER, chaSM   M: VaCuum-cleaner (×2), black-and-WHite   F: bAck, raKE, mUsic, aSK, miLK, SHRiNK, woRK

/b/   I: bAck, bAll, baT, baTH, Beans, bEEts, beLL, bOILS, bOOKS, buLB, buRST, baTHing, biGGer, biGGest, boTTLE, buBBLE, buCKLE, BLocks, bloTTer, BRead, black-and-WHite   M: rhuBaRB   F: tuB, buLB, rhuBaRB

/d/   I: Dish, daNGLE, DRum, driVing   M: WaDing, black-and-WHite   F: BReaD, clOUd, rEd, SPRead, caRD, saND

/g/   I: giFT, Goat, guM, gUn, garaGE, giGGLE, GLass, gliMPSE, graSP, GRass   M: biGGest   F: piG, icebeRG

FRICATIVES & AFFRICATES

/f/   I: Feet, fiSH, FLoWing, FRozen   M: elePHaNT   F: kniFE, mySeLF, whaRF

/θ/   I: THiNNer, THRee   M: playTHing   F: baTH, Mouth, eaRTH, heaLTH, moNTH, tweLFTH

/s/   I: sAll, saND, Seat, SoaP, sOUp, SCRatch, SLeep, SMooTH, SNow, SPoon, SPRead, SQUirt, STairs, stoNE, stOVE, STRing, SWeep, swiNG, swiNGing, SKaTing, SPLaSHing   M: mySeLF, icebeRG   F: GLass, GRass, HORse, mouSE, bEEts, BLocks, bOOKS, clOcks, gliMPSE

/ʃ/   I: shaRP, SHip, ship-aHoy, SHRink   M: SPLaSHing   F:Dish, fiSH

/v/   I: VaCuum-cleaner   M: driVing   F: stoVE

/ð/   I: THose   M: baTHing   F: SMooTH

/z/   I: ZiPPER   M: FRozen, mUsic   F: peaS, Toes, THose, Beans, bOILS, Cards, STairs

/ʒ/   M: PLeaSure   F: rouGE*, garaGE

/tʃ/   I: CHip, chuRCH, cheRRy   M: reaCHing   F:peaCH, SCRatch, chuRCH

/dʒ/   I: JumPED   M: aGing   F: paGE, caGED, laRGE

NASALS

/m/   maMa, miLK, moNTH, mouSE, Mouth, maSHER, moTHER, mUsic, mySeLF   M: maMa   F: DRum, guM, laMB, aRM, chaSM, o'poSSUM

/n/   I: kniFE, Nail, neXT, nuMBER   M: oNIon, conduCT   F: CLown, cOne, gUn, pIn, SPoon, stoNE, TRain, hoRN

/ŋ/   M: swiNGing   F: Ring, STRing, swiNG, aGing, baTHing, driVing, FLoWing, playTHing, reaCHing, swiNGing, WaDing, SKaTing

LIQUIDS & GLIDES

/l/	I: Lamb, laMP, laRGE M: elePHaNT, YeLLow F: bAll, beLL, Nail, sAll, aPPLE, boTTLE, buBBLE, buCKLE, daNGLE, giGGLE, ruFFLE, TWiNKLE, whiSTLE
/r/	I: raKE, rEd, Ring, reaCHing, rhuBaRB, ruBBER, ruFFLE M: cheRRy, GaraGE F: caR, biGGER, aSTER, bloTTER, CRaCKER, haMMER, maSHER, moTHER, nuMBER, ODOR, oFFER, ruBBER, THiNNER, VaCuum-cleaner, whiSKER, ZiPPER
/w/	I: whaRF, WaDing, whiSKER, whiSTLE M: FLoWing
/hw/	I: WHite M: black-and-WHite
/h/	I: heaLTH, heLP, hoRN, HORse, House, HaMMer M: ship-aHoy
/j/	I: YeLLow M: oNIon

* used only if 'garage' was pronounced with an affricate

scored, and these were either (a) correct, (b) omitted, (c) substitutions with other English sounds, or (d) substitutions with other sounds. A sound was considered acquired when at least 75% of the subjects in an age group produced it correctly. Templin provided a number of tables which allow manipulation of her results, although she unfortunately did not present information about the actual substitutions used by the subjects. Her results will be discussed first for single consonants and then for clusters. The discussion will concentrate on consonants because all twelve vowels which were tested reached the criterion by 3;0.

By 3;0, all the nasals were acquired, and all the stops except /-k/, /-t-,/ and final voiced ones /b,d,g/. All of these were subsequently acquired by 4;0 except /-t-/. If we look at the data more carefully, we can account for the superficially individual behavior of /-k/ and /-t-/. For /-k/, 73 percent of the 3-year-olds produced it correctly so that it just missed criterion. Also, at 4;0, it scored 87 percent compared to only 75 percent for /-t/ which did meet the criterion at 3;0. Further, /-k/ was tested in 'rake', which contains a front vowel which fronts the tongue position of the /k/ and often influences children to produce a more fronted substitute. Because of these factors, we will group /-k/ with the other voiceless stops and conclude that it is acquired by 3;0, lowering the criterion for acquisition in the process to 70 percent. Medial position /-t-/ was tested in the word 'skating'. It is a well-known fact of English that both /-t-/ and /-d-/ undergo a rule of flapping where each is produced as [ɾ]. Unfortunately, the acquisition of this rule has yet to be studied. In particular, we would want to know when children determine that the surface form [ɾ] is the surface neutralization of two phonemes. Such a study would include an examination of the use of flapping in the speech of parents to children. Templin's data indicate that the /-t-/ vs. /-d-/ contrast may be acquired late, but her scoring system is not adequate to conclude this. A child's flapping a /-t-/ would be scored as incorrect even though it is an appropriate English pronunciation.

The glides /w/, /h/, and /j/ are all acquired by 3;0. The first two are to be expected from our study of the previous period of acquisition. The sound /j/ is not particularly frequent in English and may be subject to the influences of functional load discussed in Chapter 6. The liquids /l/ and /r/ reach criterion for acquisition by 4;0, with two exceptions: /-r/ in 'car' is correct 80 percent of the time by 3;5, while /-l/ in 'bell' does not reach criterion until 6;0. Both these sounds, however, need more careful testing than in one word. As pointed out by Olmsted, /-r/ is one phoneme, but is phonetically quite variable depending on the preceding vowel. He, in fact, uses several phonetic symbols to transcribe this sound. Syllable-final /-l/ is also quite different phonetically from syllable-initial /l/ by showing a high degree of velarization (see Ladefoged 1975). The velarization of /-l/ may be so great as to reduce the sound to a vowel. Given these difficulties with /-r/ and /-l/, we will separate them from the syllable-initial liquids and conclude that the latter are acquired according to Templin's data between 3;0 and 4;0.

This leaves the fricative class. For a first look at this class, the percentages of correct responses for the three word positions in (8.7) are collapsed and are given here for each of five age groups. (The acquired sounds are in bold type.)

(8.7)   *Percentages of correct responses in Templin (1957)*

Age	/f/	/θ/	/s/	/ʃ/	/v/	/ð/	/z/	/ʒ/	/tʃ/	/dʒ/
3;0	**84**	26	**64**	44	31	20	34	15	47	35
3;5	88	32	78	63	39	23	55	23	61	41
4;0	92	49	76	**71**	51	42	58	33	**72**	**69**
4;5	97	59	77	84	54	47	66	38	83	72
5;0	91	63	78	82	62	56	64	43	84	81

As we did with the acquisition of /-k/, we will modify the criterion of acquisition from 75 percent to 70 percent. Also, for the years where half-year data are available, we will average the two. For example, the percentage of acquisition for 3;0 will be the average of the figures for 3;0 and 3;5. This loosening of the criterion is done on the grounds that 75 percent is a relatively strict criterion. Recall that the measure for matches in Chapter 6 was over 50 percent, a lower measure also used in Olmsted (1971). The revised measure shows the following acquisition. First, /f/ and /s/ are both acquired at 3;0. This is consistent with the findings of English fricatives reported for the period of the first 50 words. Next, the palatals /ʃ/, /tʃ/, and /dʒ/ are acquired at 4;0. None of the other sounds reach either Templin's or our adjusted criterion, indicating that these are the latest consonants acquired in English.

While the positions for these sounds were merged, it can be seen that at least some of the non-acquired fricatives were acquired differently in different word positions. These differences are given in (8.8):

(8.8)

Age	/v/			/z/			/ʒ/		ð/		
	I	M	F	I	M	F	M	F	I	M	F
3;0	12	60	22	30	47	25	18	12	23	17	20
3;5	30	65	23	55	75	35	25	20	32	27	12
4;0	40	75	38	62	72	42	45	22	57	45	23
4;5	47	78	38	72	75	50	48	28	60	52	30
5;0	55	80	50	65	75	53	57	28	62	67	40

The voiced fricatives /v/, /z/, and /ʒ/ all show more of a tendency to occur correctly in medial position than in either initial or final. The pattern is most obvious for /v/, but is found for the other two also. The voiced dental /ð/ shows a different pattern, in which the initial and medial positions are noticeably better than final position. There is a slight tendency for /θ/ to do this also, but not enough to suggest grouping them into a class in this regard.

(8.9) presents a summary of our interpretation of Templin's results on the acquisition of English consonants.

(8.9) *Summary of English consonant acquisition to 4;0*
   3;0 nasals /m,n,ŋ/; voiceless stops /p,t,k/; glides /w,j,h/; fricatives /f,s/; voiced stops /b,d,g/ except finally
   4;0 voiced stops in final position, palatal fricatives and affricates /ʃ,tʃ,ʤ/; liquids /l,r/ at least in initial and medial position; medial /v,z/

This summary indicates that the majority of English phonemes are acquired by 4;0. The sounds still to be acquired are the flapped intervocalic alveolar stop and several fricatives, particularly the dentals /θ,ð/ and the voiced palatal /ʒ/.

As can be seen from Table 8.6, Templin also examined a larger number of consonant clusters, 71 with two consonants and 19 with three consonants by her count. (We say 'by her count' because not everyone would classify clusters in the way Templin does. This point will be returned to below.) A brief summary of these data is as follows. (i) Active acquisition of fricatives begins between 3;0 and 4;0. At 3;0, only one cluster, /ŋk/, reached Templin's criterion; this increased to 15 clusters at 3;5 and to 35 or nearly one-half of those tested by 4;0. (ii) The clusters acquired during this time belong primarily to the following categories: (a) initial clusters with /s/ and a following stop /p,t,k/ or nasal /m,n/; (b) initial clusters with stops /p,t,k,b,d,g/ followed by a liquid /l,r/ or glide /w/; and (c) final clusters with a nasal /m,ŋ/ followed by a voiceless stop /p,k/. (iii) Those clusters which are acquired later tend to fall into the following categories: (a) clusters with three consonants – only three of the 19 tested reached criterion at 5;0, while 12 did at 6;0; (b) initial clusters which combine fricatives and liquids, e.g. /sl-/, /fr-/; (c) final clusters which combine liquids /l,r/ with obstruents, e.g. /-rb/, /lf/; and (d) final clusters which combine /s/ with stops /p,t,k/.

Templin's study provides a useful descriptive overview of English phonological acquisition. It can be used for comparison with similar studies on other languages, and as normative data for English acquisition. Here, however, we will conclude with a caution about using large sample data such as these for anything more than the most general of purposes, setting out a series of problems with Templin's study in particular and large sample studies in general. The limitations of such studies need to be emphasized since their results may be inappropriately used both for theoretical and practical purposes, the latter including cases where a child might be misidentified as being speech-delayed because of his performance of a Templin-style articulation test.

A first point that can be raised about this study is that it is an *articulation study*, not a linguistic one, that is, the results tell us something about the degree of difficulty of certain sounds, but relatively little about the phonological systems of children. The fact that children have more difficulty with one sound over another does not of itself eliminate the possibility that children may still have both sounds within their linguistic system. This is particularly possible when a high criterion of acquisition is set and the two sounds fall closely together on either side of it. The study is restricted from being a linguistic study also because grouped data are being used for the analysis: we are never talking about the language of a single child, so we can never be sure whether the general pattern is reflected in individual children. Such grouped results can only be interpreted with confidence when they are supported by single subject analyses.

Other problems arise because of the nature of the words tested and the way they are analyzed. For one thing, each sound is only tested in one word. When we say that some sound 'x' was either acquired or not at some age, what we are really saying is that this is so for this sound in the word tested. For example, when we say that /v/ is not acquired until 6;0, what we are saying is that 75 percent of children before 6 years of age cannot pronounce [v] in 'vacuum cleaner'. It may well be that children will do better with this sound in another word such as 'vase'. We will refer to such a possibility as *lexical variability*. Despite Templin's claims to the contrary, evidence exists which suggests such lexical variation is due to the influence of syllabic complexity and adjacent sounds (see Ingram 1976a: 83–5; and Ingram *et al.* 1980). This factor alone could influence greatly conclusions about the age of acquisition of a sound when just one word is used for testing. It should be pointed out that such problems are not inherent in studies of this kind. As we can see in Table 8.6, there were often several words in the test which would show each of the test sounds. If all of these data were recorded and included in the analysis it would contribute greatly to eliminating the influence of lexical variability.

A factor which interacts with lexical variability is *word familiarity*. We have already seen from the previous section that children are more likely to perceive differences between sounds in words they know than in unfamiliar ones. It is also possible that children's pronunciation of words will be influenced by this factor. A casual glance through Table 8.6 reveals several words that do not appear to be typical of very young children, e.g. 'aster', 'conduct', 'pleasure' and 'rhubarb'. Shriberg & Kwiatkowski (1980) have criticized several such tests on the grounds that the words used are also much more phonologically complex than those typical of children at the ages being tested. They demonstrate this point with percentages of different kinds of syllable structures in words used in such tests as compared with the distribution of such syllable structures in the natural speech of young children. They, in fact, reach the conclusion that the only accurate way to assess a child's phonological system is through a naturalistic language sample.

A last problem with Templin's study is the lack of *linguistic sophistication* used in selecting the test sounds and words. I have already pointed out the problem with the flapping rule for medial dentals, and the allophonic variation between final and nonfinal /r/ and /l/. A further set of such problems may arise because Templin does not distinguish syllable position from word position. Sounds which are word-medial can occur in different syllable positions; for example, medial /-f-/ and /-s-/ were tested in 'elephant' and 'myself' respectively. The [f] in 'elephant' begins an unstressed syllable preceded by an unstressed vowel, and this is a different case from the [s] in 'myself' which begins a stressed syllable. Acquisition data suggest that word-medial sounds beginning stressed syllables pattern similarly to word-initial ones in stressed syllables, yet differently from those beginning unstressed syllables. For example, the [s] in 'myself' is more likely to pattern with the [s] in 'seat' than the [s] in 'kissing'. We already observed in Templin's data a difference for several of the fricatives between sounds beginning stressed and unstressed syllables. A further difficulty concerns Templin's treatment of syllabic consonants such as /r/ and /l/ in words like 'masher' and 'whistle'. While their phonological status is controversial, many linguists would agree that phonetically these sounds should be treated as vocalic elements rather than members of clusters. If so, then words like 'apple' would not be analyzed as ending with a cluster 'pl' as Templin has done, but rather as CVCV or CVCVC structures with the [p] treated as intervocalic.

Limitations of these kinds are characteristic of large sample studies, but it should be pointed out that they are not necessarily inherent in the studies, but rather, they are characteristic of how such studies have been designed and analyzed. A large sample study done in a different way could be a valuable contribution to the study of phonological acquisition. For example, suppose that Templin had tape-recorded all of her subjects and done analyses of the kind discussed in Chapter 6 for all of the words listed in Table 8.6 for each child. Also, suppose analyses for individual children had been done within a week or two of the sampling so that follow-up visits could have pursued questionable aspects of the results, much in the way suggested for syntactic studies at the end of Chapter 7. This approach would have yielded tremendous information about the phonological acquisition of English.

Diary studies As a consequence of limitations of the kind just outlined in the analyses of data from large sample studies, the most insightful data on the emergence of phonology come from diary studies. These studies provide much more detail on the development of the phonological systems of individual children. A small number of such studies has come to form the basis of much which has been claimed about phonological acquisition. A summary of the data from a few of the most famous ones on English acquisition is presented here.

Velten (1943) Velten (1943) was the first major phonological diary to appear in support of Jakobson's (1941) theory of phonological acquisition, newly published at that time in German. Velten reports on the acquisition of his daughter Joan from her 11th to 36th month. Her words are presented in a broad phonetic transcription, and are usually dated by the month in which they appeared. No variable pronunciations are presented for individual words and it appears that Velten has presented the most typical form used by Joan for the period being discussed. Not all words are presented for the entire period studied so that it is sometimes difficult to determine how each word used was pronounced during each month of the study.

Before looking at Joan's data, it is important to discuss her linguistic background. The mother spoke American English, but other languages were also used. Velten states (p. 285):

> Since French and Norwegian are frequently spoken in the household and used to address the child (though less often than English), she acquires at an early age a large passive vocabulary, and is able to follow fairly complicated directions, in these languages ... Normally Joan responds in English when addressed in French or Norwegian.

Table 8.7 *Words acquired by Joan Velten between the 11th and 22nd months, taken from Velten (1943). Distinct phonetic types and lexical types are numbered by their order of appearance**

Word	English (month)	Word	English (month)
1. ap	1. 'up' (end of 11th)	18. ba:	15. 'pie' (15th)
2. ba	2.'bottle' (end of 11th)	19. dat	16. 'duck' (16th)
3. ba	3. 'ban' (end of 11th)	20. bap	17. 'lamb' (16th)
4. bas	4. 'bus' (12th)	21. am	18. 'M' (17th)
5. ba:'za	5. 'put on' (12th)	22. an	19. 'N' (17th)
6. baza'	5. 'put on' (later)[1]	23. n	20. 'in' (17th)
7. za	6. 'that' (12th)	24. un	20. 'in' (later)[1]
8. da	7. 'down' (13th)	25. da:	21. 'doll' (18th–20th)
9. at	8. 'out' (13th)	26. as	22. 'S' (18th–20th)
10. ba:'ba	9. 'away' (13th)	27. u:	23. 'O' (18th–20th)
11. ba:'ba'	10. 'outside' (13th)	28. a	24. 'R' (18th–20th)
12. bat	11. 'pocket' (13th)	29. nas	25. 'nice' (18th–20th)
13. af	12. 'Fuff'[2] (14th)	30. na:'na	26. 'banana' (18th–20th)
14. faf	12. 'Fuff' (later)[1]	31. wa	27. 'Y' (21st)
15. bada'	5. 'put on' (14th)	32. ats	28. 'X' (21st)
16. bus	13. 'push' (15th)	33. du'du	29. 'Doudou'[3] (21st)
17. uf	14. 'woof' (15th)	34. hwut	30. 'foot' (21st)

*[:] indicates vowel length; ['] occurs after a stressed syllable.
[1] A specific date is not given, but presumably occurs later the same month.
[2] name of family cat
[3] name of character in French children's story

Unfortunately, little more information is provided about the adult models for these languages. We speculate that Norwegian was used by Velten and probably his Norwegian parent or parents, and that French was the language of a nanny or housekeeper. The fact that French may have influenced Joan's language is an important point which we will return to later.

Joan's development is presented in essentially three parts. First, there is a detailed discussion of the slow acquisition of the first 30 words between the 11th and 21st months. Then, there is the presentation of all the words acquired during a five-week period beginning in the 22nd month when the word spurt occurred, and her language expanded from 30 to 150 words. Lastly, a series of subsequent developments are presented in detail, with special consideration given to the acquisition of vowel length.

Table 8.7 presents the words acquired by Joan before the word spurt at 22 months. One general aspect of this list is that it consists predominantly of monosyllables. The few multisyllables which occur tend to be reduplications, the only exceptions being [ba:'za],[baza'], and [bada']. The monosyllables not only dominate, but show only four syllabic shapes: VC, CV,

CVC, and V. Another feature is the way in which the voicing of consonants occurs across syllable positions. Voiced consonants occur prevocalically, and voiceless ones only at the end of the word. The only exceptions to this are [f] and [hw]. An unusual aspect of the data is the highly restricted vocalic inventory: [a] is the only vowel for several months, and only the two-vowel system [a] and [u] occurs at the time of the word spurt.

Velten points out some other features of these early words, for example, how frequent words tended to resist change. He gives the example of [ba] for 'bottle' which did not change to a CVC form [baz] until a large number of CVC words had been acquired. He states (pp. 284–5): 'from almost every stage of the development some of the most frequently used morphemes are retained without change'. Another point he makes is how words which contain a new sound seem at first like loan words, to the extent that it may be a long time before the sound becomes established as part of the child's system.

Velten's analysis of these data is that Joan has acquired nine phonemes at this point (21 months). He doesn't provide much in the way of a detailed analysis, but presents them in the discussion of the next month when Joan underwent a noticeable word spurt. Importantly, Velten emphasizes that this rapid growth of vocabulary did not result in any expansion of the phonological inventory. In fact, over a five-week period, there was only one new phoneme added, this being [h] for adult words with /h/, e.g. 'hole' [hu], 'head' [hut]. Instead, the combinations of the acquired nine phonemes increased dramatically. For example, Velten states (p. 286): 'the utilization of all theoretically possible combinations of these 9 phonemes rises, for monosyllables, from 26% to about 86%'. At least these data, then, suggest a relation of some kind between the word spurt and phonological productivity.

Table 8.8 presents Velten's summary (p. 286) of these nine phonemes, their allophones, and their correspondences to English sounds during this subsequent period of development. (Following a practice used by Smith 1973, among others, we will use | | around the proposed phonemes for the child to distinguish these from the phonemes of the adult language.) The system is relatively symmetrical, except for /f/ where there is no voiced allophone occurring prevocalically. It also fits the phonetic inventory discussed earlier for the period of the first 50 words, except for the early occurrence of [z].

Besides information on allophonic variation, the analysis also provides the adult models for the child's sounds, in which we find both general patterns and ones which are relatively unusual. The more common ones are as set out below. (We will give these correspondences names that have been used since Velten's paper, although at this point these are only meant as

Table 8.8 *Velten's analysis of Joan at 22 months*

Phoneme	Allophones	English target sounds
|p,b|	[b] before vowels	/p/,/b/;/v-/
	[p] word-final	
|t,d|	[d] before vowels	/t/,/d/;/k/,/g/;/č-/,/ǰ-/
	[t] word-final	
|f|	[f]	/f/;hw-/,/sw-/;/-v/;
		/-θ/ and /-ð/ after labials
|s,z|	[z] before vowels	/s/,/š/,/z/,/ž/;/l-/,/j-/;
	[s] word-final	/θ/ and /ð/ initially and after dentals
|m|	[m]	/m/
|n|	[n]	/n/,/ŋ/
|w|	[w]	/w/;/r-/;/-v-/
|a|	[a]	(to be discussed)
|u|	[u]	(to be discussed)

descriptive labels; when necessary, some of the examples are from the data in later samples.)

1. *Prevocalic voicing*; the voicing of obstruents before vowels, /p/ to [b], e.g. 'pocket' [bat]; /t/ to [d], e.g. 'toe' [du:]; /k/ to [d], e.g. 'cup' [dap]
2. *Final devoicing*: the devoicing of final voiced obstruents, /-b/ to [p], e.g. 'knob' [nap]; /d/ to [t], e.g. 'bad' [bat]; /-g/ to [t], e.g. 'egg' [ut]; /-v/ to [f], e.g. 'stove' [duf]
3. *Stopping*: the change of fricatives and affricates into stops, e.g. /v-/ to [b], e.g. 'vinegar' [bidu]; /č/ to [d], e.g. 'cherry' [dawa]; [ǰ] to [d], 'jam' [dab]
4. *Fronting*: the production of velar and palato-alveolar sounds as alveolars, /k/ to [t], e.g. 'duck' [dat]; /g/ to [d], e.g. 'goat' [dut]; /š/ to [z], e.g. 'shoes' [zus]; /ž/ to [z], e.g. 'rouge' [wu:z]; /č/ to [ts], e.g. 'match' [mats]; /ǰ/ to [daz], e.g. 'cabbage' [ta:budz]
5. *Gliding*: the changing of a liquid into a glide, /r/ to [w], e.g. 'rock' [wat].

Of the five patterns just named, the first two and stopping are the most prevalent in the data. Stopping appears to be marginal and primarily affects the initial affricates. This process is more widespread with other children, but Joan clearly had an ability to produce fricatives from the onset of acquisition. Gliding is restricted to initial /r/ and not /l/ according to Table 8.8. Subsequent discussion in the text, however, shows that the pattern is more widespread than this, as follows:

5. *Gliding* (revised): also affects intervocalic /-r-/ after the vowels /a/, /æ/, and /ɛ/, e.g. 'sorry' [sawa], 'Mary' [mawa], 'carry' [dawa]

Some other common patterns occur in the data which are not included in Velten's summary on p. 286, but which are mentioned later in the text. One such pattern affects certain liquids which surface as vowels, which we will refer to as vocalization:

6.   *Vocalization*: the production of syllabic or nonsyllabic liquids as vocalic elements: syllabic /r/ and /l/ as [a] or [u] (these would usually assimilate to the vowel of the preceding syllable), e.g. 'hammer' [hama], 'table' [dubu]; postvocalic /l/ after the vowels /ʌ/, /æ/, /ɛ/ to [w], e.g. 'well' [waw], 'shall' [saw], 'belt' [bawt]

There are also cases which involve deletion of either segments or syllables, labeled as follows:

7.   *Final consonant deletion*: the deletion of consonants at the end of words to preserve open syllables, /-l/ after the vowels /ɔ/, /ai/, and /aw/, (which all surface as [a]) e.g. 'doll' [da], 'while' [fa], 'owl' [aw], and after all the English vowels which surface as [u], e.g. 'peel' [pu]; /-r/, e.g. 'far' [fa]

8.   *Cluster reduction*: the simplification of consonant clusters into single segments. The direction of the reduction is often predictable:
(a) stop and liquid /l/ or /r/ combinations are reduced to stops, e.g. 'bread' [but]; 'glass' [das];
(b) /s/ and stop or nasal initial clusters are reduced to stops, e.g. 'star' [da:], 'snap' [nap];
(c) final nasal and voiceless stop clusters are reduced to stops, e.g. 'bent' [bat];
(d) final nasal and voiced stop clusters are reduced to nasals, e.g. 'hand' [han].

9.   *Unstressed syllable deletion*: delete unstressed syllables, particularly if before a stressed syllable, e.g. 'pocket' [bat], 'banana' [na:'na].

Since Joan was reasonably good at producing syllables and final consonants, neither final consonant deletion nor unstressed syllable deletion were prominent in the data.

Besides the above patterns, Joan also showed some correspondences which, based on Ingram (1981a), are less common in other children acquiring English. One of these involved the deletion of liquids. This process, *intervocalic consonant deletion*, in Joan's speech deleted intervocalic /-r-/ and /-l-/ when they followed any English vowel which surfaced as [u], e.g. 'worry' [wua], 'pillow' [pua]. Two others stand out in particular and have been the basis for later analyses, particularly in Stampe (1973). They are: (a) the change or *frication* of /ǰ-/, /l-/, /-l-/, /-r-/ and /-t-/ (presumably a flapped consonant) into [z], (for the intervocalic liquids, this only applies to cases where intervocalic consonant deletion does not apply); (b) the *denasalization* of final nasals as in 'lamb' [bap]. Denasalization occurred in words beginning with consonants or [hu], but not elsewhere. (8.10) presents some examples of these particularly interesting changes.

(8.10)

		Frication		Denasalization
/j-/		'yellow' [za:'wa]		'broom' [bub]
		'yard' [za:d]		'spoon' [bud]
/l-/		'leaf' [zuf]		'jam' [dab]
		'lady' [zudu]		'train' [dud]
/-l-/		'color' [daz]		'swim' [fub]
		'Na*pole*on' [buz]		'room' [wub]
/-r-/		'to*morrow*' [maz]		'rain' [wud]
		(later [maza])		'home' [hub]
		'Harry' [haz]		*but*:
		(later [haza])		'arm' [am]
/-t-/		'bottle' [baz]		'moon' [mun]
		'water' [waz]		'ham' [ham]

A last unusual pattern is the reduction of all English vowels into just two phonetic variants of [u] and [a]. We will present the English model vowels for these two surface vowels through the vocalic chart given in (8.11), using the phonetic symbols from Ladefoged.

(8.11)

/i/				/u/	
/ɪ/				/ʊ/	
/ei/				/ow/	
/ɛ/	(before stops			/ɔ/ before /l/	
	and spirants)	/ə/		/ɔɪ/	
/ɛ/	(before nasals	/ʌ/	/ɔ/		
	and liquids)				
/æ/	/ai/	/a/			

Generally speaking, mid and high vowels surface as [u] and low vowels as [a]. We will refer to these two patterns as *vowel raising* and *vowel lowering* respectively. These can be exemplified while pointing out another aspect of Joan's phonology. She had a small set of phonetic forms which she used for several adult words, resulting in a large degree of homonymy for them. The three most used forms in this way were [bat], [but], and [bu]. (8.12) gives adult words for these four (Velten 1943: 287–8) which can also be used as examples for the vowel correspondences in (8.11).

(8.12)

[bat]	'black, bark, spot, pocket, bought, button, bent, bite'
[but]	'brick, pig, bead, bed, break, board, boat, bird, put, boot'
[bu]	'boy, pea, beer, bare, pear, ball, blow, bowl, blue'

Table 8.9 *Summary of patterns affecting liquids (∅ = deletion)*

Pattern	/l-/	/-l-/	/-l/	/-l/	/r-/	/-r-/	/-r/	/-r/
Frication	[z]							
Gliding				[w]				
after /a, æ, ɛ/					[w]			
Vocalization					vowel			vowel
after /ʌ, e, ɛ/			[w]					
Final consonant deletion							∅	
except after /ʌ, ae, ɛ/			∅					
Cluster reduction	∅				∅			
Intervocalic consonant deletion		∅				∅		
Frication		[z]				[z]		
(if not deleted by above)								

While many of Joan's correspondences are relatively straightforward, those for the liquids /l/ and /r/ are particularly varied. This is not necessarily surprising in that we have already pointed out in relation to Templin's study that these sounds consist of several allophones. Table 8.9 is an attempt to provide an overview of the various forms that these sounds surface in, where ∅ indicates deletion.

Velten states that all of the above correspondences remained unchanged for approximately ten months, except for one important series of changes. From the 23rd to 27th months, Joan acquired the distinction between voiced and voiceless stops. This development coincided with a series of changes in Joan's use of vowel length. Velten divides these developments into five stages of change, along with substages. Table 8.10 presents a summary of this series of changes.

We have added a stage 0 to point out the situation with vowel length before these stages begin. At 22 months, the only long vowels which occur are in open syllables, with only four exceptions – words which were open but had short vowels. All vowels in closed syllables were short. The first stage brings the introduction of surface vowel length which later permeates Joan's system. The important stages are really stages 2 and 3. In stage 2, Joan introduces a surface length distinction which marks the underlying difference between voiced and voiceless consonants. This is not surprising in that English tends to lengthen vowels before final voiced consonants. The next stage shows some peculiar adjustments to this tendency. As final voiced consonants emerge, one set of previously long vowels becomes shortened, while another short set becomes lengthened. We will refer to these two unique patterns which go against the normal direction of vowel lengthening in English as *vowel shortening* and *vowel lengthening*

Table 8.10 *Stages in the acquisition of the voicing distinction for Joan Velten*

Stage	Month	Description of change	Examples
0	22nd	Only long vowels are in words with open syllables, with four exceptions.	'down' [da] vs. 'pie' [pa:] 'shut' [ba] vs. 'toe' [du:]
1.	23rd	[a:] occurs for /a/ in stressed closed syllables	'top' [da:p] vs. 'cup' [dap]
2.	24th	[a:] and [u:] occur for all vowels in stressed closed syllables before voiced stops and spirants	'bad' [ba:t] vs. 'back' [bat] 'red' [wu:t] vs. 'wet' [wut] 'bead' [bu:t] vs. 'beat' [but] 'nose' [nu:s]
3c.	24th[1]	[u] for /i, ei, ə·, ow, u/ becomes [u:] in all stressed syllables	'goose' [du:s], 'lake' [du:t] 'coat' [du:t], 'hurt' [hu:t]
3b.	24th	[a:] for /ʌ/ and /u:/ for /ɛ/ become shortened	'red' [wud][2] (from [wu:t]) 'mud' [mad][2] (from [ma:t])
3a.	24th	Final /-b/ and /-d/ are acquired	'meat' [mu:t][3] vs. 'maid' [mu:d] vs. 'moon' [mu:n] 'hat' [hat] vs. 'hug' [had][4] vs. 'hen' [han][4] *but* 'rib' [wub] vs. 'rim' [wub][5]
		final [z] is acquired for /-z, -ʒ/	'nose' [nu:z], 'rouge' [wu:z] 'hose' [hu:z]
	25th[6]	[ɪ] becomes an allophone of /ʊ/ before dentals	'foot' [fɪt] vs. 'fit' [fut][7] 'whip' [fup], 'swim' [fub]
4.	25th	the oppositions /p/–/b/, /t/–/d, and /s/–/z/ appear in initial position	'cold' [tu:d] vs. 'Joan' [du:d] 'sign' [sa:d] vs. 'yard' [za:d]
5.	27th[8]	oppositions of stage 4 also occur for medial position, except for /-t-/	'needle' [nu:du] vs. 'naked' [nu:tu], 'grocer' [du:sa] vs. 'daisy' [du:zu] vs. 'letter' [zu:zu]

[1] These three substages occur simultaneously about three weeks after 2.
[2] See stage 3a for change of [t] to [d].
[3] See stage 3c for lengthening of [u:].
[4] See stage 3b for shortening of [a].
[5] Due to denasalization, final nasal vs. stop is still neutralized in some cases.
[6] This change occurs after those of stage 3 but does not affect the lengthening rules of stage 3.
[7] This form is not attested in the data but it is hypothetically possible; we have placed it here to show the surface contrast that now occurs.
[8] This change takes over three months to spread throughout the lexicon.

respectively. The result is a four-way system of vowels which, Velten claims, lasted for nine months. Velten summarizes this system as follows:

[a] for   (a) /æ, ɔ, ai/ before voiceless consonants;
          (b) /ɛ/ before liquids, nasals, and /-t-/;
          (c) /ʌ/ in any position;
[a:] for   (a) /ae, ɔ, ai/ before voiced consonants;
          (b) /a/ in any stressed syllable;

[u] for   (a) /ɛ/ before stops and spirants;

            (b) /ɪ, ʊ/ in any position;

[u:] for   (a) /ɔl/ after initial labial;

            (b) /i, ei, ow, ɚ·, u, ɔɪ, ɪu/ in any stressed syllable.

These, then, are the major patterns discussed by Velten for the acquisition of his daughter's phonology. The only other changes briefly discussed are the loss of denasalization during the end of the third year, and the eventual development of other vowels. Velten's data show both the general aspects of early phonological acquisition during this period and the peculiarities that can be found in data from individual children. We have identified nine common patterns in the data – common in the sense that they can be found to some extent in the language of most other children acquiring English. We have also pointed out several of Joan's very unusual patterns. Four of these affect vowels (vowel raising, lowering, shortening, and lengthening), and two affect consonants (frication and denasalization). All of the patterns are striking in the detail in which they are found.

While Velten states that his data are in support of Jakobson's theory, he actually spends little time trying to justify this claim. Certainly Joan's early system does not match up particularly well with Jakobson's first stage of acquisition given in Table 6.23 on page 192. Nor does Velten attempt to show how Joan's complex patterns support Jakobson's claims about an invariant sequence of contrasts. What we have here, then, is a detailed set of descriptive data which need to be explained: later I will examine a major explanation for these data, proposed by Stampe (1969, 1973).

Leopold (1947)   I have focussed on Velten's data because of its detail and uniqueness. Before turning to the issue of explanation, two further important diary studies will be briefly considered; along with Velten, these constitute the three most frequently cited sets of data.

The next significant diary study on an English-learning child was that of Leopold on his daughter *Hildegard*. The report on Hildegard's phonological development appeared in 1947 in the second volume of Leopold's four volume work, subtitled 'Sound learning in the first two years'. Like Joan, Hildegard was not exposed just to English; she was acquiring both German and English simultaneously, and Leopold reports data for both languages. Her English data have been widely discussed, and her acquisition of her first 50 words has been analyzed in the study by Ferguson & Farwell (1975) already discussed in Chapter 6.

Leopold reports on Hildegard's development from the first words around 0;8 to the end of 1;11, with some selected remarks on later development. As reported in Ferguson & Farwell (1975), the period of the phonology of the first 50 words lasted up to 1;5 when a word spurt occurred. By the end of 1;11, Hildegard had acquired 400 words in her spoken language. Her development of phonology was similar to Joan's in the sense that she first acquired a small inventory of sounds, then expanded the combinatory potential of these during the word spurt. In other words, her development from 1;6 to 1;11 was not marked by the addition of new sounds as much as by increased use of the ones she had already acquired.

In Ingram (1985d), there was a brief report on Hildegard's phonetic inventory at 1;11, using the method presented in Chapter 6. This inventory was as follows:

(8.13) *Word-initial consonants*   *Word-final consonants*
      m- n-
      b- d-   -t   -k
      w-   h-   -ʃ

This is a strikingly small consonantal inventory for the size of her vocabulary at this age. It is even small when compared with the English phonetic inventory presented in Chapter 6 for the end of the phonology of the first 50 words. An important general aspect of Hildegard's acquisition, then, is a marked delay in phonetic acquisition compared with her lexical acquisition.

One consequence of Hildegard's slow phonetic development was the extensive existence of *homonymy*, i.e. the use of a phonetic form for two or more adult words. We pointed out that Joan also had extensive homonymy, but it appeared to be tied to the use of a small number of phonetic forms. Leopold's list of Hildegard's homonymous words (pp. 231–4) indicates that it extended throughout her lexicon. In Ingram (1985d), Hildegard's use of homonymy was measured and compared with that of two other children. The measure used was the proportion of homonymous types in each child's lexicon. A homonymous type is a word (or lexical type) which has at least one phonetic type which is homonymous with some other word in the lexicon. Some examples from Hildegard's diary are [ba] for 'ball', 'box', 'block', and 'Paul', [hat] for 'hot' and 'hat', and [titi] for 'cookie' and 'sticky'. While homonymy decreased over time for the other two children, it actually increased for Hildegard. For example, her proportion of homonymous types was approximately 0.15 at 1;7 compared to over 0.40 at 1;11. In other words, by 1;11 nearly every other word of hers was homonymous with at least one other word.

Despite some peculiarities in individual lexical items, Hildegard's substitution patterns are by and large restricted to the set of common ones mentioned in the discussion on Joan's language. (8.14) is a summary of these with some examples for each pattern.

(8.14) *Some phonological patterns of Hildegard Leopold*
1. Prevocalic voicing: e.g. 'Paul' [ba], 'toast' [dok]
2. Final devoicing: e.g. 'bug' [bok]
3. Stopping: e.g. 'Joey' [do.i], 'June' [du]
4. Fronting: e.g. 'Jack' [da]
5. Gliding: e.g. 'lie' [jai], 'rock' [wɔk]
6. Vocalization: 'bottle' [balu], 'ball' [baw]
7. Final consonant deletion: 'poor' [pu], 'big' [bɪ], 'comb' [do], 'June' [du]
8. Cluster reduction: 'stick' [dik], 'brush' [baʃ]
9. Unstressed syllable deletion: 'pocketbook' [babu]

The peculiarities which occur in Hildegard's data are restricted primarily to the acquisition of voicing and the fricatives. The early data show the use of both [p] and [b] word initially, with a later shift to only [b] with prevocalic voicing of [p]. As Leopold points out, however, this was the consequence of what he calls the 'whispering stage' (p. 208) which characterized Hildegard's first months of producing certain of her words. We have already mentioned one example of this in 6.5.4, the word 'pretty'. The [p] in these words became [b] once the vowels also were pronounced. What initially appears as a regression in development, then can actually be traced to Hildegard's tendency to whisper selected words.

Hildegard is noticeably different from Joan in her acquisition of fricatives. First, the only one in her phonetic repertoire is [ʃ] which occurs finally for /-f,/-s,/-z,/-š,/-č/. This sound not only occurs as a final substitution, but also as part of a preferred pattern for some words with a fricative elsewhere, e.g. 'stone' [doiʃ], 'story' [lɔiʃ]. When we examine her substitution patterns for initial fricatives, we find that there are very few words even attempted with them. That is, as pointed out by Ferguson & Farwell (1975), Hildegard appears actively to avoid attempting fricatives. The one exception is /f-/, which becomes [w]. Interestingly, this is a substitution that was not found in any of the 73 subjects studied in Ingram *et al.* (1980). It is a substitution which suggests some influence from her simultaneous acquisition of German.

Smith (1973)   The last diary study to be reviewed here is Smith (1973) on his son Amahl (or A as he is referred to in the book). Like Joan and Hildegard, A was raised in a multilingual environment. His father is British, and his mother Indian. The mother spoke Hindi, Bengali, Marathi, and a dialect of English referred to as Standard Indian English. Smith states that A was exposed to Hindi and Marathi, but was still raised primarily as a monolingual English speaker.

A started speaking late, around 20 months of age. Smith began his diary observations somewhat later, when A was 2;2, and continued them until 3;11. The data are divided into 20 stages for purposes of analysis. At the onset of the study, A had already acquired over 200 words. The study, therefore, provides more data on later acquisition than do either Velten or Leopold. All the data collected by Smith are conveniently given in alphabetical order in an appendix at the end of the book. Given this, it is somewhat surprising that more analyses of these data have not been done since their first appearance.

Smith's goal is to compare two kinds of analyses of A's data. One analysis assumes that the child is operating with the adult surface phonology of the language, and that the child's phonology is a set of *realization rules* which map from the adult surface form to the child's output. This position, then, assumes the complete perception theory discussed on page 357, and that the child's competence is greater than what is seen in his performance. The other analysis is one which treats the child's system as independent from that of the adult one, where the child moves 'from a more idiosyncratic and simple system to one which was more complex and more closely isomorphic with the system of the adult language' (p. 1). This alternative assumes something like the global perception theory, and a universal sequence of development which will determine the child's acquisition order independent of the adult language. The child's performance is seen as virtually isomorphic with his competence.

Smith considers these alternative theories by analysing the stage 1 sample separately for each one and following the changes that occur over time. The rules for each analysis are presented in formal notation following the general conventions of Chomsky & Halle (1968). Smith concludes that the first analysis, which proposes realization rules, accounts for the data better than the second. Here we will not go into detail over the arguments for or against each analysis. It seems to us that the second analysis (or theory) in its most general form is somewhat of a straw man. The only theories which predict idiosyncratic and autonomous development (possibly such as that in Ferguson & Farwell) are typically only for the phonology of the first 50 words, not for children as advanced as A. While Smith suggests Jakobson as one such theory, we have already discussed in Chapter 6 how Jakobson sees the influence of the adult language as always present and asserting a role very early in acquisition. Smith's observations are in fact consistent with many proposals on phonological acquisition, including the one by Stampe which we will examine in the next section.

We can get a feel for A's data and Smith's proposed realization rules by looking at Smith's analysis for the first sample (or stage 1). Table 8.11 presents a summary of this analysis along with some examples. We

Table 8.11 *A's realization rules at 2;2, taken from Smith (1973: 13–22)*

1. A nasal consonant is deleted before any voiceless consonant, e.g. 'stamp' [dɛp], 'bump' [bʌp], 'uncle' [ʌgu].

2. A voiced consonant is deleted after a nasal consonant, e.g. 'window' [winu:], 'mend' [mɛn], 'angry' [ɛŋi:], 'finger' [wiŋə].

3. The alveolar consonants /n/ and /t,d/ (but not continuants /s,z/) become velars, [ŋ] and [g], before a syllabic [l], e.g. 'handle' [ɛŋu], 'pedal' [bɛgu], *but* 'whistle' [wibu].

4. Syllabic [l] vocalizes to [u], e.g. 'apple' [ɛbu], 'nipple' [mibu].

5. A continuant consonant preceded by a nasal and a vowel, itself becomes a nasal (optional), e.g. 'noisy' [nɔ:ni:], 'smell' [mɛn], *but* 'nice' [nait], 'mice' [mait].

6. /l/ is deleted finally and preconsonantally, e.g. 'ball' [bɔ:], 'bell' [bɛ], 'bolt' [bɔ:t], 'milk' [mik].

7. /s/ is deleted preconsonantally, e.g. 'spoon' [bu:n], 'swing' [wiŋ].

8. In C₁wVC₂ syllables, C₂ assimilates to [p], [m], or [f], e.g. 'squat' [gɔp], 'queen' [gi:m], 'twice' [daif].

9. In sVC words, the /s/ is optionally deleted if the C is labial or alveolar, e.g. 'soup' [u:p], 'seat' [i:t], 'sun' [ʌn] or [dʌn], *but* 'sing' [giŋ].

10. In ʃVC words, /ʃ/ is optionally deleted if the C is labial or velar, e.g. 'sharp' [a:p], 'sugar' [ugə], *but* 'shopping' [wɔbin], 'shine' [dain], 'shirt' [də:t].

11. /z/ but not /s/ is deleted finally, e.g. 'eyes' [ai], 'nose' [nu:], 'glasses' [ga:gi:], *but* 'kiss' [gik], 'mice' [mait].

12. A nasal consonant following an unstressed vowel becomes alveolar, unless there is a preceding velar consonant, e.g. 'bottom' [bɔdin], 'driving' [waibin]; *but* 'singing' [giŋiŋ].

13. /h/ is deleted everywhere, e.g. 'hair' [ɛ], 'head' [ɛt].

14. An initial or post-consonantal unstressed vowel is deleted, e.g. 'away' [we:], 'banana' [ba:nə], 'belong' [bɔŋ].

15. /t/ and /d/ are optionally deleted before /r/, e.g. 'driving' [waibin], 'troddler' [lɔlə], 'trolly' [lɔli:] (only cases found).

16. Post-consonantal sonorants /l,r,w,j/ are deleted, e.g. 'play' [bɛ:], 'brush' [bʌt], 'new' (/nju/) [nu:].

17. Non-nasal alveolar and palato-alveolar consonants harmonize to the point of articulation of a preceding velar, e.g. 'kiss' [gik], 'coach' [go:k], but 'skin' [in].

18. /l,r,j/ (a) are neutralized as [l] when they are the only consonants in the word, e.g. 'lorry' [lɔli:], 'yellow' [lɛlu:];
    (b) become [w] or are deleted when intervocalic, e.g. 'telephone' [dɛwi:bu:n], 'follow' [wɔwo:];
    (c) elsewhere are neutralized as [d], e.g. 'light' [dait], 'write' [dait], 'yes' [dɛt].

19. Alveolar and palato-alveolar consonants harmonize to the point of articulation of a following consonant, obligatorily if that consonant is velar, optionally if it is labial, e.g. 'dark' [ga:k], 'snake' [ŋe:k], 'knife' [maip], 'nipple' [mibu], but 'stop' [dɔp], 'drum' [dʌm].

20. /f, v/ become [w] prevocalically, e.g. 'feet' [wi:t], 'fire' [wae:].

21. Post-consonantal alveolar consonants are deleted, e.g. 'empty' [bi:].

22. Alveolar consonants are optionally deleted in final position, e.g. 'moon' [mu:], 'open' [ubu:].

23. & 24. Alveolar and palato-alveolar fricatives, and affricates become alveolar [t] or [d], e.g. 'bus' [bʌt], 'zoo' [du:], 'brush' [bʌt], 'church' [də:t], 'John' [dɔn].

25. Prevocalic consonants are voiced and final ones are voiceless, e.g. 'teddy' [dɛdi:], 'kiss' [gik].

recognize many of the general patterns seen earlier in the data from Joan and Hildegard. For example, rules 1, 2, 6, 7, 15, 16, 21, and 22 are all rules of consonant cluster reduction. Smith's analysis, however, makes strong claims about the nature of such patterns. First, Smith argues that these rules are formally separate from one another and strictly ordered. For example, rule 11 which deletes final /-z/ must occur before rule 17 or else words like 'keys' would be [gi:k] instead of [gi:]. A complex set of such orderings is proposed. The general patterns, therefore, are not psychologically real rules themselves, but rather functional similarities that realization rules share. The child's actual rules will be a rather long and complex list of realization rules which carry out a small number of functions. Smith proposes that realization rules operate to perform one of the following four functions (p. 162): (i) a tendency toward vowel and consonant harmony (rules 3, 5, 8, 12, 17, 18a, 19); (ii) cluster reduction (rules 1, 2, 6, 7, 15, 16, 21, 22); (iii) systematic simplification (replacing marked sounds with unmarked ones such as replacing fricatives with stops – rules 13, 14, 18b,c, 20, 23, 24, 25); and (iv) grammatical simplification. The last function does not operate in the first sample but is found later when rule 11 becomes restricted to ungrammatical morphemes, e.g. 'nose' [nu:], 'cheese' [di:] vs. 'pages' [be:did], 'peas' [pi:d] (see Smith 1973: 67–70).

In attempting to describe A's phonological development, Smith states at the onset that he expected his task to be to account for an identifiable set of regularities in the child's spoken language. He says (p. 1): 'It soon became apparent that there were a wider range of phenomena . . . to be explained . . . In addition to the mere fact of regularity, any theory of acquisition must be able to account for at least the following classes of data observed in the acquisitional process.' He goes on to identify seven such phenomena, each of which will be briefly examined here.

The first of these phenomena is the occurrence of systematic *exceptions* to the general regularities. Exceptions can occur with individual lexical items, but they can also apply to a group of words. We have already seen cases of this, e.g. Joan's lack of final vowel lengthening in the open syllables of 'down' and 'shut'. The realization rules above show several kinds of exceptions also. For example, rule 9 deletes initial /s/ in CVC words, yet it is optional and does not apply if the final consonant is a velar. Both the optional forms like 'sun' [dʌn] and velar cases like 'sing' [giŋ] are exceptions to the generality of the rule.

There are probably several different reasons why exceptions arise. Smith in his discussion of this point suggests one cause in particular, which he calls *restructuring* (or relexicalization). He gives an example which arose when the assimilation rule 19 dropped out of A's system (p. 144). While words like 'duck' changed from [gʌk] to [dʌk], the word 'take' remained as [kʰeɪk]. This also occurred in derived forms like 'taking' and 'taken' which were [keɪkin] and [kukən] respectively. Smith proposes that this is the result of the child changing or 'restructuring' the internal lexical representation of his word from that of its adult surface form to that of the child's produced form. We have seen a related set of facts earlier from Joan Velten, where earlier acquired words resisted new sound changes. Whether we accept Smith's restructuring proposal or some other account, such exceptions need to be accounted for in some way.

The second phenomenon raised by Smith is one which was also emphasized by Velten (1943: 288):

> The child's phoneme system and the phonetic structure of English are obviously non-congruent. That is to say, not only does almost every unit of the child's system render several English phonemes, as might be expected, but, conversely, the phonetic variants of a given English unit may appear as different phonemes in the child's language.

I will refer to this phenomenon as *non-congruence*, using Velten's terminology. Smith gives the examples of A's [d] representing 13 different English phonemes, e.g. 'teeth' [ḍiːt], 'zoo' [ḍuː], 'chair' [ḍɛː], yet English /s/ surfacing in four different forms, e.g. 'sun' [ʌn], 'sock' [ġɔk], 'mice' [mait], and 'whistle' [wiḅu].

The third phenomenon concerns the observation that changes in the child's phonological system usually occur *across-the-board*. That is, when the child begins to change a particular correspondence between his sounds and those of the adult language, the change usually maintains a systematic correspondence that is narrower than the earlier one. For example, A at one point produced /w/ and /f/ as [w]. When A began to acquire the sound [f], it was consistently used for /f/ only, not for both /w/ and /f/. Such facts suggest that the child had perceived the adult distinctions, but had merged them in his own speech. This kind of observation has been used to argue against the global perception theory cited earlier. It is important to point out that across-the-board change does not imply that the change is instantaneous. It only refers to the correspondences that occur as a sound emerges in the child's system.

The next three phenomena are the occurrence of *non-native sounds*, *puzzles*, and *recidivism*. Smith observed cases where A used sounds which are not part of the phonetic inventory of English. Some examples are 'slug' [ɬʌg] with a lateral fricative, and 'Smith' [m̥is] with a voiceless nasal. The term 'puzzle' is taken from the example Smith provides in which A produced 'puzzle' as [pʌdəl] but 'puddle' as [pʌgəl]. That is, A could articulate a medial [d] but not in 'puddle' where it is required. This is a general observation pointed out long ago by Jakobson as evidence against a strictly articulatory account of phonological acquisition. Recidivism is Smith's term to refer to 'the loss of a contrast which has already been established' (p. 4). He gives the example of the words 'side' and 'light' changing over three time periods, reproduced here in (8.15).

(8.15)	Time 1	Time 2	Time 3
'side'	[ḍait]	[ḍait]	[lait]
'light'	[ḍait]	[lait]	[lait]

Superficially at least, the child appears to have taken a step backward at time 3 in the sense that a contrast between two words has actually been lost.

The last phenomenon which Smith discusses is one he observed through a clever experiment with his son. Smith tape-recorded A speaking and played it back to him. When he heard himself, A was able to recognize his reduced English words. For example, when A heard himself say 'squeeze' [ġip], he responded by squeezing a piece of cloth. This ability was also shown when Smith would say the words to A, e.g. Smith: 'What's a [sə:t]?', A points to his shirt, and Smith: 'What's a [su:]?', A points to his shoe (p. 136). Importantly, A not only recognized his reduced forms but was aware that these were different from those of the adult language. For example, when Smith pressured A to say 'ship', A responded 'No. I can only say [sip]' (p. 137). Smith refers to this situation as the 'child's *ability to understand his own speech*' (p. 5). There were two limitations on this ability. First, it only occurred when A was currently producing the word in the reduced form he heard. Once his pronunciation improved, he would not recognize his earlier form. Second, it would only occur if there wasn't an adult form that was homophonous with A's reduced form. For example, A pronounced 'mouth' as [maus] yet processed this as if it meant 'mouse' when Smith tested it in the above way.

Assessment.   The development of two of the children in the phonological diaries discussed above, Joan and A, was presented in some detail to provide an idea of the degree of complex and individual patterning that is found. They were not presented, however, to suggest in any way that they are typical of how English children acquire their phonology. In fact, it is likely that they are atypical in the sense that published diaries are usually on children who are particularly interesting in their language acquisition; for example, two of these children, Hildegard and A, both pronounced /f/ as [w], a pattern that was not found in any of the 73 children tested in Ingram *et al.* (1980).

Accounting for phonological acquisition is a formidable task. We not only need to explain the patterns or rules that children follow, but also the kinds of phenomenon described by Smith. In the next section, we turn to the issue of developing a theory of phonological acquisition.

8.2.3 The explanation of phonological acquisition

Although it is rare to see comparisons between syntactic and phonological theories of acquisition, it is obvious that the same general issues exist for the two. In our review of syntactic acquisition in Chapter 7 we touched upon several of these issues, such as continuity vs. discontinuity and the relation between the child's competence and performance. The formulation of these issues in the area of phonological acquisition will first be discussed, using Jakobson's theory as a basis of comparison. Afterwards, some specific alternative proposals will be offered.

The issue of continuity matters when it is claimed that the child begins adult-like organization of his phonological system. Jakobson's theory proposes that the child begins phonological acquisition with oppositions and the use of distinctive features. At any point in acquisition his phonology will contain a subset of the adult features. As such, it is a theory that is based on continuity and in a very general way is comparable to Pinker's view of syntactic acquisition. This view is also characteristic of the theoretical positions in Stampe (1969, 1973) and Smith (1973). An alternative view is the claim that the child undergoes one or more discontinuities or reorganizations during the course of acquisition. Probably the clearest statement of such a position is Macken (1979) who claims that the child begins acquisition with the word as the basic organizational unit, then switches to the phoneme, and lastly to the feature. There are, then, at least two reorganizations. Macken's position appears to be constructionist in the sense of Chapter 4, in that presumably the word and phoneme still play a role in the child's system when it goes through the final reorganization. (We say 'presumably' because Macken does not refer to a particular model of phonology that the child is acquiring, so that the status of the earlier units after reorganization is not clear.) Recall that the constructionist view does not deny reorganization, but only restricts its extent. Lastly, we could have total discontinuity in the sense that the child's system up to some point bears little relation to the adult system. We are unaware of anyone who takes this view for phonological acquisition.

The issue of the relation between competence and performance translates in phonological acquisition to the issue of *levels of representation*. There are a number of positions on this point, recently summarized in Stoel-Gammon (1986). Here I will simplify the possibilities to just two. One position is that there are only two levels of representation: the child's perceptual organization of the adult language (presumably an accurate phonemic representation of its surface structure) and the child's phonetic representation or output. There are then a set of realization rules (Smith 1973) or processes (Stampe 1968, 1973) which map from the underlying representation to the phonetic representation. This position argues that the child's perception is essentially adult-like at the onset of acquisition, and that there is a considerable discrepancy between the child's competence and her performance.

The alternative to this view is that there is some intervening level (or levels). Elsewhere (e.g. Ingram 1976a,b) this has been referred to as the organizational level, where the child can be said to have an underlying representation related to, but distinct from, the perceptual representation of the adult word. The mapping from the organizational level to the phonetic one is relatively close, so that in this view the child's performance is considered to be much closer to her competence.

The contrasting claims of these two viewpoints can be examplified by looking at stage 2 in Table 8.10 for Joan Velten. In (8.16) I show how each viewpoint would represent Joan's words 'bead' and 'beat'.

(8.16)   Two levels   Three levels
    Adult form: /bit/   /biːd/   /bit/   /bidːd/
                                      |bit,d| |biːt,d|
    Child form: [bit]   [biːt]   [bit]   [biːt]

In the two-level approach, the child's underlying form would be the adult phonemes, so in this case the child would have an underlying final voicing distinction. There would then be a set of rules which map between the two. The three-level approach, which is the one implied in Velten's analysis, is that the child may perceive the difference in final voicing (although this is not necessary), but does not use it phonemically in his system (see Table 8.8.). For example, there is just one phoneme |t,d| with the [d] occurring prevocalically and the [t] finally. Instead, vowel length is used to show a phonemic distinction. The level indicated by | | is the organization level referred to above. Importantly, this level is not independent of influence from the adult form. As pointed out by Jakobson, this level is constantly under pressure of the 'unifying force' to conform to the adult form, which it eventually does.

In the example just given, the influences on the child's underlying representation in the three-level approach come from the adult form. Some versions of this general model also incorporate influences from the child form (e.g. Macken 1979; Menn 1983). For example, we saw in the discussion of Hildegard's fricatives that the syllabic shape CV[ʃ] was a common form, e.g. 'kiss' [diʃ], 'knife' [naiʃ], 'much' [maʃ], which also extended itself to forms like 'stone' [doiʃ] and 'story' [lɔiʃ], distorting the normal pattern of mapping from the adult form to that of the child's. Macken (1979) refers to these as 'word patterns', and gives an example from a Spanish child referred to as Si who used the word pattern [p/b V t/d V]. This preference to produce labial consonants before dental ones has been reported elsewhere (Ingram 1974b). This pattern created some radical discrepancies between the adult form and Si's when the order of consonants in the adult words was different, e.g. 'sopa' [p'wæt'a]. This would be an example of the 'particularist spirit' mentioned by Jakobson. The child's system at the organizational level in the three-level approach can be seen as the result of the influence both of the adult form and child form.

We have interpreted Jakobson's theory as one which recognizes three levels, even though he never discussed it himself in those terms. This has also been Velten's and others' interpretation, although it has sometimes been misinterpreted to the extreme position that the organizational level bears no relation to the adult model. (It is our impression that this misinterpretation can be traced to Chao 1951, who claimed that his niece Canta was not speaking Mandarin but her own form of it, which he referred to as the Cantian idiolect.) For example, Stampe (1969: 446) states: 'Most modern students of child phonology have assumed that the child has a phonemic system of his own, distinct from that of his standard language.' This same view led Smith (1973) to his attempt to analyze A's phonology as an autonomous system without reference to the adult target sounds. We will refer to this position as 'Chao's theory' to distinguish it from Jakobson's which recognizes the importance of the adult language (see Ingram 1988 for an elaboration of this point). The disagreement with Chao's theory in the late 1960s led to two well-known attempts to argue for a two-level model (Stampe 1969; Smith 1973). Here we will look at the theory developed by Stampe which has had a great impact upon research.

Stampe (1969, 1973) Stampe, like Jakobson, approaches the explanation of phonological development from the orientation of Language Acquisition. He has developed a theory of phonology which he refers to as Natural Phonology, and uses data from acquisition and language change to support it. Publications on Natural Phonology, however, have not been abundant. Its first cited presentation is Stampe (1968), a paper which, to my knowledge, has never been published. The most cited paper is Stampe (1969), a brief work of only 12 pages. Stampe's dissertation in 1973, circulated at the time with the title 'How I spent my summer vacation', is 'a random selection of topics in phonology that occurred to me as I wrote' (p. i). Stampe refers to a book *Natural Phonology* as forthcoming, but it also has not appeared. There have been some papers since on specific topics, e.g. Miller (1972), a thesis (Edwards 1970), a dissertation (Donegan

1986), and a more recent review (Donegan & Stampe 1979). The theory has not been widely accepted among phonologists but it has had considerably more success among researchers in language acquisition.

As stated earlier, Stampe sees perceptual development as far in advance of production, with the child having an accurate phonological representation of the adult surface form of words. The child's reduced productions are the result of his applying an *innate phonological system* (Stampe 1969: 446) to the phonological representation. The innate phonological system consists of a set of universal *phonological processes* which simplify the phonological representation. These are like Smith's realization rules except that Stampe attempts to delimit the range of possible processes. It is important to understand Stampe's use of the term 'phonological process':

> A phonological process merges a potential opposition into that member of the opposition which least tries the restrictions of the human speech capacity.   (1969: 443)

> A phonological process is a mental operation that applies in speech to substitute, for a class of sounds or sound sequences presenting a specific common difficulty to the speech capacity of the individual, an alternative class identical but lacking the difficult property.
> (1973: 1)

> Although substitutions are mental in occurrence, their purpose is clearly physical: to maximize the perceptual characteristics of speech and minimize its articulatory difficulties. They are mental operations performed on behalf of the physical systems involved in speech perception and production.   (1973: 9)

As such, Stampe's theory is closest to what we referred to on page 357 as the complete perception theory I.

Stampe does not provide a list of the universal processes, which he admits is a formidable task, but does discuss several potential ones. One example concerns the data presented above in (8.16). Stampe's analysis for these data (1969: 448) is given in (8.17).

(8.17) Adult phonetic form: [bit]   [biːd]
       Child phonological representation: /bit/   /bid/
         length adjustment: bit   biːd
         final devoicing: bit   biːt
       Child form: [bit]   [biːt]

The child formulates a distinction between voiced and voiceless final consonants in her phonological representation. Two processes then simplify this representation: length adjustment, which lengthens vowels before voiced consonants, and final devoicing of obstruents at the end of words. Another example is Stampe's analysis of Joan's substitution of [z] for /l/. Rather than proposing one process of frication, Stampe gives three processes: [l] to [j] by delateralization; [j] to [ʒ] by spirantization, and lastly [ʒ] to [z] by depalatalization.

(8.18) Adult phonetic form: [lif]   [jard]   [ruʒ]

	[lif]	[jard]	[ruʒ]
Child representation:	/lif/	/jard/	/ruʒ/
delateralization:	j		
spirantization:	ʒ	ʒ	
depalatalization:	z	z	z
other processes:	u	aː	wuː
Child form:	[zuf]	[zaːd]	[wuːz]

Evidence for the separate processes for /l/ to [z] is that each one is independently supported by data from other words. 'Rouge' provides evidence for depalatalization and 'yard' for spirantization.

Besides showing three processes instead of one, the example in (8.18) shows the processes applying in a particular order. At the onset of acquisition, the order in which processes occur is 'sequential application without ordering' (1973: 60), that is, they continue to apply in any order until as many have applied as possible. The full range of processes, then, is only seen at the very onset of acquisition. The child's task in acquisition is to overcome the application of the entire innate set: 'The child's task in acquiring adult pronunciation is to revise all aspects of the system which separate his pronunciation from the standard' (1969: 444).

The child reduces the application of phonological processes in three possible ways: (i) ordering, (ii) limitation, and (iii) suppression. These are three *mechanisms of change* which operate upon the innate phonological system.

Ordering refers to imposing a restriction on the natural order of application of the processes just mentioned, such that the application of one process eliminates one of the contexts in which another process normally applies. (8.19) gives an example of this in the ordering of the processes of depalatalization and despirantization ([dʒ] to [d]) and prevocalic voicing ([tʃ] to [dʒ]) by Hildegard at 19 and 20 months (1969: 447).

(8.19) *19 months*:   'choo-choo' 'Joey'   *20 months*:   'choo-choo' 'Joey'

	'choo-choo'	'Joey'			'choo-choo'	'Joey'
[tʃ] to [dʒ]	dʒ dʒ			[dʒ] to [d]		d
[dʒ] to [d]	d d	d		[tʃ] to [dʒ]	dʒ dʒ	
	[dudu]	[doːi]			[dʒudʒu]	[doːi]

The ordering of the prevocalic voicing process before depalatalization and despirantization restricts the natural order of application, but brings the child's pronunciation closer to that required by the language.

A second mechanism of change is *limitation*, by which the child limits the range of segments or contexts in which a process applies. A crucial aspect of this mechanism is that each process contains 'various subtle and strict hierarchies, ranging from the greatest generality which is phonetically motivated, to the complete suppression of the process' (1969: 443). For example, prevocalic voicing may be more favored by stops than fricatives, or more likely intervocalically than initially. We saw an example of the first situation from Joan: all stops were prevocalically voiced while the pattern was more restricted for the fricatives. Stampe (1969: 447) gives two examples of the latter case: (i) Hildegard's development of 'papa' as [baba] to [paba] and finally [papa], and (ii) Joan's distinctions of 'paper' [pu:bu] vs. 'baby' [bu:bu] at 25 months, and 'puppy' [papu] vs. [pabu] 'probably' at 27 months.

The third kind of change is *suppression* of a process, or sequence of processes. In (8.18) the series of processes proposed for Joan's substitution of /l/ by [z] was shown. As pointed out by Stampe, it is not actually very common to find children showing each of the potential processes in a substitution. Another child, however, might begin acquisition with the pronunciations of 'leaf' [jif], 'yard' [jad] and 'rouge' [wu]. We would then say that the processes of spirantization and depalatalization have been suppressed. The claim that individual children may suppress and limit processes in different degrees is one of Stampe's major ways of accounting for individual variation in acquisition.

Stampe's processes tend to be more specific than most of the patterns identified here in Joan's speech, but less so than some of Smith's realization rules. The reason for this is his concern to propose only those processes which can be identified as natural. Stampe's work, then, goes beyond that of Velten and Smith by trying to explain the specific patterns found in the speech of children.

This point can be demonstrated by looking at one of Smith's rules for A. As descriptive accounts of A's behavior, several of A's rules do not look particularly natural. One such rule is rule 9, which deletes /s/ optionally for /s/VC words which end in labials and dentals, e.g. 'soup' [u:p] and 'seat' [i:t], but not velars, e.g. 'sing' [giŋ]. This does not have any apparent natural motivation in terms of the restrictions of the human speech capacity. Stampe would presumably identify at least the following interacting processes: despirantization ([s] to [t]), prevocalic voicing ([t] to [d]), prevocalic obstruent deletion (of [d]), and velar assimilation of coronals (or simply velar assimilation, [d] to [g]). Stampe's explanation of A's data could take one of at least two forms. One possible analysis would be that the process of prevocalic obstruent deletion has been limited to just those contexts where there are following labials and dentals. An alternative is that the process of velar assimilation is now ordered before prevocalic obstruent deletion.

Importantly, these alternatives make different predictions about acquisition in other children. If the limitation analysis is correct, then we should find children who have 'soup' [u:p], 'seat' [i:t], and 'sing' [diŋ]. If the ordering analysis is correct, then the preceding data should not be found, and the proposed limitation would not be part of the hierarchical structure of the prevocalic deletion process.

At first glance, Stampe's phonological processes are similar to Jakobson's laws of irreversible solidarity. For example, the law that fricatives imply stops (see Table 6.24 of Chapter 6) is another way to say that there is a natural process whereby obstruents become stops. Stampe recognizes this similarity and points out that Jakobson's laws are a subset of phonological processes. This subset consists of those processes which are context-free and which operate on the phonemic inventories of languages. Stampe argues, however, that there are other processes which also have to be accounted for. These are the context-sensitive processes which are commonly in conflict with context-free ones. The three mechanisms of change are needed to resolve such conflicts.

An example of such a conflict is that between the context-free process of vowel denasalization and the context-sensitive process of vowel nasalization. One of Jakobson's implicational laws is that the existence of nasal vowels in a language implies the existence of corresponding oral vowels. The corresponding phonological process is vowel denasalization, which states that nasal vowels are changed into non-nasal vowels. Evidence for this process comes from acquisition studies on languages with nasal vowels (such as French) which report that the child's first attempts at nasal vowels are oral ones (e.g. Jakobson 1941/68: 71–2). Such processes 'respond to the inner complexities of single segments' (Stampe 1973: 20). At the same time, there is the context-sensitive process of vowel nasalization which nasalizes vowels next to nasal consonants, e.g. English 'can't' [kæt] (see Ladefoged 1975: 81). Such a process responds 'to the complexity of sequences of segments' (1969: 21). Importantly both processes often coexist in a language, as in English where vowel nasalization exists at the same time as vowel denasalization occurs in loan words. Our theory, therefore, needs to account for the existence of both types of processes.

In discussing the existence of these two processes in English, Stampe (1973) also points out a potential learnability problem in English. Because of vowel nasalization (and subsequent nasal consonant deletion), children will hear pairs such as 'cat' [kæt] vs. 'can't' [kæt] and 'bees' [bi:z] vs. 'beans' [bī:z], and words like 'ant' [æt] which, unlike 'bean', do not have other surface forms that provide information about the underlying nasal consonant. These could be analyzed as having a phonemic distinction between nasal and oral vowels. Stampe's solution to this dilemma is to have

Table 8.12 *A summary of Stampe's (1973) analysis of selected forms from Joan Velten*

Adult word	Phonological processes (see below)						Child form
	A	1	2	3	4	5	
'room'	[wum]		[wūm]		[wub]		[wub]
'salmon'	[samun]		[sāmūn]		[sabud]		[sabud]
'home'	[hum]		[hum]		[hub]		[hub]
'ham'	[ham]		[ɦãm]		[ham]	[ham]	[ham]
'lion'	[lan]		[lãn]	[nãn]		[nan]	[nan]
'non'[a]	[na]					[na]	[na]
'M'	[am]		[ãm]			[am]	[am]
'bed'	[bud]	[but]					[but]

Processes
A Child's form after several phonological processes not related to the ones under analysis
1. Final obstruent devoicing (now ordered before 4).
2. Iterative regressive (vowel) nasalization: vowels, non-high nonsyllabics [ha], and non-high sonorants [l] nasalize before nasal consonants. (The nasality of vocalics is inversely related to their height, see Chen 1975.)
3. Nasalized [l] becomes [n].
4. Iterative progressive denasalization: of all nasal segments preceded by a non-nasal segment.
5. Denasalization of vocalics (context-free vowel denasalization).

[a] Joan produced a small set of French words which followed this pattern.

context-free processes innately (or naturally) ordered before context-sensitive ones. Further, the English child innately assumes that the surface nasal vowels have an underlying adjacent nasal consonant as their source, i.e. that vowel nasality is derived. The English form 'can't' /kænt/ is then correctly produced by first applying vowel denasalization and then vowel nasalization.

In looking at Stampe's explanation of English vowel nasalization, we can isolate three problems with his proposal. The first has to do with the acquisition of languages with a phonemic difference between nasal and oral vowels. It is not clear why the child would not be forced to assume that nasality is also derived in such languages. It seems that Stampe needs to treat all nasal vowels as underlying adjacent to nasal consonants, or else add some mechanism for the child to distinguish derived from nonderived nasal vowels. Based on his analysis of Joan (see below), it seems that he must take the latter step.

A second dilemma concerns the so-called natural ordering of the two processes. The first application of vowel denasalization contradicts the earlier principle which stated that the natural order of processes is to allow for their maximal application. This could be circumvented by stipulating the principle that context-free processes always follow context-sensitive ones, but then a different problem arises: such an ordering should be the first ordering used by the child. Stampe (1973) presents a very ingenious analysis of Joan's more unusual forms, which is summarized here in Table 8.12. In Stampe's own analysis, vowel denasalization is ordered after nasalization. Stampe's only remark about this inconsistency is that 'the natural order is not yet manifest' (p. 65).

The third dilemma is a more general problem for Natural Phonology. This has to do with how the child creates phonemic representations for the adult perceived forms. We have seen two examples of this problem: (i) how does the child get from 'can't' [kæt] to /kænt/, and (ii) how does the child get from 'bead' [biːd] to /bid/? That is, the theory assumes a great deal of phonological organization at the perceptual level which is never addressed. In fact, given that the phonological processes in some ways are simply performance factors in acquisition, it is these perceptual decisions which are reflecting the child's actual linguistic competence.

Stampe's work has had a major impact on attempts to understand in much more detail the range and limits to the kinds of natural correspondences that exist between the child's sounds and the adult target sounds. In some ways it can be seen as an elaboration of Jakobson's initial attempts to determine the finite set of such correspondences. It has led others to attempt to delimit the range of phonological processes, although most of this work remains primarily descriptive and contradictory (e.g. Ingram 1974a, 1976a, 1979a, 1981a; Shriberg & Kwiatkowski 1980; Hodson & Paden 1983). For example, one sees simultaneous natural processes of fronting ([tʃ] to [t]) and backing ([tʃ] to [k]) being proposed. Such contradictory processes have led others to attack the explanatory value of the theory (e.g. Dinnsen 1980).

Macken & Ferguson (1983)   Before concluding this section on explanation, one other perspective on this topic requires brief discussion. In recent years, the initial observations in Ferguson & Farwell (1975) have been expanded in a series of articles to a point where they have come to be seen as a new theory of phonological acquisition (e.g. Ferguson 1978; Macken 1978, 1979; Macken & Ferguson 1983). Unfortunately, this approach has acquired the name of a 'cognitive theory' of phonological acquisition. I say 'unfortunately' because the use of the term is not with the meaning used in this text and in child development in general; rather, it is used in a very specific way to refer to the claim that the child actively participates in the acquisition process through linguistic hypothesis testing and revision. Since this general point is arguably part of both Jakobson's and Stampe's theories (although not to the same degree), we will refer to this approach as the Stanford theory, since most of its proponents have been associated with the Stanford Child Phonology Project in one capacity or another.

Chapter 6 examined some of the observations on phonological acquisition made by Ferguson & Farwell (1975), and it was pointed out that their approach, unlike that of Jakobson or Stampe, is much more characteristic of Child Language. It arose from the detailed observations of individual children, and does not make predictions about acquisition based on a phonological theory of the adult language. To reiterate some of its aspects: the Stanford theory emphasizes individual variation in acquisition across children, and the variability of production within children. The former is established through the phone classes and phone trees approach, and the latter through the existence of lexical variability, phonetic variability, phonological idioms, and selection and avoidance. It has also been argued that much of the variability in the data they use results from their methodology, which emphasizes performance factors.

The theoretical model includes some of the following claims. Regarding perception, it proposes that some of the child's errors in production may stem from incomplete perception; as such, it is on the side of a global or partial perception theory. Macken (1980), for example, gives an analysis of Smith's rule 3 in Table 8.11 which accounts for the pattern on the basis of misperception. The theory also emphasizes the influence of the child's output or word patterns on the child's underlying representation, as mentioned above for Macken (1979). The theory, then, is like a three-level model as discussed above. Regarding change, it proposes that there are discontinuities in phonological acquisition, with the most explicit proposals those of Macken (1979), i.e. that the child's organization of phonology changes from using the word to the phoneme, and finally to the feature.

In comparing the Stanford theory with others it is necessary to realize that other theories have been aware of the kinds of observations it emphasizes. For example, both Jakobson and Stampe were aware of the extent of individual variation in phonological acquisition. Jakobson (1968: 31), for example, states:

> If all of the sound productions of the child are tossed into the same heap, it is understandable that the laws of development cannot be disclosed. By careful elimination, however, the regular succession of acquired phonemic oppositions emerges.

Stampe (1973: 11) also recognizes the extent of this diversity:

> Despite the opinion of early investigators, it is now generally recognized that different children acquire sounds and sound-patterns in

quite different relative orders ... children choose bewilderingly diverse substitutions for the sounds and sound-patterns they have not yet acquired.

While Jakobson concentrated on eliminating much of the variability by methodological means, Stampe accepted it and incorporated its potential within his theory.

It seems to us that the Stanford theory has isolated some important observations on phonological acquisition, but that it needs to address some unresolved issues before it can be considered as a serious challenger to either Jakobson or Stampe. First, it needs to provide a theory for the general aspects of acquisition: while emphasizing individual variation, it misses the fact that general patterns do occur. More generally, the theory needs to provide an explanation for the extent and limits of the individual variation it observes. A step in this direction is Macken (1986), who discusses a probabilistic component to phonological theory.

Second, the theory needs to account for the discontinuities that it proposes. For example, what does it mean to say that the child changes from words to phonemes to features? Elsewhere (Ingram 1986) I have pointed out some concerns about these proposed discontinuities. For example, does the child use the 'word' as an organizational unit for the 100 to 200 words she has in her receptive vocabulary at the onset of word production? Further, the 'word' as an organizational unit is never defined. If it were the unit of organization, we would expect units like [ba], [di], and [mu] where segments would be fused together, not the segmental patterns such as [ba], [bu], [bi] which are more typical of early phonological acquisition. Relatedly, the status of the former units during the next stage needs to be more clearly spelled out. Lastly, the theory needs to address the cross-linguistic patterns of acquisition observed in Pye, Ingram & List (1987). As pointed out elsewhere (Ingram 1988), these patterns are consistent with predictions of Jakobson's theory.

8.3 The further development of word meaning

The cognitive precursors to the onset of word meaning and the onset of early word acquisition were discussed in Chapters 7 and 8. This chapter will follow the subsequent development of word meaning from the end of the second year of life up to approximately 4 years of age, by presenting a sampling of the observations made to date on this development, and by discussing some of the theoretical proposals put forward to account for it. A comment on the limited scope of this discussion on the acquisition of meaning, however, is required here.

While tempted at times to do so, I have avoided labeling any of the sections of the book with the title 'semantic acquisition'. The reason for this is that 'semantic acquisition' comprises a wide range of topics that I could not begin to address. In fact, it is such a diverse set that no book-length treatment of the entire range has yet been attempted. What does exist, however, is a selection of books devoted to one or more of its domains.

A comprehensive treatment of semantic acquisition would need to cover at least the following topics. First, a broad distinction is made between 'lexical semantics' and 'propositional semantics', where lexical semantics refers to the meanings of individual words, and propositional semantics refers to the meaning that results from combining words. Within *lexical semantics*, we can distinguish the study of the meaning of the different word classes which occur in language. One class of such words, nominals or referring expressions (e.g. 'dog', 'flower', etc.), has been a particularly popular topic for acquisition studies. Other classes include verbs, adjectives, and adverbs. Adjectives have also proven to be a rich area for study, particularly those adjectives which refer to dimensions, such as 'big', 'little', 'long', and relations such as 'more', 'less', as well as particular domains such as color. Lexical semantics also includes the meanings of a wide range of grammatical morphemes such as pronouns, prepositions, and various inflections.

Propositional semantics is loosely used here to capture a range of phenomena which require reference to the constituent structure of sentences. For example, there are at least (i) the semantic or logical relations which underlie sentences, such as Agent and Action; (ii) the relations between pronominals and their possible antecedents, as in sentences like 'Behind him, John saw a snake'; (iii) thematic meaning (Leech 1974), referring to the marking of parts of sentences which are topics or focussed elements (for example, the thematic meaning of 'John' differs in the sentences 'It was John who I saw' and 'I saw John'); and (iv) scope relations, as in 'All of the arrows didn't hit the target'. Still other kinds of meanings include 'stylistic' meaning, the differences in using words such as 'steed' (poetic), 'horse' (general), and 'nag' (slang); and 'affective' meaning, which distinguishes sentences like 'Would you be so kind as to lower your voice' from 'Shut up!' (Leech 1974: 17–18).

The discussion in this section will be restricted to a selection of studies on lexical semantics. For this reason, the term 'word meaning' is used instead of 'semantic development'. Semantic relations have already been examined in Chapter 7, and will be returned to later in the next chapter. A discussion of the many other aspects of meaning, unfortunately, is beyond the scope of the present text.

8.3.1 Theoretical proposals: general issues

Chapter 6 discussed the child's use of overextensions as one kind of evidence that children do not always have the same meaning for a word as adults have. The discussion was somewhat cautious, however, since it appears that overextensions may result from several different causes (see Section 6.3.3). Even with such caution, it was proposed that one cause is an incomplete semantic system. Except for Piaget's views on the transition from symbols to signs, there was no examination there of how the child's semantic system develops. A review of the theories which have been attempted is now presented, beginning with some general issues in this section, and turning to some specific proposals in the next.

The general issues at stake in a theory of lexical semantic acquisition are similar to ones we have considered in other domains. Again, we are faced with the question of *continuity*. There is little in the way of proposals for stages of lexical acquisition as there are for syntactic and phonological acquisition: the single most important milestone appears to be the word spurt around 1;6. Given this situation, it is not surprising that many of the theories for lexical acquisition imply continuity of development. In such a case, the child is claimed to be using the same units and mechanisms of organization as the adult. Development, then, consists primarily in the child determining the range of meanings used by the adult for the lexicon of the language. Such theories may, at first glance, seem quite distinct from each other because they propose different units and mechanisms. Their deeper similarities appear, however, when the issue of continuity is considered.

As stated, much of the disagreement between theories can be traced to differences in the *units of organization* proposed for the child. One general difference is between theories which break down the meanings of words into features and those which do not. The former will be referred to as *featural* theories, and the latter as *holistic* ones, following Armstrong, Gleitman & Gleitman (1983). For example, we can discuss the meaning of the word 'dog' as consisting of a set of features which together construct the total meaning, much as phonological features constitute the organizational unit of phonology. The holistic alternative is that the meaning of 'dog' is the concept DOG which cannot be broken down any further. Since holistic theories require a separate concept for each word in languages, they expand greatly the number of possible units for semantic structure (see Fodor 1975). Most accounts of early lexical acquisition can be classified as featural theories.

Featural theories differ from one another on several dimensions, for example, the *kinds of features* which are assigned to words by children, and presumably adults. One widely discussed difference is between perceptual features and functional ones. *Perceptual features* are features determined for an object by the senses, e.g. shape, smell, and touch. 'Ball', for example, can be categorized by a perceptual feature [+round]. *Functional features* are those which concern the uses which objects have. A ball, for example, is something which can be thrown and bounced. Two of the most discussed theories of lexical acquisition, Clark (1973a) and Nelson (1974), propose that word meaning consists of both kinds of features, which differ in their emergence in the early months of acquisition. Clark suggests that perceptual features take precedence at the onset, while Nelson argues that functional ones do.

Another difference between featural theories is the way in which features are organized into word meanings. The traditional approach is one which has been referred to as the *definitional* view (Fodor, Garrett, Walker & Parkes 1980). The definitional view is that the meaning of a word consists of a set of invariant and necessary features. For example, the meaning of a word like 'ball' will consist of features such as [+object, −animate, +round, +throwable]. Any object identified as a 'ball' will need to have at least these features. The definitional approach to word meaning was challenged by Wittgenstein (1953), who pointed out the problems with determining an invariant set of features for any particular word. The most famous example of this is his discussion of the problem of defining a 'game'. We can identify a series of potential invariant features which all have counterexamples (shown here in parentheses), e.g. use of a board (tennis), play by at least two people (solitaire), play to win (ring around the roses). This exercise can be replicated with virtually every referential word. Wittgenstein's solution is to propose that the meaning of words is a set of *cluster concepts*. Words do not share a single set of features, but rather participate in a network of features such that different words share different features from the network.

Wittgenstein's original ideas have been picked up in recent years by Eleanor Rosch, who has developed a theoretical approach known as *prototype* theory (e.g. Rosch 1973, 1975, 1978; Rosch & Mervis 1975; Rosch *et al.* 1976). For any word meaning such as 'ball', all the members of the class will share some of the set of defining features for a ball. Those items which share the most features will be most typically balls, or the prototypes. Those objects which share fewest of the family of features associated with balls will be less likely to be so identified. A baseball, therefore, is more typically a ball than a rolled up sheet of paper that is thrown around the room. In the same way, a robin is more typically a bird than is a penguin or an ostrich. Rosch's research has consisted of asking adults to identify instances of objects as being most typical of certain words, such as 'fruit' and 'vehicle'. Adults appear to be able to grade objects in this way and agree in their ratings. Prototype theory also accounts for the observation that the boundary between categories can be somewhat 'fuzzy' when objects have features from different categories. Prototype theory had an immediate appeal to those working in language acquisition, although it has been adapted in different ways (Anglin 1977; Bowerman 1978a; Barrett 1978, 1982; Greenberg & Kuczaj 1982).

Another issue to be addressed is how the units of organization appear over time. A maturational theory of lexical development claims that the child is born with the *innate set of concepts* which can be lexicalized in human development. The child's task then is basically to map each word acquired onto the innate set. Fodor (1975) presents a theory of this kind. The other featural theories that have been proposed have been more constructionist in nature. In these, the child begins with some initial hypotheses about the meaning of words, and then gradually narrows them down. There are three different ways in which such a development might proceed. First, the child may develop from *general-to-specific* categories. For example, 'ball' might initially mean 'round thing', then 'round thing which can be thrown' and so forth (see Clark 1973a, discussed below). A second possibility is that the child may proceed from *specific-to-general* categories. In this scenario, 'ball' might mean 'this particular blue ball', with another red ball being labeled 'red'. Only after later experience with a range of balls would the term generalize (see Anglin 1970). Lastly, development could take place from some *intermediate level* of organization. For example, if children do indeed form prototypes, then the first experience with a ball might lead to an initial prototype that is neither as general as 'round thing' nor as specific as 'this particular blue ball' (Anglin 1977).

8.3.2 Specific theoretical proposals

Somewhat simplistically, the history of the study of lexical acquisition has seen the rise and fall of a series of theoretical proposals. This section provides a brief historical overview of those which have been particularly influential, using the issues just discussed as a frame of reference.

The semantic feature hypothesis The study of lexical acquisition is naturally tied to the issue of cognitive development and categorization. The meaning of a word for the child at any point in time is going to be influenced by the child's cognitive abilities. One claim about cognitive development has been that the child develops by forming general concepts and then narrowing them down, a view popular in the 1960s (Brown 1958b). Also in the 1960s, a semantic theory developed within linguistics which proposed that the meanings of words consist of a small set of universal semantic features (Bierwisch 1970). Eve Clark (1973a) combined these two proposals into a theory which she called the *semantic feature hypothesis*.

The semantic feature hypothesis is based upon a definitional view of word meaning, that is, the meaning of a word consists of a set of necessary and invariant semantic features. For purposes of discussion, we assume that the features vary from general features to specific ones. The most general features will be referred to as *superordinate* categories, and the most specific ones as *subordinate* categories. A lexical example of this distinction is 'animal' vs. 'Collie' with 'dog' at some intermediate level of generality. The corresponding semantic features might be [+animate], [+long snout], and [+canine] respectively.

The child acquires the meanings of words within this theory by first acquiring the more general superordinate features. The first meaning of 'dog' for example, might just be [+animate], and later [+animate, +four-legged]. Acquisition then goes from the more general to the more specific. Also, the first features which are acquired are those which are perceptually salient to the child. The most primitive categories involve movement, shape, size, sound, taste, and texture.

An important aspect of the semantic feature hypothesis is that it makes predictions about relational terms as well as referential ones. It predicts that various antonyms like 'same' vs. 'different' and 'more' vs. 'less' will first be acquired with the same meaning. In such cases, one of the terms is considered to be more basic or 'unmarked', so that its meaning will be acquired first. A series of predictions about the acquisition of dimension terms are also made. For example, the pair 'big', 'small' is considered to be more general than pairs like 'tall', 'short' and 'high', 'low' (H. Clark 1973), and is thus acquired before them.

The semantic feature hypothesis had the virtue of developing current views on semantics and acquisition into a coherent and testable theory of development; because of this, it stimulated a wide range of studies, and was still being critically reviewed in Carey (1982). It is very much a constructionist theory in which the child's lexical meanings are always a subset of those of the adult. Development proceeds by the addition of features to those already acquired. Its predictions about word acquisition are also relatively straightforward: words will be overextended at the onset and then eventually narrowed down until they are correct.

Functional core concept theory Katherine Nelson in Nelson (1974) puts forward a theory referred to as the *functional core concept theory*. This theory most generally differs from Eve Clark's in two ways. First, it proposes that the child first forms a concept, and then attaches a word to it, whereas the semantic feature hypothesis suggests that the child acquires a word

Table 8.13 *Four steps in the acquisition of the functional core concept 'ball', adapted from Nelson (1974: 276–8)*

1. 'Identification of an individual whole'. The child recognizes the things it acts upon as objects, not pictures or collections of features.

   A ball is recognized as an object in space and time.

2. 'Identification of important relationships of objects and assigning individuals on the basis of their functional relations to a synthesized cognitive "chunk" or "concept"'. This process can take place after experience with a single member of the class of objects.

   A ball is known as an object which enters into several relations, such as the thing that can be thrown, rolled, bounced, picked up, etc. For example, 'mother throws ball in the living room'. It is known both for its own actions and the uses it has. It does exist independent of these relations.

3. 'Identification of new concept instances by noting the salient stable ('invariant') characteristics of members included in the concept on functional grounds and forming a hierarchy of identification attributes therefore.' From experience with other members of the class, the child recognizes that certain attributes define the concept and others do not. 'For some concepts the child may retain relations that the adult regards as superfluous.'

   The child sees a boy throw a ball in the park and identifies the relation of 'throwing' as a defining feature, and location such as 'in the living room' vs. 'in the park' as not. A superfluous feature such as 'is thrown to child' may be retained as a defining feature for a while. The functional core concept of 'ball' is as follows:

BALL:	Core functions	= rolls, bounces
	Location	= L_i i.e. any place for playing
	Actor	= X_j i.e. any person
	Action	= A_k i.e. other actions can be performed that can be done to small objects
	Direction	= to child[a]

4. 'Attach a name to the concept so formed.'
   The child attaches the phonetic sequence [bɔl] to the functional core concept of 'ball'.

---

[a] This feature will need to be eliminated from the concept before this process is complete, since it is not a defining feature of 'ball'.

and then attaches meaning to it. Second, Nelson argues that there is a level of cognitive organization which exists intermediately between perception and language. She interprets Clark as mapping directly from perception to language.

Nelson outlines four processes, or steps, that the child follows in acquiring a concept. These are summarized in Table 8.13, with the acquisition of 'ball' as an example. The first process is the simple identification of the ball as a real object. The second process involves the recognition of functional features for the ball. At this point they are context-bound, and the ball is not known outside of these relations. The third process separates the core functions from the other relations which can be represented by abstract markers such as L_i 'any place for playing'. The last process involves the acquisition of a word for the concept.

We see then that the child acquires quite a bit of knowledge about a concept before attaching a word to it. Also, as pointed out by Anglin (1977), this suggests that the child has the meaning of words basically correct when they are acquired. Should the child acquire a word earlier, say during processes 2 or 3, then the error would be one of using a more narrow meaning for the word than the adult does: that is, the direction of error is in the direction of underextension. This prediction of the functional core concept theory is markedly different from that of the semantic feature hypothesis which predicts overextension of early word meanings.

It is important to point out that the functional core concept theory and the semantic feature hypothesis differ primarily in their claims about the *onset* of acquisition. The former, for example, recognizes that perceptual features will eventually be added to the child's concept, just as the latter recognizes the addition of functional features. They are both theories that approach meaning from the definitional view of word meaning and see the acquisition of word meaning as one which requires the establishment of an invariant set of features. Macnamara (1982: 10) points out the overall similarities when he states that the difference between the two theories is mainly one of emphasis.

A last point about Nelson's theory is that it is proposed for the acquisition of referring expressions such as 'ball'. It is not clear how Nelson would account for the acquisition of relational terms such as 'big' and 'little'. One of the early appeals of Clark's theory was its wider range of predictions.

Prototype theory   The basic characteristics of prototype theory were discussed in section 8.3.1. To reiterate: it is an approach developed by Eleanor Rosch and her colleagues to account for the representation of meaning by adults. The proposal is that the meaning of words is not a set of invariant features, but rather a set of features which capture family resemblances. Some objects will be most typical of the word's meaning by sharing more of the word's features than others. Certain features, then, will be more important in determining class membership than others, but none are required by all members.

This theory appeared after the two just discussed and has been adapted by several people for the acquisition of word meaning. In one version or another it is probably the most widely held theory among those who approach the topic from the perspective of Child Language. Here we will examine two of the attempts to adapt it to language acquisition – Anglin (1977) and Bowerman (1978a). Other attempts to do so can be found in Greenberg & Kuczaj (1982) and Barrett (1978, 1982).

Anglin (1977) One of the first to adapt prototype theory to child language was Anglin (1977), which still represents one of the most extensive databases on lexical acquisition. To follow Anglin's proposals it is necessary to define some of the terms he uses:

Basic definitions used by Anglin (1977:27)
1. *Term of reference*: 'a word . . . which denotes or refers to real objects';
2. *Extension*: 'all the objects which an individual is willing to denote' with a term of reference;
3. *Intension*: 'the set of properties which an individual believes to be true of the instances of the category denoted' by a term of reference;
4. *Concept*: 'all of the knowledge possessed by an individual about the category of objects denoted' by a term of reference. 'This knowledge includes both knowledge of extension and knowledge of intension.'

Like Nelson (1974), Anglin was interested in the study of referring terms or 'terms of reference'. He makes a distinction which has been made for years in semantics between a word's *extension*, i.e. the objects which a word refers to in the real world, and its *intension*, i.e. the internal representation of the word's meaning. Importantly, the concept underlying the meaning of a word contains knowledge about extension and intension.

Anglin (pp. 257–64) proposes that concepts or word meanings are acquired in the following fashion. First, the child forms a perceptual schema or representation of an object, based on his first experiences with it. This schema is analogous to a prototype, in that it is a visual image of the object that is not broken down into individual features. The child, therefore, does not begin at some superordinate level (semantic feature hypothesis) or subordinate level (functional core concept), but at an intermediate level. For example, a 'ball' is neither 'a round thing' nor 'the thing mommy throws to me in the living room', but the perceptual schema that represents the balls which the child has seen. At first, the prototype will be limited to the perceptual characteristics of the first instance so named, but will be generalized as more instances are met.

It is at this point that the distinction between extension and intension needs to be made. The child's extensional knowledge of the object will consist of the prototype which is constructed primarily from perceptual categorization. Intensional knowledge, however, will involve not just perceptual information, but also the functional characteristics discussed by Nelson. Anglin states (p. 262):

> . . . both the theory of concept formation based upon prototypes and the theory based upon function . . . have relevance for a complete description of the structure of the concepts underlying the child's

terms of reference. The former is implicated in their extension while the latter is implicated in their intension.

This account, then, incorporates the perceptual and functional aspects of early lexical development.

A key aspect of Anglin's theory is the way that extensional and intensional knowledge develop over time. For the preschool child, these two aspects of concepts are not well coordinated. That is, the child is not very efficient in using its intensional knowledge when dealing with instances of the concept, or in using its extensional knowledge when discussing its intensional knowledge. This claim is an inductive one, based on Anglin's research which indicated that children's overextensions (or identification of instances of a concept) were primarily based on perception, while their definitions of words (or intensions) were primarily functional, e.g. 'apple' is something you eat. Interestingly, the claim is also consistent with Piagetian theory, which sees coordination as an important mechanism in development.

Anglin also discusses other developments for the child. Not surprisingly, the number of concepts increases over time, as well as the amount of knowledge about each concept. More important, there is the development in the school-age child of the ability to organize his knowledge into a hierarchical system in which the child is aware of the relations between superordinate and subordinate categories. For example, the preschool child will know, at least consciously, that 'trees' are also 'plants'. This ability appears to develop quite late.

Anglin's theory is similar to Clark's and Nelson's to the extent that it is constructionist in nature. The child is using adult-like mechanisms to organize his system. The changes in time are in adding information as well as coordinating the knowledge already acquired. It differs in its predictions about the nature of the child's early word meanings: they are at an intermediate level at the onset, and develop from there to more general and more specific meanings. Also, Anglin's theory differs in its view of the relation of the child's knowledge (or competence) to his performance. By discussing two kinds of conceptual knowledge and their poor coordination, he suggests that the child's performance will only reflect *part* of the child's underlying knowledge; that is, he implies a larger gap between the two than the other theories we have discussed.

Bowerman (1978a)   Like Anglin, Bowerman developed her version of prototype theory after empirical study of the speech of children. While Anglin's data were the result of experimental research on several children, Bowerman's data consisted of her careful diary notes on the language of her own two children. Her data are the most detailed diary data presented on the topic, and will be examined more carefully later.

Bowerman believes that both Clark and Nelson have proposed theories which only account for part of the facts of lexical acquisition. In support of this view, she presents two general claims in particular about lexical acquisition. First, evidence suggests that children do not restrict themselves to just perceptual or functional features, but use at least both. For example, data indicate that the concepts behind early word meanings can be superordinate for some words, prototypical for others, and even adult-like for still others. From this she claims that children have 'a variety of methods of classification at their disposal' (p. 283). Second, one type of categorization does not necessarily replace the others over time; that is, the different kinds of classification can be used simultaneously. Therefore, one type of categorization is not more primitive than another. (We have already seen data in Chapter 6 that suggest such a situation for overextensions in the study by Rescorla 1980, as presented in Table 6.8 and the surrounding text.) From these claims, Bowerman concludes that the representation of meaning as features and prototypes needs to be incorporated into a single model.

The difference between Anglin and Bowerman represents that between two views of prototype theory. Anglin's view is that prototypes are like mental images, where the prototype is an abstract image which looks like all the members, yet is not necessarily any one in particular. As an image, it cannot be broken down into featural components. Bowerman cites a position which was expressed in Rosch & Mervis (1975) that prototypes can be viewed as consisting of features. While none of the features are required for class identification, prototypicality of any object is determined by the number of features that it shares with other members of the class. This is the version of prototype theory which was described above in 8.3.1.

The development of a prototype, in Bowerman's view, proceeds as follows: (i) the child first hears a word frequently, and possibly exclusively, in a particular context, e.g. 'night-night' while going to bed; (ii) the child first acquires and uses the word in this context (from a few days to more than a month) – presumably a preliminary prototype is formed at this time; (iii) the child imposes a featural analysis upon the word's prototypical meaning. Further, some of these features can now be recognized in other contexts without the other features with which they occurred in the previous stage. This results in the associative complexes discussed in Chapter 6 in relation to the study by Rescorla (1980). Bowerman sees the existence of such complexes as compelling evidence for a prototype model. The features selected for such overextensions can be quite variable from child to child, so universal predictions for what will occur are not possible. They can be both perceptual and functional, although the former appear to be more prominent, at least in the early stages.

Bowerman's study can only be taken as an outline of a prototype theory of lexical acquisition. There are a number of gaps in it, such as details on why some words overextend and others do not. Also, as pointed out by Barrett (1978, 1982), the theory does not account for why the child does not end up with several words for the same object through overextension. Except for the possibility of retrieval errors (see page 159), children do not usually overextend a word to objects for which other words already exist. Bowerman's initial speculations, however, have provided a basis for further refinement, as in Barrett (1982).

8.3.3 Some findings on the acquisition of nominals

Turning from theoretical speculations to look at some of the data which have resulted from attempts to test theories such as those just discussed, it can be seen from the above discussion that much of the research has focussed on the acquisition of nominal or referring expressions. To get a feel for some of the kinds of data on this topic, we will look at the most extensive report on the topic, Anglin (1977). This will be followed by a discussion of the diary data reported in Bowerman (1978a).

Anglin (1977)   Anglin reports a series of studies conducted to answer three general questions posed at the onset of the acquisition of terms of reference: (i) what is their order of acquisition; (ii) what is their extension; and (iii) what is their intension? We will look at a selection of the studies done on each of these questions.

Anglin wanted to examine the issue of *order of acquisition*, i.e. whether the child's first terms of reference indicate superordinate, intermediate, or subordinate categories. The results of such research bear on the predictions of the theories discussed in the previous section. Previous research had already provided some preliminary findings on this topic. In an important early paper, Brown (1958b) had already pointed out that children do not begin with either superordinate terms (e.g. 'thing') or subordinate terms (e.g. 'dime'), but intermediate ones (e.g. 'money'). Studies of the early vocabulary of children, such as Nelson (1973), also show this across children. Table 6.7 presented the most common terms of reference used by the subjects in Nelson (1973). The most frequent animal term, for example, was 'dog', a term intermediate between the superordinate word 'animal' and the subordinate ones like 'collie' or 'boxer'. The problem with such studies, however, is that the child might still use the terms in a more general or specific way. 'Dog', for example, might mean 'all animals' to the child, but be used instead of 'animal' because of the naming practices of adults. This was, in fact, the claim in Brown (1958b), who wanted to reconcile the use of intermediate vocabulary by children with his position that cognitive development is general-to-specific.

Anglin conducted two studies to examine this issue in more detail. The second of these (experiment 2.2) looked at the sets of terms given in (8.20).

(8.20) *Level*   I   II   III
       superordinate animal   plant   food
       intermediate   dog   flower   fruit
       subordinate   collie   rose   apple

The stimuli consisted of 36 black-and-white pictures, 12 for each set of terms. There were three pictures for each intermediate and subordinate term. The pictures of superordinate terms were divided into two sets of three, one for prototypical instances of the terms, another for peripheral ones. The pictures were selected from 146 original pictures which were shown to adults for rating of the extent to which they were typical of the test words. For example, the three pictures showing collies were those judged most like collies from 12 pictures presented. The three pictures of a prototypical animal were of a King Charles spaniel, an African elephant, and a cat. The pictures for 'animal' which were judged peripheral were of a bullfrog, a monarch butterfly, and a marsh hawk (see Table 2.4 in Anglin 1977 for a list of all the objects used and see p. 57 for the pictures used for Set I). Each set of three pictures was put on a separate poster for subsequent testing, for a total of twelve posters, four per set.

The subjects were 20 children between 2 and 5 years of age. They were first told that they would be asked to name some pictures. After a demonstration of the task with pictures testing the hierarchy 'boy-child-person', they were randomly shown the 12 posters. The experimenter pointed to each picture and asked 'What's this?' After naming each individual object on the poster, the child was then asked 'What are all these?' The children were also encouraged to give another name if they did not distinguish between objects, e.g. 'dog' for each of three dogs.

A simple summary of the major results is provided in Table 8.14, which gives the findings for the answers to the second question 'What are these?' The adults categorized the posters as expected. The responses given in the table are those which were most common for the adults and children. Two results are shown for the children: 'percent correct' represents the percentage of times that the children used the same label for each poster as the adults did, and this is followed by the most common response used by the children.

For two of the three sets, the intermediate terms 'dogs' and 'flowers' were clearly the earliest acquired. Even the specific term 'apple' is somewhat intermediate in the sense that there are varieties of apples which could be labeled. Anglin concludes (p. 67): 'There is neither a unidirectional specific-to-general progression in vocabulary development nor a unidirectional general-to-specific progression.'

In a later discussion, he proposes three factors which determine the words

Table 8.14 *Results of Anglin's experiment 2.2, reported in Anglin (1977)*

Adult	Child	
	Percent correct	Most common response
animals	50	animals
dogs	100	dogs
collies	0	dogs
plants	15	flowers
flowers	70	flowers
roses	10	flowers
foods	40	foods
fruits	20	foods
apples	95	apples

that are first acquired. One of these is *relevance*, i.e. the extent to which the object labeled is important to the child in its daily activities. This factor may override the tendency towards intermediate terms, since specific individuals like the mother and father are important to the child and will receive names. 'Dog' may be the usual intermediate term but the child will also learn the name of the family dog. The second factor is *function*, which is used to capture the fact that adults name objects at an intermediate level for a particular purpose. They group objects together when they constitute a group that the child should behave similarly toward. For example, the child might not need to be careful with all animals, but dogs might constitute such a group. Lastly, Anglin found that there was a correlation between order of acquisition and *frequency of occurrence* of the words in the speech of children. Anglin suggests that this correlation can be used as a general heuristic for determining the categories used in children's vocabularies. His subsequent analysis provides a taxonomy very similar to the one in Nelson (1973) which was reported in Chapter 6.

To answer his second research question, Anglin next examined the occurrence of *extension* by studying children's labeling in both comprehension and production. Chapter 6 already presented some studies on children's overextensions in comprehension and production. Those studies are similar to Anglin's, to the extent that they begin with spontaneous overextensions in the child's spoken language, and use these as the basis of further examination (e.g. Thomson & Chapman 1977). Anglin's studies differ in that they present a range of pictures to children and see how they label them. The pictures, however, are not selected on the basis of the child's previous naming behavior. Anglin offers a general criticism of the previous studies that they bias the study of word meaning in the direction of overextensions.

To get around the above experimental bias, Anglin used a method which would be sensitive to both over- and underextensions. His use of this method in his experiment 4.1 is examined here. Three sets of test words were used which differed in three degrees of generality: see (8.21) and compare with (8.20):

(8.21) I   II   III

I	II	III
animal	food	plant
dog	fruit	flower
collie	apple	tulip

The subjects were two groups of 18 children each, with the ages 2;6 to 4;0 (younger group), and 4;6 to 6;0 (older group). There were also 18 adults tested. Each group was divided into three subgroups of six subjects each. Within each subgroup, each subject would be shown 120 pictures distributed across three test words in the following way: 10 instances and 10 non-instances of a subordinate term, e.g. 'collie'; 20 instances and 20 non-instances of an intermediate term from a different set, e.g. 'fruit'; and 30 instances and 30 non-instances of the subordinate term from the remaining set, e.g. 'animal'. For each test picture, the child was asked 'Is this a (test word)?'

Detailed results were presented for each subject and selected pictures. The general results can be summarized as follows. The children showed both overextensions and underextensions, the latter being the more frequent. For example, the younger children underextended 29% of the possible underextensions, and overextended only 8 percent of the possible overextensions. These figures were 16 percent and 6 percent respectively for the older children. The most frequent underextension was the denial that a picture of a woman was an 'animal'. Other examples were rejecting the pictures of a praying mantis and a caterpillar as 'animals'.

There were three factors which influenced the data: (i) individual variation between children, (ii) the concept studied, and (iii) the nature of the instances and non-instances being tested. Individual variation was evident in that some terms were overextended by some children, underextended by others, and correctly used by still others. Such data support the contention of Chapter 6 that multiple factors may underlie a child's errors in extension. Despite the individual variation, there were some patterns for specific concepts. 'Flower', for example, tended to be overextended to items such as an elephant ear, a coconut, and a philodendron. 'Plant', on the other hand, was usually underextended. In particular, trees were rejected as examples of plants. Lastly, atypical or peripheral instances of a test word were more likely to be incorrectly identified than others. This point was verified by Anglin in subsequent studies.

This experiment was followed by a series of others to explore whether the child's extensional errors resulted more from perceptual or functional factors. The findings supported Clark's early findings that overextensions tend to be primarily based on perceptual similarities.

Lastly, Anglin examined the *intension* of children's early words. He studied 14 children between 2;8 and 6;7. Each child was interviewed and asked to discuss the meanings of 12 words: 'dog', 'food', 'flower', 'vehicle', 'animal', 'apple', 'rose', 'car', 'collie', 'fruit', 'plant', and 'Volkswagen'. Anglin comments as follows (p. 189) on the methodology:

> In general, we tried to ask five questions about each word in roughly the following order: (1) 'What is a ____?' (2) 'Tell me everything you can about (a) ____.' (3) 'What kinds of ____s are there?' (4) 'What kind of thing is a ____?' (5) 'Tell me a story about a ____?' However, apart from the first one, these questions were not always asked of each child for each word and quite often a variety of other questions were asked.

The method, then, was very much in the spirit of Piaget's clinical method. This particular experiment, in fact, is similar to the one in Piaget (1929).

Anglin presented his results as a series of conversational samples with individual children. Most generally, the children did not show knowledge of the ability to give a set of defining properties for a word's meaning. One interview with a child Peter, age 2;8, particularly shows the limited kinds of definitions available from young children. When discussing 'dog', Peter states that 'it goes woof, barks'. He also recalls two dogs that he has seen and what they looked like. That is, 'the very young child's expressible knowledge of a concept, as in this case, often appears to be "instance-oriented" and quite possibly is based to a considerable degree on visual imagery' (p. 191). Anglin emphasizes, however, in his analysis, that the definitions are more often based upon the functional properties of objects rather than strictly perceptual features.

Anglin cites the above findings on lexical acquisition as support for his version of a prototype theory which we have already seen. The data on the early acquisition of intermediate terms and the use of overextensions and underextensions are cited as evidence for the child establishing early prototypes which are perceptually based. The data from word definitions is given in support of the claim that the child's intensional knowledge is functionally based. The fact that both kinds of knowledge appear to be available to children leads to the proposal that a concept contains both intensional and extensional knowledge.

Bowerman (1978a)   In this paper, Bowerman presents data on the early lexical acquisition of her two daughters, Eva and Christy, to support her version of prototype theory given above. Bowerman states the following

Table 8.15 *Summary of the examples of word meaning for Eva and Christy given in four tables in Bowerman (1978a)*

Examples		Tables and their contents
Eva	Christy	
'moon'	'snow' 'money'	1. Overextensions based on perceptual similarities, counter to known functional differences
'there!' 'too tight' 'heavy'	'aha!' 'heavy'	2. Words extended to novel situations on the basis of subjective experiences
'ball' 'ice' 'off'	'on-off'	3. Words used noncomplexively for referents with shared attributes
'kick' 'close' 'open' 'giddiup' 'moon	'night-night' 'open'	4. Complexively used words with prototypical referents

about her data (p. 264): 'Fairly complete records are available on the way in which almost every word was used from its first appearance in the child's speech to about 24 months. Data on word use continue beyond that point but are more selective.' Bowerman presents her data in four tables in the form of selected examples, summarized here in Table 8.15. These examples from Eva and Christy are frequently cited in discussions on the acquisition of early word meaning.

The first table deals with the issue of whether the child's early extensions are on the basis of perceptual or functional similarity. First, Bowerman observes that most of the girls' overextensions appeared on the basis of shared perceptual features, a finding consistent with Clark's (1973a) diary analyses and the findings from Anglin (1977) presented above. She points out, however, that this finding would not be incompatible with Nelson's functional theory if the perceptual features were 'used primarily to predict the function of an object so that the object can be identified as a member of a known function-based category' (p. 265). The examples in her Table 1, however, are given to show that such was not the case in most instances. For example, Eva used 'moon' for the following situations, among others: 'for a ball of spinach she was about to eat, for hangnails she was pulling off, for a magnetic capital letter D she was about to put on the refrigerator' (pp. 265, 267). In each case, the perceptual feature of shape was similar while the actions were quite distinct.

We have already pointed out that the functional core concept theory is limited to predictions about the acquisition of nominals. Bowerman mentions this point, and turns to a discussion of the fact that Eva's and Christy's non-nominal terms could not be explained by either functional or perceptual features. She argues that the overextension of several of these words appeared to be based on the *subjective experiences* of the child. She offers the following interpretations (8.22) of the words given in her Table 2:

(8.22) 'there!'   the experience of completing a project;
      'aha!'   the experience of discovery and surprise;
      'too tight'   protest in situations involving physical restriction or interference;
      'heavy'   physical exertion, often unsuccessful, with an object, whether or not it is heavy;

Bowerman concludes from data such as that in her Tables 1 and 2 that theories of word meaning need to expand to include the possibility that overextensions can occur on the basis of several kinds of similarities, not just one. In this way, her approach is similar to Anglin's in trying to incorporate at least both perceptual and functional features.

Bowerman's next two tables turn to the issue of whether children's first overextensions are complexive or noncomplexive. We discussed this issue in Chapter 6 in relation to Rescorla (1980), where complexive uses (or associative complexes) refer to cases where the child links the use of a word from one situation to another but does not relate all the uses to one shared feature or set of features. Bowerman draws the following conclusions about this issue: (i) both complexive and noncomplexive overextensions occur from the onset of acquisition (a claim later supported by Rescorla's study); and (ii) complexive use was somewhat more common for action words than for object words, suggesting that its use cannot be directly tied to the attainment of object permanence (an issue discussed already in Chapter 6).

In presenting the examples in her Table 3 to show early noncomplexive words, Bowerman emphasizes a striking feature of her daughters' word meanings, i.e. the way in which the girls could assign very different meanings to the same words. This was particularly noteworthy since we can assume that the environment was relatively similar for the two children. The best example of this was Christy's 'on-off' and Eva's 'off' which are summarized in (8.23):

(8.23) Christy 'on-off': 'any act involving the separation or coming together of two objects or parts of an object' (p. 271), e.g. getting socks on or off; getting off a spring-horse; taking pop-beads on and off; separating stacked cups; putting phone on hook; etc.

Eva 'off': 'removal of clothes and other objects from the body' (p. 271), e.g. for shoes, car safety harness, glasses, pacifier, bib, diaper, etc.

Table 8.16 *Prototypes proposed by Bowerman (1978a) for Eva and Christy*

Word	Prototype	Features
'kick'	kicking a ball with the foot so that it is propelled forward	a. waving limb b. sudden sharp contact c. object propelled
'night-night'	person or doll lying down in bed or crib	a. crib, bed b. blanket c. non-normal horizontal position
'close'	closing drawers, doors, boxes, jars, etc.	a. bringing together two objects or parts b. cause something to be concealed
'open'	opening drawers, doors, boxes, jars, etc.	a. separation of parts which were in contact b. cause something to be revealed
'giddiup'	bouncing on a spring horse	a. horse b. bouncing motion c. sitting on toy
'moon'	the real moon	a. circular shape b. yellow color c. shiny surface d. viewing position e. flatness f. broad expanse

Such observations support the view of the child as an active organizer of her linguistic experiences.

The last of Bowerman's tables turns to examples of complexive use of words, that is, cases where the features change from instance to instance. Bowerman emphasizes that most of these cases indicated prototypical structure, that is, the instances of overextension would share at least one feature with some central or prototypical example. Such a situation is distinct from the possible one in which the child links or 'chains' words from situation to situation without any shared features across the instances. Bowerman offers the analyses in Table 8.16 of the examples in her Table 4 (see Bowerman 1978a: 274–7 for details).

We can see how diverse these activities can be by looking at some of the uses by Eva of the word 'kick'. It was used in the following situations, among others: seeing a picture of a kitten with a ball near its paw; watching cartoon turtles on TV doing the can-can; pushing her stomach against a mirror.

Bowerman's analysis leads her to conclude that her daughters were showing adult-like categories at a very early age of development. She states (p. 278): 'These findings suggest that there is less discontinuity between child and adult methods of classification than has often been supposed.' She takes the examples of early complexive words as indicative that the children were able to apply a featural analysis to the data, and that these features were similar to those used by adults. She does not discuss, however, how the child gets from its early prototypes to those of the adult language.

8.3.4 Some findings on the acquisition of relational words

While extensive attention has been paid to the acquisition of referential words, there is also a large literature on the development of relational words. These are words which 'represent abstract concepts (relationships) that cannot be directly perceived or referred in the environment' (Blewitt 1982: 153). An example would be the temporal term 'before' which places an event in relation to some other event. Here we will use the term to include dimensional words which have some physical representation, for example, spatial terms such as 'big' and 'little'. These words share the characteristic that their meaning is tied to relating one referential term to another. For example, a 'big' mouse is actually smaller than a 'small' elephant, but the meaning of each word is relative to the norms set for the sizes of the objects being discussed.

The study of relational word acquisition has differed in several respects from the study of referential words. First, the theories which have been proposed for referential words do not always work for relational words. Neither functional core concept theory nor prototype theory make claims on how such words are acquired. It is difficult, for example, to envision what a prototype for a word like 'before' is supposed to be. It is not surprising, therefore, that much of the research in this area has been concerned with testing the predictions made by the semantic feature hypothesis.

A second difference in the study of relational words concerns the focus of such studies. Referential word acquisition is often seen as a process which involves assigning the relevant features to a word in order to have the adult meaning. Importantly, these features are ones considered available to the child, so that the process is one of selection from an available set of features (as just discussed for Bowerman). The child, for example, is conceptually aware of cats, dogs, cows, etc. and needs to attach the appropriate features to the appropriate phonetic strings. Relational words, however, involve more directly the issues of complexity and cognitive ability. Regarding *complexity*, relational words can often be placed on a scale of least to most complex. For example, 'big' and 'little' can be viewed as having a relation in which 'big' is in some sense less complex than 'small' since, in the unmarked case, we ask 'How big are you?' not 'How small are you?' Such relations lead to predictions that the less complex, or unmarked, terms are acquired before more complex ones, i.e. that order of acquisition is determined by featural complexity. Such relations are less identifiable with referential words, although they do exist (e.g. 'boy' vs. 'brother').

Related to the issue of complexity is that of *cognitive ability*. There is the possibility that more complex relational words are acquired late not because they have more features to be acquired, but rather because the child has not acquired the concept which underlies them. This can be exemplified by looking at the acquisition of question words. It has been known for some time that English children acquire *wh*-question words in a relatively predictable order (e.g. M. Smith 1933; Tyack & Ingram 1977). The first question words are typically 'what' and 'where', followed by 'why', then 'how' and 'when'. This order involves increasing abstractness from the relatively concrete terms 'what' and 'where' which refer to objects and places to the more abstract temporal term 'when'. The late acquisition of 'when', therefore, may tell more about the child's cognitive development than it does about the organization of the semantic system. If order of acquisition of dimensional terms is strictly the result of cognitive development, then we could hold a view that the child's semantic classificatory processes are adult-like, and that words are acquired appropriately as concepts become available. For purposes of discussion, we will refer to this hypothetical position as the *cognition theory*.

A further characteristic of relational word acquisition concerns the child's behavior when he has to process a relational word which has not been acquired, be it due to an incomplete semantic system or incomplete cognition. It has been observed by several investigators that in such cases children will respond with some form of *non-linguistic strategy*. For example, Eve Clark (1973b) has observed that children who have not acquired the complete meanings of prepositions such as 'in' or 'on' will simply do what looks most appropriate, given the situation. For example, if handed a ball and an open container, the child will place the ball into the container rather than alongside or underneath. If the object is a card and a table, however, it is more likely that the card will be placed on the table. As work proceeded on the acquisition of relational terms, it was found that results of studies were frequently contradictory. This led to a review of the methods used in such studies, and to the further observation that children not only used non-linguistic strategies, but that these would vary according to a number of possible factors in the test situation. Much of the work in this area, then, has concentrated on determining the range of such non-linguistic or cognitive strategies.

It can be seen from this discussion of the semantic feature hypothesis and cognition theory that both approaches put the emphasis upon the child's cognitive rather than linguistic development. Further, a great deal of the discussion has been by necessity on methodological issues. The result has been that we know more about cognitive development, test methods, and the general order of acquisition of some relational words. It is not clear, however, that we know a lot more about the development of the semantic system.

In an attempt to provide a flavor of the kind of research done in this area, three kinds of relational words which have been studied in some detail will be briefly considered here. These are the temporal terms 'before'/'after', the dimensional terms 'big'/'tall', and the locational terms 'in', 'on', 'under', 'beside', 'front' and 'back'. As with other topics, specific pivotal studies will be focussed upon before discussion of subsequent research.

Before/after   One of Clark's first examinations of the semantic feature hypothesis was her study of children's comprehension and production of the temporal words 'before' and 'after' (Clark 1971). She selected these words because she felt that they are a clear case where one term, 'before', could be shown to be semantically simpler than the other, 'after'. Her semantic feature analysis of the words is presented in (8.24), where the features for 'when' are also given.

(8.24) | *Feature* | 'before' | 'after' | 'when' |
| --- | --- | --- | --- |
| time | + | + | + |
| simultaneous | − | − | + |
| prior | + | − | |

'When' is the simplest of the three terms since it is not marked for the feature [prior]. 'Before' is the next in complexity because it is positively marked for [prior]. There is minimal justification for this decision, with references to Leech (1970) and H. Clark (1970) for further argumentation. The major claim is that 'before' is more basic because 'it is used to describe the visual perceptual field, whereas its counterpart "behind" . . . is negative since it describes the area that is out of sight' (Eve Clark 1973b: 267). The predicted order of acquisition based on complexity then is 'when' > 'before' > 'after'.

'Before' and 'after' were tested in four kinds of constructions, referred to as 'before$_1$', 'before$_2$', 'after$_1$' and 'after$_2$'. Each of the constructions contained two clauses, so that the subscripts 1 and 2 refer to the position in the sentence of the clause that began with the test word. Examples of the four types of construction are given in (8.25).

(8.25) | Before$_2$ | 'He jumped the gate before he patted the dog' | E_1E_2 |
| --- | --- | --- |
| Before$_1$ | 'Before he patted the dog, he jumped the gate' | E_2E_1 |
| After$_2$ | 'He patted the dog after he jumped the gate' | E_2E_1 |
| After$_1$ | 'After he jumped the gate, he patted the dog' | E_1E_2 |

A further feature of these constructions concerns the order of the events in relation to their mention in the sentences. The 'before$_2$' and 'after$_1$' sentences mention the events in the order in which they occurred. That is, the first event, the jumping of the gate (E_1), is mentioned before the second event, the patting of the dog (E_2). Clark observes that children have been found to acquire complex sentences like this with the main clause preceding the subordinate clause. Notice that the 'before$_2$' sentence with the 'before' in the second clause also mirrors the natural order of the events, i.e. E_1E_2. She argues that these two factors make this sentence pattern easier to acquire, thus another argument for the acquisition of 'before' ahead of 'after'.

The subjects in the study were 40 children (24 girls, 16 boys), ten in each of four age groups: I 3;0–3;5, II 3;6–3;11, III 4;0–4;5, and IV 4;6–5;0. The mean ages were 3;2, 3;8, 4;3, and 4;11 respectively. Each child participated in a production task, then a comprehension task. This order of presentation is typical of studies which test both production and comprehension, since the use of a comprehension task first might provide models to the child which she could use in the production task. In the production task, the child watched two events, and then was asked a 'when' question about each event, e.g. 'When did the boy pat the dog?', 'When did the boy jump the gate?' In the comprehension task, the child was presented with a variety of toys and then asked to act out a sentence presented by the experimenter. Each of the four sentence types was presented eight times for a total of 32 test sentences in each task.

On the comprehension task, an error was recorded when the child acted out the two events in the wrong order. The measure used to score the results was the percentage of errors on each of the four sentence types. The general results on the comprehension task were as follows. First, each age group did significantly better than the previous one. The percentages of errors for the four groups were 49, 38, 28, and 17 respectively. Second, the four sentence types showed three significant degrees of difficulty: 'before$_2$' and 'after$_1$' were the easiest sentence types with only 4 percent and 11 percent of errors overall respectively, followed by 'before$_1$' with 48 percent, with 'after$_2$' the most difficult with 69 percent of errors. Since 'before$_2$' and 'after$_1$' both involved the E_1E_2 order of events, Clark interprets this as indicative that some of the children were using an *order of mention strategy*. That is, they had not yet acquired the [prior] feature for the words and were acting out the events in the order in which they were mentioned. Third, the two constructions with 'before' were significantly easier than the two with 'after', confirming Clark's prediction that 'before' was easier than 'after'.

A problem in interpreting the results was that 'after$_1$' was significantly better than 'after$_2$', and that 'before$_2$' was significantly easier than 'before$_1$',

Table 8.17 *Stages, number of subjects, and percentage of errors on four construction types for 'before' and 'after', adapted from Clark (1971)*

Stage	No. of subjects	Construction and order of events			
		before$_1$ (E$_2$E$_1$)	before$_2$ (E$_1$E$_2$)	after$_1$ (E$_1$E$_2$)	after$_2$ (E$_2$E$_1$)
A	21	80% (wrong)	4% (correct)	10% (correct)	83% (wrong)
B1	7	4% (correct)	4% (correct)	0% (correct)	89% (wrong)
B2	3	25% (correct)	8% (correct)	75% (wrong)	92% (wrong)
C	8	9% (correct)	9% (correct)	0% (correct)	6% (correct)

indicating that something else was going on in the data. Clark attempted to capture this further factor by dividing the subjects into four stages of acquisition. These stages are as follows:

Stage

A   Use the order of mention strategy to interpret sentence

B1   Correct understanding of 'before'; use order of mention strategy on sentences with 'after'

B2   Correct understanding of 'before'; interpret 'after' as if it meant 'before'

C   Correct understanding of 'before' and 'after'

The data on which these stages are based are presented in Table 8.17. The stages above also lead to strong claims about the order of acquisition of words like 'after' and 'before' which only differ in a single feature. Here we restate the four stages above in more general terms:

Proposed stages in the acquisition of antonyms

Stage   Interpretation and predictions

A   Acquisition of superordinate feature: use a non-linguistic strategy for both terms

B1   Acquisition of unmarked word: restrict use of non-linguistic strategy to marked word

B2   Acquisition of unmarked word: treat marked word as if it has the unmarked meaning

C   Acquisition of marked word: correct understanding of both words

Clark interprets the results as supporting the semantic feature hypothesis. She states (p. 275): 'children learn the meanings of words component by component, and furthermore, where these components are hierarchically related to each other, the feature hierarchy is learned in order beginning with the superordinate component, e.g. +Time, followed by +/− Simultaneous, followed by +/− Prior'.

This study inspired a great deal of discussion and further study, both on 'before' and 'after' and on other works. In Ingram (1981b) some general questions were raised about the interpretation of the data. As already mentioned, the difference between 'before$_1$' and 'before$_2$' is not explained. It appears to result from the drop in performance on 'before$_1$' at stage B2. If we look at B2, we see that this is the result of the use of an order of mention strategy that affects both 'after' and 'before'. Note that both pairs of these words have 17 percent more errors on the words with E_2E_1 order. This creates a logical problem for B1 and B2 since the child is supposed to have abandoned the order of mention strategy for 'before' at B1 and for 'after' at B2. A further problem is that there is no mechanism proposed which gets the child from B1 to B2. At B1, the child knows that 'after' is different from 'before' since it is treated differently. What causes the child to abandon this knowledge and treat them the same at the next stage? Lastly, there was no age effect between B1 and B2, and thus no independent measure for them. They thus constitute a 'stage error' in the sense of Chapter 3. It is concluded in Ingram (1981b) that there is little evidence to consider these as separate stages; they should only possibly be considered as two different ways to acquire word meaning.

Further research on these words has led to other problems with Clark's original study and further insights into the acquisition of word meaning. These studies have been excellently reviewed in Blewitt (1982), on which I will base my review here. The general findings have been as follows. First, no study has replicated the finding that for some children 'after' is interpreted as 'before'. This is a striking result which has devastating effects for the proposed stage B2. If true, it also is one that requires some explanation, in that evidence exists that such a general stage may exist for some other pairs, e.g. 'more' and 'less' (Donaldson & Wales 1970), 'tell' and 'ask' (C. Chomsky 1969), where children have been found to interpret the second word in each pair as if it had the meaning of the first one. Second, the order of acquisition of 'before' and 'after' has been controversial. Some studies have replicated Clark's result, while some others have found 'after' acquired first (Barrie-Blackley 1973; Amidon 1976; Feagans 1980), and others have found no difference in their order of acquisition (Amidon & Carey 1972; Friedman & Seeley 1976; French & Brown 1977).

Blewitt's review of these studies leads her to propose several factors which have affected children's performance on a language comprehension task. Three of these are summarized below:

(i)   *The structure of the sentence*: Amidon & Carey (1972) used sentences such as 'Before you move the green car, move the red car' where the agent is 2nd instead of 3rd person and there is one action instead of two. Children performed worse than in the Clark study.

(ii) *The syntactic role of the test word*: Coker (1978) tested with three different tasks where 'before' and 'after' were prepositions in two tasks and adverbs in the third, as in Clark's study. 'Before' was harder than 'after' on task 1, the same on task 2, and easier on task 3.

(iii) *Semantic content of the sentence*: French & Brown (1977) compared sentences with logically constrained events, e.g. 'After Raggedy Ann fills the bottle, she feeds the baby', with sentences that are not logically constrained, i.e. as in the Clark study. Children performed better on logically constrained sentences.

The first one, the *structure of the sentence*, is a factor which was also found in Carol Chomsky's study of 'ask' and 'tell'. She found that children would interpret 'ask' as if it meant 'tell', but that it would be restricted to only certain sentence patterns, at least for older children. This factor suggests that the child may have the correct meanings of the words, but that processing more complex sentence structures affects the retrieval of more recently acquired meanings. The second factor points out the crucial way in which the *syntactic role of the test word* may influence the results of a study. Coker replicated Clark's results when testing 'before' and 'after' as subordinate adverbs, but found that children did better with 'after' when they were tested as prepositions. This initially suggests the peculiar situation that the relation of markedness between two words may vary according to their grammatical role. Since the effect was influenced by the questions addressed to the child, however, it appears more likely that it was an experimentally induced bias. The third factor, the influence of the *semantic content of the sentence*, is a performance factor like the first one. That is, it indicates how earlier acquisition can be demonstrated if facilitative test sentences are used.

Big/tall   Possibly the most important claim of the semantic feature hypothesis is that the order of acquisition of relational words is based on their semantic complexity. While this claim did not hold up very well for 'before' and 'after', they are a single pair which are antonyms. It is still possible that the claim may hold between related pairs of antonyms such as 'big'/'little' vs. 'tall'/'short'. According to Bierwisch (1967), 'big'/'little' are the least complex size words because they are global and are not limited to a specific dimension. 'Tall'/'short', however, are limited to the dimension of height. Other such pairs in increasing complexity are 'high'/'low', 'long'/'short', and 'wide'/'narrow'. Because dimensional terms can be graded in this fashion, they have proved to be a rich area for the study of semantic acquisition in general and of the semantic feature hypothesis in particular.

Several studies have supported the findings that such pairs have a predictable order of acquisition based on their proposed semantic complexity. Testing children between 2;6 and 3;6 on pairs of objects, Eilers, Oller & Ellington (1974) found the acquisition order of 'big'/'little' > 'long'/ 'short' > 'wide'/'narrow'. Using the additional pair of 'tall'/'short', Bartlett (1976) replicated the results of Eilers, Oller & Ellington, with the additional finding that the pair 'tall'/'short' was acquired simultaneously with 'long'/ 'short'. Other studies with similar results include those by Clark (1972), Klatzky, Clark & Macken (1973), Brewer & Stone (1975).

In the midst of studying this issue, one peculiar finding emerged. In a series of studies on the meaning of 'big', Maratsos (1973, 1974b) found that 3-year olds correctly used 'big' as predicted by the semantic feature hypothesis, but that 4- and 5-year olds incorrectly processed 'big' as if it meant 'tall'. Further, 'tall' appeared to be correctly understood by all ages tested. This finding is interesting for a number of reasons. First, it is a problem for the semantic feature hypothesis since 'tall' seems to be easier to acquire than 'big'. Second, it poses a peculiar situation of children correctly using a word, then changing to an incorrect meaning. Third, it has been widely cited and has led to a number of subsequent studies. We will take a closer look at one of the studies on which this finding is based, then turn to a more recent study which appears to account for it.

In Experiment 1 (of four) in Maratsos (1973), 30 children between 3 and 5 years of age were tested on their understanding of 'big'. The children were presented with pairs of cardboard rectangles and toy animals, and for each pair, the child was asked 'Which one is the big one?' Maratsos states (p. 748): 'The comparative 'bigger' was not used because pilot work observations indicated that preschool children do not have a clear understanding of the comparative.' Since the stimuli for such experiments have proved to be crucial for the results, we will present them in detail. Maratsos used three test pairs and one pretest pair for each of the three types of rectangles, and three pairs of toy animals. The stimuli used are summarized below:

> *Pretest pairs*: larger rectangle is higher and wider;
> *Unequal height and width pairs*: one rectangle is higher and narrower than the other (G & H in Figure 8.1);
> *Equal height pairs*: one rectangle is wider than the other but both are equal height (C & D in Figure 8.1);
> *'Animal' pairs*: giraffe vs. hippopotamus; donkey vs. bear; policeman vs. leopard.

Facsimiles of the test pairs are shown in Figure 8.1 as pairs C, D, G, and H in the inventory of stimuli later presented by Ravn & Gelman (1984).

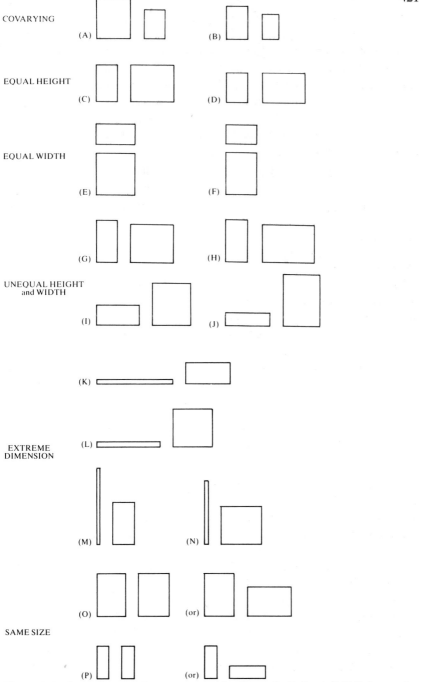

Figure 8.1 Sets of rectangles constructed by Ravn & Gelman (1984) for testing 'bigness'.

The results were scored in terms of percentages of correct responses. A correct response was to pick the member of the pair with greater overall size, e.g. the second rectangle in the pairs C, D, G, and H of Figure 8.1. The 3-year-olds show the results of the studies mentioned above where young children respond correctly to 'big'. In this case 73 percent chose the correct item. This correct response pattern, however, drops dramatically for the 4- and 5-year olds to only 37 percent and 23 percent respectively. Maratsos interprets this as indicating that the older children understood 'big' as if it meant 'tall', citing the following anecdote (p. 749) as an example:

> At one point, one boy, who consistently answered incorrectly, took the shorter animal (the leopard) and set it on its rear legs, which made it taller than the other figure. He then exclaimed, 'Look! Now it's the big one!'

This general finding was substantiated in other experiments reported in Maratsos (1973) and (1974).

This is a peculiar finding for several reasons. Besides those mentioned, there is the further question of whether this result is unique to the acquisition of 'big', or is a characteristic of semantic acquisition. We could propose that it is a general feature of acquisition when the child is acquiring words where one has a more specific meaning than another. This could be done by adapting the stages on page 417 for the acquisition of pairs like 'big' and 'tall'. If so, we would need a revised stage B, which is given below:

> Stage B:
> Loss of acquisition of unmarked word: upon acquisition of marked term, reinterpret the unmarked word as having the meaning of the marked one

As such, this proposal is very strong since it implies that the shift should occur for a wide range of words which bear this relation. Since such shifts are not widely attested in the literature, we will assume for the current discussion that it is a specific aspect of the acquisition of size words.

A recent study by Ravn & Gelman (1984) has provided an explanation for the results found by Maratsos. Ravn & Gelman picked up on an earlier suggestion by Bausano & Jeffrey (1975) that older children may not be treating 'big' as if it meant 'tall', but that another meaning might be used. Bausano & Jeffrey point out that the same results would occur for the older children if they were using a 'salient-dimensional difference rule', i.e. picking out the dimension as 'big' which was most different between the rectangles. Ravn & Gelman build upon this by proposing five possible rules which children might use in judging 'bigness'. These rules are summarized below:

Table 8.18 *Predicted patterns of response for five rules on four types of rectangle pairs from Figure 8.1, adapted from Ravn & Gelman (1984:2145, Table 2). (1st = first rectangle selected; 2nd = second rectangle selected)*

	Stimuli pairs			
Rule	K	L	M	N
Correct rule	2nd	2nd	2nd	2nd
Height rule	2nd	2nd	1st	1st
Width rule	1st	1st	2nd	2nd
Salient-dimensional difference rule	1st	2nd	1st	2nd
Salient-dimension rule	1st	1st	1st	1st

Definition

Correct rule: Biggest area in two dimensions

Height rule: 'tall'

Width rule: 'wide'

Salient-dimensional difference rule: Biggest in whichever dimension shows the greatest (most salient) difference

Salient-dimension rule: Biggest in the dimension of greatest extent

To test these rules, Ravn & Gelman constructed several sets of rectangles which have been reproduced here as figure 8.1. They were constructed in a way such that each of the five rules should lead to a different set of choices from the different sets of rectangles. Table 8.18 gives the predicted patterns of responses for each of the five rules for four of the pairs tested. These pairs proved to be the most useful ones in distinguishing between the five rules since the dimensional differences were most clear-cut.

As in the study by Maratsos, the subjects were 30 children between 3 and 5 years of age, ten at each age level. The method was also similar in that the children were asked to point out which of the rectangles was the big one. Each child's responses were coded into five scores, one for each of the rules tested. Here we will give just the results on the four pairs listed in Table 8.18. The child was assumed to be using one of the five rules if all four pairs were scored as correct for that rule. Table 8.19 gives the results for the three age groups.

The results show clearly that the children at all ages have a preference for the 'height' rule, the preference increasing with age. While the increased use of the height rule is consistent with Maratsos's results, the development of the 'correct' rule is not. Recall that Maratsos found that 3-year olds processed 'big' correctly, while here none of the 3-year olds have correct

Table 8.19 *Percentage of children who used one of five rules adapted from Ravn & Gelman (1984: 2147, Table 4)*

| | Age in years | | | |
| | 3 | 4 | 5 | All age groups |
Rule				
Correct rule	0	10	20	10
Height rule	40	60	70	57
Width rule	0	0	0	0
Salient-dimensional difference rule	0	0	0	0
Salient-dimension rule	30	20	0	17
No rule	30	10	10	17

understanding of 'big'. Ravn & Gelman account for this discrepancy as follows (p. 2147):

> This seemingly paradoxical finding can be explained by the difference in approach between our study and Maratsos's. In each of his experiments, Maratsos used a limited set of items and assumed that if children were not using the rule being tested (height or width depending on the experiment), they were using the correct rule. In contrast, we selected a range of items that would allow us to pit several rules against each other in one experiment.

To demonstrate the effect of the rectangle pairs, Ravn & Gelman scored the percentages of correct responses on the pairs C, D, G, and H, the four pairs used by Maratsos. They found the scores to be 65%, 52% and 40% for 3-, 4-, and 5-year olds respectively. These figures are somewhat higher than, but consistent with, the results reported by Maratsos. The rectangles K through N, then, proved to be a better test of the meaning of 'big' than C, D, G, and H.

Another analysis conducted by Ravn & Gelman looked at the consistency of the children's rule use. They assumed that the higher the score on a rule, the more consistently it was being used. Statistical analysis revealed that the older children were more consistent in their rule usage than the younger children. Their conclusion about the acquisition of 'big', then, is somewhat different than that drawn by Maratsos. Children do not start out with a correct understanding of 'big' and then shift to a height rule for its meaning. Rather, they begin with the height rule, but do not apply it as consistently at the onset.

While their findings differ somewhat from Maratsos's, they resemble his in being a problem for the semantic feature hypothesis. If children begin with a more narrow meaning for 'big', such as 'tall', then acquisition is not proceeding by acquiring more general (or less complex) features to more specific ones.

Given these difficulties with the semantic feature hypothesis, it is not surprising that research has begun to explore other accounts of the acquisition of relational terms. In her study of size terms, Bartlett observed that the children's responses seemed to be affected by the dimensions of individual test items, a result just seen above for rectangles. Bartlett made the following remark regarding areas for future research (1976: 214): 'One important task for future research, then, is to assess the relative effects of cognitive complexity, word frequency and perceptual salience on orders of acquisition for these dimensional features.' Research exploring the last two of these suggestions will be examined briefly here. The first suggestion will be considered in the discussion on the acquisition of spatial terms.

Keil (1979) has attempted to develop an account of semantic acquisition based on a version of prototype theory. Importantly, this work deals not only with referential words, but with relational ones. Keil & Carroll (1980) provide a useful summary of research from this perspective on the acquisition of 'tall'. A general premise is that the child first acquires a meaning for a word that is restricted to the first instances in which it is learned. That is, it is restricted to a small set of exemplars. Keil & Carroll state (1980: 21f):

> The closest view to ours is Carey's (1978) 'missing features-plus-haphazard-example-theory'. Carey suggests that the child may acquire the meanings of spatial terms such as 'tall' by first learning idiosyncratic, object-particular meanings and later learning a more general concept that applies to all objects. Thus, the word 'tall' may have different meanings for different objects.

That is, the meaning of the word for the child will be affected by the *perceptual salience* of different dimensions for different objects.

Keil & Carroll pursue this theory by contrasting its predictions on acquisition with those of the semantic feature hypothesis. If the child is acquiring semantic features for word meanings, then she should apply them consistently across objects. If the meaning is influenced by the aspects of individual objects, then the meaning should vary.

To test these alternatives, Keil & Carroll report on two experiments on the acquisition of 'tall'. In the first one, 36 children between 3 and 6 years of age were shown 18 pictures with three objects shown on each. There were 'tall items' where the objects varied in height but had the same width, and 'wide items' where the height was the same but the width varied. Keil & Carroll comment (p. 23): 'The objects ranged from familiar ones that are easy to think of as tall to ones to which "tall" cannot be so naturally applied.' The children were told the following (p. 23): 'Here are three X's (e.g. houses). Now is one of these the tallest, or are they all the same in tallness?' The results supported the predictions of Keil's prototype model. The children were correct for some items, but incorrect for others. They were significantly better at objects which had vertical lines (e.g. pencils), than they were for ones with curves (e.g. mountains).

The second study also supported this finding, but added some insight into development over time. In the second experiment, the children were shown the same pictures, but were told that they were different objects. For example, the picture of mountains was now a picture of blankets. The importance of this shift is that mountains are more naturally thought of as being 'tall' than are 'blankets'. The older children (4;6 to 7;6) were significantly more likely to make an error on the less natural objects than were the younger children. The fact that these changes in judgement occurred with the same pictures indicates that the judgements were semantic, not just perceptual, in nature. Also, the finding that older children were consistent when interpreting the pictures differently indicates that they were associating 'tall' with specific kinds of objects.

The finding of the second experiment shows that the child's linguistic experience with objects plays an important role in applying a word such as 'tall', overriding what looked like a perceptual effect in the first experiment. Blewitt (1982) discusses input *frequency* as one such factor which may influence how the child acquires such words. We have already discussed briefly at the end of Chapter 6 the possible effects of frequency of exposure. Blewitt reviews her own work as well as that of others which suggest that orders of acquisition also correlate in many cases with frequency of use. Regarding size words, she states the following (p. 169): '. . . the relative frequency with which these words are used (e.g., Kučera & Francis 1967) also matches their relative complexity. If the frequency of use in child-directed speech is comparable to the general frequencies of use, relative frequency also could account for the observed order of acquisition . . .' While presenting this possibility, she also entertains another factor, that of cognitive complexity. We turn to this aspect in the next section on the acquisition of spatial words.

Spatial words   Still another factor which could affect the order of acquisition of a set of words is the child's *cognitive* development. For example, we could propose that a child has not acquired the meaning of a particular word because he does not have the concept which underlies it. This possibility has been demonstrated in particular with the acquisition of spatial terms. There are two complementary kinds of evidence which can be brought forward to prove this possibility: one would be the demonstration of similar development in children across linguistic communities; the other would be the demonstration that children acquire certain words only after they have shown competence for their underlying concepts on a non-linguistic cognitive task. Both kinds of evidence, in fact, have been presented in a series of works by Johnston and Slobin (e.g. Johnston & Slobin 1979; Johnston 1979). An excellent summary of them can be found in Johnston (1986).

Johnston & Slobin (1979) examined the acquisition of the locative expressions 'in', 'on', 'under', 'beside', 'between', 'back', and 'front' in four languages: English, Italian, Serbo-Croatian, and Turkish. Based on Piagetian research (Piaget & Inhelder 1967), they predicted that the order of acquisition (below) should occur regardless of linguistic community if cognitive development were the sole determinant of acquisition.

Predicted order of acquisition and justification (Johnston & Slobin 1979)

1. 'in', 'on', 'under': the first spatial concepts are of containment, support, and occlusion.
2. 'beside': a purely spatial proximity relation, not dependent on the speaker's viewpoint.
3. 'front$_f$', 'back$_f$' (i.e. of objects which have inherent fronts and backs, e.g. houses): proximity to an inherent feature.
4. 'between': coordination of two proximity relations.
5. 'front', 'back' (in relation to objects without inherent fronts and backs, e.g. balls): coordination of the relative proximities of the speaker, reference object, and located object.

Forty-eight children between the ages of 2 and 4 years of age were tested in each of the four linguistic communities. Most generally, each child was tested by an experimenter who placed a 'reference object' in front of the child, and then a 'located object' in relation to it. For example, the child might be shown a plate (reference object) with a stone (located object) next to it, and then be asked 'Where is the stone standing?' Children were credited with having acquired a particular locative word if they used it more often in appropriate contexts than in inappropriate ones. The data from the study were subjected to a variety of statistical analyses. The results from one such analysis, involving Guttmann scaling procedures, are presented in Table 8.20.

The analysis results in three groups of locative terms being acquired for each language. Four of the words, 'in', 'on', 'under', and 'beside', were always acquired before the others. This was followed by a second group of 'between', 'back$_f$' and 'front$_f$'. The last two words acquired were 'back' and 'front'. This pattern is in general agreement with the cognitive predictions,

Table 8.20 *Order of acquisition of locative expressions in four languages and the percentage of subjects producing each, taken from Johnston & Slobin (1979: Table 5)*

Scale point	English		Italian		Serbo-Croatian		Turkish	
1	in	90	in	91	on	88	in	90
2	on	83	on	88	in	84	on	80
3	under	81	under	84	beside	82	under	79
4	beside	74	beside	77	under	72	beside	79
5	between	49	between	57	backᵣ	31	backᵣ	71
6	frontᵣ	30	backᵣ	42	between	26	frontᵣ	53
7	backᵣ	21	frontᵣ	41	frontᵣ	19	between	50
8	back	14	back	23	back	16	back	7
9	front	3	front	18	front	12	front	4

with less specificity for 'beside' and 'between', which were each expected to constitute a separate grouping. Also, there is variability within the groupings. For example, the English children acquired 'between' before 'back$_f$', while the Turkish children showed the opposite order.

To account for the instances where cognitive complexity did not account for the order of acquisition, Johnston & Slobin propose a second factor, that of *linguistic complexity*. They discuss five ways in which linguistic complexity might affect acquisition: (i) position of word – some evidence suggests that postpositions (e.g. Turkish) are easier to acquire than prepositions (English); (ii) lexical diversity – the number of terms available in the language for a particular proximity (for example, Turkish 'yannida' captures the meanings of English 'beside', 'by', 'next to', 'near', and 'close to'); (iii) clear etymology – the extent to which a word's meaning is semantically transparent (for example, English 'back' names an identifiable body part, while 'between' does not); (iv) morphological complexity – e.g. 'in' vs. 'on top of'; and (v) homonymity – the extent to which one term covers several meanings, e.g. 'back' in English for both featured and nonfeatured objects. Using an elaborate coding system, Johnston & Slobin score the results for the influence of these five factors and conclude (p. 541): 'Wherever conceptual complexity fails to predict actual order of acquisition, we find some pocket of relative *linguistic* difficulty.'

The second kind of evidence in support of the effects of cognitive complexity can be found in Johnston (1979). Johnston focussed on the acquisition of the English terms 'in front of' and 'in back of'. To acquire the full range of meanings of these terms, the child needs to acquire several concepts which are listed here in order of increasing complexity.

Concept	Description
PROXIMITY	The concept that two objects are in a spatial relation to each other
OBJECT FEATURE	The identification of an inherent spatial orientation for an object such as having a 'front' and 'back'
ORDER	The concept that objects can be in a particular linear arrangement with one another
PROJECTIVE RELATIONS	The conceptualization that the spatial relation between objects is relative, such as in relation to a viewer's line of sight

Johnston hypothesized that children's use of the terms 'in front of' and 'in back of' would parallel the order of complexity given above. For example, early uses of 'in front of' would be in the sense of 'next to the front of some object with an identifiable front'. This use (which we will call the *featured use*) would only require the concepts PROXIMITY and OBJECT FEATURE. Later uses with nonfeatured objects would have the meaning 'first in line of sight', which requires the concepts ORDER and PROJECTIVE RELATIONS. (Following Johnston, we will refer to this as the *deictic use* of the term.)

Johnston discusses three kinds of evidence that are necessary to demonstrate that semantic development is determined by cognitive development. First, there needs to be a correlation between performance on linguistic tasks and the nonverbal cognitive tasks of the presumed cognitive precursor. Second, the cognitive ability must precede the linguistic ability. Third, there need to be similar orders of acquisition of concepts and their linguistic forms. For example, children who use 'in front of' only to mean 'in front of some object with an identifiable front' should (i) be able to pass nonverbal tests of the concepts PROXIMITY and OBJECT FEATURE; (ii) show acquisition of PROXIMITY and OBJECT FEATURE before the use of 'in front of'; and (iii) show an order of acquisition of the meanings of 'in front of' which is similar to the order of acquisition of the related concepts.

Johnston tested the meanings of 'in front of' and 'in back of' in 33 children between 31 and 54 months of age on a variety of spatial tasks designed to explore the range of their possible meanings. She also tested the children on nonverbal tasks for the concepts listed above. She scored the results in terms of the number of children to pass or fail the task on a particular concept in relation to the number who passed or failed on the related linguistic task. These results are summarized in Table 8.21.

The first two columns of results in Table 8.21 do not provide insight into the relation between cognitive development and language use, since the

Table 8.21 *Number of subjects tested on nonverbal (concept) tasks and linguistic ('in back of' and 'in front of') tasks who either (i) passed both tasks, (ii) failed both tasks, (iii) passed only the linguistic task, or (iv) passed only the nonverbal task, on three kinds of comparisons between concept and use. Adapted from Johnston (1986: Table 1)*

		Same on both tasks		Pass only one task	
Concept and use		Pass	Fail	Linguistic	Nonverbal
PROXIMITY, FEATURE					
and featured use	'back'	9	3	1	20
	'front'	6	3	1	23
ORDER and deictic use	'back'	6	20	1	6
	'front'	0	21	0	12
PROJECTIVE RELATIONS					
and deictic use	'back'	5	9	2	17
	'front'	0	11	0	22
Totals		26	67	5	89

subjects here either passed or failed both tasks. The crucial data, however, are in the third and fourth columns under 'pass only one task'. Here 89 responses were cases where the subjects passed the nonverbal cognitive task, but failed the parallel linguistic one. The opposite result, however, only occurred five times. These results show that children consistently acquire the concepts which are related to these terms before the terms are used in related ways.

These data provide strong evidence in support of the influence of cognitive development on semantic development. In her recent review of this relation, however, Johnston (1986: 983) stops short of concluding that linguistic order of acquisition can always be determined by cognitive development. Basing her review on some of the studies discussed above as well as on Johnston & Slobin (1979), she states:

> Taken together they [the studies reviewed] provide a solid platform from which to argue that nonverbal conceptual development is an important determinant of language growth ... Further evidence from child language studies, linguistic analysis, investigations of nonverbal cognitive growth, and experimental tests of linguistic dependency did not always confirm this initial estimate. Children's learning of locative prepositions, 'more'/'less', and 'big'/'little' does seem to be affected by the evolution of spatial and quantificational knowledge. But the acquisition of dimensional adjectives other than 'big'/'little' is not yet so clearly related to parameters of conceptual growth. In that domain

factors such as frequency of input or semantic complexity may play a more dominant role.

Cognitive factors, therefore, are an important influence, but not the only one in explaining the child's acquisition of word meaning.

8.3.5 Assessment

In this section we have reviewed a range of topics on the child's acquisition of word meaning, by outlining the most cited theories which have been proposed to date, and then examining research into the areas of nominal words and relational words. In doing so we have seen that a number of predictions by the various theories have not been borne out. The semantic feature hypothesis, for example, generated a great deal of research, and yet support for it has been restricted at best. Carey (1982), for example, gives a nice review of its rise and demise.

The one theory which has managed to survive so far, in several variants, is prototype theory. This is true at least to the extent that it continues to be mentioned in recent reviews as the theory most able to account for current findings. Even prototype theory, however, is not without its critics. One problem is that it does not lend itself to an account of relational words as easily as it does to referring expressions. Another problem concerns even the results on nominals. This form of criticism of prototype theory can be found in Armstrong, Gleitman & Gleitman (1983). These authors attack prototype theory on methodological grounds. They argue that the results of numerous studies showing subjects judging exemplars as being more or less typical of some prototype is the artifact of the way in which the studies are conducted. Armstrong, Gleitman & Gleitman propose that human beings are very able to provide relative judgements when asked to do so. This does not, however, reflect their linguistic organization of the world.

Armstrong, Gleitman & Gleitman provide evidence for their claim with results from a series of studies in which subjects were asked to judge which exemplars were most typical of certain words. Some of the words tested were similar to those used in other studies in support of prototype theory, such as 'fruit' and 'sport'. Other words tested, however, were what the authors referred to as *definitional concepts*. These are terms which normally cannot be broken down into features. One such term is the phrase 'odd number', which is defined as 'an integer not divisible by two without remainder'. They found that subjects were just as able to give graded responses to definitional terms such as 'odd number' as they were to other terms such as 'sport'. The number '3', for example, was found to be the most typical odd number. They conclude that graded responses in such experiments do not reflect semantic structure, but rather an aspect of performance which operates as a heuristic to assist people in identifying instances of concepts in the real world. They go on to give a critique of featural theories in general, and argue for a holistic theory of the kind mentioned briefly at the beginning of 8.3.1.

All of this leaves the area of semantic acquisition somewhat in a theoretical hiatus. The research that continues has turned to some of the factors which have been discussed above, such as frequency of input and cognitive determinants. Some recent studies, for example, have tried to see how the linguistic presentation of words affects the child's acquisition. Carey & Bartlett (1978), for example, attempted to teach a child a new meaning by contrasting it with one the child already knew. The new word was 'chromium', which was given the meaning of the color olive-green. Subjects were shown two trays which were exactly the same except that one was red and the other was olive-green. They were then asked 'Bring me the chromium tray, not the red one, the chromium one.' Other research of this kind is reported in Dockrell (1981). The results so far have been mixed as to the extent to which such linguistic framing aids in acquisition. Such studies also often avoid discussion of broader theoretical issue.

It is difficult to predict at this time where research into semantic acquisition will direct itself in the years immediately ahead. A comment made by Armstrong, Gleitman & Gleitman about research in cognitive psychology seems equally relevant to the current state of affairs in semantic acquisition: 'we ourselves are not optimistic that a general theory of categorization, one that will answer to the serious problems (explication of functions from words to the world, and of the units that figure in phrasal meanings and in lexical entailments) is just around the corner.' The lesson so far has been caution about finding simple explanations, as well as heightened awareness of the methodological problems involved in studying this area.

Further reading

Phonemic perception

Much of the work in this area seems to have been done in a relatively short period of time around the early 1970s. It is also our impression that some have felt that Barton (1976a) was the definitive study on the topic (Clumeck 1982, for example, appears very much an extension of Barton's work). It should be clear from our discussion that we feel that this is far from true. An insightful recent study that bears this out is Johnson, Hardee & Long (1981). Edwards (1974) and Eilers & Oller (1976) remain classic studies in this difficult area. An insightful methodological review can be found in Strange & Broen (1980). A more critical overview is that of Barton (1980).

Phonological production

There are currently no textbooks devoted exclusively to phonological acquisition, although most of the general texts mentioned in Chapter 1 contain chapters on the topic. There are, however, several books on phonological disorders in children which discuss normal acquisition in some detail. The primary ones are Ingram (1976a), Edwards & Shriberg (1983) and Stoel-Gammon & Dunn (1985).

The research on phonological production has gone through several phases, based on the theoretical view popular at the time. Up until the late 1960s, most research was geared toward testing Jakobson's theory. The early 1970s were marked by an interest in determining the set of phonological processes (Stampe 1969) or realization rules (Smith 1973) that map from the adult surface form to the child's form. Much of the most recent work in this area has been from the perspective of the Stanford theory, with its corresponding emphasis on individual differences.

Overviews of phonological acquisition include Edwards & Shriberg (1983) which provides a comprehensive discussion of phonological processes, Chapter 2 in Ingram (1976a), Menn (1983) which presents the Stanford theory, and Chapters 2 and 3 of Stoel-Gammon & Dunn (1985). Their Chapter 3 provides a useful overview of current theories, updating the discussion in Ferguson & Garnica (1975) which was mentioned in our Chapter 6.

A feel for the large sample studies can be obtained from selected readings from Templin (1957). Earlier in this volume Chapters I and II were recommended; Chapter III on articulation of speech sounds should now be added. Turning to the diary studies, Velten (1943) is standard reading. Leopold (1947) is long and somewhat tedious to read, and can be scanned to get an idea of its contents. The section entitled 'General phonetic problems' (pp. 207–56) contains a number of rich observations. A brief but effective overview of Smith (1973) is found in his first chapter. Chapter 4 is the central chapter in which he discusses the results and presents a defense of his theory. Stampe's theory can be found in the short original form in Stampe (1969), or in the longer, more recent, review in Donegan & Stampe (1979). The Stanford theory is presented in a general form in Macken & Ferguson (1983). Its use in analyzing data can be seen in Macken (1979).

Word meaning

As with phonological acquisition, there is little in the way of textbooks on the topic. There are, however, some lengthy review articles, and some edited books of articles. Most introductory textbooks such as those mentioned in Chapter 1 also have chapters on this topic. One of the first edited texts is Moore (1973), which contains the first review articles presenting the semantic feature hypothesis (Clark 1973a), and prototype theory (Rosch 1973). More recent collections are Kuczaj (1982b) and Kuczaj & Barrett (1986), both of which reflect the more recent prominence of prototype theory. Nelson's own recent booklength treatment of her views in this area is Nelson (1986). A good review of the topic is that of Blewitt (1982). Carey (1982) reviews the impact of the semantic feature hypothesis, its failings, and the current lack of an accepted theory. Rice & Kemper (1984) is a highly readable discussion of the relation between cognition and word acquisition.

If time allows, reading of the first statements of the three most influential recent theories by Clark (1973a), Rosch (1973), and Nelson (1974) will provide an insight into each. The latter attempt to develop these into a more eclectic theory in Bowerman (1978a) is a widely cited article that is also basic reading. The most extensive data-based treatment of the topic remains Anglin (1977); the first chapter is an excellent review of the theories up to that time and of Anglin's viewpoint, and the last chapter is a good overview of his results and the interpretations he gives them. Of the recent reviews, I lean toward Blewitt (1982). Important recent criticisms of attempts to explain word acquisition are Carey (1982) and Armstrong, Gleitman & Gleitman (1983). A nice summary of the possible influences between cognition and language is contained in the first three chapters of Rice & Kemper (1984).

9 The period of simple sentences: the acquisition of grammatical morphemes

9.1 Introduction

We have seen in Chapter 7 that the first sentences of children consist primarily of words which belong in the adult language to lexical categories such as noun, verb, and adjective. Because of this, most studies of the period of the first word combinations have concentrated on explaining the emergence of these early lexical forms. In particular, their semantic characteristics have been emphasized. Brown (1973), for example, describes the period as one in which the first semantic relations appear. Even while arguing for early syntactic structure, Pinker (1984) has nonetheless also relied on the child's first use of semantic information to enable him to 'bootstrap' into the syntax.

In this chapter, we turn to how the child acquires the range of morphemes in language that do not have the transparent semantic meanings of the major lexical words. These morphemes are often called *grammatical morphemes* (or function words) in the sense that their meanings are either partially or totally defined by the set of rules (or grammar) of a particular language. Brown (1973: 253) refers to them as *modulations of meaning* in that they:

> ... seem to 'tune' or 'modulate' the meanings associated with the contentives in the sense that the modulation is inconceivable without the more basic meanings. Thus 'a' and 'the' make the thing referred to by a noun specific or nonspecific.

Gleitman in numerous places (e.g. Wanner & Gleitman 1982) refers to them as a *closed class* (as opposed to the 'open class' of content words) which can be defined by both syntactic (e.g. restricted membership and positions) and phonological (e.g. unstressed, often nonsyllabic) properties.

These morphemes tend to be acquired later than lexical morphemes and are usually associated with development beyond the period of the first word combinations. Brown assigns their onset to Stage II, although their development takes several years. Their study has been mostly descriptive, i.e.

Table 9.1 *A sampling of some grammatical properties not found in English, based on Comrie (1981, 1983)*

1. Regular *causative* affixation of verbs, e.g. Songhai:
Ali nga-ndi   tasu di
Ali eat-causative rice the
'Ali got someone to eat the rice'

2. *Ergativity*, where the subjects of transitive verbs are marked differently than the subjects of intransitives, e.g. Dyirbal (in which the normal word is OSV):
Transitive sentence
Balan   dʸugumbil bangul yarangu balgan
woman absolutive man   ergative hit
'the man hit the woman'

Intransitive sentence
Bayi yara   baninyu
man absolutive came-here
'the man came here'

3. *Switch reference*, the marking in one clause to indicate whether its subject is coreferential with the subject of another clause, e.g. Lenakel where SS = the morpheme which requires that the subjects refer to the same person:
Different subjects
r -im-vin   r-im-apul
he-PAST-go he-PAST- sleep
'he$_i$ went and he$_j$ slept'

Same subjects
r-im-vin   m-(im)-apul
he-PAST-go SS-PAST-sleep
'he$_i$ went and he$_i$ slept'

tracking when they occur and the kinds of error patterns in which they appear, but more recently, some attempts have been made to explain how they are acquired, both in terms of their syntactic properties and the performance factors that affect them. This introduction begins with a general discussion of the issues at stake in studying the acquisition of grammatical morphemes.

A major issue is defining the class of grammatical morphemes. As noted, several people have discussed them as a psychologically real category of grammar, distinct from the lexical morphemes. No consensus has been reached, however, on the extent to which this is true. We could, for example, deny a unified class and propose a taxonomy of classes of grammar that fall along some continuum in regard to one or more properties. The problems involved can be exemplified by looking at the status of prepositions. These are typically included in the class of grammatical morphemes, yet Chomsky (1981) has included them within a feature system that includes nouns, verbs, and adverbs. For example, they can function as heads of constructions (prepositional phrases) and, like verbs, assign grammatical case. The Government and Binding Theory of Chomsky, in fact, has yet to come up with an adequate theory of the range of possible grammatical categories. This is true, to some extent, of other theories as well; as a result, the study of the acquisition of grammatical morphemes is often theory-independent and based upon traditional category labels.

Much of the work in this area has focussed on English, but it is important to recognize at the onset the range and variability of grammatical morphemes cross-linguistically. Any account of their acquisition will need to deal with the cross-linguistic cases also. Table 9.1 presents a very brief sampling of the diversity which is involved. After reviewing the research in English, we will discuss some of the cross-linguistic data studied.

Another important step in studying the acquisition of grammatical morphemes is to establish the ways in which they differ from one another, and how these differences interact. Brown (1973) was one of the first to do this. One set of differences concern the effects of *perceptual salience*. This includes the position of a morpheme in a sentence, and whether it is free or affixed, syllabic or nonsyllabic, and stressed or unstressed. Another possible influence is *frequency of occurrence* in the parental language. As we will see later, Newport, Gleitman & Gleitman (1977) present data which suggest that children who acquire auxiliary inversion early have parents who direct more questions to them with inverted auxiliaries than do other parents. A third feature of morphemes is that they differ in *semantic complexity*. We have already seen in the previous chapter, for example, that certain spatial terms can be argued to be semantically simpler than others. Lastly, there are a number of differences between morphemes which can be placed under the category of *grammatical complexity*. These include (i) redundancy, i.e. the extent to which a morpheme is predictable, e.g. person on verbs is redundant when pronoun subjects are used; (ii) allomorphy, i.e. the number of allomorphs that occur, e.g. '-ing' has one allomorph in English but plural '-s' has three; (iii) paradigm regularity, e.g. regular verb forms vs. irregular ones such as 'to be'.

Still another issue in studying morphological acquisition is a methodological one. That is, how do we study the child's knowledge of these grammatical forms? We have an immediate problem when we try to do this exclusively from spontaneous language samples. As has been documented in several places, some of the grammatical morphemes are not very frequent even in adult language, e.g. the passive morphology on verbs. Brown (1973) has gotten around this problem to some extent by his measure of the percentage of obligatory occurrence which adjusts for frequency. Even this measure, however, requires some minimum frequency which is not always evident. Another problem with spontaneous samples is that it is not always possible to determine from the context what morpheme a child should have used. For example, if the child says 'I eat apple?', we can

Table 9.2 *A summary of the main grammatical morphemes found in English*

Inflectional morphemes	
Nominal inflections:	
plural {-s}	'two boys'
possessive {-s}	'the girl's socks'
verbal inflections:	
progressive {-ing}	'the cat is running'
present tense {-s}	'the dog sits on the rug'
past tense {-ed}	'the teacher walked to school'
passive {-en}	'the cake was eaten by the class'
perfect {-en}	'I have eaten the apple'
adjectival inflections:	
comparative {-er}	'the cat is bigger than the dog'
superlative {-est}	'this is the smallest class in the school'
Derivational morphemes[1]	
adverbial {-ly}	'Joe ran quickly to the store'
adjectival {-ful}	'May is hopeful of getting the job'
agentive {-er}	'she was the bearer of good news'
etc.	
Free morphemes	
verb negation {not}	'do not go in there'
modal auxiliaries e.g. {will, can, may}	'we will arrive by midnight'
infinitive {to}	'Mary decided to leave'
personal pronouns e.g. {I, you, it}	'they saw her near him'
possessive pronouns e.g. {his, her}	'our books'
reflexive pronouns e.g. {himself}	'they did it themselves'
demonstrative pronouns e.g. {this, that}	'I bought this book in town'
locative pronouns e.g. {here, there}	'put it down right there'
relative pronouns e.g. {which, that}	'we saw the book which was on the table'
determiners {the, a}	'the apple'
quantifiers e.g. {few, some, many}	'we only saw a few people at the dance'
complementizers {that, for..to, -ing}	'we knew that John was leaving'
gerund {-ing}	'the running of the bulls was yesterday'
participle {-ing}	'the falling leaves were lovely'

[1] Only a sampling of these are presented.

assume that an auxiliary is missing, but we can't determine which one it is, e.g. 'can', 'may', 'should', etc . . .

This area requires as much methodological caution as any other. As I will show, several innovative techniques have been developed to assist in this study, including comprehension tasks, imitation tasks, and the use of metalinguistic judgements. Since children are older at the time of morphological acquisition, it is possible to use more diverse tasks. Even so, we will see that much of what is known is still based on spontaneous language samples.

9.2 Morphological acquisition in English: a descriptive overview

I begin the presentation of findings on morphological acquisition with a historical review of some early research on English. Much of this work was done by Roger Brown and his colleagues, and they established many of the methodological procedures used. Here, studies are considered in their historical order to give a feel for how these findings became known and built upon one another. Findings will be presented for children from the onset of grammatical morphemes around age 2 years, up to children around 6 years of age.

First it is necessary to give an overview of the range of the major grammatical morphemes that occur in English and thus serve as potential targets for research (Table 9.2). This is an extensive list and no study has yet attempted to research them all in depth.

9.2.1 Three early studies

Three early studies between 1958 and 1963 provided a first insight into the patterns of acquisition of selected English morphemes. It was a time when the longitudinal study of Adam, Eve, and Sarah was underway and detailed analysis of those data was not yet completed. The studies to be reported were experimental ones which each developed a different method for the study of morphological acquisition. In retrospect, the successful development of these methodologies will be as significant as the early findings which they provided.

Berko (1958)   This study probably more than any other marked the onset of the modern era of child language studies. It is not only one of the most famous studies ever done, it is also the most replicated. Even with so many replications, its general findings remain sound.

Berko selected a variety of grammatical morphemes for experimental study. These are listed in (9.1).

(9.1) a. plural {-s}   with three allophones:
                                 [s] after [p,t,k,f,θ]
                                 [əz] after [s,z,š,ž,č,ǰ]
                                 [z] after other voiced sounds
      b. possessive {-s}   with three allophones (same as plural)
      c. present {-s}   with three allophones (same as plural)
      d. past {-ed}   with three allophones:
                                 [əd] after [t,d]
                                 [t] after [p,k,č,f,θ,s,š]
                                 [d] after all voiced sounds except [d]

    e. progressive {-ing}
    f. agentive {-er}
    g. comparatives {-er}, {-est}
    h. compounds

Here the discussion will be limited to study of the inflections selected, that is items (9a)–(9e). The five inflectional morphemes chosen give an idea of the order of acquisition of inflections. Also, the fact that the first three listed all have the same allomorphs provides an important test case of the interaction of phonological and semantic factors. For example, if inflectional order of acquisition were determined solely by phonological factors, then these three should be acquired at the same time. Lastly, the study provides the first information on the order of acquisition of specific allomorphs.

   Berko developed a technique to study these forms which has come to be known as the 'wug' procedure – as famous as the results of the study. First, Berko created a series of nonsense words which ended in sounds that would elicit one of the possible allomorphs. For example, one of her nonsense words was 'wug' which would require a [z] in the plural by the rules of English. She then created nonsense drawings which were to represent meanings for the nonsense words. A 'wug', for example, was a bird-like animal. In the case of 'wug', there were two pictures, one with one wug and one with two. The child was then tested on the following item:

(9.2) This is a wug. Now there's another one.
    There are two of them, there are two _____

The child was expected to fill in the last word. Table 9.3 gives the words tested for the five inflectional morphemes. As can be seen, there were different words for different morphemes, and some real English words used – these were added to see if the child would treat them differently from the nonsense words.

   There were two groups of children tested, a preschool group of children who were 4 and 5 years old, and a first grade group of $5\frac{1}{2}$ to 7-year-olds. There were 19 children in the preschool group and 61 in the first grade group.

   Table 9.3 gives the results in the form of the percentage of correct responses for each of the test items. Since the number of test items is small, Berko's results must be treated with some caution but one striking result is that the children showed acquisition of the single consonant allomorphs [s], [z], [t], and [d], but not the ones with schwa, i.e. [əz] and [əd]. That is, even though children may appear to have acquired an inflection, accurate use of all of its allomorphs can be quite late. A related finding concerns the differences in the scores with nonsense words requiring [əd] and [əz], and

Table 9.3 *Percentage of correct productions of children studied in Berko (1958) on words requiring one of five English inflections*

Nouns			Verbs		
Plural			*Past*		
glasses	[əz]	91	binged	[d]	78
wugs	[z]	91	glinged	[d]	77
luns	[z]	86	ricked	[t]	73
tors	[z]	85	melted	[əd]	73
heafs[1]	[s], [z]	82	spowed	[d]	52
cras	[z]	79	motted	[əd]	33
tasses	[əz]	36	bodded	[əd]	31
gutches	[əz]	36	rang		16
kazhes	[əz]	31	*3rd singular*		
Possessive			loodges	[əz]	56
nizzes	[əz]	28	nazzes	[əz]	48
bik's	[s]	87			
wug's	[z]	84	*Progressive*		
niz's	[əz]	49	zibbing		90

[1] Both 'heaves' and 'heafs' were considered correct responses.

the English words with the same requirements, that is, 'glasses' and 'melted'. The scores on the latter were markedly better than the former. This indicates that children may initially use words like these correctly, but may not yet have productive use of the allomorph being used. It is an important warning that spontaneous use is not sufficient evidence to conclude rule-based behavior. At the same time, the strength of the rule which was acquired for [d] was evident in the results for 'rang' where most of the children regularized it.

Another finding concerned the order of acquisition of the morphemes. The progressive with its single allomorph was the easiest one for the children. When we compare the scores on the three morphemes which have [əz], we see that they are not the same. The children had more difficulties using [əz] with the plural than for the possessive and 3rd singular. That is, the results suggest that there may be other factors involved than just articulatory ones.

Brown & Fraser (1963) As with Berko (1958), this study was as important methodologically as it was for its results. The study itself was very much a preliminary one, with a small set of subjects and stimuli. It presented six children between 2 and 3 years of age with a set of 13 sentences to imitate. The goal was to see if the children would process the sentences through their own grammatical system, or simply rote-imitate. The test sentences were as shown in (9.3):

Table 9.4 *Imitations of 13 sentences by the four youngest of six children tested in Brown & Fraser (1963), as reported in Brown (1973:76)*

Sentence no. Eve (25⅓ months)	Adam (28¾ months)	Helen (30 months)	Ian (31½ months)
1. I show book	(I show) book	Correct	I show you the book
2. (My) tall	I (very) tall	I very tall	I'm very tall
3. Big box	Big box	In big box	It goes in the box
4. Read book	Read book	—	Read (a) book
5. Drawing dog	I draw dog	I drawing dog	Dog
6. Read book	I will read book	I read the book	I read the book
7. See cow	I want see cow	Correct	Cow
8. Do again	I will that again	I do that	I again
9. I do apple	I do a apple	—	I do not want apple
10. To read book?	I read books?	I read books?	I read book?
11. 't car?	Is it car?	Car?	That a car?
12. Where go?	Go?	Does it go?	Where do it go?
13. Go?	—	—	Correct

(9.3) 1. I showed you the book
    2. I am very tall
    3. It goes in a big box
    4. Read the book
    5. I am drawing a dog
    6. I will read the book
    7. I can see a cow
    8. I will not do that again
    9. I do not want an apple
    10. Do I like to read books?
    11. Is it a car?
    12. Where does it go?
    13. Where shall I go?

Brown & Fraser found that the children did imitate the sentences in a systematic way. Specifically, they found that the children tended to retain the lexical or contentive words but delete the grammatical ones. Second, they found that the imitations tended to preserve the word order of the original model. Lastly, the imitations struck Brown & Fraser as being very similar to the utterances found in the spontaneous utterances of the same children. They gave the label *telegraphic speech* to this form of reduction. In general, they found that the imitations provided information about the children's grammatical systems. Table 9.4 gives the imitations that were elicited for the four youngest children.

We can see some patterns in the data by looking at the percentage of correct imitations of specific grammatical morphemes. These are given in Table 9.5 and can be compared with the Berko results in Table 9.3. Again, the plural and the progressive appear to be relatively easier to imitate than the other inflections. The past tense morpheme in particular was poorly imitated, also somewhat in support of the Berko finding that it was more difficult than the plural, progressive, and 3rd singular. The data suggest that

Table 9.5 *Imitation of grammatical morphemes, as tested in Brown &*
Fraser (1963)

Morpheme	Word(s)	% correctly imitated	
Progressive	drawing	67	(4/6)
Plural	books	67	(4/6)
Articles	the	53	(9/17)
	a	37	(11/30)
Present tense	goes	50	(3/6)
Modal auxiliaries	will	50	(6/12)
	can	50	(3/6)
	shall	50	(3/6)
Infinitive	to	50	(3/6)
Inverted copula	is	50	(3/6)
Uninverted auxiliary	am	33	(2/6)
Uninverted copula	am	17	(1/6)
Past tense	-ed	17	(1/6)

the modals may be easier than the copular and auxiliary forms of 'to be'. Lastly, there is an interesting pattern within the latter suggesting that the uninverted forms may be more difficult than the inverted ones. These preliminary results were to some degree substantiated in the in-depth research which followed.

Fraser, Bellugi & Brown (1963)   This frequently cited study set as its goal the relation between imitation, comprehension, and production. Ten grammatical contrasts were selected, and children were tested on their ability to imitate, comprehend, and produce each one. Importantly, the contrasts were selected in a way that the children would need to know specific grammatical morphemes in order to process the sentences correctly. For example, one contrast was between the sentences 'The sheep is jumping' and 'The sheep are jumping'. The authors state (p. 468): 'No one seems to have compared this kind of evidence for the passive control of grammar in normal children with evidence of active or productive control in the same children, and we have done an experiment to fill the gap.' There is no discussion of the rationale behind the selection of the ten contrasts used, and also there are no predictions made about how the children would perform with them. The ten contrasts tested with one of the sets of 40 test sentences are presented in Table 9.6.

The subjects were twelve children between 37 and 43 months of age. Each child underwent three tasks of imitation (I), comprehension (C), and production (P). The test sentences consisted of three sets of 40 sentences each. The three sets of test sentences were varied across the three tasks, and

Table 9.6 *Ten grammatical contrasts with the 40 test sentences of Set A taken from Fraser, Bellugi & Brown (1963: Table 2)*

1. Mass noun / Count noun	Some mog / A dap
	Some pim / A ked
2. Singular / plural, marked by inflection	The boy draws / The boys draw
	The kitten plays / The kittens play
3. Singular / plural, marked by 'is' and 'are'	The deer is running / The deer are running
	The sheep is eating / The sheep are eating
4. Present progressive / past tense	The paint is spilling / The paint spilled
	The boy is jumping / The boy jumped
5. Present progressive / future tense	The girl is drinking / The girl will drink
	The baby is climbing / The baby will climb
6. Affirmative / negative	The girl is cooking / The girl is not cooking
	The boy is sitting / The boy is not sitting
7. Singular / plural, of 3rd person possessive pronouns	His wagon / Their wagon
	Her dog / Their dog
8. Subject / object, in the active voice	The train bumps the car / The car bumps the train
	The mommy kisses the daddy / The daddy kisses the mommy
9. Subject / object, in the passive voice	The car is bumped by the train / The train is bumped by the car
	The daddy is kissed by the mommy / The mommy is kissed by the daddy
10. Indirect object / direct object	The girl shows the cat the dog / The girl shows the dog the cat
	The boy brings the fish the bird / The boy brings the bird the fish

the order of presentation of the three tasks was varied across subjects. A pair of pictures was designed for each pair of sentences tested. For example, for 'The sheep is jumping' the picture showed a picture of a sheep jumping, while for 'The sheep are jumping' the picture showed two sheep jumping. On the *imitation* task, the child was asked to repeat the test sentences after the experimenter. The pictures were only used in the comprehension and production tasks. In *comprehension*, the child was shown the two pictures and then heard one of the test pair of sentences. He then had to point to the picture named. Next he was given the second test sentence and again asked to select the appropriate picture. The pictures were used again for *production*, although they were a different set than those for either imitation or comprehension. 'The S is twice told the names of the two pictures but not which name goes with which picture ... After repeating the names of the pictures E points to one picture at a time and asks S to name it' (Fraser, Bellugi & Brown 1963: 469–70). Correctness was determined only in relation to the relevant morphemes in the test sentences. A correct response on any pair required that both sentences be imitated, comprehended, or produced correctly.

Table 9.7 *Percentage of correct responses on the grammatical contrasts across three tasks tested in Fraser, Bellugi & Brown (1963)*

Contrast	Imitation	Comprehension	Production	Total
6. Affirmative / negative	75	71	50	65
7. Singular / plural, of 3rd person possessive pronouns	96	63	33	64
8. Subject / object, in the active voice	79	67	46	64
4. Present progressive / future tense	83	67	24	58
3. Singular / plural, marked by 'is' and 'are'	83	50	29	54
5. Present progressive / past tense	71	54	25	50
1. Mass noun / count noun	50	54	4	36
2. Singular / plural, marked by inflection	58	29	4	31
9. Subject / object, in the passive voice	50	29	8	29
10. Indirect object / direct object	46	21	13	26

Table 9.7 presents the results in terms of percentages of correct responses on each contrast across the three tasks. One general finding was that imitation was easier than comprehension, and comprehension was easier than production. This at first glance appears to contradict the result we just saw in Brown & Fraser (1963) where the children appeared to process their imitations through their grammatical systems. The authors offer the following discussion of this contradiction:

> It is very possible, however, that this . . . outcome would reverse with still younger children. The longest sentences of the ICP Test were only eight morphemes long which means they were easily within the sentence-programming span of 3-year-old children. However, the much shorter span of children at about 2;6 should compel such younger children in the I task, to 'reduce' the model sentences . . .
> (Fraser, Bellugi & Brown 1963: 484)

That is, it will be necessary to take the child's short-term memory ability into consideration when attempting to draw conclusions from imitation tasks. As we will discuss, this was in fact done in Kuczaj & Maratsos (1975) for the acquisition of auxiliaries.

The second finding, that comprehension was better than production, supported the traditional view and the one expressed at various points in this volume. It should be pointed out, however, that this result was aided by the decision to score 'no response' in production as errors. Fernald (1972) has reanalyzed these data with a different scoring system and found the scores on the two tasks to be much closer.

There is relatively little qualitative analysis on the data discussed by Fraser, Bellugi & Brown. One observation was that the children would occasionally alter the sentences in production to fit their understanding. One example was with the contrast with indirect objects (no. 10) where five children inserted a preposition, saying for example, 'The woman gives the teddy to the bunny' instead of 'The woman gives the bunny the teddy'. This response would be scored as an error in production, but this response certainly indicates that it is understood correctly. Such examples are important for at least two reasons: they show that production data can be used to draw conclusions about comprehension, and they show how production may lag behind comprehension, indicating that some additional processing is involved.

A similar kind of observation was made in regard to the passive sentences, which received a very low score in comprehension, indicating that they were not yet understood. Five of the children responded to sentences such as 'The girl is pushed by the boy' as if it meant 'The girl pushed the boy', that is, they treated them as if they ignored the passive morphology and understood it as an agent+action+object structure. This observation has been supported by several subsequent studies which have provided more details on how these sentences develop.

The authors do briefly address the possible reasons why certain morphemes are acquired earlier than others:

> ... there does not seem to be any single dimension of the contrasts that will account for the order ... Probably the order obtained for the problems is a complex resultant of many factors that increase difficulty, including the perceptual obviousness of the contrast, the amount of redundancy in the contrast, the length of the total sentences, and the frequency with which the construction has been heard. It should be possible to investigate the importance of these variables with problems designed to that purpose. (p. 482)

The four possible variables they raise are similar to some of the ones we discussed in the previous chapter for determining the order of acquisition of words. Of some importance is the fact that the optimism of the last sentence has not completely been borne out, although we will look later in the chapter at some attempts to develop a theory that addresses these issues.

9.2.2 The analysis of Adam, Eve, and Sarah

As the 1960s progressed, the language samples collected from Adam, Eve, and Sarah were carefully analyzed for insights into English grammatical development. Two aspects of these samples were analyzed in depth. One was the development of selected grammatical morphemes, especially the inflectional ones. This was first reported in Cazden (1968), and then completed in Brown (1973). The other area was the development of the auxiliary, particularly in terms of its appearance in question words. We begin by looking at the first of these two, and return to auxiliaries in a later section.

Cazden (1968) This was the first detailed analysis of the development of inflections by Adam, Eve, and Sarah, and it laid the groundwork for Brown's later report (1973). Cazden studied the five noun and verb inflections which occur in English, i.e. the first five morphemes listed in (9.1). To do this, Cazden made several important methodological decisions which are needed in any in-depth study of grammatical development. We will look at each in turn.

The first decision concerns how to measure whether the child has a particular morpheme or not. We have already discussed the problem with counting absolute frequencies as a measure of acquisition. The problem is that we need both to see when a morpheme is used, and the number of times that it is used appropriately. Cazden reasoned (p. 227) that there are four possible ways in which an inflection could be scored for a child:

S_c: 'supplied correctly', i.e. the child used an inflection in a context for which it was appropriate, e.g. 'two dogs' in reference to two dogs;

S_x: 'supplied in inappropriate contexts', i.e. the child used an inflection in a place where it was inappropriate, e.g. 'one dogs' in reference to a single dog;

O: 'required but omitted', i.e. the child did not use an inflection in a context where it was required, based on the rules of English grammar, e.g. 'two dog' to refer to two dogs;

OG: 'overgeneralizations', i.e. use of the inflection in a context where an alternative form was correct, e.g. 'two foots' used to mean 'two feet'.

Distinctions like this enabled Cazden to see more clearly the ways in which inflections were used in the data.

A second decision concerns how one can determine when a context for appropriate use has occurred in the data. In determining transliterations for children's utterances', claims about missing morphemes have to be made. Cazden set specific criteria for determining contexts when a morpheme should be required; a feel for these can be seen by looking at her criteria for determining when a plural morpheme would be required in a sentence (p. 227):

Number – required after numbers except 1: 'two minute';

Linguistic – required on count nouns after such modifiers as 'more' or 'some': 'more page';

Interaction – required for discourse agreement: 'shoe' in response to parent's question, 'what are those?';

Normally plural – 'stair' ('upstairs');

Routines – either public, like nursery rhymes and the names of cartoon characters – 'Mr Ear' ('Mr Ears') – or private, like Eve's telegraphic version of her mother's oft-repeated explanation of father's work – 'Make penny Ema' Hall' ('He's making pennies in Emerson Hall').

As Brown (1973) later pointed out, some grammatical morphemes are easier for doing this than other. As Cazden's stated criteria show, the non-linguistic context of the utterance in very important in making such decisions.

A brief comment is in order on the three measures Cazden used to score the four kinds of uses (where S_c, S_x, O, and OG refer to the number of contexts scored as an instance of each of these categories):

Proportion of correct use $= S_c / S_c + O$

Proportion of inappropriate use $= S_x / S_x + S_c$

Proportion of overgeneralization $= OG / S_x + S_c$

One point about these measures is that all three need to be examined (Cazden does this) before claims about adult-like acquisition can be made. The child may have a high proportion of correct use, but still will not have an adult system if the other two proportions are high. A second point concerns the measure for the proportion of overgeneralization. This does not appear to me to be a very useful measure since the S_c contexts are not ones where overgeneralizations can occur in the first place. I would recommend an alternative, such as the following:

Suggested proportion of overgeneralization

$OG / OG + O_i + S_{ci}$

where $O_i =$　irregular plurals where an overgeneralization could, but did not, occur, e.g. 'two foot'

where $S_{ci} =$　irregular plurals where the irregular form was correctly used, e.g. 'two feet'

In this formula, we could also distinguish between two types of OG, those which occur on an unmarked irregular form, e.g. 'two foots', versus those which occur on the marked form, e.g. 'two feets'. Since Cazden does not provide the needed information, I cannot replace her measure of over-

Table 9.8 *Four periods in the acquisition of the English plural morpheme for Adam, Eve, and Sarah, adapted from Cazden (1968: 228, table 1)*

Period	Proportion of correct use			No. of inappropriate uses			No. of overgeneralizations		
	Adam	Eve	Sarah	Adam	Eve	Sarah	Adam	Eve	Sarah
A	—	0.00	—	—	0	—	—	0	—
B	0.36	0.15	0.13	0	0	0	0	0	0
C	0.68	0.86	0.86	25	10	4	2	8	0
D	0.94	0.98	0.98	54	1	28	40	7	23

generalization by mine. Instead, I simply replace her measure with a simpler one: the number of overgeneralizations.

A similar criticism can be raised with the second measure, the proportion of inappropriate use. In this case, it is difficult to see what kind of proportion could be used, in that the number of possible inappropriate contexts can be quite large. The only alternative I see is to use simply the number of such instances, and I therefore use this measure in the review of Cazden's results.

Using the measures discussed, Cazden found four periods in the acquisition of each inflection (while she does not say so, she appears to be using the term 'period' in a descriptive sense to avoid the implications of the word 'stage' as we have discussed in Chapter 3). These periods are defined in my words as follows:

Period definition

A The time before the appearance of any inflections
B The time of the first inflections, with no errors
C The time of widespread use of inflections, with concomitant appearance of errors and over-generalizations
D The proportion of correct use reaches 90 percent, an arbitrary measure of acquisition

Cazden states the following (p. 228):

> These three divisions do not have the same status. The break between C and D is clearly an arbitrary imposition. The meaning of the break between A and B, signaling the onset of inflection, is unclear. But the break between B and C represents a significant developmental phenomenon, because systematic errors and overgeneralizations provide convincing evidence that the child has a productive rule.

Table 9.8 presents the data for the four stages in the acquisition of the plural inflection, where we give the original proportions of correct use along with the two revised measures just discussed.

Cazden is certainly accurate in pointing to the significance of errors and overgeneralizations as an indication that a productive rule is established. We have already seen in Berko's results that correct use of a morpheme, as in 'glasses', cannot itself be taken as indicative of a rule. The fact that the child may acquire a large number of inflected words before such evidence occurs is quite striking in Cazden's data. The numbers of S_c tokens (i.e. plural inflection supplied correctly) for Adam, Eve, and Sarah at Period C are 142, 136, and 124 respectively. While these are only token frequencies, they certainly suggest a large number of words being marked correctly.

I would like to suggest that even the evidence at Period C is rather lean in regard to rule productivity. First, observe in Table 9.8 that very few overgeneralizations appear at Cazden's Period C. The average is only three across the three subjects. We interpret these results as indicating that overgeneralizations do not actually appear with any noticeable frequency until Period D. The S_c contexts for Adam, Eve, and Sarah at Period D are 927, 217, and 722, adding even more evidence to the interpretation that the child can acquire a very large vocabulary before a productive rule is established. (Recall that in Chapter 4 we discussed this as the lexical principle of acquisition.)

A possible problem for this interpretation is the fact that several inappropriate uses of inflections do appear in Period C. Recall, however, that inappropriate uses consist of using a correctly inflected word, e.g. 'dogs', where it should not be, e.g. 'one dogs' for one dog. (This, at least, is my understanding of these errors. Cazden, unfortunately, says very little about them.) Such errors are not the result of rule overgeneralizations, but rather lexical errors. If the child has acquired two semantically related words like 'dog' and 'dogs' as separate lexical items, it is not surprising to see some confusion in the process. Some cases of an inflectional omission at this period (e.g. 'two dog') in fact could be the result of the same confusion or retrieval error. I take such data at Period C, therefore, as evidence for such lexical problems rather than as indicative of a rule-based error.

Space does not allow examination of a number of other results from Cazden's study, for example, on order of acquisition of inflections, where plural and the present progressive emerge as the first two inflections acquired. Since Brown's own analysis of these data will be considered later, this topic is left until then. (Cazden also provides a useful discussion of the kinds of errors found in the data.) Two other findings of general importance may, however, be considered here.

One finding concerns the course of acquisition of the irregular forms of verbs and nouns. Cazden found that use of these usually preceded the first instances of overgeneralizations. For example, Eve used 'came' correctly 11 times between 20 and 22 months before using 'comed' three times between

25 and 27 months. Also, Cazden states (p. 238): 'Temporary coexistence of the correct irregular form and the overgeneralization is common in our records.' In other words, the use of the overgeneralized form does not appear to replace the previously acquired irregular form. This observation leads us to hypothesize three periods in the acquisition of irregular forms:

1. Acquire parts of semantically related words as separate lexical entries, i.e. the lexical principle, e.g. 'come', 'came', and 'go', 'goes'.
2. Acquire a general rule, and determine for all previously learned pairs which match the pattern and which do not; adjust lexical entries for regular pairs, and retain the irregular ones, marking them as exceptions, e.g. 'come' [−regular past], 'came' [+past].
   Overgeneralizations may occur during the period of lexical restructuring, e.g. 'comed'.
3. Attainment of adult lexical entries, which may take several months to complete.

Another finding concerns the individual patterns of acquisition for Adam, Eve, and Sarah. Eve acquired language rather quickly, and showed relatively few errors and overgeneralizations. Adam was slower, but still showed similar development to Eve's when his proportions of correct use were related to MLU. Sarah was the slowest learner of the three, at least as measured by relating age and MLU, but she supplied grammatical morphemes at a higher rate when related to MLU than either Eve or Adam. Cazden used this difference to speculate that there are two ways to acquire language: *macrodevelopment* and *microdevelopment*. She says (pp. 233–4): 'Macrodevelopment refers to the elaborateness of the semantic plan for speaking, while microdevelopment refers to the successful execution of whatever plan has been executed.' Macrodevelopment is seen as more informative, in that the grammatical morphemes are often redundant and can be supplied by the listener. This is an interesting speculation on two possible routes or individual ways to acquire language, but Cazden says little more about them, except a brief mention that they could be the result of any of the three kinds of variation I have discussed at the end of Chapter 4. The speculation has resurfaced in other places (e.g. Ramer 1976) where early accuracy in the use of semantic relations is associated with more rapid learners. A cautious review of the distinction can be found in Ingram (1981d).

Brown (1973) The most cited study of English morphological development remains that of Brown (1973). We have already seen his discussion of the semantic relations which appear in Stage I. The second half of his book is concerned with the acquisition of 14 grammatical morphemes in par-

Table 9.9   *The 14 grammatical morphemes studied by Brown and their mean order of acquisition across Adam, Eve and Sarah, taken from Brown (1973: 274, Table 38)*

Mean rank	Grammatical morphemes and general order of acquisition
2.33	1. present progressive {-ing}
2.50	2.–3. the prepositions 'in' and 'on'
3.00	4. plural {-s}
6.00	5. past irregular, e.g. 'went', 'came', etc.
6.33	6. possessive {-s}
6.50	7. *uncontractible copula {be}, e.g. 'there it is' (where the contracted form is incorrect, e.g. 'there it's')
7.00	8. articles 'the', 'a'
9.00	9. past regular {-ed}
9.66	10. 3rd person regular {-s}
10.83	11. 3rd person irregular, e.g. 'does', 'has'
11.66	12. uncontractible auxiliary {be},* e.g. 'Are you going?'
12.66	13. contractible copula {be},* e.g. 'I'm sick'
14.00	14. contractible auxiliary {be},* e.g. 'She's leaving'

* The contractible allomorphs discussed by Brown are {-s, -z, -m, -r}; the uncontractible ones are {is, am, are}.

ticular (given here in Table 9.9), which begin development in Stage II. The methodology is very similar to that used by Cazden. Linguistic and non-linguistic contextual information was used to determine contexts where the morphemes could be obligatory. Adam's, Eve's, and Sarah's use of the 14 grammatical morphemes was then measured by the *percentage of obligatory morphemes supplied*, which is more or less the same measure used by Cazden which we called the proportion of correct use. A grammatical morpheme was claimed to be acquired when this measure reached 90 percent. These 14 grammatical morphemes include the five studied by Cazden.

Brown first presents his results in terms of the order of acquisition of the 14 morphemes for each of the three children. These famous results are reproduced here in Table 9.10. Note about this table that nearly one-third of the morphemes did not reach criterion at the last samples taken at Stage V. The second point concerns the relative similarity across the children of the first morphemes acquired.

Brown pursued the latter point by looking at the rank order of acquisition of the 14 grammatical morphemes across the three children. For example, the plural morpheme was acquired first by Sarah, and fourth by both Adam and Eve for a mean rank of 3.00 (i.e. 1+4+4 = 9 divided by 3 = 3.00). Statistical analysis revealed a significant correlation between these rank orders and MLU.

Table 9.10 *The order of acquisition of 14 grammatical morphemes for Adam, Eve, and Sarah, taken from Brown (1973: 271, Figure 14)*

Stage	Ages and morphemes at each stage		
	Adam	Eve	Sarah
I	2;3	1;6	2;3
	(none)	(none)	plural {-s}
II	2;6	1;9	2;10
	progressive {-ing}	progressive {-ing}	'in', 'on'
	'in'	'on'	progressive {-ing}
	'on'	'in'	past irregular
	plural {-s}		possessive {-s}
III	2;11	1;11	3;1
	uncontractible copula {be}	plural {-s}	uncontractible copula {be}
	past irregular	possessive {-s}	articles {the, a}
		past regular {-ed}	
IV	3;2	2;2	3;8
	articles {the, a}	(none)	3rd person regular {-s}
	3rd person irregular		
	possessive {-s}		
V*	3;6	2;3	4;0
	3rd person regular {-s}	uncontractible copula {be}	past regular {-ed}
	past regular {-ed}	past irregular	uncontractible auxiliary {be}
	uncontractible auxiliary {be}	articles {the, a}	contractible copula {be}
	contractible copula {be}	3rd person regular {-s}	3rd person irregular
	contractible auxiliary {be}	3rd person irregular	contractible auxiliary {be}
		uncontractible auxiliary {be}	
		contractible copula {be}	
		contractible auxiliary {be}	

* These are listed by their order of decreasing percentages of obligatory occurrence.

Brown's results represented a significant step in our descriptive data on the acquisition of English morphemes. It expanded Cazden's earlier study by providing information on a wider range of morphemes, and also a detailed discussion about why this particular order was found. The results were also replicated in large part by a cross-sectional study conducted around the same time by de Villiers & de Villiers (1973b). The latter study examined the proportion of obligatory occurrence of the same 14 morphemes in spontaneous language samples from 21 children between 1;4 and 3;4. Like Brown, de Villiers & de Villiers found that the children showed an invariant order of acquisition. There were, however, some specific differences regarding the order of acquisition of specific morphemes. For example, if we use a difference of at least three ranks between the two studies on the individual morphemes, de Villiers & de Villiers found that the 3rd person regular and contractible copula appeared earlier, and the present progressive, possessive, and uncontractible copula appeared later. Perhaps more interesting is the fact that relatively few of the 14 morphemes showed acquisition before Stage V. Example (9.4) gives those morphemes that were acquired, where acquisition is defined as the stage at which the morpheme reaches a mean percentage of obligatory occurrence of 90 percent for that and all subsequent stages.

(9.4) *Stage*   *Morpheme acquired*
I   'on', plural
II   '-ing', 'in', past irregular
III
IV   possessive, contractible copula

This reveals that one half of these morphemes are not acquired until after an MLU of 4.00, and shows the gradual acquisition that they undergo.

Both Brown and de Villiers & de Villiers explore three reasons for these general findings: (i) frequency of the morphemes in parental speech, (ii) syntactic complexity, and (iii) semantic complexity. Neither study found any effects of (i), but both found that (ii) and (iii) had some predictive power. This was a difficult issue to pursue, since both possible causes require some theory of complexity for any effects to be determined. The following extract captures the somewhat vague conclusions that were drawn (de Villiers & de Villiers 1973b: 277):

> In conclusion, both semantic and grammatical complexity to some extent predict the order of acquisition of the morphemes, but with the analyses of these variables currently available, it is impossible to separate out the relative contributions of each type of complexity since they make the same predictions. In fact, the order of acquisition may best be predicted by some combination of grammatical and semantic complexity, frequency, and perceptibility in speech. It is possible that no one factor can be considered of primary importance in determining the acquisition of the morphemes.

9.3 The acquisition of Aux in English questions

Section 9.2 provided a general overview on the acquisition in English of a range of grammatical morphemes. It demonstrated the kinds of methods which have been applied to the study of this topic, and gave some general findings about their order of acquisition. Some general findings were also presented on the gradual process of their acquisition, which indicated that overgeneralizations appear only after a fair amount of development has taken place. There was little discussion, however, of how the rules which underlie these morphemes are acquired.

In this section we turn to a more detailed discussion of one class of grammatical morphemes which has generated a wide range of studies, the English auxiliary (or 'Aux' as it is commonly referred to in the syntactic literature). Aux has been of general interest to linguists since the first rules for its appearance were proposed in Chomsky (1957). Typically, Aux is considered to contain all of the grammatical morphemes indicated in (9.5):

(9.5) a. Tense (person, number, past)
     b. Modals (e.g. 'can', 'may', 'will', etc.)
     c. Progressive: 'be' + 'ing'
     d. Perfect: 'have' + '-en'

Issues in grammatical theory regarding Aux include whether such a class exists, and if so, where it occurs in the phrase structure of English (as well as other languages).

Much of the acquisition literature assumes that Aux exists, and has focussed on how children acquire the rules which invert Aux and subject NPs to form questions in English. In yes/no questions, Aux moves to the front of the sentence as shown in (9.6b). I will refer to this movement as Subject–Aux Inversion.

(9.6) a. John is going to the store
     b. Is John going to the store?
     c. John is doing what?
     d. What is John doing?
     e. John likes cookies
     f. Does John like cookies?

This rule also occurs in what are called *wh*-questions as in (9.6c and d). It is assumed that the *wh*- word, in this example 'what', is inserted into a place where an NP can occur. The difference between the (c) and (d) sentences is that the latter has had a second rule apply which moves the *wh*-word to the front of the sentence. I will refer to this second rule as *Wh*-Movement. A last aspect of English questions concerns 'do' and the appearance of tense. In simple active declarative sentences, the tense occurs on the verb as in (9.6e). Transformational grammar proposes a rule of Affix-Hopping which in this case moves the tense from inside the Aux onto the verb. This happens when there is no other element within Aux for the tense to attach to. Lastly, in questions where only tense exists inside the inverted Aux, a 'do' is inserted to carry tense. An example of this is given as (9.6f). We will refer to this rule as *Do*-Support. In acquiring English questions, therefore, the child needs to acquire the category Aux with its various constituents in (9.5), and four rules –, Subject–Aux Inversion, *Wh*-Movement, Affix-Hopping, and *Do*-Support.

Table 9.11 *Sentences used in Kuczaj & Maratsos (1975) and Abe's pattern of imitation*

Sentences with examples	Imitation of Aux			
	Correct	Deleted	Tense[1]	Reordered
PERIOD I				
Declaratives				
Grammatical				
'The nice monkey can kiss his little sister'	38/48			
Ungrammatical				
Tensed verb: 'The boy can pushed the elephant'	0/31	13/31	14/31	
Word order: 'The boy push will the elephant'	0/26	11/26		14/26
Wh questions				
Grammatical				
'What will the boy eat?'	1/7	5/7		1/7
Ungrammatical				
Misplacement: 'What the boy will eat?'	3/11	8/11		
Yes/no questions				
Grammatical				
'Can the boy push the elephant?'	2/16	10/16		
Ungrammatical				
Tensed verb: 'Can the boy pushed the elephant?'	0/21	19/21	2/21	
PERIOD II				
Wh-questions				
Grammatical				
'What will the boy eat?'	0/10			10/10
Ungrammatical				
Misplacement 'What the boy will eat?'	8/10			
Yes/no questions				
Grammatical				
'Can the boy push the elephant?'	10/10			
Ungrammatical				
Tensed verb: 'Can the boy pushed the elephant?'	1/10	9/10		

[1] This category records when Abe changes the tense of the verb, e.g. imitating 'The boy can pushed the elephant' as 'The boy can push the elephant.'

9.3.1 Patterns of acquisition

In this section, I review a few of the studies which have examined the acquisition of sentences like those in (9.6). First, I consider the more general patterns that have been found, and later I turn to some proposed explanations.

Kuczaj & Maratsos (1975)   This preliminary study on one child led to several consequent studies (e.g. Kuczaj 1978; Maratsos & Kuczaj 1978; Kuczaj & Brannick 1979). The study is useful in providing some more detailed facts on acquisition by a single child, as well as demonstrating a valuable technique. The subject was the first author's son Abe. Example

(9.7) gives a summary of Abe's use of Aux in his speech during the time he was studied:

(9.7) period I 2,5(21)–2,7(15) with MLU 3.01 to 3.25:
 The 3,058 sentences collected revealed only 4 with either 'will' or 'can'.
 period II 2,9(16)–(19):
 Aux was used in declaratives but not in questions.

As can be seen, Abe was not using Aux in his spontaneous speech during period I. The authors anticipated, however, that Abe might have already begun the acquisition of Aux in his receptive language. To get at this, they gave him several sentences to imitate which contained instances of 'can' and 'will'. This is the technique we saw earlier in this chapter in the study by Brown & Fraser (1963). It was hoped that Abe would show the 'filter effect', i.e. that he would change the sentences to reflect his grammatical knowledge. These sentences consisted of declarative sentences as well as *wh*-questions and yes/no questions. Each type of sentence also had sentences which were either grammatical or ungrammatical based on the rules of adult English speakers. The types of sentences used, with examples of each, are given in Table 9.11.

Abe's imitation showed a pattern indicating an underlying grammatical system. An examination of his imitations of declaratives reveals an awareness of the distribution of the English Aux. He correctly imitated it in grammatical sentences, and changed ungrammatical ones to be grammatical, either by deletion (of the Aux or tense on the verb) or by reordering. He did not, however, show an awareness of how Aux occurs in questions. In both grammatical and ungrammatical questions, he would delete the Aux. These results lead to a first conclusion that Abe acquired Aux in declaratives before questions.

Table 9.11 also presents Abe's pattern of response during period II. At this time, Abe repeats grammatical yes/no questions correctly, and also changes ungrammatical ones to be correct. This indicates that he had acquired the rule of Subject–Aux Inversion, at least for questions. The latter restriction is made because of his responses on *wh*-questions. On these, he would correctly imitate the ungrammatical ones, and change the grammatical ones into ungrammatical ones, i.e. he would change a question such as 'What will the boy eat?' into 'What the boy will eat?' It should be noted here that the study only examined the modals 'will' and 'can'.

Bellugi (1967/1971) The results of Kuczaj & Maratsos (1975) supported with a different methodology findings reported earlier by Bellugi. Bellugi had been the member of Brown's research team who had primary responsibility for the collection of data from Adam. In her 1967 dissertation, she analyzed the data from all three children and reported stages in the acquisition of questions. Brief reports can be found in Klima & Bellugi-Klima (1966) and Bellugi (1971). Ironically, the most complete published summary of these stages is in Cazden (1970). A summary of these stages, based on the latter report, is given in (9.8), which also gives Adam's age and stage at each period considered.

(9.8) period A: (I, 28 months) Children do not have Aux.
Yes/no questions marked by intonation, e.g. 'sit chair?', 'ball go?'

Wh-questions restricted to 'what' and 'where' in limited forms, e.g. 'what's that?', 'where cookie go?'

period B: (II, III, 35 months)

period C: (IV, 38 months) Aux appears throughout system. Inversion occurs in yes/no questions but not *wh*-questions. Yes/no question, e.g. 'does lions walk?', 'oh, did I caught it?', 'will you help me?'

Wh-questions, e.g. 'what he can ride in?', 'why kitty can't stand up?', 'what he can ride in?'

periods
D to F: (V and later) Gradual emergence of tag questions

These stages were widely accepted by investigators, as indicated by their citation in texts at the time (e.g. Dale 1976). The most important stage proposed is period C when children show inversion in yes/no questions but not in *wh*-questions. This is also the pattern we just saw in Abe's data.

Besides the uninverted *wh*-questions, there are two other kinds of errors that need to be pointed out. One is the occurrence of what we will call *double tense marking*, which refers to those sentences where tense is marked twice, once in the Aux and once on the verb. An example from (9.8) is 'oh, did I caught it?' Examples such as these pose an instant problem for explanation, for they require one to account for tense being copied onto the verb rather than being moved, which is the normal proposal for adult English. A related error is what we will call *double Aux marking*. Hurford (1975) cites examples of these from his daughter: 'whose is that is?' and 'what did you did?'. These differ from double tense marking in that the entire Aux is copied, not just the tense constituent. Examples of these other two kinds of errors have been noted and discussed in works by Hurford (1975), Prideaux (1976), Kuczaj (1976), Fay (1978), Maratsos & Kuczaj

Table 9.12 *The proportion of auxiliaries and proportion of inversion found in Ingram & Tyack (1979) for 21 subjects*

Period	No. of subjects	Prop. of auxiliaries		Prop. of inversion	
		Yes/no	*Wh*	Yes/no	*Wh*
A	7	0.22	0.44	0.55	0.77
B	3	0.68	0.70	0.81	0.91
C	5	0.89	0.88	0.91	0.96
D	4	1.00	0.93	0.98	0.95
E,F	2	0.99	1.00	0.97	0.98

(1978), Erreich, Valian & Winzemer (1980), and Klein (1982), among others.

Subsequent research into these patterns of acquisition has qualified the facts as they have been described. One qualification concerns the accuracy of the periods as described by Bellugi. Most of the published accounts of these periods are anecdotal in the sense that they are presented with examples rather than precise measures. One exception is Bellugi (1971) where some figures are given for Adam's use of inverted and uninverted auxiliaries. At 3;6, Adam produced only eight inverted *wh*-questions out of 30, for a proportion of 0.27. This changed to 0.87 at 3;11 (33 out of 38). Brown (1968) also gives some absolute numbers for the occurrence of these for Adam, Eve, and Sarah. He states that Adam produced 145 such questions between Stages III through V, while Eve produced seven and Sarah 18. Such data suggest that the pattern was clearly more characteristic of the speech of Adam than of the other two children.

Ingram & Tyack (1979) attempted to test these periods further by using a larger sample and more precise measures of inversion. The subjects were 21 children between 2;0 and 3;11 who were placed into periods A through F based on the MLUs given for these periods. Approximately 225 questions were collected from each child. These were then examined for (i) the use of Aux, and (ii) the occurrence of inversion. For the first point, the measure used was the proportion of auxiliaries, that is, how often did the questions have an Aux in them. The second point was measured by the proportion of inversion. This measure was applied to just those questions which had an Aux, and determined the proportion of those which showed the Aux appearing before the subject NP. Table 9.12 gives the general results.

We see the gradual emergence of auxiliaries as characteristic of grammatical morphemes, as indicated at the onset of this chapter. Of some importance is the observation that they occur even in periods A and B, at least as these can be assigned on the basis of MLU. Of more importance is the lack of a clearly marked period C, that is, at all times the children's use of inversions for *wh*-questions was as great as that for yes/no questions.

The question arises, then, of how to account for the discrepancy between these figures and the patterns reported for Abe and Adam. Ingram & Tyack discuss this point, and mention that two of their subjects did indeed show uninverted *wh*-questions of the sort reported in the literature. Their appearance, however, did not occur to such a degree as to differ substantially from the yes/no questions. Also, they tended to occur more for uncontracted auxiliaries than for contracted ones. These results, therefore, suggested that the use of uninverted Aux is not as extensive as implied in Bellugi's stages and that they may be restricted to certain contexts.

Such restrictions have been confirmed by subsequent research by Labov & Labov (1978), Kuczaj & Brannick (1979), and Erreich (1984). These first two studies are methodologically complementary in that Labov & Labov is an intensive single-subject study, while Kuczaj & Brannick is a cross-sectional study of several children. Their general results show that the inversion of Aux in *wh*-questions occurs gradually for specific *wh*-words. For example, children will show inversion for 'what' questions while having uninverted 'why' questions. Kuczaj & Brannick (1979: 43) state:

> The results suggest that children learn to apply this rule [Subject–Aux Inversion, DI] to questions beginning with one or two *wh* words, then to questions beginning with another *wh* word, and so on, rather than to all relevant question types simultaneously, indicating that the acquisition of this syntactic rule is initially relatively specific.

Another qualification concerns the generality of double tense marking and double Aux marking. As mentioned, examples of these are mostly presented anecdotally with little measurement of their pervasiveness. An exception is the report by Maratsos & Kuczaj (1978) where figures are given on the occurrence of these errors in the speech of four subjects. For two subjects, there were virtually no examples of such errors. For two others, these were restricted to forms with 'do'. These data are presented in Table 9.13. They also cite data from 15 children discussed in Kuczaj (1976) that show the same pattern. Further data in support of the restriction of such errors in questions to 'do' appear in Davis (1987).

Both Hurford (1975) and Maratsos & Kuczaj (1978) report two further aspects to these errors. One is that double tense marking is normally restricted to irregular past forms (e.g. 'broke') instead of regular pasts (e.g. 'missed') or overgeneralized past forms (e.g. 'breaked'). Also, Maratsos &

Table 9.13 *Proportion of double tense marking for five possible Aux's reported for two subjects in Maratsos & Kuczaj (1978)*

Subject	Sample size	Proportion of double tense marking for specific Aux's No. of possible contexts (in parentheses)				
		'does'	'did'	'is'	'are'	modals
D.C.	24 hours	0.40 (20)	0.18 (40)	0.00 (56)	0.00 (15)	0.00 (?)
K.R.	50 hours	0.06 (17)	0.16 (32)	0.00 (38)	0.00 (19)	0.00 (?)

Kuczaj claim that double Aux marking is extremely rare, and that it constitutes a different kind of error from double tense marking. They state (p. 344): 'Occasional errors such as 'is this is the powder' may not require any explanation at all, given their extremely low frequency . . .'

In summary, several kinds of errors in the acquisition of Aux in English have been reported. At first, these were proposed as general patterns in acquisition, but have since been seen to occur (i) in some children more often than in others, (ii) in more restricted contexts than first proposed, and (iii) with differing degrees of frequency.

9.3.2 The explanation of Aux acquisition

The facts discussed above have generated several attempts at explanation. These efforts can be placed into two general categories of competence factors vs. performance factors. In the *performance factors* approach, the child is seen as having the adult grammar, with performance factors restricting the child from fully expressing his grammatical knowledge. Those accounts which refer to *competence factors* assume that the errors above reflect the child's grammatical system, that is, the child has formed an incorrect grammar of English and needs to reformulate it. This perspective implies some form of Competence Assumption. We will briefly review some of the proposals which have been made under each of these positions.

Performance factors   The first attempts to account for Bellugi's periods are found in Bellugi (1967), Brown, Cazden & Bellugi (1969), and Brown (1968). Brown divides the child's acquisition of *wh*-questions into two general stages. Before MLU Stage III, the child's questions are seen as being either memorized routines or constructions which are nontransformational in nature. This is the time when Aux is rare, and when *wh*-questions are restricted to forms such as 'what that?'. By Stage III, however, evidence emerges for more productive rules. The general explanation of these studies is that evidence exists that the child has both

Subject–Aux Inversion and *Wh*-Movement. The evidence for the former rule is the occurrence of inverted yes/no questions, and the evidence for the latter rule is the occurrence of uninverted *wh*-questions. The general proposal is that the child has both rules, but has a performance restriction which allows him to apply only one transformation at a time. In yes/no questions only one rule is needed, Subject–Aux Inversion, so that the resultant questions look adult-like. In *wh*-questions, however, two rules are needed, Subject–Aux Inversion and *Wh*-Movement. The performance restriction results in only *Wh*-Movement occurring, so that uninverted *wh*-questions occur.

A potential problem for this explanation is why the rules are ordered for *wh*-questions as they are. That is, why couldn't the child apply Subject–Aux Inversion in *wh*-questions instead of *Wh*-Movement and say questions of the form 'can John do what?' Brown (1968) proposes that uninverted *wh*-questions occur because the child hears the parent use what he calls *occasional questions*. Brown found examples of the kinds of dialogue shown in the samples from Adam, Eve, and Sarah.

(9.9) a. Child: I want milk
      Adult: You want what?

   b. Adult: What do you want?
      Child: (no response)
      Adult: You want what?

   c. Child: I want it
      Adult: You want what?

Occasional questions like this, particularly in dialogues such as (9.9b), show the child that the *wh*-word can appear in two places, and that a movement rule must be needed in the grammar of English.

While Brown's observation about occasional questions provides the kind of positive evidence needed to form *Wh*-Movement, it still does not explain why the child chooses to select its operation in *wh*-questions instead of Subject–Aux Inversion. It also implies a noticeable discontinuity in the development of these rules. Before Stage III, the child has neither rule, and after, he has both. Another problem is that the explanation suffers somewhat in light of the newer information about the restrictions on uninverted *wh*-questions discussed above. Brown's account, it seems, would need to propose that the variation observed is in some way tied to the variation between parents in their use of occasional questions in general and with specific *wh*-questions. Brown, in fact, suggests such a possibility when he observes that Adam's mother used more occasional questions than either Eve's or Sarah's mother. Lastly, Brown's explanation still leaves the occurrence of double Aux marking as a mystery.

Competence factors   Subsequent attempts to account for these patterns of errors have often assumed that they reflect the child's grammatical system at the time (e.g. Hurford 1975; Prideaux 1976; Fay 1978; Erreich, Valian & Winzemer 1980; Klein 1982). The differences are usually in the kind of adult grammar that is assumed to be acquired, rather than disagreement over the data. Also, the focus is often on all of the error types discussed earlier.

Here we will briefly look at the proposals in Erreich, Valian & Winzemer (1980) which are characteristic of this orientation. First, they assume that the child's language at any point in time should be a possible human language. That is, the child's grammar will always need to be constrained by principles of Universal Grammar. To account for the child's double constructions, they propose that all movement rules (such as *Wh*-Movement and Subject–Aux Inversion) involve two operations: copying and deletion. Further, Universal Grammar instructs the child first to treat all cases of movement as copying, and only later as subsequent deletion. The shift from the incorrect rule to the correct one presumably occurs once the child notices that deletion always follows copying for Subject-Aux Inversion and *Wh*-Movement.

This explanation is very simple in its formulation and accounts superficially for the child's patterns of error. It has, however, certain difficulties which are typical of such approaches. Like the pro-drop parameter discussed in Chapters 4 and 7, there are problems with learnability. First, children are making these errors between Stages III and V, as found by Bellugi. It seems hard to understand how the child after so much exposure to English would not have noticed that English deletes the elements which have been copied. Second, the account requires indirect negative evidence. That is, the child will need to note that sentences with double Aux's and *wh*-words never occur in the input language. There are also data problems with these proposals. One, which is pointed out by Erreich, Valian & Winzemer, is that it predicts that children should produce sentences like 'what did you see what?', yet such sentences are not reported for children learning English. Further, it predicts that the errors should be made by all children in a wide range of sentences. We have seen above, however, that the data are much more restricted than this.

Maratsos and Kuczaj have published several studies on the acquisition of English Aux, e.g. Maratsos & Kuczaj (1978), Kuczaj & Brannick (1979), and Kuczaj & Maratsos (1983). These studies present an explanation of the errors discussed above that combines both competence and performance factors, and attempts to account for the restrictions on their occurrence.

The general orientation of their analysis is that children acquire these rules very gradually, restricting them at first to very specific contexts, and then generalizing them. Regarding uninverted *wh*-questions, Kuczaj & Brannick (1979) conclude that the child first learns the rule of Subject–Aux

Inversion for one or two *wh*-words, and only gradually generalizes it to other *wh*-words. They provide experimental results to support this conclusion.

If such is the case for *wh*-questions, then the question arises as to why the rule appears to apply quite early and generally in yes/no questions. This point is addressed in Kuczaj & Maratsos (1983), where it is argued that Subject–Aux Inversion is not as general in yes/no questions as has been assumed. The authors claim that children initially acquire the use of auxiliaries in yes/no questions separately from those used in declaratives, and only later recognize that they are the same category Aux. Two kinds of evidence are presented to support this conclusion, both argued with data from Kuczaj's two sons Abe and Ben. One is that children will show knowledge of auxiliaries in declaratives but not in yes/no questions. Abe's acquisition of four modals is exemplified in (9.10). It indicates that he would use 'would' and 'could' in declaratives for several months but would substitute 'will' and 'can' respectively in questions.

(9.10) *Abe's acquisition of 'will', 'would', 'can', 'could'*

Age	Yes/no questions	Declaratives
2;9–3;4	'will'	'will', 'would'
	'will' for 'would' (34 times)	
2;11–3;4	'can'	'can', 'could'
	'can' for 'could' (201 times)	
3;5	'could' (15 times)	
	'would' (not given)	
3;6	'could' (13 times)	
3;7	'could' (15 times)	

A second argument they give is that the children did not invert auxiliary elements in questions for declarative sentences, as in 'you better go', or similar sentences with 'gonna' and 'wanna'. These should be predicted, they claim, if the child has a general Aux category. Their account of the acquisition of Subject–Aux Inversion, then, is that the child has not yet formulated a general rule and is instead acquiring it in a very restricted way.

The explanation of double tense marking and double Aux marking is taken up in Maratsos & Kuczaj (1978). They begin by acknowledging that double tense marking is usually restricted to questions with forms of 'do' and an irregular verb. They then go on to assume that these are the result of performance factors. They state (p. 343): '... we assume that these are errors of production, rather than representing underlying rule structure, and that the child has by and large analysed the relevant sequences accurately'. The performance factor which is at stake is one of lexical retrieval, that is, in selecting the appropriate verb, the child picks the wrong one. The reason this occurs with just 'do' is presumably because the only function of 'do' is to indicate tense.

Maratsos & Kuczaj correctly point out the retrieval error solution will not work for double Aux marking since this involves inserting an Aux where one does not belong. These errors, however, are seen to be much less frequent than those of double tense marking. The implication is that errors of such minimal frequency are probably due to some other performance factor, and that their rarity is sufficient to give them secondary importance.

Maratsos & Kuczaj account for uninverted *wh*-questions through competence factors (specific learning) and double marking constructions through performance factors. More than other proposals, they also take into consideration the restrictions on the data on such errors. Despite their concern with the data, their account is still not a completely satisfactory explanation. A criticism is the same as the one directed to the discussion of distributional learning in Chapter 7: such accounts do not work from a theory of grammar and do not deal with how the child goes from specific learning to general rules. In this particular case, there are also at least two gaps in the explanation given. One concerns the claim that the child has made retrieval errors; and it seems that some theory of when such errors do and don't occur is needed. For example, they do not explain why the child wouldn't show similar retrieval problems with other Aux elements besides 'do'. Another problem is the claim that 'wanna' and 'gonna' are auxiliaries. One could also claim that they are main verbs, and that the child has their appropriate structure acquired (cf. Ingram 1985a).

9.4 Other aspects of English grammatical acquisition

This chapter has examined the acquisition of both bound and free grammatical morphemes in English. It began with an overview of their developmental patterns, and then turned to a more detailed look at the acquisition of Aux. In this last section on English, we will briefly look at a selection of other aspects of English grammar which have been investigated in recent years. In reviewing these topics, one goal is descriptive, that is, to provide the reader with information about the grammatical study of English, but as will be seen, these studies raise once more the general theoretical issue about when children acquire adult-like knowledge of English.

9.4.1 Passives

In Chapter 7, section 7.2.4 we discussed comprehension of the passive, as tested by de Villiers & de Villiers (1973a). I interpreted their results as indicating that children at age 27 months have some awareness that passives are different from actives, but that they don't yet understand the semantics of the structure. Here I will examine the development of this construction over a longer period of time, first by looking at some production data and then by turning to comprehension – a reversal of the approach in earlier chapters. Unlike the literature for earlier periods of acquisition, that on later grammatical development is more balanced in terms of the number of studies in each area. Also, the constructions under discussion are infrequent in spoken language and require careful comprehension studies.

Horgan (1978)   This is the most comprehensive study of the use of passives in spontaneous speech. Some basic information on the subjects who were observed and the methods of data collection are given below:

group I: 54 children between 2;0 and 4;2. Subjects described 44 pictures in each of two sessions, three months apart.

group II: 180 children, 30 in each age group of 5, 6, 7, 9, 11, 13 years. Subjects told stories about pictures.

group III: 262 university students. Subjects were asked to describe pictures with passives within a structured task.

We see that Horgan not only studied children in the period which we are reviewing, but also older children and adults. The adult data were obtained so that normative comparisons could be established.

The first major point that Horgan makes concerns the difference between *full passives* and *truncated passives*. These distinctions as well as others which Horgan makes are given in (9.11):

(9.11) *Types of passives*
   a. Truncated passives:
      inanimate logical objects, e.g. 'The lamp was broken'
      animate logical objects, e.g. 'The boy was chased'
      statives with 'get', e.g. 'It got broken'
   b. Full passives:
      reversible, e.g. 'The boy was chased by the girl'
      non-reversible, with agent as logical subject, e.g. 'The lamp was broken by the girl'
      non-reversible, with instrument as logical subject, e.g. 'The lamp was broken by (or 'with') the ball'

Horgan excludes truncated passives from the study on the grounds that they are a distinct structure from the full passive. That is, she proposes that the two kinds of passives are not transformationally related, but instead are generated independently of each other. She presents two arguments from

Table 9.14 *The frequency of occurrence of three kinds of full passives for three age groups of children, taken from Horgan (1978: Table 3)*

Age groups	Reversible	Non-reversible agentive	Non-reversible instrumental	Total
2–4	15	0	17	32
5–7	10	0	9	19
9–13	21	15	14	50
Total*	46	15	40	101

* Two passives were not classified because the subject was inaudible.

her data for this position. First, there is a noticeable difference in the frequency of the two passives. Truncated passives are much more frequent than full passives in the spontaneous speech of children. This observation is not consistent with the predictions of the transformational analysis, since the full passives are supposed to be more basic. The second argument is that they have different characteristics. Most truncated passives in the child data occurred with inanimate logical objects, while most full passives occurred with animate logical objects. Further, truncated passives mostly had familiar verbs like 'break' and were often used in a stative sense with 'get', e.g. 'it got broke'. Full passives, on the other hand, were used with a wider variety of action verbs.

Despite the large samples, there were relatively few full passives produced by the children. Group I produced 32 full passives and group II produced 81. If we consider that the group I children were asked to produce 88 sentences across the two sessions, then the 32 passives occurred in a sample of approximately 4,700 sentences. Table 9.14 gives a breakdown of the use of the different kinds of full passives by the children. Not only are passives infrequent, but no non-reversible agentive ones occurred until age 9.

Horgan makes the following additional observations about these data. First, 'until age 11, no child produced *both* reversible and non-reversible passives' (p. 72). That is, individual children appeared to select one way or the other to express passives. This created problems for children when they needed to express something that required the other form. For example, Horgan gives the following examples of sentences by children with only the non-reversible construction, who wanted to express a reversible meaning:

(9.12) a. 'the man was killed by the hand'
 b. 'the boy was kicked by the foot'

The second observation concerned the use of passives by the 2- and 4-year olds. Most of their reversible passives had the wrong word order, so that

Table 9.15 *Mean percentages of four kinds of responses for Stage II–V groups on the understanding of active and passive sentences, taken from de Villiers & de Villiers (1973a: Table 1)*

	Stage II (n = 7) Active	Passive	Stage III (n = 7) Active	Passive	Early IV (n = 4) Active	Passive	Late IV, V (n = 5) Active	Passive
Correct	70.0	36.3	81.0	42.3	85.5	13.3	83.3	39.4
Reversed	11.0	43.3	14.2	41.0	14.2	86.7	13.4	50.0
Child as agent	16.2	17.6	2.4	14.3	0.0	0.0	3.3	3.3
Refusals	2.8	2.8	2.4	2.4	0.0	0.0	0.0	7.3

'the cat was chased by the girl' was used to describe a picture of a cat chasing a girl. This is consistent with our impression from de Villiers & de Villiers that children have some awareness of the form of the passive, but not its meaning.

Given production data of the kind cited above from Horgan, it is not surprising that most studies on passives use more specific elicitation procedures (e.g. Smith 1970; Whitehurst, Ironsmith & Goldfein 1974) or comprehension tasks. The comprehension research will be reviewed by returning to de Villiers & de Villiers (1973a) and then by looking at the studies reported in Maratsos, Kuczaj, Fox & Chalkley (1979).

In section 7.2.3, we reviewed the study by de Villiers & de Villiers (1973a) on the acquisition of English word order in the context of children's ability to process active and passive sentences. To review, they tested 33 children across several ages on reversible active and passive sentences. They placed the children's responses into four categories: correct, reversed, child as agent, and refusals. On the basis of their results presented in Table 7.8, I concluded that the data indicated that late Stage I children show awareness of the formal characteristics of passives since they responded to them differently than they do actives (see 7.2.4 for details).

Table 9.15 presents their data for the children who were beyond Stage I. As with the late Stage I children, the older children show an understanding of the actives but not the passives. Do the data, however, provide evidence that the children are responding differently to passives than actives, as it did for late Stage I? Recall that a crucial indicator would be if the children's percentages of reversals for passives were the same as those for correct responses to actives. We see in Table 9.15 that this is not true for Stages II, III, and late IV, V. We also get marked differences in the 'child as agent' responses for Stage III. I interpret these differences as indicating that several children must be aware of the fact that passives are formally different from actives, and that other children can even interpret them correctly.

There is in Table 9.15 a striking pattern of response for the early Stage IV children: it appears that they are treating passives exactly like actives. This is a pattern which has been observed by others, e.g. Bever (1970). There are two ways in which we could interpret this. One is that this effect is due to the small sample size and to a sampling error in which children had been selected who had not yet acquired even an awareness of passives. The alternative is that children around this point in acquisition adopt a strategy for dealing with passives of treating them as corresponding actives. Note that the existence of such a performance factor does not necessarily mean that the children are unaware of the formal characteristics of passives, but rather that they have reached a cognitive level where they have better problem-solving abilities than earlier. Versions of this strategy have been around since its first proposal in Bever (1970).

In viewing results such as those in Table 9.15, there is an alternative to the claim that children either do or do not have the passive. This is that the children may have some knowledge of the grammar of passives, but incomplete knowledge. Such a possibility is suggested by the data from Horgan's study, in that truncated passives were acquired differently from full ones, and even full ones came in differently from each other. This alternative would also account for the data in Table 9.15 if we assume that children are getting some forms of passive correct but not others. The observation that children may acquire passives differently for different verbs was first made in Sinclair & Ferreiro (1970). More recently it has been argued for in Maratsos *et al.* (1979) and in Sudhalter & Braine (1985).

Maratsos, Kuczaj, Fox & Chalkley (1979) This article is an extensive discussion on the acquisition of several constructions of English. It assesses the extent to which acquisition of syntax can be accounted for solely by reference to the acquisition of formal structures independent of meaning. Reiterating a point made in Maratsos (1978), they propose that the semantic bootstrapping hypothesis combined with a purely formal rule for passives such as that in (9.13) predicts across-the-board acquisition of passives.

(9.13) NP$_1$ 'be' VERB 'en' 'by' NP$_2$

By 'across-the-board' we mean application to sentences which show a range of semantic roles for the syntactic subjects and objects, as exemplified in (9.14):

Table 9.16 *Proportions of correct responses on actional and nonactional verbs, reported in Maratsos et al. (1979)*

Age group	Actionals		Nonactionals	
	Actives	Passives	Actives	Passives
4-year-olds	0.87	0.68	0.91	0.47
5-year-olds	0.94	0.66	0.91	0.35

(9.14) a. Tables are liked by John

     INANIMATE OBJECT   EXPERIENCER

     b. John is pleased by tables

     EXPERIENCER   OBJECT

     c. Mary was kissed by John

     AGENT   ANIMATE OBJECT

          d. The door was opened by the key

     INANIMATE OBJECT   INSTRUMENT

Their purpose is to argue that passives are not acquired across-the-board, but instead show gradual acquisition from one class of verbs to another.

Maratsos *et al.* report on two studies on the acquisition of passives; while they differed in the methods used, the same general results were found. I will present a brief review of the results from the first study.

Maratsos *et al.* tested 38 4- and 5-year olds on their ability to understand passives for two main kinds of verbs: *actional verbs* such as 'find', 'hold', 'wash', 'shake', and *nonactional verbs* such as 'remember', 'forget', 'know', 'like', 'miss', 'see', 'hear', 'watch'. The children were presented with finger puppets and then told either an active or passive sentence about them – for example, a typical test sentence might be 'Donald was liked by Goofy'. After each sentence, the children were then asked 'Who did it?' While this question is appropriate for actional verbs, it is not for nonactional ones. They discuss this possible effect on their results and state (p. 11) '. . . we argue from the detailed pattern of the obtained results that the method did not prove unduly discriminatory against adequate response to nonactional passives. Another small study conducted afterwards supports further the methodological adequacy of the main study.'

The proportions of correct responses for the two kinds of verbs are given in Table 9.16. These figures are for the 31 of the subjects who were able to complete the task.

There was a significant difference in the performance on passives for each kind, indicating that passives were easier with actional verbs than non-actional ones. This finding was confirmed in the second study, and also by a later one by Sudhalter & Braine (1985). Further, there was no overlap between the individual verbs within the classes, that is, all of the actional verbs were easier to understand in the passive than any of the nonactional ones. The authors take these results as confirmation of the claim that the passive is acquired gradually over several years, and that it requires a lot of experience with individual verbs. They also see it as counterevidence for a strictly formal rule of Passive, at least up to the school years. They are not explicit as to whether they think a restructuring to a more formal rule occurs later, or that the adult rule requires semantic information. Their concern is primarily to provide data showing that there are semantic restrictions on the child's understanding of passives at least up to age 5.

Explanation. Thus far we have presented data which indicate that children may show some awareness of passives at an early age, but that it takes several years before the complete range of its application is acquired. We also mentioned in passing the implications that these data have for a theory of acquisition. Horgan implies that truncated and full passives may have different grammatical sources, at least while they are being acquired. Maratsos *et al.* emphasize the semantic restrictions of the rule during the same period. Neither, however, faces directly the implications these results have for a theory of grammatical acquisition. That is, do they indicate that a different kind of Passive rule needs to be proposed for the adult language, or that children undergo a discontinuity in development? In addition to these points, there is the issue of how the child identifies the passive construction. That is, is it the result of semantic bootstrapping or some form of distributional learning? This section will explore these issues more directly.

The question of how the child determines the meaning and form of passives is not one which has received much detailed discussion in the literature. One exception to this is the discussion found in Pinker (1984). We have already seen in Chapter 7 Pinker's proposals about the steps which the child follows in acquiring the basic phrase structure of English, and the resulting grammar he gives for Stage I. That grammar and the same steps will be used for the acquisition of passives, along with some additional machinery. We will not go into the details about how this occurs, or its concomitant problems, but will just outline the approach.

Before passives are acquired, Pinker assumes that the child already has acquired the rules which generate oblique prepositional phrases as in (9.15a). When generating the phrase structure for a passive such as (9.15b), the child has principles available which allow him to assume that the passive has the same structural characteristics as the oblique phrase (see Pinker 1984: 76–83):

(9.15) a. The cat was sitting by the fence
b. The cat was bitten by the dog

This will eventually lead to a new phrase structure rule which generates passives as well as oblique prepositional phrases. The difference between the two rules will be in the grammatical roles of the NPs. A last step will be the child's acquiring a second lexical entry for the passive form of the verb. For example, the child's lexicon will have 'bite' for active sentences and 'bitten' for passive ones.

These steps indicate a continuous development in which the child establishes the Passive rule as explained by the lexical functional approach, without any extensive discontinuity. In Pinker's discussion, in fact, there is no reference to a need for orphan categories in acquiring the passive, as there was with the oblique prepositional phrase. That is, once the structure for the oblique PPs is acquired, the acquisition of passives should follow smoothly, given appropriate input.

Given Pinker's explanation, there is then the question of whether this account fits the acquisition facts as described above. There are at least two general findings that need to be explained: (i) the treatment of passive sentences as if they were actives, and (ii) the incomplete acquisition of passives, where the rule is applied to active verbs but not to nonactive ones. A further, less well-documented observation is Horgan's, that children may express active meanings with passive morphology.

Pinker is aware of the phenomenon (i) and discusses it in his book. He does not, however, directly offer an account for it. We will therefore speculate about how he would deal with it. One possibility is to say that the child has no contextual information in this situation. That is, the child has no information which tells him that the subject is not an agent. If this occurs, however, it seems that the procedures could lead the child to a grammar where actives can have either active or passive morphology. This would account for Horgan's observations that actives may be expressed with passive formalism. Such a grammar could be restructured if it contained some orphans and the child subsequently heard passives with contextual information. Another possibility would be to consider such examples as the result of a performance factor which has intervened in the acquisition procedures. This performance mechanism would be one that operates when the child can't process all of a sentence, and yet needs to determine some meaning. In this case, it would tell the child to ignore the passive morphology and preposition, and impose some canonical expected meaning. The consequences of such a mechanism is to say that some sentences are processed for learning and others are not. This appears to be Pinker's proposal; in a general discussion of input, he states (p. 28):

I also assume that not all sentences heard by the child, nor all parts of a sentence, will be used as input to his or her acquisition mechanisms. Presumably children encode most reliably the parts of sentences whose words they understand individually, and the whole sentences most of whose words they understand.

The second set of findings concerning the restricted application of the Passive rule is directly addressed by Pinker. In his first explanation (Pinker 1982) he suggests that children initially only hear actives with semantic restrictions, and thus formulate a restricted version with the appropriate constraints. Such a rule is stated informally here:

(9.16) *Initial Passive rule*: Passive is restricted to sentences where the surface grammatical subject has the semantic role of patient and the surface grammatical object has the semantic role of agent.

He also proposes that this initial passive rule is part of Universal Grammar and the one the child first applies to passive sentences. The child could then extend the rule to more diverse semantic roles on the basis of positive evidence.

Berwick & Weinberg (1984: 215–20) have criticized the above proposal on theoretical grounds. They have pointed out that a universal rule such as that in (9.16) predicts that there should be some languages which have such a Passive rule. No such evidence, however, currently exists. They argue that if this cross-linguistic observation is true, then Pinker's proposal has a problem in accounting for the acquisition data. It would force him to a maturational model in which the child begins with such a rule, and then reaches a point where it is programmed to drop out. Such an account, however, would contradict Pinker's own assumptions about restrictions on changes in the child's grammar.

Pinker (1984: 328–33) takes an alternative approach to accounting for the restricted application of passive. He first attacks the findings themselves, citing unpublished research of his own which found children passivizing both actional and nonactional verbs. He then states (pp. 329–30): 'neither the child nor the adult entertains the hypothesis that passivization is constrained by some blanket restriction like "agentive subjects only" or "action verbs only"', effectively rejecting his earlier proposal.

The problem left is to resolve the discrepancies between Pinker's results and those of Maratsos *et al.* (1979). Pinker does this by first discussing the general constraints on passives in English. He refers to a proposal in Jackendoff (1983) called the *thematic hierarchy constraint*, which states that sentences in English can only passivize if the object has a semantic role that is lower than that of the subject on the following hierarchy: Agent–Location/Source/Goal-Theme (or Patient). This blocks passivization of a sentence such as 'The game weighs a dollar' if we assume that the subject of 'weigh' is a theme and the object is a location, both roles thus sharing the same place in the hierarchy. Presumably this is a constraint which the child acquires from positive evidence. Also, some verbs do not have clear-cut semantic roles, and require linguistic experience for the roles to be determined. Pinker suggests that several of the verbs tested by Maratsos *et al.* were such verbs. The verbs used by Pinker, however, had clearer semantic structure and could therefore be passivized. Pinker also points out that such a proposal about passives predicts that children will not over-generalize passives to verbs like 'weigh', an observation supported by the limited data available to date.

An alternative explanation for the acquisition of passives can be found in Berwick & Weinberg (1984). We have already mentioned Berwick & Weinberg's criticism of Pinker's first proposals about the acquisition of passives. They follow those criticisms with their own suggestions on how passives are acquired. Berwick & Weinberg (1984) approach language acquisition from the Government–Binding theory of Chomsky (1981, 1982, 1986). They assume that the child is born with a set of linguistic universals which are available at the onset of acquisition. As such, their general orientation is that the child's grammar is essentially adult-like from the onset, and that errors in acquisition will be restricted. One possible source of errors will be when the language is marked for some aspect of grammar and the child treats it as the unmarked case. We have already discussed this form of the parameter-setting model in Chapter 7.

In order to understand Berwick & Weinberg's account, it is necessary to have some understanding of the way in which Government–Binding theory (or GB) generates passive sentences. Here we will give an extremely brief description, referring the reader to other sources for a more detailed presentation (e.g. Radford 1981; Berwick & Weinberg 1984).

GB proposes that passive sentences like 'John was liked by Fred' have the underlying structure of (9.17):

(9.17) NP_e Past be like +en John by Fred

Unlike earlier accounts in transformational theory (e.g. Chomsky 1957), passives have an underlying structure distinct from their corresponding active sentences. NP_e stands for the occurrence of a NP which is lexically empty (hence 'e'), that is, there is no word inside it at the underlying level. The item 'en' represents the passive morpheme on the verb. A universal principle requires that all nouns in a sentence receive what is called abstract case. Nouns receive case from a restricted number of sources: subjects can receive case from the Aux, objects from the main verb, and oblique nouns from prepositions. Passives create a problem for case assignment, however, because the passive suffix 'en' is seen as blocking it. In our example, 'en' blocks the main verb 'like' from assigning case to the object 'John'. This problem is resolved by having the object move into the subject position where it can receive case from the Aux.

The child acquiring English is born with the knowledge about the properties of case assignment. In acquiring English, she is faced with two major tasks: (i) to identify the grammatical morphemes of English and (ii) to realize that the English passive morpheme 'en' blocks case assignment. The latter has to be acquired because the unmarked situation is for affixes not to affect case assignment. For example, in the active sentence 'Fred liked John', the past tense morpheme 'ed' does not stop the main verb 'like' from assigning case to the object 'John'.

Berwick & Weinberg argue that the problem in acquiring the passive resides in the passive affix 'en'. First, this morpheme has a common allomorph 'ed' which is homophonous with the past tense morpheme 'ed'. This will create problems with identifying 'en' as a distinct morpheme which is also marked for blocking case assignment. Because of this problem, children will be very cautious when they begin to acquire this morpheme. Berwick & Weinberg state (p. 219): 'The result is a drive to limit the scope of this rule's affixation as much as possible. Hence the initial hypothesis that the rule applies to the most minimal class of verbs consistent with the data that is heard.' Since the first verbs heard with passives are action verbs, only they will have the passive morpheme associated with them. The account differs from Pinker's in placing the restriction on the association of the passive morpheme to a particular class of verbs, rather than on the Passive rule itself.

As with Pinker's analysis, we can ask if the Berwick & Weinberg explanation is consistent with the acquisition facts. Recall that our first finding was that children initially treat passives as actives. Berwick & Weinberg do not offer an account of why this occurs, and we can only speculate that there is a performance factor at work of the kind discussed by Pinker. This is a problem because their model assumes at the onset that the child 'knows about word segmentation and morphology, for example, that 's' is a plural morpheme in "cats"' (p. 203). This difficulty reflects a general one with their proposal which is that it is so incomplete that it immediately becomes difficult to assess.

This difficulty continues with the second set of data, on the restricted use of passives. There is no principle of acquisition given which tells the child to restrict the passive morpheme to active verbs. Further, the account is highly dependent on the child only hearing passives with active verbs, a point still to be substantiated. The model suffers the same problem that all strong nativist models have: if the child has the principles available, then slower acquisition needs to be tied to lack of input. A last point concerns the lack of discussion about the nature of the input that leads the child to assume that the passive morpheme blocks case assignment.

9.4.2 Relative clauses

Up to now, we have examined aspects of English grammar which can be described as part of the acquisition of simple sentences. In these last two sections, we look at a few other aspects of grammatical acquisition which concern complex sentences. *Complex sentences* are those sentences where one sentence (the subordinate clause) occurs within another sentence (the main clause). Example (9.18) gives two kinds of complex English sentences (where the subordinate clauses are shown within square brackets):

(9.18) a. Relative clause: We saw the boy [who left]
       b. Verb complement: We know [that Mary left]
                                    We asked [Bill to leave]
                                    We promised Bill [to leave]

(9.18a) is an example of a relative clause, which is a clause that modifies an NP. Such clauses are introduced by *relative pronouns* such as 'who', 'that', and 'which'. The examples in (9.18b) demonstrate clauses which function as complements to the verb. Such clauses are introduced by *complementizers* such as 'that'. Tenseless complement clauses have the infinitive 'to' which marks the clause as such. Here we just look at the acquisition of relative clauses.

A striking feature of the spontaneous speech of children between 2 and 5 years is that there are relatively few relative clauses. Instead of embedding one clause into another, children tend to string clauses together with numerous insertions of 'and'. This can be exemplified by the following passage from my daughter Jennika at 4;4 when she was asked to tell the story of Little Red Riding Hood.

> A little girl goes for a walk and her mom tells her not to talk to visitors and she saw a big ole wolf. The big blue wolf said do you want to pick some flowers for your grandmother? Where do you going to? Just somewhere in the woods and let's see who gets there first and then he puts on the grandma's clothes . . .

This lack of relative clauses in spontaneous speech was confirmed in Ingram (1975). There I examined the grammatical structures which children used to begin stories. The onset of children's stories is a context where a relative clause is normally used. Since such stories typically begin with an introductory sentence such as 'There once was an old lady who lived in a shoe', with the introduction of the main character, e.g. 'There once was an old lady', and then a relative clause which provides the qualification, e.g. 'who lived in a shoe', it was expected that children would also use relative clauses in their own stories if the construction was part of their grammar.

To study this, I looked at the first sentence of 360 stories told by 210 children between the ages of 2 and 5 years. The data were taken from a collection of stories collected by Pitcher & Prelinger (1963). I found that there were three ways with which children began their stories: these are shown in (9.19) along with examples of each.

(9.19) a. *Juxtaposition*
'A bus. He went up a hill.' (Dale 2;8)
'Boy fell out of car. He went in car again.' (Cass 2;8)
'Once there was a house. Peter lived in the house.' (Porteus 2;10)
b. *Conjunction*
'Once there was a little boy and he went for a walk in the woods.' (Kurt 3;1)
'Once there was a little boy and he hit someone on the head.' (Marla 3;4)
c. *Relative clause*
'Once there was a kitty named Cindy.' (Tina 5;0)
'Once there was a big scarey man with lots of faces' (Emmet 5;0)
'Once upon a time there was a little girl who went for a walk to a restaurant.' (Chloe 4;2)

These three patterns show a gradual fusion of the introduction and qualification of a story. *Juxtaposition* is a very loose connection between these parts. Some children just named the main character, as in the first example, and then placed the qualification as a separate sentence. The second example has the two together, but as one main clause. The third example shows an appropriate introduction, but the qualification as an independent clause. *Conjunction* shows a closer relation by the inclusion of an 'and', but the two parts still have equal status. It is only in the use of *relative clause* that the appropriate subordination of the qualification occurs.

Table 9.17 presents the proportion of times each of these three beginnings were used by the children. For the youngest children, juxtaposition is clearly the dominant pattern. This preference decreases over time, but is still the most used for all groups except the 5-year olds. We also see that relative clauses are very rare for the first two age groups, and are only beginning to be frequent for the oldest children. Even for these children, many of the examples are formulaic such as 'kitty named Cindy' and 'man with lots of faces'. Non-reduced relative clauses with relative pronouns and verb phrases were never frequent in the data.

Table 9.17 *The proportion of use of three ways in which children begin stories, taken from Ingram (1975: 112, table 3)*

Relation	Age groups			
	2;0–2;11	3;0–3;11	4;0–4;11	5;0–5;11
Juxtaposition	0.75	0.57	0.40	0.25
Conjunction	0.22	0.40	0.37	0.40
Relative clause	0.03	0.03	0.23	0.35

Sheldon (1974) There have been several studies on children's comprehension of relative clauses, e.g. Gaer (1969), H. Brown (1971), de Villiers, Tager-Flusberg, Hakuta & Cohen (1979), Hamburger & Crain (1982). The study by Sheldon (1974), however, remains the one which initiated extensive discussion on the acquisition of relatives.

Sheldon studied the comprehension of relative clauses by 33 children divided into three age groups of 11 children each: I (3;8–4;3), II (4;6–4;11), and III (5;0–5;5). The children were tested on four types of sentence with relative clauses, shown in (9.20):

(9.20) *Subject relatives*
    SS The dog *that jumps over the pig* bumps into the lion
    SO The lion *that the horse bumps into* jumps over the giraffe

Object relatives
    OS The pig bumps into the horse *that jumps over the giraffe*
    OO The dog stands on the horse *that the giraffe jumps over*

The sentences differed depending on (i) whether the subject or object of the main clause contained the relative clause, and (ii) whether it was the subject or object of the relative clause which was relativized. SO, for example, indicates that the relative clause modified the subject of the sentence (or S), and that the object of the relative clause (or O) was relativized. The children were also given coordinate sentences which corresponded to each of the relative clause sentence types. A coordinate sentence corresponding to OS, for example, was 'The pig bumps into the horse and the horse jumps over the giraffe'. These were given to see if the children were treating the relative clauses sentences the same as coordinations or not. Each child received three sentences of each of the eight types for a total of 24 sentences.

Each child was presented with a collection of toy animals appropriate for the sentences and asked to act out the test sentences. For a sentence to be scored correct, the child needed to carry out both acts correctly, but could

Table 9.18 *Mean number of correct answers by age groups on relative sentences and coordinate sentences, taken from Sheldon (1974: Tables 3 and 4) (A perfect score would be 3, since there were three sentences per type)*

	Relative sentences				Coordinate sentences			
Age group	SS	SO	OS	OO	SS	SO	OS	OO
I (3;8–4;3)*	1.0	0.18	0.54	1.36	1.75	1.75	1.63	2.13
II (4;6–4;11)	1.45	0.73	0.91	1.64	1.82	2.0	1.82	2.0
III (5;0–5;5)	2.27	0.64	1.17	1.55	2.64	2.0	2.27	2.55
Total average	1.58	0.52	0.88	1.52	2.1	1.93	1.93	2.23

* Three children in group I did not complete the coordinate sentences.

do so in any order. While responses with only one action were scored as incorrect, Sheldon comments that these never were more than 4–5 percent of the total responses for any sentence type.

Table 9.18 gives the results on the eight sentence types tested. Statistical tests revealed the following results:

(a) The coordinate sentences were easier than the relative ones, and showed no differences across the age groups. *Conclusion*: the children were aware that relative sentences are different from coordinate ones. This finding reminds us of the one by de Villiers & de Villiers (1973a) on actives and passives, where the children showed an awareness that passives were different even though they hadn't determined their actual features.

(b) The SS and OO relative sentences were significantly easier than SO and OS relatives. *Conclusion*: sentences are easier to understand when the NP which has a relative and the NP which is relativized have the same grammatical function. Sheldon refers to this as the *parallel function hypothesis*.

(c) SS relatives show significant improvement across age groups, but the OO relatives do not. *Conclusion*: there must be some additional factor which causes this effect.

The first finding has been verified by other research and has not been particularly controversial. The opposite has been the case, however, concerning the second finding. A useful review of this issue can be found in Bowerman (1979). This literature, in fact, has been so contradictory that Bowerman has commented (p. 292) that it 'presents a tangled web of conflicting findings and alternative interpretations'. The criticisms can be grouped into two categories. First, there are those who question whether the data support the conclusion. Some studies have found results which show different patterns of difficulty, e.g. de Villiers *et al.* (1979). Others (e.g. Hamburger & Crain 1982) have noted that the parallel function hypothesis does not account for the fact that SS relatives are easier than OO ones (although Sheldon has a proposal for this which will be discussed shortly). Second, others have questioned the parallel function hypothesis on theoretical grounds. It is not clear what role this function plays in the acquisition of relatives. While it appears to be a performance factor, it could operate under two possible conditions: (a) the child has acquired the grammar of English relatives, but uses this as a processing constraint when short-term memory fails, or (b) the child has not acquired the grammar of English relatives, and uses this as a heuristic for responding while acquiring them. As pointed out by Hamburger & Crain (1982), this is a claim about the performance factors affecting relatives rather than one about how the child's competence emerges. Tavakolian (1981b) has rejected the parallel function hypothesis in that it assigns too much competence to the child and claims instead that the children are treating these sentences as if they were simply two conjoined clauses.

Sheldon does offer a proposal to account for the third finding which addresses the child's linguistic competence. She argues that the pattern in the third finding given above results from the child's overuse of the English rule of Extraposition. This is a rule in the adult language which moves a relative clause from a subject NP to the end of the sentence. This rule, for example, would operate on (9.21a) to produce (9.21b):

(9.21) a. The boy *who left* was sick
    b. The boy was sick *who left*
    c. The dog bumps into the horse *that the giraffe jumps over*
    d. The dog *that the giraffe jumps over* bumps into the horse

Sheldon proposes that children have this rule, and thus treat OO sentences like (9.21c) as if they were an SO sentence as in (9.21d). The distribution of the children's responses, then, was as follows (figures are percentages):

	SS	SO	OS	OO
Correct	52	17	29	50
Parallel function	14	69	14	12
Extraposition			44	32
Other	33	13	12	5

An important set of evidence in support of the Extraposition argument is that approximately one-third of the children only made this error on the object relatives. Even more importantly, the same subjects virtually never got any of the object relatives correct. The main criticisms of the proposal are (i) that there is little other evidence to date that children have such a rule at this point in acquisition, and (ii) doubt as to why the child would ever form it this way since it is not a pattern found in the adult language. If it were the result of overgeneralization of the rule, as Sheldon suggests, then the children would require indirect negative evidence to overcome their mistakes.

Sheldon's study was important in drawing attention to children's emerging ability to understand relatives, and it suggested some possible ways to account for it. It also influenced the study on relatives reported in Hamburger & Crain (1982).

Hamburger & Crain (1982) Hamburger & Crain approach the topic from the perspective of Language Acquisition as discussed in Part I of this volume. They are quick to point out that Sheldon's study is more a study of performance factors than competence factors. Their own orientation is along the lines of what we have called a strong inclusion hypothesis. They set out to show that children may have a better knowledge of relative clauses than is indicated by research to date. Since they are in agreement with Sheldon's implicit claim that children have rules for relatives, they are more concerned about the extent of errors found in the data. In particular, they want to construct the experiments on the acquisition of relative clauses in such a way as to minimize the conditions that encourage the use of performance factors.

Hamburger & Crain studied the comprehension of relative clauses by having children act out sentences, as Sheldon did. They adjusted other aspects of Sheldon's methodology in the following ways:

(a) Several exemplars are presented of the toy which is referred to by the head of the relative clause. This is done because relative clauses served to delimit a set of objects, and having a choice from this set should make the task more natural or consistent with conversational requirements, that is, we normally only use a relative clause if there is a need to select one specific member of a set.

(b) The order in which the child performs the two actions in the sentences is recorded and included in the analysis. Sheldon did not take order into consideration, but it has implications for the child's interpretations (see below).

(c) Sentences of only one type were tested, the OS ones. They were selected for two reasons: (i) they had resulted in the most errors in previous studies (although note that the SO ones were the most difficult category in Sheldon 1974); (ii) they show an order of mention that is opposite to the conceptual order. For example, in the OS sentence 'The pig bumps into the horse *that jumps over the giraffe*' it is assumed that the horse jumps over the giraffe' before the pig bumps into it. No independent psychological evidence, however, is presented to support this claim.

The subjects were 18 children divided into groups of 3-, 4-, and 5-year olds. Their results were scored in the following way. Each NP in the test sentences was assigned a number as in (9.22):

(9.22)   1   2   3
The duck stands on the horse that jumps over the pig

The child's actions were then coded according to their order and the NPs used. For example, 23, 12 means that the child had the horse jump over the pig, and then the duck stand on the horse. Only two numbers were used if only one action was performed.

Table 9.19 *Percentages of use of three response patterns for OS sentences, adapted from Hamburger & Crain (1982: 267, Table 7.2)*

Age groups	Patterns of response			Other	Sheldon's scoring (perfect score = 3)
	12,23	23,12	12		
3 years	42	27	0	31	2.07
4 years	18	43	13	26	1.83
5 years	5	35	55	5	1.2
Average	22	35	23	21	1.7

Table 9.19 presents the major results of the study. Hamburger & Crain treat the three patterns given in Table 9.19 (excluding 'other') as all correct, i.e. indicating correct processing of the sentence. They see the patterns 12,23 and 23,12 as differing in that the latter reflects more accurately the natural order of the events. They also score 12 as correct because it indicates that the child is aware that the relative clause is functioning to help delimit which toy to select, and that the main action is having the main clause subject act upon the main clause object. By these measures, then, the children can be interpreted as showing good ability at OS structures, since the percentages of correct response are 60, 74, and 95 for the three groups.

In Table 9.19, I have also entered the score which the children would have received if Sheldon's scoring methods had been used. By her measure, both 12,23 and 23,12 would have been correct, but 12 would not. We then multiplied by 3 the percentages obtained, to get an equivalent score. By comparing these scores with those in Table 9.18, it is seen that the Hamburger & Crain's children did do better than those tested by Sheldon.

There appear to be two major differences in the two studies which led to the better performance of the children: several exemplars of the head of the relative clause were used, and only one sentence type with relatives was tested. One can propose that these two changes made it much easier to do the task, which indeed was the goal of the study. The general conclusion is that at least some younger children can be shown to have more knowledge of relative clauses than has been proposed (at least by some) when optimal test conditions are involved.

While the above conclusion appears to be a reasonable one, I would like to point out an alternative interpretation. If all three response types above are correct ones, then one would expect a gradual improvement in all three across time. This, in fact, is not the case. The 12,23 and 12 patterns are actually going in opposite directions. A different interpretation results if we assume that 12,23 results from incorrect processing and 12 results from correct processing. This is also reasonable, in that 12,23 could also result from treating the sentence as a form of coordination whereby the child treats the last NP mentioned before the second verb as its subject. Under this alternative, relative clause comprehension does not look as well developed in children younger than 5 years.

A second study conducted by Hamburger & Crain involved the production of relative clauses, which, as we observed earlier, are not common in the speech of children at these ages. As in the above study, Hamburger & Crain wanted to create an optimal situation for the elicitation of relatives. To do this, they placed children in a situation where they had to describe something to someone who was blindfolded. The child had to tell this person to pick up one of a set of objects which was doing something. For example, there could be a set of walruses where one was seen tickling a zebra. An appropriate response would be 'Pick up the walrus that is tickling the zebra'. Ten of the 12 children responded and 72 percent of their responses used some form of an OS sentence.

Summary.   The results of the above studies demonstrate several points about the acquisition of relative clauses. They do not appear to be abundant in the speech of young children in this age range. There is evidence, however, that they have some awareness of their existence in the language, and that they can comprehend and even produce them under certain conditions. We are reluctant, however, to conclude that children have acquired relative clauses by the end of this period around age 4;0. It appears that their acquisition has begun, but that the productivity in their use which is characteristic of adult speech has still not occurred. The results, then, are similar to those found in our review of passives.

9.4.3 Pronominal reference

Pronominal reference concerns the conditions under which English (and languages in general) will allow pronouns to refer to surrounding noun phrases. The study of this topic is one that has received a great deal of attention in recent years in both linguistic theory and language acquisition. It has been found to be an area that is extremely complex in the range of phenomena which it affects, and one which varies from language to language. While linguistic theory has begun to study the range of such conditions across languages, much of the work on language acquisition has been restricted to English.

We will look at English pronominal reference by first distinguishing three general conditions, adapted from Chomsky (1981). These will be referred to as reflexive, pronominal, and nominal conditions on reference. They are exemplified by the sentences given in (9.23).

(9.23) *Conditions on coreference*
    a. Reflexive
       1. John thinks that Bill likes himself (= Bill)
       2. *John thinks that Bill likes himself (= John)
       3. *Himself likes Bill
    b. Pronominal
       4. John thinks that Bill likes him (= John)
       5. *John thinks that Bill likes him (= Bill)

    c. Nominal
      Blocked backwards pronominalization
      6. He (John) thinks that Bill left
      7. *He (= Bill) thinks that Bill left

      Backwards pronominalization
      8. When he (= Bill) left, Bill was hungry

      Blocked forwards pronominalization
      9. In front of Bill, he (= John) saw a snake
      10. *In front of Bill, he (= Bill) saw a snake

Reflexives are pronominal forms in English which add the morpheme 'self' to English pronouns. Their use in English has a requirement that the NP (or antecedent) to which they refer must occur in the same clause. Further, the NP antecedent must precede it in the sentence. These general facts are exemplified in the sentences in (9.23). Sentences 1 and 2 show that the reflexive 'himself' can only refer to 'Bill' because only 'Bill' is in the same clause. ('John' is in the higher clause which has the form 'John thinks

X'.) Sentence 2 is therefore ungrammatical under the interpretation where 'himself' is meant to refer to 'John'. Sentence 3 shows that the reflexive cannot precede the antecedent.

Pronouns are referential forms in English that are normally divided into subject, object, and possessive cases, e.g. 'I', 'me', and 'my'. Their conditions of reference are generally complementary to those of reflexives. That is, pronouns cannot refer to an antecedent in the same clause. This is shown in sentences 5 and 6 above, where 'him' can refer to 'John' but not 'Bill', where 'John' is outside the clause in which 'him' occurs but 'Bill' is not.

The conditions on the possible order of pronouns and their antecedents are more complex than the condition for reflexives. While reflexives cannot precede their antecedents, pronouns can precede their antecedents under certain conditions. There are also certain conditions under which pronouns cannot follow their antecedents, but need to precede them. These sets of conditions are exemplified in (9.23) as nominal conditions on reference. They are grouped under the term 'nominal' because it appears that they can best be described by referring to the position of the nominal antecedent in relation to the pronoun.

The nominal condition on coreference can be seen by looking at the relations between the pronouns and their potential antecedents in the three types given in (9.23c). Blocked backwards pronominalization is a case where the pronoun cannot precede its antecedent. This is similar to the condition on reflexives and might initially lead one to propose that it is the same for pronouns. The existence of backwards pronominalization, however, indicates that the condition is not one of simple linear order. In sentence 8, the pronoun precedes the antecedent 'Bill', and yet may refer to it. Such sentences have led linguists to propose that the condition needs to include reference to the relative position of the pronoun and the NP in the structure in the sentence. Observe that the pronoun occurs in a higher position than 'Bill' in sentence 7, but not in sentence 8: 'He' is the main clause subject in 7, whereas 'Bill' is the main clause subject in 8. That is, it appears that coreference is possible as long as the pronoun does not occur in a higher place in the hierarchical structure of the sentence than does the antecedent NP. This observation is supported further by the cases of blocked forwards pronominalization. Here the NP cannot precede the pronoun as shown in sentence 10. Note in 10 that the pronoun, as in 7, occurs as the main clause subject. We can summarize the conditions discussed as:

(9.24) (a) Reflexive: a reflexive pronoun must refer to an NP which precedes it within the same clause;

(b) Pronominal: a pronoun cannot refer to an NP which occurs within the same clause;

(c) Nominal: a nominal cannot be the antecedent for a pronoun which occurs in a higher position in the structure of the sentence.

The facts on pronominal reference have been overly simplified in order to provide a general feel for the range of phenomena which are involved. The exact conditions require more careful specification of the grammatical roles of the pronominal and nominal forms as well as the grammatical structure of the relevant constructions. Also, it needs to be pointed out that languages differ from English in the way in which reference is handled. Japanese, for example, allows what we can call 'long distance reflexives': it allows a sentence like 2 in (9.23) where the reflexive refers to 'John'. Further, while it allows long distance reflexives, Japanese imposes a 'subject condition' on reflexives, that is, the antecedent for the reflexive can only be the subject of the sentence. Other languages will show still further differences, and the facts on such variation are still being gathered (see Wexler & Manzini 1987).

Linguists differ in the ways they attempt to explain such facts. There are two general issues that arise. One concerns whether or not *linear order* needs to be stated as part of the conditions. In (9.24) I mention restrictions on ordering in (a) and (b), but not (c). A more theoretical approach could eliminate any reference to order whatsoever by restricting the account of reference to structural conditions between the antecedent and the pronominal form.

The most commonly discussed structural relation of this kind is that of c-command (Reinhart 1976, 1981, 1983). C-command, very simply stated, is a relation between two constituents in a grammatical structure such that they share a particular relation to some other grammatical category, let's say G. Under one definition, we can say that one category c-commands another if the G that is directly above it is also above the other category. There are two features of this relation that need to be made explicit. One concerns the possible grammatical categories of G. These are usually restricted to S (for sentence), and VP (for verb phrase). The other is the notion of 'directly above'. The constituent which is c-commanding another needs to have a relation to the G category such that no other G category intervenes.

We can demonstrate the use of c-command in accounting for the facts in (9.24). In a simple English reflexive sentence like 'John likes himself', the antecedent c-commands the reflexive since the first S over 'John' is also over 'himself'. 'Himself', however, does not c-command 'John' because the first G category over 'himself' is VP, and 'John' occurs outside the VP. These relations can be seen by examining the grammatical structure in (9.25):

(9.25)

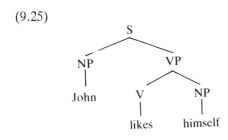

We can now eliminate the linear condition on reflexives in (9.24) by referring to c-command. We can say that a reflexive cannot c-command its antecedent. Further, we can make the nominal condition of reference more explicit by using c-command. (9.24c) can be stated simply as 'a pronoun cannot c-command its antecedent'. This can be seen by comparing sentences 7 and 8 in (9.23). In sentence 7, the pronoun c-commands the antecedent and is therefore ungrammatical. In sentence 8, however, the pronoun does not c-command the antecedent 'Bill', because the S immediately over the pronoun is the one for the clause 'When he left', and 'Bill' is not inside of that clause. Hence, the coreference is allowed.

Many theoretical accounts of pronominal reference have attempted to eliminate the need to refer to the linear order of constituents and use c-command exclusively. The most famous of these is that of Chomsky (1981) where the three kinds of conditions in (9.24) are stated in formal terms using solely c-command. They are referred to as 'binding conditions' and labeled A–C respectively. (For example, a reference to 'condition A' in the theoretical literature refers to the conditions on English reflexives. Condition B refers to the condition on pronouns, and condition C is that on nominals.) The term 'binding' simply refers to the situation where one constituent is c-commanded by another. A reflexive, for example, is 'bound' by its antecedent, because it is c-commanded by it. While this is a dominant trend, other attempts exist where linear order is retained in the explanation of reference (e.g. O'Grady 1986).

A second issue in the theoretical explanation of pronominal reference is the *generality* of the conditions on coreference. The appeal of a notion like c-command is that it is a simple account of how reference is handled. We can propose that Universal Grammar is such that all conditions on reference are handled by c-command. The child then needs only to determine the appropriate c-command conditions for its language. (Presumably the range of possible languages is also restricted, as we will discuss further below.) Chomsky's binding conditions are stated in such a way that a simple statement about c-command relations applies to a wide range of constructions. Take the three kinds of constructions given in (9.23) under nominal conditions on reference (these are actually just a subset of the possible constructions which are involved): all three are handled by condition C of the binding conditions which states roughly that a pronoun cannot c-command its antecedent. Carden (1986), however, has argued against a general account of these constructions, using a range of linguistic and psycholinguistic arguments. In particular, he has focussed on blocked forwards pronominalization, where, under closer examination, the c-command account has problems.

The topic of pronominal reference is of particular interest for language acquisition because it provides a testing ground for a number of the major issues in the field. This point was briefly discussed earlier in Chapter 4. One general issue is the predictions that particular theories make about *acquisition data*. It turns out that data from pronominal acquisition have been interpreted as support for each of the general theories we have treated. Related to this point is the extent to which data from pronominal acquisition can be used to support one theory over another. Another issue is the *learnability* of pronominal reference. There are important questions that arise concerning what constitutes positive evidence for its acquisition, and what the child needs as part of Universal Grammar for it to be acquired. Each of these issues will be briefly reviewed here.

Data on the acquisition of pronominal reference   Studies on pronominal reference have been conducted primarily during the 1980s (see under 'Further reading' at the end of this chapter). There was, however, a much earlier study by Carol Chomsky (1969) which provided some preliminary data and interpretations. I will begin with that study and then turn to the more recent work.

Carol Chomsky (1969)   This study is a classic in the field for several reasons. At the time of its appearance, there was a general impression that language acquisition was complete by age 4 or 5 years. Chomsky demonstrated that several of the more complex aspects of English syntax may not be acquired completely until the primary school years. The study was also important for isolating the areas which may be acquired later. She conducted studies on children's ability to process complex sentences with the verbs 'easy to see', 'promise', 'ask', and 'tell'. She also proposed stages that children appear to go through in acquiring such constructions.

The last study reported by Chomsky was one on pronominalization. It looked at the ability of 40 children between 5 and 10 years of age to process three specific constructions, exemplified here in (9.26). Chomsky simply refers to these as 'types', and we have provided the labels for them, based on terminology used in Ingram & Shaw (1981).

(9.26) type 1   *Blocked backwards pronominalization*
              He found out that Mickey won the race
      type 2: *Backwards pronominalization*
              Before he went out, Pluto took a nap
      type 3: *Forwards pronominalization*
              Pluto thinks he knows everything

Each child took a 15-item comprehension test, with five sentences for each of the three types. First the child was presented with two dolls, Mickey and Pluto. Then the child was read the test sentence followed with a question about its interpretation, e.g. 'Pluto thinks that he knows everything. Pluto thinks that *who* knows everything?' The child then would answer with the name of one of the dolls. Each response was then recorded as either coreferential or non-coreferential.

Since the responses on types 2 and 3 could be either coreferential or non-coreferential, Chomsky only considered the scores on type 1, i.e. blocked backwards pronominalization. She considered this construction to be acquired when all five test sentences were answered correctly, i.e. as being non-coreferential. Of the 40 subjects, 31 (or 78 percent) showed acquisition of type 1. Further, with just three exceptions, it was at age 5–6 years that children began to meet her criterion for acquisition. She noted that 36 subjects also showed at least some coreferential responses on type 2. From these results she concluded (p. 109): 'the principles of pronominalization appear to be acquired by the majority of children at about the same age'. Importantly, her interpretation of the results is a maturational one. She proposes that the principle (or principles) which children use for pronominal reference matures around age 5 or 6, and its emergence is independent of 'linguistic elaboration in the environment, intelligence, and rate of general cognitive development' (p. 110). This principle, using N. Chomsky's more recent proposals, would be condition C of the binding conditions.

Chomsky has little to say about the children's performance before the maturation of the appropriate grammatical principle. She does, however, mention four subjects who got type 1 correct and never responded with coreferential responses on Type 2 – backwards pronominalization. The pattern of these subjects could result from a simple rule of linear order rather than one of c-command. Chomsky, in fact, leans in this direction by saying that these subjects 'seem to be operating with the simple principle that the basic function of a pronoun is to refer to what precedes, without further refinements' (p. 109). This opens the possibility that the structural principle needed for backwards pronominalization is preceded in acquisition by a simpler rule based on the order of appearance of the pronoun and its antecedent.

Chomsky's study was one which was clearly ahead of its time. The development since then of linguistic theory on pronominal reference makes it possible to restate her findings in more current terminology. Her maturational explanation implies that c-command is a principle which matures at a point around age 5 or 6. Before then, without that principle, children rely on a rule which uses only the linear relation of the pronoun and the antecedent. The result of this situation is a marked discontinuity in the acquisition of pronominal reference.

More recent research has attempted to expand the range of constructions studied (Ingram & Shaw 1981; Solan 1983, 1987; Crain & McKee 1985), as well as to examine other languages (O'Grady, Suzuki-Wei & Cho 1986). This research has also included an extension of the topic to reflexive constructions (Wexler & Chen 1985).

One line of this research has been from a nativist perspective. The primary support for the maturational explanation of C. Chomsky has come from the research by Wexler & Chen (1985). They have found that the proposed condition B, i.e. the pronominal condition in (9.24b), does not appear to be consistently acquired until around age 6. They imply that the principle matures around that time. Much of the other work, however, has been in a direction away from a maturational explanation. Crain & McKee (1985), for example, have adjusted the task conditions used and have been able to get correct responses from children as young as 3 years of age. Their research is in the same spirit as that reported earlier on relative clauses by Hamburger & Crain (1982). They hope to prove, by showing correct performance by young children, that the child's grammar is essentially adult-like.

A somewhat paradoxical study from the same perspective is that of Solan (1983). Solan studied a range of constructions with pronominal reference in four experiments on 36 children between 5;2 and 8;5. He found that the children did well on cases of backwards pronominalization and concludes a version of the strong inclusion hypothesis which is reproduced here:

The restrictive model
Children will have little difficulty using notions such as c-command, d-command, precedence and clausematedness. Once they have learned that backward anaphora is possible at all, they will quickly hypothesize restrictions based on the correct definitions.

(Solan 1983: 92)

Solan contrasts this model with one which he calls the 'developmental model'. We find this paradoxical in that Solan's results seem very much interpretable within the constructionist perspective discussed in this text. First, he acknowledges an early stage in the acquisition of pronominal reference when children rely solely on linear order. Second, the use of linear order (or precedence) does not drop out when structural properties such as c-command appear, but remains as part of the rule. He thus adapts the binding conditions of the adult grammar to include earlier properties used by the child. This is very much in keeping with the Constructionist Assumption of Chapter 4. Lastly, the subjects are relatively old, and at an age when results in Carol Chomsky (1969) and Ingram & Shaw (1981) show backwards pronominalization is acquired. Their use of a structural rule at that point of acquisition is accepted in research from a developmental perspective.

More explicit claims for a developmental or constructionist model of the acquisition of pronominal reference can be found in Ingram & Shaw (1981) and in work by O'Grady and his students (Taylor-Browne 1983; O'Grady 1986; O'Grady, Suzuki-Wei & Cho 1986). Ingram & Shaw (1981) examined both backwards pronominalization and blocked forwards pronominalization in 100 children between 3;0 and 8;0. O'Grady, Suzuki-Wei & Cho (1986) looked at pronominal reference in separate studies on Korean and Japanese. These studies, as well as the review in Carden (1986), generally propose four descriptive stages in the acquisition of pronominal reference. They are summarized below, adapted from Ingram & Shaw (1981; see also O'Grady 1986: 146–7):

Four stages in the acquisition of pronominal reference
stage 1: *Use of coreference*: a pronoun may refer to an NP in a clause which may either precede or follow it;
stage 2: *Use of linear order*: a pronoun may only refer to a preceding NP;
stage 3: *Use of dominance*: a pronoun may refer to a following NP if the appropriate structural conditions exist, i.e. children acquire backwards pronominalization;
stage 4: *Use of dominance*: a pronoun cannot refer to a preceding NP under certain structural conditions, i.e. blocked forwards pronominalization is acquired.

As in Solan's work, these studies show children moving from the exclusive use of linear order to a system which takes into account the structural properties of the sentence. Ingram & Shaw do not express a position on the nature of the latter properties while Solan and O'Grady both do. The fact that backwards pronominalization and blocked forwards pronominalization are acquired at separate times has to be taken as evidence against the generality and nature of condition C of Chomsky's binding conditions.

Learnability   Learnability has to do with how the child is able to determine the conditions of pronominal reference from the sentences which it hears.

One issue is what constitutes positive evidence for pronominal reference. Coreference is clearly an example of positive evidence, telling the child that coreference is possible. What, however, about non-coreference? Since many cases of coreference are optional, the child could assume that an instance of non-coreference is just an optional application of a rule which allows coreference. This can be circumvented by allowing indirect negative evidence, or by arguing that non-coreference is itself a form of positive evidence.

Another issue is how the child formulates the rules underlying pronominal reference. The potential problem here has to do with the possibility that the child will overgeneralize a pattern and have no way to learn that the rule is incorrect. For example, suppose that children do have a stage such as Stage 1 described above, where the rule is simply that a pronoun can refer to any pronoun. How does the child narrow this rule down to the one in stage 2 where the pronoun can only refer to a preceding noun? Numerous other such problems could potentially arise if children generalize patterns of coreference. These problems are also compounded when we consider the variability in pronominal reference across languages.

One approach to this problem is to argue that children are quite conservative in the ways that they formulate rules for complex grammatical processes like pronominal reference. This perspective is argued for in O'Grady (1986), among others. The basic argument is that children acquire the rule on a construction by construction basis, and do not overgeneralize as they seem to do in morphology and semantics. It is somewhat ironic that such piecemeal acquisition has normally been associated with Child Language theories rather than those of Language Acquisition.

The problem with cross-linguistic acquisition has been addressed in Wexler & Manzini (1987). Wexler & Manzini have discussed the possibility that languages differ from each other on some grammatical construction in such a way that the contexts of application in one language are always a subset of those in another. For example, I have already mentioned that Japanese differs from English by restricting reflexive antecedents to subjects. The contexts for antecedents in Japanese are therefore a subset of those for English. I also mentioned that Japanese allows long distance reflexives whereas English does not. In this case, then, the English contexts are a subset of the Japanese ones.

Wexler & Manzini, like Chomsky (1981), accept the parameter-setting model of language acquisition. On any particular parameter of grammar, Universal Grammar will allow a restricted range of possibilities. The child is born with knowledge about these, and a principle of acquisition which Wexler & Manzini refer to as the *subset principle*. This principle is summarized as:

Subset principle: for any parameter of grammar, assume initially in acquisition that the unmarked case is that which has the most restricted range of application.

We can see how this principle operates by looking at the English and Japanese differences on reflexives. Since the subject condition of Japanese is more restricted than the one for English, it will be the unmarked case. Conversely, the English clausemate restriction is more limited than the long distance reflexives in Japanese and is thus the unmarked case. The child is therefore born with the following two expectations about reflexives: (i) the antecedent is restricted to subjects, and (ii) the antecedent must be in the same clause as the reflexive (the clausemate condition). The sentences in any language which have a wider range of application will constitute positive evidence. For example, the English child will know that English does not have a subject condition when it hears antecedents for reflexives which are not subjects. So too, a Japanese child will realize that Japanese does not have a clausemate restriction when it hears sentences with long distance reflexives.

The subset principle is obviously a very powerful claim about how the diverse patterns of language are acquired. An important point is that it is also potentially testable as long as one does not take the maturational view of acquisition, that is, we can test children in the relevant linguistic contexts to see if the subset principle is at work.

9.5 Cross-linguistic morphological acquisition

Thus far our coverage of morphological acquisition has focussed on English. As stated at the onset, however, languages differ greatly from one another in their morphological structure. Further, since English has a relatively limited morphology, it is not the best choice for the study of morphological development – the concentration of studies on English is more the result of demographic reasons than theoretical ones.

There are, in fact, a large number of studies on morphological acquisition in languages other than English. A recent two-volume work edited by Slobin (1986), for example, is devoted to the general issue of cross-linguistic development. There is not, however, any in-depth review and assessment of this wide range of data, although some selective comparisons have been made (e.g. Slobin 1982). The reports are often primarily descriptive in nature, and often not easily comparable to other studies as a result of various methodological differences. Much of these data, therefore, have gone largely unnoticed.

Here it is useful to take a brief look at just one aspect of these data, on the acquisition of languages with greater morphological complexity than English. As we have seen earlier, English children tend to acquire morphological endings after they have established some basic grammatical relations. We have also seen this pattern used to support the semantic bootstrapping view of acquisition. The question then naturally arises whether or not children acquiring more morphologically complex languages will nonetheless show the same general sequence. This question may be addressed by providing brief reports of studies on five diverse languages: Dutch, Estonian, Greenlandic Eskimo, Hindi, and Quiché.

Dutch As a language closely related to English, Dutch is not as rich in bound morphology as the other languages we will consider. (It does, however, have a rich system of diminutive suffixes, whose acquisition is discussed in Snow, Smith & Hoefnagel-Hohle 1980.) In fact, since it is close to English, one would expect that the pattern of its acquisition should be similar to the English data. A study by Arlman-Rupp, van Niekerk de Haan & van de Sandt-Koenderman (1976) (henceforth ANS), however, has concluded that such is not the case.

ANS examined four children longitudinally between 2;0 and 2;3. The data from each child consisted of approximately four-and-a-half hours of spontaneous language collected in five sessions at six-week intervals. The children's sentences were then classified into the ten semantic relations for Stage I speech proposed by Brown (1973). Recall that this was done at a time when Brown's semantic taxonomy was having a significant impact on the field.

ANS found that the semantic classification accounted overall for less than half of the children's sentences. The actual percentages were 48, 49, 50, and 36. Many of the unclassified utterances contained what ANS referred to as 'modal' elements. They listed five of these, reproduced here in (9.27):

(9.27) a. adverbs of negation and affirmation, e.g. 'niet' (not), 'nee' (no), 'ja' (yes);
    b. quasi-temporal adverbs, e.g. 'nou' (now);
    c. other adverbs, e.g. 'dan' (then), 'maar' (just);
    d. the interjection 'hoor' (hear, listen);
    e. modal auxiliaries, e.g. 'kan' (can), 'wil' (will).

They also say (p. 273): 'Other non-terms such as copulas, articles and prepositions contribute yet more surplus to these utterances.' In other words, it was not apparent that the acquisition of a small basic set of semantic relations was the primary motivation behind the acquisition of the first sentences in Dutch.

Of importance in interpreting this result is the difference in basic sentence structures between English and Dutch. Like German, Dutch uses the surface word order of Subject-Aux-Object-Verb. One possibility is that the position of the Aux between the subject and object and away from the main verb may draw the child's attention to it more than in English. ANS's own explanation is that the modal elements receive more frequent use in Dutch and so are more prominent in the language. They state (p. 274): 'The strikingly early, frequent and appropriate use of modal elements by children learning Dutch is very likely a reflection of the fact that modality is much more frequently expressed in modal adverbs and other modal elements by adult speakers of Dutch than in other languages studied.'

There are two features of these results which are of particular importance: (i) they suggest some basic cross-linguistic differences in acquisition; (ii) they indicate that type frequency may play an important role in syntactic acquisition. (Note that we have already discussed the role of type frequency in phonological acquisition.)

Estonian   A Finno-Ugric language, Estonian is characterized by a rich system of case suffixes on nouns, several verb inflections, and postpositions instead of prepositions. It is also an *agglutinative* language, i.e. 'words are typically composed of a sequence of morphs with each morph representing one morpheme' (Lyons 1968: 188). Given the findings on morphological development in English, one would expect that this complex system would be difficult to acquire. Some preliminary data reported in Lipp (1977), however, suggests that this may not be the case.

Lipp collected spontaneous language samples from three Estonian children, Avo, Karen, and Erik, ranging from 2;6 to 3;0 at the onset of the study. They were observed four times over an eight-week period. For comparative purposes, 250 utterances were selected from each sample for subsequent analysis. The MLUs for each of the three children for the first and last sessions were 1.87–2.91 (Avo), 2.75–2.68 (Karen), and 2.62–3.36 (Erik). Using Brown's stages, Avo went from Stage I to III, Karen was at Stage III throughout the study, and Erik went from Stage III to IV. A range of grammatical morphemes was analyzed for each session, using frequency and percentages of obligatory occurrence. A morpheme was considered as acquired when it occurred at least four times in a session and was used correctly in 90 percent of its obligatory contexts.

The first general finding was that 20 of the morphemes studied reached the criterion of acquisition during the period of observations. This is a much higher figure than that obtained by Brown for English. Karen, for example, acquired ten morphemes while at MLU stage III. Another finding concerned the order of acquisition of the morphemes. Lipp divided them into an early and a late group. She found that the early group shared several similarities with the early morphemes acquired in English. One of the exceptions was the Estonian copula in the 3rd person singular form. This form was acquired much earlier than its English counterpart. In comparing the late morphemes with the English data, however, Lipp found very little overlap. The major characteristics of the late Estonian morphemes were: (i) they consisted of combinations of several morphemes of agreement; and (ii) 'combined with fewer nouns and verb stems, and generally occurred less frequently in the data' (p. 318). Lipp also found several differences in the order of acquisition for Estonian and Latvian, using the Latvian data in Rūķe-Draviņa (1973).

Greenlandic Eskimo   The North American languages constitute a rich and diverse range of languages which have been studied in some detail. Due in part to the fact that many of them are, or are on the verge of, becoming extinct, their acquisition has not often been studied in detail. For example, a recent attempt by Pye to study two native languages of British Columbia, Thompson and Chilcotin, did not turn up a single subject acquiring either as the first and only language (see Pye 1987). There are, however, a few of these languages which are still being acquired as first languages and can be studied if the investigator can overcome the geographic and political problems which may be involved.

One such study is Fortescue (1984/85) on the acquisition of Greenlandic Eskimo, or henceforth Eskimo. Eskimo constitutes a range of mutually intelligible dialects that cross a vast geographical area in the north-most regions of North America. (In recent years it is referred to as Inuit, the preferred name of its native speakers). The language has been known for years to be a *polysynthetic language*, that is, one which is very rich in its morphological structure. Fortescue comments (pp. 101–2):

> ... the typical word form consists of a stem followed by from zero to at least eight derivational affixes then an obligatory inflexional ending (followed in turn by optional clitics), all bound together by complex morphophonemic patterns of morpheme attachment and falling under one potential intonational tone unit.

It is also *agglutinative*, in that there tends to be a single meaning attached to each of the many morphemes. This is distinct from languages like Polish where several grammatical meanings may be attached to a morph.

Fortescue examined a half-hour language sample from a 2-year-old boy, Aqissiaq, acquiring Greenlandic Eskimo as a first language. He found that Aqissiaq had already acquired a wide range of the numerous affixes of the language. He states that the sample revealed 24 derivational affixes, 40 grammatical inflections (25 verbal and 15 nominal), and three enclitics. Most importantly, he states that they were productive. By this he means,

'All of these occur attached to more than one stem or on stems elsewhere appearing with other productive affixes or zero following them' (p. 103). He is cautious in this interpretation and recognizes that some holistic learning may also be taking place. Also, he acknowledges the limitation of the sample size used. Overall, however, his data are very suggestive that grammatical morphemes are used from the earliest stages of the acquisition of Eskimo. Furthermore, they are supported by other data reported on synthetic languages, e.g. Solberg (1978) on Quechua, Pye (1983a) on Quiché.

Hindi   Varma (1979) reports on the spontaneous language of his daughter Chopti, between the ages of 1;4 and 1;10. The child's MLU was 1.05 at the beginning of the observations and 3.43 at the end. This particular article focusses on the child's Stage I speech (in the sense of Brown's stages). This period lasted approximately 13 weeks, with the MLU in the last session at 1.88.

Varma states (p. 167): 'One of the most interesting aspects is the rapid development of verbal endings in Chopti's speech.' During Stage I, the child showed evidence of using the imperative, present progressive, past, and future suffixes. Also, the copula appeared during this period and 'is well established and used correctly by the end of Stage I' (p. 168). One example shows the copula being used along with the present progressive. With nouns, Chopti uses some, but by no means all, of the possible postpositions of Hindi. The earliest one acquired was the form 'ka' which marks possessives. Of particular interest is the observation that Chopti did not use noun combinations of the kinds reported for English children to express semantic relations.

Varma's general conclusion is that Chopti is acquiring Hindi by using single inflected lexical categories rather than combinations of lexical categories. That is, she is more concerned with acquiring function words than semantic relations. The following summarizes his findings (p. 170): 'it is clear that Chopti's MLU in Stage I increases generally as functors are added, and not by concatenating relations as one would expect from previous work on this stage'.

Quiché   I have already discussed the research by Pye on Quiché in Chapter 5 in relation to linguistic input, and in Chapter 6 in relation to phonological acquisition. Here the patterns of its early grammatical acquisition will be considered.

Pye (1983a) reports on the first morpheme combinations of four Quiché children between 2;0 and 3;0. Naturalistic samples were collected for an hour every two weeks for approximately a nine-month period. Though a little older than comparable English children, they were at the onset of multi-morphemic utterances at the beginning of the study. Recall from our earlier discussion that Quiché mothers are not as verbal with their infants as English ones, leading to a later onset of language (see Pye 1986).

Like Greenlandic Eskimo, Quiché is polysynthetic in that the verb takes several prefixes and suffixes. The prefixes indicate person and aspect, while the suffixes mark transitivity and termination. The termination affixes constitute a complex set of facts that require some explanation. The choice of particular termination morphemes is influenced by several factors including the sentence's aspect, root morpheme, and transitivity marker. There are two phonological facts of importance about the termination markers. One is that they do not always have their own syllable but result in resyllabification of the verb. For example, the sentence 'you see it' has the following morphemic structure: k-∅-aw-il-oh (where 'il' is the verb 'see' and 'oh' is the termination suffix), but it has the following syllabic structure: ka-wi-loh'. That is, the syllable which has the termination suffix begins with the final consonant of the verbal root. A second feature is that the stress tends to fall onto the final syllable. In the above example it is on the syllable 'loh'.

Pye discusses Quiché as a good test case of semantic versus distributional theories of acquisition, although he doesn't use these particular terms. He states (p. 591) '... there are two possible parts of the verb with which Quiché children might begin: the semantically salient but perceptually weak verb root, and the perceptually salient but semantically complex verb suffixes'. His analysis indicates that the children consistently chose perceptual saliency over semantic complexity. From their first appearance, the verbal suffixes were used correctly and apparently productively (we say 'apparently' because no strict productivity measure was applied). He makes the following comment about the children's use of the verbal suffixes (p. 593):

> There is also no indication that the children had any trouble distinguishing transitive from intransitive endings. Finally, the vowel in the transitivizing suffix is lexically determined – it follows no regular pattern. The children, however, seldom got the vowel wrong in the utterances. All this indicates that the children had indeed learned to use the status markers freely and appropriately at an early stage in their linguistic development.

This pattern of acquisition is supported by similar results reported for Dakota in Nokony (1978).

9.6 The explanation of morphological acquisition

Much of the theoretical discussion on morphological acquisition has been done by identifying the factors which seem to be at work. A theory of such acquisition, however, will require a more detailed model of how the child identifies and processes grammatical morphemes. There have been two major attempts to provide such a model: MacWhinney (1978) and Pinker (1984).

MacWhinney (1978)   This monograph attempts to develop a psychologically real model of morphological acquisition. We have already seen in Chapter 7 MacWhinney's six strategies of early word combinations (section 7.4.2). The 1978 monograph is an earlier attempt to focus on morphological development, and refers to three of the six strategies: rote, analogy, and combination.

MacWhinney refers to his approach as the *dialectic model*. It consists of three major aspects: application, correction, and acquisition, which are linked in a cyclic fashion, as in (9.28):

(9.28)

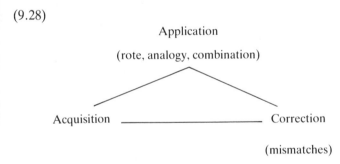

These three aspects will operate in the child's perception of language as well as his production.

Application refers to the child's initial step in the process of using and/or acquiring grammatical morphemes. In reception, the goal is to understand the semantic/syntactic meaning of morphemes, while in production it is to retrieve and use them. In either modality, the child uses the three strategies of rote, analogy, and combination in that order. For example, a word like 'cats' may initially be stored as a holistic unit. Next, it will be separated into two parts, 'cat' and 's', but the use of 's' will be restricted by analogy to a few similar words, e.g. 'bat' and 'mat'. Later still, combination will result through the use of a general rule.

A crucial feature of following a child's application is how he proceeds from one strategy to another. These changes are apparently the result of the child being able to segment morphemes and place them into one of three categories: (1) words, (2) affixes, and (3) roots. At an early stage, for example, a word like 'cats' may be placed in the word category with no further segmentation. Later, 'cat' will be put in the root category and 's' in the affix category. During acquisition, specific kinds of potential errors may be made, for example, having words in different categories: the child could have 'cats' as a whole item as a word (category 1), and also as a root 'cat' (category 2). This could result in the error of taking 'cats' from 1 and adding the plural from 2, creating 'cats + s'. To avoid this, MacWhinney proposes that the child has a process of *affix checking* which restricts the child from creating a meaning for a new category when that meaning already exists in another category. Notice that this will restrict the child from producing 'feets' if 'feet' already exists as a word.

As the child identifies roots and affixes, he will also need to deal with the existence of words with different roots, e.g. 'wife', 'wives', and also the allomorphs of grammatical morphemes, e.g. 'cats' [s] vs. 'dogs' [z]. The major problem here is one which arises in linguistic theory in general – what is the nature of the child's morphological system? There are some rules of combination which are phonetically motivated, such as the English plural, and others which are not. An example of the latter would be gender in languages such as French and German where the child needs to select the correct form of some grammatical class to go with the gender of the noun being used. MacWhinney does not provide a linguistic theory as a framework, but falls back on the three strategies mentioned above – that is, the child progressively works toward the general rules of the language being acquired, whatever those rules may be.

The application phase of MacWhinney's model only provides the child with the ability to segment words into classes. This is not sufficient, however, to acquire rules or avoid potential errors. For example, the child still can select words like 'foot' and add 's' to get 'foots', a well-documented kind of error. Application does not have the necessary mechanisms for complete acquisition and correction. For that to occur, the next two phases must operate.

The first step is referred to as *correction*. This step occurs when some mismatch takes place in the perception or production of a morphological combination. This state is somewhat like Piaget's idea of disequilibrium, in the sense that the child's system may not conform to that of the input. MacWhinney's notion of mismatch, however, is broader because it also refers to mismatches within the child's system itself. Such mismatches draw the child's attention to the fact that there is a potential error in his system. This can be seen by looking at the kinds of mismatches which can occur.

MacWhinney discusses four types of mismatches (or what he calls disequilibrated pairs), listed below:

> *Type 1: Self corrections.* The child overgeneralizes a rule when the correct rule is available within the system, e.g. child says 'wifes', and then 'wives';
>
> *Type 2: Semantic mismatches in production.* The child expresses an incomplete meaning, e.g. saying 'dog' to mean 'dogs';
>
> *Type 3: Semantic mismatches in reception.* The child hears something said which does not communicate the complete meaning intended, e.g. hearing 'dogs' and only recognizing 'dog', yet seeing two dogs in the context;
>
> *Type 4: Auto-instruction.* A productive combination becomes a role item, and elicits adults' corrections, e.g. saying 'foots' and being corrected to say 'feet'.

MacWhinney is not completely clear how these kinds of mismatches lead to correct acquisition, nor what mechanisms underlie each. Type 1 assumes some kind of self-monitoring of production in relation to the current competence. This mechanism, however, could have negative effects if the child's competence is incorrect for it would wrongly mark an incorrect production as correct. Type 4 brings direct positive evidence into the process, although MacWhinney acknowledges that the child will resist such corrections.

The real key to the child's ability to correct itself lies in types 2 and 3. These direct the child to seek out meanings for the speech it hears and uses. Unfortunately, it is not clear how this takes place. The problem with type 2 is delimiting how the child knows that what it wants to express exists within the language being acquired. Type 3 is clearer to follow. It implies a mechanism which leads the child to identify repeated stretches of speech and to seek a meaning for them. No information is given, however, on how this segmentation and identification takes place.

If the child uses a form and no mismatch results, then the form can undergo *acquisition*. Acquisition here is used in a way roughly similar to the notion of 'strengthening' that was discussed in Chapter 7 for syntax. As acquisition of any form proceeds, the three strategies of rote, analogy, and combination will compete for the way the form will be stored. In particular, rote will constantly attempt to override analogy and combination.

MacWhinney lays out five potential cycles that forms can follow in being applied, corrected and acquired, summarized below:

> Cycle 1: *Amalgams.* The child looks for forms to express the meanings of its semantic system. When a form is heard which

appears to express that meaning, the child acquires it as an unanalyzed whole.

Cycle 2: *Allomorphs*. The child identifies the meaning of an affix and finds that there is another affix with the same meaning. They are flagged as being allomorphs. As they are used, correct usages strengthen the rule being acquired, and mismatches weaken it.

Cycle 3: *Modification productions*. The child identifies that a mismatch has occurred in his use of some allomorph. He compares his form with the correct one and reformulates the rule used to create it.

Cycle 4: *Selection productions*. The child determines that a particular mismatch resulted because the child generalized a minor pattern. The rule is then flagged as a minor rule.

Cycle 5: *Implicational table*. When general or minor rules are not adequate to capture the morphological patterns in the language, the child resorts to lexical principles, that is, he memorizes that certain morphemes are used with certain classes. This can be captured through the use of an implicational table.

Cycle 1 occurs in response to type 2 and 3 mismatches. For example, the child may wish to express 'dogs', but may only have 'dog'. If he should hear 'dogs', it gets identified as a single form which expresses the plural of 'dog' and is stored as such. Cycle 2 involves the identification of allomorphs. The next two cycles concern how the child forms a rule to use these allomorphs. To understand these, we need to distinguish between general and minor rules. A general rule is one which will apply to most forms which have the required phonological shape. For example, the use of plural [s] after certain voiceless consonants is a general rule. A minor rule is one which only applies for a small class of words in the language. For example, the change of 'wife' [waif] to 'wive' [waiv] in the plural is a minor rule in that words with final 'f' will not all normally change in this fashion. Cycles 3 and 4 allow the child to determine through the examination of mismatches whether a rule is general or minor.

The last cycle concerns what happens for those cases where the morphological selection is predominantly lexical. MacWhinney proposes that the child sets up implicational tables of the relevant morphemes. He exemplifies this process with the articles in German. Example (9.29) gives an adaptation of MacWhinney's implicational table for German singular definite articles, based on his Table 2 (p. 14).

(9.29) *Roots*	*Class*	*Nominative*	*Dative*	*Accusative*
Mann, etc.	1	'der'	'dem'	'den'
Frau, etc.	2	'die'	'der'	'die'
Pferd, etc.	3	'das'	'dem'	'das'

MacWhinney concludes his general discussion of his model with a section on the major determinants of the child's order of acquisition. His claims in this regard are very straightforward: the sequence of acquisition of the first amalgams 'will be determined largely by the functional importance . . . of the amalgams within which the affixes are embedded . . . as well as the intonational packaging of these units' (p. 16). Their subsequent productive acquisition is determined primarily by their functional importance. He concludes (p. 17): 'Nowhere in the model is there a role for either semantic or grammatical complexity per se. Rather, the emphasis is on functionality as a determinant of morpheme acquisition.' The rest of his monograph is a demonstration of the application of his model to data from Hungarian and Finnish.

Despite a lack of specifics at several points, MacWhinney deals with the major issues required for a model of morphological acquisition. There are three particular aspects needing further development. First, he is not working from any particular theory of the adult system: from our earlier discussion of his competition model, it was clear that he is more disposed to develop processing models than to test current linguistic theories. Another aspect is what we will call the 'segmentation' problem: he points out that the child needs to identify the morphemes, but says relatively little about how that occurs. Lastly, there is the 'identification' problem: how exactly does the child determine the appropriate grammatical/semantic meaning which underlies the specific morpheme being acquired?

Pinker (1984)   In Chapter 7 Pinker's views on early syntactic development were discussed. In its general orientation, his approach to morphological development shares the same features. He outlines a series of specific steps that the child follows in reaching the adult system. These steps allow the child to formulate some incorrect rules, but limit the range of incorrect rules which are possible. This is done in detail, presenting arguments and examples along the way.

Pinker deals with each of the three areas just mentioned for MacWhinney's model. As we noted earlier, he works from a particular theory of grammar, Lexical Functional Grammar. In doing so, he also develops the theory to make it more compatible with the facts of language acquisition. He also addresses the segmentation problem, although he does not offer a detailed account. He postpones this 'for more precise notions to be taken from a theory of phonology' (p. 188). The identification problem, however, occupies a central place in Pinker's treatment of morphological acquisition, and demonstrates the manner in which he approaches the topic.

Pinker outlines three specific proposals for handling the identification problem, eventually rejecting the first two for the third. The process, in fact, appears to be a historical account of Pinker's own stages of thought on the subject.

The first proposal is called *exhaustive hypothesization* and suggests that the child first attaches a universal set of possible grammatical meanings to a newly identified morpheme. The child then compares each possible meaning with the context and rejects those meanings which are not compatible. By this process of elimination, the child eventually narrows down the meaning to the correct set. Pinker correctly points out three serious problems for this proposal. First, it requires an enormous amount of calculation: assuming the list of possible meanings can be quite long, the child would be faced with an extensive range of possible meanings to be checked out. Second, the proposal makes the false prediction that morphemes with several grammatical meanings (syncretic ones) will be acquired before ones with just one or two, since there would be fewer to be eliminated. Facts from acquisition, however, indicate that the opposite is the case. Third, the proposal makes false predictions about overgeneralizations, since it predicts that morphemes should be first undergeneralized. In particular, the child should not overgeneralize a morpheme to a false context if it is initially flagged with a range of appropriate possible meanings. Such kinds of overgeneralizations, however, do occur.

The second proposal is one of *hypothesis sampling*. In this approach, the child does not assign all possible meanings to a morpheme, but rather just one at a time. Further, the list of possible meanings is weighted so that more likely ones are tested first. For example, a language is more likely to have a verbal affix which indicates aspect than one which indicates the definiteness of the object, as is found in Hungarian. Pinker presents seven arguments against the viability of the hypothesis-testing proposals, only a few of which can be examined here. First, it doesn't account for how zero morphemes are acquired. It also 'makes the implausible assumption that the child sooner or later hypothesizes out of thin air every feature equation that languages in the world can use' (p. 173). Pinker feels that the model needs some mechanism that actually draws the child's attention to particularly unusual meanings. Another difficulty is that the proposal does not account for *morphological imperialism* (Slobin 1973), when the child uses one morpheme based on one feature (e.g. nominative case) and then abandons it for another morpheme based on a different feature (e.g. gender). Indeed, the problems that Pinker points out for this proposal are also problems for the earlier extensive hypothesization proposal and are important questions that all accounts of morphological development need to address.

This brings us to Pinker's own account of morphological acquisition. The approach actually is rather similar to that already discussed by MacWhinney. In particular, it builds upon the notion that the child constructs implicational tables of grammatical morphemes. The latter are called 'paradigms' by Pinker, and the idea is developed much more extensively. As in Chapter 7 Pinker's approach will be outlined by assigning a series of 'steps' to the acquisition process, even though he does not quite present it in this fashion. The numbers for his procedures are indicated within parentheses. While Pinker discusses several acquisition procedures, his approach will be simplified here to two major steps.

Step 1: Establish word-specific paradigms (I1, I2). The child begins acquiring grammatical morphemes by acquiring the stem and the affix as a complete unit. This is similar to MacWhinney's first step of acquiring amalgams and assigning them to the class of words. The child at the onset has not segmented the affix from the stem. The difference from MacWhinney is that the child at the onset sets up paradigms for these. Example (9.30) gives one such paradigm for the verb 'walk'.

(9.30) *Progressive*   *Present*   *Past*
      walking   walks   walked

This presumably also can occur for independent morphemes such as the German determiners in (9.29). At first, the paradigms are given a single dimension, but new dimensions can be added as new entries are added (I2). The advantage that this step has over MacWhinney is that it allows the child to begin morphological identification before the affixes are actually determined. It creates a system, therefore, for them to be placed in once they are segmented. A further point about this step concerns the criteria used for establishing paradigms. Pinker allows for the possibility of using both semantic and phonological features.

Step 2: Form general paradigms and word structure templates (I5, I6). In this step the child abstracts away from the individual word paradigms and creates general paradigms in which individual grammatical morphemes are entered. This requires the child to scan the words in the word-specific paradigms and separate out the stems and affixes (roughly MacWhinney's cycle 2). Further, as required by the grammatical model that Pinker is using, a word structure template is set up (I6). Example (9.31) shows this for 'walk'.

(9.31) *Class*   *Progressive* *Present* *Past*
      'walk', etc.   ing   s   ed
      Word structure template: [$_V$ stem + affix]

While these steps appear straightforward enough, there are numerous specific problems which the child will face, including syncretic morphemes, the acquisition of class differences, and paradigm splitting (the latter is the situation where a morpheme will fill more than one place in a paradigm). Pinker addresses all of these and offers procedures for accomplishing them.

Summary. The research on morphological development has resulted in a number of observations on patterns of development. The models by Mac-Whinney and Pinker are the most extensive attempts to date to explain in more detail how these patterns emerge. Together they have identified much of what has to be accounted for. The model needs to be able to segment morphemes, identify grammatical meanings and allomorphs, and group morphemes into their appropriate patterns of arrangement. Both approaches also share the feature of trying to develop a process model of acquisition. A very interesting extension of some of MacWhinney's original ideas can be found in Rumelhart & McClelland (1986), where an account of English verbal endings is given.

9.7 Linguistic input and grammatical acquisition

We last discussed the role of the linguistic environment in Chapter 6, section 6.6, where we presented some information on early conversational development, methodology, and effects on lexical development. Here we turn to the issue of the role of the linguistic environment in the young child's grammatical development.

Throughout this text we have addressed the issue of the interplay of the innate ability of the child and the effects of the environment. Gleitman, Newport & Gleitman (1984) have summed up very nicely where the controversy does and does not occur on this issue. They point out that there is not much disagreement that 'the way caretakers talk, and the circumstances under which they talk, affect learning' (p. 44). The controversy resides in the extent to which the internal state of the child intervenes and influences the issue. In this sense, the positions tend to fall upon some point of a graded view of the influence of the linguistic environment.

We can examine this issue in the context of the three general theories we have considered throughout. The behaviorist wants to demonstrate a direct relation at all points of acquisition, so that the child's behavior can always be traced to adult variables. The nativist positions we have discussed will vary on this point. A maturationist will minimize the influence of the environment: if a principle of grammar has not yet matured, then no amount of linguistic input will lead to its acquisition; if it has matured, then presumably some minimal exposure will be sufficient. The position of strong inclusion proposes that the child's readiness is set very early in acquisition so that only a sufficient range of constructions need to be heard. Lastly, a constructionist perspective falls between the two positions: readiness will be a factor, and thus the child will not acquire a form until the child's system is ready for it, but at the same time, the development of a structure will involve a set of interactions between the child's internal system and the linguistic environment.

A look at the literature on this topic in recent years suggests that most of it has sought to demonstrate environmental effects of some kind. As such, it has had a constructionist and even behaviorist flavor to it. The earlier research was primarily interested in demonstrating that at least English parents adjust or reduce their speech to children. Later, the obvious question arose as to whether or not such adjustments contribute to acquisition or not. It is this latter question which has dominated most recent work.

Two distinct research programs into the effects of the linguistic environment on English grammatical acquisition will be considered here. The first is the research of Lila Gleitman and her colleagues. Gleitman's perspective is primarily maturational in nature, as can be seen in Gleitman (1981). Her position is that the course of acquisition is more determined by the child's internal state than by the language environment but that the latter does play a role in the acquisition of language-specific grammatical morphemes. The other approach is that of Keith Nelson and his colleagues. (References to his work are indicated as K. E. Nelson to distinguish him from Katherine Nelson.) K. E. Nelson takes what I interpret as a more constructionist perspective. He sees acquisition as the interplay between facilitative adult behavior and the child's internal readiness.

Gleitman, Newport & Gleitman (1984)   In the middle 1970s, researches were very actively describing the attributes of the speech which parents direct to their children. This literature often implied that these adjustments were facilitative and even necessary for the child's linguistic development. This research was set back, however, by an influential study reported in Newport, Gleitman & Gleitman (1977; henceforth NGG). NGG compared the speech of children and their parents and found very few instances where the parent's behavior seemed to influence the child's subsequent development. They did suggest, however, that such influences occur with the English auxiliary as it appears in yes/no questions. This led them to a position that the effects of the linguistic environment are only found with the more language-specific morphemes.

The NGG findings resulted in a new caution in drawing causal implications between adult linguistic behavior and language acquisition. Their findings were also aided by the cross-linguistic research which was beginning to appear and which indicated that some cultures did not have adult speech adjustments. (The latter literature was briefly reviewed in Chapter 5 of this volume.) Since then, adult speech adjustment to children has been seen as at most potentially facilitative, but by no means necessary and sufficient. They also directed research toward more detailed work on what might be facilitative and what might not.

The results in NGG were challenged by Furrow, Nelson & Benedict (1979; henceforth FNB). FNB criticized a number of methodological aspects of NGG, and reported their own results which indicated more adult influences than found by NGG. As discussed in Chapter 6, they looked at correlations of the mother's speech at Time 1 (when the children were around 1;6) and Time 2 (when the children were around 2,3), with the children's speech at Time 2 (around 2;3). Importantly, they found that the correlations at Time 2 could not predict the correlations found at Time 1. They conclude from this that the possible correlations will be affected by the child's stage of development. They looked at correlations between several measures of adult language and four measures of child behavior: MLU, number of verbs per utterance, number of noun phrases per utterance, and number of auxiliaries per verb phrase. Some of the significant correlations they found between adult speech at Time 1 and the children's speech at Time 2 are summarized here:

Facilitative aspects
(a) Greater adult use of yes/no questions leads to:
   i. more child use of auxiliaries,
   ii. greater child MLU.
(b) Greater adult use of nouns leads to:
   i. more child use of verbs,
   ii. greater child MLU.
(c) Greater adult use of interjections leads to:
   i. more child verbs per utterance.
Prohibitive aspects
(d) Greater adult use of pronouns leads to:
   i. less child use of verbs,
   ii. shorter child MLU.
(e) Greater adult use of different words leads to:
   i. shorter child MLU,
   ii. fewer verbs and noun phrases per utterance.
(f) Greater adult use of verbs and copulas leads to:
   i. less child use of verbs,
   ii. shorter child MLU.

FNB interpret their results as supporting the position that simpler adult speech aids children in their acquisition. They manage this by offering the following scenario. Simple speech will be characterized by salient aspects of the grammar (such as fronted Auxs as in yes/no questions), simple semantic messages (such as having more nouns than verbs), and pauses which shorten the sentence (interjections). These aspects all proved to lead to more advanced child measures. Complex speech, on the other hand, will have more pronouns, complex vocabulary, verbs, and copulas. Greater use of these led to poorer child performance on the measures used.

The FNB results were a strong challenge to the earlier results in NGG. The latter responded in great detail in Gleitman, Newport & Gleitman (1984). First, they accepted the methodological criticisms of FNB and provided an in-depth discussion of methodology. This was followed by a reanalysis of their original data, as well as the data in FNB. Further, they imposed a much stricter statistical measure of correlation to eliminate what they refer to as 'spurious correlations', i.e. correlations which are found but which seem to make little sense. Their results after this elaborate procedure ended up being quite similar to those in NGG. All of the significant correlations which they found are given below:

For younger children (18 to 21 months)
(a) Greater adult use of declaratives leads to more verbs per utterance.
(b) Greater adult repetition leads to fewer child auxiliaries.
(c) Greater adult use of complex sentences leads to more child auxiliaries.
(d) Adult unintelligible speech leads to more child verbs (interpreted as a spurious correlation).
For older children (24 to 27 months)
(a) Greater adult use of yes/no questions leads to more child verbs and greater MLU.

Gleitman, Newport & Gleitman conclude from their study that there are fewer effects than indicated in FNB once better statistical procedures are used. Also, if such effects exist, they tend to be restricted to the younger group of children – this partially supports the claim of FNB that such effects may differ depending on the language level of the child. They emphasize, however, that their reanalysis provides little support for most of the correlations found in FNB, and thus for the FNB theory concerning the role of the linguistic input. Lastly, they emphasize that the earlier finding about the use of yes/no questions was replicated even with the revised statistical procedure.

The finding about yes/no questions is important because it is at the core of the Gleitman, Newport & Gleitman view of language acquisition. They propose that the child acquires language most easily when the linguistic input provides a range of grammatical constructions. They argue on logical grounds against the FNB view about simple speech. They state (p. 69):

... it is relatively easy to show that the language is learnable if the input includes complex sentences; it is awesomely harder to show learnability if the input is restricted to the simplest sentences. This position should not really come as a surprise.

This point is supported by their findings that they did not get the correlations in their data which are predicted by FNB. The fact that the yes/no questions in adult speech lead to more child auxiliaries is because yes/no questions place auxiliaries in a very prominent place in the sentence. It is because of the prominence of the Aux that the effect occurs.

Gleitman, Newport & Gleitman (as well as NGG) go on from auxiliaries to language in general. Auxiliaries are one member of a general class they refer to as the *closed class*. They do not give a formal definition of these, but say (p. 71) 'Closed-class items, roughly, are the inflections and functors, those items that can occur unstressed in the languages of the world.' It is because of their language-specific, and unstressed nature that these items tend to be acquired later. They propose that adult speech can contribute to the acquisition of these items if it places them in some more prominent position for acquisition. This is the case for English yes/no questions.

The studies by Gleitman *et al.* and by FNB serve to highlight two distinct views on the role of adult speech in the child's acquisition. While FNB want to assign importance to simplified speech, Gleitman *et al.* want to play down its importance, and emphasize instead the importance of hearing a range of constructions. In the latter view, the adult speech can contribute if the constructions used contain closed class items in prominent positions.

Nelson & Baker (1984)　The studies just reviewed, as well as many of the others on this topic, are based on the analysis of spontaneous language. Such data are always difficult to assess, due to problems with sampling and sample sizes. (Gleitman, Newport & Gleitman 1984, for example, criticize FNB for using only 100 utterances per mother and child, while they used an average of 513 per mother and up to 300 per child.) It is possible, however, to examine this question from a more experimental perspective. Such a line of research, in fact, has been pursued in research years in a series of studies by K. E. Nelson and his colleagues.

The theoretical perspective which underlies Nelson's experimental work can best be seen in two review papers, K. E. Nelson (1981) and K. E. Nelson, Denninger, Bonvillian, Kaplan & Baker (1984). (We refer to Nelson here but assume his perspective has been developed with and is shared by his several co-authors.) Nelson refers to this theory as a *rare-event comparison theory* of acquisition (K. E. Nelson 1981). The theory accepts the cross-linguistic research of recent years which indicates that many features of parental speech adjustment are not necessary for children's grammatical development. He emphasizes, however, that such findings, as well as those in NGG, only indicate that 'high quantities' of linguistic input may not be needed. Nelson's view on frequency is that there is not a directly linear relation between adult frequency and acquisition rate (as is claimed in FNB, for example). Rather, Nelson et al. state (1984:49): 'in our view, whether more frequently presented examples in input are more rapidly acquired by the child than less frequent examples in input depends entirely upon *how* those examples are embedded in the fabric of conversation'.

In Nelson's approach, there are two additional factors besides frequency which need to be considered. One is that the child has to be ready to acquire the form under consideration. If the child is linguistically at a point where a particular form can be acquired, the frequency of exposure to it can be quite minimal. The other factor is the way in which the parent presents the form to the child. Nelson has argued that there are two facilitative responses that parents can make. One is what he calls a *simple recast*, a reply by the adult which continues 'reference to the central meanings in the child's preceding utterances' but which departs 'structurally by slight or moderate changes' (p. 37). Such changes are limited to one major component of a child's utterance, e.g. the subject, verb, or object. For example, the child utterance 'broke' can be recast as 'the truck broke'. The other facilitative feature is that the recast be a *continuation* of the discourse. A continuation is an adult response which does not meet the definition of a recast but which continues the topic under discussion. The claim is that constructions are acquired more rapidly when the child hears them in the form of recasts and continuations.

Nelson's theory has been experimentally tested in a series of studies, e.g. K. E. Nelson (1977), K. E. Nelson & Baker (1984), K. E. Nelson et al. (1984). The general procedure is to pretest children on a construction (or constructions) to be sure that it is not yet acquired. Next, there is an experimental period from four to eight weeks when an experimenter meets with the child on a regular basis and recasts the child's speech, using the construction(s) under study. At the same time, there is a control group which receives no such intentional recasting. Finally there is a post-test to see if the construction has been acquired. The results reported have in general supported the theory.

We will present this experimental approach in more detail by focussing on Study 2 in K. E. Nelson & Baker (1984) on the acquisition of passives, relative clauses, and auxiliaries. The subjects were six children (four girls and two boys) between 2;6 and 3;2 with MLUs from 3.07 to 4.17. In the month before the study began, spontaneous language samples were collected from conversations between the children and their mothers. The

Table 9.20 *Number of spontaneous productions for six normal children of passives, relative clauses, and 'may' and 'could', taken from Nelson & Baker (1984: Tables 5 and 6)*

Session	Passives	Relative clauses	'may' and 'could'
1	0	0	1
2	0	0	2
3	1	0	–
4	2	2	2
7	3	0	1
9	1	4	1
11	2	1	7
12	7	3	5
Total	16	10	19

children were then placed into three pairs based on similarities on three measures: MLU, noun and verb complexity, and use of complex forms. Each was randomly assigned to two treatment groups with each member of a pair assigned to a different group. One group (C/E) heard their sentences recast while the other did not (E/E). The E/E group, however, did hear the experimenter recast her own utterances.

The syntactic forms tested were passives, relative clauses, and two auxiliaries, 'may' and 'could'. Although data are not given regarding the pretest samples, it is implied that none of these forms was used at that point. The experimental phase of the study consisted of four weekly sessions for three weeks, or 12 sessions. The first sessions consisted of 15 minutes of recasting and five minutes of observations. The last session was for post-testing. An additional language sample was subsequently collected in each child's home. Proportions of the use of each syntactic form were calculated after each session to ensure that the number of recasts was comparable for both groups.

Table 9.20 presents a summary of the spontaneous use of the syntactic forms tested across a selection of tape-recorded sessions. The results for both groups have been collapsed although there was a tendency for the C/E group to produce more forms than the E/E group. The main effect is that the spontaneous use of these forms increased over the test sessions. For example, none of the children produced a passive sentence until the third session, but 16 were produced by the end. Also, full passives (eight) were nearly as frequent as truncated passives (nine). The results indicate that the use of these recasts by the experimenter can lead to increased spontaneous use in the child.

To support their conclusions, Nelson & Baker also compared their results to the data collected in Horgan (1978), whose study was summarized in section 9.4.1. They calculated the proportion of different types of passives used and compared figures with those in Horgan for the children aged between 2 and 4 years. These results are summarized in (9.32):

(9.32) Type of passive	Horgan	Nelson & Baker
Reversible	47%	63%
Agentive non-reversible	0%	25%

Horgan found that agentive non-reversible passives were not used until age 9. Also, none of the children she studied produced both reversible and non-reversible passives until age 11. The Nelson & Baker subjects had higher percentages of both of these types, and one-half of their subjects produced both reversible and non-reversible passives.

Further reading

English morphological acquisition
This area has generated a massive literature. In particular, the classic study by Berko (1958) has been replicated, with various modifications, literally hundreds of times. It remains a valuable article which is probably required reading in just about everyone's course on child language. Much of the cited literature is the work of Brown and his colleagues. The study by Cazden (1968) presents an important early analysis of the Brown data which was the basis for the subsequent report in Brown (1973). Brown (1973) is an important but very long discussion of the acquisition of 14 English morphemes. A feel for the data and the results may be obtained from reading pp. 249–73.

Aspects of English grammar
While many aspects of English have been studied from an acquisition standpoint, the few areas reviewed in the text have received most attention.

Aux. The acquisition of auxiliaries in questions was first studied in detail by Bellugi in her unpublished doctoral dissertation (1967). Her original observations have led to a range of studies trying to replicate the pattern and explain its causes. An excellent review and theoretical treatment of the topic is Davis (1987).

Reading in this area should begin with looking at Bellugi's original stages of question acquisition. This can be gotten from Bellugi (1971), or Cazden (1970) which is one of the clearest summaries ever written on the topic. The study by Kuczaj & Maratsos (1975) presents an important methodology and lays out the relevant issues at stake. Ingram & Tyack (1979) and Labov &

Labov (1978) provide grouped and single subject data respectively that suggest that some caution is necessary in assuming the generality of the stages proposed by Bellugi. A feel for the theoretical implications of auxiliary acquisition can be gotten from Brown (1968) and from Erreich, Valian & Winzemer (1980).

Passive. The passive is another pattern which has been studied numerous times, initiated in the late 1960s by studies by Turner & Rommetveit (1967), Slobin (1968), Huttenlocher, Eisenberg & Strauss (1968). Other areas such as relative clauses and pronominal reference have only been studied in more recent years as syntactic research has expanded, despite the early research by Carol Chomsky (1969). Pronominal reference especially has received much recent discussion, e.g. Solan (1983), Lust (1986).

The first findings on passives were reported in Turner & Rommetveit (1967) and Slobin (1968). Bever (1970: 303–12) is a frequently cited report of when children begin to use strategies to cope with the passive construction. Horgan (1978) gives a wealth of data on the use of passives in spontaneous speech. The diverse theoretical interpretations on passives can be seen by comparing the discussion in Maratsos *et al.* (1979) with the nativist perspectives in Berwick & Weinberg (1984: 212–22) and Borer & Wexler (1987).

Relative clauses. The first observations on relative clauses were made by Limber (1973). The experimental work by Sheldon (1974) has inspired a number of subsequent studies, such as Tavakolian (1981b). The development viewpoint in Ingram (1975) can be contrasted with the nativist one in Hamburger & Crain (1982).

Pronominal reference. Reading here should begin with Carol Chomsky's original study (1969: 102–11). Conveniently, Carden (1986) provides an excellent review of much of the recent literature, as well as his own interpretation of the results. A recent two-volume work on the topic is Lust (1986). We also recommend looking at the cross-linguistic data presented in O'Grady, Suzuki-Wei & Cho (1986).

Cross-linguistic morphological acquisition
Slobin's bibliography (1972) gives separate indices for cross-linguistic research up to that time. References are given for African, Algonquin, Amerindian, Arabic, Bantu, Bulgarian, Burmese, Chinese, Comanche, Czech, Danish, Dutch, English, Estonian, Finnish, French, Garo, German, Gilyak, Greek, Hebrew, Hopi, Hungarian, Icelandic, Iroquois, Italian, Japanese, Korean, Latvian, Malay, Marathi, Navaho, Norwegian, Pidgin, Polish, Polynesian, Portuguese, Romanian, Russian, Ruthenian, Samoan, Serbian, Slovenian, Spanish, Swedish, Ukrainian, Welsh, Wolof, and Yiddish. His more recent edited work (1986) provides more up to date information on a smaller selection of languages.

Recent projects by Berman (e.g. Berman 1981a, b, 1982) and Weist (e.g. Weist 1983; Weist *et al.* 1984; Weist & Konieczna 1985) provide insightful new information on Hebrew and Polish respectively. Slobin (1982) gives a nice review of his own research comparing English, Italian, Serbo-Croatian, and Turkish. A comparison of English, Hungarian, and Italian can be found in MacWhinney & Bates (1978).

It is insightful to read one or two descriptive papers on the acquisition of a language which is very different from English to see how the pattern of acquisition can vary. A reading of any of the articles reviewed in the text can provide this, as well as numerous others. We feel that Pye (1983a) does this very well, in addition to Slobin (1982) and MacWhinney & Bates (1978), mentioned above. An excellent assessment of the implications of these kinds of data is Bowerman (1986).

The explanation of morphological acquisition
We looked at just two attempts to develop a processing model for the acquisition of morphology: MacWhinney (1978) and Pinker (1984). An overview of MacWhinney's approach is found in pp. 1–20 of his monograph. Pinker's discussion is in his Chapter 5, entitled 'Inflection'. A more recent work which has generated a great deal of interest is that of Rumelhart & McClelland (1986).

Linguistic input
There have been a series of debates in the various attempts to demonstrate causal effects between parental and child speech. The text discussed the one between Furrow, Nelson & Benedict (1979) and Gleitman, Newport & Gleitman (1984). Other reports have appeared which differ from these two in various ways. Barnes *et al.* reports several correlations between adult and child measures, but interpret the effects as reciprocal rather than unidirectional. Scarborough & Wyckoff (1986) reanalyze their data and find virtually no effects, that is, even fewer than Gleitman, Newport & Gleitman.

A less prominent debate occurred after Moerk (1980). Moerk suggested that the effects of parental speech may be more subtle than had been suggested. In particular, he suggested that parents may increase their use of specific forms for just a short period around the time that the child shows evidence of acquiring them. This elicited a critique from Pinker (1981), as well as a response from Moerk (1981).

A helpful review of this literature is that of Hoff-Ginsburg & Shatz (1982). The article by Gleitman, Newport & Gleitman (1984) is not easy reading, but it provides an in depth discussion of the relevant issues. Keith Nelson's views are probably most accessible in Nelson (1981).

10   Concluding remarks

I began this text with the goal of presenting an in-depth introduction to the field of child language acquisition. This was to be done by providing a balance between method, description, and explanation. We would like to conclude by giving a brief assessment of where we now stand in regard to these three aspects.

As should be apparent, the field has evolved tremendously in the area of method, and should continue to do so in the years ahead. It has gone beyond the simplistic view that a child's linguistic knowledge can be adequately assessed by collecting a spontaneous language sample. An obvious way in which the approach has changed is the development of diverse experimental methods to get at the many aspects of language that are not immediately apparent from spontaneous speech. These have included the use of imitation as in Kuczaj & Maratsos (1975), comprehension tests as in Thomson & Chapman (1977), and elicitation procedures as in Berko (1958). Indeed, studies such as these across a range of linguistic behaviors suggest that seemingly impossible aspects of language can be studied as long as one brings a creative mind to the task.

While such experimental approaches have held great promise, their details are still being developed. We have discussed cases where studies have not been replicated, or where different methods of analysis have been proposed. The area of environmental effects, for example, is still in the midst of determining the appropriate methodological procedures needed to determine causality. Another example is in the area of infant speech perception where I presented the methodological debate between the nativists and the developmentalists. So too, we are still attempting to resolve the kinds of discrepancies that occur when an area is tested in both comprehension and production: that is, which kinds of data are to be considered most reliably an indication of a child's linguistic ability? With regard to the use of experimental techniques, therefore, particularly in combination with each other, there are still a number of issues to resolve.

Methodological research has also sought to develop better ways to use spontaneous speech. One effective means has been the improvements made

516

in the use of parental diaries to study the general aspects of early vocabulary acquisition. Another concerns refinements in the linguistic methods used to analyze language samples. We have addressed two areas in particular. In the area of phonological acquisition, we discussed the need to set some criteria for productivity as well as ways to separate individual from general patterns. These same general issues returned when we discussed the analysis of children's early word combinations. Again the question of productivity arose. In both domains we want to eliminate random and memorized speech forms from the set of data being used to make claims about a child's rule system. I am somewhat concerned that the limitations of spontaneous samples have led some to consider them to be of no value. Instead, while recognizing such limitations, I believe that a better methodology can still lead to new insights into the developmental patterns of both areas.

The descriptive aspect of the text deals with a review of the relevant literature in the field. As stated in the Introduction, I have tried to limit this aspect in the sense of restricting the range of studies discussed. Instead, I have gone for a more intensive survey of a small set of relevant studies. The tone of the review, therefore, is highly different from other attempts such as McCarthy (1954).

A goal of the literature survey has been to present the reader with a feel for the richness of the research which has already been done in the field. I have presented a historical overview, and have opted to focus on what I perceive to be classic studies, though, of course, including current work which is perceived to be of importance. There is a concern among at least some from the Child Language perspective that this literature is being lost. This is true not only for older studies but even for more recent ones. I pointed out, for example, the lack of any discussion of McNeill's work in the 1970s in Pinker (1984), despite some very general similarities in the two approaches.

The lack of interest in previous research among at least some current researchers can be traced to two causes. One concerns the fact that current linguistic theory has discovered new and interesting patterns of language which have not been known before and there was no previous research, therefore, which directly examined them. A related cause is the feeling that the previous research was by and large descriptive. I acknowledge that there may well be a range of linguistic phenomena which will require entirely new research studies, particularly those phenomena which tend to be acquired later in childhood. At the same time, however, I believe that a number of previous studies can be reinterpreted in the light of more recent research. I discussed, for example, the relevance of the data in Rodd & Braine (1970) to current discussions about the acquisition of subject pronouns. While it is true that some of the earlier research was descriptive, much still contains insightful and speculative theoretical suggestions. It just may not be characterized by the current linguistic jargon.

Certainly the attention to explanation has expanded and now is central to most research currently underway. I have tried to capture the directions of this work by comparing these different general approaches to the question. The more traditional developmental view that children go through progressive stages of acquisition has been contrasted with two nativist views. One of these, which I have called 'maturational', allows maturational milestones and is quite comfortable with discontinuities in acquisition. The other, which I labeled a 'strong inclusion' view, sees the child as essentially adult-like from the onset of acquisition.

These differences of opinion are currently being assessed by all sides as to their predictions about language acquisition. I have some concern about the polarization which may result from these differences, and have contrasted Child Language and Language Acquisition as a way to characterize the respective camps. I have some worries about the future in this regard, but see no inherent differences in the general goal of all sides to better understand the child's language acquisition process. Indeed, I believe that the disagreements may come down to whether one assigns a child's linguistic behavior as the result of its performance or competence. If such is the case, we may all be satisfied at some point with the data, and only debate its interpretation.

The more serious point perhaps, at least as concerns the future of our field, is the interest in data at all. If language acquisition shows little about the child's emerging linguistic competence, then linguists will presumably lose interest in child language data altogether. This does not mean, of course, that there will be no more issues of interest to study. Certainly an account of the performance mechanisms at work will be a primary issue. So too, the logical problem of how specific constructions can be acquired from positive evidence will keep us busy for many years to come. Even so, much of the research in the field has been driven by the assumption that children's patterns of speech reveal something of interest about their linguistic rules. It is certainly this interest which has led me to highlight the constructionist perspective in this text. The resolution of this point, to my mind, will constitute the single most important event in the history of the field.

Bibliography

Abrahamsen, A. 1977. *Child language: an interdisciplinary guide to theory and research*. Baltimore, Md.: University Park Press.

Abrahamsen, D. 1938. The function of language and its development in early childhood. *Acta Psychiatrica et Neurologica* 13: 649–58.

Ament, W. 1899. *Die Entwicklung von Sprechen und Denken beim Kinde*. Leipzig: Ernst Wunderlich.

Amidon, A. 1976. Children's understanding of sentences with contingent relations: why are temporal and conditional connectives so difficult? *Journal of Experimental Child Psychology* 22: 423–37.

Amidon, A. & Carey, S. 1972. Why five-year-olds cannot understand before and after. *Journal of Verbal Learning and Verbal Behavior* 11: 417–23.

Anastasi, A. & D'Angelo, R. 1952. A comparison of Negro and white preschool children in language development and Goodenough Draw-a-Man I.Q. *Journal of Genetic Psychology* 81: 147–65.

Anglin, J. 1970. *The growth of word meaning*. Cambridge, Mass: MIT Press.

1977. *Word, object, and conceptual development*. New York: Norton.

Anisfeld, M. 1984. *Language development from birth to three*. Hillsdale, NJ: Lawrence Erlbaum.

Antinucci, F. & Miller, R. 1976. How children talk about what happened. *Journal of Child Language* 3: 167–89.

Antinucci, F. & Parisi, D. 1973. Early language acquisition: a model and some data. In Ferguson & Slobin (1973: 607–19).

Arlman-Rupp, A., van Niekerk de Haan, D. & van de Sandt-Koenderman, M. 1976. Brown's early stages: some evidence from Dutch. *Journal of Child Language* 3: 267–74.

Armstrong, S., Gleitman, L. & Gleitman, H. 1983. What some concepts might not be. *Cognition* 13: 263–308.

Aslin, R. & Pisoni, D. 1980. Some developmental processes in speech perception. In Yeni-Komshian, Kavanaugh & Ferguson (1980b: 75–102).

Atkinson, M. 1982. *Explanation in the study of language acquisition*. Cambridge: Cambridge University Press.

Bach, E. & Harms, R. (eds.) 1968. *Universals in linguistic theory*. New York: Holt, Rinehart & Winston.

Baker, C. L. 1979. Syntactic theory and the projection problem. *Linguistic Inquiry* 10: 533–81.

Baker, C. L. & McCarthy, J. (eds.) 1981. *The logical problem of language acquisition*. Cambridge, Mass.: MIT Press.

519

Baldie, B. 1976. The acquisition of the passive voice. *Journal of Child Language* 3: 331–48.

Bar-Adon, A. & Leopold, W. (eds.) 1971. *Child language. A book of readings.* Englewood Cliffs, NJ: Prentice-Hall.

Barnes, S., Gutfreund, M., Satterly, D. & Wells, G. 1983. Characteristics of adult speech which predict children's language development. *Journal of Child Language* 10: 65–84.

Barrett, M. 1978. Lexical development and overextension in child language. *Journal of Child Language* 5: 205–19.

1982. The holophrastic hypothesis: conceptual and empirical issues. *Cognition* 11: 47–76.

Barrie-Blackley, S. 1973. Six-year-old children's understanding of sentences adjoined with time adverbs. *Journal of Psycholinguistic Research* 2: 153–65.

Bartlett, E. 1976. Sizing things up: the acquisition of the meaning of dimensional adjectives. *Journal of Child Language* 3: 205–20.

Barton, D. 1975. Statistical significance in phonemic perception experiments. *Journal of Child Language* 2: 297–8.

1976a. The role of perception in the acquisition of phonology. Doctoral dissertation, University of London.

1976b. Phonemic discrimination and the knowledge of words in children under three years of age. *Papers and Reports on Child Language Development* 11: 61–8.

1978. The discrimination of minimally-different pairs of real words by children aged 2;3 to 2;11. In Waterson & Snow (1978: 255–61).

1980. Phonemic perception in children. In Yeni-Komshian, Kavanaugh & Ferguson (1980b: 97–116).

Bateman, W. 1916. The language status of three children at the same ages. *Pedagogical Seminary* 23: 211–40.

Bates, E. 1976. *Language and context: the acquisition of pragmatics.* New York: Academic Press.

1979. *The emergence of symbols: cognition and communication in infancy.* New York: Academic Press.

Bates, E., Camaioni, L. & Volterra, V. 1975. The acquisition of performatives prior to speech. *Merrill-Palmer Quarterly* 21: 205–36.

Bates, E. & MacWhinney, B. 1979. The functionalist approach to the acquisition of grammar. In Ochs & Schiefflin (1979: 167–211).

1982. The development of grammar. In Wanner and Gleitman (1982: 173–218).

Bates, E. & Rankin, J. 1979. Morphological development in Italian: connotation and denotation. *Journal of Child Language* 6: 29–52.

Bateson, M. C. 1975. Mother–infant exchanges: the epigenesis of conversational interaction. In D. Aaronson & R. Rieber (eds.) *Developmental psycholinguistics and communication disorders. Annals of the New York Academy of Science* 263: 21–9.

Bausano, M. K. & Jeffrey, W. E. 1975. Dimensional salience and judgements of bigness by three-year-old children. *Child Development* 46: 988–91.

Bavin, E. & Shopin, T. 1985. Children's acquisition of Walpiri: comprehension of transitive sentences. *Journal of Child Language* 12: 597–610.

Bellugi, U. 1967. The acquisition of the system of negation in children's speech. Doctoral dissertation, Harvard University.

1971. Simplification in children's language. In Huxley & Ingram (1971: 95–119).

Bellugi, U. & Brown, R. (eds.) 1964. The acquisition of language. *Monographs of the Society for Research in Child Development* 29.

Benedict, H. 1979. Early lexical development: comprehension and production. *Journal of Child Language* 6: 183–200.

Berko, J. 1958. The child's learning of English morphology. *Word* 14: 150–77.

Berko-Gleason, J. 1975. Fathers and other strangers. In Dato (1975: 289–97).

Berman, R. 1981a. Regularity vs. anomaly: the acquisition of Hebrew inflectional morphophonology. *Journal of Child Language* 8: 265–82.

1981b. Language development and language knowledge: evidence from the acquisition of Hebrew morphophonology. *Journal of Child Language* 8: 609–26.

1982. Verb-pattern alternation: the interface of morphology, syntax, and semantics in Hebrew child language. *Journal of Child Language* 9: 169–91.

Berwick, R. & Weinberg, A. 1984. *The grammatical basis of linguistic performance.* Cambridge, Mass.: MIT Press.

Bever, T. 1970. The cognitive basis for linguistic structures. In Hayes (1970: 274–353).

Bierwisch, M. 1967. Some semantic universals of German adjectivals. *Foundations of Language* 3: 1–36.

1970. Semantics. In J. Lyons (ed.) *New horizons in linguistics.* London: Penguin, pp. 166–84.

Blewitt, P. 1982. Word meaning acquisition in young children: a review of theory and research. In H. Reese & L. Lipsitt (eds.) *Advances in child development and behavior,* vol. 17. New York: Academic Press, pp. 140–95.

Bloom, L. 1970. *Language development: form and function in emerging grammars.* Cambridge, Mass.: MIT Press.

1971. Why not pivot grammar? *Journal of Speech and Hearing Disorders* 36: 40–50.

1973. *One word at a time.* The Hague: Mouton.

(ed.) 1978. *Readings in language development.* New York: John Wiley.

Bloom, L. & Lahey, M. (eds.) 1978. *Language development and language disorders.* New York: John Wiley.

Bloom, L., Hood, L. & Lightbown, P. 1974. Imitation in language acquisition: if, when, and why? *Cognitive Psychology* 6: 380–420. Reprinted in L. Bloom (1978: 452–88).

Bloom, L., Lifter, K. & Hafitz, J. 1980. Semantics of verbs and the development of verb inflections in child language. *Language* 56: 386–412.

Bloom, L., Lightbown, P. & Hood, L. 1975. Structure and variation in child language. *Monographs of the Society for Research in Child Development* 40 (2, serial no. 160).

Bloom, L., Miller, P. & Hood, L. 1975. Variation and reduction as aspects of competence in language development. In A. Pick (ed.) *Minnesota Symposia on Child Psychology* 9: 3–55. Reprinted in Bloom (1978: 169–216).

Bloom, L., Rocissano, L. & Hood, L. 1976. Adult–child discourse: developmental interaction between information processing and linguistic knowledge. *Cognitive Psychology* 8: 521–52.

Bloom, L., Lahey, M., Hood, L. Lifter, K. & Fiess, K. 1980. Complex sentences: acquisition of syntactic connectives and the semantic relations they encode. *Journal of Child Language* 7: 235–61.

Bloomfield, L. 1933. *Language*. New York: Henry Holt.

Blount, B. 1969. Acquisition of language by Luo children. Doctoral dissertation, University of California, Berkeley.

1972. The prelinguistic system of Luo children. *Anthropological Linguistics* 12: 326–42.

Bohn, W. 1914. First steps in verbal expression. *Pedagogical Seminary* 21: 578–95.

Borer, H. & Wexler, K. 1987. The maturation of syntax. In Roeper & Williams (1987: 123–72).

Bowerman, M. 1973a. *Early syntactic development: a cross-linguistic study with special reference to Finnish*. Cambridge: Cambridge University Press.

1973b. Structural relationships in children's utterances: syntactic or semantic? In Moore (1973: 197–213).

1974. Learning the structure of causative verbs: a study in the relationship of cognitive, semantic and syntactic development. *Papers and Reports on Child Language Development* 8: 142–78.

1975. Commentary, In Bloom, Lightbown & Hood (1975: 80–90).

1976a. Commentary. In Braine (1976: 98–104).

1976b. Semantic factors in the acquisition of rules for word use and sentence construction. In Morehead & Morehead (1976: 99–179).

1977. The acquisition of rules governing 'possible lexical items': evidence from spontaneous speech errors. *Papers and Reports on Child Language Development* 13: 148–56.

1978a. The acquisition of word meaning: an investigation into some current conflicts. In Waterson & Snow (1978: 263–87).

1978b. Semantic and syntactic development: a review of what, when, and how in language acquisition. In Schiefelbusch (1978: 97–189).

1978c. Systematizing semantic knowledge: changes over time in the child's organization of meaning. *Child Development* 49: 977–87.

1979. The acquisition of complex sentences. In Fletcher & Garman (1979: 285–305).

1981. Beyond communicative competency: from piecemeal knowledge to an integrated system in the child's acquisition of language. *Papers and Reports on Child Language Development* 20: 1–24.

1986. What shapes children's grammars? In Slobin (1986: 1257–319).

Boyd, W. 1913. The beginnings of syntactical speech: a study in child linguistics. *Child Study* 6: 21–4 and 47–51.

Braine, M. D. S. 1963a. The ontogeny of English phrase structure: the first phase. *Language* 39: 1–13.

1963b. On learning the grammatical order of words. *Psychological Review* 70: 323–48.

1971a. On two types of models of the internalization of grammars. In Slobin (1971: 153–86).

1971b. The acquisition of language in infant and child. In C. E. Reed (ed.) *The learning of language*. New York: Appleton-Century-Crofts, pp. 7–95.

1973. Three suggestions regarding grammatical analyses of children's language. In Ferguson & Slobin 1973: 421–9.

1974a. On what might constitute a learnable phonology. *Language* 50: 270–99.

1974b. Length constraints, reduction rules, and holophrastic processes in children's word combinations. *Journal of Verbal Learning and Verbal Behavior* 13: 448–56.

1976. Children's first word combinations. *Monographs of the Society for Research in Child Development* 41 (1, serial no. 164).

Braine, M. D. S. & Hardy, J. 1981. Case categories. In Deutsch (1981: 201–22).

1982. On what case categories there are, why they are, and how they develop: an amalgam of a priori considerations, speculation, and evidence from children. In Wanner & Gleitman (1982: 219–39).

Braine, M. D. S. & Wells, R. 1978. Case-like categories in children: the Actor and more related categories. *Cognitive Psychology* 10: 100–22.

Brainerd, C. 1978. The stage question in cognitive-developmental theory. *The Behavioral and Brain Sciences* 2: 173–213.

Brandenburg, G. 1915. The language of a three-year-old child. *Pedagogical Seminary* 22: 89–120.

Branigan, G. 1979. Some reasons why successive single word utterances are not. *Journal of Child Language* 6: 411–21.

Braunwald, S. 1978. Context, word and meaning: towards a communicational analysis of lexical acquisition. In Lock (1978: 485–527).

Bresnan, J. 1978. A realistic transformational grammar. In Halle, Bresnan & Miller (1978: 1–59).

(ed.) 1982. The mental representation of grammatical relations. Cambridge, Mass.: MIT Press.

Bretherton, I., McNew, S., Snyder, L. & Bates, E. 1983. Individual differences at 20 months: analytic and holistic strategies in language acquisition. *Journal of Child Language* 10: 293–320.

Brewer, W. & Stone, J. 1975. Acquisition of spatial antonym pairs. *Journal of Experimental Child Psychology* 19: 299–307.

Brown, H. D. 1971. Children's comprehension of relativized English sentences. *Child Development* 42: 1923–6.

Brown, R. 1958a. *Words and things*. Glencoe, Ill.: Free Press.

1958b. How shall a thing be called? *Psychological Review* 65: 14–21.

1968. The development of *wh* questions in child speech. *Journal of Verbal Learning and Verbal Behavior* 7: 277–90.

1970a. *Psycholinguistics: selected papers of Roger Brown*. New York: Free Press.

1970b. The first sentences of child and chimpanzee. In Brown (1970a: 208–31).

1973. *A first language: the early stages*. Cambridge, Mass.: Harvard University Press.

1977. Introduction. In Snow & Ferguson (1977: 1–27).

Brown, R. & Bellugi, U. 1964. Three processes in the child's acquisition of syntax. *Harvard Educational Review* 34: 133–5. Also in Lenneberg (1964).

Brown, R. & Fraser, C. 1963. The acquisition of syntax. In C. Cofer & B. Musgrave (eds.) *Verbal behavior and learning: problems and processes*. New York: McGraw-Hill. pp. 158–201.

1964. The acquisition of syntax. In Bellugi & Brown (1964: 43–79).

Brown, R., Cazden, C. & Bellugi, U. 1969. The child's grammar from I to III. In J. P. Hill (ed.). *Minnesota Symposium on Child Psychology*, vol. 2. Minneapolis, Minn.: University of Minnesota Press, pp. 28–73.

Brown, R. & Hanlon, C. 1970. Derivational complexity and order of acquisition. In Hayes (1970: 11–53).

Brown, R., Fraser, C. & Bellugi, U. 1964. Explorations in grammar evaluation. In Bellugi & Brown (1964: 79–92).

Bruner, J. 1975. The ontogenesis of speech acts. *Journal of Child Language* 2: 1–21.

Bruner, J. & Sherwood, V. 1976. Peekaboo and the learning of rule structures. In J. S. Bruner, A. Jolly & K. Sylva (eds.) *Play – its role in development and evolution.* Harmondsworth, Middx: Penguin, pp. 277–85.

Buhler, C. 1931. *Kindheit und Jugend.* Leipzig: Hirzel.

Burroughs, G. 1957. *A study of the vocabulary of young children.* Edinburgh: Oliver and Boyd.

Butterfield, E. & Cairns, G. 1974. Discussion summary – infant reception research. In Schiefelbusch and Lloyd (1974: 75–102).

Bybee, J. 1979. Child morphology and morphophonemic change. *Linguistics* 17: 21–50.

Campbell, D. & Stanley, J. 1963. Experimental and quasi-experimental design for research in teaching. In N. Gage (ed.) *Handbook of research on teaching.* Chicago, Ill.: Rand McNally.

Caramazza, A. & Zuriff, E. (eds.) 1978. *Language acquisition and language breakdown.* Baltimore, Md.: The Johns Hopkins University Press.

Carden, G. 1986. Blocked forwards anaphora: theoretical implications of the acquisition data. In Lust (1986: 319–57).

Carey, S. 1978. The child as word learner. In Halle, Bresnan & Miller (1978: 264–93).

1982. Semantic development: the state of the art. In Wanner & Gleitman (1982: 347–89).

Carey, S. & Bartlett, E. 1978. Acquiring a single word. *Papers and Reports on Child Language Development* 15: 17–29.

Carter, A. L. 1975a. The transformation of sensorimotor morphemes into words: a case study of the development of 'here' and 'there'. *Papers and Reports on Child Language Development* 10: 31–47.

1975b. The transformation of sensorimotor morphemes into words: a case study of the development of 'more' and 'mine'. *Journal of Child Language* 2: 233–50.

1978a. The development of systematic vocalizations prior to words: a case study. In Waterson & Snow (1978: 127–38).

1978b. From sensorimotor vocalizations to words: a case study of the evolution of attention-directing communication in the second year. In Lock (1978: 309–49).

1979. Prespeech meaning relations: an outline of one infant's sensorimotor morpheme development. In Fletcher & Garman (1979: 71–92).

Caudill, W. & Weinstein, H. 1969. Maternal care and infant behavior in Japan and America. *Psychiatry* 32: 12–43.

Cazden, C. 1968. The acquisition of noun and verb inflections. *Child Development* 39: 433–48.

1970. Children's questions: their form, functions, and roles in education. *Young Children*, March, pp. 202–20.

1972. *Child language and education.* New York: Holt, Rinehart & Winston.

Chamberlain, A. & Chamberlain, I. 1904. Studies of a child. *Pedagogical Seminary* 11: 264–91, 452–83.

1905. Studies of a child. *Pedagogical Seminary* 12: 427–53.

1909. 'Meanings' and 'definitions' in the 47th and 48th months. *Pedagogical Seminary* 16: 64–103.

Chao, Y.-R. 1951. The Cantian idiolect. *University of California Publications in Semitic Philology* 2: 27–44. Reprinted in Bar-Adon & Leopold (1971: 116–30).

Chapman, R. 1981a. Cognitive development and language comprehension in 10–21-month-olds. In Stark (1981: 359–91).

1981b. Mother–child interaction in the second year of life: its role in language development. In Schiefelbusch & Bricker (1981: 201–50).

Chapman, R. & Thomson, J. 1980. What is the source of overextension errors in comprehension testing of two-year-olds? A response to Fremgen & Fay. *Journal of Child Language* 7: 575–8.

Chen, M. 1975. An areal study of nasalization in Chinese. In C. Ferguson, L. Hyman & J. Ohala (eds.) *Nasalfest: Papers from a symposium on nasals and nasalization.* Palo Alto, Calif.: Stanford University Press.

Chomsky, C. 1969. *The acquisition of syntax in children from 5 to 10.* Cambridge, Mass.: MIT Press.

Chomsky, N. 1957. *Syntactic structures.* The Hague: Mouton.

1959. Review of *Verbal behavior*, by B. F. Skinner. *Language* 35: 26–58.

1964. Formal discussion. In Bellugi & Brown (1964: 35–9).

1965. *Aspects of the theory of syntax.* Cambridge, Mass.: MIT Press.

1968. *Language and mind.* New York: Harcourt Brace Jovanovich.

1972. *Studies on semantics in generative grammar.* The Hague: Mouton.

1975. *Reflections on language.* New York: Pantheon.

1981. *Lectures on government and binding: the Pisa lectures.* Dordrecht: Foris.

1982. *Some concepts and consequences of the theory of government and binding.* Cambridge, Mass.: MIT Press.

1986. *Barriers.* Cambridge, Mass.: MIT Press.

Chomsky, N. & Halle, M. 1968. *The sound pattern of English.* New York: Harper & Row.

Clark, E. 1971. On the acquisition of the meaning of 'before' and 'after'. *Journal of Verbal Learning and Verbal Behavior* 10: 266–75.

1972. On the child's acquisition of antonyms in two semantic fields. *Journal of Verbal Learning and Verbal Behavior* 11: 750–8.

1973a. What's in a word? On the child's acquisition of semantics in his first language. In Moore (1973: 65–110).

1973b. Nonlinguistic strategies and the acquisition of word meanings. *Cognition* 2: 161–82.

Clark, H. 1970. How young children describe events in time. In G. Flores d'Arcais & W. Levelt (eds.) *Advances in psycholinguistics.* Amsterdam: North-Holland.

1973. Space, time, semantics, and the child. In Moore (1973: 27–63).

Clark, H. & Clark, E. 1977. *Psychology and language: an introduction.* New York: Harcourt Brace Jovanovich.

Clark, R. 1974. Performing without competence. *Journal of Child Language* 1: 1–10.

1977. What's the use of imitation? *Journal of Child Language* 4: 341–58.

1982. Theory and method in child-language research: are we assuming too much? In Kuczaj (1982b: 1–36).

Clumeck, H. 1982. The effect of word familiarity on phonemic recognition in preschool children aged 3 to 5 years. In C. E. Johnson & C. L. Thew (eds.) *Proceedings of the Second International Congress for the Study of Child Language. Vol. 1.* Washington, DC: University Press of America, pp. 58–77.

Coker, P. 1978. Syntactic and semantic factors in the acquisition of before and after. *Papers and Reports on Child Language Development* 12: 81–8.

Comrie, B. 1981. *Language universals and linguistic typology.* Chicago, Ill.: University of Chicago Press.

1983. Switch-reference in Huichol: a typological study. In J. Haiman & P. Munro (eds.) *Switch-reference and universal grammar.* Amsterdam: John Benjamins, pp. 17–37.

Crain, S. & McKee, C. 1985. Acquisition of structural relations on anaphora. *NELS* 16: 94–110.

Cruttenden, A. 1970. A phonetic study of late babbling. *British Journal of Disorders of Communication* 5: 110–18.

Crystal, D., Fletcher, P. & Garman, M. 1976. *The grammatical analysis of language disability.* London: Edward Arnold, pp. 200–7.

Culicover, P. & Wilkins, W. 1984. *Locality in linguistic theory.* Orlando, Fla.: Academic Press.

Dale, P. 1976. *Language development: structure and function.* New York: Holt, Rinehart & Winston.

1985. Productivity analysis of early child language (PANEL): user's guide. IBM versions. Unpublished paper.

Dale, P. & Ingram, D., (eds.) 1980. *Child language: an international perspective.* Baltimore, Md.: University Park Press.

Darwin, C. 1877. A bibliographical sketch of an infant. *Mind* 2: 285–94.

Dato, D. (ed.) 1975. Developmental psycholinguistics: theory and application. *Georgetown University Round Table on Languages and Linguistics 1975.* Washington: Georgetown University.

Davis, E. 1937. The development of linguistic skills in twins, singletons with siblings, and only children from age five to ten years. *University of Minnesota Institute of Child Welfare, Monograph Series* 14.

Davis, H. 1983. Restructuring in child language. Paper presented to the Canadian Linguistic Association annual meeting, Vancouver, BC.

1987. The acquisition of the English auxiliary system and its relation to linguistic theory. Doctoral dissertation, University of British Columbia.

Day, E. 1932. The development of language in twins: 1. A comparison of twins and single children. 2. The development of twins: their resemblances and differences. *Child Development* 3: 179–99.

de Boysson-Bardies, B., Sagart, L. & Durand, C. 1984. Discernible differences in the babbling of infants according to target language. *Journal of Child Language* 11: 1–15.

de Laguna, G. 1927. *Speech: its function and development.* New Haven, Conn.: Yale University Press.

Della Corta, M., Benedict, R. & Klein, D. 1983. The relationship of pragmatic dimensions of mothers' speech to the referential–expressive distinction. *Journal of Child Language* 10: 35–43.

de Saussure, F. 1922. *Cours de linguistique générale.* Paris: Pavot, 5th edn 1955. (1st edn 1916). English translation by Wade Baskin, 1955. *Course in general linguistics.* New York: Philosophical Library, 1959.

Deutsch, W. (ed.) 1981. *The child's construction of language*. New York: Academic Press.

Devereux, G. 1949. Mohave voice and speech mannerisms. *Word* 5: 268–72.

de Villiers, J. (1980). The process of rule learning in child speech: a new look. In K. E. Nelson (1980:1–44).

de Villiers, J. & de Villiers, P. 1973a. P. Development of the use of word order in comprehension. *Journal of Psycholinguistic Research* 2: 331–41.

   1973b. A cross-sectional study of the acquisition of grammatical morphemes in child speech. *Journal of Psycholinguistic Research* 2: 267–78.

   1978. *Language acquisition*. Cambridge, Mass.: Harvard University Press.

de Villiers, J., Tager-Flusberg, H., Hakuta, K. & Cohen, M. 1979. Children's comprehension of relative clauses. *Journal of Psycholinguistic Research* 8: 499–518.

Dinnsen, D. A. 1980. Phonological rules and phonetic explanation. *Journal of Linguistics* 16: 171–91.

Dockrell, J. E. 1981. The child's acquisition of unfamiliar words: an experimental study. Unpublished doctoral dissertation, Stirling University, Scotland.

Donaldson, M. & Wales, R. 1970. On the acquisition of some relational terms. In Hayes (1970: 235–68).

Donegan, P. J. 1986. *On the natural phonology of vowels*. Outstanding Dissertations in Linguistics series. New York: Garland.

Donegan, P. J. & Stampe, D. 1979. The study of natural phonology. In D. A. Dinnsen (ed.) *Current approaches to phonological theory*. Bloomington, Ind.: Indiana University Press, pp. 126–73.

Dore, J. 1975. Holophrases, speech acts and language universals. *Journal of Child Language* 3: 22–39.

   1979. What's so conceptual about the acquisition of linguistics structures? *Journal of Child Language* 6: 127–37.

Dore, J., Franklin, M., Miller, R. T. & Ramer, A. 1976. Transitional phenomena in early acquisition. *Journal of Child Language* 3: 13–28.

Dresher, E. 1981. On the learnability of abstract phonology. In Baker & McCarthy (1981: 188–210).

Drummond, M. 1916. Notes on speech development, 1–2. *Child Study* 9: 83–6, 95–9.

Edwards, M. L. 1970. The acquisition of liquids. MA dissertation, Ohio State University.

   1974. Perception and production in child phonology: the testing of four hypotheses. *Journal of Child Language* 1: 205–19.

Edwards, M. L. & Shriberg, L. D. 1983. *Phonology: applications in communication disorders*. San Diego, Calif. College-Hill Press.

Eilers, R. 1980. Infant speech perception: history and mystery. In Yeni-Komshian, Kavanaugh & Ferguson (1980b: 23–39).

Eilers, R. & Gavin, W. 1981. The evaluation of infant speech perception skills: statistical techniques and theory development. In Stark (1981: 185–213).

Eilers, R. & Oller, D. K. 1976. The role of speech discriminations in developmental sound substitutions. *Journal of Child Language* 3: 319–29.

Eilers, R., Gavin, W. & Oller, K. 1982. Cross-linguistic perception in infancy: early effects of linguistic experience. *Journal of Child Language* 9: 289–302.

Eilers, R., Gavin, W. & Wilson, W. 1979. Linguistic experience and phonemic perception in infancy: a cross-linguistic study. *Child Development* 50: 14–18.

Eilers, R., Oller, D. K. & Ellington, J. 1974. The acquisition of word meaning for dimensional adjectives: the long and the short of it. *Journal of Child Language* 1: 195–204.

Eilers, R., Wilson, W. & Moore, M. 1976. Discrimination of synthetic prevoiced labial stops by infants and adults. *Journal of the Acoustical Society of America* 60, Supplement 1, S91 (abstract).

  1977. Developmental changes in speech discrimination in infants. *Journal of Speech and Hearing Research* 20: 766–80.

Eilers, R. Oller, D. K., Bull, D. & Gavin, W. 1984. Linguistic experience and infant perception: a reply to Jusczyk, Shea & Aslin (1984). *Journal of Child Language* 11: 467–75.

Eimas, P. 1974. Linguistic processing of speech by young infants. In Schiefelbusch & Lloyd (1974: 55–73).

Eimas, P., Miller, J. & Jusczyk, P. In press. On infant speech perception and the acquisition of language. In S. Harnad (ed.) *Categorical perception*. Cambridge: Cambridge University Press.

Eimas, P., Siqueland, E., Jusczyk, P. & Vigorito, J. 1971. Speech perception in infants. *Science* 171: 303–18. Reprinted in Bloom (1978: 87–93).

Elbers, L. 1982. Operating principles in repetitive babbling: a cognitive continuity approach. *Cognition* 12: 45–63.

Elkonin, D. B. 1971. Development of speech. In A. Va. Zaporozhets & D. B. Elkonin (eds.) *The psychology of preschool children*. Cambridge, Mass.: MIT Press, pp. 111–85.

Emonds, J. 1976. *A transformational approach to English syntax: root, structure-preserving and local transformations*. New York: Academic Press.

Erreich, A. 1984. Learning how to ask: patterns of inversion in yes–no and *wh* questions. *Journal of Child Language* 11: 579–92.

Erreich, A., Valian, V. & Winzemer, J. 1980. Aspects of a theory of language acquisition. *Journal of Child Language* 2: 157–79.

Fay, D. 1978. Reply to Kuczaj (1976). *Journal of Child Language* 5: 143–9.

Feagans, L. 1980. How to make sense of temporal/spatial 'before' and 'after'. *Journal of Child Language* 7: 529–37.

Ferguson, C. A. 1964. Baby talk in six languages. *American Anthropologist* 66: 103–14.

  1978. Learning to pronounce: the earliest stages of phonological development in the child. In Minifie & Lloyd (1978: 237–97).

Ferguson, C. A. & Farwell, C. B. 1975. Words and sounds in early language acquisition. *Language* 51: 49–39. An earlier version appeared in 1973 in *Papers and Reports on Child Language Development* 6: 1–60.

Ferguson, C. A. & Garnica, O. K. 1975. Theories of phonological development. In Lenneberg & Lenneberg (1975: 153–80).

Ferguson, C. A. & Slobin, D. (eds.) 1973. *Studies of child language development*. New York: Holt, Rinehart & Winston.

Fernald, C. 1972. Control of grammar in imitation, comprehension, and production: problems of replication. *Journal of Verbal Learning and Verbal Behavior* 11: 606–13.

Fillmore, C. 1968. The case for case. In E. Bach & R. Harms (eds.) *Universals in linguistic theory*. New York: Holt, Rinehart & Winston, pp. 1–88.

Fisher, M. 1934. Language patterns of preschool children. *Child Development Monographs* 15. New York: Teachers' College, Columbia University.

Flavell, J. 1963. *The developmental psychology of Jean Piaget.* New York: Van Nostrand.

Fletcher, P. & Garman, M. (eds.) 1979. 2nd edn 1986. *Language acquisition.* Cambridge: Cambridge University Press.

Fodor, J. 1975. *The language of thought.* New York: Crowell.

Fodor, J., Garrett, M., Walker, E. & Parkes, C. 1980. Against definitions. *Cognition* 8: 263–67.

Fónagy, I. 1972. À propos de la génèse de la phrase enfantine. *Lingua* 30: 31–71.

Fortescue, M. 1984/5. Learning to speak Greenlandic. *First Language* 5: 101–13.

Francis, H. 1969. Structure in the speech of a 2½-year-old. *British Journal of Educational Psychology* 39: 291–302.

Fraser, C., Bellugi, U. & Brown, R. 1963. Control of grammar in imitation, comprehension, and production. *Journal of Verbal Learning and Verbal Behavior* 2: 121–35.

Freedle, R. & Lewis, M. 1977. Prelinguistic conversation. In M. Lewis & P. Rosenbaum (eds.) *Interaction, conversation and the development of language.* New York: John Wiley, pp. 157–85.

Fremgen, A, & Fay, D. 1980. Overextensions in production and comprehension: a methodological clarification. *Journal of Child Language* 7: 205–11.

French, L. & Brown, A. 1977. Comprehension of 'before' and 'after' in logical and arbitrary sequences. *Journal of Child Language* 4: 247–56.

Friedman, W. & Seeley, P. 1976. The child's acquisition of spatial and temporal word meanings. *Child Development* 47: 1103–8.

Furrow, D., Nelson, K. & Benedict, H. 1979. Mothers' speech to children and syntactic development: some simple relationships. *Journal of Child Language* 6: 423–42.

Gaer, E. P. 1969. Children's understanding and production of sentences. *Journal of Verbal Learning and Verbal Behavior* 8: 289–94.

Garnica, O. K. 1971. The development of the perception of phonemic differences in initial consonants by English-speaking children: a pilot study. *Papers and Reports on Child Language Development* 3: 1–29.

1973. The development of phonemic speech perception. In Moore (1973: 214–22).

1977. Some prosodic and paralinguistic features of speech to young children. In Snow & Ferguson (1977: 63–88).

Gazdar, G., Klein, E., Pullum, G. & Sag, I. 1985. *Generalized phrase structure grammar.* Cambridge, Mass.: Harvard University Press.

Gilbert, J. 1982. Babbling and the deaf child: a commentary on Lenneberg *et al.* (1965) and Lenneberg (1967). *Journal of Child Language* 9: 511–15.

Ginsberg, H. & Opper, S. 1969. *Piaget's theory of intellectual development: an introduction.* Englewood Cliffs, NJ: Prentice-Hall.

Givón, T. 1979. *On understanding grammar.* New York: Academic Press.

Gleitman, L. 1981. Maturational determinants of language growth. *Cognition* 10: 103–14.

Gleitman, L., Newport, M. & Gleitman, H. 1984. The current status of the motherese hypothesis. *Journal of Child Language* 11: 43–79.

Gleitman, L., Shipley, E. & Smith, C. 1978. Old and new ways not to study comprehension: comments on Petretic & Tweney's (1977) experimental review of Shipley, Smith & Gleitman (1969). *Journal of Child Language* 5: 501–19.

Goad, H. & Ingram, D. 1988. Individual variation and its relevance to a theory of phonological acquisition. *Journal of Child Language* 14: 419–32.

Goertz, C. 1973. The impact of the concept of culture on the concept of man. In C. Goertz, *Interpretation of cultures*. New York: Basic Books, pp. 33–54.

Goldstein, U. 1979. Modeling children's vocal tracts. Paper presented at the 97th Meeting of the Acoustical Society of America, Cambridge, Mass., June 12–16.

Gottlieb, G. 1976. Conceptions of prenatal development: behavioral embryology. *Psychological Review* 83: 215–34.

Graham, L. W. & House, A. S. 1971. Phonological oppositions in children: a perceptual study. *Journal of the Acoustical Society of America* 49: 559–66.

Greenberg, J. & Kuczaj, S. Towards a theory of substantive word meaning acquisition. In Kuczaj (1982: 275–311).

Greenfield, P. & Smith, J. 1976. *The structure of communication in early language development*. New York: Academic Press.

Greenfield, P. & Zukow, P. 1978. Why do children say what they say when they say it? An experimental approach to the psychogenesis of presupposition. In K. E. Nelson (1978).

Grégoire, A. 1937, 1947. *L'apprentissage du langage*. Vol. 1 (1937); Vol. 2 (1947). Liège, Paris: Droz.

Grimshaw, J. 1981. Form, function, and the language acquisition device. In Baker & McCarthy (1981: 165–82).

Gruber, J. S. 1967. Topicalization in child language. *Foundations of Language* 3: 37–65. Reprinted in Bar-Adon & Leopold (1971: 364–81).

   1975a. 'Topicalization' revisited. *Foundations of Language* 13: 57–72.

   1975b. Performative–constative transition in child language. *Foundations of Language* 12: 513–27.

Grunwell, P. 1985. *Phonological assessment of child speech (PACS)*. San Diego, Calif.: College-Hill Press.

Guillaume, P. 1927/28. First stages of sentence formation in children's speech. In Bloom (1978: 131–48).

Gvozdev, A. 1949. *Formirovanie u rebenka grammaticheskogo stroya russkogo yazyka (Formation in the child grammatical structure of the Russian language)*, parts 1 & 2. Moscow: Akad. Pedag. Nauk RSFSR.

Halle, M., Bresnan, J. & Miller, G. (eds.) 1978. *Linguistic theory and psychological reality*. Cambridge, Mass.: MIT Press.

Halliday, M. A. K. 1975. *Learning how to mean: explorations in the development of language development*. London: Edward Arnold.

Hamburger, H. & Crain, S. 1982. Relative acquisition. In Kuczaj (1982b: 245–74).

Harding, C. & Golinkoff, R. 1979. The origins of intentional vocalizations in prelinguistic infants. *Child Development* 50: 33–40.

Hayes, J. R. (ed.) 1970. *Cognition and the development of language*. New York: John Wiley.

Hayhurst, H. 1967. Some errors of young children in producing passive sentences. *Journal of Verbal Learning and Verbal Behavior* 6: 634–9.

Hill, J. 1984. Combining two-term relations: evidence in support of flat structure. *Journal of Child Language* 11: 673–8.

Hills, E. 1914. The speech of a child two years of age. *Dialect Notes* 4: 84–100.

Hodson, B. & Paden, E. 1983. *Targeting intelligible speech: a phonological approach to remediation*. San Diego, Calif.: College-Hill Press.

Hoek, D., Ingram, D. & Gibson, D. 1986. An examination of the possible causes of children's early word extensions. *Journal of Child Language* 13: 477–94.
Hoff-Ginsburg, E. & Shatz, M. 1982. Linguistic input and the child's acquisition of language. *Psychological Bulletin* 92: 2–26.
Hogan, L. 1898. *A study of a child, illustrated with over 500 original drawings by the child.* New York: Harper.
Holmes, U. 1927. The phonology of an English-speaking child. *American Speech* 2: 219–25.
Hood, L. & Bloom, L. 1979. What, when and how about why: a longitudinal study of expressions of causality in the language development of two-year-old children. *Society for Research in Child Development*, serial no. 181, vol. 44, no. 6.
Horgan, D. 1978. The development of the full passive. *Journal of Child Language* 5: 56–80.
Howard, R. 1946. Language development in a group of triplets. *Journal of Genetic Psychology* 69: 181–9.
Howe, C. 1976. The meanings of two-word utterances in the speech of young children. *Journal of Child Language* 3: 29–47.
Hoyer, A. & Hoyer, G. 1924. Uber die Lallsprache eines Kindes. *Zeitschrift für angewandte Psychologie* 24: 363–84.
Humphreys, M. 1880. A contribution to infantile linguistics. *Transactions of the American Philological Association* 11: 5–17.
Hurford, J. 1975. A child and the English question formation rule. *Journal of Child Language* 2: 299–301.
Huttenlocher, J. 1974. The origins of language comprehension. In R. Solso (ed.) *Theories in cognitive psychology.* New York: Erlbaum, pp. 331–68.
Huttenlocher, J., Eisenberg, K. & Strauss, S. 1968. Comprehension: relation between perceived actor and logical subject. *Journal of Verbal Learning and Verbal Behaviour* 7: 527–30.
Huxley, R. & Ingram, E. (eds.) 1971. *Language acquisition: models and methods.* New York: Academic Press.
Hyams, N. 1983. The acquisition of parameterized grammars. Doctoral dissertation, City University of New York.
  1984. Semantically based child grammars: some empirical inadequacies. *Papers and Reports on Child Language Development* 23: 58–65.
  1986. *Language acquisition and the theory of parameters.* Dordrecht: D. Reidel.
Ingram, D. 1971. Transitivity in child language. *Language* 47: 889–910.
  1972. The development of phrase structure rules. *Language Learning* 22: 65–77.
  1974a. Phonological rules in young children. *Journal of Child Language* 1: 49–64.
  1974b. Fronting in child phonology. *Journal of Child Language* 1: 233–41.
  1975. If and when transformations are acquired by children. *Monograph Series on Language and Linguistics. Georgetown University* 27: 99–127.
  1976a. *Phonological disability in children.* London: Edward Arnold.
  1976b. Phonological analysis of a child. *Glossa* 10: 3–27.
  1978. Sensori-motor intelligence and language development. In Lock (1978: 261–90).
  1979a. Phonological patterns in the speech of young children. In Fletcher & Garman (1979: 133–49).

1979b. Stages in the acquisition of one-word utterances. In P. French (ed.) *The development of meaning*. Hiroshima: Bunka Hyoron, pp. 256–81.

1981a. *Procedures for the phonological analysis of children's language*. Baltimore, Md.: University Park Press.

1981b. The notion of 'stage' in language acquisition studies. *Proceedings from the Second Wisconsin Symposium on Research in Child Language Disorders* 2: 1–16. Revised version to appear in H. Wittje (ed.) *Festschrift Els Oksaar*. Tübingen: Gunter Narr.

1981c. The transition from early symbols to syntax. In Schiefelbusch & Bricker (1981: 259–86).

1981d. Early patterns of grammatical development. In Stark (1981: 327–52).

1981e. On variant patterns of language acquisition. Paper presented to the Biennial Meeting of the Society for Research in Child Development, Boston, Mass.

1981/2. The emerging phonological system of an Italian-English bilingual child. *Journal of Italian Linguistics* 2: 95–113.

1985a. The psychological reality of children's grammars and its relation to grammatical theory. *Lingua* 66: 79–103.

1985b. [v]: the acquisition. Paper presented to the Western Conference of Linguistics, University of Victoria, October. Revised version to appear in *Language and Speech*.

1985c. The acquisition of Dative Movement from positive evidence. Unpublished paper.

1985d. On children's homonyms. *Journal of Child Language* 12: 671–80.

1986. In defense of the segment in phonological acquisition. Paper presented to the Linguistic Society of America, New York.

1988. Jakobson revisited: some evidence from the acquisition of Polish phonology. *Lingua* 75: 55–82.

Ingram, D. & Mitchell, G. to appear. A longitudinal comparison of French and English phonological development.

Ingram, D. & Shaw, C. 1981. The comprehension of pronominal reference in children. Unpublished paper, University of British Columbia. Revised version to appear in *The Canadian Journal of Linguistics*.

Ingram, D. & Tyack, D. 1979. The inversion of subject NP and Aux in children's questions. *Journal of Psycholinguistic Research* 4: 333–41.

Ingram, D., Christensen, L., Veach, S. & Webster, B. 1980. The acquisition of word-initial fricatives and affricates in English by children between 2 and 6 years. In Yeni-Komshian, Kavanaugh & Ferguson (1980a: 169–92).

Inhelder, B. 1963. Some aspects of Piaget's genetic approach to cognition. In Kissan & Kohlman (eds.) *Thought and the young child*, pp. 17–32.

Inhelder, B. & Piaget, J. 1964. *The growth of logic in the child: classification and seriation*. London: Routledge & Kegan Paul.

Irwin, O. C. 1941–49. See references in McCarthy (1954).

Jackendoff, R. 1977. *X̄ syntax: a study of phrase structure*. Cambridge, Mass.: MIT Press.

1983. *Semantics and cognition*. Cambridge, Mass.: MIT Press.

Jakobson, R. 1939. The sound laws of child language and their place in general phonology. Communication prepared at Charlottenlund, Denmark, in the summer of 1939 for the 5th International Congress of Linguists at Brussels, September, 1939. Reprinted in Bar-Adon & Leopold (1971).

1941/68. *Child language, aphasia, and phonological universals*. The Hague: Mouton. Translation by R. Keiler of original German version of 1941.

Jakobson, R., Fant, G. & Halle, H. 1963. Preliminaries to speech analysis: the distinctive features and their correlates. Technical Report 13, MIT Acoustics Laboratory, 1952. Cambridge, Mass.: MIT Press.

Jakobson, R. & Halle, M. 1956. *Fundamentals of language*. The Hague: Mouton.

Jegi, J. 1901. The vocabulary of a two-year-old child. *Child Study Monthly* 6: 241–61.

Jenkins, J. & Palermo, D. 1964. Mediation processes and the acquisition of linguistic structure. In Bellugi & Brown (1964: 141–69).

Jespersen, O. 1922. *Language: its nature, development, and origin*. London: Allen & Unwin.

Johnson, C. 1983. The development of children's interrogatives: from formulas to rules. *Papers and Reports on Child Language Development* 22: 108–15.

Johnson, C. J., Hardee, W. P. & Long, S. H. 1981. Perceptual basis for phonological simplification. Paper presented to the American Speech, Language, and Hearing Association, Los Angeles, California.

Johnston, J. 1979. A study of spatial thought and expression: 'in back' and 'in front'. Doctoral dissertation, University of California, Berkeley.

1986. Cognitive prerequisites: the evidence from children learning English. In Slobin (1986: 961–1004).

Johnston, J. & Slobin, D. 1979. The development of locative expressions in English, Italian, Serbo-Croatian, and Turkish. *Journal of Child Language* 6: 529–45.

Jusczyk, P. 1981. Infant speech perception: a critical appraisal. In P. Eimas & J. Miller (eds.) *Perspectives on the study of speech*. Hillsdale, NJ: Erlbaum.

Jusczyk, P., Shea, S. & Aslin, R. 1984. Linguistic experience and infant speech perception: a re-examination of Eilers, Gavin and Oller (1982). *Journal of Child Language* 11: 453–66.

Kaczmarek, L. 1953/71. A general view of the formation of child language. In Bar-Adon & Leopold (1971: 133–4). Translation of original Polish.

Kahn, L. 1986. *Basics of phonological analysis: a programmed learning text*. San Diego, Calif.: College-Hill Press.

Kamil, M. L. & Rudegeair, R. E. 1972. Methodological improvements in the assessment of phonological discrimination in children. *Child Development* 43: 1087–91.

Kaplan, E. & Kaplan, G. 1971. The prelinguistic child. In J. Eliot (ed.) *Human development and cognitive processes*. New York: Holt, Rinehart & Winston, pp. 358–81.

Karmiloff-Smith, A. 1979. *A functional approach to child language: a study of determiners and reference*. Cambridge: Cambridge University Press.

Katz, N., Baker, E. & Macnamara, J. 1974. What's in a name? A study of how children learn common and proper names. *Child Development* 45: 469–73.

Kaye, K. 1980a. Why don't we talk 'baby talk' to babies. *Journal of Child Language* 7: 489–507.

1980b. The infant as a projective stimulus. *American Journal of Orthopsychiatry*.

Kaye, K. & Charney, R. 1981. Conversational asymmetry between mothers and children. *Journal of Child Language* 8: 35–49.

Keil, F. C. 1979. *Semantic and conceptual development: an ontological perspective.* Cambridge, Mass.: Harvard University Press.

Keil, F. C. & Carroll, J. J. 1980. The child's acquisition of 'tall': implications for an alternative view of semantic development. *Papers and Reports on Child Language Development* 19: 21–8.

Kent, R. 1981. Articulatory–acoustic perspectives on speech development. In Stark (1981: 105–26).

Kernan, K. 1969. The acquisition of language by Samoan children. Doctoral dissertation, University of California, Berkeley.

Kiparsky, P. & Menn, L. 1977. On the acquisition of phonology. In Macnamara (1977: 47–78).

Klatzky, R., Clark, E. & Macken, M. A. 1973. Asymmetries in the acquisition of polar adjectives: linguistic or conceptual? *Journal of Experimental Child Psychology* 16: 32–46.

Klee, T. & Fitzgerald, M. D. 1985. The relation between grammatical development and mean length of utterance in morphemes. *Journal of Child Language* 12: 251–69.

Klein, S. 1982. Syntactic theory and the developing grammar: reestablishing the relationship between linguistic theory and data from language acquisition. Doctoral dissertation, UCLA.

Klima, E. & Bellugi-Klima, U. 1966. Syntactic regularities in the speech of children. In Lyons & Wales (1966: 183–208). Reprinted in Bar-Adon & Leopold (1971: 412–24).

Kučera, H. 1983. Roman Jakobson. *Language* 59: 871–83.

Kučera, H. & Francis, W. 1967. *Computational analysis of present-day American English.* Providence, Rhode Island. Brown University Press.

Kuczaj, S. A. 1976. Arguments against Hurford's 'Aux copying rule'. *Journal of Child Language* 3: 423–7.

1978. Why do children fail to overgeneralize the progressive inflection? *Journal of Child Language* 5: 167–71.

1982a. On the nature of syntactic development. In Kuczaj (1982b: 37–71).

(ed.) 1982b. *Language development. Vol. 1. Syntax and semantics.* Hillsdale, NJ: Lawrence Erlbaum.

Kuczaj, S. A. & Barrett, M. (eds.) 1986. *The development of word meaning: progress in cognitive development research.* New York and Berlin: Springer-Verlag.

Kuczaj, S. A. & Brannick, N. 1979. Children's use of the *wh* question modal auxiliary placement rule. *Journal of Experimental Child Psychology* 28: 43–67.

Kuczaj, S. A. & Maratsos, M. 1975. What children 'can' say before they 'will'. *Merrill-Palmer Quarterly of Behavior and Development* 21: 89–111.

1983. Initial verbs of yes–no questions: a different kind of general grammatical category. *Developmental Psychology* 19: 440–4.

Kuhl, P. 1980. Perceptual constancy for speech-sound categories in early infancy. In Yeni-Komshian, Kavanaugh & Ferguson (1980b: 41–66).

1981. Auditory category formation and development of speech perception. In Stark (1981: 165–83).

Kuhl, P. & Miller, J. D. 1975. Speech perception by the chinchilla: voiced–voiceless distinction in alveolar-plosive consonants. *Science* 190: 69–72.

Labov, W. & Labov, T. 1978. Learning the syntax of questions. In R. Campbell & P. Smith (eds.) *Recent advances in the psychology of language: language development and mother–child interaction,* vol. 4b. New York & London: Plenum, pp. 1–44.

Ladefoged, P. 1975. *A course in phonetics.* New York: Harcourt Brace Jovanovich.

Lange, S. & Larsson, K. 1973. Syntactic development of a Swedish girl, Embla, between 20 and 42 months of age, I: age 20–25 months. *Report No. 1, Project Child Language Syntax.* Stockholm: Institutionem for nordiska sprak, Stockholms Universitet.

Lasky, R. E., Syrdal-Lasky, A. & Klein, R. E. 1975. VOT discrimination by four to six-and-a-half month old infants from Spanish environments. *Journal of Experimental Child Psychology* 20: 215–25.

Leech, G. 1970. *Towards a semantic description of English.* Bloomington, Ind.: Indiana University Press.

1974. *Semantics.* Harmondsworth, Middx: Penguin.

Lenneberg, E. H. (ed.) 1964. *New directions in the study of language.* Cambridge, Mass.: MIT Press.

1967. *Biological foundations of language.* New York: Wiley.

Lenneberg, E. H. & Lenneberg, E. (eds.) 1975. *Foundations of language development.* New York: Academic Press.

Lenneberg, E., Rebelsky, G. & Nichols, I. 1965. The vocalizations of infants born to deaf and to hearing parents. *Human Development* 8: 23–37.

Leonard, L. 1976. *Meaning in child language: issues in the study of early semantic development.* New York: Grune & Stratton.

Leonard, L., Newhoff, M. & Mesalam, L. 1980. Individual differences in early phonology. *Journal of Applied Psycholinguistics* 1: 7–30.

Leonard, L., Rowan, L., Morris, L. & Fey, M. 1982. Intra-word phonological variability in young children. *Journal of Child Language* 9: 55–69.

Leopold, W. 1939–49. *Speech development of a bilingual child: a linguist's record.* Vol. 1: Vocabulary growth in the first two years (1939). Vol. 2: Sound learning in the first two years (1947). Vol. 3: Grammar and general problems in the first two years (1949). Vol. 4: Diary from age two. (1949). Evanston, Ill.: Northwestern University Press.

1952. *Bibliography of child language.* Evanston, Ill.: Northwestern University Press.

Lewis, M. M. 1936/51. *Infant speech: a study of the beginnings of language.* 2nd edn. New York: Harcourt Brace. (First edition published in 1936.)

1937. The beginning of reference to past and future in a child's speech. *British Journal of Educational Psychology* 7: 39–56.

Lieberman, P. 1975. *On the origins of language.* New York: MacMillan.

1980. On the development of vowel production in young children. In Yeni-Komshian, Kavanaugh & Ferguson (1980a: 113–42).

Lightfoot, D. 1979. *Principles of diachronic syntax.* Cambridge: Cambridge University Press.

1982. *The language lottery. Towards a biology of grammars.* Cambridge, Mass.: MIT Press.

Limber, J. 1973. The genesis of complex sentences. In Moore (1973: 169–85).

1976. Unravelling competence, performance and pragmatics in the speech of young children. *Journal of Child Language* 3: 309–18.

Lipp, E. 1977. The acquisition of Estonian inflections. *Journal of Child Language* 4: 313–19.

Lisker, L. & Abramson, A. S. 1967. The voicing dimension: some experiments in comparative phonetics. *Proceedings of the Sixth International Congress of Phonetic Sciences*, Prague.

Loban, W. 1976. *Language development: kindergarten through twelve*. Urbana, Ill.: National Council of Teachers of English.

Lock, A. (ed.) 1978. *Action, gesture and symbol: the emergence of language*. London: Academic Press.

Locke, J. L. 1971. Phonemic perception in 2- and 3-year-old children. *Perceptual and Motor Skills* 32: 215–17.

1983. *Phonological acquisition and change*. New York: Academic Press.

Lovell, K. & Dixon, E. 1967. The growth of the control of grammar in imitation, comprehension and production. *Journal of Child Psychology and Psychiatry* 8: 31–9.

Lukens, H. 1894. Preliminary report on the learning of language. *Pedagogical Seminary* 3: 424–60.

Lust, B. 1986. *Studies in first language acquisition of anaphora: defining the constraints*. Boston, Mass.: D. Reidel.

Lynip, A. 1951. The use of magnetic devices in the collection and analysis of the preverbal utterances of an infant. *Genetic Psychology Monographs* 44: 221–62.

Lyons, J. 1968. *Theoretical linguistics*. Cambridge: Cambridge University Press.

Lyons, J. & Wales, R. (eds.) 1966. *Psycholinguistic papers*. Edinburgh: University of Edinburgh Press.

MacKain, K. S. & Stern, D. N. 1985. The concept of experience in speech development. In K. E. Nelson (1985: 1–33).

Macken, M. A. 1978. Permitted complexity in phonological development: one child's acquisition of Spanish consonants. *Lingua* 44: 219–53.

1979. Developmental reorganization of phonology: a hierarchy of basic units of acquisition. *Lingua* 49: 11–49.

1980. The child's lexical representation: the 'puzzle-puddle-pickle' evidence. *Journal of Linguistics* 16: 1–17.

1986. Representation, rules and overgeneralization in phonology. Unpublished paper, Stanford University.

Macken, M. A. & Ferguson, C. A. 1983. Cognitive aspects of phonological development: model, evidence, and issues. In K. E. Nelson (1983: 256–82).

Macnamara, J. 1972. Cognitive basis of language learning in infants. *Psychological Review* 79: 1–13. Reprinted in Bloom (1978: 390–406).

(ed.) 1977. *Language learning and thought*. New York: Academic Press.

1982. *Names for things: a study of human learning*. Cambridge, Mass.: MIT Press.

MacWhinney, B. 1975. Rules, rote, and analogy in morphological formations by Hungarian children. *Journal of Child Language* 2: 65–77.

1976. Hungarian research on the acquisition of morphology and syntax. *Journal of Child Language* 3: 397–410.

1978. Processing a first language: the acquisition of morphophonology. *Monographs of the Society for Research in Child Development* 43, no. 174.

1982. Basic syntactic processes. In Kuczaj (1982b: 73–136).

MacWhinney, B. & Bates, E. 1978. Sentential devices for conveying givenness and newness: a cross-cultural developmental study. *Journal of Verbal Learning and Verbal Behavior* 17: 539–58.

Malrieu, P. 1973. Aspects psychologiques de la construction de la phrase chez l'enfant. *Journal de Psychologie* 70: 157–74.

Marantz, A. 1982. On the acquisition of grammatical relations. *Linguistische Berichte* 80–82: 32–69.

1983. The connection between grammatical relations and lexical categories in language acquisition and linguistic theory. In Otsu *et al.* (1973: 165–7).

1984. *On the nature of grammatical relations*. Cambridge, Mass.: MIT Press.

Maratsos, M. 1973. Decrease in the understanding of the word 'big' in preschool children. *Child Development* 44: 747–52.

1974a. Children who get worse at understanding the passive: a replication of Bever. *Journal of Psycholinguistic Research* 3: 65–74.

1974b. When is a high thing a big one? *Developmental Psychology* 10: 367–75.

1978. New models in linguistics and language acquisition. In M. Halle, J. Bresnan & G. Miller (eds.) *Linguistic theory and psychological reality*. Cambridge, Mass.: MIT Press, pp. 247–63.

1982. The child's construction of grammatical categories. In Wanner & Gleitman (1982: 240–66).

1984. The acquisition of syntax. In J. Flavell & E. Markman (eds.) *Carmichael's handbook of child psychology*, vol. 3, 4th edn. New York: Wiley.

Maratsos, M. & Abramovitch, R. 1975. How children understand full, truncated, and anomalous passives. *Journal of Verbal Learning and Verbal Behavior* 14: 145–57.

Maratsos, M. & Chalkley, M. A. 1980. The internal language of children's syntax: the ontogenesis and representation of syntactic categories. In K. E. Nelson (1980: 127–214).

Maratsos, M. & Kuczaj, S. A. 1978. Against the transformational account: a simpler analysis of auxiliary overmarkings. *Journal of Child Language* 5: 337–45.

Maratsos, M., Kuczaj, S. A., Fox, D. & Chalkley, M. A. 1979. Some empirical studies in the acquisition of transformational relations: passives, negatives, and the past tense. In W. Collins (ed.) *Children's language and communication*. Minnesota Symposia on Child Psychology. Hillsdale, NJ: Erlbaum, pp. 1–45.

Mazurkewich, I. 1982. Second language acquisition of the dative alternation and markedness: the best theory. Doctoral dissertation, Université de Montreal.

1984. The acquisition of the dative alternation by second language learners and linguistic theory. *Language Learning* 34: 91–109.

Mazurkewich, I. & White, L. 1984. The acquisition of the dative alternation: unlearning overgeneralizations. *Cognition* 16: 261–83.

McCarthy, D. 1930. The language development of the preschool child. *Institute of Child Welfare Monograph Series* 4. Mineapolis: University of Minnesota Press.

1954. Language development in children. In Carmichael (ed.) *Manual of child psychology*. New York: John Wiley, pp. 492–630.

McNeill, D. 1966a. Developmental psycholinguistics. In Smith & Miller (1966: 15–84).

1966b. The creation of language by children. In Lyons & Wales (1966: 99–115).

1970a. *The acquisition of language.* New York: Harper & Row.

1970b. The development of language. In P. Mussen (ed.) *Carmichael's manual of child psychology*, vol. 1, pp. 1061–1161.

1971. The capacity for grammatical development in children. In Slobin (1971: 17–40).

Mead, M. 1963. *Sex and temperament in three primitive societies.* New York: Morrow.

Menn, L. 1971. Phonotactic rules in beginning speech. *Lingua* 26: 225–51.

1978. *Pattern, control and contrast in beginning speech, a case study in the development of word form and word function.* Bloomington, Ind.: Indiana University Linguistics Club.

1980. Phonological theory and child phonology. In Yeni-Komshian, Kavanaugh & Ferguson (1980: 23–41).

1983. Development of articulatory, phonetic, and phonological capabilities. In B. Butterworth (ed.) *Language production: development, writing and other language processes.* Vol. 2. New York: Academic Press, pp. 3–50.

Menyuk, P. 1969. *Sentences children use.* Cambridge, Mass: MIT Press.

1971. *The acquisition and development of language.* Englewood Cliffs, NJ: Prentice-Hall.

Menyuk, P. & Anderson, S. 1969. Children's identification and reproduction of /w/, /r/, and /l/. *Journal of Speech and Hearing Research* 12: 39–52.

Menyuk, P. & Menn, L. 1979. Early strategies for the perception and production of words and sounds. In Fletcher & Garman (1979: 49–70).

Mervis, C. & Canada, K. 1983. On the existence of competence errors in early comprehension: a reply to Fremgen & Fay and Chapman & Thomson. *Journal of Child Language* 10: 431–40.

Miller, G. & McNeill, D. 1969. Psycholinguistics. In G. Lindzey & E. Aaronson (eds.) *Handbook of social psychology.* Reading, Mass: Addison-Wesley, pp. 666–794.

Miller, J. 1981. *Assessing language production in children.* Baltimore, Md.: University Park Press.

Miller, J., Chapman, R., Bronston, M. & Reichle, J. 1980. Language comprehension in sensorimotor stages V and VI. *Journal of Speech and Hearing Research* 23: 284–311.

Miller, J. & Yoder, D. 1974. An ontogenetic teaching strategy for retarded children. In Schiefelbusch & Lloyd (1974: 505–28).

1984. *Language comprehension text (clinical edition).* Baltimore, Md.: University Park Press.

Miller, P. D. 1972. Vowel neutralization and vowel reduction. *Papers from the Eighth Regional Meeting, Chicago Linguistic Society*, pp. 482–9.

Miller, W. & Ervin, S. 1964. The development of grammar in child language. In Bellugi & Brown (1964: 9–34).

Minifie, F. & Lloyd, L. (eds.) 1978. *Communicative and cognitive abilities in early language assessment.* Baltimore, Md.: University Park Press.

Moerk, E. 1980. Relationships between input frequencies and children's language acquisition: a reanalysis of Brown's data. *Journal of Child Language* 7: 105–18.

1981. To attend or not to attend to unwelcome reanalyses? A reply to Pinker. *Journal of Child Language* 8: 627–31.

Moffitt, A. 1971. Consonant cue perception by 22 twenty-four-week-old infants. *Child Development* 42: 717–32.

Moore, T. (ed.) 1973. *Cognitive development and the acquisition of meaning*. New York: Academic Press.

Morehead, D. M. & Ingram, D. 1973. The development of base syntax in normal and linguistically deviant children. *Journal of Speech and Hearing Research* 16: 330–52.

Morehead, D. M. & Morehead, A. E. (eds.) 1976. *Normal and deficient child language*. Baltimore, Md.: University Park Press.

Morse, P. 1974. Infant speech perception: a preliminary model and review of the literature. In Schiefelbusch & Lloyd (1974: 19–53).

Moskowitz, A. 1970. The two-year-old stage in the acquisition of English phonology. *Language* 46: 426–41.

1971. Acquisition of phonology. Doctoral dissertation, University of California, Berkeley.

Mowrer, O. 1960. *Learning theory and symbolic processes*. New York: John Wiley.

Muma, J. 1986. *Language acquisition: a functional perspective*. Austin, Texas: Pro-Ed.

Munson, J. & Ingram, D. 1985. Morphology before syntax: a case study from language acquisition. *Journal of Child Language* 12: 681–4.

Nelson, K. 1973. Structure and strategy in learning to talk. *Monographs of the Society of Research in Child Development* 38, no. 149.

1974. Concept, word and sentence: interrelations in acquisition and development. *Psychological Review* 81: 267–85.

1975. The nominal shift in semantic–syntactic development. *Cognitive Psychology* 7: 461–79.

1986. *Event knowledge: structure and function in development*. Hillsdale, NJ: Erlbaum.

Nelson, K. E. 1977. Facilitating children's syntax acquisition. *Developmental Psychology* 13: 101–7.

(ed.) 1978. *Children's language. Vol. 1*. New York: Gardner Press.

(ed.) 1980a. *Children's language. Vol. 2*. New York: Gardner Press.

1981. Toward a rare event cognitive comparison theory of syntax acquisition: insights from work with recasts. In Dale & Ingram (1981: 229–40).

(ed.) 1984. *Children's language. Vol. 4*. Hillsdale, NJ: Erlbaum.

(ed.) 1985. *Children's language. Vol. 5*. Hillsdale, NJ: Erlbaum.

1981. Toward a rare-event comparison theory of syntax acquisition. In Dale & Ingram (1981).

Nelson, K. E. & Baker, N. 1984. Recasting. *First Language* 5: 3–21.

Nelson, K. E. & Bonvillian, J. (1973). Concepts and words in the 18-month–old: acquiring concept names under controlled conditions. *Cognition* 2: 435–50.

Nelson, K. E., Carskaddon, G., & Bonvillian, J. 1973. Syntax acquisition: impact of experimental variation in adult verbal interaction with the child. *Child Development* 44: 497–504.

Nelson, K. E., Denninger, M., Bonvillian, J., Kaplan, B., & Baker, N. 1984. Maternal input adjustments and non-adjustments as related to children's linguistic advances and to language acquisition theories. In A. D. Pelligrini & T. D. Yawkey (eds.) *The development of oral and written languages: readings in developmental applied linguistics*. New York: Ablex, pp. 31–56.

Newmeyer, F. 1983. *Grammatical theory: its limits and its possibilities.* Chicago, Ill.: University of Chicago Press.

Newport, E., Gleitman, H. & Gleitman, L. 1977. Mother, I'd rather do it myself: some effects and non-effects of maternal speech style. In Snow & Ferguson (1977: 101–49).

Nice, M. 1917. The speech development of a child from eighteen months to six years. *Pedagogical Seminary* 24: 204–43.

1920. Concerning all-day conversations. *Pedagogical Seminary* 27: 166–77.

1925. Length of sentences as a criterion of child's progress in speech. *Journal of Educational Psychology* 16: 370–9.

Ninio, A. & Bruner, J. 1978. The achievement and antecedents of labelling. *Journal of Child Language* 5: 1–15.

Nokony, A. 1978. Word and gesture by an Indian child. In Lock (1978: 291–307).

Ochs, E. 1979. Transcription as theory. In Ochs & Schefflin (1979: 43–72).

1982a. Ergativity and word order in Samoan child language. *Language* 58: 646–71.

1982b. Talking to children in Western Samoa. *Language in Society* 11: 77–104.

Ochs, E. & Schefflin, B. (eds.) 1979. *Developmental pragmatics.* New York: Academic Press.

O'Donnell, R. C., Griffin, W. J. & Norris, R. C. 1967. *Syntax of kindergarten and elementary school children.* Champaign, Ill.: National Council of Teachers.

O'Grady, W. 1986. *Principles of grammar and learning.* Chicago, Ill.: University of Chicago Press.

O'Grady, W., Suzuki-Wei, Y. & Cho, S. W. 1986. Directionality preferences in the interpretation of anaphora: data from Korean and Japanese. *Journal of Child Language* 13: 409–20.

Oksaar, O. 1983. *Language acquisition in the early years.* New York: Saint Martin's Press. Translated from the German original of 1977.

Oller, D. K. 1980. The emergence of the sounds of speech in infancy. In Yeni-Komshian, Kavanaugh & Ferguson (1980: 93–112).

1981. Infant vocalizations: exploration and reflexivity. In Stark (1981: 85–103).

Oller, D. K. & Eilers, R. 1982. Similarity of babbling in Spanish- and English-learning babies. *Journal of Child Language* 9: 565–77.

Oller, D. K., Eilers, R., Bull, D. & Carney, A. 1985. Prespeech vocalizations of a deaf infant: a comparison with normal metaphonological development. *Journal of Speech and Hearing Research* 28: 47–63.

Oller, D. K., Wieman, L., Doyle, W. & Ross, C. 1976. Infant babbling and speech. *Journal of Child Language* 3: 1–11.

Olmsted, D. 1971. *Out of the mouth of babes.* The Hague: Mouton.

Olsen-Fulero, L. 1982. Style and stability in mother conversational behaviour: a study of individual differences. *Journal of Child Language* 9: 543–64.

O'Shea, M. 1907. *Linguistic development and education.* London: Macmillan.

Otsu, Y., van Riemsdijk, H., Inoue, K., Kamio, A. & Kawasaki, N. (eds.) 1983. *Studies in generative grammar and language acquisition.* Tokyo: Editorial Committee. (Inside jacket states that copies can be ordered from N. Kawasaki, c/o Division of Languages, International Christian University, Tokyo.)

Park, T.-Z. 1978. Plurals in child speech. *Journal of Child Language* 5: 237–50.

Pelsma, J. 1910. A child vocabulary and its development. *Pedagogical Seminary* 17: 328–69.

Penman, R., Cross, T., Milgrom-Friedman, J. & Meares, R. (1983). Mothers' speech to prelinguistic infants: a pragmatic analysis. *Journal of Child Language* 10: 17–34.

Perlmutter, D. 1983. *Studies in relational grammar 1*. Chicago, Ill.: University of Chicago Press.

Perroni Semoes, M. & Stoel-Gammon, C. 1979. The acquisition of inflections in Portuguese: a study of the development of person markers on verbs. *Journal of Child Language* 6: 53–67.

Peshkovskiy, A. M. 1925. Desyat' tysyach Zvukov. Sb statey.

Peters, A. 1977. Language learning strategies. *Language* 53: 56–73.

   1983. *The units of language acquisition*. Cambridge: Cambridge University Press.

Petretic, P. & Tweney, R. 1977. Does comprehension precede production? The development of children's responses to telegraphic sentences of varying grammatical adequacy. *Journal of Child Language* 4: 201–9.

Piaget, J. 1929. *The child's conception of the world*. New York: Harcourt Brace.

   1948. *Play, dreams and imitation in childhood*. New York: Norton.

   1952. *The origins of intelligence in children*. New York: International Universities Press.

   1954. *The construction of reality in the child*. New York: Basic Books.

   1955. *The language and thought of the child*. Cleveland, Ill.: World Publishing Co.

   1971. *Biology and knowledge*. Chicago, Ill.: University of Chicago Press.

Piaget, J. & Inhelder, B. 1967. *The child's conception of space*. New York: Norton.

   1969. *The psychology of the child*. New York: Basic Books.

Piattelli-Palmarini, M. (ed.) 1980. *Language and learning: the debate between Jean Piaget and Noam Chomsky*. Cambridge, Mass.: Harvard University Press.

Pinker, S. 1981. On the acquisition of grammatical morphemes. *Journal of Child Language* 8: 477–84.

   1982. A theory of the acquisition of lexical interpretive grammars. In J. Bresnan (ed.) *The mental representation of grammatical relations*. Cambridge, Mass.: MIT Press.

   1984. *Language learnability and language development*. Cambridge, Mass.: Harvard University Press.

Pitcher, E. G. & Prelinger, E. 1963. *Children tell stories*. New York: International Universities Press.

Pollock, F. 1878. An infant's progress in language. *Mind* 3: 392–401.

Prather, E. M., Hedrick, D. L. & Kern, C. A. 1975. Articulation development in children aged two to four years. *Journal of Speech and Hearing Disorders* 40: 179–91.

Preyer, W. 1889. *The mind of the child*. New York: Appleton. Translation of original German edn of 1882.

Prideaux, G. 1976. A functional analysis of English question acquisition: a response to Hurford. *Journal of Child Language* 3: 417–22.

Pye, C. 1980. The acquisition of grammatical morphemes in Quiché Mayan. Doctoral dissertation, University of Pittsburgh.

   1983a. Mayan telegraphese: intonational determinants of inflectional development in Quiché Mayan. *Language* 59: 583–604.

   1983b. Mayan motherese: an ethnography of Quiché Mayan speech to young children. Unpublished paper.

1985. Review of *Language learnability and language development* by Pinker. *Language* 61: 903–7.

1986. Quiché Mayan speech to children. *Journal of Child Language* 13: 85–100.

1987. Language loss in the Chilcotin. Unpublished paper, University of Kansas.

Pye, C., Ingram, D. & List, H. 1987. A comparison of initial consonant acquisition in English and Quiché. In K. E. Nelson & A. Van Kleeck (eds.) *Children's language, vol. 6*: 175–90 Hillsdale, NJ: Erlbaum.

Radford, A. 1981. *Transformational syntax: a student's guide to Chomsky's Extended Standard Theory*. Cambridge: Cambridge University Press.

Ramer, A. 1976. Syntactic styles in emerging speech. *Journal of Child Language* 3: 49–62.

Ratner, N. & Bruner, J. 1978. Games, social exchange, and the acquisition of language. *Journal of Child Language* 5: 391–401.

Ravn, K. E. & Gelman, S. A. 1984. Rule usage in children's understanding of 'big' and 'little'. *Child Development* 55: 2141–50.

Reinhart, T. 1976. The syntactic domain of anaphora. Doctoral dissertation, MIT.

1981. Definite NP anaphora and c-command domains. *Linguistic Inquiry* 12: 605–35.

1983. *Anaphora and semantic interpretation*. Chicago, Ill.: University of Chicago Press.

Rescorla, L. 1980. Overextensions in early language development. *Journal of Child Language* 7: 321–35.

Rice, M. L. & Kemper, S. 1984. *Child language and cognition*. Baltimore: University Park Press.

Rodd, L. & Braine, M. D. S. 1970. Children's imitations of syntactic constructions as a measure of linguistic competence. *Journal of Verbal Learning and Verbal Behavior* 10: 430–43.

Rodgon, M. 1976. *Single-word usage, cognitive development and the beginnings of combinatorial speech*. Cambridge: Cambridge University Press.

Rodgon, M., Jankowski, W. & Alenskas, L. 1977. A multi-functional approach to single-word usage. *Journal of Child Language* 4: 23–44.

Roeper, T. 1981. In pursuit of a deductive model of language acquisition. In Baker & McCarthy (1981: 121–50).

Roeper, T. & Williams, E. (eds.) 1982. *Parameter setting*. Dordrecht: D. Reidel.

Rosch, E. 1973. On the internal structure of perceptual and semantic categories. In Moore (1973: 111–44).

1975. Cognitive representation of semantic categories. *Journal of Experimental Psychology: General* 104: 192–233.

1978. Principles of categorization. In E. Rosch & B. Lloyd (eds.) *Cognition and categorization*. Hillsdale, NJ: Erlbaum.

Rosch, E. & Mervis, C. 1975. Family resemblances: studies in the internal structure of categories. *Cognitive Psychology* 7: 573–605.

Rosch, E., Mervis, C., Gray, W., Johnson, D. & Boyes-Braem, P. 1976. Basic objects in natural categories. *Cognitive Psychology* 8: 382–439.

Roussey, C. 1899–1900. Notes sur l'apprentissage de la parole chez un enfant. *La Parole* 1: 790–880, 2: 23–40, 86–97.

Rūķe-Draviņa, V. 1973. On the emergence of inflection in child language: a contribution based on Latvian data. In Ferguson & Slobin (1973: 252–67).

Rumelhart, D. & McClelland, J. 1986. On learning the past tenses of English verbs. In J. McClelland & D. Rumelhart (eds.) *Parallel distributed processing: explorations in the microstructure of cognition. Vol. 2. Psychological and biological models.* Cambridge, Mass.: MIT Press, pp. 216–71.

Ryan, J. (1973). Interpretation and imitation in early language acquisition. In R. Hinde & J. Hinde (eds.) *Constraints on learning: limitations and predispositions.* London: Academic Press, pp. 427–44.

Sachs, J. 1977. The adaptive significance of linguistic input to prelinguistic infants. In Snow & Ferguson (1977: 51–61).

Sachs, J. & Truswell, L. 1978. Comprehension of two-word instructions by children in the one-word stage. *Journal of Child Language* 5: 17–24.

Samarin, W. 1967. *Field linguistics: a guide to linguistic field work.* New York: Holt, Rinehart & Winston.

Sander, E. K. 1961. When are speech sounds learned? *Journal of Speech and Hearing Disorders* 37: 55–63.

Scarborough, H. & Wyckoff, J. 1986. Mother, I'd still rather do it myself: some further non-effects of 'motherese'. *Journal of Child Language* 13: 431–7.

Schaerlaekens, A. 1973. *The two-word sentence in child language development.* The Hague: Mouton.

Schiefelbusch, R. (ed.) 1978. *Bases of language intervention.* Baltimore, Md.: University Park Press.

Schiefelbusch, R. & Bricker, D. (eds.) 1981. *Early language: acquisition and intervention.* Baltimore, Md.: University Park Press.

Schiefelbusch, R. & Lloyd, L. (eds.) 1974. *Language perspectives: acquisition, retardation, and intervention.* Baltimore, Md.: University Park Press.

Schiefflin, B. 1979. Getting it together: an ethnographic approach to the study of the development of communicative competence. In Ochs & Schiefflin (1979: 73–108).

Schlesinger, I. M. 1971. The production of utterances and language acquisition. In Slobin (1971: 63–101).

  1974. Relational concepts underlying language. In Schiefelbusch & Lloyd (1974: 129–51).

  1977. *Production and comprehension of utterances.* Hillsdale, NJ: Erlbaum.

  1982. *Steps toward language: toward a theory of native language acquisition.* Hillsdale, NJ: Erlbaum.

Schwartz, R. & Camarata, S. 1985. Examining relationships between input and language development: some statistical issues. *Journal of Child Language* 12: 199–207.

Schwartz, R. & Leonard, L. 1982. Do children pick and choose? An examination of phonological selection and avoidance in early acquisition. *Journal of Child Language* 9: 319–36.

Schwartz, R. & Terrell, B. 1983. The role of input frequency in lexical acquisition. *Journal of Child Language* 10: 57–64.

Scollon, R. 1976. *Conversations with a one year old.* Honolulu: University Press of Hawaii.

Sheldon, A. 1974. The parallel function in the acquisition of relative clauses in English. *Journal of Verbal Learning and Verbal Behavior* 13: 272–81.

Sherrod, K., Friedman, S., Crawley, S., Drake, D. & Devieux, J. 1977. Maternal language to prelinguistic infants: syntactic aspects. *Child Development* 48: 1662–5.

Shibamoto, J. S. & Olmsted, D. 1978. Lexical and syllabic patterns in phonological acquisition. *Journal of Child Language* 5: 417–57.

Shipley, E., Smith, C. & Gleitman, L. 1969. A study in the acquisition of language: free responses to commands. *Language* 45: 322–42.

Shirley, M. M. 1933. The first two years: a study of twenty-five babies. Vol. 2. *Institute of Child Welfare Monograph Series*. Minneapolis, Minn.: University of Minnesota Press.

Shriberg, L. & Kwiatkowski, J. 1980. *Natural process analysis (NPA)*. New York: John Wiley.

Shvachkin, N. 1948/73. The development of phonemic speech perception in children. In Ferguson & Slobin (1973: 91–127).

Sinclair, H. 1971. Sensorimotor action patterns as a condition for the acquisition of syntax. In Huxley & Ingram (1971: 121–30).

Sinclair, H. & Ferreiro, E. 1970. Etude génétique de la comprehension, production et répétition des phrases à mode passif. *Archives de Psychologie* 40: 1–42.

Skinner, B. F. 1957. *Verbal behavior*. New York: Appleton-Century-Crofts.

Slobin, D. 1966. Abstracts of Soviet studies of child language. In Smith & Miller (1966: 361–86).

(ed.) 1967. *A field manual for cross-cultural study of the acquisition of communicative competence*. Berkeley, Calif.: University of California.

1968. Recall of full and truncated passive sentences in connected discourse. *Journal of Verbal Learning and Verbal Behavior* 7: 876–81.

1970. Universals of grammatical development. In G. Flores D'Arcais & W. Levelt (eds.) *Advances in psycholinguistics*. Amsterdam: North-Holland, pp. 174–86.

(ed.) 1971. *The ontogenesis of grammar*. New York: Academic Press.

1972. *Leopold's bibliography of child language*. Bloomington, Ind.: Indiana University Press.

1973. Cognitive prerequisites for the development of grammar. In Ferguson & Slobin (1973: 175–208).

1977. Language change in childhood and history. In Macnamara (1977: 185–214).

1982. Universal and particular in the acquisition of language. In Wanner & Gleitman (1982: 128–70).

(ed.) 1986. *Cross-linguistic study of language acquisition*. Hillsdale, NJ: Erlbaum.

Smith, C. 1970. An experimental approach to children's linguistic competence. In Hayes (1970: 109–35).

Smith, F. & Miller, G. A. 1966. *The genesis of language*. Cambridge, Mass.: MIT Press.

Smith, M. 1926. An investigation of the development of the sentence and the extent of vocabulary in young children. *University of Iowa Studies in Child Welfare* vol. 3, no. 5.

1933. Grammatical errors in the speech of preschool children. *Child Development* 4: 183–90.

1935. A study of some factors influencing the development of the sentence in preschool children. *Journal of Genetic Psychology* 46: 182–212.

Smith, N. V. 1973. *The acquisition of phonology: a case study*. Cambridge: Cambridge University Press.

1982. Review of *Language acquisition*, by P. Fletcher & M. Garman (eds.). *Language* 58: 470–4.

Snow, C. E. 1977a. Mothers' speech research: from input to interaction. In Snow & Ferguson (1977: 31–49).

1977b. The development of conversation between mothers and babies. *Journal of Child Language* 4: 1–22.

Snow, C. E. & Ferguson, C. A. 1977. *Talking to children: language input and acquisition.* Cambridge: Cambridge University Press.

Snow, C. E. & Goldfeld, B. 1983. Turn the page please: situation-specific language acquisition. *Journal of Child Language* 10: 551–70.

Snow, C. E., Smith, N. S. & Hoefnagel-Hohle, M. 1980. The acquisition of some Dutch morphological rules. *Journal of Child Language* 7: 539–53.

Snyder, L., Bates, E. & Betherington, I. 1981. Content and context in early lexical development. *Journal of Child Language* 8: 565–82.

Solan, L. 1983. *Pronominal reference: child language and the theory of grammar.* Dordrecht: D. Reidel.

1987. Parameter setting and the development of pronouns and reflexives. In Roeper & Williams (1987: 189–210).

Solberg, M. E. 1978. Constant and structure contingent characteristics of the language array. In R. Campbell & P. Smith (eds.) *Recent advances in the psychology of language: language development and mother–child interaction.* New York: Plenum.

Stampe, D. 1968. Yes, Virginia . . . Unpublished paper presented to the 4th Annual Regional Meeting of the Chicago Linguistic Society.

1969. The acquisition of phonemic representation. *Proceedings of the Fifth Regional Meeting of the Chicago Linguistic Society*, pp. 433–44.

1973. A dissertation on natural phonology. Doctoral dissertation, University of Chicago.

Stark, R. 1980. Stages of development in the first year of life. In Yeni-Komshian, Kavanaugh & Ferguson (1980: 73–92).

(ed.) 1981. *Language behavior in infancy and early childhood.* New York: Elsevier North-Holland.

Stark, R., Rose, S. & McLagan, M. 1975. Features of infant sounds: the first eight weeks of life. *Journal of Child Language* 2: 205–21.

Starr, S. 1975. The relationship of single words to two-word sentences. *Child Development* 46: 701–8.

Stern, C. & Stern, W. 1907. *Die Kindersprache.* Leipzig: Barth.

Stern, D., Spierker, S., Barnett, R. & MacKain, K. 1983. The prosody of maternal speech: infant age and context related changes. *Journal of Child Language* 10: 17–34.

Stern, W. 1924. *Psychology of early childhood up to the sixth year of age.* New York: Holt.

Stockman, I., Woods, D. & Tishman, A. 1981. Listener agreement on phonetic segments in early childhood vocalizations. *Journal of Psycholinguistic Research* 10: 593–617.

Stoel-Gammon, C. 1986. Underlying representations in child phonology: current models, sources of evidence, and future research. Unpublished paper, University of Washington.

Stoel-Gammon, C. & Cooper, J. 1984. Patterns of early lexical and phonological development. *Journal of Child Language* 11: 247–71.

Stoel-Gammon, C. & Dunn, C. 1985. *Normal and disordered phonology in children.* Baltimore, Md.: University Park Press.

Strange, W. & Broen, P. A. 1980. Perception and production of approximant consonants by 3-year-olds: a first study. In Yeni-Komshian, Kavanaugh & Ferguson (1980b: 117–54).

Streeter, L. A. 1976. Language perception of two-month-old infants shows effects of both innate mechanisms and experience. *Nature* 259: 39–41.

Strohner, J. & Nelson, K. E. 1974. The young child's development of sentence comprehensions: influence of event probability, nonverbal context, syntactic form, and strategies. *Child Development* 45: 564–76.

Sudhalter, V. & Braine, M. D. S. 1985. How does comprehension of passives develop? A comparison of actional and experiential verbs. *Journal of Child Language* 12: 455–70.

Taine, H. 1877. On the acquisition of language by children. *Mind* 2: 252–9.

Tavakolian, S. (ed.) 1981a. *Linguistic theory and language acquisition.* Cambridge: Mass.: MIT Press.

1981b. The conjoined-clause analysis of relative clauses. In Tavakolian (1981a: 167–87).

Taylor-Browne, K. 1983. Acquiring restrictions on forward anaphora: a pilot study. *Calgary Working Papers in Linguistics* 9: 75–100.

Templin, M. 1957. *Certain language skills in children.* University of Minnesota Institute of Child Welfare Monograph Series 26. Minneapolis: University of Minnesota Press.

Thomson, J. R. & Chapman, R. 1977. Who is 'Daddy' revisited: the status of two-year-olds' over-extended words in use and comprehension. *Journal of Child Language* 4: 359–75.

Thorndike, E. & Lorge, I. 1944. *The teacher's word book of 30,000 words.* New York: Teachers College, Columbia University.

Trehub, S., Bull, D. & Schneider, B. 1981. Infant speech and nonspeech perception: a review and reevaluation. In R. Schiefelbusch & D. Bricker (1981: 9–50).

Trubetzkoy, N. 1969. *Principles of phonology.* Berkeley and Los Angeles: University of California Press. Translation of original German version.

Tse, S.-M. 1982. The acquisition of Cantonese phonology. Doctoral dissertation, The University of British Columbia.

Turner, E. & Rommetveit, R. 1967. The acquisition of sentence voice and reversibility. *Child Development* 38: 649–60.

Tyack, D. & Gottsleben, R. 1974. *Language sampling, analysis, and training.* Palo Alto, Calif.: Consulting Psychologists Press.

Tyack, D. & Ingram, D. 1977. Children's production and comprehension of questions. *Journal of Child Language* 4: 211–24.

Uzgiris, I. & Hunt, J. McV. 1975. *Assessment in infancy: ordinal scales of psychological development.* Urbana, Ill.: University of Illinois Press.

Varma, T. 1979. Stage I speech of a Hindi-speaking child. *Journal of Child Language* 6: 167–73.

Velten, H. 1943. The growth of phonemic and lexical patterns in infant speech. *Language* 19: 281–92.

Vihman, M. 1981. Phonology and the development of the lexicon: evidence from children's errors. *Journal of Child Language* 8: 239–64.

Vinson, J. 1915. Observations sur le développement du langage chez l'enfant. *Revue Linguistique* 49: 1–39.

Vygotsky, L. 1962. *Thought and language*. Cambridge, Mass.: MIT Press. Translation of original Russian version of 1934.

Wall, R. 1972. Review of *Language development: form and function in emerging grammars*, by L. Bloom. *Language Sciences* 19: 21–7.

Wang, W. & Crawford, J. 1960. Frequency studies of English consonants. *Language and Speech* 3: 131–9.

Wanner, E. & Gleitman, L. (eds.) 1982. *Language acquisition: the state of the art*. Cambridge, Mass.: MIT Press.

Wasow, T. 1983. Some remarks on developmental psycholinguistics. In Otsu *et al.* (1983: 191–6).

Waterson, N. 1970. Some speech forms of an English child: a phonological study. *Transactions of the Philological Society* 1: 1–24.

  1971. Child phonology: a prosodic view. *Journal of Linguistics* 7: 179–211.

Waterson, N. & Snow C. (eds.) 1978. *The development of communication*. New York: John Wiley.

Watt, W. 1970. On two hypotheses concerning psycholinguistics. In Hayes (1970: 137–220).

Weiner, F. 1979. *Phonological process analysis*. Baltimore, Md.: University Park Press.

Weir, R. 1962. *Language in the crib*. The Hague: Mouton.

Weist, R. 1983. Prefix versus suffix information processing in the comprehension of tense and aspect. *Journal of Child Language* 10: 85–96.

Weist, R., Wysocka, A. Witkowska-Stadnik, K., Buczowska, E. & Konieczna, E. 1984. The defective tense hypothesis: on the emergence of tense and aspect in child Polish. *Journal of Child Language* 11: 347–74.

Weist, R. & Konieczna, E. 1985. Affix processing strategies and linguistic systems. *Journal of Child Language* 12: 27–36.

Wellman, B., Case, I., Mengert, I. & Bradbury, D. 1931. Speech sounds of young children. *University of Iowa Studies in Child Welfare* 5.

Werker, J. & Tees, R. 1984. Cross-language speech perception: evidence for perceptual reorganization during the first year of life. *Infant Behavior and Development* 7: 49–63.

Werner, H. & Kaplan, B. 1963. *Symbol formation*. New York: John Wiley.

Wexler, K. 1982. A principle theory for language acquisition. In Wanner & Gleitman (1982: 288–315).

Wexler, K. & Chen, Y.-C. 1985. The development of lexical anaphors and pronouns. *Papers and Reports on Child Language Development* 24: 138–49.

Wexler, K. & Culicover, P. 1980. *Formal principles of language acquisition*. Cambridge, Mass.: MIT Press.

Wexler, K. & Manzini, M. R. 1987. Parameters and learnability in binding theory. In Roeper & E. Williams (1987: 77–89).

White, L. 1982. *Grammatical theory and language acquisition*. Hingham, Mass.: Kluwer.

Whitehurst, G., Ironsmith, M. & Goldfein, M. 1974. Selective imitation of the passive construction through modelling. *Journal of Experimental Child Psychology* 17: 288–302.

Wilkinson, A. 1971. *The foundations of language: talking and reading in young children.* Oxford University Press.

Wilson, L. 1898. Bibliography of child study. *Pedagogical Seminary* 5: 541–89.

Winitz, H., 1969. *Articulation, acquisition and behavior.* New York: Appleton-Century-Crofts.

Wittgenstein, L. 1953. *Philosophical investigations.* New York: Macmillan.

Yeni-Komshian, G., Kavanaugh, J. & Ferguson, C. (eds.) (1980a). *Child phonology. Vol. 1. Production.* New York: Academic Press.

(eds.) 1980b. *Child phonology: Vol. 2. Perception.* New York: Academic Press.

Young, F. 1941. An analysis of certain variables in a developmental study of language. *Genetic Psychology Monographs* 23: 3–141.

Zarębina, M. 1965. Ksztaltownaie sie systemu jeszykowego dziecka. Krakow. Oddzial w. Krakowie: Polska Akademia Nauk.

Zukow, P. 1982. Transcription systems for video-taped interactions: some advantages and limitations of manual and computer rendering techniques. *Journal of Applied Psycholinguistics* 3: 61–79.

Zwicky, A. 1970. A double regularity in the acquisition of English verb morphology. *Papers in Linguistics* 3: 411–18.

Author index

Edwards, M. L., 1970: 386
1974: 233, 344–5, 350–4, 356, 432
Edwards, M. L. & Shriberg, L. D.,
1983: 433
Eilers, R., 1980: 87
See Oller, D. K.
Eilers, R. & Gavin, W., 1981: 95
Eilers, R., Gavin, W. & Wilson, W.,
1979: 93–5
Eilers, R. & Oller, D. K., 1976: 233,
344, 353–60, 432
Eilers, R., Oller, D. K., Bull, D. &
Gavin, W., 1984: 95
Eilers, R., Oller, D. K. &
Ellington, J., 1974: 420
Eilers, R., Wilson, W. & Moore, M.,
1976: 88
1977: 88
Eimas, P., 1974: 137
Eimas, P., Siqueland, E., Jusczyk, P.
& Vigorito, J., 1971: 87, 90–3
Eisenberg, K.: see Huttenlocher, J.
Elbers, L., 1982: 138
Elkonin, D. B., 1971: 232
Ellington, J.: see Eilers, R.
Emonds, J., 1976: 73
Erreich, A., 1984: 460
Erreich, A., Valian, V. &
Winzemer, J., 1980: 459, 463, 514
Ervin, S.: see Miller, W.

Fant, G.: see Jakobson, R.
Fay, D., 1978: 458, 463
Feagans, L., 1980: 418
Ferguson, C. A., 1964: 132
1978: 392
See Macken, M. A.; Snow, C.;
Yeni-Komshian, G.
Ferguson, C. A. & Farwell, C. B.,
1973: 199–200
1975: 200–4, 207, 210–14, 233, 376,
378, 392–3
Ferguson, C. A. & Garnica, O., 1975:
233, 433
Ferguson, C. A., & Slobin, D. (eds.),
1973: 30, 180, 232, 338
See Antinucci, F. & Parisi, D.;
Braine, M. D. S.

Fernald, C., 1972: 445
Fey, M.: see Leonard, L.
Fillmore, C., 1968: 61, 279–80
Fisher, M., 1934: 14
Flavell, J. 1963: 138
Fletcher, P. & Garman, M. (eds.),
1979: 4
See Bowerman, M.
Fodor, J., 1975: 396, 398
Fodor, J., Garrett, M., Walker, E. &
Parkes, C., 1980: 397
Fonagy, I., 1972: 239–40
Fortescue, M., 1984/5: 496
Fox, D.: see Maratsos, M.
Francis, H., 1969: 69
Franklin, M. see Dore, J.
Fraser, C.: see Brown, R.
Fraser, C., Bellugi, U. & Brown, R.,
1963: 443–6
French, L. & Brown, A., 1977:
418–19
Friedman, W. & Seeley, P., 1976: 418
Furrow, D., Nelson, K. &
Benedict, H., 1979: 132, 226, 508,
515

Gaer, E. P., 1969: 478
Garman, M.: see Fletcher, P.
Garnica, O. K., 1971: 344–5
1973: 233, 344–5
1977: 132
See Ferguson, C. A.
Garrett, M.: see Fodor, J.
Gavin, W.: see Eilers, R.
Gazdar, G., Klein, E., Pullum, G. &
Sag, I., 1985: 331
Gelman, S. A.: see Ravn, K. E.
Gibson, D.: see Hoek, D.
Gilbert, J., 1982: 112
Ginsberg, H. & Opper, S., 1969: 138
Givón, T., 1979: 304
Gleitman, H.: see Armstrong, S.;
Gleitman, L.; Newport, M.
Gleitman, L., 1981: 507
See Armstrong, S.; Newport, M.;
Shipley, E.; Wanner, E.
Gleitman, L., Newport, M. &
Gleitman, H., 1984: 506–10, 515

General index